||||||||||||||||||||||||||||||||||||||||||||||||

IO788190

AMERICAN BETRAYAL

ALSO BY DIANA WEST

THE DEATH OF THE GROWN-UP:
HOW AMERICA'S ARRESTED DEVELOPMENT
IS BRINGING DOWN WESTERN CIVILIZATION

AMERICAN BETRAYAL

THE SECRET ASSAULT ON
OUR NATION'S CHARACTER

DIANA WEST

ST. MARTIN'S PRESS ✷ NEW YORK

AMERICAN BETRAYAL. Copyright © 2013 by Diana West. All rights reserved. Printed in the United States of America. For information, address St. Martin's Press, 175 Fifth Avenue, New York, N.Y. 10010.

www.stmartins.com

Design by Meryl Sussman Levavi

Library of Congress Cataloging-in-Publication Data

West, Diana, 1961–
    American betrayal : the secret assault on our nation's character / Diana West.
—First Edition.
        p. cm
    ISBN 978-0-312-63078-2 (hardcover)   *5199 5594   06/13*
    ISBN 978-1-250-01755-0 (e-book)
    1. United States—Politics and government—1933–1953.   2. Political culture—
United States—History—20th century.   3. Socialism—United States—History—
20th century.   4. United States—Foreign relations—Soviet Union.   5. Soviet Union—
Foreign relations—United States.   I. Title.
    E743.5.W39 2013
    973.917—dc23   2013000632

St. Martin's Press books may be purchased for educational, business, or promotional use. For information on bulk purchases, please contact Macmillan Corporate and Premium Sales Department at 1-800-221-7945 extension 5442 or write specialmarkets@macmillan.com.

First Edition: May 2013

10 9 8 7 6 5 4 3 2 1

For Mother and Jed

CONTENTS

For every one that doeth evil hateth the light,
neither cometh to light, lest his deeds be reproved.
But he that doeth truth cometh to the light,
that his deed may be made manifest,
that they are wrought in God.

—JOHN 3:20–21

INTRODUCTION "THE BEGINNING"

S ometime in 1934, two men got off separate trains at Union Station in Washington, D.C. They had arrived in the nation's capital to fight on different sides of a war. It was a war few Americans knew, or even now know, was raging all around the capital. One man, in his early thirties, had come to expand the reach of the secret Communist apparatus already entrenched inside the U.S. government. The other man, age sixty, had come to expose it. The name of the younger man was Whittaker Chambers. Later, he would become the most famous ex-Communist to bear witness to the conspiracy he had served. The older man, William A. Wirt, would die in obscurity.

Chambers, who was working directly for Soviet military intelligence, had come late that spring or early summer of 1934 for an appointment with Harold Ware, leader of a secret, tightly organized Communist network based in the new government agencies that had mushroomed since President Franklin D. Roosevelt had embarked on his "New Deal."[1] Chambers met Ware at the Childs Restaurant on Massachusetts Avenue NW, not far from the Hotel Bellevue (now Hotel George), where Soviet general Walter Krivitsky, another great ex-Communist witness-to-be, would die by violent means six years later. He was murdered, Chambers would later write, "by the same party which he and I both devotedly served, but from which we had both broken."[2]

In 1934, Chambers's break was still five years away—an eternity. For now, he was conferring with Ware and, later, with another underground party leader, J. Peters, about his new mission to help move "career Communists" out of the New Deal agencies, such as the AAA (Agricultural Adjustment Administration) and the NRA (National Recovery Administration), to reorganize them in the main government departments. The party's first objective: the State Department. Later that same afternoon, Chambers would meet the first member of his new cell. His name was Alger Hiss.

William A. Wirt, traveling with his wife to the nation's capital from Gary, Indiana, in April 1934, knew nothing of this key vector of the Soviet-directed assault on the American republic about to take shape. Wirt, a nationally noted schools superintendent, didn't know who Whittaker Chambers was, let alone Harold Ware and Alger Hiss. He knew nothing about other secret Communists at the AAA—Lee Pressman, John Abt, Charles Kramer, and Nathan Witt, for example. Wirt nonetheless believed a secret revolution was under way, and he was in Washington to testify before a select House committee about his unexpected brush with it.

His evidence came from a series of conversations he'd had with government personnel in meetings and at a soon-to-be-notorious dinner party regarding their "concrete plan" for the "proposed overthrow of the established American social order," as Wirt put it. These officials, it bears notice, were mainly employed by the same New Deal agencies from which Whittaker Chambers was to marshal forces to fan out across the U.S. government. Wirt's assessment of the radicalism within the folksily titled New Deal had preceded him to Washington, having made it into the *Congressional Record* and then the newspapers. *"The fundamental trouble with the Brain Trusters,"* he wrote, *"is that they start with a false assumption. They insist that the America of Washington, Jefferson and Lincoln must first be destroyed and then on the ruins they will reconstruct an America after their own pattern."*[3] Out of the political pandemonium that ensued, a select House committee emerged to investigate—or, as the Democratic New Deal majority preferred, to lay the matter to rest.[4]

On April 10, 1934, in the same caucus room where Whittaker Chambers would testify fourteen years later, witness Wirt would have his say, but barely. The powers that be understood that Wirt's story of radicalism in the Roosevelt administration might distract from or even halt their political momentum. Thus the select committee of three Democrats and two Republicans would merely go through the motions—and not even all of them. Contrary to custom (and by party-line vote, 3–2) Wirt wouldn't be allowed to read his ten-minute opening statement, wouldn't have benefit of counsel (3–2), and wouldn't be permitted to rebut charges against him (3–2)—not even after he was falsely accused of having been jailed for German sympathies during the World War (1917–18).[5] Hitler, too, would be invoked to smear Wirt. Most important of all, the committee voted (3–2) not to call any of the key administration officials Wirt cited in his testimony—not the Agriculture Department official who told him about talk in the AAA about retarding the economic recovery in order to speed up the revolution, nor the housing officials planning to collectivize American workers in government-planned communities, nor the "brain trusters" advocating the seizure of the economy and the destruction of laissez-faire. House

Democrats preferred, in the words of the scathing minority report on the Wirt investigation, to leave Wirt's testimony as hearsay. Then it could be smacked down by denials in the press and majority rule.

Indeed, within an hour of Wirt's hearing, such denials "followed in rapid order."[6] So, too, did a countercharge from the dinner party attendees, all mid-level government officials (five U.S. and one Soviet) Wirt had cited for what he described as revolutionary statements. Not only, they told the press, had they not made any of the statements Wirt alleged, Wirt himself had monopolized all conversation to the point where no one else had been able to say anything at all. As they told it, he just never stopped talking.

The world laughed. William Wirt became the butt of jokes throughout the administration and press corps. This front-page *Miami Daily News* story, head-lined LAUGHING THROUGH, is not untypical.

> It is hard on the good Dr. Wirt and hard on the politicians who sought to use him to make political capital, but it has been a blessed relief for the nation. A nation needs a good laugh now and then . . . Laughing again, the country can resume its march, not to revolution, but to prosperity.[7]

The piece also showcased a few lines of widely published doggerel by brain truster Donald Richberg:

> *Cuttle-fish squirt;*
> *Nobody hurt;*
> *And that's the end*
> *Of Dr. Wirt.*

FDR, too, got into the comedy act a few days after Wirt testified. On return-ing to Washington from a fishing trip, the president addressed an improbably colossal welcoming committee at Union Station—cabinet secretaries, thirty senators, two hundred representatives, three thousand people, and the Marine Band playing his campaign theme song, "Happy Days Are Here Again." Play-fully, the president chided the legislators for, in his absence, having gone "from bad to Wirt." "When he made the pun about Dr. Wirt," *The New York Times* noted, "he paused to let the crowd follow his meaning, but only a few responded."[8]

After the next round of hearings devoted to the dinner party, everybody was in on the joke. The dinner guests all reprised under oath the stories they had already told the press. As hostess Alice Barrows put it, "As a dinner party it was not a success because Dr. Wirt talked all the time."[9] Of course, this meant that Wirt, silenced by committee rules and looking on at the witnesses with "clinched hands," was not just an old bore, he was also a liar.[10] Which must have been devastating. Barrows, a U.S. Education Office official, had been Wirt's secretary for many years. But Barrows was also a secret member of the American Communist Party and a KGB source dubbed "Young Woman." She would continue to serve the KGB for years, even if her Moscow masters chided her for engaging in serial love affairs with Soviet diplomats.[11] Whom was she serving under oath in 1934, truth or Stalin?

The same question might be asked of the next dinner guest to testify, Hildegarde Kneeland, a senior economist at the Agriculture Department. Kneeland might not have had so colorful a file as Barrows, but she, too, is ID'd in KGB archives as a secret party member and "intelligence contact/informant" who would be "in contact with Victor Perlo," leader of the notorious Perlo Group, another Communist underground apparatus.[12] "I want to say that it was impossible for me or for anyone else to have taken part in the talk that followed dinner," Kneeland told the committee. "The evening was his, I mean, Dr. Wirt's."[13]

Really? Or was the fix in? Naturally, the other guests—Mary Taylor, editor of an AAA publication that pushed government-planned agriculture as part of a government-planned economy,[14] Robert Bruere of the NRA, and David Cushman Coyle of the PWA (Public Works Administration)—concurred with their friends. The final guest, Laurence Todd of the USSR propaganda agency TASS, also denied Wirt's story, including the charge that Todd had described Roosevelt as "only the Kerensky of the revolution," who would later be replaced by "a Stalin." "It was a most wearying experience," Todd told the committee.[15]

How tiresome. How ridiculous. How could "Todd and a few little women," as Chairman Alfred L. Bulwinkle (D-NC) put it, be leading a revolution? The morning papers dubbed Wirt the "4-Hour Monologist."[16] It was all a big joke, which is how posterity remembers William Wirt—if, of course, it remembers him at all.

There was nothing funny going on, however, at least as far as the committee Republicans were concerned. Refusing to sign the majority "opinion" that Wirt's statements "were not true," the minority members scored the Democrats for refusing to permit any witnesses besides the dinner guests to be called, which prevented a bona fide investigation of Wirt's charges. Thus "the majority members made it inevitable that the proceedings would be a suppression of the truth rather than an uncovering of the truth."[17] This, alas, would not be the last time, and such suppressions of the truth—cover-ups—would involve Republicans and Democrats alike.

Wirt continued to press his case, at least for a while. After being branded a liar by the committee (3–2), Wirt addressed the American Legion in Chicago. Two radio stations planned to broadcast his speech warning that the New Deal would lead America to socialism or Communism, but then abruptly did no such thing. WMAQ "found it advisable" not to broadcast, according to a Legion official, while WIND, after appearing to introduce the Wirt broadcast on the air, suddenly discovered the necessary telephone wires were not in place.[18] After that, Wirt disappears from the public record until 1938, when he died of a heart attack, by some accounts broken by his experience.

That wasn't quite the end of the William Wirt story, though. On April 10, 1940, the sixth anniversary of Wirt's testimony, one of the three Democrats who had effectively run the select Wirt committee published an extraordinary confession in the newspapers—or, at least, in some newspapers (not *The New York Times, The Baltimore Sun,* or *The Washington Post*).

From *The Observer-Dispatch*, Utica, New York:

O'Connor Admits Helping to Discredit Dr. Wirt

Former Representative John. J. O'Connor (D-NY) "confessed" in a statement today that he had helped prevent a thorough investigation in 1934 of charges by the late Dr. William A. Wirt that a group of New Dealers were plotting a new American revolution.

O'Connor, who was defeated for renomination in President Roosevelt's 1938 "purge," said he was sorry for "turning the thumbscrews" on Wirt and expressed belief that most of the latter's charges had come true.

Wirt, a Gary, Ind. schools superintendent, created a national furor six years ago by asserting that there was a deliberately conceived plot among New Dealers to overthrow the established social order in this country and substitute a planned economy.

O'Connor ranked next to Chairman Bulwinkle (D-NC) in a special House committee which investigated Wirt's charges.

In his statement entitled "Confession is Good for the Soul," O'Connor said his participation in the Wirt incident was "in my early, rubber stamp support of the New Deal."

Soon after its appointment, he declared, *the committee met "and discussed rules as to how to handle Dr. Wirt and to prevent the minority Republican members from converting the hearings into an investigation of the truth of the charges."*

"The procedural motion, which I personally presented," he said "limited the hearings to an examination of Dr. Wirt under oath to bring out the names and the exact statements of his informants. Over the protests of the minority members, any examination of the other persons, connected in any way with said activities was precluded . . . [ellipsis in original].

"Dr. Wirt was not allowed to have his counsel cross-examine witnesses, nor was he called in rebuttal after they had presented their 'well-staged' denials.

"I use the word 'well-staged' advisedly because it was known that at least six of them met and rehearsed their denials of what they had told Dr. Wirt."

The former Congressman, now a Washington lawyer, recalled the famous dinner, given at the home of Alice Barrows, office of the education executive, which Wirt attended. It was there, Wirt said, that he heard a boast that President Roosevelt was "The Kerensky of the coming American Revolution."

For his charges, O'Connor said, Wirt was "dishonored and purged and retired."

"The pack got the smell of blood and tracked down the prey: A great job was done. Little did we know that most of the happenings which Dr. Wirt said the plotters had predicted would come to pass" [emphasis added].[19]

This mea culpa of collusion, witness tampering, and character assassination is extraordinary. It is also obscure—a single voice of vindication for a singular voice. It's not so much that O'Connor has thrown into question whether a careful investigation of William Wirt's charges might have averted the Communist infiltration of the U.S. government that marks the middle decades of the twentieth century and beyond. More revealing is the harsh light he shed on the political mechanism by which elected U.S. officials automatically sought to shield an apparent conspiracy from investigation, against an airing of the facts, even as they also casually sacrificed a good citizen to do so. This was, alas, the beginning of an era—an era of American betrayal. In such an era, O'Connor's confession, too little too late, would be buried as well, lost from what we retain of the historical record.

O'Connor would also write:

Maybe in our hearts we knew the plot was not idle gossip and we lunged at the discloser to appease our conscience.

Many times privately have I apologized for my part in turning the thumbscrews, and I take this occasion to do so publicly.

May Dr. Wirt's honest, patriotic soul rest in peace.

His was "the voice of one crying in the wilderness."[20]

More "voices of one" would follow William Wirt, some famous, most of them quickly forgotten, each recklessly attempting to break the conspiracies of silence, suppression, and obfuscation arrayed against them.

What follows is dedicated to them all.

CHAPTER ONE

Once I used to hope that experience of life could be handed on from nation to nation, and from one person to another, but now I am beginning to have doubts of this.

—ALEXSANDR SOLZHENITSYN[1]

Having lamented "the death of the grown-up" in a previous book, it may seem odd to begin here with a paean to "the child"—a perfectly guileless but curious and also innately logical child. This is the very young person in Hans Christian Andersen's "The Emperor's New Clothes," who entered posterity by speaking out, free and heedless of consensus, careerism, peer pressure, personal safety, legal repercussions, and even, freest and most heedless of all, "giving offense."

If you recall, the procession of the naked emperor, arrayed in what was put over, flimflam style, as rich and sumptuous attire, was a great success so long as the crowd played along and participated in the charade. "Nobody would let on that he couldn't see anything," Andersen writes, "because then he would have been unfit for his job or very stupid." It was at this point that the little child—boy or girl, we never know which—said its famous line:

"But he hasn't got anything on!" . . . And it was whispered from man to man what the child had said . . .

"Why, but he hasn't got anything on!" they all shouted at last.

And the emperor winced, for he felt they were right. But he thought to himself: "I must go through with the procession now." And he drew himself up more proudly than ever, while the chamberlains walked behind him, bearing the train that wasn't there.[2]

So ends one of the great cliff-hangers. Will the emperor and his chamberlains brazen it out, cowing the people into acquiescence and thus maintaining their power? Or will the people have the courage to trust their own eyes and, relying on the evidence before them, call the emperor and his men to account? In considering these possibilities, never underestimate the influence of those invisible-train-bearing chamberlains, each one of whom has everything to lose if the empire of lies goes down.

There is hope, at least, in the open question. There is inspiration, too, in the example of the child who tells the truth. However, the forces of illusion and self-delusion are formidable foes against such outbursts of reality. The odds are against any public reckoning. More likely than not, the free-speaking child will be hushed up or badly shunned until it, too, either learns "better" or loses heart in the reeducation process. After all, it's not easy to continue shouting out what is in plain sight when surrounding society is determined to ignore, overlook, or even hide it. When "everyone" agrees there is nothing there, what is there becomes invisible by consensus, and the Big Lie lives. At some point, even this child may buy into it.

Not a chance.

This child, too, is a force in history, as the following chronicle of Big Lies will tell us, its voice calling out the nation's betrayal in a desperate struggle to pass on dangerous knowledge that is too often suppressed. We must listen for these voices. You will hear them time and again in the following pages. Sometimes the child has bad teeth and mumbles. Sometimes he pierces the echo chamber of lies with a funny accent. Sometimes he sports a yachting cap and hails from the Social Register. Sometimes she—for, yes, there were such women, too—is careworn, eyes seared by unimaginable hell on earth. Sometimes she is quirky. But the child is always true, always real. It is the rest, the emperors and chamberlains all around, who are as false and hollow as the historical narrative they create, assuming we will follow along. As, in fact, we do. That is our problem today. Heirs to a false and hollow history, we become unwitting participants, perpetuating and entrenching many, many lies as we take our places in a secretly subverted pageant—and never know it.

That's partly because this subversion of our history, this assault on our nation's character, has no visible markers or specific constituencies. From the inner rings of the Pentagon to the principal's office in a local grammar school, we see nothing amiss. Our people still look, speak, and comport themselves just as they should, snapping salutes and schooling the young. What's changed here is on the inside. Forced to reckonings that require gathering facts and drawing conclusions about ourselves or others, we do not fall back on a vital store of survival instinct and moral code; we fall back on a perversion of both. It is in this moment of free fall when we must look more closely to understand what has happened to us.

Let me illustrate with a true story about a real-life U.S. Navy admiral that first crystallized the syndrome for me several years ago. You know the type: steel-gray hair, clipped; military ribbons, bristling; dutiful, loyal, the works. One day in this long-drawn-out post-9/11 era, this admiral received a lengthy, extensively documented briefing on the Islamic doctrine of jihad (Islamic war) from Maj. Stephen C. Coughlin, U.S. Army Reserves. Coughlin is an expert on the legal-religious doctrine that Islamic terrorists claim as the justification for campaigns of violence against infidels and rival Muslims.[3] His briefings, which I've attended multiple times, are legendary in security circles in Washington and elsewhere for their comprehensive, if not overwhelming, compilation of factual, Islamic-sourced evidence, which demonstrates, for example, that Islamic terrorists are not "hijacking" Islamic law (sharia) when they engage in jihad. On the contrary, they are executing it. Nor are they "twisting" the foundational principles of Islam as codified in each and every authoritative Islamic source. They are exemplifying them.

For reasons that should become clearer over the following pages, this briefing on these basic facts of jihad doctrine is typically our top military leaders' *first exposure* to what is known in Pentagon parlance as the "enemy threat doctrine." I am not exaggerating. Years of battle—even worse, years of battle *planning*—have passed without our leadership having studied, or even having become acquainted with, the principles and historic facts of Islamic war doctrine. Four years into the so-called war on terror, then–Joint Chiefs Chairman Peter Pace even pointed this out in a speech at the National Defense University on December 1, 2005.[4]

Notwithstanding Pace's concern, the study and analysis of Islam and jihad remained de facto forbidden in policy-making circles inside the Bush White House, which even codified a lexicon in 2008 to help government officials discuss Islamic jihad without mentioning "Islam" or "jihad."[5] The Obama administration would carry this same see-no-Islam policy to its zealous limit, finally mounting a two-front assault on the few trainers and fact-based training materials that were sometimes (sparingly) used by law enforcement agencies and the military to educate personnel about Islam and jihad. What history should remember as the Great Jihad Purges of 2012 began at the Justice Department, affecting domestic law enforcement agencies, and spread to the Pentagon, affecting the entire U.S. military.

First, the FBI eliminated hundreds of pages of "anti-Islam" educational material from its own training programs and those of other law enforcement agencies. Several Muslim advocacy groups applauded these purge results at the briefing at the bureau on February 15, 2012, "unexpectedly" attended by FBI Director Robert Mueller himself.[6] Next, on April 24, 2012, Joint Chiefs Chairman Gen. Martin E. Dempsey ordered a similar scrub, calling on the entire

U.S. military to "review" its educational and training classes, files, and rosters of instructors to ensure that no members of the armed services were studying material "disrespectful of the Islamic religion."[7]

What exactly does the U.S. government and its Muslim advisers consider "anti-Islam" or "disrespectful," or, as a Pentagon spokesman put it on Al Jazeera TV, "warped views"?[8] One trophy of this so-called Islamophobia that made it into *Wired.com* (whose reportage seems to have energized if not triggered these government purges) was a PowerPoint slide created by Stephen C. Coughlin about the "permanent command in Islam for Muslims to hate and despise Jews and Christians and not take them as friends."[9]

Pretty disrespectful and warped for sure—*but only if Coughlin's premise and supporting documentation were untrue.* The statement and the documentation, however, are incontrovertible. There *is* a permanent command in Islam for Muslims to hate and despise Jews and Christians and not take them as friends. The slide in question includes citations of the most authoritative Islamic texts, the Koran and the hadiths (the sayings and deeds of Mohammed, which Muslims hold sacred) to document its veracity.[10]

Veracity is not the issue here, though. *Evidence* is not the issue here. *Reality* is not the issue here, either. The issue is a commandment from on high in government—"Islam is a religion of peace." It is the Big Lie that is the basis of the prevailing ideology, and, above all, the Big Lie must live. No one in the leadership contradicts it "because then," as Hans Christian Andersen tells us, he would be "unfit for his job or very stupid."

Admiral X certainly didn't want anyone to think that. So what did he make of his Coughlin briefing, an introduction to the central Islamic doctrine of jihad and its role in driving global jihad? How did he react to the spectacular if not shattering array of information contained in the authoritative Islamic texts and books of authentic, mainstream Islamic jurisprudence before him, which shattered the Islam-is-peace mantra?

He said, and I quote, "I'll have to check with my imam on that."

I was staggered when I first heard this story, and, in a way, I still am. Was the admiral kidding? Did he not have the wit to make up his own mind based on the ample, annotated, inconvenient evidence before him? Witlessness, however, wasn't the admiral's problem, just as witlessness wasn't the problem in the Justice and Defense Departments. If the admiral was announcing that he would be deferring to "his imam"—in other words, to an Islamic interpreter of things Islamic—on the matter of Islamic war-making doctrine, there was a reason for this, and it had nothing to do with IQ. Similarly, if FBI Director Mueller and Joint Chiefs Chairman General Dempsey were deferring to the wishes of an array of Muslim advocacy groups—including groups designated by the U.S. government as Muslim Brotherhood front groups[11]—regarding education about Islam, something else had rendered them, and countless others like them in military, security, and civilian leadership, incapable of assessing facts and passing judgment.

What was it?

This is the leading question that guided the research going into this book. What, in a nutshell, throughout eight years of George W. Bush and four years of Barack Obama, caused our leadership to deny and eliminate categorically the teachings of Islam from all official analysis of the global jihad that has wracked the world for decades (for centuries), and particularly since the 9/11 attacks in 2001? This omission has created a scrupulously de-Islamized, and thus truly "warped," record for future historians to puzzle over. What will they make, for example, of a 2007 ninety-slide briefing on "the surge" in Iraq presented by counterinsurgency guru David Kilcullen that failed to mention Islam (let alone jihad war doctrine) once? Instead, the militarily, politically, and academically elite audiences for whom the presentation was created were asked to *"think of the [Iraqi] environment as a sort of 'conflict ecosystem.'"*[12] How will they explain Gen. Stanley McChrystal's 2009 "assessment" of the war against Islamic jihadists in Afghanistan, which, in sixty-six pages, contained not one discussion of Islam, jihad, or how they fit into both the Taliban struggle and the Afghan people's antipathy for Western forces? How will they explain why "everyone" agreed to fight blind?

To be fair, there is one passing reference to Islam in the McChrystal assessment. Calling for an improved communications approach, the commander demanded that insurgents and jihadist militias be "exposed continually" for their "anti-Islamic" use of violence and terror. The report elaborates, "These include their causing of the majority of civilian casualties, attacks on education, development projects, and government institutions, *and flagrant contravention of the principles of the Koran*" (emphasis added).[13]

It would be easy to toss off a derisive quip at this point and move on, but it's well worth mulling over how it could be that eight years after 9/11, a West Point–trained, battle-hardened, and by all accounts capable commander fighting jihad forces in the Islamic Republic of Afghanistan could assume the role of an apologist for Islam rather than an expert analyst of holy war as waged against his own forces. Flagrant contravention of the Koranic principles of jihad? Au contraire. Between the Koran's teachings against befriending Christians and Jews (noted above) and its teachings that it is a "grave sin for a Muslim to shirk the battle against the unbelievers," as the scholar and critic Ibn Warraq explains ("those who do will roast in hell"), it is also perfectly Islamic to wage jihad against any and all infidel "education, development projects," not to mention against Muslims not actively fighting or supporting jihad.[14]

Don't just take my word for it. Back in 2003, the man who used to be described as Osama bin Laden's "spiritual guide" castigated President Bush along similar lines, and rightly so. In response to Bush's repeated slander of the religion of jihad as the "religion of peace," Abu Qatada said, "I am astonished by President Bush when he claims there is nothing in the Koran that justifies jihad or violence in the name of Islam. Is he some kind of Islamic scholar? Has he ever actually read the Koran?"[15]

If Bush, or McChrystal for that matter, ever did crack the book, he read only the "good parts"—the 124 verses of tolerance—that are rendered meaningless according to the rule of "abrogation." The rule of abrogation is the key that Islamic scholars use to resolve contradictions within the Koran. By means of this doctrine, Koranic passages are "abrogated," or canceled, by any subsequently "revealed" verses that convey a different meaning. In other words, when there is a contradiction (e.g., don't kill the infidel vs. yes, kill the infidel), whatever was "revealed" to Islam's prophet, Mohammed, more recently trumps whatever was "revealed" before it. This technique comes from Mohammed himself at the Koran's sura 2:105: "Whatever verses we [i.e., Allah] cancel or cause you to forget, we bring a better or its like."

It's a simple concept, unforgettable once taught—but our elected officials, our military and other security providers, our pundits and other public voices seem never to have learned it, much less explained it to the rest of us. Or worse, they are ignoring it on purpose. In this ignorant morass, then, We, the People are left on our own to make sense of misinformation and disinformation. Why? Why haven't they sought and told the truth?

There are reasons. In his book *What the Koran Really Says,* Ibn Warraq explains that while abrogation resolves the abundant contradictions to be found in the Koran, it "does pose problems for apologists of Islam, since all the passages preaching tolerance are found in Meccan (i.e., early) suras, and all the passages recommending killing, decapitating and maiming, the so-called Sword Verses, are Medinan (i.e., later)." His conclusion: " 'Tolerance' has been abrogated by 'intolerance.' "[16] Just to be clear: Islamic tolerance in the Koran has been *canceled* by Islamic intolerance in the Koran.

Like Coughlin's slides and presentations, this fact contradicts the Big Lie at the root of the prevailing ideology: "Islam is a religion of peace." Therefore, our leaders don't want us to know it. They also don't want to know it themselves. So they don't, as the Kilcullen "surge" presentation and the McChrystal Afghanistan "assessment" demonstrate. Such knowledge would collapse their deceitful balloon of "universal" values, which rises on the hot air of "Kum-bay-a"-interchangeable sameness. Such a collapse would, in turn, doom the relativism, moral and cultural, that currently drives these same utopian fantasists to undermine liberty in their quest to order or even rule our world and beyond.

Suppression of the facts, then, becomes the only way to keep this enterprise of lies buoyant, something for which there is ample precedent in our past, as the pages ahead will show. Under both the Bush and Obama administrations, then, any fact-driven discussion of Islamic religious, legal, and historical imperatives to make holy war until the world is governed by Islam threatened this same enterprise and had to be, in effect, outlawed and later officially forbidden. "Cultural sensitivity" had to become the name of the game. Thus, as Joint Chiefs Chairman Gen. Martin Dempsey wrote in April 2012, U.S. military programs must "exhibit the cultural sensitivity, respect for religion and intellectual balance that we should expect of our academic institutions."[17] In plain English: Whitewash Islam or else.

Why? And how did the whitewashing of Islam become the business of the United States government? This is another question that inspired this book. It is also a question which, true confession, has driven me to distraction for more than a decade. Sometimes I despair. Sometimes I play it for laughs, or at least revel a little in the absurdity. You have to. Imagine the following scenario coming across your desk: Kifah Mustapha, a known Hamas operative and unindicted coconspirator in the landmark Holy Land Foundation trial, gets invited into the top secret National Counterterrorism Center (NCTC) and then to the FBI's training center at Quantico.[18] The auspices were a six-week "Citizens' Academy" hosted by the FBI in 2010 as part of the agency's "outreach" to the Muslim community.

You look at the story and rub your eyes. A Hamas operative? An unindicted coconspirator? Must they "reach out" quite so far? Here we see the U.S. officials charged with fending off the jihad that Mustapha's activities supported (as laid out in court documents filed by federal investigators) flinging open the doors to this man *on their own terror watch lists.* How could this even be happening?

"The plugs had to be pulled" on the watch system just to get Mustapha in the NCTC door, Patrick Poole wrote online at *PJ Media,* quoting a Department of Homeland Security official. After all, "the NCTC has Kifah Mustapha on the highest watch list we have."[19]

Unbelievable. So who pulled those plugs? Wouldn't it be great to get a bunch of national security pooh-bahs into one room and ask them?

It would be—and so it was. In September 2010, at a Washington conference on domestic intelligence, I took the opportunity to ask as many of these officials as possible this very question. First up was James Clapper, director of national intelligence, who would later make history, or, rather, antihistory, by proclaiming the Muslim Brotherhood to be a "largely secular organization."[20] During a question-and-answer session, I asked him about FBI "outreach" to Mustapha. "I think the FBI will be here later," Clapper boldly punted (laughter in the room). Meanwhile, he continued, there is "great merit in outreach, to engage as much as possible with the Muslim community." Subtext: Bringing a Hamas op into a top secret security installation is no big deal.

Between panels, I buttonholed panelist Sean Joyce, a senior official with the FBI. What did the FBI executive assistant director for national security think about the Mustapha incident?

"We don't comment on individuals," he told me.

OK. How about commenting on a blanket policy regarding FBI tours of sensitive installations for unindicted coconspirators and terrorist group operatives?

"Again, we don't comment on individuals."

It's not every day that you notice a former director of the Central Intelligence Agency standing around, so I asked Michael Hayden for his overall opinion of the speak-no-Islam policy that let jihadists through the door. "People I trust"—uh-oh—"say to be careful not to use the term 'jihadist' because it does have a broader use across the Islamic world," he said, referencing the definition of jihad as "inner struggle."

Oh, please. This is another Grand Pulling of Wool over Infidel Eyes. Why? There is precisely one explicit reference in the Koran to jihad ("ja-ha-da") "as an inner, spiritual phenomenon, not as an outwardly (usually military) phenomenon." So writes Tina Magaard, a Sorbonne-trained linguist specializing in textual analysis. "But," she continues, "this sole reference does not carry much weight against the more than 50 references to actual armed struggle in the Koran (and even more in the Hadith)."[21]

Unfortunately, I didn't have a Magaard cheat sheet with me when I happened on the former CIA director, so I just erupted, politely: So what? That doesn't affect the accuracy of "jihadist" as a description of the enemy!

Then again, not using the word "Islamic," he continued, "obfuscates the issue (and) neuters our understanding" of Islamic terrorism *"however perverted it might be."* Hayden continued, meaningfully: "This is in no way a comment on the Islamic faith."

Heaven forfend. The Islamic faith can inflict censorship, death for leaving Islam, marital rape, polygamy, and slavery on the world, but please, none of the above is in any way a comment on the Islamic faith. Or so the American "intelligence" community has determined. What we inadequately label "political correctness" has obfuscated and neutered fact-gathering and conclusion-drawing powers to the point where the "political correctness," too, is obfuscated. To wit: NCTC Director Michael Leiter next took the podium to address the conference and declared "there was no PC-ness" on his watch. "If someone is inspired by Islamic ideology—" he began, then stopped. "Let me rephrase that: al Qaeda ideology . . ."

Poor baby.

Later, I had an opportunity to ask Leiter what he thought about the FBI bringing Mustapha into NCTC. "Ask the FBI," he suggested helpfully.

Isn't NCTC your shop? I asked.

"Actually," he explained, "the building isn't owned by us. Three organizations have offices there."

When I picked myself up off the floor, he was still talking. "It's more complicated—talk to the FBI. They've got a lot more information than I do."

The FBI better be good, right? They should be prepared, anyway. Indeed, on taking my Mustapha question, FBI Director Robert Mueller, the conference's final speaker, said he'd been briefed to expect it. His response? "I'm not sure I agree with the predicate of your question, and we're not going to debate it here."

He continued discussing the Citizens' Academy program, which he described as "exposing the FBI to a variety of communities."

"Exposing" is right.

He, too, wouldn't discuss individuals, he said, but added, "We do look into the individuals that we invite into the Citizens' Academies." The man who pulled the plugs had spoken, but he explained nothing. Soon, the FBI director would make his way out of the conference hall, his security detail in tow. *And he drew himself up more proudly than ever, while the chamberlains walked behind him, bearing the train that wasn't there.*

I magine a World War II Allied military staff briefing on the Shintoism that animated Imperial Japan. (Shinto war doctrine and Islamic war doctrine are similar in many ways.[22]) Would a WWII-era commander have deferred to the judgment of "his Shinto priest" to assess the validity of a briefing on the expansionist ideology of Imperial Japan?

No.

Would he, alternately, have invited a German American Bund leader into sensitive security installations as a matter of "fascist outreach"?

No again.

Would he have suspended judgment on a briefing on the principles of Marxism-Leninism pending consultation with "his commissar"?

Pause.

Not exactly. However, there were always Communist agents and apologists steering the U.S.-Soviet relationship away from the inevitable rocks of incompatibility, just as today there is an all-encompassing force field blocking the realization that freedom and Islam are similarly incompatible.

The many parallels between America's struggle with Communism and with Islam are striking. Once upon a time, Washington was penetrated by Communist networks and agents to the point of occupation, as I will argue in the chapters ahead. In 1938, five or six or twenty years into this complex underground assault directed by Moscow, the indomitable Rep. Martin Dies (D-TX) took it upon himself to crank up the House Un-American Activities Committee to investigate totalitarian infiltration, whether Communist or fascist. Pressured by FDR himself from day one to halt investigations into Communist infiltration—"Several of the best friends I have are Communists," FDR told Dies[23]—the Dies Committee finally ran into a brick wall a few years later when the outbreak of World War II and the Western alliance with Stalin kicked off a newly intensive period of "Communist outreach," to be discussed ahead. Only in the late 1940s, after the war had ended and Soviet intentions to communize as much of Europe and Asia as possible became bitter reality, and as the great witnesses, ex-Communists Elizabeth Bentley and Whittaker Chambers, defected to the FBI, did a willing and quite able Congress begin to get its arms around at least some of the extensive Soviet-directed operations against this country, which had by then been going on for nearly two decades. Thus began a short-lived heyday of House and Senate investigations into Communist penetration that come down to us as an enduring historical record we would not otherwise have.

Today, we are again allies with adherents of a totalitarian ideology whose agents and apologists have penetrated Western institutions, both overtly and covertly. Just as simultaneous Communist alliance and penetration once disabled our defenses, today, simultaneous Islamic alliance and penetration do so again. Once upon a time, our forebears came to a breaking point with Communism with the advent of what we call the Cold War. There is no comparable breaking point with Islam in sight. In fact, simply pointing out the incompatibility of a civilization based on individual liberty (the West) and a civilization based on collectivism (Islam), for instance, can get a body fired and, even worse, branded a dread "Islamophobe." To date, we have not seen the emergence of investigators among our elected officials to fill the shoes of Reps. Martin Dies and Carroll Reece, Senator Patrick McCarran, and others including, yes, above all, Senator Joseph McCarthy. For *writing a letter* to the State Department inspector general that hoisted a red flag over the close, dense, demonstrable, ongoing family ties to Muslim Brotherhood organizations of Huma Abedin, a top aide to Secretary of State Hillary Clinton, Rep. Michele Bachmann (R-MN) was crucified in the summer of 2012 by the media and political Establishment, Right and Left, as the second coming of Joe McCarthy, Antichrist—a smear campaign as unfair to McCarthy, who, as we will see, has been vindicated by the historical record, as it was to Bachmann, who was entirely correct and measured in merely asking an inspector general to examine the alarming connections of someone so highly placed.[24] Meanwhile, the jihadist penetration of our institutions continues apace.

Don't believe me? Guess who said the following. "The earliest defenders of Islam would defend their more numerous and better-equipped oppressors because the early Muslims loved death—dying for the sake of almighty Allah—more than the oppressors of Muslims loved life. This must be the case when we are fighting life's other battles."

I know I haven't asked a fair question. As former federal prosecutor Andrew C. McCarthy has put it, "That leitmotif—*We love death more than you love life*—has been a staple of every jihadist from bin Laden through Maj. Nidal Hasan, the Fort Hood killer."[25]

McCarthy, who successfully prosecuted Omar Abdel Rahman, the "Blind Sheikh" behind the 1993 attack on the World Trade Center, elaborated: The "Supreme Guide" of the Muslim Brotherhood, Muhammad Mahdi Akef, while praising Osama bin Laden, urged teaching young people "the principles of jihad so as to create mujahideen who love to die as much as others love to live."[26] In 2004, the 3/11 bombers in Madrid left behind a tape saying, "You love life and we love death."[27] Jihad expert Andrew Bostom points out that the noted Muslim historian and Koranic commentator al-Tabari recorded this statement, circa 634, from the Muslim commander to Hurmuz, the Persian leader in Iraq: "Now then. Embrace Islam so that you may be safe, or else make a treaty of protection for yourself and your people, for I have brought you a people who love death as you love life."[28]

Just to be sporting, here's more of the same mystery quotation. "What are our oppressors going to do with a people like us? We are prepared to give our lives for the cause of Islam." Chilling, but not helpful, right? Similar death-cult code could come from any jihadist, from Mohammed Atta, in his night-before-9/11 instructions (oddly not included in the 9/11 Commission report), to the late and unlamented Anwar al-Awlaki, in his e-mails "ministering" to the underpants bomber, Umar F. Abdulmutallab.

Could it also come from a former Bush administration appointee? A member of the board of directors of the American Conservative Union (ACU), sponsor of the well-known CPAC convention in Washington, D.C., where every single GOP presidential hopeful comes to speech-o-flex before thousands of grass-roots activists?

The surprising answer is yes.[29] The former Bush official and ACU board member I am quoting above is Suhail Khan, a close associate of the extremely influential antitax activist Grover Norquist. Khan's shocking quotation—shocking, that is, for a classical conservative, but not for a classical jihadist—comes from a 1999 speech he gave at another convention, that of the Islamic Society of North America (ISNA).

As Suhail Khan has said himself, his father, Mahboob Khan, helped found and was very active in ISNA. He said so in that same 1999 speech, further pledging as his "life's work, inspired by my dear father's shining legacy . . . to work for the *umma*," or transnational Islam. According to a key internal 1991 document of the Muslim Brotherhood entered into evidence at the 2008 Holy Land Foundation trial, ISNA is a Muslim Brotherhood front, the largest one in America. Which means that Khan's father was a founding member of the Muslim Brotherhood in America.

That's right, America. The Brotherhood isn't merely a Tunisian or Libyan or Egyptian or Syrian movement committed to Islamic world government (caliphate) and sharia (Islamic law); the Brothers are here. According to government evidence in the Holy Land Foundation trial, the Muslim Brotherhood claims twenty-nine front and "friendly" organizations in North America, all of which remain unindicted coconspirators. The Council on American-Islamic Relations (CAIR)—which was founded by members of Hamas, which is the Palestinian wing of the Muslim Brotherhood—also remains an unindicted coconspirator in this landmark trial.

What do our elites do with such information?

I'll have to check with my imam on that . . . in spades. They ask members of these same front groups for advice about homeland security. They bring sympathizers of such radical groups into the Pentagon to help formulate policy. They tap them to organize Muslim chaplains for the military and to help set up a mini-sharia-state at Guantánamo Bay. They invite them onto Fox's *O'Reilly Factor* to comment on the affairs of the day. What we're watching begins to look like an influence operation to rival that of the old days of the Communist Kremlin, only this time around the hostiles proceed much of the time in plain sight. So how does it all go unnoticed, unremarked upon?

To look for the answer, let's return to Admiral X—not to mention FBI Agent Y and Congressman Z—and the way in which they all are prone, primed, and *conditioned to withhold judgment.* Despite their sworn duty to preserve and protect the Constitution of the United States of America, such leaders find nothing amiss in *outsourcing* their understanding of the enemy threat doctrine to a likely agent, proponent, or sympathizer of that same enemy threat doctrine (and then inviting them into sensitive security installations). Mastering the objective facts of the matter and drawing their own conclusions never seems to enter their minds. Why? The short answer is that *they don't have it in them* to make up their own minds. The longer answer will lead us back through nearly a century's worth of Big Lies to a place where their corrosive source should become clear.

For the moment, though, let's turn from paralysis in the capital over jihad to paralysis in a small California school district over what historian Robert Conquest might call the "residual muck" of Marxism-Leninism—another enemy doctrine targeting Western beliefs.

In the run-up to Thanksgiving 2008, a small-town elementary school in Southern California received a letter. It was from a parent whose daughter was enrolled in the school's kindergarten. This parent, later described as a university English professor "specializing in Native American literature," wrote in to say she had just learned that, according to local custom some forty years old, the school's kindergartners would be joining kindergartners from another local school for a Thanksgiving feast, with one class dressed up as Indians and the other class dressed up as Pilgrims.

Costuming the children this way was "demeaning," she wrote, adding, "I'm sure you can appreciate the inappropriateness of asking children to dress up like slaves (and kind slave masters), or Jews (and friendly Nazis), or members of any other racial minority group who has struggled in our nation's history." The first Thanksgiving thus equated with mealtime at Buchenwald served up by Simon Legree, the parent demanded the schools *abolish the celebration,* which meant up to and including the macaroni Indian necklaces and the black paper Pilgrim hats.[30]

Before considering the official response of the schools, it's worth recalling that in the case of the Plymouth Colony harvest feast of 1621 that Americans have commemorated as a day of national thanksgiving since the nineteenth century, the "minority group" who "struggled" was in fact the group of Pilgrims and other passengers who had made the arduous Atlantic crossing in 1620. Half of these English Separatists had died since setting sail from Plymouth, England, mostly during that first Massachusetts winter, and it was largely due to the aid of two English-speaking Indians, Squanto and Samoset, that the 53 (out of 102) who survived were able to bring in a good harvest the following fall. It was then, according to a contemporaneous account by Edward Winslow, "amongst other Recreations, we exercised our Armes, many of the Indians coming amongst us, and amongst the rest their greatest king Massasoyt, with some ninetie men, whom for three dayes we entertained and feasted."[31] Here lies the basis of our foundational act of thanksgiving to God and comity among men—not to mention bona fide cultural duality, if not technical diversity.

One politically correct push, however, and those charged with passing on this legacy gave way. Just as our admiral above was unable to draw on reason and knowledge at his core to render judgment on the threatening doctrine of Islamic jihad, the administrations of both elementary schools were similarly incapacitated when it came to rendering judgment on this Marx-inspired, "multicultural" assault on American legitimacy. The educators couldn't muster the most elementary defense of themselves or their tradition based on what was once a bedrock, intuitive, and practically atavistic understanding that, at the very least, the Indian-Pilgrim relationship at Plymouth Rock bore no resemblance to either the slave-master relationship or the Jew-Nazi relationship.

How hard would it have been to explain to the parent that the costume party tradition was an age-appropriate way both to illustrate the historic unity of peoples, purpose, and thankfulness that we rightly celebrate to this day and to connect these young schoolchildren to founding mythology that happens to be true? Instead, the schools surrendered their judgment without hesitation, let alone a fight. They subordinated not only their understanding of history but also their understanding of themselves—namely, their ability to differentiate between right and wrong—to an interpretation specifically engineered to eradicate and replace their own. They then trumpeted their surrender in a letter they sent home with the kids.

"Dear Kindergarten Parents," the principal of one of the two schools wrote. "This year we continue the wonderful tradition of sharing a feast with the students . . ."

But.

She continued, obviously without proofreading, "It has been brought to our attention that by dressing the students in an Indian costume may be perceived as a negative caricature of Native Americans. In order to be sensitive to the Native American culture, we will not celebrate our feast together in costume. We will instead dress in Mountain View and Condit t-shirts."[32]

Goodbye, "Pilgrim" hats and "Indian" necklaces; hello, Happy T-Shirt Day. In yielding our nation's historical symbols, in depriving the students of their cultural heritage, the educators exposed their own subverted core. There, facts are no match for the magnetic draw of ideology, which causes our culture to collapse in on itself. Over the black hole that remains, the last standard flying is a pair of stupid T-shirts.

What—who—brought us here?

This is the mystery. The clues lie scattered behind us, somewhere along the rocky course of a voyage of transformation, which, I find, has never been completely tracked, sounded, and mapped. Along this still uncharted way are the familiar landmarks of World War II and what we think of as the Cold War, the era of hostilities that gave way to, or, at least, was superseded by, a war with Islam that goes on officially unacknowledged. As enemies of the West, godless Communism and godcentric Islam are strangely, eerily similar, in their collectivist, totalitarian natures, in their dysfunctional ideological reliance on the Eternal Foe for forward thrust, and, above all, in *our blindness* to all related and resulting implications of our struggle against them. In the following quotation, Robert Conquest, circa 2005, is retrospectively considering the animus of Soviet Communism, but what he describes sounds much like the timeless drive of Islamic jihad:

> The confrontation with the West was, like the ruin of the [Soviet] economy, a product of the mental distortions of the Soviet order. The 'insane militarization' Gorbachev spoke of was a symptom of the mind-set that prevailed, which required *an unceasing struggle with all other cultures* [emphasis added].⁵⁵

One salient difference is that the Soviets only had "rope" to sell the West; Islam has oil.

While there is reasonable consensus on the link between the Soviets' "unceasing struggle" with others (climaxing in the Reagan-driven arms race) and the ultimate ruin of the Soviet economy, we hardly consider the impact that this same "unceasing struggle" had on ourselves. The fact is, wars change combatants, and we, the West, did not emerge unscathed from the better part of a century of accommodating, appeasing, enabling, opposing, fighting, tolerating, accepting, and assisting the influence and power of the Soviet regime. Indeed, the changes wrought by this continuous entanglement of Communist Russia and the Free World are deep, if also grossly and dangerously unappreciated.

Take the reputation in the West of Communism itself. It may not be trumpeted as the coming thing—not specifically by name, anyway—but, in the burn pit for catastrophic ideologies, its aura today is not blackened to the same crisp as Nazism and fascism. Not even close. Despite Soviet "defeat" in 1991, the ideas associated with Communism remain shockingly reputable throughout what we still know as the Free World.

Consider class warfare. This basic tenet of Marx 101 has been a staple of President Barack Obama's rhetoric—only, again, not by name. Euphemism here, as always, is key. Meanwhile, to have served, nonrepentant, as an identified Communist or fellow traveler during the MAD-fraught years of the Cold War is no bar to continuing public service in the supposedly anti-Communist, or, at least, non-Communist West. In fact, it often seems to be an asset.

We see this all over the European Union, once the central battlefield of the Cold War. With a new constitution known as the Lisbon Treaty, the EU has become a supranational federal state led by an unelected president and foreign minister, exerting concrete control over the rights of over five hundred million citizens. With its rigid centralization, unelected ruling body, flagrant corruption, and, recently, colossal states of bankruptcy, the governing structure the EU most closely resembles is the old USSR—"though admittedly only a pale copy," as onetime Soviet dissident Vladimir Bukovsky is quick to explain. Still, Bukovsky, a self-described "ex-convict," sees chilling parallels, for example, in the police powers of Europol, particularly in the force's diplomatic immunity. Bukovsky writes, "A policeman with diplomatic immunity can come in, take whatever he likes, beat you up, and you can't even sue him. EuroPol will police us on 32 criminal counts, 2 of which are particularly interesting because they don't exist in the penal codes of any other country. One is 'racism' and the other is 'xenophobia.' "[34]

Bukovsky further notes that "the authorities"—the unelected commissioners (commissars?) who run the EU—have already indicated that opposition to EU immigration policy, for example, may count as "racism," while opposing further integration of Europe may trigger a "xenophobia" alert. With Europol up and running—and did I mention that the EU has also streamlined country-to-country extradition?—who needs to go to the trouble of setting up a Gulag?

After all, one thing the rise and fall of the Soviet Union demonstrates is that the Gulag is a cumbersome means of social control—in the end, more trouble than it was worth to the dictatorship. (Then again, as a source of slave labor, the Gulag remains unsurpassed.) Today, turning one individual into an example seems to be all that's necessary to keep the citizenry in line. We've already seen a series of recent precision prosecutions for speech "violations" in the Netherlands (Geert Wilders), Denmark (Lars Hedegaard), Austria (Elisabeth Sabaditsch-Wolff), and elsewhere. Even when these trials end in acquittal, the time, expense, and wear and tear on the spirit do wonders to check the voice of the people, any people. On these relatively narrow shoulders of repression, then, central state power rises.

According to the Soviet-era archive Bukovsky amassed by copying thousands of classified Kremlin documents in 1992, these Soviet-lite developments in Europe are not accidental. Rather, as Bukovsky discovered in the minutes of secret meetings that would continue until shortly before the December 1991 collapse of the Soviet Union, we are seeing the results of "convergency" planning by Mikhail Gorbachev in 1987 to create an EU-USSR "counterbalance" to the United States. In an extraordinary Moscow meeting in January 1989 between Gorbachev and members of the Trilateral Commission—David Rockefeller, Henry Kissinger, Yasuhiro Nakasone, and Valery Giscard d'Estaing—recreating Europe from "the Atlantic to the Urals," as Kissinger sweepingly put it, was discussed there before the treaties to make such a European superstate were drafted.[35] Twenty years later, after the Lisbon Treaty was finally ratified—after being rejected in three separate referenda—English-language *Pravda,* of all publications, published a column highlighting similarities between the EU government and the USSR government, in particular their powers to check individual rights. The headline was an attention grabber: TWENTY YEARS AFTER THE FALL OF THE BERLIN WALL, THE EU IS A REINCARNATION OF THE FORMER SOVIET UNION.[36]

Given that Europe was the primary theater of the Cold War—a war that was plenty "hot" at times[37]—this is quite a mind-boggling concept. Then there's the leadership. The EU's first foreign minister—appointed in Politburo-style secrecy by its governing body, the European Commission—is Baroness Catherine Ashton. Not even the baronial crest awarded her by Tony Blair's Labor government in 1999 hides the fact that Ashton is the former treasurer of the British organization Campaign for Nuclear Disarmament (CND), a Marxist-infiltrated, Communist-led organization deemed "communist and subversive" by MI5 for its Cold War–era efforts to disarm Britain, force U.S. cruise missiles off British bases, and decouple Europe generally from the U.S.-led NATO alliance—the latter a point of Soviet strategy documented in Bukovsky's blessedly purloined archive.[38] Ashton's tenure coincided with the final, covert Soviet drive of the Cold War, the Moscow-orchestrated and Soviet-bloc-funded "peace movement" to strip the West of its tactical superiority in nuclear weaponry. In other words, in answer to the question, "What did you do in the Cold War, Mummy?" the baroness would have to include the fact that she advanced the cause of the Other Side. Then again, has "convergency" reached a stage where we still recognize there was one?

Gerard Batten, member of the European Parliament for the United Kingdom Independence Party, laid out the case against Ashton's appointment publicly, concluding, "CND was, knowingly or unknowingly, the Soviet Union's Fifth Column, and its senior members were either traitors or what Lenin called 'useful idiots.' " As for Baroness Ashton, he wrote, "She, who would have unilaterally removed Britain's nuclear defenses, will now direct the foreign and defense policies of Europe's nuclear powers: Britain and France."[39] Not only did Batten's plaint not stir outrage, it failed even to lift an eyebrow.

Meanwhile, if Ashton denies she was herself ever a Communist, not so seven of twenty-seven members of the European Commission, the unelected

supercouncil Bukovsky likens to the old Soviet Politburo.[40] Among the commission's recycled revolutionaries is its president, José Barroso, who, while
Baroness Ashton was a top official of the CND in Britain, was himself a leader
of an underground Maoist revolutionary party in Portugal in the 1970s. This
was a period, Batten notes, "when such parties were directed from Beijing in
the same way as the Communist Parties were controlled by Moscow." Another
commissioner, Joaquín Almunia, who currently belongs to the Marxist wing of
the Socialist Workers Party in Spain, was a minister (1986–91) in the "fanatically pro-Kremlin" government of Felipe González. Batten writes that this
Spanish government "enthusiastically supported the Soviet project of the creation of a 'common European home,' [and] also opposed the independence of
the Baltic states." The should-be shocking litany goes on, as Batten elaborates
on six more EU commissioners with notable Communist associations.[41]

The European Parliament, to say the least, was unmoved by Batten's toc-
sin, validating Bukovsky's comparison of that body to the old USSR's mori-
bund, rubber-stamp Supreme Soviet.[42] Indeed, the empowerment of longtime
Communists and Soviet sympathizers in Europe's new superstate is nonnews
everywhere. Maybe the apathy is itself another consequence of our struggle-
cum-encounter with Communism: The West has been down-to-the-nub exhausted, bored, or to-its-very marrow co-opted by the whole experience.

Such ennui, if that's the right term, is no match for the persistent animus
toward capitalism, individualism, and "bourgeois" culture that, again, seemingly paradoxically, has long outlasted the rotted Soviet superstructure. Indeed,
in the person of President Barack Hussein Obama, two decades after the disintegration of the USSR, such animus pulses through his administration.

Of course, here I am talking about Barroso the Maoist, and Ashton the fellow traveler, and Almunia the Marxist, and assorted apparatchiks running
Megastate Europe, and I imagine readers nodding along, not registering any
upset at all over the terminology I've chosen. In other words, the ideological
labels I have affixed to these European figures have violated no intense, doctrinal taboos.

On the other hand, even now, if I were to critique Obama as a "Marxist," a
"socialist," or a "fellow traveler," something quite different would be likely to
happen. Even if I offered quotations from Obama himself about "spreading the
wealth" and income redistribution, like Pavlov's dog, most readers would be
instantly overtaken by the conditioned reflex of rejection, becoming instantly
derisive and scoffing in disbelief. I would be automatically discredited for attempting to affix descriptive labels on the man or even on his Marxist, socialist,
or fellow-traveling policies—including his plan for socialized medicine, that
definitively Marxist program applauded by Bolsheviks, "progressives," statists,

socialists, and fellow travelers alike. I would hear either that I don't understand Marxism, that I am imprecisely characterizing socialism, or that it is historically out of context to invoke "fellow traveling." What is being rejected is definition itself, labeling, even with a factual basis. The preference for imprecision, for "nuance," has the effect of denying us the clearest understanding of reality possible, and thus becomes more dangerous than Marxism itself. It is bad enough to consider the fact that two decades after the fall of the Berlin Wall, the forty-fourth president of the United States of America could be accurately thumbnailed by the term "Marxist" (or "socialist" or "fellow traveler"); it is somehow worse when one can't broach the topic without triggering an avalanche of opprobrium.

Even beyond the question of how Americans elected a man incubated in a radical comfort zone peopled by Stalinists, Maoists, card-carrying Communists, socialists, and postmodern revolutionaries unhelpfully obscured as "Alinskyites," and who first ran for elected office as both a Democrat and socialist (New Party) "fusion" candidate, how did this topic of crucial public interest became a conversation ender, something to wave off, frantically, like a bad smell? Or, alternately, how did a topic so important to the future of the nation become a laugh-track prompt? There was something unnatural about the taboo from the start.

Jonah Goldberg noted the phenomenon as a matter of fact in a 2010 *Commentary* magazine essay called "What Kind of Socialist Is Obama?" He wrote, "Republicans believed they had hit a rhetorical mother lode with this line of argument, but *their efforts to make hay of Obama's putative socialism proved unedifying, if not outright comic*" (emphasis added).[43]

To be sure, back in 2008 many conservatives believed that simply unmasking Obama's inner Marxist, really laying it out in plain sight for voters to see, would inevitably trigger a dramatic shift in support away from Obama and toward a GOP ticket that was at least a marginally safer bet than the anti-American abyss Obama beckoned toward. Surely, the *facts* would lead Americans to *conclude* that a candidate who embraced Frantz Fanon, the "Marx of the Third World," and assorted anti-American revolutionists rather than philosophers of free enterprise and liberty was *wholly unsuitable for the presidency*. I know I felt that way even over noxious revelations about Obama's close, twenty-year-long association with the Rev. Jeremiah "God damn America" Wright. Funny to say "even." I actually thought it was all over for Obama. (I even predicted it on national television.) It was hard to let the notion go. In the waning days of the campaign, *The New Criterion*'s Roger Kimball gallantly argued that an abiding belief that ideology—Obama's—mattered. The occasion was the late-breaking emergence online (never in the mainstream media) of a

2001 radio interview with Obama on WBEZ in Chicago. In a real tour-de-Marx performance, Obama is heard bemoaning constitutional restraints on state powers and the fact that the Civil Rights–era Warren Court "never ventured into the issues of redistribution of wealth." He also plugs "community organizing activities on the ground" that create "coalitions of power through which you bring about redistributive change."[44]

Got that? Not *hope* and change—*redistributive* change.

Referencing some of the exemplars of extremism associated with Obama (Bill Ayers, Rev. Wright), along with his alarmingly sealed past (e.g., Obama's refusal to release his college and law school transcripts), Kimball wrote, "For reasons that I find difficult to comprehend, such elements in Obama's political DNA so far seem to have made little impression on the public at large. People cannot seem to get their minds around *the implications of these alliances.*" (emphasis added).

Or maybe, Kimball continued, people couldn't get their *hearts* around the implications, so emotionally committed were they to the "hope and change" candidate. "All that, I suspect, is about to change, and change fast," he wrote. "Credulity is a wonderful thing. So long as you maintain the illusion of benevolence, all is well. Once that begins to crack, the façade shatters and disillusionment rushes in like a tempest-driven tide."

He was so certain, adding, "Here at last you witness the real Barack Obama. The sound you hear in the background is the cracking of Obama's nimbus of benevolent moderation. This is not 'change we can believe in.' It is left-wing radicalism aimed at the foundations of the American system of government."[45]

Kimball really cared. Well, so did I and some insufficient number of our fellow Americans. The majority of us did not. As Goldberg would later note, the political impact of revelations about Obama's radical ideology (so far as they went, sans mainstream media coverage) was "unedifying if not outright comic."

Why not "edifying" and "outright alarming"?

I have come to believe the apathy and especially the laughter are conditioned responses, trained responses designed to short-circuit the thinking process and other natural reflexes. Who or what did the conditioning? Who or what taught us to yawn at or mock overtly anti-American subversion? Did I just say "anti-American subversion"? That's another howler for most of us postmoderns. So howl at this: Barack Hussein Obama, by associations, by actions, by stated beliefs—by rights—should not have been given a government security clearance, let alone the highest government security clearance. Short of having been elected president, the shocking paradox is, it is extremely unlikely he would ever have received it. Of course, is it a paradox if it doesn't even rate a newspaper story? Meanwhile, it's difficult to be shocked if you've been conditioned never to widen your eyes and gasp. Ever.

Frankly, we were lucky to get as close as we did to the whole socialism issue. It was only the unexpected and electrifying emergence of "Joe the Plumber" about three weeks before Election Day 2008 that put Obama's belief in economic redistribution on display, briefly, for the wider public. "I think when you spread the wealth around, it's good for everybody," Obama famously told Joe Wurzelbacher, during a televised campaign stop in Ohio on October 12, 2008. Obama's "postpartisan" mask had slipped. Did it reveal the Marxist underneath? Did this would-be emperor wear antidemocratic clothes?

If so, no one wanted to look too closely, John McCain's fainthearted jabs and Sarah Palin's full-throated sloganeering aside. The MSM, clutching their candidate's invisible train, decided that what American voters wanted to know—or, rather, should have wanted to know—was not whether the next president was a Marxist but rather whether Joe was a *licensed plumber.* Stranger still, significant conservative voices downplayed the socialism issue, too.

The timing was critical. Recall that in the 2000 presidential election, a late-breaking wavelet of outrage crested over carefully leaked "news" that George W. Bush had been DUI in 1976, likely causing him to lose the popular vote, and very nearly the election. The socialist issue (Marxist, collectivist, statist, Communist), had it caught fire, might well have frightened some measurable percentage of Obama voters, particularly among his more conservative or independent voters. The MSM seemed to hold its breath. On October 24, 2008, however, with less than two weeks before Election Day, Fox News's *Special Report with Brit Hume* took up the issue in a panel discussion featuring Mara Liasson, Fred Barnes, and the quasi-oracular Charles Krauthammer.

The conversation kicked off promisingly enough with a question from Hume as to whether Obama's recent comment to Joe the Plumber had "raised legitimate questions about whether he has a socialist or socialistic policy." Conversation stalled with Barnes, who seemed more intent on fending off similarly justifiable questions regarding the socialist underpinnings of both John McCain's and George W. Bush's taxation and banking policies, ignoring the Obama story altogether. As a legitimate line of inquiry, however, the topic dead-ended when it got to Charles Krauthammer. "Since the word 'socialism' has reared its ugly head," he began, "let's dispose of it."[46]

Think of it. The presidential front-runner—the supposedly *"postpartisan"* presidential front-runner—says, "When you spread the wealth around, it's good for everybody," and the leading pundit of what passes for conservatism knocks the issue down on the first go-round. On the contrary, he wants to explain why socialism could not possibly be at issue. His reasoning? Socialism just isn't "socialism," Krauthammer explained, unless the government owns the means of production. So, presumably, because Obama didn't tell Joe that it's good for everybody when you spread the wealth around *and* as President, he would take over two of the Big Three automakers, one-sixth of the economy (health care), and much of the student loan and home mortgage industries, there was no reason to wonder what type or even whether a Socialist was about to be elected president. (Meanwhile, the extent to which the social engineer and megaregulator George W. "I've abandoned free-market principles to save the free market" Bush had already "pre-socialized" the economy, to use Michelle Malkin's term, shouldn't be forgotten, and he was hardly the first, as we will see.)[47]

Rather than consider "spreading the wealth around" in the context of Obama's lifelong ties to card-carrying Communists, Marxists, Maoists, and socialists, Krauthammer introduced an irrelevant and distracting historical context. He said, "What Obama is talking about is what we have had for a long time, progressive taxation." Progressive taxation "for a long time" should present a conservative with a problem, not the Adam Smith stamp of approval.

But back to Krauthammer: "Now, he wants to raise the marginal income tax rate from about 36 percent today to about 39.5 . . . But let's remember, under Eisenhower, the marginal income tax rate was 91 percent . . . [Such tax rates] are not the Supreme Soviet, it's not Sweden, and it isn't even Eisenhower's America."

A sound bite is sometimes just a sound bite, but this one still reverberates. In pairing these late-breaking glimpses of Obama's redistributionist beliefs with "Eisenhower's America," Krauthammer invoked the worn Rorschach prompt for plain vanilla conservatism, which could hardly be more inaccurate. Eisenhower may have been elected on his solemn pledge to roll back the New Deal and war-inflated spending and taxes, but he did neither. That doesn't change Ike's chiseled-in-stone reputation for "conservative" stability, however. By referencing Eisenhower's America, Krauthammer was promoting a sense of politics as usual. Quite possibly, it reflected his own desire to believe in politics as usual. Joe the Plumber aside, this emperor does wear clothes. Nothing subversive here. The center *can* hold.

The electorate, of course, was similarly undisturbed. Just as revelations about Obama's lifelong involvement with anti-American radicals failed to resonate beyond remote outposts of the Right, Obama's breaking-news espousal of Marxist theory fell completely flat. The possibility that the next president of the USA might be a not-so-crypto Marxist didn't alarm or distress many voters. Why not?

One plausible explanation put forward by author and professor Paul Kengor is this simple fact: "The history and truth about communism are not taught by our educators."[48] Americans are not equipped, not prepared, to regard anything resembling Communism—Marxism, socialism, statism, collectivism, and other such terms that are much more interchangeable than we are taught to think—as an existential threat to liberty. Ignorant of Communism's history of blood and terror, we are susceptible to its false promises. In fact, we are continually conditioned to embrace Communistic principles, all serving to expand the power and authority of the state over the individual—and it all started long before Barack Hussein Obama came on the scene.

Again, which side was it that won the "ideological" battle of the century?

It was one thing for the liberal likes of *The New York Times* to wait until two months *after* Obama was inaugurated to get around to asking him "whether his domestic policies suggested he was a socialist, as some conservatives have implied."[49] It was another for Fox's flagship pundits, in essence, to stow the subject, pre–Election Day, before it could be even partly aired. We knew from Stanley Kurtz, writing as early as June 2, 2008, at the mainstream conservative Web site *National Review Online,* that on the eve of Obama's first election in 1995 (he won an Illinois State Senate seat), Obama said the following:

> In America, we have this strong bias toward individual action. You know, we idolize the John Wayne hero who comes in to correct things with both guns blazing. But individual actions, individual dreams, are not sufficient. We must unite in collective action, build collective institutions and organizations.[50]

Obama could not have been clearer about his intentions to replace what he denigrated as the old "right-wing," "individualistic bootstrap myth" with a collectivist order—pure Marx. Such sentiments were underscored by other statements from his career, including that "redistributionist" radio interview unearthed by bloggers and mentioned above. Media on the left and most media on the right just let these choice scoops lie, flopping on the Internet, denying them the mainstream oxygen that would have turned them into living, breathing campaign issues. This same blanket of silence lay heavily on those of us who judged the evidence as it lay there, untrumpeted, unheralded, almost entirely unreported, subtly pressuring us not to break ranks. *If a story broke in the forest and no one reported it . . .* It was as if the s-word (socialist) came with a gag. I remember feeling that way at CNN. I remember thinking extra long and hard before one of my regular appearances on the political roundtable of the old Lou Dobbs show about whether to use the word "socialist" on the air (I'd already used it in my column), triple-checking already double-checked facts, reevaluating the evidence, almost as though I didn't trust myself. If no one else was talking about it, could it be true? If no one else was bringing it up, did it matter? Such questions are unavoidable in the silence of a sound booth. What I was responding to, however, was the force of taboo—the unspoken vow of silence. No one in the mainstream media, liberal or conservative, wanted to talk about it. Finally, I overcame the ultrasensitivity and wondered aloud on CNN whether as president "Obama will lead the country in a socialist direction" and was instantly accused of "Red-baiting" by the next panelist. Coincidentally or not, I never resumed regular appearances on Dobbs after that, and my contract was not renewed. Even *National Review*'s Kurtz, with his clear-cut and ground-breaking reportage, at that time danced around directly calling Obama or his New Party affiliation "socialist," arguing that what was important here was not the label, but rather the fact that Obama and the New Party were clearly far to the left of mainstream liberalism.

I disagree. The label, the clarity, is always of paramount importance.[51] Of course, with Krauthammer at Fox summarily disposing of the label that set off the cry of "Red-baiting" at CNN, little wonder mum remained the word. It still does. As long as Obama, or anyone else, isn't correctly identified and discussed as being "socialist" or "Marxist," his place and that of others like him in the continuum of American liberalism is secure; the same goes for the socialist tenets of American liberalism in general. (In 1933, the Democratic Party should have changed its name to the Democratic Socialist Party. The Republican remnant would have done well to take the name Constitutionalist Party.) This is the identical argument I frequently make about our failure to speak freely about Islam—and yes, absolutely, our deferential attitudes toward the two ideologies are deeply and tragically related.

I much appreciated the counsel of a British writer named Adam Shaw. Describing the wide range of socialists, so labeled, in British and European politics, and commenting on the contortions of the American media, particularly conservatives in the media, to avoid the "obvious fact [that] President Obama is quite clearly a socialist," he tried to shine a little wisdom across the water: "To call someone a socialist is not conspiratorial, and it is not fear-mongering; it is simply the truth, and it is time for some in the conservative media to take a deep breath and admit it—America has a socialist leading the country. Welcome to the club: It stinks!"[52]

Why our neo-Victorian recoil at such frankness? The answer has something to do with what Andrew C. McCarthy has described as "fog from the vaporous arsenal to which Alinskyites resort when they know clarity would betray their radicalism."[53] This is key: the use of confusion, obfuscation, deception . . . *when they know clarity would betray their radicalism.* Of course, I would argue that the use of the term "Alinskyite," in reference to community organizer Saul Alinsky, is itself a shot of fog. All of these weapons of semantic confusion from the "vaporous arsenal" go straight back, past Alinsky, to Lenin and Marx.

From *The New York Times,* March 7, 2009, Exhibit A: "Obama has always sought to avoid being defined by labels, presenting himself as open to ideas from the left and the right . . . Asked to describe his philosophy in a word, he said, 'No, I'm not going to engage in that.' "[54]

Of course not. "Engaging in that" might burn off the fog, which, in this same story, Obama actually tries to sink more deeply into. On *Air Force One* earlier in the day, the *Times* reporter had asked the new president whether his domestic policies could be described as socialist. " 'The answer would be no,' he said, laughing for a moment . . . As the interview progressed, Mr. Obama never returned to the question." About ninety minutes after the plane landed, though, he called the reporter from the Oval Office and said he had been thinking about it. "It was hard for me to believe you were entirely serious about that socialist question," the president said.

Notice the implication of ridicule, the suggestion that such a question was so unworthy as to be a punch line.

He then dismissed the criticism, saying that large-scale government intervention in the markets and the expansion of social welfare programs had begun under his Republican predecessor, George W. Bush.

As Charles Krauthammer told us, large-scale government was part of "Eisenhower's America."

"It wasn't under me that we started buying a bunch of shares of banks," Mr. Obama said. "And it wasn't on my watch that we passed a massive new entitlement, the prescription drug plan, without a source of funding."

He added, "We've actually been operating in a way that has been entirely consistent with free-market principles, and some of the same folks who are throwing the word socialist around can't say the same."

Aside from that parting whopper about his own administration operating on "free-market principles," Obama never spoke truer words. George W. Bush did indeed ramp up the socialization of the U.S. economy with colossal government bailouts in the banking, auto, and insurance industries. Further, the Bush administration's intervention into the home loan industry capped one of the great, bipartisan social engineering disasters of all time. His reputation as a conservative, however, seems secure—if only, as Jonah Goldberg has noted, as a foil for the Left and, I would add, a talisman of the Right, a Buddha to rub for reassurance and corroboration. The thinking goes: *Since I'm a conservative and supported Bush, Bush must be a conservative, too.* Or: *Since Obama's planned tax increases are more modest than Eisenhower's, Obama must not be a socialist.* Call it innocence—conservatism—by association.

Obama's socialism did become a topic on conservative talk radio for a time, notably driven by Mark Levin, while Glenn Beck on Fox News explored what amounts to a century-old "progressive" assault on the nation's founding principles. Such antisocialist rhetoric reached a crescendo during the Obamacare debate, which probably explains why Obama himself entered the fray. During a televised January 2010 meeting with House Republicans, out of the blue, he made the following point: "The component parts of this thing [Obamacare] are pretty similar to what Howard Baker, Bob Dole, and Tom Daschle proposed at the beginning of this debate last year. Now, you may not agree with Bob Dole and Howard Baker, and, certainly, you don't agree with Tom Daschle on much, but that's not a radical bunch."

Another declaration of innocence by association. Then this: "But if you were to listen to the debate and, frankly, how some of you went after this bill, *you'd think that this thing was some Bolshevik plot*" (emphasis added).[55]

Here we see an epic act of self-vaccination, a public declaration designed to ward off any political harm caused by mounting discussion of whether nationalized health deserves to be called socialist or Marxist. (Yes.) We never heard the term "Bolshevik" invoked during the health care debate, but I think the president chose the label for being the most antique and, to the twenty-first-century-ear, most outlandish, and thus the most likely to cue reflexive laughter.

To wit: A smattering of applause arose from the Republican ranks at the mention of "Bolshevik plot," as though some Republicans actually believed Obama had delivered a witty zinger. On the contrary, the president had put them on notice as to what was politically incorrect and thus diss-able, which is quite different. Suggesting that nationalized health care had "Bolshevik" origins was ridiculous, he was saying, while arguing that it was a "plot" was crazy. Further, such talk was only one step away from conspiracy theory (total looney tunes!). Bolshevik plot? Bob Dole? Are you crazy? Yuk, yuk, yuk.

Would that some Republican, any Republican, had replied, *Not necessarily a "plot," sir, but a program that is indeed "Bolshevik" in conception, design, and purpose nonetheless. Government control of private sector activity, as the American people well know, is aptly described as Bolshevik—or Marxist, socialist, collectivist, statist, and, for that matter, fascist, too. Indeed, nationalized health care was one of the first programs enacted by the Bolsheviks after they seized power in 1917. (Banks, insurance companies and means of communications were also taken over by Soviet authorities immediately.*[56] *Further, it is worth noting that one of the most prominent early champions of nationalized health insurance and socialized medicine in this country, Henry Sigerist, was a notorious apologist for Stalin, including his state-engineered famine in the Ukraine. According to historian John F. Hutchinson, Sigerist "shared with the architects of Soviet health policy under Stalin an outlook best described as medical totalitarianism. He really believed that humanity would be better off if every individual were under the medical supervision of the state from the cradle to the grave . . . Sigerist's belief in the necessity for state control over all aspects of medicine ultimately made him an apologist for state control over most aspects of human life."*[57]

But no.

It's always no. Such rejoinders, such logical deductions from the conservative side, the side left to defend the republic as founded, come few and far between. At almost every challenge, the bastions of tradition run up a white flag. It's almost as if they've been neutralized, neutered even, as though there were nothing left on the inside. Could it be that emptiness, reluctance to stand on and defend tradition and its institutions, a shaky hold on principle, a failure to draw conclusions and make judgments, are the real legacy of the "American Century"?

If so, who really won all of those wars?

CHAPTER TWO

For equilibrium's sake, the solid ground of conventional wisdom, circa 1989, holds great attraction. That was the year the captive nations of the USSR's "Eastern Bloc" began to reconstitute themselves as free-standing states for the first time since the Soviets forced what Winston Churchill famously named the "Iron Curtain" over half of Europe at the end of World War II. Climactically, 1989 was also the year that the Berlin Wall, erected twenty-eight years earlier, with its checkpoints, mines, trip wires, and bunkers, crumbled in a stupendous preview of the pending implosion of the evil empire itself.

Remarkable how the phrase "evil empire," particularly when framed in the quotation marks of irony, still evokes the indelible image of cartoonish "cowboys" playing at "Star Wars." Under battering assault by an arsenal of psychological weapons that began with Soviet propaganda and ended with domestic peer pressure, the West was made more uncomfortable by the *phrase* "evil empire" than by the evil of the empire itself. It still is.

"All Chekists," Lenin instructed his secret police on December 25, 1919, "have to be on the alert to shoot anyone who doesn't turn up to work because of 'Nikola' [St. Nicholas's Day]."[2] Seventy-two years later, on another December 25, the USSR officially dissolved. It was 1991, and the United States could suddenly lay claim to a shotless final triumph over Lenin's police state. It was a grand victory that seemed to be due at least partly to the ascendance of a more robust wing of the American Right in the preceding decade. Anti-Communist aspects of U.S. foreign policy had finally repulsed Soviet Communist expansionism, it seemed, thanks in decisive part to the fortunate happenstance of Ronald Reagan. The conventional chorus lists other factors—the deep rot of Communist "planned economies," the advent of the so-called reformer Gor-

bachev and his policies of perestroika and glasnost, Poland's Solidarity movement and the Pope John Paul II effect—but within this same context it seems
fair to say Reagan was the singular catalyst, not to mention a lucky break, a political foundling who was only uneasily adopted by the Republican Establishment after he made it to the White House. This was something he accomplished
without following (or leaving behind) a line of political bread crumbs. At the
same time, however, these seemingly victorious policies ("peace through
strength," support for anti-Soviet forces in the third world, "trust but verify,"
Strategic Defense Initiative) promulgated by Cold Warriors far from home
proved wholly impotent stateside.

   Here, since even before the earliest days of the twentieth century, the riddling, boring penetration of Marxian beliefs—through the influx of true believers from Europe and Russia, through the conversion to true belief of new
Marxists at home, and through campaigns of Soviet disinformation and other
"active measures"—advanced mainly unchecked. The ideological war abroad,
or, more accurately, the *anti*-ideological war abroad—because, as Robert Conquest reminds us, the West, unlike the USSR, "did not have a universal and
exclusively defined mind-set"—was lost on all fronts in the battlespace at home:
in the academy, in the media, in the popular culture, in the arts, and in the
zeitgeist up and down Main Street and even, or perhaps especially, along capitalism's main thoroughfare, Wall Street.[3] It was as if we opposed an enemy
Over There without noticing that great chunks of his ideology had taken root,
flourished, and borne collectivist and thus anti-American fruit Over Here.

   I'm not just referring to those most radical elements of the early Soviet
agenda (the original "Bolshevik plot," as President Obama might have said)
that became Western fixtures even as they were, ironically, reversed under Stalin in the 1930s when they proved to be destabilizing to the young regime.
These would include the de-sacralization and legal diminishment of marriage
(state boosterism of marriage became apparent in 1936 when wedding rings
became available in state-run stores), quick 'n' easy divorce (curtailed in 1936,
largely abolished in 1944), "freedom of abortion" (abolished in 1936), and the
elevation of children's rights to the detriment of parental authority ("respect"
for elders became a theme in state-controlled press by 1935).[4]

   Such "antibourgeois" ideas, however, would become the basis of Western
manners and mores. Sometimes specifically ascribed to the 1920s writings of
Italian Marxist Antonio Gramsci or the later teachings of the so-called Frankfurt School, other times seen as spillover from the wellspring of early twentieth-
century "socialist" and "progressive" political and educational movements, in
recent times repackaged as "Alinskyite," such ideas, rising from the same Marxian wellspring, have flooded, saturated, and finally warped those bastions of

Western civilization that conservatives, by definition, feel compelled to defend—*just as though those bastions of Western civilization were still bastions.* Secure places. Enduring repositories. Eternally unchanged by all the meticulously, continuously documented breaching. In fact, the biggest problem today is with the bastions. They're not secure, they're not enduring, and they have been breached.

Broadly, these bastions include Christianity itself, the concept of "patriarchy" and family, and all safeguards of nationhood and traditional culture. My purpose is less to trace the weblike and overlapping origins of the ideas that have undermined these institutions than it is to recognize their common endgame—a place, a world, where these same core Western institutions are no more.

Funny, but wasn't that the endgame of the defunct USSR, the raison d'être of junk-heaped Marxism-Leninism? That's a serious question, something to ask while tripping over the strong bonds and common cause shared by America's enemies and their American friends. The sugarcoater of my enemy, the empathizer with my enemy, the enabler of my enemy, is my . . . what?

Whatever he is, he's still with us. Failing to see in Soviet collapse the failure and corruption of the overbearing state, the statist Left has in fact been buoyant, both in spirit and at the polls in these first post-Soviet decades. I don't mean to suggest that Communist Party members have been winning elections—at least not in the United States. Then again, they don't have to *win* to win: The collectivist agenda advances. (It was a positively crowing CPUSA leader Sam Webb who in May 2010 addressed his assembled masses in New York City to take stock of Communist Party gains—all policies or actions initiated by President Barack Obama.[5]) In fact, David Horowitz argues that "the one consequence of note" of the disappearance of the Soviet bloc has been to reenergize the Left's assault on the West: "It has lifted the burden of having to defend . . . an indefensible regime. Because the utopian vision is no longer anchored in the reality of an actually existing socialist state, the left can now indulge its nihilistic agenda without restraint."[6]

That sounds good, very neat, but I think something else is going on. Something in the wider society and across the political spectrum is permitting the Communistic Left an untrammeled indulgence: the gross fraud of sundering Communist theory from Communist practice, of detaching support for Communism from any moral responsibility for its crimes, of exempting those same crimes from judgment and punishment. The overlooked fact is that so much of the "utopian vision" that Horowitz refers to is now deeply anchored in the *reality of our own actually existing state*—and state of mind—and bastions as defended by the political Right. It is the success of the Marx-inspired drive deep into the tissues of the West that is connected to the perplexing vitality of that Marx-inspired agenda.

A clue to the extent of the penetration may be extracted from the seeming oddity that we Americans, as a free people, as Westerners, as a civilization idealizing the autonomy of the individual, never sought to claim "victory," ideological or otherwise, over superstate Communism at the apparent end of the Cold War. No consensus clicked over signs that an unalloyed U.S.-led triumph over Communism had taken place, that a truly moral victory of freedom over totalitarianism had occurred, that the forces of good—for sure, the forces of *better*—had at last triumphed over the forces of a demonstrable, nonabstract evil as attested to by all objective examinations of Gulag or Chekist or famine or purge history.

Was this hollow reaction due to the "crisis of confidence" we hear about, that "PC"-inculcated failure to believe in the worth of the West? I used to think exactly that and no more, that the postmodern West, conned past a point of sheepish self-effacement to wallow, gratefully, in a slough of self-loathing, no longer saw anything of value in itself and was thus no longer able to take pride in or even succor at the demise of its nemesis. *After all, who's to say the Western system is qualitatively better than any other?*

However, the crisis itself doesn't tell the whole story. That is, recognizing the disease isn't the same as identifying its cause, how and when it was contracted, its full impact, or the patient's prognosis. After all, there comes a point at which the crisis has passed—even a crisis of confidence—and then what? Has that point come and gone? When I look at the out-and-out antagonism the West directs toward its own foundational pillars, I see not a West that simply fails to appreciate itself anymore, but rather a West that *isn't itself anymore.*

This concept offers another perspective from which to see the fact that even as the walls of Communism came tumbling down in the final decade of the twentieth century, the official American tone was noticeably reticent; there was almost an air of embarrassment over witnessing the USSR at such a colossal disadvantage. This tortured psychological condition was not unlike "the embarrassment widely felt in some American circles about possession of the atom bomb," as Cold War historian Adam Ulam wrote in 1972. Ulam was describing the immediate aftermath of World War II when, as he put it, some people had "the feeling that somehow it was *not fair* for the U.S. to enjoy a monopoly of this weapon" (emphasis added).[7] Of course, due to the success of a vast, Soviet-directed conspiracy, that monopoly didn't last more than the four years between the U.S. atomic test in 1945 and the USSR atomic test in 1949. By 1953, Julius and Ethel Rosenberg were executed for their roles in the conspiracy, triggering an open-ended argument over their culpability that became ingrained in the American psyche to a point where even archival documentation of their guilt fails to fill in the worn cultural groove entirely. Meanwhile, the argument went, the Russians would have gotten the bomb by themselves eventually, so what's the difference?

The question mark here masks a complete lack of comprehension when it comes to discerning any possible distinction between nuclear-enhanced Gulag might and nuclear-enhanced constitutional rights. Instead, the question mark here perversely signals the train of thought's terminus in the brick wall of "moral equivalence."

What's the difference? USSR, USA, they're both big bullies.

The successful Soviet atomic test in 1949 thoroughly unnerved Americans, generating jitters over international Communist aggression and new fears of domestic Communist penetration that would be investigated most sensationally, but by no means uniquely, by Senator Joseph McCarthy beginning in 1950. It also had tangibly cataclysmic results. On April 5, 1951, Judge Irving R. Kaufman stated, in sentencing the Rosenbergs to death, that the scientific consensus of the day was that the theft of atomic secrets in the 1940s accelerated the development of a Soviet atomic bomb by several years. This accelerated Soviet acquisition of atomic capability, Kaufman continued, "caused the Communist aggression in Korea, with the resultant casualties exceeding 50,000 and who knows but that millions more of innocent people may pay the price of your treason."[8] It was Kaufman's conclusion that the treachery of these American Communists and their accomplices had directly led to the 1950 outbreak of the Korean War.

Today, archival evidence, unearthed by researchers in Russia and released in the United States, proves Judge Kaufman to have been correct. "Absent an atomic bomb, Stalin would not have unleashed Pyongyang's army to conquer the entire Korean peninsula," Herbert Romerstein and Eric Breindel, authors of *The Venona Secrets: Exposing Soviet Espionage and America's Traitors,* concluded in 2000. "Confident that his possession of atomic weapons neutralized America's strategic advantage, Stalin was emboldened to unleash war in Korea in 1950," John Earl Haynes, Harvey Klehr, and Alexander Vassiliev, authors of *Spies: The Rise and Fall of the KGB in America,* wrote in 2009. These latter authors further contended that Soviet espionage, which ended up crippling America's ability to read Soviet military communications, also ensured that the invasion of South Korea was a surprise "for which American forces were unprepared."[9]

I'm guessing this revelation—that Soviet possession of an atomic bomb in 1949, due to the treachery of American Communists, helped *precipitate* the Korean War in 1950—is new to many readers, particularly those who have long been taught to believe that Rosenberg guilt, even when ultimately if reluctantly acknowledged, was largely a matter of "personal conscience" or political conviction, and not in any way an issue of national security. This is the typical response to this day. For example, even the landmark work *The Haunted Wood,* the 1999 book by Allen Weinstein and Alexander Vassiliev that amasses voluminous evidence of American treason on Moscow's behalf during the New Deal (1930s) and war years (1940s), ultimately assesses this same evidence in the most personal terms: namely, the impact of this concerted and aggressive campaign of theft and subversion *on the agents themselves.* Their "enduring legacy," the authors sum up in their final line, "remains one of inglorious constancy to a cruel and discredited cause."[10] Such minimization of the link between personal cause and global effect is typical, even among the greatest scholars of Soviet espionage. There has been scant attempt, to continue with the Rosenberg example, to connect their treachery with its impact: to connect the theft of nuclear technology with 36,940 Americans killed, 91,134 wounded, and 8,176 still missing in action in a war that claimed at least two million civilian lives on both sides.[11]

Instead, we look back on an exhausting struggle over *whether* such Communist penetration existed in the first place. Communist penetration existed—the historical record amply and redundantly confirms this—but endless wrangling even today wards off a comprehensive reckoning of the impact of that penetration. Undoubtedly, this is the purpose of some of the wranglers. Like a magic word denoting an atavistic taboo, the term "McCarthyism," used as an epithet, still stymies debate, while the nagging phrase "looking for a Communist under every bed" still dampens the blazing import of declassified revelations from the archives. The fact that there *were* hidden Communists practically everywhere, and probably under the bed, too, remains stuck in the limbo between old, discredited theories, and new, confirmed realities. Somehow, we never get around to judging the effects, the impact of Communism itself, whether that impact is something as concrete as a body count or something as vaporous as a sensibility. That's why after seventy years of diligently chronicled crime, cataloged, sourced, witnessed, and experienced (the luminous names of Elinor Lipper, David Dallin, Victor Kravchenko, and, of course, Aleksandr Solzhenitsyn spring to mind, as well as Robert Conquest), the recent confirmations of guilt often show up as mere technicalities, relegated to footnotes, small type, and back pages. The reckoning eludes us.

So it *still* wasn't fair, this time in 1989, to bear exacting witness to the unraveling of seven-plus decades of Communist horror, terror, perversion, and epochal loss—and especially not from the fat and happy vantage point of the "Reagan 1980s." Better to extend to the Soviet Union the official courtesy of not acknowledging, not noticing, the systemically rotten reasons for Communist decay, as though nothing more significant were occurring on the world stage than a colossal wardrobe malfunction. Writing in April 1991, eight months before the USSR's official dissolution, *New York Times* columnist William Safire noted, "We are so careful to avoid the appearance of triumphalism—with Mr. Bush murmuring his twin mantras of 'mustn't gloat' and 'mustn't get sucked in'—that we risk watching the triumph of capitalism over Communism turn into a series of internal disasters posing external dangers."[12]

Oh, right. That would have been George H. W. Bush presiding. Funny how the mind's eye sometimes sees Reagan in the Oval Office for these events. No, it was Bush père, all right, and he, as Leader of the Free World, quickly set the scrupulously nonjudgmental and even supplicating tone that marks the era. This began with Bush's very first post–Berlin Wall conference with Mikhail Gorbachev, the last dictator—or, as they were more tastefully titled, the last "general secretary"—of the USSR.

Two decades after the historic Bush-Gorbachev shipboard get-together off the island-state of Malta, the transcripts released by the Gorbachev Foundation (the U.S. record, shockingly, remains classified at the George H. W. Bush Library in Texas[13]) make for revealing, if also startling reading. If you didn't know better, you might think the United States had just lost a war or something.

"I hope you have noticed that while the changes in Eastern Europe have been going on, the United States has not engaged in condescending statements aimed at damaging the Soviet Union," Bush was quick to point out in that first meeting with Gorbachev aboard the Soviet cruise ship *Maxim Gorky*. Indeed, in opening remarks, Bush offered Gorbachev an array of economic carrots and no sticks—i.e., no quid pro quo. Such carrots included Most Favored Nation status and eased access to Western credit. That wasn't all. Bush then stressed America's desire to continue to *safeguard Soviet prestige*: "We have attempted to construct our proposals in a way that does not give the impression that America is 'saving' the Soviet Union. We are not talking about a plan of assistance but about a plan for cooperation."[14]

The extent of this "cooperation" to keep the USSR intact would become publicly embarrassing for Bush when in August 1991 in Kiev, Ukraine, he gave a speech panning "suicidal nationalism" and urging the Soviet "republic" not to vote itself independent of the Moscow monolith. In Safire's words, this became immortalized as the "Chicken Kiev speech." In 2004, the columnist would reveal that Bush had not spoken to him since.[15]

Bush, of course, saw—or wanted to see, or wanted the world to see—Gorbachev as a "reformer" he could work with. He staked his presidency on it, as national security expert Angelo Codevilla has noted, and thus acted to preserve the status quo, i.e., Gorbachev's power.[16] The context of Soviet decline—the blood, the sweat, the fear-stained annals of Communist history—all of that was just some extraneous "vision-thing." As far as this forty-first president of the United States was concerned, the apparent U.S.–USSR endgame was no more significant than a Toyota-Ford contest: Ford had taken a big hit, and Toyota "mustn't gloat" while they both set out together to expand market share. This approach to the crisis in totalitarianism depended on continuity in all things, and that included maintaining the official silence that left the millions killed and ruined by Communists in open-ended and unmarked anonymity.

Thus it is that in reading the 1989 Malta transcripts we glimpse an eager-to-please Bush encountering a downright insolent Gorbachev. Think of it. The Soviet dictatorship is foundering on top of a "planned economy" in ruins even as its captive nations are breaking away. Incredibly, Gorbachev proceeds to admonish Bush about "the export of American values" and "Western values." (This was the same point of pique Gorbachev had raised a day earlier in a meeting at the Vatican with Pope John Paul II.[17]) *Even more incredibly, Bush takes it.* In what is described as a private, one-on-one session with Bush, Gorbachev said, "I cannot accept it when some American politicians say that the process of overcoming the split in Europe—should be based on Western values."[18]

I cannot accept it? Bear in mind that what Gorbachev is calling "the split in Europe" is the apparent breakaway of nations ruined by Communism, territories seized nearly a half century earlier by the USSR, as British historian Gregor Dallas has pointed out, exactly according to the brutish division of Europe as laid out in the secret protocol of the 1939 Nazi-Soviet Pact—sans Nazis.[19] Gorbachev "cannot accept" that such societies, at that moment deep in death throes, should be "split" from Moscow and saved by "Western," i.e., free-market, freedom-based principles. Nonetheless, he would soon find a way to accept the $45 billion in aid that would be gushing his way, a massive flow of largesse created by those same robust Western values.[20] It was all "take" and no "give," and might well have prompted Lenin himself to posit his trademark power question: "Who—whom?" Who had prevailed over whom?

Gorbachev went on to push a related point. "It seems that earlier we were blamed for the 'export of revolution,' and now they speak about the export of American values. I believe this goes against the spirit of today's changes."[21]

Here, just at the precise historical date when what you might call the consumer nations of the Eastern Bloc appeared to be returning all Communist imports to sender—ideology, police state, poverty, secrecy—Gorbachev was still pressing ahead with a corollary of "moral equivalence": If the Soviets "were blamed" for exporting "revolution" (police state), then the Americans were equally at fault for exporting "American values" (rule of law). It was as though dictatorship and constitutional government were interchangeable, a fallacy that Gorbachev (b. 1931), a blinkered, censored, molded creation of the Soviet state narrative, had no reason to question.

Yes, the "visionary reformer" gloss on "Gorby" was thin from the start. As far back as November 1985, six months after Gorbachev "took" office, *The New York Times* reported, almost incredulously, on Gorbachev's apparent internalization of Soviet disinformation about the United States. It was during the run-up to Gorbachev's first meeting with Ronald Reagan in Geneva, and the paper quoted unnamed diplomats noting how closely Gorbachev's conversation echoed *Pravda* editorials. One added, "There may be an element of posturing and calculated propaganda, but *all the evidence suggests that the man sincerely believes these things*" (emphasis added).

Such evidence includes this nugget: "The diplomats said Mr. Gorbachev, who was more combative and argumentative than he had been in previous meetings with Americans, challenged almost every statement made by [Secretary of State George Shultz] about the United States. They said, for example, that *he refused to accept Mr. Shultz's depiction of the United States as a source of military hardware and other aid to the Soviet Union in World War II, belittling the lend-lease program*"[22] (emphasis added).

When I read this, I knew from long-ago history classes and reading ever since that Gorbachev was plain dead wrong (brainwashed himself) and/or flat-out lying (brainwashing others). George Shultz's "depiction" of Uncle Sam as "a wartime supplier" to the USSR was a fact. It was also a gross if not also grotesque understatement. What's known as Lend-Lease, now dimly recalled (usually in association with Britain's war effort and rarely as the program FDR sold to Congress as a means to keep America *out* of the Second World War[23]), was crucial to the Soviet Union's World War II victory over Hitler's Germany.

But did I know that FDR gave Lend-Lease aid to Russia a priority that superseded all Allied military needs—*including American military needs?*

No.

Did I know that the Lend-Lease program provided much more than war supplies to the USSR—that massive lots of *post*war supplies (which quickly became Soviet Cold War supplies) were thrown in with the deluxe deal?

No.

Did I know that such supplies also included the materials that go into making an atomic bomb—chemicals, metals, minerals *up to and including uranium?*

Again, no. Why were these salient details not included in the standard narratives? This question became as intriguing as the lost record itself, which exists, or rather languishes, on a dust heap of history all its own.

"After Hitler invaded the USSR in June [1941], U.S. war supplies flowed to

the Soviet Union as well [as Britain], despite American hostility to communism," says the one single sentence on the subject of Lend-Lease to Russia in
the current AP U.S. history textbook—the one concept Americans are ever
expected to know on the subject. I'm going to leave aside, just for the moment,
that supposed "American hostility to communism," a problematic statement
given the crippling extent to which we know *without doubt* that all echelons of
the United States government were riddled with Moscow-loyal agents and fellow travelers—and when I say "all echelons," I mean *all* echelons, something
I'll be getting to.

War supplies didn't just "flow" to the Soviet Union, they flooded it, with
over half a million trucks and jeeps, nearly $1 billion worth (1940s dollars) of
ordnance and ammunition, thousands of fighter aircraft, bombers, and tanks,
13 million pairs of winter boots, 1.7 million tons of petroleum products, a merchant fleet, 1,000 steam locomotives, 581 naval vessels including minesweepers,
landing craft, submarine chasers, frigates, torpedo boats, floating dry docks,
pontoon barges, river tugs, and a light cruiser.[24] There were also icebreakers,
which were essential to keep the northernmost ports of the Gulag Archipelago
supplied with fresh slaves, another "lost" fact.[25] American Lend-Lease didn't
just keep the Soviet police state humming along internally, either. As Nikita
Khrushchev would say to *Life* magazine in 1970 of those half a million trucks
and jeeps, "Just imagine how we would have advanced from Stalingrad to Berlin without them!"[26]

OK, I'm game. Let's imagine. What Khrushchev seems to have been saying
is that without all those American wheels, the Soviets *wouldn't have been able
to advance the roughly 1,400 miles from Stalingrad to Berlin,* occupying the nations of Eastern Europe in between for the next four and a half decades.

Clearly, on challenging Shultz about Lend-Lease, Gorbachev should have
had his knuckles rapped, diplomatically speaking, what with all the made-in-
USA munitions stockpiles, diesel engines, entire prefab factories, and hydroelectric plants that he must have tripped over as a youngster in the postwar
Soviet Union. Hundreds of thousands of patents—literally, as estimated by a
congressional committee[27]—made their way to the Soviet Union under Lend-
Lease, including secret military blueprints (more on that below) and, of course,
those atomic research goodies. And I'm barely scraping the surface of the Soviet Lend-Lease catalog, which, as noted above, also included plenty of non-
military supplies: for example, a tire plant, an oil refinery, an unstated number
of pipe-fabricating works, nearly one million miles of copper wire (that would
remain on a twenty-acre lot in Westchester County until shipment to the USSR
near the very end of the war), tens of millions of dollars' worth of switchboard
panels and parts, lathes and power tools for metal working, machinery for

textiles, woodworking, and typesetting, cranes, hoists, derricks, elevators, air compressors, coal cutters, and rock drills, not to mention $152 million in women's "dress goods," 18.4 million pounds of writing paper, and assorted cigarette cases, compacts, jeweled watches, lipstick, liquor, ten bathtubs, two pianos, and, intriguingly, one tobacco pipe. As George Kennan would write, understating, at the war's endgame, there was "no adequate justification for continuing a program of lavish and almost indiscriminate aid to the Soviet Union at a time when there was increasing reason to doubt whether her purposes in Eastern Europe, aside from the defeat of Germany, would be ones which we Americans could approve and sponsor."[28]

Was the continuous Lend-Lease supply line to Soviet Russia, then, a case of government inertia, or was there some other justification worth ferreting out from our lost history? Could it have had anything to do with the curious priority the U.S. government attached to Soviet Lend-Lease superseding other Allied and *even American military needs*? (As for American civilian needs, the 217,660,666 pounds of butter shipped to the USSR during a time of strict stateside rationing offers a quick read on U.S. government priorities.[29]) Here, for example, from orders issued on January 1, 1943, to Maj. George Racey Jordan, a supervisory "expediter" of Soviet Lend-Lease aid who was stationed at the Great Falls, Montana, hub of the Soviet pipeline, is what that priority looked like in black and white:

> 1. The President has directed that "airplanes be delivered in accordance with protocol schedules by the most expeditious means." To implement these directives, the modification, equipment and movement of *Russian planes have been given first priority, even over planes for U.S. Army Air Forces* [emphasis added].[30]

Jordan would tell Congress in December 1949 that he kept this presidential directive on his person to show presumably incredulous fellow servicemen, such as the U.S. Air Force colonel who, Jordan notes in his essential 1952 memoir of Lend-Lease, *From Major Jordan's Diaries,* was flummoxed when Jordan informed him that his mission would be held up due to Soviet "first priority." "He went around muttering, '*First* priority! I'll be damned.' He asked me whether many Air Force pilots knew about this. I told him that they found out about it when they hit Great Falls and tried to enter the [Russian] Pipeline" (emphasis in original).[31]

What does it mean that FDR gave Soviet supply this singular urgency as soon as it was politically feasible following Nazi Germany's invasion of Soviet Russia on June 22, 1941?

The search for answers to this admittedly offbeat question is not a comforting exercise. Items such as the following about the rush of military supplies to the USSR during the fall of 1941 start popping up. Paul Johnson writes in *Modern Times* that this yeoman supply effort to Moscow tipped the balance for Stalin "during that first desperate winter"—but at what cost? As Johnson notes, such supplies "included 200 modern fighter aircraft, intended originally for Britain's highly vulnerable base in Singapore, which had virtually no modern fighters at all. The diversion of these aircraft (plus tanks) to Russia sealed the fate of Singapore."[32]

Singapore, which would fall on February 15, 1942, a giant morale crusher, was in the Pacific. From the start, the Pacific War didn't count. From the start, the Soviet war counted more.

Even after December 7, 1941, when Japan attacked Pearl Harbor?

Yes.

Even after December 8, when Japan attacked 151,000 Americans and Filipinos stationed in the U.S. protectorate of the Philippines?[33]

Yes. Why?

On December 10, 1941, eighty-six Japanese bombers attacked and sank the British battleship *Prince of Wales* and battle cruiser *Repulse* north of Singapore. This was a stunning disaster costing the lives of more than eight hundred British sailors, including Admiral Sir Tom Phillips, the highest Allied officer to die in action during the war. As Churchill's physician and biographer Lord Moran noted on more than one occasion, these appalling losses always haunted Churchill, who had insisted on this mission.[34] The warships had no air cover.

Of course, Russia did. Remember the two hundred modern fighters Paul Johnson noted were diverted from Singapore to the USSR? "The diversion of these aircraft (plus tanks) . . . sealed the fate of Singapore," he writes, the implication being such air support would have been crucial to a successful effort to repulse or even forestall the Japanese onslaught on Singapore. "Thus," Johnson concludes, "by one of the great ironies of history, Churchill, the last major British imperialist, may have sacrificed a liberal empire in order to preserve a totalitarian one."[35] When Singapore fell to the Japanese on February 15, 1942, more than one hundred thousand British forces surrendered. This haunted Churchill, too.

Washington, meanwhile, only had eyes for Moscow. "The need to meet monthly protocol schedules and shipping dates took precedence over everything else," notes George C. Herring in his 1973 history of Soviet Lend-Lease. As no-strings, zero-interest supplies earmarked for Moscow became available, Herring continues, "they were set aside for the Russians under absolute priority over the competing demands of Britain and the United States." No military misgivings based on *national interests* slowed the gears of war production for the Soviet Union as ordered by FDR. Again, quoting Herring, "He [FDR] left no doubt of the importance he attached to aid to Russia. 'I would go out and take the stuff off the shelves of the stores,' he told [Treasury Secretary Henry] Morgenthau on March 11, 1942, 'and pay them any price necessary, and put it in a truck and rush it to the boat . . . Nothing would be worse than to have the Russians collapse.' "[36]

Nothing would be worse? Not even, for example, the collapse of those 151,000 American and Filipino troops who, at this touching moment of solicitude in the Oval Office for the Red Army, had just begun their fourth month of unreinforced, unsupplied, death-defying resistance to a massive, concentrated Japanese assault on Bataan and Corregidor? It just happens that also on March 11, 1942, under Roosevelt's order, Gen. Douglas MacArthur was attempting to slip through the Japanese blockade and leave the American island protectorate to take up command of the Southwest Pacific in Australia. By Morgenthau's account, however, Roosevelt's thoughts were still elsewhere: "I would rather lose New Zealand, Australia or anything else than have the Russian front collapse."[37]

Why? What accounts for this unusual level of anxiety? And why does it matter now? To take the last question first, it matters now because FDR is included among the top American presidents every time a newspaper or university or blue-ribbon committee assembles "experts" to vote; and because there are in FDR's solicitude clues to important lessons we've never learned about ourselves as a nation. Quite unexpectedly, it turns out, the search for the lost history of American betrayal takes an unexpected detour through World War II. There is something in what I can now only think of as Roosevelt's "Soviet First" policy—Lend-Lease was just the beginning—that I believe offers a key to understanding much that has always puzzled me about subsequent American history. It's not hindsight alone that brings this into focus now, but rather a new, archivally informed hindsight. In other words, the evidence gleaned from archives in Moscow and Washington, which opened after the USSR dissolved in 1991, explains more than Cold War secrets. I believe it enables us to see into the murky beginnings of cultural relativism and other conditions that mark us to this day.

"They were the only Americans in the world at this time who were fighting the enemy, yet the flood of weapons from their country's arsenals was being rushed to every other battle front but theirs." So wrote Col. Warren J. Clear, an intelligence officer under MacArthur at Bataan.[38] In his 1962 book *Reminiscences,* Gen. Douglas MacArthur revealed details about the crisis on the Philippines unknown to the American public for the two decades since it took place:

Although Admiral King felt the fleet did not have sufficient resources to proceed to Manila, it was my impression that our Navy deprecated its own strength and might well have cut through to relieve our hard-pressed forces. The bulk of the Jap Navy was headed south to seize Borneo, Malaya, and Indo-China. American carriers having escaped destruction at Pearl Harbor could have brought planes to the Philippines. The Navy fought the next two years and had great victories without any new ships.

But a top-level decision had long before been reached that the Atlantic war came first, no matter what the cost in the Far East. President Roosevelt and Prime Minister Churchill, in a Washington conference after the attack on Pearl Harbor, reaffirmed a policy to concentrate first on the defeat of Germany . . . Unfortunately, I was not informed of any of these vital conferences and believed that a brave effort at relief was in the making.[39]

As MacArthur only later found out—"truth," John Hersey wrote, came in "mean little doses"[40]—the Allied strategy focused on dispatching Nazi Germany, which resulted in the "Soviet First" policy. Defeating Japan could wait. So, too, it seemed, could MacArthur's forces. They would fight the Japanese on the Philippines from December 8, 1941—a day that does *not* "live in infamy" or really anything else in our collective memory—until their surrender six terrible months later. Hitler's Germany simply had to be stopped before it destroyed Stalin's Russia—or is it that Stalin's Russia had to be *saved* before Hitler's Germany destroyed it?—and at any cost, including those 151,000 troops in the Pacific.

Then there were the catastrophic Allied losses along the North Atlantic shipping supply route to the USSR. Washington may have determined that it was too dangerous to supply Americans and Filipinos in the Philippines, but no losses were too high to stop supplying the USSR. And were they ever high. In July 1942, for example, only eleven out of thirty-five merchant ships in the supply convoy to Murmansk known as PQ-17 survived unceasing German attacks.[41]

Could a supply effort to MacArthur have possibly cost more in men and matériel? Is there something wrong, really wrong, with this picture as drawn by the intelligence officer and the general—something that evades the frame of national memory? I realize these questions take shape outside the scope and boundary of popular history—the bestselling books, the moist-eyed reminiscences, the landmark photographs, the Oscar-winning movies, the acclaimed TV miniseries—all of which fuel the residual glow around American involvement in World War II. Even today, Americans recall with practically eyewitness certitude a war narrative that unspools with the attack on Pearl Harbor, somehow overlaps the Battle of Britain (which ended in 1940), and climaxes with

D-day. Images such as the flag raising at Iwo Jima, the mushroom cloud over Hiroshima, and the kiss in Times Square pop up to disconnected but powerful effect.

My questions make me uneasy even as I ask them, even as I know at least some of the answers. My quandary is not unlike that of a mystery writer. The difference is I'm trying to lay a trail of clues that identify not just an unnoticed criminal but an unnoticed crime. An unimagined crime. An unnoticed, un-imagined crime of Communist penetration *and therefore influence,* not only on the course of American postwar policy—a story we grasp, if only incompletely, as the notorious "betrayal at Yalta" that left Eastern Europe to Soviet designs, circa 1945—but also on the formation of America's shining moment on the world stage. I refer to World War II, even now our talisman of a moral, mighty past unbowed by postmodern doubt and multicultural division.

I might as well begin by saying we don't know the half of it, which, in an odd way, takes some of the sting out of Gorbachev's Lend-Lease lie. That is, we have our own narrative of gross omission, and it turns out to be just as factually challenged as his. Whether Gorbachev disbelieved in the indisputable fact of Lend-Lease (testament to the powers of Soviet propaganda to twist even its own dictators), or simply wanted the West to disbelieve in it (testament to the Soviet resolve to spread disinformation whenever and wherever possible), or even both at the same time, history as a record of real events itself long ago disappeared from view in Communist Russia. It was either imprisoned, liter-ally, in the shackled witness of millions of prisoners in the Gulag Archipelago, or it was hidden in the resulting and no less terrifying Gulag of the furtive, fearful mind. Or, more prosaically, it was simply locked away in secret state files. History became verboten when Soviet Man was compelled to sacrifice truth to fear.

So what is our excuse? If Soviet overlords brutally and forcibly locked the truth and the truth tellers away, we in the West freely blind ourselves to facts while ignoring or deriding our truth tellers out of existence.

Why?

One answer is that it is easier to muffle truth than act on it, definitely more pleasant. Better to inhabit a faux-sophisticated atmosphere free of Koestler's "Cassandra cries," where, in the luxe-y limbo of "moral equivalence," no one had to do anything heroic, or plan or even think anything confrontationally challenging. So much easier to stifle the occasional and always tiresome voice of dissent. In this way, the default position of moral equivalence became the or-thodoxy of twentieth-century elites, driving editorials, political platforms, so-cial activism, and even pop culture. Take the espionage fiction of British author

John le Carré, which appeared periodically throughout the Cold War beginning in 1961. Le Carré's fiction, which includes such titles as *The Spy Who
Came In from the Cold* and *Tinker, Tailor, Soldier, Spy,* did two things. First, it
painted the Cold War divide between West and East from a palette of "nuanced" "shades of gray," depicting an unresolved, unresolvable battlescape of
tonal shadows. This ideological morass "blurred" any and all distinctions between the two sides, even, remarkably, the fact that the Cheka and its spawn,
including the KGB, were central to the conduct of Soviet foreign policy, as well
as to running the one-party state, in ways Western intelligence organizations
never were and couldn't be.[42] Second, these books reliably hit Western bestseller lists. Tastefully cynical and conveniently amoral, the le Carréllian message was: East, West, Communism, capitalism, mirror images, no difference.
The impact of this message was huge. I still remember a sinking feeling when I
saw Senator Pat "Leaky" Leahy boarding a flight out of Washington, D.C.,
clutching le Carré's *A Perfect Spy.* The 1986 book is about a double agent who
languishes in exquisite torment, living a tissue of lies and all that, not knowing
one side from the other anymore. At the time, Leahy was chairman of the Senate Intelligence Committee.

Just a few years later at Malta, Gorbachev gave voice to this same familiar
fiction. "Some are beginning to speak about the 'Bush doctrine,' that is replacing the 'Brezhnev doctrine,' Gorbachev declared in 1989."[43] The implication
was, this was equally bad: that is, if the Brezhnev doctrine was out, the so-called
Bush doctrine should be out, too. George H. W. Bush failed to disagree. The
forty-first American president's response was to reassure Gorbachev he would
not be jumping "up onto the [Berlin] Wall" to hasten German reunification.

To which Gorbachev replied, "Well, jumping on the Wall is not a good activity for a president."

Transcript: "Laughter."[44]

In a later Malta session, Gorbachev again returned to this pet Soviet
peeve: "I am under the impression that U.S. leaders are now quite actively
advancing the idea of conquering the division of Europe on the basis of
'Western values.' "[45]

Again, by "the division of Europe" Gorbachev meant the Soviet-usurped
sovereignty of about one dozen nation-states. "Conquering" that "division" is
Politburo-speak for introducing rule of law, freedom of speech, and other
"Western values" in place of rule by threat and thugocracy.

Gorbachev continued, "If this premise is not solely for propaganda purposes, and they are intending to make it the basis for practical policy, then I will
say bluntly that they are committing many follies. At one time in the West there

was anxiety that the Soviet Union was planning to export revolution. But the aim of exporting 'Western values' sounds similar."

Soviet revolution (police state) vs. Western values (Bill of Rights): What's the diff?

The phrase "Western values" popped up in the American briefing books for Malta, so maybe Gorbachev's attack triggered something in the president's cranial nooks. Bush said, "What are Western values? They are, if you will, free speech, openness, lively debates. In the economic realm—stimulus for progress, a free market. These values are not something new, or of the moment . . . They unite the West. We welcome changes in [the USSR and Eastern Europe] but by no means set them against Western values."

Mild, but something at least. The Soviet ruler, however, was not assuaged. In fact, what already feels like heat on the transcript page seems to intensify. Gorbachev hotly interjected a question from his chief Marxist-Leninist theorist: "A. N. Yakovlev is asking: Why are democracy, openness, [free] market 'Western values'"?

As with Gorbachev and his reflexive denial of Lend-Lease, it's quite likely that Politburo member Yakovlev—a collective-farm boy who became a Marxist-Leninist ideologist and propagandist, head of the Communist Party propaganda department, and, later, Central Committee secretary of ideological matters—didn't know, couldn't know, the correct answer. It's possible that as a Communist propagandist he was ill equipped to trace the history of liberty in the Western world as the precious legacy of Greece and Rome, of Judaism and Christianity. Because Yakovlev, post Gorbachev, would later work to excavate the hidden toll of Soviet state crime and human suffering (atonement?), would that it were possible to interview him about this historic exchange; he died in 2005. In 1989, however, there was his question, tossing George H. W. Bush a golden educational, if not also political, softball.

Did the American president pull out a well-worn pocket edition of the Declaration of Independence and begin reading aloud?

When, Gorby, in the course of human events . . .

Or tell the Soviets the story of the English barons who in 1215 instituted rule of law by forcing the Magna Carta on tyrannical King John?

Many centuries ago, Comrade Yakovlev, in a place called Runnymede . . .

None of the above, naturally. Instead:

BUSH: It was not always that way. You personally created a start for these changes directed toward democracy and openness. Today it is really much clearer than it was, say, 20 years ago that we share these values with you.

GORBACHEV: There is no point in entering into propaganda battles.

YAKOVLEV: When you insist on "Western values," then "Eastern values" unavoidably appear, and "Southern values" . . .

GORBACHEV: Exactly. And when that happens, ideological confrontations flare up again.

BUSH: I understand and I agree. Let us try to avoid *careless words* and talk more about the content of these values. From the bottom of our hearts we welcome the changes that are taking place [emphasis added].

Those "careless words" Bush abandoned so readily stood for precise and precious facts—the truth. In the face of conflict—a Commie hissy fit—the president of the United States negotiated away that truth in exchange for Moscow's false narrative.

From the bottom of our hearts, Bush surrendered the core principles that distinguished the American republic from the "union" (vise) of "Soviet" "socialist" ones (dictatorships). In other words, Bush there and then gave away the store. In this first meeting of wasted East and robust West since the fall of the Berlin Wall, Bush conceded to Gorbachev the right to set all parameters of discussion, to control the language itself, and, therefore, crucial historical and political understandings of events. Of course, to be fair, Bush was merely sealing the deal, offering yet another extension of the legitimacy with which the United States had endowed the criminal Communist enterprise since official relations began. Gorbachev had won *again*. He replied:

That is very important. You see, as I said, the most important thing is that the changes lead to greater openness even in our relations with each other. We are beginning to become *organically integrated,* freeing ourselves from everything that divided us. What will this be called in the final analysis? I think it is a new level of relations. For that reason, for my part, I support your proposal; let us not conduct the discussion at the levels of the Church. In history this has always led to religious wars [emphasis added].

Big difference: The tragedy of religious wars within "the Church" was that all combatants worshipped the same deity. This is not the case with Communism and the West. Communism enshrines the state. The West, according to its central principles, protects the rights of the individual. There is nothing that the West—or at least the individual—gains by blurring this distinction in order to worship at a phony altar with dictators.

None of this mattered to George H. W. Bush. The day after the Malta meeting, Bush channeled his "new" U.S.-USSR understanding in an address at

NATO headquarters in Brussels. He duly emphasized that "the end to the un-natural division of Europe and Germany" should "proceed in accordance with and be based upon the values that are becoming universal ideals."[46] There was no talk, no mention, of "Western values."

In the end, Gorbachev would fail to retain Soviet power; nonetheless, he had successfully averted a crucial "Western" victory over the seven-decade-long ideological catastrophe the USSR had inflicted on the whole world, both free and unfree.

Did "universal" values fare well in the new, post-Soviet day? In Freedom House's *Freedom of the Press 2012* survey, Russia is ranked "not free." Ranked 172 out 197, Russia shares the bottom tier with Saudi Arabia, China, and Iran, trailing Pakistan and Sudan.[47] ("Not safe" is another apt designation, since fifty-three journalists have been killed in Russia since 1992.[48]) Meanwhile, "Re-ligious freedom conditions in Russia continue to deteriorate," said the 2012 annual report of the Commission on International Religious Freedom, which returned Russia to its "watch list" in 2009.[49] As for monitored Russian elections, such as the 2008 presidential election, they are increasingly deemed unfree and unfair.[50] Human rights? The Gulag network of prison camps has not reopened, but two dozen political prisoners are under lock and key, writes Vladimir Bu-kovsky, who also has called attention to the attempted resurrection in Russia of psychiatric hospitals as tools of political repression.[51] In the spring of 2012, op-position activists presented a list of thirty-nine "political prisoners."[52] Such depredations are widely noted, but merely clucked over at international gather-ings.[53] Maybe all those Russian state-owned gas and oil assets pipelining into Europe have a gagging effect.

In answer to the 64,000-ruble question—"What went wrong?"—Bukovsky cites the failure to render judgment on the Soviet system on its dissolution: "We were given a chance to win in 1991. To do it we needed a Nuremberg trial, but not a trial of people. In a country like the Soviet Union, if you tried to find all the guilty, you would end up with 19 million people, and who needs another Gulag? This isn't about punishing individuals. It's about judging the *system*."[54]

As the transcript reveals, Bush of Malta wasn't about to judge or even ac-knowledge "the system." Ultimately, neither was Boris Yeltsin, who became the first president of the new Russia. But Yeltsin's reasons, according to Bukovsky, were different from those of George Bush. Yeltsin actually enabled Bukovsky to help prepare a court case against Communism. Looking back on the period he spent digging around and extracting documents from those Soviet archives to which he was granted access, Bukovsky writes:

I spent a lot of time trying to persuade the Yeltsin government to conduct such a trial. Yeltsin finally said, "No." The reason he had to say no was *the enormous pressure he felt from the West not to have such a trial.* I've seen the cables he received from all over the world, mostly from Russian embassies, explaining that local politicians and governments were against any trials or disclosure of crimes of opening of archives. Finally Yeltsin just gave in [emphasis added].[55]

How bizarre: the enormous pressure Yeltsin felt *from the West*? After witnessing the theater of appeasement Bush staged at Malta, it's hard to be entirely surprised. Still, it does remain baffling, particularly without preparatory context. The Free World, as I began this chapter arguing, had every reason to put Communism on trial in some way: to vindicate and showcase the free-market system, to justify treasury-draining military and related expenditures throughout the Cold War, to memorialize the tens of millions of people lost to Communism's inhumanity. "Never again," however, became the vow never taken. Why?

Once again, the West as we think of it just isn't the West *as it is.* Bukovsky explains:

Because of the documents I recovered [in Soviet archives], we now understand why the West was so against putting the communist system on trial. It is not only that the West was infiltrated by the Soviets much deeper than we ever thought, but also that there was ideological collaboration between left-wing parties in the West and Soviet Union. *This ideological collaboration ran very deep* [emphasis added].

Deeper Soviet infiltration and deeper Western ideological collaboration made all the difference. On a pop cultural level, what Bukovsky describes sounds more like the premise of *The Invasion of the Body Snatchers,* the sci-fi cult classic about the secret infiltration and subversion of an entire town via alien "pods," than any Cold War history or thriller I can think of. The horror of *Body Snatchers* stems from the pod-people's surface normalcy, which masks their transformation within. Increasingly, they are on or of the Other Side. Seeing this story as a metaphor for the eroding West, we might see that with so many "pod-people," declaring victory over the Soviet Union became impossible. How could a society, a people, a civilization have been "turned"? Apathy has made the answer elusive—and could that be another effect of the compromised condition? It would certainly explain our failure as a society to pass judgment on the crimes of Communism, which, as tabulated in the seminal 1999 work *The Black Book of Communism,* destroyed some one hundred million lives. Ditto for our failures to pass judgment more generally on the array of Marx-inspired assaults and threats against bedrock, traditional society. These include assaults on social pillars ("traditional" marriage, "traditional" family) and constitutional principles (individual liberty). These gigantic manifestations of nonjudgmentalism, a kind of society-wide suspension of moral acting that is crucial to the spread, by the way, of cultural relativism, are the distinctive social phenomena of our time.

All of which makes Nuremberg an extremely ironic example for Bukovsky to have cited as the judgmental model of choice. Indeed, it was at this international tribunal, a veritable judicial Camelot, so the annals do tell, that Western nonjudgmentalism was publicly and officially institutionalized, a form of justice so very blind that crimes (on all sides) that should have been weighed impartially went unseen altogether, subsequently vanishing from our own historical context. Even to participate in these trials, the Western Allies had to overlook Stalin's crimes and pretend they had not taken place within the timeline of the war whose very outbreak was precipitated by the infamous 1939 Nazi-Soviet nonaggression pact negotiated by German foreign minister Joachim von Ribbentrop and Soviet foreign minister Vyacheslav Molotov. After all, the Nazis and Soviets had begun World War II together as allies with the invasion of Poland. The Germans invaded Poland from the west on September 1, 1939—a well-known date—and the Red Army invaded from the east on September 17, 1939.

Not a well-known date.

Why?

Given the USSR's 1939–41 attacks on Poland, Finland, Lithuania, Latvia, Estonia, and Bessarabia alone, as John Laughland writes in his 2008 book *A History of Political Trials,* "the Communists were therefore guilty of exactly the same crimes against peace as the Nazis. They were also guilty of numerous atrocities."[56]

At first, this was another concept that brought me up short, another point of clarity that should have been obvious but had somehow been obscured by the fog of that vaporous arsenal clouding our understanding of the past. It wasn't right to convict Hitler's successors of charges that Stalin was equally guilty of and call it not only justice but Perfect, Lodestar Justice for the Ages. One of the many proofs of the corruption of Nuremberg lies in the fact that when a German defense counsel named Alfred Seidl brought forward the first public evidence of the secret protocol to the 1939 Nazi-Soviet pact that divided the nations and peoples of Europe between Hitler and Stalin—evidence of Stalin's guilt of committing "conspiracy to wage aggressive war," one of the key charges against the German high command—Seidl's evidence, a verified copy of the protocol, was ruled inadmissible. In open court—and not just any open court, but the model court of a new international order—the Western Allies signed on to a Soviet *conspiracy of silence* conceived of and directed by Stalin. Meanwhile, Stalin, it turns out, had empowered a secret commission at Nuremberg "to prevent at all costs any public discussion of any aspects of Nazi-Soviet relations in 1939–1941, and, first and foremost, of the actual existence, let alone contents of the so-called secret protocols," writes Arkady Vaksberg in his 1990 biography of Andrei Vyshinsky, *Stalin's Prosecutor.* Vyshinsky headed that secret commission. "However, all his [Vyshinsky's] worries proved unfounded; the foreign members [of the tribunal] were quite kindly disposed toward their [Soviet] Allies and certainly had no desire to strain relations."[57]

In this cozy court, Seidl set off an unanticipated eruption of the facts, which the U.S. government, already in possession of the Nazi archives, might well have known even before the German lawyer made his case. Quite by chance, Seidl had overheard von Ribbentrop in the prison yard revealing the secret protocol and its contents to Hermann Göering. Seidl then embarked on a very vocal search for the document, up and down channels, eventually and clandestinely receiving a photostat of the document from an unnamed U.S. officer, who we might assume was fed up with Nuremberg "justice," too. While the evidence wasn't admitted in court, it entered the equally important court of public opinion. On May 22, 1946, the day after Seidl was overruled at Nuremberg, *The St. Louis Post-Dispatch* published the once-secret protocol in its entirety, thus thwarting the conspiracy of silence.

It's possible that without Seidl's "indomitable" efforts, as the *Post-Dispatch* described them, we might never have learned about the secret protocol—certainly not for some time. The fact is, not a jot about of the Soviet criminal case came to judgment at Nuremberg—not the NKVD massacre of some twenty thousand Polish officers known as the Katyn Forest Massacre (charged to the Germans), not the forced "repatriation" of some two million Soviet-claimed refugees, which occurred thanks to essential assistance from British and U.S. troops—our very own war crime—which was still under way in Germany and elsewhere even as Nuremberg unfolded. Yes, as we've seen, Vyshinsky, Stalin's all-purpose fixer and prosecutor at the notorious Moscow show trials of the 1930s (the Great Purge that liquidated tens of thousands of Soviet citizens[58]), kept showing up to ensure, minder-style, "that everything went off as planned, and especially to ensure that no discussion of the Nazi-Soviet Pact was allowed in the courtroom."[59] However, as we've also seen, the presence of the man Britain's chief prosecutor Sir Hartley Shawcross called "Stalin's foremost proxy" was likely unnecessary, what with "the Tribunal," as Telford Taylor, chief American counsel at Nuremberg, writes in his *Anatomy of the Nuremberg Trials,* "doing its best to protect [the Soviets] from embarrassment."[60]

Shades of George Bush at Malta, forty years later.

Taylor's 1992 "personal memoir" of Nuremberg only skimmed what he called the trials' "political warts," the "biggest wart" being "the presence of the Soviet judges on the bench." Why? By way of explanation, Taylor invoked the "hatred and fear of communism and the Soviet Union . . . voiced throughout the United States," which is no explanation at all. As for the Moscow show trials, he gently broke it to readers on page 639 that the trials "had a very bad name." Then there was that "very ticklish matter" of the Nazi-Soviet Pact, Taylor writes. Even a practically kindly passing reference to the perfidious agreement by prosecutor Shawcross was infamously omitted in deference to Soviet sensibilities.[61] These were the lies and hypocrisy that led to such ghastly scenes as when, with Hermann Göring and Rudolph Hess in the dock, the Soviet prosecutor Roman Rudenko spoke on February 8, 1946. Taylor writes, "Rudenko described the [German] invasions of Czechoslovakia, Poland, Yugoslavia, and then . . . the Soviet Union. *Certain events contemporaneous with the destruction of the Polish state seemed to have been erased from Rudenko's memory*" (emphasis added).

"Certain events," of course, referred to the massive, simultaneous and, at that moment in the proceedings, ongoing Soviet role in said Polish destruction. Taylor's account continued, quoting the words of the Soviet prosecutor, "On September 1, 1939 the fascist aggressors invaded Polish territory in treacherous violation of existing treaties," [Rudenko] declaimed, and read from a document . . . to show "how the gangster assault of Hitler's Germany on Poland was *prepared in advance*" (emphasis added).

"Prepared in advance"? Even Taylor doesn't fail to notice Rudenko's omission, writing, "Of course, the crucial 'preparation in advance' was the Nazi-Soviet treaty."[62] Taylor makes no additional comment on this brazen hypocrisy, an altered state of mind that the West dysfuntionally tolerated to a point where even as late as 1986, Soviet officials could with impunity denounce references to the historical consequences of the 1939 Nazi-Soviet pact as being "disinformation about the prewar policy of the USSR" and a "hackneyed lie that the Soviet-German Treaty of 1939 opened the path to the second world war."[63] Never mind that it did. Taylor does, however, note a memorable observation made by Nuremberg psychologist Dr. G. M. Gilbert: "Gilbert recorded that Goering and Hess, in disgust, took off their headphones. During the lunch break, Goering was scornful: 'I did not think that they [the Russians] would be so shameless as to mention Poland.' "[64]

When Göring and Hess have the moral high ground, you know you're in trouble—or at least you should. Knowing or not, everyone who participated in the charade at Nuremberg was complicit. In a 1962 essay titled "Who Betrays Whom?" the British writer and ex-Socialist Malcolm Muggeridge, who had famously and to the detriment of his journalistic career borne early witness to the horrors of Soviet collectivization and forced famine in the 1930s, had this to say: "Let us hope that mankind will sometime recover sufficient equanimity to get a laugh out of the spectacle of English and American judges sitting alongside Soviet ones, and solemnly pronouncing Germans guilty of the use of forced labour and of the partition of Poland."[65]

Germans, but not Soviets.

No such knowing derision has ever compromised the solemn regard in which Nuremberg is still held, still respected as a civilizational milestone. Given the travesty of Soviet immunity alone, this vaunted tribunal gives off the noxious fumes of a *Western* show trial, albeit one conducted not to establish the phony guilt of defendants but rather to establish the phony legitimacy of the court itself—specifically the Soviet Union's rotten central role in it. How else to regard a judicial proceeding where Moscow show trial judge Iona Timofeevich Nikitchenko presided?[66] In his Nuremberg memoir, Telford Taylor opaquely introduced late-twenty-century readers to Nikitchenko as "an army judge advocate," but in 1936, Nikitchenko made mass murderers' row as one of the judges who signed the spurious death sentences of the "old Bolsheviks" in the first of Stalin's public show trials that initiated the Great Purge decimation of a generation of Russians.[67] "We might agree, at least retrospectively," Robert Conquest wrote in 2005 regarding Nikitchenko's blood-soaked spot on the Nuremberg bench, "Nuremberg can be pronounced defective on this basis alone."[68]

But we do not so agree, retrospectively or otherwise. Such a thought doesn't enter our minds. Nuremberg "justice" as jointly apportioned by "Allies" who included hardened criminals-against-humanity from the USSR lives on as "a moral reference point."[69] How can that be? How can we look at darkness and see purity? Once again, Mikhail Gorbachev's failure to accept the reality of half a million trucks and jeeps wasn't and isn't the only amazing game of denial in town.

Indeed, Bukovsky's notion of Western "ideological collaboration" to serve Soviet ends has a long and storied tradition that, as the example of the 1946 Nuremberg Trials indicates, certainly goes back further than 1991. In both cases, in Moscow in 1991 and at Nuremberg in 1946, Communist doctrine and its leading agent, the Soviet Union, were allowed to slip away unrecognized, unjudged, unpunished. Perhaps it's possible to say that the difference is that in 1946, the main motivation to protect Communism, while enabled and acquiesced to due to Allied expediency, still came from within the USSR, a co-victor, after all, in World War II. In 1991, with the USSR in tatters, the decisive block on passing judgment against the USSR, the Cold War loser, *came from the West itself.*

Now, what was it I said at the beginning of this chapter about finding equilibrium in the conventional wisdom about the 1989 breakup of the Soviet bloc?

I was just leading you on.

CHAPTER THREE

A tyrant has fallen in the Germany of Hitler, where we have seen Dachau and Buchenwald. But I say to you, that over there are hundreds of Dachaus and hundreds of Buchenwalds.

—VASSILI LUJNA[1]

It is as if the West actually does not want to know the truth until the moment when this knowledge has ceased to be of use.

—ALEKSANDR SOLZHENITSYN[2]

Warning: Reading this chapter may be hazardous to your worldview. Writing it was to mine.

What I discovered, or, rather *un*covered—for what I was doing was tracing references and footnotes backward along a well-mapped historical route that had simply fallen into disuse—reads like the history of a mirror-image universe. Certainly not like the history of the United States of America as I knew it. Or even as I knew it through the distorting prism of "political correctness," multiculturalism, cultural relativism, and the undermining rest—and that's saying something.

I am specifically referring to a largely overlooked chain of events that took place during the span of history preceding, including, and immediately following World War II. This is the climactic era that still serves as the American touchstone, the "Good War" (grating term) we "won," thanks to Franklin Delano Roosevelt, our "great" if not "greatest" modern president—at least according to all of those blue-ribbon polls, which, unbidden, continually roll out predictable tallies of legacy, reputation and lore.[3] FDR is always up there with George Washington and Abraham Lincoln, the two perennial presidential medalists. Of course, when it comes to any reckoning of this era, there's no omitting Winston Churchill, the embodiment of fully half of what we still, atavistically, invoke as the "special relationship" between the United States and

Great Britain. It would no doubt frost FDR to know that Churchill gets the moniker "Man of the Century" for his role in vanquishing Nazism. By the final year of the war, it seems, FDR had grown jealous and weary of Churchill, although we don't usually perceive such fissures from our rosy vantage point.[4] Looking back, we see history aglow with their gigantic reputations, lighting a veritable Eden of patriotic unity fostered by the war against Germany, and also Japan (sometimes we almost forget), which didn't fade and fragment until the 1960s.

That last point, the one about the 1960s, particularly the mid- to late 1960s, marking the decisive break with all that had come before is something I have previously tried to debunk in *The Death of the Grown-Up.* In this earlier book, I argue that the political, artistic, racial, sexual, and youth liberation movements for which we remember the decade were already under way before campus "radicals" took over their first building at Berkeley in 1964. For example, *Playboy* magazine, flagship of mainstreamed pornography, sailed forth in 1953, the year before the milestone desegregation ruling, *Brown v. Board of Education.* Rosa Parks took her famous bus ride two years later, in 1955. *Lady Chatterley's Lover* made its unexpurgated American debut in 1959; women were taking "the Pill" by 1960. James Meredith was desegregating the University of Mississippi by 1961, the same year comic Lenny Bruce (b. 1925) started beating obscenity raps. The "Port Huron Statement" bemoaning youth's ennui came out in 1962. By 1963, a full year before the sex, drugs, and rock 'n' roll generation descended on Sproul Hall at Cal, Timothy Leary was booted from Harvard for promoting the use of LSD. Indeed, the logic of the timeline makes a compelling case for an essential continuity between what is remembered as having been the "boring" 1950s and the "countercultural" 1960s.

How did that happen? That is, if, under the retrospective lens, the 1950s are not as stable and "normal" as eyewitness accounts of *Ozzie and Harriet* episodes would attest, what triggered the overlooked upheaval? Something must have happened in the preceding period to lay the foundations—or, better, to demolish the foundations—for what would turn out to be near-total social breakdown and reconfiguration. What?

It is at this junction where most of us—certainly most conservatives, the group preoccupied with this abiding cultural mystery—find ourselves stumped. We may chronicle civilizational change, note shifting fault lines of behavior, highlight their deleterious impact on society, but walking back along the trail, we hit a dead end at the basic question: Why? Why did all of these things begin to happen in the first place? The common reply (I've made it myself) comes down to this: We lost our cultural confidence. We don't believe in ourselves, our values, anymore.

Why don't we? There are reasons, proximate causes, economic, educational, and pop cultural developments, but no ultimate explanation. And *"c'est la vie"* just isn't enough. The fact is, the loss of cultural confidence explains many things, but it doesn't explain the loss of cultural confidence itself. Neither do theories of attrition that posit a cyclical ebb and flow by which civilizations flourish and then die off on autopilot. Such an approach rests on a nonexistent natural law of inevitability, as though human beings have no more impact on forestalling or triggering the collapse of their societies than they have on forestalling or triggering sunrise.

The question then becomes, What if that loss of cultural confidence weren't the result of an "inevitable" progression from traditional morality to cultural relativism? What if there were in fact some culprit, or some culprit act or movement, behind the downward spiral of events that has been acutely and repeatedly examined and analyzed? What if the resulting "death of the grown-up" were in fact . . . a murder?

This is the only half-whimsical conclusion I've come to since digging into some of the deeper, less accessible layers of the past, initially seeking some explanation for our chronic indifference over the demise of the Soviet Union, over the colossal transgressions of the Communist system. At a certain point in this research, I found myself exploring what began to look more and more like a historical crime scene, a notion I first broached in the previous chapter. A distinct pattern of deceit emerged from heretofore invisible, unnoticed, discarded, or suppressed clues, evidence overlooked or hidden so long that the criminals themselves are long forgotten. Indeed, this was the perfect, perfect crime because not only did the perpetrators get off scot-free, their crimes have never been detected. Here, in light of information and documentation not publicly available until four and five decades after the fact, was a cold case with quite staggering implications—and my worldview was rocked.

So what was this crime of the century? Logical, reasonable question, but I find myself reluctant to pull the pin and let the bomb explode just yet. This ground requires preparation, some retracing of the steps I followed back through the evidence by which the light dawnethed, revealing a ghastly scenario every American should now bear retrospective witness to.

That so seriously said, I must emphasize that it was with no such foreknowledge that I set out to fill in the blanks about why it was that we had recently witnessed triumph in the Cold War abroad (the demise of what we knew as the Soviet Union, anyway) even as that same Cold War at home—the riddling, corrupting drive against what we now regard as "traditional" morality, Enlightenment logic, and cultural memory—had gone so badly, and with strange, corrosive effects. As a result of losing, or, at least, not winning the Cold War at home, according to the outline I presented to my publisher, "even the over-whelming moral imperative to oppose totalitarianism as exemplified by Soviet power became a source of vague discomfort, if not outright embarrassment." Having gone through college and entered journalism during the last decade of the Cold War, this I recall personally. I wanted to probe the origins of that lurking discomfort and embarrassment, that Pavlovian trigger that always prompted a moment's hesitation or hitch, discomfiting the average anti-Communist on giving voice (or not) to the anti-Communist point of view during much of the last century, at least in any circles counting as "intellectual"—artistic, academic, even journalistic or mainstream (read: liberal) political.

These were the enlightened circles, the "cool" circles, clubby and powerful in the sense of owning the dominant professional territory. Intriguingly, they also occupied—or, better, seized and held—the moral high ground. Over the decades, whether the Communist crime du jour was blood purge, invasion, show trial, assassination, atomic espionage, subversion, deception, treason, Gulags, boat people, "reeducation" camps, or genocide, such circles remained, at base, redoubts of a morally pristine "anti-anti-Communism." The bizarre effect of such nonsullyable purity was to take all the crimes of Communism, or of a Communist agent, right off the table, simultaneously thrusting the nearest anti-Communist into the hot seat.

Epically, Whittaker Chambers experienced this same syndrome at its punishing extreme. Chambers, probably the most famous American ex-Communist ever, was a former courier for Soviet military intelligence, subsequently an editor at *Time* magazine, and, in passing, curiously, the English translator of the 1923 Austrian novel *Bambi,* which became the 1942 Disney cartoon. His exceedingly wise decision to retain hard evidence attesting to his espionage work in the 1930s helped convict, most sensationally, Alger Hiss—the Ivy-educated, well-connected former State Department official and progenitor of the United Nations, president of the Carnegie Endowment for International Peace, and all-around poster boy of the Liberal Establishment. Starting in 1950, Hiss served four years in jail for perjury charges related to Soviet espionage.

Then what happened? Did a thankful President Truman crown Chambers in laurels and congratulate him on behalf of a grateful nation for exposing a Communist conspiracy metastasizing at the highest levels of the federal government?

Never has a simple "no" been less adequate. Fortunately for us, Chambers's 1952 landmark book, *Witness,* explains in painstaking and also painful detail the cauterizing ordeal he underwent for what was widely and weirdly regarded as his own "crime" of calling out the Communist machine. At one point in his testimonial, Chambers encapsulates the physics of anti-anti-Communism this way: "I had been warned repeatedly that the brunt of official wrath was directed, not against Alger Hiss as a danger, but against me for venturing to testify to the danger."[5]

It bears restating: Officialdom was enraged not by the danger posed by Hiss, a Soviet military intelligence agent "continuously since 1935," but by Chambers for testifying to the danger.[6] This may be a pattern familiar to us since Cassandra, but it repeats itself with frantic frequency throughout the past century, up to and beyond when Ronald Reagan named the Soviet empire "evil," and the world expressed more outrage over the phrase "evil empire" than over the evil of the empire itself. Of course, Reagan was President. Chambers was nobody. For him, "the brunt of official wrath" meant the vengeful response of the Truman administration, beginning with a statement from Truman himself in which he famously dismissed the whole case against Hiss as a "red herring." This, Chambers would later write, was "the most unexpected and, to me, the most stunning" development of all.[7]

As stunning as the drive against putting Communism on trial coming *from the West* would be forty years later.

Important to note is that with a twist of the timeline, Chambers could just as easily have been subjected to the "wrath" of the Roosevelt administration or the "wrath" of the Eisenhower administration. Both of these administrations shared with Truman's the same propensity for suppression when it came to the touchy subject of domestic Communist conspiracy. In the end, this had the effect of protecting the Communist conspiracy itself. In FDR's case, for example, the president personally tried to shut down Rep. Martin Dies's investigations into Communist conspiracy—and later his political career.[8] In Eisenhower's case, as president he was personally involved in efforts to shut down Senator Joseph McCarthy's quite similar investigations.[9] In all such cases, as with the Hiss case, this meant that both the extent and the impact of the conspiracies were officially downplayed, denied, suppressed, and/or ignored by those elected leaders directly responsible for defending the Constitution. In each and every instance, it was the anti-Communists, the ex-Communists, and the Cassandras who were punished and castigated by the Washington Establishment, and then ostracized for their "crimes" of exposing treason.

Why?

This question drove me further past the pat narratives that have sufficed for too long. It is particularly pertinent today as we watch the same Establishment forces coalescing anew to suppress logical and, indeed, patriotic questions about hostile Islamic penetration of the U.S. government particularly since 9/11.[10] When did this ugly stuff really get going? A related question: When did anti-Communism itself—the philosophical and political drive against state domination of the individual—become a radioactive inheritance of perceived bigotry and mass hysteria to be passed down, gingerly, generation to generation? It must be here where the origins of our indifference to the plight of the anti-Communist witnesses and to Cold War victory and Communist crime lie. What I was looking for, then, was the beginnings of the greatest propaganda coup and flimflam operation in history: the hocus-pocus transformation of liberty-loving anti-Communism into a force of repression to be reviled—not always by the people, who were reflexively anti-Communist, but certainly by the elite expression of public conscience. There was a flip side to the phenomenon, too: the hocus-pocus transformation of totalitarian Communism into a force of liberalism, later liberation, to be shielded or even fully embraced by that same public conscience. It was almost as if a giant syringe of novocaine had been injected into the body politic at some unknown point and with permanent effect: the numbed sensibility that reflexively reviles the evil of Hitler but calmly accepts that of Stalin, Mao, and other Red thugs and killers. Among the many manifestations of this weirdly insenate state, my symbolic favorite is the eye-catching frequency with which Warhol's silkscreen of Chairman Mao pops up as an aspect of chic in lavishly decorated homes, glorious fruits of the freeish market as celebrated in four-color, glossy shelter magazines. And no, irony is not a fig leaf for the mass murderer over the mantelpiece. His pride of place is more evidence of internal rot and betrayal.

The so-called McCarthy Era is the obvious place to search for answers, since the narrative we can all recite tells us that the Red-hunting Republican senator from Wisconsin was himself singlehandedly responsible for the evisceration of ideological opposition to Communism—anti-Communism—rendering said anti-Communism into a kind of disease. The remedy was said to be a steadying dose of anti-anti-Communism, despite the often heavy pro-Communist side effects. McCarthy accomplished all of this, the same narrative goes, with his crude zealotry and wild overreach, hectoring and destroying American innocents who had the misfortune to be dragged before his investigatory Senate committee *for nothing*. "Name one Communist or Soviet agent ever identified by McCarthy," goes the perpetual challenge to this day, regardless of evidence from both Soviet and American archives that corroborate FBI reports, sworn testimonies, and other facts amassed in support of innumerable McCarthy investigations into the Soviet penetration of the federal government.[11] The accusatory catchphrase "Have you left no sense of decency?" still vibrates tremulously on a historical wavelength of inexhaustible outrage.[12]

The sequence of events, however, suggests a rat. Two years *before* McCarthy's 1950 kickoff speech in Wheeling, West Virginia, ex-Communist couriers

Whittaker Chambers and Elizabeth Bentley had already struck body blows for exposure, breaking the Communist creed of omertà—mob silence—in separate public appearances before the House Committee on Un-American Activities. (They had both already been extensively debriefed by the FBI starting in 1945.) The committee itself had already been up and running for a decade. In other words, as the seminal, groundbreaking, and essential *Blacklisted by History: The Untold Story of Senator Joe McCarthy and His Fight Against America's Enemies* (2007) by M. Stanton Evans makes clear, anti-Communism was in bad odor with the powers that be and make noise long before McCarthy decried still unaddressed security risks inside the State Department in his 1950 speech. In certain ways, McCarthy's investigations might almost be seen as the end of something, not the beginning—the end phase of an arduous anti-Communist effort to demonstrate, once and for all, not just the existence of domestic Communist incursions but also *the reluctance of the federal government under both Democrats and Republicans to do anything about it.* With the political fall of McCarthy, the brief, intense popularity enjoyed by anti-Communist investigations came to a halt. Still, investigations would grind on for another highly productive twenty years in both the House Committee on Un-American Activities and the Senate Subcommittee on Internal Security, where McCarthy never played a role.[13] Following the invention of dread "McCarthyism," however, these investigations always seemed to begin from a defensive crouch.

More relevant to the search for origins, then, might be the precedent set by Martin Dies, the House Democrat from Texas who in 1938 founded what would be known as the House Committee on Un-American Activities, or, under his chairmanship which lasted until 1944, the Dies Committee. "Before Joe McCarthy, there was Martin Dies," Evans writes. "Virtually everything that would later be said about Joe McCarthy was said first of Martin Dies, that he was conducting 'witch hunts,' smearing innocent victims, using the Communist issue to advance his own malign agenda, spreading hysteria about a nonexistent menace . . . It was the same routine from start to finish."[14]

Pre-McCarthy "witch hunts" in 1938? I promptly began mining Evans's footnotes for related material. These included *The Red Decade* by Eugene Lyons, *Martin Dies' Story* by Martin Dies, and *The Red Plot Against America* by Robert E. Stripling.

Or, rather, across the Stripling book's red cover, emblazoned in white capitals with black contrast: *THE RED PLOT AGAINST AMERICA.*

In smaller letters, the author's name: Robert E. Stripling, Chief Investigator, House Un-American Activities Committee, 1938–1948. The rest of the cover of the old book was equally striking—jarring, even, to the modern eye. Standing out on a red and black map of the outline of the USA is a white hammer-and-sickle from which phrases explode, like rays: IN THE WHITE HOUSE! IN LABOR! IN THE STATE DEPARTMENT! IN HOLLYWOOD!

What was that faint noise I thought I heard as I examined the cover art? Was it the sound of . . . snickers? ("Ha-ha! A Communist under every bed!") Catcalls? ("Dirty rotten Commies!") It was almost as if some late-night host, deadpan, held up this relic of the "Red Scare" before the cameras without comment, prompting his ever-primed studio audience to let off guffaws on cue.

I know those guffaws. They're born of conditioning over several generations to regard a "Red plot" against America as something so ridiculous as to be utterly laughable and beyond all reason. Closed-minded, too, and even indecent. From this same bent of mind, this same consensus, came the Establishment ire at Whittaker Chambers in 1948, not at Alger Hiss; outrage over the "evil empire" label by Ronald Reagan in 1983, not the USSR; and, more recently, ridicule over but also suppression of the Marxist inclinations and associations of Candidate Obama in 2008. (They didn't really surface at all in 2012.) More official outrage welled up again against Rep. Michele Bachmann for raising elementary questions about Muslim Brotherhood penetration of the U.S. government in 2012. The same routine from start to finish.

Even if I was prepared for this McCarthy-revisited routine—make that, McCarthy *pre*visited routine—I was still taken aback by the bitterness with which Stripling recounts the decade he served as the chief investigator for the Un-American Activities Committee. "I want to tell in detail the price that men must pay for the dubious privilege of being reviled in print and on the air," he writes, for their labors in "what amounts to a necessary sewer project" of Communist investigations. This is his "attempt to outline, without conjecture, the scope of the Communist conspiracy against the government and people of the United States," he writes, although "to do so is to invite the charge of Fascist, Red-baiter, witch-hunter, smear-artist. To fail to do [so] is to capitulate to a resourceful enemy who can endure any counter-attack *except exposure*" (emphasis added).[15]

There are those words again: "Fascist, Red-baiter, witch-hunter" . . . and there is that same soft spot of "exposure" again, the desperate trigger of character assassination by poisonous invective. This lexicon of political profanity developed to enforce what ex-Socialist journalist Eugene Lyons called the "irrational and indefensible taboo against criticizing the Great Experiment in Stalin's Russia or its extensions and machinations in our own country."[16] Like today's cries of "Islamophobia," like the still-current cry of "McCarthyism," the cry of "Red-baiting" in the 1930s, 1940s, and 1950s denoted taboo, requiring an immediate cease to all debate—and thus a continued block against "exposure."

Interestingly enough, Stripling notes that Dies Committee investigations into German, Japanese, and Italian subversive activities in the run-up to World War II were widely lauded, even inspiring government action—as when an investigation into Adolf Hitler's use of German diplomatic and consular officers as spies in this country led FDR to shut German consulates down. "But," Stripling continues, "whenever we cast an inquiring eye on the equally subversive activities of the Communist Party, we were instantly assailed, though the strongest microscope could not differentiate between the nature of the Party's conspiracy and that of the Germans, Japanese and Italians."[17]

Lyons, too, observed this same double standard at work, noting the favorable reception studies of fascism and Nazism in America typically received. "We have yet to hear their authors denounced as brown-baiters, black-baiters or silver-baiters," he writes, noting the colors adopted by fascist and Nazi followers. On the contrary, "the charges [against fascists and Nazis] are assayed on the basis of their truth or falsity. They are not arbitrarily dismissed with a hackneyed epithet. There is yet among us, it happens, no taboo against examining and if necessary condemning the operation of Mussolini, Hitler and their direct or indirect agents."[18]

Not so Communism in the 1930s, Lyons's "red decade," or the 1940s, which Stripling would look back on, noting, "Of course, we fully expected to be smeared by leading Communists and by 'The Daily Worker' and its abusive carbon copies. But we did not expect what often became an avalanche of abuse from more conservative quarters—from men as high in public esteem as Franklin D. Roosevelt."[19]

Neither Stripling nor Dies was prepared for this realization as they encountered active White House hostility to the committee's anti-Communist activities. A decade later, Whittaker Chambers wasn't prepared for it, either. I doubt Joseph McCarthy knew what he was heading into later still. In his memoir, Martin Dies describes a chance meeting he had with McCarthy and his wife-to-be, Jean Kerr, at the venerable and vanished Harvey's Restaurant, which used to stand next door to Washington's Mayflower Hotel on Connecticut Avenue. It was 1952, and Dies had just been reelected to the House of Representatives after an eight-year hiatus. McCarthy would soon become chairman of the Senate Committee on Government Operations and, as Dies put it, "contemplated investigating Communism." Matter of fact, Dies wrote, "Joe wanted suggestions and advice."

Did the world hang in the balance for a pregnant pause while a trial by fire was ignited by bolts of lightning in the gathering storm—or something? Dies doesn't mention augurs of heaven or hell. He continued, "I told him of my own experiences and warned him to expect abuse, ridicule, and every known device of 'character assassination' and mental torture. I told him to move cautiously until he was sure of his footing; to beware of unsupported charges that would soon be flooding his offices, and never to underestimate the cleverness and resourcefulness of the Communists and their fellow travelers."[20]

Clearly—at least, clearly at a remove of more than a half century—this was war. A hidden army was in place—a secret insurgency—and much of the local population was sympathetic or even in league with it. When McCarthy came along, as M. Stanton Evans documents, he was entirely correct to suspect, track, and attempt to expose the extensive and *ongoing* conspiracy that Dies had probed before him, that Chambers had participated in and witnessed, that official Washington, for reasons to be discussed (none of them good), sought to keep under wraps. The historical fact is, secret Soviet forces had made massive incursions into the federal government following FDR's first election in 1932 and reached every kind of inner sanctum during the United States' wartime alliance with the Soviet Union (1941–45)—the one really and truly "special relationship," as I have learned. As Evans lays out in detail, much of it drawn from newly declassified FBI and Senate records, the United States wasn't just riddled by Communist agents; we were for all intents and purposes occupied by a small army—a small army being just what this kind of war requires. Expert estimates now peg the number of Americans assisting Soviet intelligence agencies during the 1930s and 1940s as exceeding five hundred.[21] Not *one* Aldrich Ames. Not *two* Rosenbergs. Not *five* "magnificent" Cambridgers. More than five hundred willing and variously able American traitors, many operating at the very highest levels of the federal government, with who knows how many more in support roles. This was a national security fiasco of a magnitude that has never, ever entered national comprehension.

There is something else Evans makes clear that must be understood: what he calls "the parlous state of the historical record."[22] It turns out that the historical record—*our* historical record—is in fragments. Much of it still remains classified. That which is declassified remains heavily censored. Other parts of the record, thousands of intercepted Soviet cables that make up the so-called Venona project, for example, have *never been decrypted and deciphered,* while We, the People have no way of knowing whether everything decrypted and deciphered from Venona has in fact been released. Meanwhile, the identities of numerous Soviet agents whose activities are tracked in Venona cables remain unknown. "Salient among the mysteries of 'Venona' are the hundreds of unbroken cryptonyms that stud the cables, protecting the identities of agents and informants even when the messages have been deciphered," wrote U.S. Air Force historian Eduard Mark.[23] In other words, we still don't fully know what, or even who, hit us.

There are other stunning gaps in the record that became evident to Evans as he attempted to assemble his own McCarthy archive of primary sources. For example, on many occasions he discovered that some person or persons unknown had preceded him on this document hunt to *delete the record*. This had the unmistakable effect, if not also the intent, of thwarting, or at least delaying, Evans's plans. Scads of primary sources—dozens of State Department documents pertaining to Soviet penetration, letters listing Communist security risks from the Senate and the CIA, even newspapers of the era—have selectively vanished from their archival repositories. In one instance, Evans was searching for a memorandum by a State Department official named Samuel Klaus. The 106-page memorandum, written in 1946, listed and detailed security risks at State, including names of suspected Soviet agents on the department payroll. A copy of this document, at McCarthy's behest, was obtained by a Senate committee in 1950. Today, neither the original State Department document nor the Senate's copy is to be found. At the National Archives, Evans discovered a letter of transmittal attesting to the memo's entry into the Senate committee's files, and an index listing the memo in Klaus's personal papers. In both cases, in the Senate committee files and the Klaus files, the document was gone.

Another example: When Evans traveled to Wheeling, West Virginia, to examine the *Intelligencer*'s coverage of the famous, and famously disputed, February 1950 speech McCarthy gave in town, kicking off the McCarthy Era, he was directed to the local library where the newspaper archives on microfilm are stored. There, Evans discovered that the newspaper editions for January and February 1950—and only those editions—were *missing from the collection*. Incredibly, it was the same creepy story at the Library of Congress: Those same *Wheeling Intelligencer* editions had vanished. Sandy Berger may be the first man to become famous for scrubbing the archives to set the record crooked, but he is far from the first. Who were these secret thieves of history? Anti-McCarthy authors protecting their (phony) turf from marauding facts? Soviet spies? The relative of an erstwhile "security risk" seeking to protect Grandma or Grandpa from infamy for the ages? These mysteries endure.

While some primary documents have made all-too-easy pickings in open archives, others remain overly protected. Declassified FBI files, which Evans describes as "a treasure trove of information on Communist penetration of American life and institutions, suspects tracked down by the Bureau, countermeasures taken, and related topics," remain heavily censored. "In case after significant case," Evans writes, including the most famous investigations into the Communist activities of high-ranking government officials such as Alger Hiss

(State Department), Lauchlin Currie (White House), and Harry Dexter White (Treasury), "entries have been held back or heavily 'redacted' (blacked out), sometimes for dozens of pages at a stretch." Much more remains classified and thus under government lock and key. Evans writes, "Without the documents referred to, and without the items blacked out in the records, attempts to chronicle our domestic Cold War, while not entirely futile, are subject to the most serious limits."[24]

This is astonishing. After all, we're not talking about three-thousand-year-old cuneiform tablets, fragments of ancient papyrus, or shards of pre-Columbian pottery. These are essential documents of relatively recent vintage. They date back to an era some of us were actually born into, and some of us still predate. It was concurrent with radar, sonar, atomic energy, and the jet engine, not to mention good old Smith Corona typewriters and carbon paper, and it featured functioning institutions equipped with archivists and protocols for record keeping and the like. There is simply no good reason for these missing links, nor is there any sound purpose for the U.S. government's continuing to withhold so much evidence from Us, the People. There must be a reason and purpose behind the continued secrecy, but it is neither good nor sound. That's because such secrecy only preserves the life of the lies that the release of the documents would destroy.

From what you might still call the Communist perspective, there remains every reason and purpose to keep the historical record hidden. That's because it is by now an observable axiom: The more the tightly held record is dislodged from secret archives at home and abroad—even piecemeal, requiring both the analytical and foraging talents of scholar-detectives like M. Stanton Evans—the more once-reviled anti-Communists such as Martin Dies, such as Whittaker Chambers, such as Joseph McCarthy, are vindicated, and the more the false narrative we have been taught as truth is debunked as Communist agitprop. The kind of document poaching Evans discovered in his own hunt for the record and the continuing government-sealed secrecy only benefit that same Other Side.

Evans observes, "It's not too much to say . . . that the loss of so many primary records has created a kind of black hole of antiknowledge in which strange factoids and curious fables circulate without resistance."[25]

Maybe in this black hole of antiknowledge lies the epicenter of American betrayal. Of course, Evans's entire book stands as bold correction of such "antiknowledge." With hard-won facts, he reconstructs McCarthy's career without the dirty smears that the Establishment used to depict "the caveman in the sewer," as Evans describes the elite consensus on McCarthy, that "Red"-hunting monster of the liberal demonology who preyed on such pure souls of chivalric progressivism that they were besmirched even by proximity to his fetid clutches. On the contrary, it is a singular American patriot who emerges from Evans's efforts, a genuine martyr, the proverbial lightning rod who withstood, for as long as he humanly could, the surging currents of the death-house switch as flipped by the most genteel and privileged members of the Attack Left.

I've read that last sentence over several times just to make sure the metaphor hasn't taken on an overly vivid life of its own, too independent of the thought process that inspired it. No, it hasn't. The sentence conveys what I consider to be the appropriate intensity. McCarthy was a patriot. McCarthy was a martyr. As a colossal and popular force of exposure—the Gallup poll ranked him the fourth-most-admired man in America at the beginning of 1954—McCarthy had to be utterly and completely neutralized, then destroyed. Just as there was extreme caricature in his demonization, there should be an operatic flourish to his redemption. He deserves it.

But McCarthy remains a special case. Historical reevaluation continues to pass him by—Evans's tome the most obvious exception—in most of what might be termed post-Venona "exposure" research.[26] Conducted by notable scholars and intelligence historians, such research counters the bulk of the "antiknowl-edge" still circulating about Soviet espionage, infiltration, and subversion in the West by providing new proofs of their existence from previously unavailable archival materials. McCarthy himself, the man best remembered and worst damned for his efforts to expose this same espionage, infiltration, and subver-sion, remains history's Lost Man. Events recede and conditions change—the forbidding Berlin Wall, for example, became rubble marketed as souvenirs—but the venomous sting of McCarthy, or, rather, *McCarthyism,* remains as deadly as ever.

Evans explains the reluctance to reevaluate McCarthy's role as an anti-Communist warrior: "Such reluctance to tackle McCarthy in light of the new information may seem odd, but is understandable in context. 'McCarthyism' is the third rail in Cold War historiography—and of our political discourse in general—and any contact with it could prove fatal to writers trying to get their work accepted in academic or mainstream media circles."[27]

Any contact could prove fatal. This should tell us the war isn't over, not by a long shot. This should tell us it goes on, now, against an enemy who still controls vital territory—academic or mainstream media circles—to such a degree that research diverging from this party line cannot be published with-out dire consequences to the author. That's because the cause these remnant or reflexive anti-anti-Communists championed in the absence—or, rather, the suppression—of facts has never been discredited to a point of acknowledged surrender. On the contrary, having successfully warded off attacks of the facts

led by individuals of singular courage, having successfully maintained the vacuum of deception, they long ago usurped the prerogative of the victor—the
writing of history—to produce the antihistory we rely on to this day.

McCarthy, bad.

Communists, good and/or nonexistent.

Anti-Communism, terrible.

Who cares what Venona says, outside of a few academics? *Have you left no
sense of decency?*

To put it another way: "There was a certain magnificence in its un-
abridged cynicism, its defiance of . . . common sense . . . The roles of leading
historical figures were perverted or altogether erased. New roles were invented for others . . . All books, articles, documents, museum materials which
contradicted this extraordinary fantasy parading as history—and that means
nearly all historical and political writings and documentation—disappeared
throughout the country!"[28]

All true, an apt description of the replacement of facts with a false narrative.
However, this heated passage addresses something else entirely—the sweeping,
devastating psychological impact of the publication of the *History of the Communist Party,* a 1938 work of propaganda by the Soviet government. The description is by Victor Kravchenko, who, by my count, became perhaps only the
third Soviet regime defector in American history when, in the spring of 1944,
he walked away from his privileged position as an economic attaché with the
Soviet Government Purchasing Commission at 3355 Sixteenth Street NW,
Washington, D.C., the Soviet administrative hub of Lend-Lease to the USSR.
His purpose? To contribute his firsthand knowledge of Communist crime to
the FBI. Obviously, in the above excerpt from his 1946 international bestseller
I Chose Freedom, he didn't have the American history of the Cold War in
mind—particularly as it had yet to unfold. Still, when I read Evans's description
of Cold War "antihistory," it was Kravchenko's words that I heard, sounding a
jarringly concordant note.

Kravchenko continues, describing the Soviet regime's rewrite of Russian
history, "Shamelessly, without so much as an explanation, it revised half a century of Russian history. I don't mean simply that it falsified some facts or gave a
new interpretation of events. I mean that it deliberately stood history on its
head, expunging events and inventing facts. It twisted the recent past—a past
still fresh in millions of memories—into new and bizarre shapes, to conform
with the version of affairs presented by blood-purge trials and the accompany-
ing propaganda."[29]

As the previous chapter attests, I have never been one for mirror imagery
that regards the United States and Soviet Union as equivalents, or geopolitical

twins of any kind. At the same time, I can't now ignore disturbing parallels that exist between Kravchenko's description of Soviet propaganda-as-history and, beginning with this period of Soviet infiltration under consideration, American-history-as-Soviet-propaganda. Given what we now know, both from old evidence and new, it is this inversion of our own history that requires rapt attention.

Of course, what distinguishes the two national rewrites of history is blood—a factor of a colossal differentiation, but also a puzzlement. That is, how is it that mere propaganda, sans force or threat of the Gulag, was enough to stand our history on its head? Mulling the landmark works of historical correction assembled since the 1990s by John Earl Haynes and Harvey Klehr, Christopher Andrew and Vasily Mitrokhin, Herbert Romerstein and Eric Breindel, Allen Weinstein and Alexander Vassiliev, Jerrold and Leona Schecter, and more, it becomes painfully clear that Kravchenko's contemptuous description of the Communist narrative as "bold, specious, conscienceless fiction" and "extraordinary fantasy parading as history" quite aptly defines what we naively regard as our own transparent, truthful, good-faith narrative. The citizens of this country have been deceived on a massive scale, often by the U.S. government, regarding the reach and impact of the secret war of aggression the USSR waged in the United States with American proxies.

Not all of us were deceived, of course. Publicly available evidence was voluminous from the start, becoming a colossal and ever-expanding dossier of eyewitness testimonies and investigations, proof of the reality that somehow—again, how?—faded away while a vivid and grotesque fantasy lived on. Kravchenko describes the Soviet process by which reality in his homeland disappeared, a process that included the physical removal of the very officials and staff who had presided over Communist Party doctrine and propaganda in the first place. He writes:

> To brand the shame more deeply on our minds, "study" of the new version was made obligatory for all responsible Party people. History classes met nearly every night in this period and lecturers from Sverdlovsk came to our town to help hammer home the lies, while most of us fumed inwardly. Whatever human dignity remained in our character was humiliated. *But even the most gigantic lie, by dint of infinite repetition, takes root; Stalin knew this before Hitler discovered it.* As I looked on I could see terrible falsehoods, at first accepted under pressure, become established as unquestioned "facts," particularly among younger people without personal experience to the contrary to bother them [emphasis added].[30]

It can't happen here, right? Nevertheless, something very much like it did happen here, and is still happening, from the schoolroom, where "political correctness" dictates curriculum, to the workplace, where "sensitivity training" conditions behavioral and thought patterns that didn't take back in the school-room. The Communist origins, the Communist inspiration, for this top-down transformation of the human condition may be the ultimate secret that the archives have disgorged, even as it sits, raw and unclaimed, in plain sight.

Of course, there was so much else to see after the Soviet government dissolved on December 25, 1991, and select Soviet archives opened, briefly, to eager, intrepid scholars. The earliest forays into the stacks were transformational for many, leading John Earl Haynes and Harvey Klehr, for example, to publish *The Secret World of American Communism* (1995), a book in which they revealed the existence of an archive of evidence in the USSR confirming what Cold Warriors had been arguing (shouting) for decades: that the Communist Party in America (CPUSA) had "maintained an underground arm, a fact long denied by many historians." (The word "denied," of course, doesn't begin to conjure the adamantine refusals of "many historians" who, kicking and screaming, failed to face already overwhelming evidence to the contrary—and still do.[31])

There was more: This American Communist underground, in the words of Haynes and Klehr, "cooperated with Soviet intelligence in espionage against the United States," while the CPUSA as a whole "was indeed a fifth column working inside and against the United States in the Cold War."[32] Like a Soviet Frankenstein, the CPUSA was the creation of Moscow masters, and now, finally, there was overwhelming documentary proof to see at the source.

To say Cold Warriors knew such things all along is to miss the devastating point. For the forty years since the end of World War II—or, to use that more instructive historical marker, for the sixty-two years since the United States recognized the USSR in 1933 in exchange for promises that, among things, the Soviet Union would not wage a clandestine war against the United States from within—this crucial fact of Soviet-directed subversion was, to varying degrees, in play. Contested. Derided. Denied. The anti-anti-Communists denied it existed; the anti-Communists argued that it did exist, suffering the slings and arrows—"witch hunters!" "Red-baiters!"—of outrageous slander. What is worse, however, is the discovery that the U.S. government, almost from the start, knew the truth about the existence of the Communist conspiracy, having amassed its own evidence, a secret archive of irrefutable documentary confirmation of Soviet-orchestrated espionage. These top secret decryptions of intelligence cables from KGB agents in Washington and New York to superiors in Moscow between 1943 and 1948 would become known to the public as the Venona archive, but not until 1995—and only *after* findings from Soviet archives had already begun to be published.[33]

Question: Why did the U.S. government allow this destructive, corrosive civil war—the "debate" over whether Communist conspiracy existed—to rage on even as it continued to enlarge its own secret archive of proof?

On this crucial question there is mainly conjecture about what was for fifty years an unbroken wall of official silence. Like all such silence, it only served the Communist conspiracy itself, the Other Side, desperate to shield itself from all glints of light on its treasonous activities. Typically, intelligence historians make only desultory arguments to justify the U.S. government's Silence Was Golden Policy, but I'm not buying. Since the rationales the experts offer are speculation, we don't have to.

What do you do with the disturbing evidence, brought forward by Jerrold and Leona Schecter and reinvestigated and affirmed by the late Robert Novak, that Harry S. Truman, for example, was informed *as early as 1950* that findings from the Venona project confirmed both Assistant Treasury Secretary Harry Dexter White and former State Department official Alger Hiss as Soviet agents? The Schecters further reveal that according to their source a select group of Washington movers and shakers were similarly informed of Venona's early findings. Included in this group was Philip Graham, publisher of *The Washington Post,* the newspaper Whittaker Chambers would later describe as "the most implacable of the pro-Hiss newspapers."[34] (Haynes and Klehr reject this hypothesis.[35]) If true, however, this means "the brunt of official wrath" that Chambers and other anti-Communists continued to bear could not have arisen from official ignorance. Suddenly, we have evidence of a deeply troubling level of official complicity in the Communist conspiracy of silence.[36] Why would Truman and later Eisenhower have done nothing with the Venona revelations? Why would they have uniformly failed to reveal the truth and disperse the political poison in the body politic?

These aren't just questions about what took the government so long. They are more urgently questions about what moral compass, what petty political considerations, allowed these powerful men to permit American citizens such as Chambers, Bentley, and many, many others including their defenders (elected representatives, lawmen, investigators, and journalists, not to mention anti-Communist citizens and refugees), to be pilloried, undermined, and personally destroyed, hounded from a public square scrubbed clean of the truth. What role, if any, did the Communist penetration of the U.S. government play in their decision to prolong the confusion and subterfuge? What does the extent of this penetration mean for our own history—or, rather, what we have always thought of as our own history (but which clearly was rather more intertwined with that of our Main Adversary than we have previously understood)? Assessing the impact, the effect, the toll of the penetration, then, is the vital exercise that is long overdue. Even the most virtuostic intelligence researchers, perhaps concentrated as they are on locating, extracting, verifying, analyzing, and assembling the data themselves, seem loath to attempt this. Indeed, the Grand Historical Impact of the very subversive activities they labor to chronicle, working from clues and secrets as cryptic as those of ancient civilizations, is left more or less hanging. Of course, maybe Grand Historical Impact isn't part of their job description. Or maybe they, too, remain subject to the false framework in which the focal point of controversy turns narrowly on whether active Soviet espionage networks existed in the United States in the first place. Anti-Communists recognized all along that they did indeed exist, and tried to expose them; anti-anti-Communists swore all along that they didn't, or didn't amount to much, and attacked the anti-Communists for their efforts.

This particular argument is now settled once and for all, and spread the word. In their monumental 2009 book *Spies: The Rise and Fall of the KGB in America,* Haynes, Klehr, and Alexander Vassiliev, for example, after nearly two decades of research, arrive at the bottom line—literally—on page 548, the final page of their book:

> It was no witch hunt that led American counterintelligence officials to investigate government employees and others with access to sensitive information for Communist ties . . . but a rational response to the extent to which the Communist Party had become an appendage of Soviet intelligence. And, as the documents in Vassiliev's notebooks make plain, they only knew the half of it.[37]

It was no witch hunt. It was a rational response. They only knew the half of it. With these very simple sentences, a universe, if not a galaxy, is inverted—or, rather, is turned right side up again. End of book, end of story.

But . . . isn't something missing? Aren't some apologies in order? Some rather extravagant wreaths of orchids and rosebuds for the lonely graves of unsung heroes? Putrid heaps of scorn to dump, liberally, on the heads of their tormentors? The fact is, under the sheer and unstoppable weight of the new evidence, a war has reversed outcomes. Due to fresh and confirming documentation, a verdict of history has been overturned. However, there has been no real reckoning. No tangible crystallization. No click of realignment. No truth commission. *And no mea culpas.* A most extensive pattern of Soviet infiltration is a documented fact, but the old pantomime goes on even as it no longer makes sense on its own terms.

McCarthy, bad.

Communists, good and/or nonexistent.

Anti-Communism, terrible.

Venona is interesting and everything, but . . . *Have you left no sense of decency?*

The pretense will endure as long as we allow it to, until the point arrives at which we finally dare face the logical implications of these newly mined, polished, glittering, glaring, blinding facts.

Their implications being what precisely?

Their implications being that for many crucial years, American statecraft was an instrument of Soviet strategy.

CHAPTER FOUR

Thousands who do not hesitate to speak their minds vigorously about other social philosophies or political regimes stop short, panic-stricken, when it comes to speaking their minds on communism.

—EUGENE LYONS[1]

Honestly, I anticipated a smoother landing, a gentle glide path coming to rest in a deep cushion of seamlessly interlocking historical arguments. Instead, there it is, washed up like some great, beached sea creature requiring emergency resuscitation: American statecraft as an *appendage* of Soviet strategy. What does that mean?

I like to think the answer is readily manifest in the mountains of intelligence evidence that have come into view in the last twenty years like a heretofore undiscovered range. That's because I've already been out and about in them, clambering through the documentation scholar-explorers have amassed on their travels into virgin archival territory on my own quest to explain permanent apathy over Communism's crimes and Soviet dissolution, and reflex animus toward anti-Communism's "crimes" of exposure. Such "crimes," from anti-Communist investigations to anti-Communist military campaigns, would rate as gallant, good-guy pushback were it not for that permanent apathy.

We can quickly get our bearings, at least, from these same mountains of evidence, old and new: "old" meaning, for example, the scores of U.S. government officials ID'd as Soviet agents by Elizabeth Bentley and Whittaker Chambers sixty-plus years ago, and "new" meaning, for example, recent confirmation that those chance, voluntary, could-just-as-easily-never-have-happened revelations were correct. In fact, as Haynes, Klehr, and Vassiliev like to put it, Bentley and Chambers "only knew the half of it," adding, "KGB sources of whom they were unaware honeycombed the federal government and its scientific laboratories."[2]

That debate, at least, is over. That is, Washington, D.C., was, yes, a giant hive of Soviet intelligence activity. A massive Communist conspiracy did, in fact, exist. There was indeed a "Red plot against America," orchestrated by the KGB and related Soviet branches and executed by an extensive network of American traitors. Cold Warriors, who, notes Robert Conquest, were supposedly "opposed to the Soviet system because of some irrational predisposition" (hence the tag "rabid" anti-Communist), *were right all along.*[3]

That last bit still tears it, probably. While this is the logical implication of these newest sets of facts haltingly working their way into national consciousness, it devastates what is still, despite those facts, the conventional wisdom and venerated mythology. The earth is flat. McCarthy was wrong. A legacy of denial remains.

At the same time, a new paradox has emerged. Many of the bunk-busting experts seem to regard the recently opened book on Soviet penetration activities (the very book these same experts themselves opened) as a simultaneously closed chapter. That is, the so-called golden age of Soviet espionage, 1933–45, which coincides exactly with FDR's White House years, comes across as an era with a beginning and, more important, an end. It stands as a long national nightmare we were fortunate enough to wake up from and leave behind. As Daniel Patrick Moynihan is quoted summing up, elder-statesman-style, in *The Haunted Wood* (2000), Allen Weinstein and Alexander Vassiliev's masterful account of this golden age, "by the onset of the Cold War, the Soviet attack in the area of espionage and subversion had been blunted and turned back." That means "blunted and turned back" by 1946, the conventional starting point of the Cold War. Moynihan further wrote, "By the close of the 1940s, Communism was a defeated ideology in the United States, with its influence in steep and steady decline, and the KGB reduced to recruiting thieves as spies." In other words, case closed, and what a relief: Now readers are free to relish all of these perfectly thrilling, true tales of deception in books such as *The Haunted Wood* as guilt-free entertainments from history's vaults, solutions to forgotten riddles and nothing more.

Weinstein and Vassiliev concur with Moynihan's sweeping release, offering as corroborating evidence their assessment that the 1945 defections of both Elizabeth Bentley and Igor Gouzenko, a former Soviet code clerk in Canada, destroyed the Soviet spy structure, ending most Soviet spying.[4] Nine years later, even the subtitle of *Spies* by Haynes, Klehr, and Vassiliev drives the same point home: *The Rise and Fall of the KGB in America.* Operative word: "fall."

I don't mean to suggest that Soviet espionage activities were *not* checked by the revelations and investigatory efforts of a motley crew of anti-Communists on watch and in the spotlight, or coming in from the cold. Certainly, though, Moynihan's claim that Communist "influence" was over and done with by

1950, as well as the expert conclusion that the KGB withdrew from the secret American battlefield altogether, conveys a sense of both ideological and operational victory that is unwarranted. Such misplaced, dare I say, "triumphalism" is belied by the ever-flickering flames of Communist sympathy on the Left, flames that would supercharge the Marx-inspired "Long March" through America's institutions that characterize the postwar era,[5] and that continue to shape (betray) our national character, our outlook as a people, to this day. It is a creaky kind of closure that leaves the question open as to the malevolent source and poisonous nature of this ongoing ideological assault.

Indeed, the authors of *Spies* make note of the loose ends. Calling Elizabeth Bentley's defection to the FBI "the single most disastrous event in the history of Soviet intelligence in America," they describe its profound impact. Not only did Bentley correctly identify scores of Soviet sources—M. Stanton Evans pegs the total at around 150 network members or collaborators[6]—she also had the effect of refocusing the FBI's counterespionage efforts. Her timing was just right. It was on November 7, 1945, when she presented herself to the FBI—coincidentally or not, an anniversary of Lenin's 1917 takeover of the Russian Revolution. Both World War II and the US-USSR wartime alliance had come to an end, and hundreds of agents previously working on German and Japanese counterespionage were free and, more important, politically unleashed to focus on Communist networks. The authors continue:

"Her revelations triggered a wholesale withdrawal of experienced KGB officers that left the agency's American stations woefully unprepared for the opening years of the Cold War, led to the public exposure of links between the American Communist Party and Soviet intelligence that destroyed the former's use as an espionage Fifth Column, and additionally tainted the Communist movement with treason, contributing to its political marginalization."[7]

If so—and it's worth remembering that the links between the American Communist Party and Moscow were open to question if not disbelieved in many quarters when Haynes and Klehr dragged the evidence out of Soviet archives in the 1990s—why doesn't this great American woman have a statue somewhere? Her alma mater, Vassar, would do nicely for starters. Just as Yale pays monumental homage to its own renowned spy, Nathan Hale, Vassar should pay homage to Bentley. Why not? The answer, of course, is obvious: On the American college campus, hothouse of Marxist pedagogues and incubator of American elites, a spy against the colonial British monarchy merits celebration whereas a spy against the colonial Communist dictatorship is anathema. In that Marx-influenced outlook lies our greatest problem: the anti-anti-Communist stranglehold on the narrative. Thus, not only is Elizabeth Bentley reviled in the academy, but Bard College in upstate New York has set up the

"Alger Hiss Professor of Social Studies," and Columbia University boasts the "Corliss Lamont Chair of Civil Liberties." The University of Washington is home to the "Harry Bridges Center for Labor Studies," which showcases "a celebration of Communists in Washington [State] history as well as a condemnation of anyone who dared criticize communism."[8]

Furthermore, say Haynes and Klehr, "FBI investigations and voluminous congressional testimony supported Bentley's story. The documents in Vassiliev's notebooks, as well as the KGB cables deciphered by the Venona project, *demonstrate unequivocally that Bentley told the truth*" (emphasis added).

Vindication, yes; justice, no.

"Yet the consensus of several generations of American historians (backed by many journalists and other opinion leaders) routinely mocked, ridiculed, and dismissed her as a fraud and mountebank."[9]

They still do. Which takes us back to Square One, or, rather, Stumbling Block One: the mentality—make that the *psychosis*—of historians, journalists, and opinion makers impervious and hostile to facts. Pages and books and stacks of facts. They are also even more impervious and even more hostile to the logical, often ineluctable *implications* of these facts, which are devastating to the conventional wisdom and venerated mythology. In this impaired mindset I think we see the ultimate impact of Communist influence, Communist conspiracy. The complete subversion of logic is what it *did* to us. In this sundering of fact from implication lies the end of Enlightenment thinking, the seedbed of cultural decline, the rise of the godless but nonetheless cultishly religious Left, and the disintegration of a faltering, also damaged Right. Into this same breach between fact and implication, between implication and judgment, has rushed antilogical, contrafactual "political correctness" and also amoral cultural relativism.

To grapple further with this concept, it's crucial to understand that this secret assault, this domestic front of the Cold War—which I suggest we backdate to 1933, the onset of both Soviet espionage's "golden age" and the Sovietophile Roosevelt administration (which conferred diplomatic recognition on the Soviet Union that year)—was always about far more than eavesdropping and filching scientific formulas or battle plans. The "other" side of espionage—subversion, deception, disinformation, provocation, and influence—has an intangible impact compared to "spying," but its effects can be every bit as significant if not much more so. Nonetheless, history consistently minimizes or overlooks them altogether, and not just in the entertainment-oriented Spy Museum in Washington, D.C., where the entire history of espionage is almost exclusively depicted as the literal theft of secrets. Despite their centrality to the forward thrust of the USSR—or, come to think of it, probably *because of* their centrality to the forward thrust of the USSR—these stealth tactics have never entered our understanding of our historical experience. When it comes to what we know as a people, with lore to remember and stories to pass on, and, more urgently, when it comes to how we react and act as people, with occasions to rise to and crises to solve, we tend to draw a big, fat blank.

Let's examine that blank more closely. One simple, concrete measure of the success of Soviet subversion in America is the near-total absence of movies that dramatize arguably the primary historical drama of the last century: the struggle—military, guerrilla, spiritual, artistic, personal—against spreading Communist totalitarianism. It wasn't until *The Lives of Others* came out in 2006 that we even saw the first serious cinematic treatment of Communist dictatorship in Europe—and that was made by a young German writer-director, Florian Henckel von Donnersmarck, who was born in 1973. His youth was an indictment of one, two, three generations' failure to withstand, let alone overcome, the influence of the Other Side on the most essential modes of thinking and expression.

In *Hollywood Party: How Communism Seduced the American Film Industry in the 1930s and 1940s*, Kenneth Lloyd Billingsley plumbs the movie vaults to rattle around these gaping holes in celluloid memory. Thousands of Germans alone risked their lives to break out from behind the barbarically inhuman Berlin Wall and find freedom in the West, he writes, but only a single Hollywood offering (*Night Crossing* from Disney, 1982) ever dramatized this inhuman scenario. Similarly, the screen goes dark on perilous escapes closer to home—from Fidel Castro's Cuba, a Marxist regime that executed political rivals, imprisoned poets, and persecuted homosexuals. For serious depictions of the Soviet Union as a giant jail, there is *Never Let Me Go* (1953), starring Clark Gable and Gene Tierney, about an American journalist fighting the Soviet state for a visa for his Russian wife, but what else? While screen heroes inspired by Marxist sensibilities or Nazi villainy still abound, who can name one anti-Communist good guy from the movies? Meanwhile, Billingsley writes, "not a single Hollywood film has ever shown Communists committing atrocities." Given the toll—an estimated one hundred million dead of Communism in the twentieth century according to *The Black Book of Communism*—that's a mind-boggling omission. So far, I've only found one exception: *Knight Without Armor,* a gem of a 1937 movie starring Robert Donat as a British agent and Marlene Dietrich as a Russian aristocrat. In a raw scene of terror, Red Army forces mow down White Russian prisoners. Instead, when it came to the Terror Famine in the Ukraine or the Moscow show trials, Hollywood spewed out pro-Soviet propaganda with *North Star* (1943) and *Mission to Moscow* (1943).

Nicknamed "Submission to Moscow," this latter movie was a landmark achievement in made-in-the-USA Soviet propaganda, and with good reason. It was based on the 1941 bestselling book of the same title by U.S. ambassador to the Soviet Union Joseph E. Davies, and Davies was a Soviet apologist's Soviet apologist. For example, Davies was quick to reassure Washington in 1938 that when it came to the Moscow show trials, public travesties (enabled by future Nuremberg dignitaries) in which Stalin liquidated his political rivals on false charges, there was "proof beyond reasonable doubt to justify the verdict of guilty of treason."[10] Far from losing his career over such base propaganda, Davies remained a senior adviser on Soviet affairs to FDR and, later, to Harry Truman. Davies was not only a liar, however; he was also an ignoramus on such affairs, as he himself admitted to the State Department's Elbridge Dubrow, who dutifully and officially recorded Davies's comments in early 1943. What amounts to an extraordinary personal confession is worth quoting at length:

> Mr. Davies in a very frank frame of mind stated he had been "very lucky" in the attitude he had deliberately adopted regarding the Soviet Union. He added that predicting international events and trends was really a matter of speculation and that he had been lucky in his speculation on the Soviet Union . . .

Remember, this is the go-to guy on Things Soviet.

> In expanding this theme to some length Mr. Davies explained that because of his lucky predictions regarding the Soviet Union and particularly the prowess of the Red Army he had gained the reputation of being an expert on the Soviet Union. He stated that while he had endeavored to the best of his ability to learn all he could about that country during his comparatively short stay there [as ambassador!] he realized fully he did not have a complete and basic knowledge of the country.

Notice, however, that this didn't stop him from dispensing advice.

> He stated that because of this fact he felt that at the present time, particularly in connection with his statement of last Sunday regarding the trustworthiness of Stalin, he was "whistling by the graveyard" since he realized that in making such a prediction he was going contrary to the facts of the past *but felt it was necessary to make such a statement in order to try to prepare the ground for a basic understanding* [emphasis added].[11]

If wishing wouldn't make it so, maybe a statement "going contrary to the facts" would.

So runs the thinking process of an influential American official in the midst of creating a lie with enormous implications—Stalin is trustworthy—and what do we discover? He's operating on desperation, chicanery, and delusion. By chance, we have seen how a leading Soviet "expert" of the day abandoned the solid ground of facts for the perilous, looking-glass world of what-might-be-if, where even good intentions become a perverted basis for evil actions. We see it here in 1943, vis-à-vis the Soviet Union; we see similar thinking processes nearly seventy years later vis-à-vis Iraq and Afghanistan, where what-might-be-if strate-gies running contrary to Islamic realities have disastrously prevailed.[12]

I am not suggesting Davies's intentions were good, however. He knew too much about the facts he saw fit to dismiss, and indeed appears to have been garishly compensated to dismiss them. How? Drop in on Hillwood, the Wash-ington, D.C., estate of the late Marjorie Merriweather Post (Toasties), sometime and see. Open to the public, the Georgian-style mansion houses the largest col-lection of Russian decorative art outside Russia—Fabergé boxes and eggs, reli-gious icons, tiaras, samovars, paintings, tea sets, Cossack daggers, jewelry, and stacks and stacks of gilded porcelain dishes. Much of it was picked up—no, shoveled up—by Post and Davies during their marriage in what Davies himself described as an "orgy" of buying that coincided with his tenure as Soviet am-bassador from 1936 to 1938.[13]

Didn't that coincide with the Moscow show trials?

You betchum. There's a connection, too, as Robert C. Williams notes in his book *Russian Art and American Money*: "The wave of terror of 1937 had flooded the art market with items that could compromise their owners as being bour-geois, religious, or worse. The desperate were divesting themselves of incrimi-nating evidence; the Davies were among the foreign beneficiaries."[14]

The Davieses were well aware of the "desperate" and their "divestments." On March 22, 1937, Joseph wrote a letter to his daughter describing the "inter-esting" state-run "commission shops." They resemble "our antique shops," he wrote, and "sell all manner of things brought in by their owners, *including those taken over by the government from the 'purged' high officials.*" (emphasis added). This disclosure is edited out of this letter as it appeared four years later in Da-vies's book *Mission to Moscow,* Williams notes[15]—one more act of denial to make the world go around. Life, dinner parties—blood purges, rummaging through the art of the "purged"—went on.

Example: Davies wrote in his journal on March 13, 1938, that ho, hum, Bukharin was sentenced to death today, and that he and Marjorie had gone to the commission shop and "picked up a few odds and ends." Two days later, Williams notes, Marjorie received for her fiftieth birthday, among other trin-kets, a Fabergé topaz box set with gold and diamonds, an eighteenth-century gold perfume bottle, a malachite and lapis lazuli cigarette box, a silver samovar, and "a large painting of some happy collective farm workers"—nice socialist-realist ballast.[16] Tim Tzouliadis IDs this painting as *Peasant Holiday in the Ukraine* in *The Forsaken*, his unforgettable 2008 account of American citizens abandoned in the Gulag by the U.S. government. The painting, Tzouliadis writes, "a cultural negation of a famine that killed five million" on view at Hillwood in the dining room, is "waiting for someone with sufficient grace to take it down." When I checked in 2012, it was in storage.[17]

Marjorie, by the way, knew the score, too. Thirty years later, she told an interviewer she used to hear vans pulling up in the middle of the Moscow night, followed by women and children screaming as the NKVD made arrests and carted off loved ones. Marjorie also said she was regularly awakened by the sound of gunfire. "I know perfectly well they are executing a lot of people," she told her husband the ambassador. "Oh no," he replied. "I think it's blasting in the new part of the subway."[18]

I've wandered through Hillwood's public rooms. The docents will tell you that this largest collection of Russian decorative art outside of Russia came together during those years *Marjorie* spent in Moscow trolling the commission shops. Davies, who was Husband No. 3 out of four, gets scant mention. It's almost as though he has been purged from her biography. Speaking of purges—which the docents do not—Williams writes that during this period of Moscow show trials and blood purges, "the commission shops had about them the scent of death."[19] With that in mind, a visit to the collection becomes an unnerving experience. Display case upon display case of dishes—luminously colored porcelain, gold-leafed and often with royal crests—still give off the whiff of terror and doom Williams mentioned. It is too easy to imagine the great houses that were emptied of these luxuries, their owners murdered by the regime that helped the Davieses acquire them by the gross at a bargain price. Judging by the merely impressed faces of museum visitors, the treasures have become no more than an art lover's pleasure, sundered from their bloody political provenance. This, too, has become just more "facts" to ignore, as Davies discussed back in 1943, to "prepare the ground for a basic understanding."

What of the Davies statement, the one that prompted his personal confession to Dubrow, the foreign service officer who then placed it in the official State Department record? A few days earlier, on January 30, 1943, Davies had been quoted in *The New York Times* as having "deplored the 'damned poor judgment' of those who expressed fears at the time that if Russia's army went through to Berlin, Premier Josef Stalin would dictate the terms of the peace and communize Europe."

Such talk, Davies declared, was "bunk."[20]

Really?

Such talk was clairvoyant, but what did it matter to those on a "mission" to and from Moscow? Both the Davies book and movie, conceived of as a means of persuading a reluctant U.S. public to support Lend-Lease aid to the USSR, were, as historian Todd Bennett writes, "conscious instruments" of White House foreign policy.[21]

Or was that conscious instruments of Soviet foreign policy?

"The only task of literature was that of fulfilling the social directions of Stalin," said a Soviet poet quoted by Nicholas S. Timasheff in *The Great Retreat: The Growth and Decline of Communism in Russia,*[22] by way of explaining the role of the Soviet artist in the school of Socialist Realism. This was a role the Hollywood Ten, Twenty, Thirty, Hundred—proud "Stalinists"—took equally seriously. Which is another reason why we have no cinematic offerings on Patton's Washington-thwarted push to liberate Prague in 1945, the 1944–47 forced repatriation to Soviet custody (and often death) of two million Soviet-claimed nationals who thought they'd escaped to freedom in the West, the 1956 Hungarian uprising against the Soviet military . . . Both the epic drama of Prague Spring (1968) and the Soviet-backed crackdown on Poland's Solidarity movement (1981) seem to be backdrops for just one film apiece: the former in a fleeting sequence in *The Unbearable Lightness of Being,* and the latter in *To Kill a Priest,* which, as Billingsley points out, "failed to detail the politics involved."[23]

These aren't "American" stories, you say?

What about the "lost" heroics of CIA agents the world over? Rambo aside, what about the truly lost Americans, thousands of American POWs from every American war involving the USSR, beginning with World War I, whom the U.S. government unconscionably and reprehensibly left behind, often to languish as medical guinea pigs in Soviet hell?[24] Or the American citizens, unemployed Depression pilgrims and, worse, their American children, whom the U.S. government allowed to live out their time on earth as prisoners of the Gulag Archipelago?[25] Stateside, what about the flatfoots, the G-men, who shadowed honest-to-goodness Communist conspirators? We have *The House on 92nd Street,* an interesting 1945 movie with FBI heroes trailing a Nazi spy ring operating on Manhattan's Upper East Side, but no movie features FBI heroes trailing myriad Communist spy rings operating in New York and Washington. What about the spies who came in from the cold, the ones forced into a life of unjust ignominy, and the ones who committed "suicide"? Or the congressional investigators who took intensive White House heat (à la Rep. Martin Dies) and press vilification to expose what they knew, despite the wall of liberal static, was treason? What about Joe McCarthy, who loved his country, tried to defend the Constitution, and, as the evidence, increasingly collected and sorted, tells us, was right every time?

These are American dramas, all right, but they all went down the memory hole, discarded as tainted goods unfit for public consumption, let alone dra-

matic treatment and thus a place in cultural memory. At this point, I must interject a personal note—so deeply personal I almost forgot to include it, not from
shyness exactly, but due to its internalized place in my psyche. My father, Elliot
West, a novelist and Hollywood writer, was a veteran of World War II. He cast
his first vote for FDR somewhere in northern Europe in 1944 and his second
vote for Henry Wallace in New York City in 1948. He later signed a petition
against the execution of the Rosenbergs in 1953 and refused to sign a CBS loyalty oath around that same time (my mother doesn't remember exactly when).
No later than 1960, however, he had become unreservedly and outspokenly
anti-Communist. Indeed, some of my earliest memories are of loud voices rising
up the stairs from the living room, where a dinner party had become a heated
argument over the Vietnam War, "youth" protests, rock 'n' roll, Watergate, racial
quotas—the greatest political hits of a tumultuous time.

In 1969, he sold a story to Houghton Mifflin to write a novel about a Berkeley professor and Spanish Civil War veteran who had had an Orwell-like epiph-
any on the evils of the Communist Left, which the professor saw reconstituted
around him in the Vietnam antiwar movement. Within a week of signing the
deal, some large number of Houghton Mifflin editors, presumably sympathetic
if not linked to this same movement, *threatened to resign en masse* if this one
book with a viewpoint they did not share stayed on the Houghton Mifflin list.
To make a short story shorter, my dad wrote a completely different book that
year—and never got back to that Berkeley novel. Later, in 1978–79, despite
high-profile agency representation, he got nowhere faster with another anti-
Communist novel, this one set amid what he called *The Third Front*—the Communist infiltration of Europe during World War II—and the forced "repatriation"
of 2 million Soviet-claimed nationals, most of them to death and imprisonment
in the USSR. The IBM Selectric–typed manuscript, two-thirds complete, sits in
a box behind my desk—the perfect metaphor for all of the anti-Communist
stories that remain unincorporated into our lore. Such masses of evidence have
accumulated in odd, unsorted piles outside and separate from the narratives we
"know." I don't think it is inapt here to quote Solzhenitsyn, who, considering
the muzzled state of Russians still in the shadow of the Gulag, wrote, "And if
we do not show that loathsomeness [of the state] in its entirety, then we at once
have a lie. For this reason I consider that *literature did not exist* in our country
in the thirties, forties, and fifties. Because without the *full* truth it is not literature" (emphasis in original).[26]

We Americans didn't show "that loathsomeness" in its entirety, either, and,
as I've noted before and remain struck by, we weren't operating under

threat of the Gulag. How did our process of literary selection, which certainly wasn't always natural, take shape? Billingsley points, for example, to the efforts of one John Weber, a Marxist labor organizer whose party work in Hollywood included organizing the Screen Story Analysts Guild, a Communist-dominated group that read—i.e., vetted or nixed—movie scripts. Just for good measure, the vice president of the guild was another Communist Party member, Lillian Bergquist, who also served as the chief script analyst for the Bureau of Motion Pictures (BMP), the Hollywood branch of the Communist-dominated Office of War Information (OWI).[27]

Incredibly, disastrously, Weber went on to head the literary department at the William Morris Agency, then the preeminent talent agency in town, another choke point from which to monitor the flow of work and workers (writers). Such control was a point of strategy, but it was also a point of pride, prompting the odd indiscreet revelation—and thank goodness. One prize gaffe came from Oscar-winning screenwriter and Communist Dalton Trumbo, later a poster boy for Hollywood martyrdom during what we think of as the Hollywood Blacklist days, the period in the 1950s during which studios and producers officially "blacklisted" Hollywood Communists conspiring with Moscow to overthrow the U.S. government.

But . . . isn't that treason?

Trumbo's statement, made in 1946 in *The Worker* (petted Hollywood screenwriters are "workers," too!), brags about a de facto *anti-Communist blacklist* that effectively prevented stories told from the anti-Communist perspective from getting to the silver screen. There might be a dearth of "progressive" movies on-screen, Trumbo admits, "but neither has Hollywood produced anything so untrue or reactionary as *The Yogi and the Commissar, Out of the Night, Report on the Russians, There Shall Be No Night,* or *Adventures of a Young Man.*" He goes on to tick off a few more significant anti-Communist manifestos, gloating over their never-to-be-exploited commercial value. "Nor does Hollywood's forthcoming schedule include such tempting items as James T. Farrell's *Bernard Clare,* Victor Kravchenko's *I Chose Freedom,* or the so-called biography of Stalin by Leon Trotsky."[28]

Clearly, there existed a Hollywood blacklist before there existed *the* Hollywood Blacklist. Trumbo's statement breaks down to a basic message: Even if "progressive" (read: Stalinist) movies are tough to put over, take heart, comrade; every "untrue," "reactionary," "Trotskyist" hot property that comes along and gets rejected is a victory for Mother Russia. Some of those titles, it's important to note, preceded the U.S. wartime alliance with the USSR (1941–45), coming along during the time of the Nazi-Soviet Pact (1939–41). This is something to keep in mind the next time tears are ordered up for a Hollywood Blacklist pity party. The fact is, Dalton Trumbo, martyr of the 1950s "Red Scare," hero to the 1960s Berkeley Free Speech Movement, was himself "a blacklister before he was himself blacklisted."[29]

Further, the Communist Party maintained an index of proscribed works Party members were not "allowed" to read. In *I Chose Freedom,* Victor Kravchenko describes the inner life of "totalitarian subjects abroad" who "remained the terrorized subjects of a police-state" and, as such, had to contend with censorship and other restrictions even while stationed in America. Any indiscretion—reading a Russian-language publication deemed "counterrevolutionary" was the worst offense, but almost any American newspaper was suspect (exceptions: *The Daily Worker, PM, The Nation,* and *The New Republic*)—could mean political suicide or even worse.[30]

Even more shockingly, similar restrictions were supposed to apply to *American* Communists—even tanned and lotus-eating Hollywood types. Ex-Communist Hollywood director Edward Dmytryk relates in his 1996 memoir *Odd Man Out: A Memoir of the Hollywood Ten,* the following exchange he had with producer Adrian Scott near the beginning of their fruitful collaboration that produced such films as *Cornered, Crossfire,* and *Murder, My Sweet.* There they were, two young princes of Hollywood, strolling across the RKO lot one day, when Dmytryk mentioned he'd been reading an interesting book.

"What book," asked Scott.

"Koestler's *Darkness at Noon,*" I replied.

Adrian stopped short, and, as I turned to face him, he spoke in a subdued voice. "Good God!" he said. "Don't ever mention that to anyone in the group!"

"Why not?" I was honestly puzzled.

"It's on the *list!*" he breathed, looking a little embarrassed. "Koestler is corrupt—a liar. He is an *ex*-communist, and no member of the Party is allowed to read him."[31]

Dmytryk was flabbergasted. Not only had he been unaware of such a "list," he hadn't known Scott was a Party member. (That this was a revelation demonstrates the effectiveness of "cells" in maintaining Party secrecy.) *Allowed by whom?* Dmytryk wanted to ask, but he writes that he didn't say anything. In the end, of course, no movie fan was "allowed" to see Koestler's gripping indictment of Communism on the silver screen, either—or any other anti-Communist story like it.

The backstory of *Out of the Night,* another title on Trumbo's blacklist, is similarly revealing. Although it is a forgotten book today, Princeton literature professor John V. Fleming includes this memoir of Communist and Nazi intrigue and adventure by the pseudonymous Jan Valtin, whose real name was Richard Krebs, among the four "anti-communist manifestos" that shaped the Cold War.[32] Appearing in January 1941, *Out of the Night* was a publishing sensation, teased in two successive issues of *Life* magazine, featured by the Book of the Month Club, and chosen as a *Reader's Digest* book selection. It would be a bestselling book of 1941. It would also be one of the last trade book exposés of Communist crime published until 1945, an information vacuum that neatly coincided with our wartime alliance with Stalin.

In 1942, Bennett Cerf, the storied chief of Random House, would actually propose that the American publishing industry *withdraw from sale* all books critical of the Soviet Union.[33] While this frankly totalitarian proposal to pull pre-"politically incorrect" books from the shelves did not go into effect, it highlights both the receptivity to Soviet propaganda and the hostility to the anti-Communist critique that were prevalent in literary circles. Indeed, in December 1941, publishing titan Cass Canfield of Harper & Brothers, pulled back *already distributed* review copies of Leon Trotsky's critical biography of Stalin (so contemptuously dismissed by Oscar-winning Commie flack Trumbo).

The story of the publication of the Trotsky book was an epic in itself. As the editor's note to the edition finally released in 1945 rather sanguinely notes, "Like most authors, Trotsky was more optimistic than accurate about the expected date of completion, and his case was aggravated not only by the excessive optimism of the revolutionist and military leader but by continual harassments and *attempts on his life*" (emphasis added).

On August 20, 1940, Trotsky was still at work on his Stalin biography when an assassin sent by Stalin plunged an ice pick into his head, splattering his manuscript with his own blood. Some parts of the book were utterly destroyed in the ensuing struggle. Still, Harper assembled, edited, and published a finished book by December 12, 1941, when—historical significance, epic effort, blood, and murder aside—the publisher decided to consign it all to the memory hole. Stalin murdered Trotsky? Cass Canfield murdered Trotsky's *Stalin,* But with finesse. In his note calling back the Trotsky book from public view, flagged by George Orwell in a letter to his English publisher (shortly before Orwell began writing *1984),* Canfield rather elegantly wrote to prospective reviewers, "We hope you will co-operate with us in the matter of avoiding any comment whatever regarding the biography and its postponement."[34]

Any comment whatever. The Trotsky recall took place just days after the attack on Pearl Harbor that drew the United States into World War II. Harper also withdrew *My Year in the USSR* by *New York Times* correspondent G. E. R. Gedye, while Doubleday, Doran canceled the spring publication of *One Who*

Survived, the reminiscences of ex-Soviet diplomat and military officer Alexander Barmine. These publishing recalls were reported in the March–April 1942 edition of *Partisan Review,* which, decrying the wartime pressures being exerted on political speech, also announced the creation of a new department, "Dangerous Thoughts," to "give publicity to the more significant instances of suppression of free thought from month to month."[35]

Did these appalling acts of censorship serve the "greater good"—namely, the wartime alliance with USSR to defeat Hitler? That's the consensus, but I reject it. Why? The effect, intended by all too many, was to harness the evil of Hitler to deny the evil of Stalin. In the end, it was a big, fat load of this "greater good" argument that strengthened and perpetuated a greater evil—the USSR, the true victor of World War II due in large part to the successful campaign in the West to whitewash Communist crime and to coddle Communist criminals.

This wasn't just an American whitewash. Across the pond, Churchill's 1932 book *Great Contemporaries,* a collection of biographical essays, was crudely bowdlerized in a 1941 reprint that cut out—purged—two opponents of Stalin, Trotsky and Boris Savinkov. It further censored an acerbic critique of George Bernard Shaw's notorious 1931 visit to the Communist regime in Moscow in which no Soviet lie was too big to swallow. This brings to mind the famous story of how in 1953, following the trial and execution of Lavrenty Beria, former NKVD chief, editors of the *Great Soviet Encyclopedia* sent out a notice to subscribers urging them to cut out the Beria entry "with a small knife or razor blade" and replace it with an essay on the Bering Sea, which the editors thoughtfully provided. So how can we deride the Soviets as heavy-handed censors without also deriding ourselves?[36]

Returning to *Out of the Night,* from the Hollywood perspective, it had it all—"adventure, danger, suspense, violence, tear-jerking romance, steamy sex," writes Fleming, besides being "an eventually patriotic and morally uplifting true story for our times." In terms of anti-Communist appeal it had everything, too: a vast criminal conspiracy directed by Moscow; Party orthodoxy rigidly enforced from within by internal spies and purges; parallels between Stalin's regime and Hitler's regime, which were (and remain) the biggest no-no of all. In Trumbo's Hollywood, this book was DOA—"untouchable," Fleming writes, and even before Nazi Germany attacked Communist Russia on June 22, 1941.

Three days later, on June 25, noted Hollywood producer and director Albert Lewin wrote a letter describing what Fleming would later call the "informal censorship" that suppressed anti-Communist works in Hollywood: "Although 'Out of the Night' would not be an easy book to make into a picture, I thought it would surely have sold long before this because of the enormous popularity of the book. I have made some inquiries and have been told that there was considerable interest among some producers, but that *Washington indicated its disapproval out of a desire not to offend Russia*" (emphasis added).

No word, alas, on how "Washington indicated its disapproval," or who did the indicating. Lewin's letter continues, "Evidently the attack on Russia will make it still more unlikely that anyone would want to market an anti-Communist picture now."[37]

Due to the German attack on the USSR, Lewin predicted it would be "still more unlikely" that *Out of the Night* would ever have any Hollywood takers. This suggests the Washington campaign against the book had begun earlier, during the period of Soviet-Nazi alliance as codified in the Molotov-Ribbentrop pact of 1939. Somebody, as Trumbo implied, didn't want anti-Communist stories made into movies no matter what. So they weren't.

The net effect of these pro-Soviet machinations? In plain Brooklynese, we wuz robbed. As a culture, we were stripped of defining events and people, markers and guides that should have been familiar signposts along the nation's path, not historical specialties waiting to be discovered (or not) via academic research. These books, these stories, all of these people, were ideological casualties of the Communist conspiracy, and their losses reflect our own. These omissions contribute to the funhouse-mirror reflection of our distorted worldview. We struggle to make sense of an artificially incomprehensible void, unenlightened by the repetition of empty buzz words ("McCarthyism") and the appearance of 2-D villains ("Red-baiters"). Truly, this is "the black hole of anti-knowledge," where the twentieth-century struggle against Communism—against the "Red menace," the "Communist peril"—is sucked in and swallowed up. Recent research may validate the use of such terminology as "menace" and "peril," but it is "Have you left no sense of decency?" that echoes on in our collective consciousness, even if it makes no sense at all—*and never did*.[38]

Welcome to the culture of omission, with gaps, blanks, and disconnects throughout. Such holes tend to go unnoticed, but sometimes they trip us up, and perplexingly so. At the end of *The Sword and the Shield* (1999), a landmark compendium of files copied from KGB archives, Cambridge don and doyen of intelligence historians Christopher Andrew and ex-KGB archivist Vasily Mitrokhin note the fact, apparently puzzling to them, that most historians ignore intelligence history, including Venona and other such archives. This has meant, they continue quite logically, that the standard studies of the Cold War, biographies of Stalin, and histories of the Soviet Union in general have overlooked the central role played by the operations and achievements of the intelligence and security organs of the Soviet state, chief among them the KGB. Listing some historical works notable for such omissions, the authors further note, "In many studies of Soviet foreign policy, the KGB is barely mentioned."[39]

This fact is not only astonishing, it is nonsensical—"physics without mathematics, if you will," as KGB historian John J. Dziak wrote, describing exactly the same phenomenon a decade earlier in *Chekisty: A History of the KGB*.[40] Andrew and Mitrokhin go on, almost ingenuously, to take a stab at analysis: "Though such aberrations by leading historians are due partly to the overclassification of intelligence archives . . . , they derive at root from what psychologists call 'cognitive dissonance'—*the difficulty all of us have in grasping new concepts which disturb our existing view of the world*. For many twentieth-century historians, political scientists and international relations specialists, secret intelligence has been just such a concept" (emphasis added).[41]

It's impossible to say whether Andrew and Mitrokhin realize what a damning indictment of "twentieth-century historians" they have just issued, despite the ameliorating tag of empathy: *the difficulty all of us have in grasping new concepts . . .* It's as if to say, there these twentieth-century historians were, poor babies, busily fitting the facts into their "existing view of the world," when, all of a sudden, KGB history reared its view-changing head. What else could they do? Like a Hollywood producer turning down *Out of the Night* in deference, direct or indirect, to the local Hollywood and White House commissars, or like an Allied prosecutor at Nuremberg editing his indictment to protect Stalin's legal and moral vulnerabilities, historians have scotched evidence that would displease these same masters—and would also undermine their own "existing view of the world." Andrew and Mitrokhin sum up this existing worldview this way: It is "the common assumption of a basic symmetry between the role of intelligence in East and West."[42]

This "common assumption" requires either taking a chain saw to the record or wearing a blindfold permanently. So what if we miss the KGB effect on Soviet foreign policy? Undermining that "common assumption" of "basic symmetry" would mean shattering the mirror imagery between the U.S. and the USSR in general, and we mustn't have that. End of mirror imagery, good-bye nuanced palette of le Carréllian grays with which such historians have painstakingly painted a murky age of moral and other equivalences between the Free World and totalitarianism. End of nuanced palette, good-bye age of moral and other equivalences. *Maybe even good-bye moral relativism, too.*

So what if, as Andrew and Mitrokhin point out, "the Cheka and its successors"—GPU, OGPU, NKVD, KGB (today FSB)—"were central to the functioning of the Soviet system in ways that intelligence communities never were to the government of Western states"? So what if, as the authors write, they "were central to the conduct of Soviet foreign policy as well as to the running of the one-party state"?[43]

One-party state?

Heavens, get that one-party state out of my existing view of the world. It's wrecking my common assumption of basic symmetry.

Soldiering on, Andrew and Mitrokhin seem fairly hip to the problem, but then soft-soap its cause: "The failure by many Western historians to identify the KGB as a major arm of Soviet foreign policy is due partly to the fact that many Soviet policy aims did not fit Western concepts of international relations."[44]

That's some failure. That's some way to dress up the cause of that failure, too. "Western concepts of international relations" is a nice way of describing the alternate reality created by Soviet "agitprop"—agitation and propaganda—which, to varying degrees, is precisely what was devastated by the evidence Andrew and Mitrokhin amassed in their own book. It is such evidence that so discombobulated the intellectual elite's "existing view of the world," from Hollywood studios to New York publishing houses to faculty lounges, with precious few exceptions.

British historian Robert Conquest is one such magnificent exception. Conquest's special branch of Soviet history might well be called Soviet exterminationism—a new "ism," perhaps, but one that fittingly encapsulates the history of mass murder Conquest has immersed himself in, cataloging and analyzing the boggling scale of murder and tragedy deliberately wrought by the Communist regime in Russia. His macabre exercise began, most notably, with his history of Stalin's purges of the 1930s, *The Great Terror.* The book came out in 1968, a time when no other historians were even acknowledging the existence of this hulking wound of a subject, a time when, amazingly, Joseph E. Davies's twenty-seven-year-old pro-Stalin tract, *Mission to Moscow,* was still the first and last word on the subject. Noting the Conquest book's uniqueness in 1968, Andrew and Mitrokhin called it "a sign of the *difficulty* encountered by many Western historians in *interpreting* the Terror" (emphasis added).[45] When Conquest finally marshaled the available research and put a number on the horror—twenty million killed during the Stalin period—it was as though the historian had additionally become a cold-case criminologist and, further, by implication, a hanging judge. As crunched by columnist Joseph Alsop, commenting in 1970 on a particularly callous review of the Conquest book and its themes, those twenty million souls killed by the regime represented one-eighth of the entire Russian population "of that period, in peacetime and without provoking a whisper of protest."[46]

How could that be? Without understanding the extent of Communist penetration into the decision-and-opinion-making echelons of the West—and, as important, into the decision-and-opinion-making *minds* of the West—the question is baffling, a mystery without clues, a historical brick wall. From our vantage point, blanks and all, it is almost impossible to comprehend how it could have been that our relatives and forebears, apparently sentient, apparently decent Americans, could have looked on in neutral silence as the Soviet state, year after year, starved and brutalized and enslaved millions of its own people to death—news of which did indeed spread throughout the West despite Soviet censorship and prevarication, although it remained outside consensus.[47] Dalton Trumbo, as we've seen, took pride in the silence on the Hollywood front. He's hailed as a martyr of idealism. Historians, as we've seen, looked the other way, strenuously, to protect their precious "basic symmetry." They remain figures of respect and authority. How—and when—did these and other inversions of logic and morality, common sense and common decency, begin to take place?

Two extraordinary and very different works by journalist Eugene Lyons take us a little closer to the answer. One is *The Red Decade* (1941), "an informal account of Bolshevism in our country," as he described it, and the other is *Assignment in Utopia* (1937), his memoir of his personal odyssey from committed fellow traveler of Communism and dedicated apologist of the Soviet experiment to outspoken and remorseful anti-Communist. Where *The Red Decade* surveys the Communist penetration of the opinion-and-decision-making echelons of the West, *Assignment in Utopia* examines its effect on the Western opinion-and-decision-making *mind*—Lyons's own—and how the ideology, once internalized, acts on conscience, reason, and also the survival instinct. His experience is singularly instructive.

Through Lyons's reflections we see from the inside looking out what we usually try to understand from the outside looking in. As a general memoir of disenchantment with Communism, Lyons's book is by no means unique; there is a rich literature on the subject.[48] However, as a working journalist, a gentleman of the press ("mainstream media" came much later), Lyons, who served as United Press Agency's Moscow correspondent between 1928 and 1934, offers an uncommon perspective on ghastly, seminal events, and how and why they were reported to the outside world, or not.

As Lyons's fervor for the Soviet experiment waned, his insights into the Communist state's use of terror—and American willingness to excuse such terror—grew and sharpened until they became personally unbearable. Not the typical reaction, alas. In tracing the fissures of doubt that would slowly develop into crevasses large enough to swallow up his Communist loyalties, Lyons adds to our understanding of how the culture of omission we have inherited evolved, and how its creators actually operated.

Lyons perfectly sums up the internal workings of what we know now as

"media bias," at that time a largely new phenomenon in terms of both ideological impetus and global impact:

> In the first year or so of my Russian sojourn [1928], my imported convictions
> were a sieve that sifted events for me; reporting was no more than a physical job
> of finding and transmitting "desirable" information; I needed only a little dex-
> terity in wishing away or explaining away the rejected materials.

Kind of like one of Andrew and Mitrokhin's see-no-KGB historians.

> Later, when doubts obtruded themselves and my instincts were more and more
> hurt, the sifting became more and more a mental effort, paid for in self-
> reproach.[49]

Such "self-reproach" turned out to be the undeniable thorn of conscience,
but it could just as easily have been the ever-gratifying tickle of masochistic torment. Had things gone differently, he writes, had he not, specifically, returned
to Russia after a 1931 sojourn in the States for his final, ultimately therapeutic
dose of Communist reality, he might have "evolved a new, if badly scarred and
patched enthusiasm." Later, he would think that by returning for ultimate disillusionment he had "escaped something vaguely shameful," and that had he not
returned to Russia for the second half of his Moscow tour, "I might have
ended by contributing high-minded lies to the New Masses and slept happily
ever after."[50]

Still, self-extrication was a long process. Lyons writes of self-censoring pressures that sound like a set of adolescent anxieties: "the anxiety to 'belong' in the
dominant social circles in Bolshevik Moscow, the fear of being rejected by the
only circles that mattered to me at home." These "played their roles in keeping
me 'friendly,'" he writes, along with more concrete, professional concerns.[51]
Only "friendly" correspondents could remain in Russia. The slightest deviation
from the Party line could draw a meaningful official warning, for example, in a
sudden inaccessibility of Soviet officials, or a delay in obtaining travel visas.
Indeed, the totalitarian culture of censorship that Westerners—press, diplomats, businessmen, industrialists—came all too quickly to accommodate was
probably the key source of lasting and corrosive moral compromise. Which reminds us of the crucial role free speech plays in a moral society.

S. J. Taylor, in her frank biography of *New York Times* correspondent Walter
Duranty, the most notorious Soviet apologist in the Moscow press corps, reveals an early example of this phenomenon. In mid-1932, she writes, after British business interests sent a Canadian agricultural expert named Andrew

Cairns to study the effects of forced collectivization on Soviet agriculture, the results of the study—"a record," British ambassador Sir Esmond Ovey wrote at the time, "of over-staffing, overplanning and complete incompetence at the centre; of human misery, starvation, death and disease among the peasantry . . . Workers are left to die in order that the Five Year Plan shall at least succeed on paper"—was suppressed by this same British ambassador. Taylor writes, "In a somewhat puzzling statement, Ovey wrote, 'The pity of it is that this account cannot be broadcast to the world at large as an antidote to Soviet propaganda in general.' "

Why ever not? Weren't these facts exactly what the world desperately needed as an antidote to poisonous Soviet propaganda? Wasn't this report exactly what the peasants, already dying of starvation by the tens of thousands, were owed? Taylor duly explains the apparent reason the publication of Cairns's report was "postponed" (à la Trotsky's Stalin bio censored by Cass Canfield). The British Foreign Office wanted to send Cairns back to Russia the following spring—presumably to write another report that would be similarly "postponed"—"but because of the controversial nature of Cairns's first report they feared he would be refused a return visa if it were published."[52] In the end, Cairns did not return; the report languished unpublished. Western complicity in the Terror Famine, the Stalinist assault on the peasantry that killed an estimated six million people between 1930 and 1933, may be seen as having been, from the start, a matter of business as usual.

Where true believers such as Eugene Lyons were concerned, however, self-censorship wasn't only a matter of narrow tactical calculation. He writes of "the bugaboos of loyalty and consistency, the need to safeguard my faith; a frantic desire to save my investment of hope and enthusiasm in the Russian revolution"[53]—motivations that more than anything else speak to an unbecoming human weakness for self-validation, an ego-driven cause all too many find irresistible even as they end up clinging to fraud like an anchor of self-esteem. A man's faith in Communism must be justified simply because it is his faith. It is his "investment," as Lyons put it, that must be protected along with his "consistency." *How could I have been so dumb* is the neon-flashing subtext to be blacked out by heavy overlays of falsehood or "carefully sifted" truth. Thus Lyons safeguarded his faith, and he succeeded, publicly, for some years after doubts had set in.

On returning home to the U.S. in 1931, Lyons was something of a celebrity for having scored the first, two-hour, sit-down interview with the elusive Stalin himself (much to *Times*man Duranty's consternation). "It was," Lyons writes, describing the 1930s equivalent of 24/7 media coverage, "front-paged throughout the world, quoted, editorialized, put on the radio by the 'March of Time' as one of the ranking 'scoops' in recent newspaper history." It was also, he confesses, "a magnificent opportunity frittered away." Amid the flood of congratulatory telegrams from around the world, Lyons confesses to having been "far from exultant."

> I thought of all the searching questions which I might have asked but had been too idiotic and too timid and too grateful to ask and I was overwhelmed with a conviction of failure. I had failed to confront Stalin with the problems which were by this time weighing on my own conscience—the use of terror as a technique of government, the suppression and punishment of heretical opinion within the ranks of devoted communists, the persecution of scientists and scholars, the distortion of history to fit the new politics, systematic forced labor, the virtual enslavement of workers and peasants in the name of the socialism which was to emancipate them.[54]

From this extraordinary mea culpa comes a sense of the grotesque mismatch that pit vain and weak mortals against the inhuman, supernatural evil of Stalin, starkly and terrifyingly apparent in 1931 even as the majority of his twenty million victims still lived. But maybe that's giving the journalist a sentimental pass. I confess to liking Lyons from his work, and admiring his post facto honesty that drove him to reveal himself in such a brilliantly unflattering light. Such revelation helps us learn how these omissions, these collusions, these twistings of the truth come about.

"In my purely professional thrill of a Stalin interview, I had been content to remain politely on the lacquered statistical surface of the Soviet scene."[55]

All the way home across Europe and the Atlantic in 1931—the land and sea odyssey back to the safe haven of the Statue of Liberty, New York City—Lyons "wrestled with the problem of how much of what I had seen and what I had thought I should tell," a problem that reveals his internalization of the totalitarian taboo. Such candor is refreshing if also disturbing. As a vital source of public information, Lyons was torn by a dilemma that was in fact no private matter, particularly once United Press dispatched its star correspondent on a public lecture tour (having plugged his recent series summing up his three years in Russia in foot-high letters on delivery trucks: THE TRUTH ABOUT RUSSIA). It was here that Lyons succumbed to emotional currents he felt emanating from his Depression-era audiences. "I had intended to paint a more realistic picture," he writes of a lecture stop in Youngstown. "But the simple believing people, their eyes pleading for reassurance, . . . could not be denied."[56] And remember, Lyons had already concluded (and declared privately) that the USSR was a terror-state.

It all seemed far away from Youngstown and the other twenty cities in the throes of economic crisis that Lyons toured in the northeast, so far away that, he writes, "your mind imposed its own favorite designs upon the Soviet contradictions, choosing, discarding, arranging, hastily repairing the damage wrought by three years of immersion." He continues, "Whatever your American lectures may have done to the listeners, they almost convinced the lecturer. By compromising with your experiences you nearly sneaked back into the comfortable groove of uncritical faith . . . [The] dead are dead and the maimed are dying, and what if another million dung-colored Russians are driven into the marshes and forests and deserts, if the great idea marches forward."[57]

Chilling words. After all, "What if?" here means "So what?" Anything to keep the "great idea" moving forward—particularly if it were only millions of "dung-colored Russians" standing in the way. It's hard not to hear a shocking echo: *The dead are dead and the maimed are dying and what if another million dung-colored Jews are driven into the ovens just a few years later, if the great idea marches forward . . .*

But that's different.

Is it?

The difference I see is that the Nazi totalitarian "great idea" was always inseparable from its toll, but the Soviet totalitarian "great idea" was *always separated and protected from its toll.* We never ask why one Holocaust matters when multiple holocausts do not, why one "great idea" of totalitarianism was only totalitarian and the other was only great. We condemn the German population of a police state for looking the other way from and doing nothing about Jewish annihilation under way in Nazi concentration camps; we never think to question ourselves living large in a free world and looking the other way from and *saying nothing* about ethnic, political, class, and religious annihilation under way in Soviet concentration camps. This split vision derives from the triumph of Communism's unceasing world revolution against "traditional" morality, objective morality, a morality of fixed standards by which men navigate, or at least perceive the shoals of evil and treacherous behaviors. Such morality tells us there is no separating the idea from its toll. This is the lesson we have erased from our slate.

In Malcolm Muggeridge's 1934 novel *Winter in Moscow,* a bitter send-up of the expat community in Moscow and its indifference to what Robert Conquest would later document as the Terror Famine that killed millions in the Ukraine in the early 1930s, one character observes starving peasants begging for bread. To Muggeridge, who had arrived in Moscow in 1932 "effervescing with Soviet sympathies" that would rapidly go flat (within just a few months, as fellow journalist William Henry Chamberlin observed[58]), "the idea," which others used to justify or ignore the famine, meant nothing, as his character in the novel makes clear: "Whatever else I may do or think in the future, he thought, I must never pretend that I haven't seen this. Ideas will come and go, but this is more than an idea. It is peasants kneeling down in the snow and asking for bread. Something I have seen and understood."[59]

On his real-life return to the USSR, Eugene Lyons would see and eventually understand. He writes of finding the familiar old mind games, the sifting techniques, no longer effective on his return. "With every week after my return I came to feel more ashamed of my mealy-mouthed caution while at home," he writes. "Deep under those excuses I had made for myself, I now was forced to admit, had been the subconscious desire to remain persona grata with the masters, retain my job. I was protecting my status as a 'friendly' correspondent. And at that I had just about crawled under the line."[60]

There Lyons was to stay at least long enough to participate in a seminal event in Soviet crime and Western turpitude: what Robert Conquest would much later identify as the very first successful implementation of the "Big Lie"—the concerted assault on truth to form world opinion, in this original case, to deny the regime-engineered Famine in the Ukraine. It was a Faustian turning point.

Conquest writes:

On the face of it, this [deception] might appear to have been an impossible undertaking. A great number of true accounts reached Western Europe and America, some of them from impeccable Western eyewitnesses . . .

But Stalin had a profound understanding of the possibilities of what Hitler approvingly calls the Big Lie. He knew that even though the truth may be readily available, the deceiver need not give up. He saw that flat denial on the one hand, and the injection into the pool of information of a corpus of positive falsehood on the other, were sufficient to confuse the issue for the passively instructed foreign audience, and to induce acceptance of the Stalinist version by those actively seeking to be deceived.

Flat denial plus a corpus of positive falsehood: Sounds like another black hole of antiknowledge, another corroding attack on the basis of the Enlightenment itself. Conquest describes this concerted effort to deceive the world about the truth of the state-engineered famine, Stalin's brutal war on the peasantry, as "the first major instance of the exercise of this technique of influencing world opinion."[61]

This instance, then, was a seminal moment in the history of the world. *The* seminal moment, perhaps, of the twentieth century, a moment in which history itself, always subject to lies and colorations, became susceptible to something truly new under the sun: totalitarianism; more specifically, the totalitarian innovation of disinformation, later expanded, bureaucratized and, in effect, weaponized, by KGB-directed armies of *dezinformatsiya* agents.

What do I mean by "armies"? Ion Mihai Pacepa, former chief of intelligence in Communist Romania, told me, "During the Cold War, more people in the Soviet bloc worked for the dezinformatsiya machine than for the Soviet army and defense industry put together. The bloc's intelligence community alone had over one million officers (the KGB had over 700,000) and several million informants around the world. All were involved in deceiving the West—and their own country—or in supporting the effort."[62]

That came later. It had to start somewhere, though, and so it did. By 1936, after civil war broke out in Spain, George Orwell could sense a sea change in the writing of history, of news, of information, of the handling of what he called "neutral fact," which heretofore all sides had accepted. "What is peculiar to our age," he wrote, "is the abandonment of the idea that history *could* be truthfully written." Or even that it should be, I would add. For example, he wrote, in the *Encyclopedia Britannica*'s entry on World War I, not even twenty years past, "a respectable amount of material is drawn from German sources." This reflected a common understanding—assumption—that "the facts" existed and were ascertainable. As Orwell personally witnessed in Spain, this notion that there existed "a considerable body of fact that would have been agreed to by almost everyone" had disappeared. "I remember saying once to Arthur Koestler, 'History ended in 1936,' at which he nodded in immediate understanding. We were both thinking of totalitarianism generally, but more specifically of the Spanish Civil War." He continued, "I saw great battles reported where there had been no fighting, and complete silence where hundreds of men had been killed . . . I saw newspapers in London retailing these lies and eager intellectuals building emotional superstructures over events that had never happened."

Then he hits it precisely: "I saw, in fact, history being written not in terms of what happened *but of what ought to have happened* according to various 'party lines'" (emphasis added).[63] Ideology over all.

That had to start somewhere, too. The confession-minded Eugene Lyons seems to know where. In fact, he was present at the creation. Chapter 15 in Lyons's book *Assignment in Utopia* is called "The Press Corps Conceals a Famine." It lays out the basics about what he called in 1937 "the whole shabby episode of our failure to report honestly the gruesome Russian famine of 1932–1933." This group failure is best but by no means exclusively characterized by the eye-rolling bunk Pulitzer Prize–winning Walter Duranty would cable home as news to *The New York Times,* which was in fact Soviet-sanctioned propaganda

designed to justify a brutal and unprecedented war to destroy millions of peasants. To familiarize ourselves with Duranty's techinque, here from March 1,
1933, is how he rationalized the forced, violent uprooting of one million peasant
families to all but certain death in penal colonies in the north:

> The Russian masses may and do grumble about shortages and other difficulties,
> but there is no sign they are horrified, alarmed or even disapproving at the sight
> of "removals" of recalcitrant peasants . . .
>
>   They accept the Bolshevist explanation that "class enemies" must be de-
> feated and made powerless, and, as far as this writer can see, they accept it read-
> ily as a natural and indeed excellent thing.[64]

Thus, Westerners, free men as defined by the Magna Carta, the Rights of Man,
the Constitution, the Bill of Rights, and the American Way (even though Duranty himself was English), capitulated to the totalitarian machine. They listened to and amplified the agitprop of the "Bolsheviki" and the *nomenklatura*
(priviledged bureaucracy). When it came time to face the Terror Famine, they
preferred to construct their own, pre-Orwell memory hole to rid themselves of
the truth.

   It is an extraordinarily wide press conspiracy that Lyons goes on to describe,
all of it designed to undermine the veracity of one man, one outlier, a lone truth
teller who came, who saw, who reported—and, most important, made headlines. This singular person was twenty-seven-year-old Gareth Jones, a brilliant,
Russian-speaking, Welsh journalist who had served as David Lloyd George's
secretary, and whose initial, attention-grabbing statements to the press on
reaching Germany, after extensively debriefing his journalistic colleagues in
Moscow and completing a secret trek through the starving areas of the USSR,
brought the famine into the light. Exposure. His sensational report was carried
in many newspapers including *The New York Evening Post, The London Evening Standard,* and *The Manchester Guardian,* where another, ultimately more
enduringly famous truth teller, Malcolm Muggeridge, had just published several mainly overlooked articles about the state-organized mass starvation in
progress.[65]

   "Everywhere was the cry, There is no bread. We are dying," Jones told the
world, which drove frantic editors back home to send a flurry of cables asking
their Moscow correspondents why they couldn't hear that same cry. "But the
inquiries coincided with preparations under way for the trial of the British engineers," Lyons explains, referring to the now-forgotten Metro-Vickers show
trial that would see six British engineers convicted of espionage and ejected
from the country. This, according to Lyons, became the correspondents' over-

riding concern because there was a "compelling professional necessity," he writes, to remain on "friendly" terms with the censors, at least for the duration of the trial.

A paper-thin excuse, it would seem, but the cover-up organized to discredit Gareth Jones was airtight. Lyons writes, "Throwing down Jones was as unpleasant a chore as fell to any of us in years of juggling facts to please dictatorial regimes—but throw him down we did, unanimously and in almost identical formulas of equivocation."[66]

Like a scene out of *Comrade X*—a classic romantic comedy starring Clark Gable and Hedy Lamarr set amid the Moscow press corps (which, believe it or not, packs grim elements of truth about the Soviet regime, no doubt to Dalton Trumbo's consternation)—the real-life correspondents gathered in one reporter's Moscow hotel room one evening in the spring of 1933. There, chief censor Comrade Umansky, "the soul of graciousness," Lyons writes ironically, joined them. Due to the upcoming British engineers' trial, incredibly, Umansky had leverage over the correspondents' famine coverage, or so the men believed—or so they *wanted* to believe. Indeed, in Lyons's eyes, "it would have been professional suicide to make an issue of the famine at this particular point." So, he writes, through "much bargaining in a spirit of gentlemanly give-and-take . . . a formula of denial" was worked out among them.

"We admitted enough to soothe our consciences, but in roundabout phrases that dismissed Jones as a liar. The filthy business having been disposed of, someone ordered vodka and *zakuski* [hors d'oeuvres], Umansky joined the celebration, and the party did not break up until the early morning hours."[67]

A more morally sordid scene is hard to imagine. As for that "formula of denial" the correspondents worked out, Duranty would take the lead, as usual, and write a first-person smackdown of Jones in his next-day report—headline: RUSSIANS HUNGRY, BUT NOT STARVING—dismissing the Welshman's "big scare story" in *The New York Evening Post* as hasty, wrong-headed, anti-Soviet thinking. Duranty admitted there was a lack of bread in the villages but put this fact down to mismanagement, inexperience, even "conspiracy." He also inserted his chilling, trademark line: "But—to put it brutally—you can't make an omelette without breaking eggs." Indeed, Duranty went on to compare the Soviets' indifference to "casualties" in their "drive toward Socialization" with that of generals who might order a costly battlefield attack. Of course, he overlooked the potentially extenuating circumstance that generals are typically driving an enemy from the homeland, while the Soviet regime was fighting its people on their farms. Classic bottom line in prevarication: "There is no actual starvation or deaths from starvation, but there is widespread mortality from diseases due to malnutrition."[68]

Got that? No deaths from starvation, but widespread mortality from diseases due to malnutrition. To understand this episode is to understand the extent to which Orwell's "Newspeak" had its birth in the pages of the free press as much as in the totalitarian censor's office.

Naturally, Gareth Jones objected to Duranty's personal attack on his credibility and published a strong response in which he underscored both the veracity and the variety of his sources and evidence. In so doing, Jones also noted his discussions with "between twenty and thirty consuls and diplomatic representatives of various nations" whose testimony supported his own. Jones continued:

> But they are not allowed to express their views in the press, and therefore remain silent.
>
> Journalists, on the other hand, are allowed to write, but the censorship has turned them into masters of euphemism and understatement. Hence they give "famine" the polite name of "food shortage," and "starving to death" is softened down to read as "widespread mortality from diseases due to malnutrition." Consuls are not so reticent in private conversation.[69]

That's no saving grace in my book. These consuls Jones refers to were not only as intimidated by Soviet censorship as the journalists were, they were equally as culpable in aiding and abetting this first, crucially significant Big Lie. Looking back over more than three-quarters of a century of Big Lies to follow, this initial instance, this first time, demands a level of scrutiny and reflection it doesn't ordinarily receive, not having been widely recognized as the Original Sin that would ultimately corrupt us all. It was as if society suddenly became incapable of making the most elementary if also vital connections between facts and conclusions, logic and judgment, ideas and implications, and truth and morality.

More than three decades later, in 1968, when Robert Conquest came along with his testimonies, his figures, and his footnotes attesting to the colossal horror of the Soviet regime, first regarding the Moscow show trials, and then, in 1985, with his testimonies, his figures, and his footnotes attesting to the Terror Famine in the Ukraine, there was no need to meet in a hotel room with a Soviet censor and work out a conspiracy of denial and drink to it with vodka. Nor was there consciousness of such a need. The legacy of denial had become so powerful in the interim as to have become imperceptible and stunningly effective. "The main lesson seems to be that the Communist ideology provided the motivation for an unprecedented massacre of men, women and children," Conquest wrote, but class was incapable of learning.[70]

"People accepted his facts, but they didn't accept his conclusions," British writer Neal Ascherson said to the British newspaper *The Guardian* in 2003, perfectly crystallizing the intelligentsia's permanent reaction to Conquest.[71] This facts-sans-implications formulation is key. It sounds so reasonable. *Come, come, dear boy; no one is rejecting your facts, just your conclusions.* There may indeed be extreme "food shortages," but widespread mortality is due to diseases associated with "malnutrition," not famine. Facts, yes. Conclusions, no. However, such facts *are* conclusions because they are *crimes*. Soviet *exterminationism* is *Soviet* exterminationism (emphasis on Soviet), just as Nazi *genocide* is *Nazi* genocide (emphasis on Nazi). Reject the conclusion and the facts, the crimes, become meaningless. Indeed, such facts demand judgment, just as such crimes demand a verdict. As Conquest put it:

> The historian, registering the facts beyond doubt, and in their context, cannot but also judge. *Die Weltgeschischte ist das Weltgericht*—World History is the World's Court of Judgment: Schiller's dictum may seem too grandiose today. Yet the establishment of the facts certainly includes the establishment of responsibility.[72]

The Left tried to drive a wedge between the facts as Conquest marshaled them and the conclusions as he drew them, making efforts to taint both due to his evident "dislike" of purges, terror, and death camps—or, as Eugene Lyons might have put it ironically, his middle-class liberal "hang-overs of prejudice" against dictatorship, mass slaughter, and the crushing of the human spirit. Conquest writes:

> It was believed that a "Cold Warrior" became opposed to the Soviet system because of some irrational predisposition . . . The idea seems to be that if one can show that opposition to the Soviet threat was in part based on dislike of Soviet actualities and intentions—that is, "emotions"—then the opposition cannot have been objective. But, of course, the Soviet system was indeed disliked, even detested, *because* of its record and intentions.[73]

What Conquest's detractors dismissed as "emotions"—namely, "dislike of Soviet actualities and intentions" (including twenty million killed by Stalin)—was in fact a historian's verdict of responsibility regarding such crimes. Visceral feelings aside, it is a judgment based on evidence, logic, and moral analysis. These are the same underpinnings of any rational investigation into Nazi "actualities and intentions" and subsequent finding of their detestable nature. No one would pause over the following slight reworking of a Conquest line quoted above: "The main lesson seems to be that the Nazi ideology provided

the motivation for an unprecedented massacre of men, women and children"—
but insert "Communist ideology" into the sentence and boy, look out.

"No one could deal with this," he writes of his *Great Terror* research, "or
other themes I wrote of later, unless judgmental as well as inquisitive; and those
who denied the negative characteristics of Soviet Communism were deficient in
judgment and in curiosity—gaps in the teeth and blinkers on the eyes."[74]

To be able to "deal with" the evil of Communist extermination history,
then, as Conquest writes, is to be judgmental as well as inquisitive. This suggests a continuum between such fruits of curiosity and academic labor—the
repugnant facts of Communist extermination history—and our judgment of
them. The gap-toothed and blinkered ones, however, set out to interrupt this
continuum, to sunder these facts from their conclusions, to explode the whole
logical exercise that begins in facts and ends in conclusions into senseless fragments—to *decontextualize* it (and everything else while they're at it). Yes, the
Nazi system killed six million people (fact), and yes, the Nazi system was evil
(conclusion); and yes, the Soviet system killed twenty million people (fact), but
how dare that "cowboy" Ronald Reagan call the Soviet Union the "evil empire"?

Like postmodernism itself, this massive inconsistency on Nazism and Communism doesn't make a shred of sense. If making sense were the goal, the
phrase "evil empire" would have been a trite truism, a hoary cliché long before
Ronald Reagan uttered the words, which, like the most potent incantation,
drove tribes of intelligentsia the Western world over into fits of mass hysteria
and rage—*against evil Reagan,* not the empire. If the words today no longer
conjure the same teeth-gnashing indictment of Old West simplicity they once
did, they still manage to strike a spark or two of faux outrage. Also, the quotation marks of irony have yet to fall away.

I went back to the original Reagan speech recently, realizing I'd never heard
or read any more of it than that signature phrase. Reagan was addressing evan-
gelical Christians at a time when the so-called nuclear freeze, which we now
know to have been a colossal Soviet influence operation,[75] was under debate in
Congress and Reagan was proposing to deploy Pershing missiles in Europe.
Two weeks later, he would announce his Strategic Defense Initiative (SDI),
which, even as it became the obsession that would drive the final Soviet dictators to exhaust the Communist system in their futile efforts to compete, was
endlessly caricatured in Western media as a "cowboy's" comic-book ray gun of
choice straight from *Star Wars*—no doubt a Soviet-encouraged moniker.

The speech is surprisingly mild. I was surprised to learn that by the time
Reagan gets around to mentioning the "evil empire," he was not inveighing
against the USSR directly but rather against the creed of moral equivalence, at
the time the very definition of intellectual chic. It's hard to convey the intensity

of the drumbeat for moral equivalence in those days. It was background noise and op-ed commentary, the premise of debate ("Resolved: There is no moral difference between the world policies of the United States and the Soviet Union," Oxford Union debate, February 23, 1984) and the endings of movies (*Three Days of the Condor* [1975], *Apocalypse Now* [1979], *Reds* [1981]). The era Reagan was trying to end was one of entrenched belief in "ambiguities" between capitalism and Communism, between liberty and tyranny. It was too much for one man to do, even Ronald Reagan.

"We're all the same, you know, that's the joke," East German agent Fiedler remarks to British agent Leamas in *The Spy Who Came In from the Cold,* le Carré's stunningly successful 1963 novel that instituted the le Carré brand. This joke was an old story by the 1980s, the conventional wisdom, the Establishment point of view. It still is. By 2008, le Carré was confiding to *The Sunday Times of London,* over fragrant, amber-colored glasses of Calvados, as the waves crashed at the foot of the cliffs below the author's Cornwall home, that he had himself been tempted to defect to the Soviet Union.[76]

> "Well, I wasn't tempted ideologically," he reasserts, in case there should be any doubt, "but when you spy intensively and you get closer and closer to the border . . . it seems such a small step to jump . . . and, you know, find out the rest" [ellipses in original].

The rest about the twenty million killed? Heavens, no. *The Times* explains:

> This is maybe less surprising than at first it seemed: we are in true le Carré territory, *nuanced and complex,* where the spying is sometimes an end in itself and *where there is rarely an easy, Manichaean split between the good guys and the bad guys.* Defecting was a temptation the writer resisted, to our good fortune [emphasis added].

To each our own. What is remarkable here is less the "news" about le Carré than the ease with which the reporter absorbs this point of moral cretinhood, conveying the author's view as a beguilingly piquant eccentricity even as it skirts the charnel houses the man found himself fascinated and not repelled by. Such enthusiasm would not have greeted a thriller writer who expressed a temptation to "jump . . . and, you know, find out the rest" about, say, the Third Reich.

If an unhealthy attraction to the Soviet Union was still respectable as recently as 2008, imagine how outrageous the phrase "evil empire" sounded twenty-five years earlier. This is what Reagan actually said:

In your discussions of the nuclear freeze proposals, I urge you to beware the temptation of pride—the temptation of blithely declaring yourselves above it all and label both sides equally at fault, to ignore the facts of history and the aggressive impulses of an evil empire, to simply call the arms race a giant misunderstanding and thereby remove yourself from the struggle between right and wrong and good and evil.[77]

Reagan's exhortation to face "the facts of history" was a broad challenge, his reference to "the aggressive impulses of an evil empire" an "Emperor's New Clothes" moment. The cataclysmic histories of Ukraine, Finland, Bessarabia, Lithuania, Latvia, Estonia, Poland, Bulgaria, Romania, Czechoslovakia, Hungary, Austria, Korea, East Germany, Vietnam, China, Cuba, Angola, and on and on were not the shining raiment becoming an empire of peace. Reagan was challenging us to acknowledge the *implications* of this fact, to fight the paralysis of "moral equivalence," and see not two bullies in a playground, as the East-West struggle was repetitiously framed, but one aggressor seeking to impose a totalitarian system over as much of the world as possible. Good and Evil. Reagan may have had to struggle to explain this to the West, but the Soviets, as Robert Conquest reminds us, looking back from the vantage point of 2005, were never unclear, morally or otherwise, about their intentions:

The Soviet Union, right up to the eve of its collapse, was committed to the concept of an unappeasable conflict with the Western world and to the doctrine that this could only be resolved by what Foreign Minister Andrey Gromyko described, as officially as one can imagine (in his 1975 book *The Foreign Policy of the Soviet Union*) as world revolution: "The Communist Party of the Soviet Union subordinates all its theoretical and practical activity in the sphere of foreign relations to the task of strengthening the positions of socialism, and the interests of further developing and deepening the world revolutionary process."[78]

As Conquest added, "one could hardly be franker."

Ah, Gromyko. In the outraged uproar *in the West* over Reagan's "evil empire" speech in the spring of 1983, the Soviet foreign minister called an unusually extended press conference to offer his response. As reported by *The New York Times*'s Serge Schmemann, the resulting story ran under the eye-catching headline GROMYKO NEWS CONFERENCE: A "VIRTUOSO PERFORMANCE."[79] The quotation in the headline comes from the reporter himself, who wrote that unnamed "Western experts agreed that his [Gromyko's] performance was virtuoso." You can almost see the *Times* reporter nudging a colleague in the room and saying,

"Hey, wasn't that a virtuoso performance?," getting a nod back, then duly noting the "expert" consensus.

Gromyko's performance was virtuoso, all right, exceeding all boundaries of veracity, all measure of reality. "Mr. Gromyko poked the air with his forefingers as he condemned Mr. Reagan's statements on the Soviet Union," a separate *Times* news story reported. " 'If it were possible to start compiling charts of the amount of evil in the two systems,' he said, 'I want to assure you that the height of the curve for the United States would be *hundreds of times higher than ours*' " (emphasis added).[80]

No report I've seen indicates that the correspondents received this comment with anything other than rapt attention, quiet professionalism, and serious consideration. As that world-class whopper took shape, rose, and broke over the room, it's easy to imagine the scratch of pens on steno pads, the spinning tape recorders, the furrowed brows, the nodding heads. I can also imagine the murdered millions, for whose deaths the Soviet Union was never tried, and who did not rise, could not rise, from mass graves beneath the permafrost to condemn this new lie. Maybe that's because there really is no such thing as ghosts. Or maybe it's because the gravitational force of the zombie-millions who never act or think to condemn the Soviet Union, Communism, and their agents, prevented them. Their apathy, their silence was just too much. It truly was a virtuoso performance.

Weren't they all.

CHAPTER FIVE

When people renounce lies, they simply cease to exist. Like parasites, they can only survive when attached to a person.

—ALEKSANDR SOLZHENITSYN[1]

A truth that disheartens, because it is true, is still of far more value than the most stimulating of falsehoods.

—MAURICE MAETERLINCK[2]

I'm not quite done with "Virtuoso" Gromyko, who first pops into this story nearly forty years before a president of the United States finally pronounced the Soviet empire "evil." It was 1944, and Gromyko was the new, wartime ambassador to Washington, a survivor of the 1930s purges that had decimated Soviet elites. No doubt Gromyko's rapid climb was due to what Conquest would later describe as Stalin-requisite "servility and ruthlessness."[3]

There he was, the thirty-four-year-old ambassador, likely ensconced in the elegant Soviet embassy, a Beaux Arts mansion built near the White House by the wife of the American capitalist whose fortune came from Pullman cars, when, on Tuesday, April 4, 1944, the defection of Victor Kravchenko sensationally made the front page of *The New York Times.*

SOVIET OFFICIAL HERE RESIGNS; ASSAILS "DOUBLE-FACED" POLICIES.

Within the next several years, Kravchenko would write two enduringly significant books on the totalitarian horrors of life in the USSR that prefigure Solzhenitsyn; he would also, in the course of the world-famous libel suit he would bring against a Communist publication in Paris, effectively put the Soviet system itself on trial for these same horrors, and win. Whether clairvoyance figured into the Soviets' panic, the spare facts of that first news story were threatening enough to the Soviet masquerade as American "ally": Kravchenko, for twenty-two years a Communist Party apparatchik, then an economic attaché at the Soviet headquarters of Lend-Lease in Washington—in today's dollars, the $300 billion pipeline to our wartime allies[4]—had flown the Communist coop.

Say, wasn't that the same Lend-Lease aid program that officially gave "first priority" to Russian planes "even over planes for U.S. Army Air Force," as Maj. George Racey Jordan's January 1, 1943, orders said; and that sent to the USSR those half a million trucks and jeeps that Khrushchev declared in 1970 were indispensable to the Red Army sweep across Eastern Europe, pulling the Iron Curtain down behind them? And the same program that a brainwashed or mind-gaming Mikhail Gorbachev refused even to acknowledge when George Shultz brought it up in 1985?[5]

The very same. Now, it's possible that when Gorby first denied Lend-Lease, he didn't know better. He might not have grasped, or even been have able to conceive of, anything more closely approximating reality than the Soviet propaganda he was raised on. (Us, too, come to think of it.) Lend-Lease boss Harry Hopkins—FDR's alter ego, co-president, or Rasputin, depending on who's talking—might well have proclaimed in 1942 to Russia, the world, and Madison Square Garden, that "nothing shall stop us from sharing with you all that we have and are,"[6] but there was no audible, credible Soviet acknowledgment of the influx of massive American aid in the Soviet Union during World War II (or after). In fact, with those hundreds of thousands of Dodge trucks, rolling off the ships ("with instructions in Russian stenciled in Detroit"[7]), there is a sense in which the U.S. government, vassal-like, effectively conspired in its own deprecation. By going along with the ruse, the United States bolstered Stalin's propaganda that the USSR fought the war alone, while simultaneously snowing the American people with happy talk about Stalin to make the case for more—indeed, unlimited—aid. American statecraft as Soviet strategy? That's how it strikes me, and Stalin was always in the driver's seat.

"Is that a German jeep or an American jeep?" an American correspondent asked at the Russian front [in the summer of 1944].

"Neither one," said the [Red Army] lieutenant, "it's a Russian jeep. Your American jeeps are too flimsy . . . Five thousand kilometers and they fall to pieces. Here we only use Russian jeeps."[8]

So went the psychological subtext of World War II: a codependent's policy of appeasement based, it was thought, said, and believed, on a tangle of heightened emotions driven by the fear that Stalin would cut a deal with Hitler, and the hope that Stalin was, or would some better day become, our bestest friend. In the war's aftermath, military expert Hanson Baldwin analyzed such delusions in *Great Mistakes of the War,* a slim, instructive book outlining what the

Pulitzer Prize–winning war correspondent called the "four great—and false—premises" of the war.

Great, false premises of the war? The Good War? The American Victory? Baldwin's is an eye-widening, counterconventional concept. It brought me up short, as I think it probably would anyone raised on the rah-rah narrative of World War II as pure American triumph. Sure, Yalta was a disaster, the Iron Curtain was an epic tragedy, and China went Red, but, but . . . that was all postwar aftermath, Cold War origins stuff. The main event was that Hitler was licked and the world was safe again for democracy.

Or was that safe for "people's democracy"?

On a more gimlet-eyed second glance, the postwar map doesn't look so good, what with the Soviet Union having engorged itself on a European continent divided according to the war-igniting Nazi-Soviet Pact—only "with the Nazis conveniently excluded," courtesy Allied intervention.[9] Which was, when you think of it, quite a generous contribution to the Soviet cause. From Finland to the Baltics to the Balkans, from East Germany, which was permitted to encircle "partitioned" Berlin, to Poland, whose invasion by Germany and the USSR brought England and France to war in the first place, all was lost to the evil empire. As for Asia, where the Soviet Union declared war on Japan on August 8, 1945 (thanks a lot), the Soviets claimed and received Manchuria, which had been promised to the Chinese at Yalta. The Soviets also got Japan's Kuril Islands and half of Korea on a plate. That worked out well.

Regarding the globe this way isn't just a glass-half-empty exercise. It is a massive conceptual twist that forces what we "know" about "victory" into reverse. Hanson Baldwin's 1949 book provides a good, solid point of analytical departure, particularly given that his four great and false premises of the war all have to do with our (incorrect) assessments and (mis)perceptions of the Soviet Union—head fakes, all—rather than conventional military blunders, as one might expect. They were:

1. That the Soviet Union had abandoned its policy of world revolution.
2. That "Uncle Joe" Stalin was a "good fellow," someone we could "get along with."
3. That the USSR might make a separate peace with Germany.
4. That the Soviet Union's entry into the war against Japan was essential to victory or necessary to save thousands of American lives.

Such premises, in other words, all fall into the category we would later identify as Soviet *dezinformatsiya*—disinformation purposefully planted, fed, primed, echoed, and amplified according to Kremlin plan. Accepting Baldwin's list, then, we might consider two possible explanations. We, ourselves, arrived at these false premises. Or we, subverted from within by hundreds of agents loyal to a foreign power and aided and abetted by exponentially more fellow travelers and useful fools, were *convinced* to arrive at these false premises and were *duped* by a massive Communist influence operation into making these and many, many other mistakes. This is the shocking new scenario that begins to take shape with the overlay of intelligence history onto diplomatic, military, and cultural history.

Circa 1949, the basic evidence of Soviet infiltration of the U.S. government was fresh, hot off the hearings, following the 1948 appearances of Elizabeth Bentley and Whittaker Chambers before the House Committee on Un-American Activities. News of such infiltration has no discernible impact on Baldwin's analysis. This could be due to delay built into the publication schedule. It could also be due to the rawness of the evidence, not to mention the intensive controversy it ignited.

Sixty years later, we have no such excuses. As Haynes, Klehr, and Vassiliev point out in their nearly one-hundred-page chapter in *Spies* on government infiltration, the Vassiliev notebooks, copied from KGB archives, confirm that the dozens of officials the two ex-spies named were Soviet sources, while most of these same names also appear in the Venona cables. (Remember, Chambers and Bentley, these two greatest network sources, "only knew the half of it."[10]) This leaves it to us to reexamine the old lore with eyes open to the long-hidden implications of Communist penetration at every echelon of the U.S. wartime government—White House, Treasury, State, War, OSS, Office of War Information, and more. We need to walk back over our battlegrounds, pore over old strategies, and ask ourselves whether it is the case that our forbears made honest-to-goodness *American* mistakes to make the USSR the true victor of World War II, or whether it is possible instead that they became instruments, willingly or not, of long-term Soviet strategy.

To make the question concrete for a moment, were all of those hundreds of thousands of Lend-Lease jeeps and trucks really the awesome output of a sovereign American state acting in its own best interest? Or even a sovereign state of mind thinking about its own survival? Or is there some way in which those trucks symbolize a tithe, a tax, an offering of a serflike nation? Were they a sweetener or bribe? That's how the two-hundred-million-plus pounds of butter Uncle Sam shipped to the USSR looks in light of strict stateside rationing at the time. Such notions may sound outrageous, I know; and I may be asking these questions too soon, before I have marshaled all of the arguments. Nevertheless, it's important to mark the trail through the looking-glass early in order to see where we're going.

Of course, it wasn't just an atmosphere of deception created by agents of

Soviet influence that undermined American strength. After the war, Victor Kravchenko would testify before Congress to the effect that the Soviet Lend-Lease operation he defected from—the Soviet Purchasing Commission, located about three miles due north of the front door of the White House—was in reality the Soviet Spying Commission, the Soviet Thieving Commission, and the Soviet Ransacking Commission, with its thousand-plus employees under orders to filch as many industrial and military secrets as possible for the upcoming struggle between the USSR and the USA. This struggle, they were all told, would inevitably follow World War II. We may have been numb to the chill, but what we call the Cold War was under way long before historians tell us it began.

All the signs of struggle were there for anyone to see—anyone, that is, who could believe his own eyes, who could close his ears to the incessant propaganda. "Russian aims were good and noble. Communism had changed its stripes," Hanson Baldwin writes, recapping the stream of wartime hooey. He continues, "A study of Marxian literature and of the speeches and writings of its high apostles, Lenin and Stalin, coupled with the expert knowledge of numerous American specialists, should have convinced an unbiased mind that international Communism had not altered its ultimate aim; the wolf had merely donned a sheep's skin."[11]

"Islamic aims are good and noble. What stripes could possibly need changing? Extremists are trying to hijack one of the world's great religions, a religion of peace," a military analyst of the future will write of our own era's propaganda stream. "A study of Mohammed's law (sharia) and the speeches and writings of Islam's authorities, Hassan al-Banna and Yusef al-Qaradawi, coupled with the expert knowledge of American specialists, should have convinced an unbiased mind that international Islam posed a dire threat to liberty."

Don't think we aren't penetrated today by new totalitarians who look to Mecca, not Moscow.

Baldwin says we became "victims of our own propaganda," but what if it's more accurate to say we became victims of *Soviet* propaganda as shaped and disseminated by Soviet agents within our Soviet-penetrated government? Above a certain level of infiltration by the other side, a group, a body, or an institution is no longer viably "ours"; it's "theirs." I believe the infiltration of the United States soared past that danger level to the point of de facto occupation, where *national* interest was no longer paramount but Soviet interests were. The emperor, in other words, wore *Soviet* clothes. This is more than a theoretical gambit or flight of fancy. If I have drawn the correct conclusions from what I have assimilated from the gargantuan body of research on view, we must overhaul and revamp our understanding of our historical universe.

To appreciate the level of infiltration/occupation I am talking about, let's take the Office of War Information, one of those government bureaus set up in the early stages of the war. The OWI's mission called for pro-American and pro-Allied propaganda at home and abroad, but it tended to push Communistic policy at home and the Soviet line abroad.[12] Or, to quote the more peppery 1954 description by Chesly Manly, longtime Washington correspondent of *The Chicago Tribune,* a bitterly anti-Roosevelt paper in those days, OWI "was loaded with draft dodgers, red revolutionists, and a scum of European refugees who pretended to sell America to the world but made it their business to sell Communist Russia to America."[13]

Periodically, OWI drew the equivalent of dirty looks from congressional Republicans and even censure once from FDR himself for an outbreak of Sovietophilia beyond even White House bounds.[14] As M. Stanton Evans writes, having "scrambled to recruit personnel numbering in the thousands with little time, and apparently less desire, for anti-Red security vetting," units such as OWI were "custom-built for penetration."[15] They worked like a dream—Soviet dream, American nightmare.

That's a lot to accept on faith, I know. So here follows a sampling, extracted from several volumes of spy-tracking research by our leading scholars, of OWI personnel under OWI directors Robert Sherwood, Pulitzer Prize–winning playwright and Harry Hopkins crony and biographer, and Elmer Davis, a popular pre-Cronkite radio commentator whose tenure is aptly summed up by his yeoman efforts to cover up Soviet responsibility for the Katyn Forest Massacre, setting the story for domestic broadcasts, which would bar commentators who spoke the truth about Soviet guilt.[16]

There was Joseph F. Barnes, OWI assistant director of overseas reporting. For starters, Barnes was an alumnus of the 1933 Moscow correspondents' conspiracy to suppress news of the Terror Famine and the takedown of Gareth Jones described in the last chapter. According to Romerstein and Breindel, Barnes "had a long relationship with Soviet intelligence." In the fall of 1944, a Venona cable mentions Barnes, noting that while recruiting him for the NKVD "is obviously not only inadvisable but unrealizable . . . It is desirable to use him without signing him up." One explanation for this, Romerstein and Breindel posit, "may be that he was already working for the GRU" or Soviet military intelligence.[17] In open congressional hearings in 1951, four witnesses would identify Barnes as a Communist, including ex-Communists Whittaker Chambers and Louis Budenz and former Soviet intel officer Alexander Barmine.[18]

There was Owen Lattimore, the ardently pro-Communist director of OWI's Pacific operations. Lattimore's status as a spy remains contested, although not for want of expert opinion. Chiang Kai-shek conveyed to the FBI in 1948 he believed Lattimore, while acting as his Roosevelt-supplied wartime adviser, was supplying information to Communist forces, and Alexander Barmine knew of Lattimore as a Soviet agent.[19] Meanwhile, his function as an agent of Communist influence is impossible to contest. Lattimore would be described in 1952 by Senator Pat McCarran's Internal Security Subcommittee as "a conscious, articulate instrument of the Soviet conspiracy." Having studied his recently declassified FBI files, M. Stanton Evans reports that "Lattimore spent an inordinate amount of time swimming in a veritable Red sea of officially Communist spies and Moscow agents." Not surprisingly, his "files are replete with data about his links to Communists and Soviet agents, allegations that he stacked his Pacific office of OWI with pro-Red staffers, that he belonged to Communist fronts, that his writings were pro-Soviet propaganda."[20] Barmine would testify publicly that Soviet intelligence regarded *both* Barnes and Lattimore as "our men."[21] Barnes would later help Lattimore write *Ordeal by Slander,* his 1950 counterattack on Joseph McCarthy, which popularized the epochal term (likely published first in *The Daily Worker*) "McCarthyism."[22]

There was David Karr, formerly of *The Daily Worker,* who served in OWI as a foreign language specialist.[23] Long suspected of being a Soviet agent—Martin Dies brought him before his committee in 1943, where Karr pleaded innocent-lambdom and falsely claimed to have been working for the FBI all along—Karr resigned from this government job to serve as legman and reporter to Drew Pearson, the leading anti-anti-Communist columnist of the mid-twentieth century and, later, the "central figure for mobilizing attacks on McCarthy in the Washington press corps."[24] Later denounced as an agent working on behalf of Moscow in what M. Stanton Evans describes as one of McCarthy's "bitterest speeches" in 1950, Karr was roundly defended from all charges, including by another senator. If Karr was pro-Communist, Pearson replied in *The New York Times,* "the Washington Monument is a hole in the ground."[25] Well, Karr was—appearing both in Venona as a source and in Soviet archives as a confirmed agent—and the Washington Monument isn't.[26] As Evans concludes, all of this "indicates McCarthy knew whereof he spoke."[27]

There was Cedric Belfrage, an alumnus of both British and U.S. intelligence, who, as a member of OWI's "de-Nazification" team, drew McCarthy's notice (correctly) for work on behalf of U.S.-funded Communist publications. Portrayed as a hapless victim of "McCarthyite excess" when he took the Fifth Amendment rather than answer whether he had been a Communist, Belfrage, as Evans reports, was in truth a KGB agent who appears in "numerous" Venona cables reporting back to Moscow with highly sensitive information from the office of British spy chief William Stephenson (the man Churchill called "In-

trepid"). Haynes, Klehr, and Vassiliev further describe him as "fanatically devoted to Chinese communism."[28]

There was journalist James Aronson, Belfrage's OWI "sidekick" in
Communistification-as-de-Nazification and other ventures, who later took the
Fifth Amendment when asked about membership in the Communist Party.

There was Julia Older Bazer, who handled OWI's cable file to Moscow, who
also invoked the Fifth Amendment, on being asked about Party membership.
Bazer, Evans notes, was the sister of columnist Drew Pearson's legman Andrew
Older, ID'd by the FBI as a Communist agent.[29]

There was journalist Peter Rhodes, "unambiguously a KGB agent," Haynes,
Klehr, and Vassiliev write, who, according to an October 1941 KGB memo,
"has been hired for a government job and is travelling to London . . . as head of
the information office, which will supply information to the president, Donovan, the 2nd Department (army intelligence, a.k.a. G-2), naval intelligence, and
the FBI." The memo continues: "Peter has been given the right to hire employees for the aforementioned office. This is a pretty good find for us." Rhodes,
later identified by Elizabeth Bentley as a member of the "Golos network,"
would became chief of the Atlantic news section.[30]

There was labor correspondent Travis Hedrick, who would leave OWI to
what you might call graduate to the Soviet government news agency TASS (and
take the Fifth Amendment when asked if he had been a Communist Party
member).

There was Robin Kinkead, an OWI analyst of foreign propaganda, who the
FBI reported in 1944 was a contact of Gregori Kheifetz, whom Romerstein
and Breindel ID as "NKVD Rezident in San Francisco and active in atomic
espionage."[31]

There was William Hinton, sent by OWI to "assist" Chiang Kai-shek and
Allied forces in China, who would also take the Fifth Amendment when asked
by Congress if he were a Party member, and would later return to China to
work for Mao's revolution.

There was Paul Hagen, a leading light on the OWI German desk. Hagen
was a member of the Communist Party in his native Germany and later "identified by the FBI as a Soviet agent" active in Communist front organizations in
the United States. (Presidential aide Lauchlin Currie appeared as a sponsor for
a visa application of Hagen's. Sounds crazy until you find out Currie, too, was a
bona fide Soviet mole.[32]) A 1943 Venona cable further identified Hagen as
"close" to Eleanor Roosevelt, part of the coterie of Communists and collaborators she allowed herself to be surrounded by.[33]

Louis Adamic, an "informal guru" on the Yugoslav desk, pushed the pro-Tito

Communist propaganda campaign that destroyed the reputation of the genuinely anti-Nazi, anti-Red Serbian leader, Gen. Draja Mihailovich, helping convince the Allies that Mihailovich was a collaborator and traitor. Mihailovich's isolation and, later, execution by Tito mark one of the most notorious Soviet deception campaigns and Allied disgraces.[34]

Carlo a Prato was on the OWI Italian desk. His résumé included being "expelled from Switzerland for life as a Soviet agent who received and disbursed funds from Moscow."[35]

Haynes and Klehr further note that after the war, "several members of OWI's Polish-language section emerged as defenders of the Communist takeover in Poland and as close relatives of officials in the new Polish Communist regime." For example, Arthur Salman would "graduate" from the OWI's Polish desk to become editor-in-chief of *Robnotnik* (Worker), a big paper in Communist Warsaw.

Flora Wovschin was an almost frantically active KGB agent within OWI (her Soviet intelligence activities there and, later, at the State Department take up some twenty Venona cables).[36]

Irving Lerner, an employee of OWI's motion picture division, was caught red-handed trying to photograph the cyclotron used in the creation of plutonium at Cal Berkeley without authorization.[37] Speaking of the OWI's motion picture division, along with the White House, it was deeply involved in the making of *Mission to Moscow* (1943), summed up by producer Robert Buckner as that "expedient lie for political purposes."[38]

The question is, *whose* political purposes—ours or the Soviets'?

Kenneth Lloyd Billingsley notes *Mission to Moscow* was known as "the first Soviet production from a major [American] studio."[39] That was originally meant ironically, but it is very nearly literally true. Remember, the thing was written by Moscow-show-trials superapologist Joseph Davies, who would be praised, also in 1943, by Soviet ambassador to the United States Maxim Litvinov as "in effect an envoy of the Soviet Union in Washington."[40] Naturally, the first in-effect-Soviet-envoy in Washington would make the first in-effect-Soviet-production in Hollywood. As the old Soviet socialist realist said, "The only task of literature was that of fulfilling the social directions of Stalin."[41] *Mission to Moscow* succeeded.

What of poor Kravchenko, dangling in the limbo of defection for the past eight pages? He, too, figures into the story of OWI penetration. Christina Krotkova, an NKVD agent who insidiously became Kravchenko's typist, translator, and KGB informant, was also on Uncle Sam's payroll as an OWI employee.[42]

Still the dossier is incomplete. Haynes and Klehr, for example, point out that not all Soviet intelligence assets inside OWI and code-named in Venona have even been identified. It's not the biggest leap of logic to see that this Office of War Information could well have been named the Office of *Soviet* War Information. Suddenly, Chesly Manly's wild talk of Red revolutionists and scum of Europe becomes merely descriptive, almost humdrum. It's that official U.S. government stamp of approval—the perfect cover—that suddenly seems lurid, dangerous, and confounding.

Back along the Lend-Lease supply line, thousands of miles west of OWI and Kravchenko's post in Washington, D.C., U.S. Army Maj. George Racey Jordan, a Lend-Lease "expediter," found himself thinking along similar lines in the months before Kravchenko's defection. Having bought the "United Nations" propaganda at least for the duration, Jordan was nonetheless perplexed by what he saw going down the Lend-Lease supply line—what he, himself, as an expediter, had orders to speed along. Even with Uncle Sam's sanction, the increasing amounts of secret cargo bound for the Soviet Union under protection of "diplomatic immunity" bothered him more and more, finally kicking him into the kind of action that transformed this everyday, unsuspecting patriot, a businessman in his forties who had flown with Eddie Rickenbacker in the First World War, into one of our rare fellow citizens—a rare human being—who takes a step out of line, who says No to the Machine, who loves his country more than its Establishment, ultimately ascending to what ex-Socialist Max Eastman once called the "moral aristocracy."[43]

Jordan's official role was to "expedite" the air transport of thousands of tons of cargo and hundreds of U.S. warplanes, first out of Newark, New Jersey, and later out of Gore Field, the big wartime airbase in Great Falls, Montana. He may have been officially on the outside looking in, but as "liaison officer" to the Soviet Lend-Lease representatives, Jordan found himself in quarters so uniquely close he was practically expediting Lend-Lease *en famille*. For instance, once, when Jordan stopped by the apartment of the Soviet chief, Col. Anatole Kotikov, and his wife-secretary to drive the pair to work—already kind of cosy—he saw Mrs. Kotikov pull her husband's treasured "Experimental Chemicals" dossier, the one the Russian official brought back and forth to work every day, from "a hiding-place under the mattress, while her husband was pulling on his handsome boots of black leather."[44]

All very homey, but what was in that file?

Turns out, it had to do with everything you need, courtesy Lend-Lease, to cook up a brand-new and experimental atomic pile.

Jordan got along well with Colonel Kotikov—they worked at desks side by side—but not so well that he didn't smell a Lend-Lease rat. A lot of them, in fact, all skittering through Great Falls under "diplomatic immunity" to Russia. It wasn't diplomatic "pouches" that were going through; these questionable cargoes usually shipped in large, cheap, shiny black suitcases, sealed with red wax and bound with white cord. What came out later was that back in Washington, D.C., Victor Kravchenko himself helped pack up some of the very suitcases Jordan saw moving down the pipeline. Of course, "pipeline" doesn't do this supply effort justice. It was more like a vacuum cleaner.

Jordan argues that Lend-Lease was "the greatest mail-order catalogue" ever, and he proves it in his 1952 book *From Major Jordan's Diaries*. A precious memoir of life along the Lend-Lease pipeline, the book contains the most complete lists of Soviet Lend-Lease matériel ever published, I do believe, to this day.[45] There was that nearly million miles of copper wire that lay coiled in spools in Westchester County for *postwar* Russian use (but at a higher priority under Lend-Lease than refitting war-damaged U.S. Navy ships) mentioned in chapter 2, along with other sundries (the oil refinery, the hydroelectric plants, the pianos . . .). The list goes on—

> Railway car axles, without wheels, 69,818,310 lbs., $2,520,778
> Railway car axles, with wheels, 45,900,258 lbs., $2,392,165 . . .
> Power metal working machine tools, 5,773 lbs., $6,461,539 . . .
> Power machines, tools and parts, $60,313,833

—in tiny type for twenty-five pages. One entry that stopped me cold—in between three "Electric fans" ($33) and, lucky Politburo wives, 204 "Electric domestic vacuum cleaners" ($6,752)—was an entry for more than $6 million worth of "Searchlights and airport beacons" and "Floodlights." Imagine: When a slave-prisoner of the Gulag made a midnight break for the Arctic tundra, Soviet jailers zapped his cover of darkness with a searchlight made in the USA.[46]

Jordan's list includes more than $13 million worth of aluminum tubes, necessary for "cooking" uranium into plutonium; 834,989 pounds of cadmium metal, necessary for controlling the intensity of an atomic pile ($781,472); 13,440 pounds of thorium in 1942 ($22,848); and other ingredients for an atomic pile. Another 11,912 pounds of thorium shipped out in January 1943, Jordan notes, but none thereafter "due undoubtedly to General Groves' vigilance." Jordan was referring to Gen. Leslie Groves, the chief of the Manhattan Project. Groves would later testify before Congress in 1949 that his operation came under *continuous* pressure to release experimental atomic materials to the USSR from the Lend-Lease office.[47]

If George Racey Jordan is remembered at all—sorry; let me start over: If Jordan *were* to be remembered at all, it would be for the compilation of reports, orders, journal entries, and jottings on envelopes that Jordan compiled between May 1942 and June 1944 that comprise a unique record of the Lend-Lease experience—of what, in effect, was the national looting, far above and beyond the exigencies of war supply, that the U.S. government enabled on behalf of the USSR during and even for some time after World War II.[48] Not that the United States didn't receive something in return. After Jordan took on the role of Great Falls's de facto immigration official, he recorded the names, ranks and functions of some 418 Russians who deplaned and illegally entered the United States. "The list proved to be of value, I was told, in tracing Communist espionage in America during the war," he wrote in his 1952 book.

Jordan couldn't do much with the nameless Russians he watched land in Great Falls and *make a run for it,* just as though they knew where they were going, Jordan always thought. "I would see them jump off planes, hop over fences, and run for taxicabs . . . It was an ideal set-up for planting spies in this country."[49] Quite a contrast to Americans who made anything like an unauthorized landing in the Soviet Union. I'm thinking of one crew from the famous Doolittle Raid, who, after their stunning bombing run over Tokyo on April 18, 1942, landed their B-25 at a Red Army Air Force base in Vladivstok. Dangerously low on fuel, having had to launch prematurely from the USS *Hornet* after the aircraft carrier had been sighted by a Japanese fishing craft, this crew, under Capt. Edward J. York, hoped to refuel and continue on to their designated Chinese base to reunite with the rest of the raiders as planned. For the next miserable year, this American crew was interned by the Soviet government.

Wait, the Russians were our "allies." We were in this together, weren't we?

It had to be that way, the Soviets explained, for fear of provoking an "international incident" with Japan, with whom the Soviet Union was not at war, despite having secretly destroyed the Japanese 6th Army in Mongolia in August 1939.[50] Notice how the Soviets had no fear of provoking an international incident with the USA—or even causing a hiccup in Lend-Lease—*by holding our men prisoner.*[51]

As for the lost raiders, York and his crew, suffering from malnutrition and dysentery, ended up working as day laborers in South Russia, where they lived in mud huts on a diet of black bread and cabbage. Eventually, they were able to make a harrowing escape into Soviet-occupied Iran, where their ultimate path to freedom would lie through the British consulate in Mashad. This is an unseen dark side of the "Good War," something discarded from our recollections. To be sure, it is not hinted at in *Thirty Seconds over Tokyo,* the stirring 1944 movie—screenplay by Red blacklister Dalton Trumbo—based on the memoir of the April 1942 Doolittle Raid by Capt. Ted W. Lawson. Enthralled moviegoers who watched Lawson's crew execute the attack on Tokyo (depicted with fascinating documentary footage of the raid) and crash-land in China saw Chinese allies tend to the crew's injuries and transport them beyond the reach of conquering Japanese forces—even as, in reality, their brother bombers lay rotting in Soviet custody; as our navy was sustaining terrible losses convoying Lend-Lease matériel to the Soviet Union through U-boat-thick North Atlantic waters; as our own army lay besieged in the Pacific, deprived of desperately needed supplies—and, don't forget, as Jordan began compiling his curious record of Lend-Lease.

This included notes on cargo and personnel, which and whom Jordan saw with his own eyes, evidence we must now weigh carefully against his credibility as a witness. After all, he is the only person we know of taking Russian passenger names, or spot-checking the contents of those black suitcases, which, at a certain point, started shipping through the airfield, fifty at a time, and under armed Russian guard. The mystery of these suitcases particularly troubled Jordan. Even in this insistently halcyon era of official, no-questions-asked-and-that's-an-order amity between the United States and the USSR, Jordan "repeatedly raised hell" about them, as one senior officer put it.[52] He could get no rise from above. It drove him a little nuts.

One midwinter night, Jordan writes, he slipped away from a vodka party in town hosted by his Russian comrades (the only such party ever staged) and raced the four miles back to the airport, where, as he suspected, a Lend-Lease plane was warming up, clearance pending. Jordan pushed and ducked his way past "a barrel-chested Russian," as he wrote, one of two armed couriers aboard, to clamber into the plane's cabin.

> "It was dimly lighted by a solitary electric bulb in the dome. Faintly visible was an expanse of black suitcases, with white ropes and seals of crimson wax . . . My first thought was: 'Another bunch of those damn things!' The second was that if I were ever going to open them up it was now or never."[53]

As Jordan made his intentions clear, he and the guards began to scuffle, the Russians shrieking probably the one English word they knew: "Deeplomateek!" Jordan pulled out a safety razor, yanked one of the suitcases into his hands, and began to open it. Quite suddenly, he realized he needed an American witness, and quick, to prevent what he imagined might be passed off as a "deplorable accident."

> I called to a Yank soldier who was on patrol thirty feet away. He crunched over through the snow. Bending down from the plane I asked him if he had had combat experience. He answered that he had, in the South Pacific. I stooped lower and murmured:
> "I'm going to open more of this baggage. I want you to watch these two Rus-

sians. Both are armed. I don't expect any trouble. But if one of them aims a gun at me, I want you to let him have it first. Understand?"

After a moment's thought, he looked me in the eye and said, "Sir, is that an order?" I replied that it was an order.

In the frigid, black night, Jordan, gloveless, using a flashlight, proceeded to examine roughly every third suitcase.

Using one knee as a desk, I jotted notes with a pencil on two long envelopes that happened to be in my pocket. There was usually one entry, or phrase of description, for each suitcase inspected. These scrawls were gathered into a memorandum.

What a memorandum it was. It listed the road maps he found pinpointing American industrial sites ("Westinghouse," "Blaw-Knox"). Maps of the Panama Canal Zone. Documents related to the Aberdeen Proving Ground, "one of the most 'sensitive' areas in the war effort." Folders stuffed with naval and shipping intelligence. Stacks of papers on oil refineries, machine tools, steel foundries, and the like. Groups of documents on stationery from the Departments of Agriculture, Commerce, and State, "trimmed close to the text," Jordan noted, perhaps to save weight—or remove "Secret" or "Restricted" stamps (or both). Folders from the State Department Jordan claimed were marked "From Sayre"—that would be Francis Sayre, who hired Alger Hiss—and "From Hiss," Soviet spy Alger Hiss himself. Engineering and scientific treatises that "bristled with formulae, calculations and professional jargon." Something very, very interesting I will describe a little farther down attached to a thick map bearing the legend that Jordan recorded as "Oak Ridge, Manhattan Engineering District" (remember, this was taking place sometime in the winter of 1943–44, before the invention, or public knowledge, of the atomic bomb). He also found a carbon copy of a report from "Oak Ridge" containing a series of "outlandish" words Jordan made a note to look up later: "cyclotron," "proton," "deuteron." There were also "curious" phrases, he wrote, "energy produced by fission" and "walls five feet thick, of lead and water, to control flying neutrons."

Then, Jordan writes, "For the first time in my life, I met the word 'uranium.'"

Why, in all of our inherited historical legacy, has there been no room for this wartime witness to the plunder of atomic secrets just as they were being spirited out of the country on a U.S.-government-sponsored flight? Not that Jordan understood at the time that this was what was going on. He did, however, have that gut-checking hunch that these documents, so many of them obviously classified (including, for example, confidential reports to the secretary of state originating in the U.S. Embassy in Moscow), shouldn't be heading out of the country to a foreign power. Jordan didn't know it, but he was witnessing the last days of the pre–Atomic Age, when the Manhattan Project was the biggest state secret the United States had. Or thought it had. As we now know, Stalin was not at all surprised when Truman informed him of the atomic bomb at Potsdam in 1945. Turns out, Russian knowledge of the effort was surprisingly widespread. Noted war correspondent W. L. White wrote of a 1944 exchange he had with a Soviet guide who specifically referenced "cyclotrons," "splitting of atom," and the "Manhattan project" in casual conversation. White didn't know what he was talking about and put his misunderstanding down to the language barrier.[54]

Knowing that the Communist regime controlled its press, it's easy to understand how even half a million made-in-Detroit Dodge trucks might disappear from Soviet memory—but by what mechanism did Jordan and his sensational findings completely vanish from U.S. consciousness? Then again, was what Jordan said legit? Was he crazy? Was any of this for real?

Here was my next step: to determine whether Jordan's claims were ever proven or disproven, whether he himself had been vetted as a witness. As I had learned, conventional "history books" would be inadequate, barely hit and mostly miss. Relevant chronicles mainly overlook Jordan's evidence altogether despite the significant attention, both media and political, that his charges drew at the time. Indeed, it turned out his claims, which originally aired over a national radio broadcast, were subject to thorough FBI investigation and congressional questioning under oath. In those cases where posterity does record Jordan's contributions at all, however, they are almost invariably smeared or discounted. For example, George C. Herring's *Aid to Russia, 1941–1946*, a 1973 study I have found otherwise useful, had this to say: "In 1949 one disgruntled former lend-lease official even issued sensational accusations that Roosevelt and his pro-communist advisers had given the Russians the raw materials and technical information necessary to produce an atomic bomb." Herring goes on to identify Jordan as the "disgruntled" official in his endnotes. He continues, "Congressional investigations proved these most extreme charges without foundation."[55]

Really? I quote from the March 3, 1950, testimony of Donald T. Appell, former FBI agent and investigator for the House Committee on Un-American Activities, specifically concerning Jordan's charges regarding the Lend-Lease shipment of atomic materials to the Soviet Union: "As to the shipment of uranium and heavy water, two specific shipments of uranium oxide and nitrate and shipments of heavy water have been completely documented to include even the number of the plane that flew the uranium and heavy water out of Great Falls."[56]

Appell testified to further corroboration on four out of five Jordan claims at issue in these hearings (the fifth, to be discussed, stands unconfirmed but not, by any means, ruled out). Clearly, Jordan has vaulted the initial threshold of credibility, prompting the question: What happened to this man in the historical record? What are the implications of his claims? What does it mean for the historical record that his claims, his testimony, almost without exception, have receded into, at best, anonymous limbo?

The fate of Jordan's testimony might seem like a small thing, but it shows, in a defined and demonstrable example, how it is that waves of misinformation wash away the facts, leaving behind a false trail and debris of doubt. We went from "completely documented" atomic-related transfer in 1950 to "disgruntled official" in 1972. By 2004, in Albert Weeks's *Russia's Life-Saver: Lend-Lease Aid to the U.S.S.R. in World War II*, a book drawing on Russian revisionism—i.e., newly available archival material in Russia attesting to the existence of vital American Lend-Lease aid—Jordan's evidence of atomic aid had evanesced into unverifiable myth.[57]

In between come the obliterating layers of disinformation. It began, first, with what Jordan described in the preface to his 1952 book as the "efforts of the character assassins and the press experts *to keep the implications of this story from being brought into proper focus.*"[58] I may be a sucker for italics, but this point about implications (Jordan's word in this case, not mine) is so important to the progression of our mortal illness as a civilization—nonjudgmentalism regarding mortal threats—that I have to flag it. The effort to keep implications from coming into relevant focus is the story of our lives.

The assassination attempts on Jordan's character—for example, spurious allegations that he was being paid by the GOP—began right after the first public airing of his story on Fulton Lewis's radio show on December 2, 1949. This was just a couple of months after President Truman announced on September 23, 1949, that the Soviets had exploded an atomic bomb. The president's announcement, Jordan wrote, left him "shocked and stunned to the depths of my being," and made him realize that he, personally, must have "expedited" the transfer of key parts of the Soviet atomic program. He had to do something. "There was evidence in my possession, I was convinced," he wrote, "proving that the disaster was chargeable *not only to spies but to actual members of the Federal hierarchy*" (emphasis added).[59] Soon, Jordan was able to bring his story to the attention of Senator Styles Bridges (R-NH) and Lewis, a popular national radio personality. Lewis's staff investigated the story, after which Lewis broke it on the air. FBI investigators methodically, exhaustively vetted the same charges. This was a far cry from the dead-end apathy that greeted Jordan back in 1944 when he attempted to alert his superiors in Washington to his suspicions. A few days after the radio broadcast, Jordan would testify before the Un-American Activities Committee, returning to testify a second time in 1950.

Question: In light of the evidence Jordan provided, which has been corroborated, is it possible to continue to regard the creation of the Soviet bomb as solely resulting from the thievery associated with known, KGB-directed espionage rings? Jordan's evidence proves there was more to the story, that the U.S. government itself, via Lend-Lease, played a key role outside the criminal channels we know about.

Or was the U.S. government acting inside criminal channels, too? That is, just because Lend-Lease, in effect, said everything was all right—even as Lend-Lease cogs Jordan and Kravchenko knew what was going on wasn't all right—was the Lend-Lease atomic flow, indeed, all right, kosher, and aboveboard from the point of view and national interest of Uncle Sam? Or was Lend-Lease covering up a rogue operation? Was Lend-Lease, as run out of the White House by the president's top adviser Harry Hopkins, itself a rogue operation?

Before attempting to answer these questions, there is more recent confirmation of George Racey Jordan's credibility to cite. In his 1995 book *Dark Sun: The Making of the Hydrogen Bomb,* Pulitzer Prize–wining author Richard Rhodes mines Jordan's memoir as a reference, reproducing Jordan's list of twenty-three atomic materials (including nearly fourteen million pounds of aluminum tubes) as extracted from Lend-Lease tallies the Soviets gave Jordan. Rhodes describes these ingredients as "useful in constructing and controlling a nuclear reactor."[60] He also relates Jordan's eyewitness account of the illegal entry into the country of all those undocumented Soviet espionage workers spilling out of Lend-Lease planes arriving from Moscow and into surrounding Montana, citing corroborating evidence from a retired general. He even reprises the highly cinematic action sequence Jordan recounted that leads up to Jordan's single-handed assault on "the black suitcases," which I included above.

Rhodes also quotes, as Jordan himself does, from the dramatic testimony of Victor Kravchenko, who in 1950 told the Un-American Activities Committee that he helped pack some of the very suitcases George Racey Jordan saw moving down the Lend-Lease pipeline to the USSR. This was a key piece of the puzzle. Kravchenko recalled working behind closed doors at the Soviet Purchasing Commission in northwest Washington with Communist colleagues, including Semen Vasilenko, an expert metallurgist who was in charge of pipe and tube production in the Soviet Union. Vasilenko, according to Kravchenko, was in the United States for the sole purpose "of finding some special information." (As Jordan would explain parenthetically, "The gaseous diffusion plant at Oak Ridge and the Hanford Plutonium Works use many miles of pipes." Hence those millions of pounds of aluminum tubes.[61]) Kravchenko recalled

helping Vasilenko pack six suitcases filled with assorted industrial plans—
"found in an unofficial way," as Kravchenko put it. Jordan's diary offered independent evidence that Vasilenko had transited through Great Falls with some
four thousand pounds of "diplomatic mail." In his sworn testimony, Kravchenko
dated Vasilenko's trip back to Russia to February 1944—the same time frame
noted in Jordan's diary entry. Jordan further reported that while in Great Falls,
Vasilenko also picked up for transit to Moscow Colonel Kotikov's dossiers, including his treasured "Experimental Chemicals" folder.

Rhodes writes, "Jordan's story of Soviet espionage shipments through Great
Falls has never been corroborated in its entirety, but enough pieces of it have
found independent confirmation to establish its general credibility."[62]

The Rhodes citations mark a crucial step in what should be Jordan's rehabil-
itation—or, rather, initial inclusion—as an important historical source. Why
not? Meanwhile, it's worth nothing that Rhodes, a noted historian of the nuclear age, happens also to be a laurel-crowned Establishment figure, a visiting
scholar at Harvard and MIT, a PBS host and correspondent, and a recipient not
just of the Pulitzer Prize but of grants from the Ford, Guggenheim, and Mac-
Arthur Foundations. In other words, this is no McCarthyite anti-Communist
vouching for Jordan from the loneliest corners of the Right.

Rhodes further underscores Jordan's veracity in an additional note on his
sources, writing, "George Racey Jordan's account of wholesale espionage shipments through Great Falls under cover of Lend-Lease was widely discounted
when it first appeared."

Widely discounted in the echo chamber of the Left, that is. Rhodes continues, "I discuss its several corroborations in my text; based on those corroborations, it appears to me to be *largely credible.* Soviet espionage was indeed
wholesale, and obviously successful; *Jordan's black suitcases explain how the ten
thousand pages of secret documents that shocked Yakov Terletsky might have been
transported*" (emphasis added).[63]

Rhodes is referring to the postwar moment when Terletsky, a young KGB
physicist engaged in the Soviet atomic espionage department, was amazed to
find ten thousand pages of mainly American and some British top secret nuclear documents in the Lubyanka, KGB headquarters. According to Terletsky,
this voluminous cache, which seemed to have materialized from nowhere, outlined the "content of the basic experiments in determining the parameters of
nuclear reactions, reactors, and the descriptions of various uranium reactors,
the description of gaseous-diffusion installations, journal entries on the testing
of the atomic bomb and so on."[64]

In sum, what can be confirmed in Jordan's testimony has been confirmed,
or, in the case of Terletsky's archive surprise, supported. It was not knocked

down. It was not poked full of holes. It is still standing, still relevant, even after all these years. Jordan was one hell of a witness.

Remember that.

It's now April 4, 1944. Victor Kravchenko is on the front page of *The New York Times,* and Virtuoso Gromyko is choking on his morning kasha. Kravchenko said he had "resigned" to alert America to the fact that Uncle Joe Stalin was playing a "double-faced" game, talking democracy abroad while practicing totalitarianism at home and planning to bring it to Europe. Jordan may have been thwarted by his own chain of command ("I returned to Great Falls in low spirits," he writes after an unsuccessful trip in January 1944 to blow the whistle in Washington), but Kravchenko had gone straight to the American public. This set off alarms in official Soviet circles. David J. Dallin, an ex-Menshevik leader and Russian émigré and scholar who helped Kravchenko make his break, describes the panic: "We soon learned that in Kravchenko's division of the Purchasing Commission, all work ceased on that Tuesday: people raced in and out; small conferences were held; telephone calls about the 'traitor' went on incessantly; everyone was excited and presumably indignant."[65]

I think it's safe to assume that at least some of the time, maybe even "incessantly," it was Gromyko on the line. The thirty-four-year-old ambassador would spend much of the following year, the final year of World War II, "repeatedly prodding" FDR's State Department, personally lobbying the State Department to deport "deserter" Kravchenko to the Soviet Union and absolutely certain death.[66] The one thing that wasn't "virtuoso" about this early Gromyko performance was that it didn't work. If Kravchenko remained free, though, it was not for want of teamwork. Venona cables reveal that in addition to Gromyko's high-level diplomatic efforts, NKVD chief Lavrenty Beria took personal control of the case. Various NKVD agents (including the OWI employee mentioned above) successfully penetrated Kravchenko's circles in and around New York City. Mark Zborowski, a KGB agent who gained admittance to the Kravchenko sanctum, it came out later, had previously infiltrated Trotskyist circles and was involved in the apparent assassination of Trotsky's son in Paris in 1938.[67] Mainly, though, these Soviet stooges watched and harassed, uncertain what else could be done with or to Kravchenko in America while they awaited his return to Soviet clutches.

What we have here is an extensive, foreign, secret police network operating in our midst, a most deadly franchise, as the corpses of defector Walter Krivitsky, Danish diplomat Paul Bang-Jensen and others proved, with branch offices in Washington, New York, Chicago, and Connecticut. No such network of trusted American "émigrés," "refugees," and well-placed moles was similarly set up in Moscow, Leningrad, and the Ukraine to inform, to terrorize, to assassinate defecting Americans and their allies gone rogue.[68] Nor were there agents of American influence at the highest levels of the Kremlin influencing Stalin. It was not the USSR that was occupied by a secret army. It was the USA.

Question: Who led that secret army? Who cheered it on? Or, more immediately ascertainable, who, in this salient and instructive case, made common cause with the NKVD on the return of Kravchenko, this one lone truth teller who, prodded by an impulse stronger than survival, more cryptic than uncracked genetic code, was determined, at the risk of life and limb, to bear public witness to Stalin's deception?

Answer: The highest, most powerful official to make common cause with the NKVD on Kravchenko's defection was Harry Hopkins. He was also Roosevelt's most intimate and ubiquitous adviser. He was also, as well noted at the time, America's co-president, who, not at all incidentally, in another acid-rinse of the historical record, barely surfaces in our cultural consciousness today. As well he should. A body of evidence has accumulated over the decades indicating that Hopkins was at least an asset, at least an ally, and quite possibly an agent of the Kremlin. That demands our attention.

How Harry Hopkins made his exit, or, perhaps, made his *escape,* from the historical record is just the beginning of the mystery. Unlike Major Jordan, for instance, Hopkins was a world-famous figure, the dominant player in the Roosevelt administrations, a mainstream media darling of the day. Harry Hopkins was so big he wore Winston Churchill's fedora. He was such a White House presence that reporters could tell when he was out of town because the president's appointment list suddenly lengthened. He was so powerful that, unelected, unconfirmed, he negotiated one-on-one with Churchill and Stalin. "Few men of this century have exerted more influence upon American politics, domestic and foreign, than Hopkins," wrote noted American diplomat Robert Murphy about this man you've never heard of.[69] When Soviet foreign minister Molotov made his first visit to Washington in May 1942, Secretary of State Cordell Hull handed *Hopkins* a memorandum indicating the things he wanted taken up with Molotov.[70] When FDR placed Russia under Lend-Lease through a cable Hopkins drafted in October 1941, Secretary of War Henry Stimson, Hopkins wrote, "was obviously unhappy because he is not consulted about the strategy of the war."[71]

Harry Hopkins was a one-man cabinet. That's how *Life* magazine accurately put it in a Hopkins spread that ran on September 22, 1941, just as Lend-Lease was getting into high gear. Being *Life* magazine, the story includes lots of photos: Harry in a wing chair in the White House's Lincoln Bedroom, where he lived between May 1940 and December 1943; Harry's childhood home, a frame house (with outdoor privy) in Grinnell, Iowa; Harry in a robe recuperating from one of his many, many, *many* illnesses at the Miami Biltmore Coral Gables (not bad); Harry at the racetrack two-dollar betting window; Harry in suspenders at the 1940 Chicago convention (index finger extended at "Boss Kelly"); Harry in white tie with movie star Errol Flynn and socialite Liz Whitney; Harry with flood victims in Mississippi; Harry with his little girl, Diana, virtually a foster child of Eleanor Roosevelt after the death of Harry's second wife; and Harry's three sons from his first marriage, which ended in divorce. *Life* explained the star treatment:

> As boss of the Lend-Lease program, his control of the destiny of empire is second only to Mr. Roosevelt's own. As the President's familiar and constant traveling companion, he is a perfect mirror of executive policy who can make or break a plan or its proponent with as little effort as a grunt or a frown. In the kind of personalized one-man government that war has made of the administration of Franklin D. Roosevelt, that man has the greatest influence who has easiest access to the Chief of State's ear. *Harry Hopkins sees the President early, late and frequently in between. He is at Roosevelt's bedside before the President goes over to the Executive Office to begin his grueling business day. And more often than not he can be found about 11 o'clock at night in his shabby blue-silk dressing gown, sitting on the side of the President's bed discussing tomorrow's problem just before the bigger and wearier man in the flannel shawl drops off to sleep* [emphasis added].[72]

What unimpeded access for an agent of Soviet influence! Not pillow talk, of course, but a uniquely intense and sustained intimacy. Unprecedented, for sure. "During the fourteen days Churchill was in the White House he and Roosevelt and Hopkins had lunch and dinner together every day but one," Hopkins's official biographer, Robert Sherwood, would write of "Arcadia," code name of the first wartime Washington Conference of Roosevelt and Churchill that took place following Pearl Harbor in December 1941–January 1942. "It was at the lunches where most of the major problems were thrashed out,"[73] and usually to Hopkins's approval. Indeed, in January 1945, when Hopkins would *not* convince FDR to return Kravchenko to Soviet custody, he could console himself with a remarkable record of successes. In the end, FDR balked on Kravchenko because he couldn't expect a meaningful guarantee from Stalin that on the defector's return he wouldn't be shot. Hopkins replied to FDR that once Kravchenko was in Soviet custody, no one would know if he had been shot or not, but there the matter lay.[74]

I don't think FDR was squeamish. Just as he knew that publicly supporting free Poland—the casus belli for Britain and France back in 1939—while privately acquiescing to Stalin's installation of a Communist puppet government was good politics in an election year (as FDR himself explained to Stalin at Tehran in December 1943), I think he also knew that returning a defector to a Soviet firing squad was bad politics, especially before the Senate considered ratification of the United Nations agreement.[75] Better to leave the messy matter in limbo; let Kravchenko take his chances. Certainly, that's what happened over more than a year of diplomatic wrangling following the front-page walkout. Kravchenko wouldn't gain the right of asylum until the day of FDR's death on April 12, 1945.[76] Coincidence?

As the surviving scraps of this tawdry record reveal, Hopkins spoke of Kravchenko as a "deserter" exactly as the Soviets did. He pressed FDR to return Kravchenko to Soviet custody, and blew his top when he learned from Joseph "Submission to Moscow" Davies that the FBI was trying to recruit Kravchenko as a spy, that Secretary of State Hull knew about it and, presumably, didn't disapprove. "My God," Hopkins exploded, "what if Stalin knew that a member of the President's family had been a party to this desertion!"[77]

A queer reaction. Or, a queer reaction if the speaker is a devotee of liberty, the Rights of Man, and the Spirit of '76. It makes perfect sense if the speaker is a devotee of Marx, of statism—

"Farmers have for the first time in history become conscious of their relationship to the Government through direct contact with it and help from it," he said in 1939, *looking over new crops on the 388-acre Iowa farm he rented in a dead-end presidential probe of his own.*[78]

—of redistribution—

"When a democratic victory is won," Hopkins wrote in 1941, *"then the great wealth of the world must be shared with all people.*[79]

—and of self-loathing:

"The days of the policy of 'the white man's burden' are over," Hopkins wrote in 1942. *"Vast masses of people simply are not going to tolerate it and for the life of me I can't see why they should. We have left little in our trail except misery and poverty for the people whom we have exploited."*[80]

Ten days after he penned the above statement in a letter to the U.S. ambassador to Britain, Hopkins followed up with a stemwinder before a pro-Russia rally of twenty thousand in Madison Square Garden. He said:

I believe we are fighting for a new world. Because there can be no real freedom without economic freedom. The world can be freed from the economic oppressions that have nourished misery among hundreds of millions of people. There is enough wheat to feed the world. There is enough stone and brick and lumber to house the world. There is enough cotton and wool to clothe the whole human family. But no Utopia was ever won without struggle and the struggle to abolish poverty in the world . . . is a struggle to which every freedom loving person can wholeheartedly subscribe.[81]

Who knew World War II was a "war on poverty"?

Later that same day, Harry would follow his own trail of misery and poverty to swanky El Morocco, zebra striped and celebrity studded, where he would sup with Louise Macy, his third-wife-to-be, a former Paris editor of *Harper's Bazaar.* Hopkins and his date took the 1:00 A.M. train back to Washington, where, the following evening, he felt sufficiently unexploited and unburdened to ask Louise to marry him in "the Averell Harriman suite" of the Mayflower Hotel before dining at the British Embassy with Winston Churchill.

Harry soldiered on, according to the in-depth reportage of a two-part *New Yorker* profile where these details of his life are preserved. I offer it by way of illustrating Hopkins's personal strategies for coping with his share of the "white man's burden." Not that his life was all Utopia and nightclubs. There were real aggravations. Kravchenko, for instance. Our source for Hopkins's angry comment on Kravchenko's "desertion" is Joseph Davies's journal entry of December 22, 1944, via George McJimsey's sympathetic biography of Hopkins. Interestingly enough, December 22, 1944, is also the date of one of the most shocking documents M. Stanton Evans ever fished out of the FBI files. It bears witness to just how close Kravchenko came to *American* capture, and it's hard not to wonder whether Hopkins was involved. Fortunately for Kravchenko, even before his bestseller, *I Chose Freedom,* appeared in 1946, he already carried the small shield of a public profile. He had published several magazine articles and was writing his book with the well-known American journalist Eugene Lyons, our friend from chapter 4. (The Soviets no doubt knew this because one of their agents in the OWI was acting as Kravchenko's translator.[82]) More importantly, Kravchenko was cooperating with the FBI and, having entered the country as a civilian, did not, in the eyes of the attorney general, merit deportation as a military deserter. Still, this FBI memo indicates Kravchenko's arrest was imminent at the hands of unknown U.S. "government representatives." Even in the just-the-facts-ma'am style of the FBI memo, the 1944 warning is quite emphatic:

On Friday, December 22, Mr. Ugo Carusi, Executive Assistant to the Attorney General, advised . . . that Mr. [Edward] Stettinius and the State Department were putting the pressure on the Department of Justice to bring about the surrender of Victor Kravchenko to the Russians for return to Russia. Mr. Carusi stated that undoubtedly the pressure was also being put on the State Department by the Soviets . . . Later that afternoon, Mr. Carusi advised that the Attorney General believed the Bureau should discreetly tip off Kravchenko to the fact that "the heat was on" and that he should flee and carefully hide himself so that he would not be found by government representatives.[83]

Stettinius was the new secretary of state, having just replaced the long-serving and long-out-of-the-loop Cordell Hull. Stettinius would serve eighteen months in all, a stint now noted mainly for his relationship with senior aide Alger Hiss as the FBI was closing in on the prized GRU agent.

"I hope it isn't you," Stettinius would say to Hiss in April 1945.[84]

This period is also notable given Stettinius's relationship to Harry Hopkins. We begin to get the gist from the following cable from Britain's Washington ambassador to the Foreign Office (filched by a Soviet agent in London and passed to Stalin, Molotov, and Beria). Stettinius's appointment to head the State Department was "a victory by Harry Hopkins," the cable said. "Stettinius is a loyal protégé of Hopkins and never forgets it . . . Since the important strategic posts have been filled by such people as [James] Forrestal, Harriman and now Stettinius, the White House and *Hopkins in particular are getting more complete control than ever.*"[85]

So what else is new? Back in 1941 when Stettinius became the figurehead administrator of Lend-Lease, Robert Sherwood, Hopkins's official biographer, writes, "Hopkins knew that policy governing Lend-Lease would still be made in the White House and that the President would continue to delegate most of the responsibility to him. Stettinius was his friend and they could work together—and that was that."[86]

That was always that. It was the Hopkins modus operandi to work through proxies, and this pattern repeats itself throughout his unconstitutional quasi-regency. "Such people," as noted by the British ambassador—Forrestal, Harriman, Stettinius—were all Hopkins picks. In some significant measure, they all owed their administration positions, often their career trajectory, to him.[87] This list goes on, a Who's Who of the Roosevelt years: Army Chief of Staff George C. Marshall, White House Chief of Staff Adm. William D. Leahy, Vice President Henry A. Wallace, and other officials including Charles Bohlen, Joseph Davies, Gen. James H. Burns, Donald Nelson . . . If you were Victor Kravchenko, "the heat" really was on.

We have to go back to Lend-Lease to begin to understand why the Kravchenko case might have meant as much as it did to Hopkins and the Soviets. Lend-Lease, which Kravchenko could (and ultimately did) blow the whistle on, was more than the lifeline to the Soviet war effort and beyond. Lend-Lease was also the private bridge to the Kremlin from inside the Roosevelt White House, manned and overseen by Hopkins, most of the time from his White House digs in the Lincoln Bedroom. What if, as I asked some pages ago, Lend-Lease, as run out of the Roosevelt White House by Harry Hopkins, was a rogue operation?

Certainly it sailed into law in March 1941 under false colors, sold by FDR to the American public as a means to keep the United States out of war in Europe—as a *substitute* for U.S. military involvement, not a means by which to enter the war. Supposedly circumventing neutrality laws (but in reality breaking them), Lend-Lease "gave the president exclusive power to sell, transfer, lend, or lease such war matériel" to Great Britain and China, writes Albert L. Weeks, although it was envisioned from the start by the White House as a means to assist the USSR as well.[88] The legislation endowed the president with unprecedented powers to bypass the Senate and other checks and balances. For example, Lend-Lease allowed FDR to set the terms of the most massive U.S. expenditures in foreign aid in history and their repayment, or nonrepayment. Who, then, needed a Senate to advise and consent on related treaties? Who needed treaties? The State Department, too, took on attributes of a governmental fifth wheel as Hopkins helmed Lend-Lease *and* U.S. foreign policy from the White House. With the passage of Lend-Lease, "Hopkins became identified as 'Roosevelt's own personal Foreign Office,'" Sherwood writes, and "more violently controversial than ever."[89] The real-life and official Foreign Office—a.k.a. the State Department—was in many ways knocked out of power for the duration. It's astonishing to learn, with the exception of interpreters and note takers, neither Secretary of State Cordell Hull nor any other State officials *ever attended any of the wartime conferences with Churchill and Stalin.*[90] The British sent Anthony Eden, foreign secretary; the Soviets sent Vyacheslav Molotov, foreign minister; and the Americans sent Harry Hopkins, Roosevelt's own personal Foreign Office. Only at Yalta in February 1945 did the brand-new U.S. secretary of state, Edward Stettinius, attend—Hopkins's "loyal protégé"—ably assisted by top aide Alger Hiss.

With the creation of FDR's "Map Room"—the White House military information center and communications office that would morph into the White House Situation Room—the consolidation of powers at the White House was complete. Only the president, Harry Hopkins, and the president's chief of staff, Admiral William Leahy (as noted earlier, another Hopkins selection[91]), had access. Churchill, too, when he was in town. Now, all presidential communications with the major wartime allies (Britain, the USSR, and China) entirely bypassed the State Department, which—don't fall out of your chair—in those days included a roster of knowledgeable anti-Communist analysts. (These anti-Communists would be successively purged under direct Soviet pressure in what M. Stanton Evans has referred to as a "rolling coup d'etat."[92]) The Joint Chiefs, too, were often "kept in the dark ... until the die was cast," said Maj. Gen. John R. Deane, former secretary to the Joint Chiefs, who would become the Moscow-based administrator of Lend-Lease and write an important book about the experience called *The Strange Alliance*.[93]

Lend-Lease did more than transform the power structure of the U.S. government. It also introduced a revolutionary principle into our foreign policy. I'll just put it out there in the words of "Junior Stettinius," the Hopkins protégé whom we just saw putting the heat on Kravchenko in 1944—or at least *conducting it,* since Stettinius was, by all accounts, the emptiest of well-tailored suits.[94] As Stettinius wrote—or, perhaps better, in words attributed to Stettinius:

> The principle was contained in the words defining eligibility for Lend-Lease aid—"any country whose defense the President deems vital to the defense of the United States." The word "vital" was the heart of the matter. To favor limited aid to the allies as an expedient device for saving friendly nations from conquest was one thing. To declare that the defense of those nations was "vital" to our own national security was quite another. *If we adopted the bill with those words, we would, in effect, declare the interdependence of the American people with the other freedom-loving nations of the world* in the face of Axis aggression [emphasis added].[95]

We did indeed adopt the Lend-Lease bill with those words.[96] This makes March 11, 1941, the day the Lend-Lease bill passed after three months of raucous congressional debate, America's Interdependence Day. It was the first day of a new global order under which all manner of international intervention is automatically declared "vital"—i.e., essential to life—to U.S. interests. It no longer even draws comment when American presidents routinely declare the destinies of far-flung peoples "vital" to that of the United States, whether in Saudi Arabia (Roosevelt), Iraq (Bush), or Afghanistan (Obama).[97]

So how did Lend-Lease, this de facto American declaration of global interdependence—this de facto reversal of nonbelligerence if not also this de facto declaration of war—come about? Notably, the dispensers of conventional wisdom draw a stunning blank on its origins. Roosevelt biographer Doris Kearns Goodwin's explanation is typical: "How Roosevelt arrived at this ingenious idea, which cut through all the stale debates in Washington about loans and gifts, is unclear," she writes in her 1995 Pulitzer Prize–winning book *No Ordinary Time*.[98]

Goodwin goes on to quote Robert Sherwood, who, citing Harry Hopkins, described Roosevelt's unseen, supposedly creative mode by which policy was hatched—a mysterious "refueling process," as Sherwood described it. "Then one evening," Hopkins told Sherwood, recalling a two-week postelection fishing trip he accompanied FDR on in December 1940, "he suddenly came out with it [Lend-Lease]—the whole programme."

Sounds like a fish story, but Sherwood happily took the bait from Hopkins's hook: "One can only say that Roosevelt, a creative artist in politics, had put in his time on this cruise evolving the pattern of a masterpiece."[99] Then again, according to Labor Secretary Frances Perkins, the "masterpiece" didn't take any time at all. She wrote that Lend-Lease was a "flash of almost clairvoyant knowledge and understanding," describing FDR's quasi-divine policy revelation as being akin to when a musical genius suddenly perceives "the structure of an entire symphony or opera."[100]

In fact, the evidence suggests Lend-Lease was a con job, and a really big one, put over by another Soviet tool: Soviet go-between, Soviet money-launderer, Soviet hobnobber Armand Hammer. So reports Edward Jay Epstein, who, in his groundbreaking 1996 biography of Hammer, assembled a convincing record indicating that Hammer was the person who floated the original Lend-Lease notion back in 1940. As Epstein discovered, Hammer had transformed himself "virtually overnight . . . from a businessman specializing in importing art and barrel staves from Stalin's Russia to a geopolitical strategist concerned with helping Great Britain get immediate aid from the United States." Before *Dossier,* incidentally, Epstein's Hammer biography, which establishes Hammer as a traitor with revelations of Hammer's pro-Soviet activities, the "international businessman" was generally billed as a nice old philanthropic "man of peace."[101]

That quick transformation of Hammer's back in 1940 is odd on its face. Given that Hammer had Soviet interests at heart (and in the bank), why would he start beating the drum—taking out newspaper ads urging British aid, contributing money to pro-British funds—for Britain? Meanwhile, given the only marginal profitability of Hammer's businesses at that time, Epstein notes "it was not clear where he was getting the funds for his campaign." While Hammer wrote of his concerns as a Jew regarding Nazi Germany, Epstein notes Hammer was simultaneously helping to facilitate oil trade into Germany—scoring a 10 on the hypocrisy meter. The fact is, helping Britain at this early stage in hostilities helped the Kremlin, and was in fact the Communist Party line du jour. "The longer the British pursued the war" against Hitler, Epstein explains, "the more time Stalin would have to prepare the Red Army" for what he considered to be an inevitable war with Hitler. After all, they had read Hitler's plans for them in *Mein Kampf,* and even had plans of their own.

Epstein tells us Hammer not only launched a PR campaign on Britain's behalf but also lobbied the British Embassy in Washington with an idea that resembled the initial Lend-Lease policy, under which the United States "lent" destroyers for the "lease" of British bases, which famously eliminated the need for money to procure aid. The British were cool to Hammer's query, already having established that he was part of the Soviet "secret regime" in the West. Too bad they didn't mention that to us. Then again, maybe they did and the intelligence somehow found its way to that nice, quiet bureaucratic dead end where all too much anti-Soviet intelligence disappeared. Undeterred, Hammer tried the U.S. Senate, where he convinced a friendly Senator William H. King (D-UT) to present, unsuccessfully, aid legislation that Hammer himself had drafted in September 1940. Finally, Hammer briefly met with FDR himself at the White House on November 28, 1940. Epstein calls this meeting the "five minute summit." It seems to have done the trick. FDR and Hopkins embarked on that postelection two-week "refueling" cruise in December, which Sherwood mentioned above, immediately after which FDR announced the plan for Lend-Lease in a press conference. He followed up in a Fireside Chat with the Hopkins-crafted declaration that the United States must now become "the arsenal for democracy."[102] Epstein further notes that FDR dispatched "deputy President" Hopkins to New York City at least two times to confer with Hammer further on this aid idea. Like a cuckoo's egg, then, Lend-Lease was laid inside the White House nest by Hammer the Soviet tool, where Stalin's best friend Hopkins had only to keep it in place so the president could hatch and crow about it.[103]

Still, there were details to work out. Who better to work them out than Assistant Secretary of the Treasury Harry Dexter White? Albert Weeks tells us that White was "one of the main drafters of the administration's side of the Lend-Lease particulars, especially as Lend-Lease was to be extended to the Russians."[104] Harry Dexter White was also signed, sealed, and delivered by copious documentation a Soviet spy.

From Hammer to Hopkins to White and back again to Hopkins: The question now becomes, How could Lend-Lease *not* have been a rogue operation?

In short, Lend-Lease was a slam-dunk-victorious Soviet influence operation, carried out and executed by Uncle Sucker.

Now, where were we?

It's not hard to imagine Hopkins on that December day in 1944, gunning for Kravchenko, grim. The four-poster bed in the Lincoln Bedroom littered with papers. The dramatic, floor-to-almost-ceiling windows overlooking the winter-parched South Lawn. The historic desk on which Abraham Lincoln signed the Emancipation Proclamation. Was it Hopkins himself, sitting at that same hallowed desk, who picked up the phone to put "the heat" on Kravchenko?

If so, it's also not hard to imagine the hapless Secretary of State Stettinius on the other end of the line—he who was unforgettably described by an aide at one time as not having a desk in his office, just a table and telephone, because, Stettinius said, deadpan, "the papers should be with the man who is doing the job."[105]

Were Davies and Hopkins together "doing the job" if (when) it was Hopkins who phoned Stettinius?

Or maybe Davies had already left Hopkins, returning to Tregaron, his Rock Creek Park mansion (now an outbuilding of the Washington International School), where perhaps he sat in his library to write in his journal.

Did a dark-eyed Romanov portrait, souvenir of his Moscow posting, eye Stalin's leading public apologist as he wrote up the events of the day? More likely, it was the silver-framed and autographed photo of Stalin himself that oversaw Davies at work, a last-minute gift at the train station along with a plea from Litvinov—he who toasted Davies as Moscow's envoy in America—for "unbiased judgments" on Soviet life in anything Davies might ever write.[106] Not to worry, as *Mission to Moscow* would prove. Davies would prominently display his framed Stalin in the library for years to come. Yes, it was probably Stalin's gaze on Davies as he duly recorded Hopkins's outrage over Kravchenko's "desertion."

"Hopkins's job with the president was to represent the Russian interests. My job was to represent the American interests." So, disconcertingly, stated George C. Marshall, Army chief of staff (1939–45), secretary of state (1947–49), and secretary of defense (1950–51), to Forrest Pogue, his official biographer, on January 22, 1957.[107] That's a statement to shock anyone. Hopkins and Marshall were the two top wartime advisers to FDR. They may have had differences, but what Marshall describes isn't normal. *Harry's job was to represent the Russian interests; Marshall's job the American interests; and the president would choose between the two?* I can just see the Norman Rockwell illustration of this triumvirate dominated by a quizzical FDR, the American representative (Marshall) at one ear, the Soviet representative (Hopkins) at the other. American interest vs. Soviet interest. Whatever did Marshall mean by that—and whose interests, American or Soviet, did he think won the day? Should it concern us that Marshall was yet another Hopkins protégé? Hopkins biographer McJimsey tells us Marshall "always believed that Hopkins had been responsible for his appointment as chief of staff."[108]

Unfortunately, Pogue wasn't able, didn't want to, or couldn't imagine his way to seize the moment and find out the answers to such questions, which harken back, sub rosa, to George Racey Jordan's 1949–50 Lend-Lease testimony before Congress. In addition to testimony on black suitcases, atomic materials, and the continuous Soviet-American "deeplomatik" runaround, Jordan, a 14-karat witness as established above, had leveled two sensational charges about Harry Hopkins.

The first pertained to a note on White House stationery signed with the initials "H.H."—maybe not an exact transcription, Jordan would later write, but close, which Jordan took to denote Harry Hopkins. Jordan said he found the note inside one of the black suitcases he searched on that winter night when he raced back to the airfield. Given Hopkins's role as Lend-Lease chief, there was nothing odd about a note from Hopkins in a shipment of Lend-Lease supplies. Indeed, from day one of Jordan's mission as a Lend-Lease expediter, he said, Harry Hopkins's name was invoked daily by the Russians, as many others attested. Similarly, there was nothing odd about the second charge Jordan brought to the committee regarding a telephone conversation Jordan said he had had with Hopkins. It was about expediting a "certain shipment" through Great Falls. Nothing necessarily eyebrow-raising about that, either. Jordan was the lead expediter, after all.

What was odd—what was more than passing strange—was the content of both the note and the phone call. According to Jordan, both the note and the phone call concerned atomic-related shipments to Moscow. The "H.H." note was affixed to two documents. One was a thick map, "as wide as the span of my extended arm," Jordan wrote, with a legend he recorded as "Oak Ridge Manhattan Engineering District," which, completely unbeknownst to Jordan at the time, was the top secret headquarters of the U.S. atomic project. The other was a carbon copy of a report, presumably for Harry Hopkins (his name was stamped or typed on the front, Jordan said), which was filled with those "outlandish" words ("cyclotron" and "deuteron") and "curious phrases" ("energy produced by fission" and "walls five feet thick") mentioned above. This was where Jordan met the word "uranium" for the first time.

Then came the Hopkins phone call. One day in April 1943—a most critical month in the history of "American betrayal," as we shall see—Jordan said his Soviet colleague Colonel Kotikov handed him the receiver. On the phone was Harry Hopkins. This, Jordan told Congress, was the first and only contact Jordan had with the Lend-Lease head in twenty-four months of service.

"Big boss, Mr. Hopkins, wants you," Kotikov said.

Jordan had no reason to believe it was anyone other than Hopkins on the line, as some would later suggest, particularly after "Hopkins" inquired whether Jordan had received a windfall supply of scarce pilots to break up a logjam of two hundred antitank Air Cobras destined for bases in the USSR that had piled up at the airfield. Only Hopkins, Jordan believed, could have known about this snafu.

Hopkins went on to tell Jordan about "a certain shipment of chemicals" that would be coming through Great Falls and would need expediting.

OK, boss.

But . . .

"I don't want you to discuss it with anyone," Hopkins said, "and it is not to go on the records. Don't make a big production of it, but just send it through quietly, in a hurry."

"Yessir" was the essence of Jordan's reply. After all, Hopkins, as Jordan wrote, was "a legendary figure of the day, the top man in the world of Lend-Lease in which I lived." Jordan later quizzed Kotikov as to what these chemicals might be and where they'd be coming from. Kotikov pulled out a folder called "Bomb Powder."

"Presumably, after the talk with Hopkins, I had been accepted as a member of the 'lodge,'" as an aside. Jordan dryly commented.

"'I show you,' [Kotikov] announced . . . He drew out a paper sheet and set a finger against one entry. For a second time my eyes encountered the word 'uranium.'"[109]

This uranium would come to Great Falls, Montana, from a mine in Canada.

If you know anything about U.S. uranium stocks during the war—not a burning topic of contemporary interest, I know—that last line about Canada is a clincher, a denouement-style revelation that could well be punctuated with an ominous, wavering organ chord.

Let me explain.

This uranium shipment—news of which Jordan first brought to the public in December 1949 following that first, successful, and shocking Soviet atomic test—was confirmed to have been pushed through to the USSR by federal agencies led by Lend-Lease. In fact, a thorough document search yielded a paper trail of freight bills and other items definitively tracking the uranium's progress. This shipment, which Hopkins apparently tipped off Jordan to, was the second of three shipments totaling nearly three-quarters of a ton. (A fourth research-related shipment of heavy water was also later confirmed.) What is notable—what is organ-chord ominous—about the Hopkins tie-in here is its timing. At the very point Hopkins was on the phone with Jordan in April 1943, the Manhattan Project under General Leslie Groves had already placed an embargo on the export of uranium chemicals from the United States. Groves did so after the first Soviet shipment of uranium chemicals had passed through Great Falls (without drawing Jordan's attention) in March 1943. It wasn't until after the war ended that the general even learned (from House investigators) that the Soviets had thwarted his embargo on uranium exports by tapping Canadian stocks.

Sure enough, when the Hopkins-tipped shipment finally arrived in Great

Falls in June 1943, it came in under Russian guard from Toronto. Jordan copied down the guard's name, identifying him with the initials "C.C." for "Canadian Courier."

After Jordan made this story public in December 1949, the air force pilot of the plane, Ben L. Brown of Cincinnati, came forward to identify himself, adding not only corroboration but a colorful stroke to the story. After taking off from Great Falls and unloading in Fairbanks, Alaska, one of the wooden boxes fell from the plane, the pilot said. A corner broke open from which some chocolate brown powder spilled. Out of curiosity, Brown picked up a handful, whereupon a Soviet officer slapped the crystals from his hand, explaining, "No, no—burn hands!"[110]

Nice, vivid detail, but it doesn't detract from the glaring import of Jordan's story. He wrote in his 1952 memoir, "My share in this revelation was testimony under oath leading to one conclusion—*that the Canadian by-pass was aided by Mr. Hopkins.* At his direction, Lend-Lease issued a certificate of release without which the consignment could not have moved. Lend-Lease channels of transportation and Lend-Lease personnel such as myself were used. Traces of the scheme were kept off the books by making it a 'cash' transaction" (emphasis added).[111]

A kingdom for Marshall's biographer to have asked, What do you know about Harry Hopkins's role in helping the Soviets obtain vital materials and scientific data related to our atomic program? Were you aware of it at the time? Was the president aware of it? Why do you think Harry Hopkins would illegally conspire to thwart the embargo designed to protect America's most precious war secret?

Instead, Pogue's question to Marshall was "During the Congressional hearings in the late 1940s, early 1950s, one or two witnesses indicated that the army's efforts to prevent critical material from going to the Russians was overridden by Mr. Hopkins. Any comment on this?"

Marshall's reply: "I don't remember just what the reaction was in hearings in relation to giving items to Russia."

Sounds as if the old Washington hound was buying a little time to think, because, of course, he hadn't been asked to recall the reaction in hearings or elsewhere to such testimony, but rather for his own comments. He added, "Hopkins's job with the president was to represent the Russian interests. My job was to represent the American interests, and I was opposed to any, what I call, undue generosity which might endanger our security. I thought we gave too much at times and Hopkins thought we gave too little, which would always be the case."

Sounds like a "yes, Hopkins overrode the embargo," but Pogue didn't push it. Instead, he asked, "Do you feel the administration was over-generous with the Soviet government?"

Marshall: "I have answered that question just now."

Well, no, not exactly, General . . . but the moment passed even as a multitude of questions formed and hung there.

Just to confirm, General: It sounds as if you are obliquely confirming the allegation that Hopkins helped the Soviets procure materials for their nuclear program, including uranium, that General Groves had designated off-limits for export. Correct? And what exactly do you mean by saying Hopkins's "job" was representing "the Russian interests"? Are you saying Hopkins in some way worked for the Russians, had a special dossier from the Russians? Do you think it was in the best interests of the United States that the closest adviser to the president "represented" the Russian interests? Or that he elevated two men to run Lend-Lease about whom U.S. ambassador to Moscow Admiral William H. Standley would write, "General [James] Burns is of the same beliefs as [General Philip] Faymonville; Russian interests come first, last and all the time"?[112] Did you ever wonder about such things? Worry about them? Seek to learn anything more about them? Do something about them? You yourself have said you owed your elevation to military chief to Harry Hopkins. Looking back, do you think this sense of gratitude adversely affected any of your actions?

Of course, not even the surface of this subject was disturbed, and the whole matter sank to the bottom and went dormant.

I do mean dormant. Dead. More than thirty years passed—forty-four years since the ever-ailing Hopkins finally died in 1946—before a trusted KGB defector, Oleg Gordievsky, a former KGB colonel and KGB London chief who later served as an undercover British secret agent in Moscow (1974–85), really churned things up. In 1990, Gordievsky reported that as a young KGB agent in the 1960s, he had heard Iskhak Akhmerov, the most spectacular of the secret Soviet spymasters or "illegals" in wartime America, devote most of a lecture at KGB headquarters "to the man whom, he alleged, was the most important of all Soviet wartime agents in the United States: Harry Hopkins."[113]

Not only was Akhmerov, responsible for the oversight of spies including Lauchlin Currie, Nathan Gregory Silvermaster, Elizabeth Bentley, and Harry Dexter White, calling Harry Hopkins a "Soviet agent." He was calling him the most important of all. More important than the far more infamous Alger Hiss or the Rosenbergs. More important even than ultradamaging White, whom Haynes, Klehr, and Vassiliev label "the most highly placed asset the Soviets possessed in the American government."[114] White's Soviet-directed input ("Operation Snow") helped, first, to provoke the Japanese attack on Pearl Harbor and, later, through the Morgenthau Plan, to prolong German resistance to the bitter end. Germany's utter destruction, an important Soviet goal, came about as a result.[115] No less than Elizabeth Bentley testified to White's role "to push the devastation of Germany" through the Morgenthau Plan "because that was what the Russians wanted."[116] How could anyone be more important than that? Hopkins was, though, said Akhmerov. Gordievsky went on to discuss this revelation with "a number of officers" in Soviet intelligence, and "all believed that Hopkins had been an agent of major significance."[117]

Akhmerov, Gordievsky said, also spoke of his "occasional meetings" with Hopkins, which he said preceded Hopkins's historic first visit to the USSR in July 1941. When exactly did they take place? We don't know. As a temporal point of reference, Hopkins, practically the original New Dealer, was by May 1933 already ensconced in the first Roosevelt administration as the head of federal unemployment relief (supposedly, his own and a colleague's idea). MONEY FLIES, said the Washington Post *headline under a front-page photo of Hopkins, as Hopkins gave away five million Depression dollars in his first two hours on the job.*[118] More significant, by the fall of 1933, Hopkins biographer McJimsey tells us, Hopkins was participating in a Communist-organized study group at the Department of Agriculture.

Not that McJimsey describes it that way; this interpretation comes from intelligence experts Romerstein and Breindel. McJimsey put it more antiseptically. "Hopkins entered liberal circles in the fall of 1933, when he and Aubrey Williams began attending informal meetings with a group from the Department of Agriculture, including Paul Appleby (whom Hopkins had known at Grinnell College), Gardner Jackson, Lee Pressman, Jerome Frank, and Rex Tugwell."[119]

We're left to our own devices to evaluate Hopkins's Ag-mates, who, in McJimsey's telling, were brought together by a shared interest in "projects to help the poor." The first time through, my eyes skimmed over the names as though I were searching for something else in the phonebook: didn't register. Later, after reading both Martin Dies's and Robert Stripling's memoirs, I recognized Gardner Jackson as the instigator of an attempt in 1940 to discredit Rep. Martin Dies, chairman of the House Un-American Activities Committee, with a document later unmasked as a forgery.[120] Rexford Tugwell, whose name sounds like someone out of F. Scott Fitzgerald, vaguely resonated. McJimsey notes that Tugwell had the most "trenchant ideas," which, extra research revealed, arose from the young Columbia econ professor's swoony, steely admiration of what was still called the "Soviet experiment." Such ideas included putting the government in total control of the economy: production controls, price controls, profit controls, the works. In case there's any doubt where Tugwell was coming from, he predicted in 1931, "Business will be logically required to disappear."[121] The end of the free market—"the abolition of 'business'"—was one of his hobbyhorses. TUGWELL SEES END OF LAISSEZ-FAIRE, *The New York Times* headlined in 1934.[122]

"That fall," McJimsey writes of 1933, "Hopkins tried to persuade Roosevelt to articulate a New Deal philosophy along Tugwell's lines, but the president was reluctant."[123] No wonder: Congressional elections were coming up, and the president didn't want to blow them by going completely Bolshevik. Better, I'm thinking, to preserve a good-cop (FDR), bad-cop (Tugwell) deniability.

When Romerstein and Breindel looked at McJimsey's list, the tip-off for them was the presence of Lee Pressman, who happened (if that's the right word) to be a Harvard Law School classmate of Alger Hiss. In 1948, Whittaker Chambers identified Pressman as a very big Communist cheese: one of seven leading members of a Communist apparatus within the U.S. government, each of whom was charged with organizing a study group/cell in his respective agency. The way it worked was that members would be further evaluated by Communist cell leaders, after which they might be selected to join the Communist underground and work in Soviet espionage. Pressman's agency was Agriculture. Suddenly, McJimsey's study group looks less revival meeting and more Marxist conspiracy meet-and-greet.

Was Hopkins tapped for advanced work here? We have no evidence. Which, of course, isn't to say it didn't happen. My hunch is that if Hopkins were in fact an Akhmerov agent—and, as we will see, his contact with Akhmerov is confirmed—he may have belonged to a network we don't know about, or a network of one. This little Ag group, by the way, with the exception of Pressman, remains clean when it comes to official espionage links, but they were all fellow travelers active in Communist or Soviet causes, which is, after all, what fellow travelers do. Take Jerome Frank, who was Rexford Tugwell's housemate. Frank was a drafter of the New Deal law that ushered in the Agricultural Adjustment Administration, the New Deal agency empowered to compel farmers to limit or destroy their output in exchange for government subsidies.

"More Bolshevistic than any law or regulation existing in Soviet Russia," said Rep. Fred Bitten (R-IL). *"We are on our way to Moscow,"* said Rep. Joseph W. Martin (D-MA).[124]

Frank became the AAA's general counsel, an appointment Arthur M. Schlesinger Jr. in his book *The Coming of the New Deal* called a triumph for the "liberals."[125] Liberals? I look at Frank's hires for the counsel's office and see some of the most notorious Communists of the day mixed in among the liberals—or is that vice versa? From Harvard Law School alone, Frank hired Alger Hiss, Lee Pressman, John Abt, and Nathan Witt, all members of the secret Communist apparatus known as the Ware Group, later identified by Whittaker Chambers as a hardened espionage unit. Hopkins's little study group appears to be a low-impact offshoot.

Maybe not so low-impact. Tugwell, after all, Frank's housemate, was a radical's radical and the foremost member of FDR's so-called brain trust—one of the leaders William A. Wirt attempted to bring to Congress's attention in May 1934 for allegedly plotting revolution from within. Arthur Schlesinger relates an anecdote about an overnight visit from a friend of Frank's from his, yes, corporate law days to the Frank-Tugwell home. The friend, in Schlesinger's words, became "shocked by Tugwell in a mood of early morning intensity." (Tugwell probably read him selections from his latest oeuvre, something about how the solution to the "central problem of subordinating the profit motive to social welfare" lay in "genuine economic planning and social control."[126]) After departing, the friend cabled Jerome Frank with a warning about Tugwell: BEWARE COMMA JEROME STOP THIS MORNING AT BREAKFAST I SAW THE FACE OF ROBESPIERRE.[127]

Such was the red-hot Washington scene Akhmerov found on arriving to take control of the secret intelligence network in the middle 1930s—we don't know exactly when—until he was recalled to Moscow in late 1939. Having survived Stalin's show trials and purges, he returned to the United States in December 1941. Hopkins, a fixture of the Roosevelt administration since 1933, first traveled to the USSR in July 1941. As Romerstein and Breindel note, this timeline tells us "Akhmerov must have worked with Hopkins in the 1930s before Akhmerov returned to the Soviet Union in 1939."[128]

While we can't pinpoint the initial date of Akhmerov-Hopkins contact, there is a crucial significance to the relationship. "Illegals" such as Akhmerov always operate outside official channels, always operate under cover. (Think of the ten "illegals" bagged and returned to Russia in 2010.) In other words, they have none of the protections of the embassy, including diplomatic immunity. On the contrary, using false identities, they pose as ordinary persons simply residing in their host country. Akhmerov, for example, on his return to the United States in December 1941, held a phony U.S. passport, avoided all contact with CPUSA chief Earl Browder (even though he was married to Browder's niece), and, in March 1942, moved to Baltimore to open a fur and clothing business in partnership with a local Soviet agent from which to run his agents based in Washington. As Romerstein and Breindel explain, an illegal's identity as a Soviet intelligence official is a secret *from everyone except his espionage contacts.* This, as the authors underscored in their 2000 book, is a weighty factor in favor of the argument that Hopkins was a *conscious* Soviet agent. Hopkins had plenty of workaday contacts with open Soviet officials, and, indeed, they make appearances in Sherwood's biography. Not Akhmerov. In dealing with "Baltimore furrier" Akhmerov, Hopkins, the president's right hand, was dealing with an undercover superspymaster, someone who, according to Mitrokhin and Andrew, "controlled most political intelligence operations in the United States."[129] His premiere stable of agents included Nathan Gregory Silvermaster, who ran the Silvermaster network, Laurence Duggan, Alger Hiss, Michael Greenberg, and more. Given the stakes, maintaining his cover was crucial, and so he did. It would take decades for American intelligence to identify this spymaster whom they simply knew as "Elizabeth Bentley's 'Bill.'" Akhmerov, Romerstein and Breindel write, had no reason to break "cover" as a middle-class businessman and reveal himself as an intelligence officer of the Kremlin to Hopkins *unless Hopkins were an agent himself.*" (emphasis added).[130]

Here we see the stunning significance of Gordievsky's claim take shape. So then what happened? Not much, really. The revelation that pulled the pin on the biggest grenade in American history turned out to do little lasting damage. FDR's right hand and alter ego, the co-president and Svengali who was always there for lunch with Churchill, dinner with Stalin, breakfast, lunch, poker, gin rummy, and fishing with Roosevelt, was said, on credible authority, to have been a Kremlin agent, the supreme Kremlin agent in the United States during World War II—and no one cared.

Of course, it was almost as if Gordievsky and Andrew didn't want a large explosion themselves. "Gordievsky," they write, "gradually came to the conclusion that, *despite his clandestine meetings with a Soviet illegal,* Hopkins had never been a conscious agent" (emphasis added).[131]

Really? How did Gordievsky "gradually" arrive there? Had he gradually gathered additional evidence?

No, not any that he and his coauthor develop in the book, gradually or otherwise. Rather, as Andrew and Gordievsky, rather abruptly write, "that interpretation"—Hopkins as *un*conscious agent, or "useful fool"—"best fits the evidence on his career available in the West."[132]

What "evidence" is that? The evidence that Hopkins lobbied for the "deserter" Kravchenko's return to certain death? The evidence that Hopkins pulled strings to send uranium and nuclear know-how to the Kremlin? Or could it be, for the intelligence historians, that that pesky existing view of the world was blocking their line of sight again? Amazingly, with few exceptions (Romerstein and Breindel, for instance), Hopkins got a pass.

"The probability is . . . [Hopkins] was never a conscious agent."[133]

Probability based on what preponderance of fact? None is offered. The sentence should more accurately read: We surely hope Hopkins was never a conscious agent because that would change everything.

"Hopkins did not depart from what he saw as American interests . . . Hopkins acted from determination to prevent a Nazi victory rather than from a secret commitment to the Communist cause."[134]

Again, more declarations of wishful thinking. If anything, Andrew's defense of Hopkins has intensified even as the evidence, which he, to his craft and credit, has continued to present in subsequent works, has mounted. Noting KGB boasts that Hopkins had been a Soviet agent, Andrew (with Mitrokhin) writes in 1999, "These boasts were far from the truth. Hopkins was an American patriot with little sympathy for the Soviet system."[135]

Far from the truth? Hopkins the American patriot? No sympathy for the Soviet system? There is simply no evidence of Hopkins's patriotism other than the fact that he worked in the White House. There is only an assumption here, a faith based in wishful thinking, which is hardly the tool of good spycraft.

In 1998, the late U.S. Air Force historian Eduard Mark published a breakthrough in the Hopkins analysis, a meticulous examination of what appears to be the first damning document to emerge from the Venona record against Hopkins: specifically, a partly decrypted Venona cable, believed to have been authored by our friend Akhmerov, in which a very senior Roosevelt administration official, code-named "Source 19," conveys the contents of a private, top secret conversation between FDR and Churchill in late May 1943 about the invasion of Normandy, which at that time was still a year off. By process of painstaking elimination, Mark determines that it is "probable virtually to the point of certainty" that "Source 19" is Harry Hopkins.[136] I read it (and recommend that others do the same), and I buy his meticulously marshaled logic. Far more important, of course, experts Romerstein and Breindel buy it, too, *and both Christopher Andrew and Vasily Mitrokhin buy it*, at least in endnotes, calling Mark's study "detailed, meticulous and persuasive."[137] Haynes and Klehr, however, remain agnostic, which has the unfortunate effect of eliminating the story, even the suggestion of the story, from their influential works. For example, their 650-page compendium *Spies* doesn't even footnote it. True, Vassiliev found little about Hopkins in the finite number of KGB files he was allowed to view and copy—although given the controversy, even that might merit a footnote. Leaving all Hopkins analysis out of the research has the unfortunate effect of both suspending what should be an ongoing investigation and retarding curiosity.

In his endnotes—peculiarly enough, endnotes are where much of the scholarly debate about Hopkins takes place—Eduard Mark regards the state of the scholarship since Gordievsky first lobbed the Hopkins-Akhmerov revelation into the field nearly a decade earlier, which intitally prompted vigorous debate in reviews of the book. Mark writes, "Since that time, however, scholars have published scores of books and articles on facets of American foreign policy related to Hopkins's activities. As far as I know, not one of these studies has dealt with Akhmerov's allegations."[138]

Mark, again, was writing in 1998. Today, more than ten years later, two decades since the original claim, more than sixty years since Jordan offered his evidence, sworn testimony that Hopkins sent atomic plans to the Kremlin and pushed uranium shipments past the Manhattan Project embargo, we are still counting down to a real reckoning. Others have since pulled the same pin—Romerstein and Breindel, of course, in their 2000 analysis in *The Venona Secrets;* investigative journalist Cliff Kincaid in his AIM report; Paul Kengor in his 2010 book *Dupes*—but, to date, the *implications* of the evidence have yet to be grasped by the lapels and shaken. A Soviet spy and American traitor advised the president and himself made policy before and during World War II: This is a thesis that demands further confrontation even if it might shift the balance of our historic understanding.

Mark cites the "indifference of American diplomatic historians to intelligence [history]," which by now is an old refrain in this book. He also notes "their predominantly liberal political orientation." This, he writes, "has led them to ignore the whole question of the relationship between security and foreign policy as smacking of 'McCarthyism.'"[139]

Ah so—we're back to that old vampire, still sucking our past dry, destroying the vital flow of evidence that links facts to conclusions. Keeping the Hopkins story and the rest of our intelligence history in the dark, then, prevents the truth from coming in from the cold, and keeps the national imagination from igniting, from throwing light into the black hole of antiknowledge, from blowing up our totally phony consensus narrative.

What follows is my own attempt. This will include my own dossier on Hopkins—the facts as I have found them, an admittedly fragmentary record culled from multiple sources—and my own try at assessing *the implications,* and how they bear on something larger than any one man, something that seems to be missing, and inexplicably so, in the moral life and times of our society. This is our own hidden history, our stolen history, precisely the sequence of events we have lost virtually all trace of. Reclaiming it, then, becomes an archaeological exploration of the past where our Kravchenkos, our Jordans, our Lyonses, our Joneses, our Dieses, Conquests, and McCarthys lie buried, lost from our view of history. Little wonder we have lost our bearings, too.

CHAPTER SIX

Who reads the Communist press? Only a few people who are already Communists. We don't have to propagandize them. What is our object? Who do we have to influence? We have to influence non-Communists if we want to make them Communists or if we want to fool them. So, we have to try to infiltrate the big press.

—VYACHESLAV MOLOTOV[1]

The Soviets live and breathe deception. You cannot understand what they are doing without understanding this. Indeed, you can't even begin to understand Communism without understanding deception, which is very rarely mentioned in textbooks on Communism *[emphasis added].*

—JOSEPH D. DOUGLASS JR.[2]

Who stole our history?

Because stolen it was, diverted from its natural course and re-channeled to the point where the beaten path became a shortcut from reality to deception. This, I believe, is confirmed every single time one of those gigantic corrections of the false record, flagged by scholars shouting "Eureka!," fails to enter our general histories, fails to capture popular imagination, fails to become part of our popular understanding, and fails to occur to us as a mainstream thought. Like a skiff on a dry creek bed, these corrections go nowhere.

Thus, when it comes to Harry Hopkins, for example—after Andrew and Gordievsky's stunning revelation (1990), after Mark's meticulous Hopkins-Venona study (1998), after Andrew and Mitrokhin's endnote endorsement of Mark's conclusions (1999), after Romerstein and Breindel's extended analysis (2000) (and even more evidence of Hopkins's treason, as I will argue below), Cambridge University Press can offer *Yalta 1945* by Fraser J. Harbutt, 468 pages published in 2010, in which Harry Hopkins lives into posterity as simply that "close aide" FDR relied on. There is not even an asterisk to indicate the small but expert school of thought that attests to Hopkins's activities on the

Kremlin's behalf, which require consideration in any study of this final and momentous (disastrous) meeting of the so-called Big Three. (Even worse is the tome's black hole on GRU Agent Alger Hiss, who was all over Yalta like flypaper but rates exactly two mentions in passing.[3]) All we get by way of elucidation is that Hopkins's "monitoring and energizing talents were applied far and wide throughout the governmental bureaucracy and on the multiple boards and commissions that were conceived, often on very short notice, to fill unanticipated gaps and discharge urgent critical tasks."[4]

This isn't untrue; it just ignores the central, unresolved controversy: *on behalf of whom* he was applying those talents. This omission is typical. To sample some of recent bios of FDR, in the 1,360 pages of *Franklin Delano Roosevelt: Champion of Freedom* by Conrad Black (PublicAffairs, 2003), in the 896 pages of *Traitor to His Class* by H. W. Brands (Doubleday, 2008), and in the relatively svelte 560 pages of *Franklin and Winston: An Intimate Portrait of an Epic Friendship* by Jon Meacham (Random House, 2003), the ubiquitous co-president, foreign secretary, and uranium snatcher Harry "Rasputin" Hopkins, is depicted as that most "intimate" of Roosevelt intimates, the most "versatile," and most "indispensable." Again, none of this is untrue. All of these recent histories, however, completely ignore the still-burning question about Hopkins that was first raised by experts a quarter century ago: indispensable to whom?

Such professional incuriosity is staggering. Then again, considering the amount of feet-of-clay-revealing spadework that a serious correction of the record will entail, perhaps it is also disappointingly understandable. It's that "existing view of the world" again: No one wants to admit it's a total phony. Once we finally incorporate the facts of Soviet-directed penetration of the U.S. government—the Communist-agent-occupation of the U.S. government—which began in earnest in 1933, everything we know about ourselves as a nation will also have to rearrange itself, our history taking on a brand-new pattern of revelation.

It starts small, like a single click of a kaleidescope: Since Harry Hopkins was so close to FDR, as the biographies/hagiographies usually note in passing, *and Harry Hopkins served as an agent of Stalin's influence,* where does that leave the motives, the judgment, and the keystone legacy of the "great" Roosevelt?

The questions fragment and multiply. What about those momentous decisions Hopkins influenced Roosevelt to make? That is, what about the economic policies and, later, the war strategies Hopkins helped set in place and personally kept in motion? These same economic polices and war strategies made the postwar world.

Suddenly, our own preexisting view from the Tidal Basin vantage point of FDR's sprawling memorial blurs. Of course, this new way of looking at things isn't just about Harry Hopkins. His example is neither singular nor even singularly blatant. Scads of devilish Kremlin agents with dossiers stuffed with confirmed Venona references still manage to retain their masks and smile for the history books, or, more often, disappear into the woodwork of the past as though the Red hunts of old and the massive evidence spills of late never happened. So long as the Red hunters remain lost to us in the toxic black fog of "McCarthyism," who will notice that they were right all along? Always, correction of the record, *exposure* of the record, stalls against a formidable force field surrounding the status quo of conspiracy, an ancien régime of lies.

The case of Lauchlin Currie illustrates how history's cloak of invisibility works, how a perfectly, loftily placed Soviet agent with the trust of and access to the president of the United States can remain an anonymous, unknown, unreckoned presence in our histories despite the epic damage he did to the nation. The truth is, Benedict Arnold should have an awful lot of company in those recesses of the American mind where a name rings a bell and the free-association word choice is "traitor." Even before Currie started working in the White House in 1939, where his activities on behalf of the Kremlin appear in nine Venona cables (KGB code name "Page"), I would argue that this Harvard PhD was already undermining free markets and liberty as the original champion of a brand-new macroeconomic policy we now know as "stimulus spending."[5] No archival evidence to date confirms that Currie's pre-Keynesian championing of "public expenditure as a stimulus to the economy" was, in fact, a Red Plot to Destroy America, but the fact that its initial booster inside the Roosevelt administration was a Soviet agent should draw our eye.

Currie wasn't alone with his Soviet sympathies in the West Wing. Venona tells us Currie's assistant, Michael Greenberg, was a Soviet agent, too. Moreover, David K. Niles, another Roosevelt executive assistant, appears in Venona, noted for his intervention to procure visas for a KGB husband-wife team—with the final paperwork, Romerstein and Breindel report, being handled by another Soviet agent named Michael W. Burd.[6] Was Niles an agent, too? The record establishes Niles's close connections to other agents, but no more. These connections, by the way, included Harry Hopkins. When Hopkins test-drove his own presidential candidacy in the run-up to 1940—Roosevelt's third term in the end—Niles was, in Sherwood's words, Hopkins's "chief political adviser and campaign strategist."[7] There were other even closer connections. According to a story Whittaker Chambers heard from another Soviet agent (these people got around), Niles at one time threatened to expose the activities of a Communist group in Washington that included a Soviet agent—Niles's homosexual lover—unless the man left his wife. The man was ordered out of Washington immediately by the Communist underground, then under "illegal," or undercover, spymaster J. Peters.[8] Quite a Red barrel of monkeys, the Roosevelt White House.

To be sure, such evidence was a U.S. government secret before the mid-1990s release, unpredicted but serendipitous, of nearly three thousand fully or only partly decrypted Soviet cables from the Venona archive. Still, it's important to understand that much of what Venona confirmed had been in the public domain for half a century. In 1948, our heroine Elizabeth Bentley publicly named Currie among dozens of government officials who were also agents of Soviet infiltration. Currie, she said under oath before the House Committee on Un-American Activities, was a leading member of a spy network known as the Silvermaster Group. (Whittaker Chambers would testify later that he knew Currie to be close to Silvermaster and arch Soviet spy Harry Dexter White, No. 2 man at Treasury.) In 1944, Bentley recalled, Currie tipped off the Soviets that American codebreakers were cracking a secret Soviet code (ironically, the very code used in the Venona cables); and, further, that Currie had thrown his White House weight around to protect Nathan Gregory Silvermaster from a government security investigation. He also, Bentley testified, simultaneously promoted and helped place other Soviet agents.[9] All nose-of-the-camel stuff, as it turned out.

What was also true—*and the FBI knew it from 1945 wiretaps*—was that Currie interceded not just to save other Communist agents from exposure but also to save himself. I refer to his role in the most important espionage case that never came to trial, the *Amerasia* case, named for the pro-Communist magazine owned and edited by Philip Jaffe, a friend of CPUSA chief Earl Browder. *Amerasia* was publishing classified information. OSS (Office of Strategic Services), the precursor to the CIA, wanted to know how. On June 6, 1945, the FBI arrested six people on espionage charges in the case, including owner-editor Jaffe and a State Department official named John Stewart Service. A whopping thousand pounds of classified documents would be impounded from *Amerasia's* offices and elsewhere, including Service's State Department office.[10] About one-quarter of these documents concerned military matters, while many were marked with the warning that possession of them was a violation of the Espionage Act. Little wonder FBI Director J. Edgar Hoover considered *Amerasia* an "airtight case."[11]

However, as M. Stanton Evans documents, *Amerasia* would never come to trial. Why? The fix was in. A dirty plot "to throw the case and free John Service" was hatched and executed by Lauchlin Currie, veteran New Dealer-wheeler Thomas 'Tommy the Cork' Corcoran, and "higher-ups at Justice," including Truman's newly named attorney general (and later Supreme Court justice) Tom Clark. It was all on tape.[12] Stuff like this:

CORCORAN: What I want to do is get the guy [Service] out.

CURRIE: Yeah, the important thing is to get him out . . .

CORCORAN: . . . I think our problem is to take care of this kid, isn't it?

CURRIE: That's right.

That this shocking exchange and others like it were recorded for posterity (fat lot we've done with it) was entirely accidental. Suspicious of Roosevelt loyalist Corcoran, Truman had ordered the FBI to listen in on him, warrantless-wiretap-style, to see what Corcoran was up to. The G-man on the other end of the line must have blown his top when he realized he was listening to a conspiracy in action—not just a conspiracy theory—to rig a grand jury espionage case. *Meanwhile, back on Okinawa*—just to add a little context—soldiers and marines were just then fighting for gains of "up to" one thousand yards of mud a day. Who was really knee-deep in the muck?

The implications of *Amerasia* are staggering. It wasn't just "the kid" and his five *Amerasia* codefendants who got "taken care of." It is no exaggeration to say that it was practically the entire secret Communist occupation of the U.S. government itself, kit and caboodle, that these Washington fixers saved from disruption and dispersal, from the mortal blow of exposure. It is also no exaggeration to say that millions of lives would be lost due to this effective and corrupt maneuver to shield this Red Plot in Progress to communize China. That is, here, in mid-1945, quite suddenly poking into the light, was the jagged edge of the dark sword aimed at China by Moscow and ably carried forward by Soviet agents within the U.S. government. The Washington fixers, led (rolled) by Soviet agent Currie, managed to push everything back into the shadows, but the Communist jig could well have been up in open court, even before Elizabeth Bentley came in from the cold five months later. Evans explains, "Because the fix was in, there was no serious effort to track down the confederates of the *Amerasia* culprits threaded throughout the State Department, Treasury, the White House, and other influential places, all diligently working to shape the course of Cold War history in Asia."[13]

Threaded, knotted, and tangled throughout the government is more like it. This thicket of Communist occupation is overwhelming to behold, even now, with the lights up and the curtain partly lifted. At the time, however, everything went dark again with the *Amerasia* "fix," and the Red conspirators played on unseen. There would be no probe of *Amerasia's* owner, Philip Jaffe—for example, his meetings with CPUSA chief Earl Browder, Chinese Red leader Tung Pi-wu, officials at the Soviet consulate in New York, and Soviet agent Joseph Bernstein (KGB code name "Marquis"). There would be no routine investigation of John Stewart Service to net the fact that two slam-dunk Soviet agents had been his housemates in China: Solomon Adler and Chi Chao-ting, both instrumental in the sabotage of the Nationalist Chinese government under Chiang Kai-shek, and the Red-rigged triumph of Mao Tse-tung and his so-called People's Republic. Worst of all, the sprawling Institute of Pacific Relations (IPR), an intimately linked and leading player in the Chinese tragedy (under the Red-toadying tutelage of Owen Lattimore), which regarded *Amerasia* as one of its publications,[14] would be allowed to continue its massive influence operations. IPR would continue to shade and shape U.S. policy in support of what it promoted as the "agrarian" Chinese—Mao's Red Army. Following a monumental investigation, Senator Pat McCarran's (D-NV) Internal Security Subcommittee report boiled down the IPR essence thus: "The IPR was a vehicle used by the Communists to orientate American far eastern policy toward Communist objectives."[15] That was in 1952, and the news was too late. All of this and more could have come out in 1945.

It didn't, thanks in large part to Lauchlin Currie.

Did I mention Currie's "special program" at the White House was Far Eastern affairs? As a smart Soviet mole in a White House office—which, cozy thought, Currie shared with his assistant, Soviet agent Michael Greenberg, himself an IPR man[16]—Currie's notion of "special" meant such projects as maneuvering Japan away from an attack on Siberia and later communizing China.[17] That meant a close association with IPR. Indeed, Lauchlin Currie personally (and without consulting Secretary of State Cordell Hull[18]) installed the IPR's Owen Lattimore, "a conscious, articulate instrument of the Soviet conspiracy,"[19] as a White House adviser to Chiang Kai-shek—or, as Chiang himself suspected, Communist eyes and ears.[20] So neat. Obviously, Currie couldn't let something as inconvenient and dangerous as an FBI investigation and a grand jury proceeding mess everything up. As the Red Plot's top in-house White House adviser on China, he had to do everything in his considerable power to ensure that Service walked. If Currie hadn't succeeded, Mao's Long March might well have been frozen in its tracks.

What a concept. Of course, the march tramped on, assisted in part by Washington's Soviet proxies. Service housemate Solomon Adler, a Venona-identified spy in the Silvermaster network, remained under cover as a Treasury staffer working to throw China, while Service housemate Chi remained under cover as a Maoist agent inside the Chinese Nationalist government until it fell in 1949, "at which point," Evans writes, "mission completed, he would abscond to Beijing."[21] After Senator Joe McCarthy, *bless him,* started unpacking the stinking corruption that had gutted the *Amerasia* case, much to the benefit of world Communist revolution, the U.S. Treasury Department's Adler also absconded to Beijing. By 1960, amid the hustle and bustle of Mao's Great Leap Forward (which killed eighteen million to forty-six million Chinese), Adler was spending his days translating Mao's writings into English.[22]

Words fail.

There was something else that should have happened in 1945 that didn't: the unmasking of Lauchlin Currie himself. No such luck. How could luck—how could the FBI, how could a grand jury—compete against the Communist occupation of Washington? Currie, Adler, Chi, and the rest kept their cover, even their cool. They carried on, their networks of spies and traitors remaining in place until, Evans explains, "Joe McCarthy in his rough-and-ready fashion set about dragging into public view, case by painful case, in 1950."[23] Really dirty work, but someone had to do it. It is only when the malignancy, range, and ruthlessness of the Soviet infestation are understood that the requirements of fumigation make sense.

Funny, 1950 was when Adler left the country; Currie, too—and about time. Five damaging years had passed since the *Amerasia* arrests. Currie, for one, had resigned from his White House job shortly after the arrests. By July of 1945, not long after that wiretapped *Amerasia* conversation about "the kid" took place, he had, according to a brief story in *The New York Times*, already taken up a position in a company. Whether that was due to *Amerasia*, I can't say. Salient point is, though, Currie went out with his head high, confident enough of his "protected status," as Evans calls it—and, I would add, his laughable disguise as a loyal public servant—to bluff his way through a historic House committee hearing in August 1948 where he and the rest of the secret agents called in to testify categorically denied all of Elizabeth Bentley's charges.[24]

Mr. Currie also denied that he had disclosed any "inside information" concerning China to any person not authorized to receive it . . .

Mr. Currie also denied he had interceded for Mr. Gregory Silvermaster when he was under a loyalty investigation.[25]

As for the infamous photo lab in the basement of Silvermaster's house? The one that Elizabeth Bentley had told Congress was used by Silvermaster and William Ludwig Ullmann, another federal employee-cum-spy (who jointly owned the Silvermaster house[26]), to photograph secret government documents for dispatch to Moscow?

To the befuddlement of the House committee, Silvermaster had earlier invoked the Fifth Amendment against self-incrimination to answer whether his basement contained photographic equipment; Ullmann had, too. Ullmann even invoked the Fifth to refuse to answer whether he'd ever been in the basement of the house he'd lived in for ten years.

It turned out the FBI had been there and already knew everything there was to know about the photo lab. "On November 29, 1945, a detailed observation of the basement of the Silvermaster residence . . . was made," an entry in the voluminous declassified Silvermaster FBI file reads. It goes on to describe the lights, reflectors, enlarger, tripods, camera, and well-stocked supplies that were observed,[27] but you didn't need to be a G-man or a Soviet spy to figure it out. On May 3, 1947, a real estate listing in *The Washington Evening Star* announced the "price for quick sale" of the Silvermaster house. "Interior of this fine brick house must be seen to be appreciated," the real estate copy ran beneath a picture of the house. Among its attributes: "an excellent photographic room in the basement."[28]

This ad, not the FBI's "detailed observation," went into congressional record presumably in response to Silvermaster's and Ullmann's stonewalling. Maybe that's why the Communists' story on the Silvermaster basement changed by the time Lauchlin Currie was called to testify.

In an extraordinary daylong hearing in August 1948 where the witnesses were "persons accused in the Soviet spy-ring investigation," as *The New York Times* put it—and which, in Venona-vetted fact, featured various heavy hitters of the Silvermaster lineup (Currie, Harry Dexter White, Frank Coe, who soon would be translating Mao into English with Solomon Adler, Sonia and Bela Gold, Donald Hiss)—Currie and White both played indignant, owl-eyed bureaucrats with nothing to hide. Former assistant treasury secretary White, now recognized as the highest-ranking U.S. government official to serve Stalin covertly, even had the gall to speechify about democratic principle (printed verbatim by the pro-Communist publication *PM*[29]). No pleading the Fifth Amendment for these cool customers. Matter of fact, they both admitted visiting Silvermaster's home, *even visiting the basement.* They also admitted that they "understood" that Ullmann—mentioned in an impressive twenty-four separate Venona cables—was an amateur photographer. They just didn't notice whether he had a photo lab in the basement.

Too busy, apparently. "Mr. White said that he went there to play Ping-Pong . . . Mr. Currie said he had gone with his son, who was interested in power tools, to see Mr. Ullmann's collection."[30]

Three days later, on August 16, 1948, Harry Dexter White was dead of a heart attack, age fifty-five. "His death completed my sense of human disaster," Whittaker Chambers writes in *Witness,* describing his thoughts on hearing the news of his former confederate's sudden death. "White is luckier than the rest of us. He at least is well out of it."[31]

Chambers was right. We, as a nation, were just entering those muddy trenches, thanks to the Curries and Whites and Silvermasters and Hisses. So much damage had been done and was still being done; so many lives were already lost, with more, many more, Americans included, still to be lost—from Siberia to Korea, from Hungary to Vietnam. As Evans reminds us, "in the five-year span between the *Amerasia* fix and the McCarthy blow-up of 1950," China fell. The rise of Mao was assured; the death sentences of tens of millions of Chinese had only to be written; wars in Korea and Vietnam were just waiting to be fought. Would Adler and Coe, busy scribbling Mao's evil aphorisms into English, even notice? Do we even notice? What do we retain of these momentous events? What understanding or artifact do we have to recall the tortuous trail of corruption, betrayal, bloodshed, tears, terror, and waste that seems to follow so very directly from that Corcoran-Currie-Clark conspiracy to "fix" *Amerasia* in June 1945?

Nothing.

"The bride is a great-granddaughter of the late Harry Dexter White, an economist who helped create the World Bank and the International Monetary Fund," *The New York Times* effervesced *in 2009.[32] An economist whose epic treason against this country is documented in fifteen Venona cables, more than two dozen KGB documents unearthed from the archives, and notes in his handwriting found in the Whittaker Chambers "Pumpkin Papers."[33]* What about that?

Nothing.

More people "know" that J. Edgar Hoover wore a red dress around the Plaza Hotel—a total fabrication—than know the first thing about Lauchlin Currie, Harry Dexter White, and their epic treason against this country that delivered millions of people to misery and death. As a society we gaze, stupefied, at those Warhol portraits of Murderer Mao over the gas logs in the fireplace, and think they make life soigné; we snarl, reflexively, at a demonology centered around Senator Joe McCarthy, inhaling with salubrious indignation over the dastardly deeds of the Evil One. "Had McCarthy done nothing more during his uproarious heyday in the Senate," Evans writes, "his role in blowing the lid off the *Amerasia* scandal would deserve the plaudits of a grateful nation."[34]

Yes. The nation should indeed be grateful to McCarthy for his determination to *expose Amerasia,* to wrest the facts of the matter *from the darkness* of conspiratorial deception, to *reveal* the *hidden* workings of a case "replete with cover-up, perjury and grand-jury-rigging," as Evans neatly sums up. In retrospect, this case, among many others, should finally recalibrate our historical gaze from the bull's-eye wrongfully painted on McCarthy's hide to the phony halo awkwardly clamped over the Truman White House. It was the Truman administration, after all, that kept John Stewart Service on the State Department payroll, along with, as noted, his housemate Solomon Adler at Treasury, both men repeat champions of multiple Truman-instituted "loyalty tests" despite their fattening FBI dossiers.

Strange. When given the choice, the Truman White House always chose concealment over revelation, squelching a security breach rather than sounding an alarm. This would seem to make it, in effect, a coconspirator in Communist infiltration, and a lousy defender of the Constitution. I don't know how to conclude otherwise. The fact is, when we say Venona was a secret before 1995, that means it was a secret to us—Us, the People. Long before the entirely haphazard sequence of events that led to the declassification of the Venona archive—or some portion thereof (we don't know for sure)—these ciphers were broken. They were read. At some point, then, long before 1995, Lauchlin Currie's Soviet record was obvious. At some point, then, long before 1995, Alger Hiss's Soviet record was obvious, too. Ditto for Harry Dexter White and Gregory Silvermaster and William Ludwig Ullmann *and hundreds more.* After a codebreaker read it first—the electrifying flicker of comprehension coming as payoff for the skull-cracking days, months, years of study—the Kremlin's secret wasn't a secret anymore; it was disseminated very strictly to American officials, military and civilian. Was it now . . . an American secret?

While it would seem that some very wild cats were out of the bag, they were immediately locked back up in a cage where, the idea was, they could do no harm. The truth is, when these secrets were locked back up, *they could do no good.* They could shed no light on the bitterly, dangerously divisive controversies that would tear this country apart for decades, probably forever. They could offer no succor to the pilloried Cassandras who had no protection but a stubborn grasp of the facts as they knew them *and as the government knew them, too.* But refused to say so. The continued hush-hush classification of Venona could help no one except, irony of ironies, the spies and traitors who served that murderous and revolutionary junta in Moscow, ardently, volubly supported by the useful fools ("useful morons" seems more apt) in their thrall who created, controlled, and amplified the echo chamber of Communist apologetics.

The raucous career of Drew Pearson, political gossip columnist, radio personality, and one-man cottage industry, demonstrates the echo chamber in action.

By 1950, when McCarthy began trying to reconstruct the hidden means by which the U.S. government had been secretly infiltrated and occupied, the senator picked up on the trail of Lauchlin Currie. As noted above, it was around this same time (I don't know if it was before or after McCarthy was on the case) that Currie took a powder to Colombia—or, as his apologists prefer, accepted a position with the Colombian government. This was somewhat bad luck for Pearson, whose hugely litigious and influential columns and broadcasts carried their fair share of Currie "tips" through the years.[35] Indeed, they were sometimes conveyed to him through John Stewart Service.[36]

Only met the man at a party once, Pearson stipulates in his diaries, *lying*. Why did he say that? "Currie arranged for Service to meet the renowned political columnist Drew Pearson in a little bar in the basement of the Hay Adams hotel . . . They met several times," writes Laura Tyson Li in her 2006 biography *Madame Chiang Kai-Shek,* explaining that Currie wanted Service to "build a backfire" against Madame Chiang's soaring popularity in the United States. "Pearson grew increasingly acerbic [read: anti-Chiang] on the subject of China."[37] Service wasn't, as he put it himself in an interview with Harvey Klehr and Ronald Radosh in 1985, Lauchlin Currie's "designated leaker" for nothing.[38]

On June 13, 1951, with the McCarran Committee in full investigatory mode, Pearson wrote in his diary, "Tipped off Lock Currie that the McCarran Committee was about to brand him as one of the top Russian informants in the Roosevelt administration . . . He looked as if the ground had fallen out from under him . . . Lock is a meek and mild little man who I think would have been the last to have played ball with the Russians."[39]

Tipped off Lock Currie? One of the scores of out-of-print books that now stand in stacks in my study is *Drew Pearson: Diaries, 1949-1959.* Examining the black-and-white head shot of Pearson filling the cover of the 1974 book (a face familiar enough at sell books at one time), I look for some telling break in the intently smug stare, the furrowed brow, the Kronkite mustache (then again, Kronkite's mustache was probably a Pearson mustache). My question is, Did Pearson buy his own blather? He sure sold a lot of it. "Lock" Currie wasn't the only little man "to have played ball with the Russians" Pearson went to the mat for; Pearson also vouched for *Amerasia*'s star, John Stewart Service. "I doubt whether there was any real reason to doubt his loyalty,"[40] he wrote on December 9, 1951, the day Service was finally fired by the State Department (after somehow passing "loyalty reviews" for six years). He vouched for Mao's Red Army—"Northern Chinese" or "an agrarian party," as he called them.[41] Then there was his vouching for Owen Lattimore, the Big Daddy link in the pro-Communist chain to turn China Red. Pearson assured the nation, via coast-to-coast radio hookup, "I happen to know Owen Lattimore personally, and I only wish this country had more patriots like him."[42]

Patriots? Owen Lattimore never met a purge, show trial, or violent Communist takeover he couldn't and didn't apologize for. Pearson got his wish, though. The country *did* have more "patriots" like Lattimore—in spades—and that was precisely the problem. For starters, there was Pearson's legman and reporter David Karr, an alumnus of the Communist-occupied Office of War Information.[43] Karr's the one about whom Pearson said that if the charges against him were true, the Washington Monument was a hole in the ground.[44]

The record tells us that David Karr was indeed a Communist agent—"a competent KGB source," as the KGB described him in a file unearthed by Russian journalist Yevgenia Albats in 1992.[45] Come to think of it, Karr's predecessor as Pearson legman, Andrew Older, was also a Party man, identified by undercover agent Mary Markward, while Andrew's sister, Julia Older Bazer, handler of Moscow cables at OWI , would later invoke the Fifth when asked if she was a Party member.[46] Too bad Pearson died before KGB files fingered his longtime cocolumnist Robert S. Allen as a paid NKVD agent in the 1930s—exactly when the duo came to national prominence for their widely syndicated "muck-raking" feature, "The Washington Merry-Go-Round."[47] Pearson would have had to eat his hat.

All of which is to say that Drew Pearson was a man who batted 1.000 when it came to misplaced Communist sympathies—or misplaced sympathies for Communists. The puzzle on Pearson's page is whether he was just a blowhard who vouched for the Communist agents who happened to be clustered around him or whether he was actively agenting himself. "Virtually every scandal that opponents used to besmirch McCarthy's reputation . . . can be traced to a Drew Pearson column," writes Arthur Herman.[48] True, but was it thrill-seeking empathy or strict dogma that drove the man? I can't find the answer, although it's part of the record now that Pearson and his journalist brother Leon both became sufficiently palsy-walsy with an important NKVD agent named Samuel Krafsur—a TASS "correspondent" who trolled for NKVD recruits in the Fourth Estate[49]—to pop up in a 1944 Venona cable because the NKVD was considering inviting Leon aboard. No further Venona or other word on what happened next, but Leon would accompany Secretary of State James Byrnes to Moscow in 1945, which somehow is a less than comforting thought.[50]

Those Krafsur-Pearson-Pearson tête-à-têtes sound intriguing, probably great Hollywood material—although reel life, as we've seen, was rigidly controlled with ideological purpose. So, too, was real life, where the alternate reality created and dominated by the Drew Pearsons of the day supplanted life as it was, and as it should have and would have been apparent had basic facts been revealed and acknowledged—basic facts about the sworn testimonies and other evidence against, for example, Lauchlin Currie. In this case, I don't blame the media so much as I blame the government. Uncle Sam. In keeping the growing archive of Venona's secrets from the American people for four decades—not to mention burgeoning, bursting FBI dossiers—the U.S. government played a shocking role in perpetuating what is more and more obviously a fantasy world at war with reality: a crazy place where Communist infiltrators were not, *in fact,* under every bed; where Red hunters did not, *in fact,* deserve the plaudits of a grateful nation; where the Curries and Whites and Adlers and Hisses did not, *in fact,* play ball with treason every time. Because the U.S. government withheld so much vital information, we learned to laugh at Communist "bugaboos," loathe uptight "Red-baiters," and cluck sadly over all those "martyrs" of congressional "overreach." Which reminds me, one of Pearson's more risible defenses of Soviet agent Karr was that he only worked for the Communist newspaper *The Daily Worker* so he could cover the New York Yankees and see them play for free.

It is in exactly this kind of fantasy world where what Orwell called "neutral fact" could not exist. As we have seen, he dated its disappearance to 1936 in Spain, where battles were being misreported for *ideological* ends—whether they were won or not, whether they took place or not—something Orwell noted was not a problem as recently as World War I. With the injection of Communist ideology into the world's nervous system, "neutral fact," unshaded fact, unvarnished fact, objectivity, or absolutes couldn't exist anymore. Moral absolutes couldn't exist anymore, either. Patriotism, for example, would no longer be "good," just as treason would no longer be "bad." Treason is no more when fact and morality are fungible. The concept itself disappeared from our lexicon, and even, I think, from our thoughts altogether. The phrase "betrayal of the nation" has an archaic quality to most of us, the word "betrayal" itself an act of exaggeration somehow inappropriate to any set of circumstances, and "nation"—what's that?

A 1996 review of Edward Jay Epstein's biography of Armand Hammer made the eradication of treason as a concept plain. As noted earlier, Epstein's book reveals the billionaire philanthropist and magnus art collector to have been, yes, a traitor. The reviewer considered the notion a retro novelty. "That word," the reviewer wrote of "traitor," "to modern ears, sounds as quaint as 'victrola.' But Epstein gives it teeth by putting Hammer's perfidy in context."[51]

Context—bingo. It is precisely such vital context that the U.S. government deprived us of and that, astonishingly, we lack to this day. In their book *Sacred Secrets,* Jerrold and Leona Schecter examine the short, tight flow of revelation from within the Venona project, beginning in 1945, to the Truman White House. There, it hit not just a brick wall but high ramparts with battlements behind which President Truman himself crouched, armed with buckets of boiling oil to stop it from entering his partisan political domain. From Truman's fifteen-minute meeting with Gen. Carter W. Clarke and his aide Col. Ernest Gibson of army intelligence (G-2) on June 4, 1945, when, the Schecters argue, Truman was first informed that army codebreakers had been attempting to read secret Soviet cables from Moscow to Washington since 1943, the happy heyday of the anti-Hitler alliance, Truman didn't want any of it. Shockingly and

disappointingly (to Truman fans), this wasn't even a matter of this president accepting the facts, old boy, just not the implications. Truman didn't want the
facts, period; the implications never had a chance.

The Schecters cite three concerns Truman may have been guided by in the
following order: Truman's concern about whether decoded cables could be introduced in court as evidence to prosecute Soviet agents; concern about damage to FDR's place in history that such revelations of Soviet infiltration would
cause; and concern about political damage to the Democratic Party as the party
in charge that had let the country down. Even without Venona's confirmation,
Republicans were running on the platform that Democrats were "soft on security," a perennial GOP issue; at that time, of course, as Haynes and Klehr might
say, they only knew the half of it.[52]

I've concluded that the Schecters' order of concerns should be reversed.
Truman doesn't seem to have regarded the revelations of Venona—confirmation
of Communist infiltration of the U.S. government under FDR—as anything
other than a partisan political problem, a cudgel Republican security hawks
could use to bash Democrats in elections and, therefore, would have to be deprived of. Mainly for this petty reason, the sensational body of information,
which belonged to a betrayed nation, remained on political ice at all costs. That
didn't just mean national security costs. There was also the incalculable cost of
continued concealment to the creation of a cogent, factual, reality-based record
of history.

It's true there were legal issues to be resolved regarding the use of the secret,
fragmentary decryptions as courtroom evidence, but Truman's efforts to squelch,
minimize, and negate non-Venona sources of corroboration—Elizabeth Bentley's and Whittaker Chambers's testimonies spring to mind—make evident the
president's appalling indifference to his basic constitutional responsibilities to
safeguard the nation. There was also, I would add, his indifference to his obliga-
tion as a human being and American citizen, let alone president, to support the
truth tellers twisting nightmarishly in a funhouse-mirrored world where truth
had no context and lies predominated. Remember, Truman's initial reaction to
Whittaker Chambers's testimony about Alger Hiss was to dismiss it as a "red
herring." This plunged Chambers into despair, as he later wrote in *Witness,*
because it told him he "was not only deprived of official good will in testifying
against Communism" but also guaranteed "active hostility among the most
powerful sections of the Administration." Indeed, Chambers was soon informed by several sources that the Justice Department was "actively *making
plans to indict me, and not Alger Hiss,* for perjury on the basis of my testimony
before the House Committee" (emphasis added).[53]

Chambers was not, in the end, indicted, but his sources correctly picked up on active administration animus in that direction. The Schecters quote a memo recounting an August 16, 1948, meeting between George M. Elsey, aide to White House Chief of Staff Clark Clifford, and Attorney General Tom Clark—he of the *Amerasia* "fix"—where such efforts were discussed. It had been a chaotically crippling couple of weeks—if, that is, your idea of "crippling" is the exposure of Soviet agents in the U.S. government. In fact, it had been a chaotically crippling day. Also on August 16, 1948, accused (and copiously and redundantly confirmed) Soviet spy Harry Dexter White had died of a heart attack. Only three days earlier, he had denied under oath in Congress all espionage charges against him made by Chambers and Bentley.

This White House memo makes it clear that the concerns of the Truman White House centered not on what White and other Soviet agents might have done or were still doing to the U.S. government, but rather on what impact the exposure of their deeds might have on the Democratic Party and the 1948 presidential election. When political advantage is of greater concern than national security, the restorative action is reconcealment to try to make it all go away. This was the course the Truman administration was looking to take. The August memo advised the president to avoid addressing the espionage investigations altogether and to consider referring the matter to a "bi-partisan commission"—which, of course, is political slang for punting. Here's the Chambers bit: It also recommended that "Justice . . . make every effort to ascertain if Chambers is guilty of perjury" and to investigate Chambers's "confinement in mental institution," a story that was pure Communist propaganda, by the way.[54] Nor was Elizabeth Bentley neglected. The memo further noted that the Justice Department would provide a description of Bentley's evidence so the White House could "endeavor to determine how much of the information was freely available to the Soviet government" during the wartime alliance. "The purpose," the memo continued, "would be to make it clear that Miss Bentley was not successful in transmitting secret material to the Russians that they did not already have."[55]

Deflect, destroy, and deny—and that was the reflexive response of the "Good Guys." It didn't stop there. In December 1948, several months after Bentley and Chambers first appeared before the House Committee on Un-American Activities, and one month after Truman's stunning upset victory over Republican presidential candidate Thomas Dewey, Truman asked Attorney General Tom Clark whether the FBI could draw up a statement of fact slamming the "meddling efforts" of the House Committee on Un-American Activities as "a 'red herring'"—that cliché again!—"not only to detract attention from the shortcomings of the 80th Congress but also [for contributing] to the escape of certain communists who should have been indicted." The memo is signed "HST."[56] No record of follow-up exists, the Schecters note, which is hardly surprising given FBI Director J. Edgar Hoover's respective feelings for both the committee (positive) and the Truman White House (strained, to say the least).

I must point out that Haynes and Klehr reject the Schecters' assertion that Truman all this time knew about Venona, believing it "unlikely" he would have embarked upon his attack on Chambers's and Bentley's credibility with such knowledge. They write, "Had [Truman] been aware of Venona, and known that Soviet cables confirmed the testimony of Elizabeth Bentley and Whittaker Chambers, it is unlikely that his aides would have considered undertaking a campaign to discredit Bentley and indict Chambers for perjury, or would have allowed themselves to be taken in by the disinformation being spread by the American Communist Party and Alger Hiss's partisans that Chambers had at one time been committed to an insane asylum."[57]

So we would all of us hope. Is there a case to be made, however, for Truman's state of graceful ignorance of Venona? Haynes and Klehr made their initial claim for Truman's innocence in their 1999 book *Venona,* writing, "The evidence is not entirely clear, but it appears that Army Chief of Staff Omar Bradley, mindful of the White House's tendency to leak politically sensitive information, decided to deny President Truman direct knowledge of the Venona Project."[58]

The footnoted source of this statement is twofold, the first being Daniel Patrick Moynihan's 1998 book *Secrecy.*[59] Moynihan's "smoking gun," as columnist Robert Novak would write in 2003 when he entered this fray in support of the Schecters, was a 1949 FBI memo from an FBI agent to J. Edgar Hoover's assistant, Mickey Ladd, "regarding the dissemination of [Venona] material to the Central Intelligence Agency."[60] Bringing the CIA into the loop was something General Clarke of army intelligence was vehemently against, as the Schecters note in their book, because Clarke believed Elizabeth Bentley's charges that her own nest of agents, some of whom were alumni of the wartime intelligence agency OSS, might well have entered the newly created CIA (she was right). Clarke was afraid to let the CIA know what American codebreakers knew about Venona—so the Soviets wouldn't thereby know it, too.[61]

The 1949 FBI memo Moynihan relies on to prove Truman had no knowledge of Venona recounts a discussion between General Clarke and Adm. Earl E. Stone. Stone was "disturbed" by the progress Venona codebreakers were making, which he'd only just been briefed on, and he wanted the president and the director of the newly created CIA to be alerted "to the contents of all of these messages." The memo states that Clarke said he "vehemently disagreed," telling Stone that the only people entitled to know about Venona "were [deleted] and the FBI."

Alas, we don't know who "deleted" was. Since the subject of the memo specifically addresses whether the CIA should be brought into the Venona loop, I wonder if "deleted" could be Truman himself.

Back to the memo, for its key, supposedly Truman-exonerating quotation. Clarke said he informed Stone that Army Chief of Staff Omar Bradley agreed with Clarke and "stated that he [Bradley] would personally assume the responsibility of advising the President or anyone else in authority if the contents of any of this material so demanded."

Unless my command of the English language has suddenly failed, Clarke simply indicated that Bradley had taken responsibility for briefing the president or anyone else in authority as needed. It beats me how Moynihan could reprint this memo in full as the "smoking gun" *proving* Truman never heard word one about Venona. Moynihan concludes, triumphantly, "Army 'property.' And so Truman was never told."[62]

Far more accurate to have written: "Army" property. We simply don't know from this memo what, or even whether, Truman was told about Venona. Moynihan was a brilliant man, but Bradley's assumption of responsibility for briefing Truman about Venona as needed in no way allows us to conclude that *therefore* Truman never heard a word about the content of the Venona archive. It just doesn't add up, at least not without the artificial and ultimately empty boost of wishful thinking.[63]

In the late 1990s, the Schecters interviewed Oliver Kirby, a crack American cryptanalyst who was assigned during the war to the renowned British decoding center at Bletchley as both a linguist and cryptanalyst, later parachuting into Germany on intelligence work, which included recovery and analysis of Nazi cryptographic records. After the war, Kirby joined what became known as the Venona project and, as his National Security Agency Web page says, "was one of the few selected to distribute VENONA products to the small group of authorized readers."[64] As a result, he participated in some of these rather frantic discussions over what to do with the increasingly horrifying "Venona products"—facts—emerging as the Soviet codes were being broken. He later told the Schecters that in 1950, Harry Dexter White and Alger Hiss were both "positively identified" as Soviet agents by Venona codebreakers, a date Robert L. Benson and Michael Warner affirm in their Venona study.[65]

Kirby himself claimed to have brought this information to the attention of General Bradley, White House point man, as noted, on Venona. Kirby said, "When Bradley called me back later he said, "The President was most upset

and agitated by this. Bradley reported President Truman's words, 'That G——
D—— stuff. Every time it bumps into us it gets bigger and bigger. It's likely to
take us down.'" The Schecters add, "Kirby said there was no doubt the President understood."[66]

In other words, President Truman took in and grasped revelations that, according to Soviet secret cables, the most senior-level, trusted, and powerful
U.S. government officials had been working on behalf of the Soviet Union, and
then he, as president, *did nothing about it.* Suddenly, Truman's domestic anti-
Communism program starts to look like a giant act of misdirection. Rather
than follow these intense, high-beam revelations to their logical ends—that the
U.S. government under his predecessor during depression and war had been
penetrated and compromised to a point, I maintain, of occupation captained by
an army of painstakingly revealed agents—Truman apparently preferred to
treat the whole thing like a "fairy story." He preferred to generalize a very specific threat by instituting "loyalty boards" for all and sundry. Rather than focus
on Venona-ID'd traitors specifically, he ordered that the patriotism of millions
of Americans be questioned generally.[67]

No evidence has emerged to contradict Kirby, whose assessment of Truman's visceral aversion to Venona's revelations comes from notes he made at the
time, now in the Schecters' possession.[68] It certainly fits the demonstrated government predilection for concealment over revelation, the pattern of papering
over facts with fantasy. Truman's consistent efforts to quash any and all information pertaining to the Communist infiltration of the U.S. government—
whether emanating from the FBI's confidential reports that started coming
across his desk in the spring of 1945, from defector testimonies extracted by
counsel before the House Committee on Un-American Activities climactically
in 1948, or from Joseph McCarthy's one-man fumigations of the government's
dirty laundry beginning in 1950—lend ample credence to Kirby's observations
as a young man. "That G——D—— stuff," particularly as it pertained to government penetration, remained officially under lock and key for the next forty
years, arguably the most successfully maintained American state secret of all
time, preserved and upheld through every administration to follow.

Why?

It should be noted that a number of espionage prosecutions were secretly
assisted by Venona, beginning with that of Soviet agent Judith Coplon, a young
Justice Department analyst who in May 1949 became the first spy to be identified and arrested due to Venona revelations; Robert Soblen and Jack Soble followed. It was Venona clues that led to the linchpin conviction of British atomic
spy Klaus Fuchs in 1950, and Venona decrypts "unmistakably identified Julius
Rosenberg as the head of a Soviet spy ring and David Greenglass, his brother-

in-law, as a Soviet source at the secret atomic bomb facility at Los Alamos, New Mexico," Haynes and Klehr write.[69]

"Unmistakably." The word peals like a steel bell, cold, penetrating, and troubling. *Venona decrypts unmistakably identified Julius Rosenberg . . .* "Unmistakably"—and the U.S. government let that secret evidence sit in a vault as our citizens tore each other up over this case for decades? Exactly the same question goes for the Hiss case, the other split-view lodestar by which what became two distinct peoples took their bearings. The U.S. government knew the truth about Hiss and withheld it, too.

Why?

It's worth noting that Hiss, unlike Coplon and the other atomic spies, was in no way prosecuted with the help of Venona. Indeed, Hiss was already in jail serving four years for perjury related to the lies he told Congress about Chambers before analysts deciphered his name in Venona. It was in the contentious aftermath of his imprisonment, however, during the battle over Hiss and White and Silvermaster and the rest on the one hand, and Bentley and Chambers on the other, that every scrap of information belonged in the center of the public square under bright lights, with Uncle Sam playing town crier:

Hear ye, Hear ye . . .

Instead Uncle Sam mumbled to himself and hid away the precious proof against the traitors, protecting the traitors against the soundings and probes of investigators hot on their trail. Let them grope and stagger blind, Uncle Sam said, let them sift through the good info and the bad, let them rely on their gut hunches to go on, let them fall back on their political courage until it gives out, let them get knocked down, smeared, destroyed. Let the country go to hell. Given what the executive branch knew and when it knew it, this was the greatest betrayal of all.

So, yes, M. Stanton Evans is right about the nation owing plaudits to Joe McCarthy, and more. We owe all of these intrepid public servants our undying gratitude. Sensing the massiveness of the assault on our republic—yes, a conspiracy so immense, to give McCarthy his due—they kept at it, seeking, hunting what their many detractors, many inside the government, never stopped screaming was a mythological beast, a figment, a "witch hunt." It was just something "under the bed," a silly "bugaboo," which became the White House term of choice.

"Mr. Congressman, you must see a bugaboo under every bed," President Roosevelt chided Rep. Martin Dies, founding chairman of the House Committee on Un-American Activities,[70] during a 1940 meeting in which Dies outlined for the president what his committee had discovered about Communists on the government payroll and in control of labor unions and other front organizations.

"The people are very much wrought up about the Communist bugaboo," Harry S. Truman wrote in a letter to former Pennsylvania governor George H. Earle in 1947, in response to a very similar warning from Earle.[71] Truman would switch to "red herring" when it came to the Hiss case in 1948.

Bugaboo? Red herring? Alger Hiss was neither. He was a bona fide enemy of the American republic, but the U.S. government didn't want anyone to know that, not even after Venona confirmed Hiss's treason sometime in 1950, as the Schecters report. Why? Oliver Kirby recounted a revealing exchange with Defense Secretary James Forrestal two years earlier, in 1948, about disclosure in general. The way the Schecters tell it, "Kirby raised with Forrestal the idea of publicly releasing the news that American intelligence had broken the Soviet code." The Soviets, aware American codebreakers were reading them since 1945 (thanks to the treason of Drew Pearson's meek little "Lock" Currie), would only be further inhibited by the announcement, Kirby argued. More important, "Kirby believed that revealing the full extent of Soviet penetration"— complete exposure—"would remove the issue from politics" and limit a "Red Panic" (Truman's political concern) "because the cases would be acted upon and fully resolved."

Call it the Sunshine Strategy. Forrestal nixed the notion in no uncertain terms. "Forget that. No. Hell, no"—that kind of thing. His reaction was not unlike what Kirby had already heard from the State Department when he attempted to bring Venona-fingered Communist infiltration to its attention. Or what he would later hear from Gen. Omar Bradley, who, Kirby said, would urge him not to brief other administration officials on Venona's findings.[72]

It begins to sound like a lot of other things. What George Racey Jordan heard in early 1944 when he went to the State Department wondering about whether he really should be "expediting" military secrets ASAP to Moscow. What U.S. Army Maj. John Van Vliet heard after expeditiously filing a report of his eyewitness assessment of Soviet responsibility for the Katyn Forest Massacre in May 1945. Or what German defense lawyer Alfred Seidl would hear at Nuremberg in 1946 when trying to introduce to the world evidence of the secret division of Europe that Stalin and Hitler had prearranged in the Nazi-Soviet Pact of 1939. Sunshine was the last thing the powers that be—the powers that accommodated, the powers that served—wanted when it came to any aspect of Communist crime and deception. The Establishment wanted its shadows deep, dark and undisturbed. Maybe that was because too many of its members were in them. Maybe that was why they always argued against exposure because, the rationale went, it might upset the Soviets, might worsen relations, might play into the hands of the "hardliners." These are variations on the same arguments, not at all incidentally, that we hear today to squelch the truth about Islam and its agents' penetration of the U.S. government.

This Iron Curtain of secrecy left it to the Great Red Hunters to investigate the old-fashioned way, the hard way, the rough way, their suspicions more often than not, it now may be fearlessly declared, confirmed by evidence that just continues to mount to the skies. Evidence that condemns not just the agents of our destruction *but our own government, too.* With Venona in a vault, the U.S. government became an agent of concealment, and thus, in effect, a part of the Communist conspiracy, despite itself (or perhaps not). The struggle that characterized what we know as the McCarthy Era, then, pit the forces of full disclosure and transparency—personified by Senator Joseph McCarthy—against the more powerful forces of deception and obfuscation, which included the Truman and Eisenhower White Houses. That's not at all how we think about it, of course. We're conditioned, Pavlov's-dog-style, to invert the paradigm.

This is demonstrably wrong, but it is also our most fervent and reflexive belief as a society. Given how many millions lost their lives due to Communists, it may not be correct to say that the American cover-up that supported this inversion was worse than the Communists' crimes. The cover-up, however, was in no way a victimless crime. It did something to us. It wrought a transformation of us as a people from which we have never recovered. Or did it consolidate a transformation that was already upon us? After all, I pushed off on this roller coaster pointing out that Lauchlin Currie's record was plenty troubling decades before Venona's release. In October 1944, more than a year before Elizabeth Bentley walked into an FBI office in New Haven, Connecticut, with her hair-curling tale to tell, Currie was publicly invoked as a marquee name for Communist subversion by one John Bricker, the GOP nominee for vice president running with Thomas E. Dewey.

Coming six months before the end of World War II, Bricker's salvo may seem surprising given the general but false impression that it was only after Bentley and Chambers testified in 1948 that this kind of stuff was "out there." Not so. Bricker, at the time a third-term Republican governor of Ohio, in this final stretch of the presidential campaign, was raising the roof on the myriad connections between FDR, the New Deal, and "radicals and Communists," who, "boring from within," as Bricker put it, were attempting to "take over our American government."

The rhetoric of the unfairly forgotten John Bricker sounds a lot like the rhetoric of the unfairly notorious Joseph McCarthy from a few years later. Bricker even had a list of names, only not in his hands.

Will anyone who has read to this point be surprised to learn that M. Stanton

Evans couldn't locate this particular list of 1,124 names of radicals and Communists "[vanished] from the public record"? Assembled by Rep. Martin Dies in 1941, it included the names of Alger Hiss, Harry Dexter White, and Harold Glasser. Evans never locatd the five supplemental volumes chronicling the activities of those named that were compiled by the FBI in 1942.[73]

Bricker explained that such connections and influences, Currie's among them, were evidence of a "foreign fifth column," which was, for the first time in U.S. history, trying to swing a U.S. election.

Quoting the ex-Communist journalist and author William Henry Chamberlin, Bricker declared, "The all-out Communist support for the fourth [FDR] term admits of no other interpretation. There has never been anything like this before because no American party or group has been willing to serve as the obedient instrument of the policies of a foreign power."[74]

Bricker couldn't have been clearer, but the American people weren't listening. To be sure, the ongoing war in Europe and the Pacific had a lot to do with this; FDR's campaign slogan, "Don't change horses in the middle of the stream," was a powerful admonition to a nation with millions of men—sons, brothers, husbands—under arms. However, it is also the case that years of incessant propaganda promoting "Uncle Joe" and the Soviets as a bunch of All Right Guys had softened up the American psyche—we were "victims of our own propaganda," as military analyst Hanson Baldwin later put it.[75] *Enemy infiltration as described by Bricker didn't make sense, couldn't make sense.* If all the news, via the Communist-riddled OWI, Drew Pearson, Hollywood, and the local bookstore, depicted the Red Army as Boy Scouts with stars, Bricker's description of the American Communist Party as a "fifth column" of a hostile power came out of left field. There was no *context* in the public square to bolster it.

Here's the truly amazing thing: In so many ways, there still isn't. We still tag history's hardened agents of Moscow "idealists"; we still romanticize their Leftist acolytes, their enforcers, as "freethinkers." The Hollywood Ten ("Rat Dmytryk" excepted) were "martyrs" who got standing O's till they dropped. Bricker's warning from that long-ago whistle-stop campaign to nowhere zings through the eras without answering echoes. It's as if we were always deaf to it.

Or were we? In 1950, Supreme Court Associate Justice Robert H. Jackson used language similar to Bricker's and even more forceful in a Supreme Court opinion in which he made clear the crucial distinctions that separated the Communist Party from all other American political parties. Jackson was discussing the section of the Taft-Hartley Act that required officers of unions to take an oath avowing they were not Communists. Among the six key differences Jackson cited—also among them were Party aims to seize power by and for a minority, Party membership secrecy, and Party requirement of unconditional obedience to Party authority—he wrote, "The Communist Party alone among American parties past or present is dominated and controlled by a foreign Government."[76] He continued, "The chain of command from the Kremlin to the American party is stoutly denied and usually invisible, but it was unmistakenly disclosed by the American Communist party somersaulting in synchronism with shifts in the Kremlin foreign policy" in the run-up to World War II.[77]

Seeing was believing. In that span of years, then, between Bricker's political speech and Jackson's Supreme Court opinion, a span in which Bentley and Chambers testified truthfully, Currie and White lied under oath, China turned Red, and the Soviet Union occupied half of Europe and got "the bomb," is it fair to say a consensus had taken hold that the CPUSA was, at least, the instrument of a foreign power? If so, it didn't last. By the time Harvey Klehr became the first American to examine the Moscow archives of the Communist International (Comintern) in the summer of 1992 (where he found not only "extensive" correspondence and reports detailing the Comintern's tight and dominant relationship with the American Communist Party but also the first "direct archival confirmation" of Elizabeth Bentley's charges), and by the time Stephen Haynes became the first American to examine the heretofore unknown Moscow archives of the American Communist Party in January 1993 (where he found more than 435,000 pages of material shipped by the CPUSA to Moscow attesting to Moscow's control of what was demonstrably an American outpost of Soviet power), any such consensus that the Kremlin controlled a Communist party and espionage in the USA had broken up. It had completely vanished in academia. Indeed, on Haynes and Klehr's publication of the primary documents from Moscow that copiously, redundantly supports these unmistakable links, American academia recoiled en masse against the researchers, firing at will, the stunning experience driving the authors to write a separate book in 2003 called *In Denial.* In it, they catalog exactly "how contemporary scholars and intellectuals have failed to confront new evidence about the history of American communism and Soviet espionage"—including the history of American Communists in Soviet espionage.[78] They haven't just failed to confront the new evidence. These "scholars" also engaged in "misshaping cultural memories to fit the ideological biases." This, of course, is exactly the same problem Andrew and Mitrokhin observed: *"the difficulty all of us have in grasping new concepts which disturb our existing view of the world."* It is not an attribute of the open-minded.

Maybe Bricker on the right and Jackson on the left were too reasonable, too mainstream, too respectable, too easy to drown out. Jackson, lead Nuremberg prosecutor, is well known. Bricker, just for the record, was no slouch. Résumé highlights include: U.S. Army first lieutenant and chaplain in World War I; assistant attorney general of Ohio; attorney general of Ohio; three-time governor of Ohio; GOP vice presidential nominee; and later two-term U.S. senator who authored the Bricker Amendment, a proposed amendment curtailing the president's treaty-making powers, which sounds like a still-needed restraint on the presidency post-FDR. Still, when it comes to American history as it has been written to fit the Left's "existing view of the world," these two are both Invisible Men. Mute as wallpaper. Passed over when it comes to posterity's favored heirs, the ones selected *by the victors* to tell "our story." *There's no connection between Moscow and the CPUSA, and Communist subversion was a "bugaboo"*—that's "our story" and they're sticking to it.

It's as if "two plus two make five," as George Orwell explained in *1984,* the author likely seizing on a chapter of the same name in Eugene Lyons's 1937 memoir *Assignment in Utopia.* In the novel, which came out in 1949, less than six months after Bentley and Chambers testified, Orwell explores the impact of such thought control, analyzing how "the very existence of external reality" could be "tacitly denied" by ideology. He concludes, "In the end the Party would announce that two and two made five, and you would have to believe it. Not merely the validity of experience, but the very existence of external reality, was tacitly denied by their philosophy."

The mind could adapt, though. Orwell: "And what was terrifying was not that they would kill you for thinking otherwise, but that they might be right. For, after all, how do we know that two and two make four? Or that the force of gravity works? Or that the past is unchangeable? If both the past and the external world exist only in the mind, and if the mind itself is controllable—what then?"[79]

What then? Here's what then: Whittaker Chambers is relegated to purgatory; there was no Lend-Lease to the Soviet Union; McCarthy is the Great Satan; John Bricker is remembered as "an amiable and photogenic figure of no remarkable qualities."[80] Lauchlin Currie et al.—and I mean *all*—keep their cover in posterity's mainstream without even a teeny, tiny, scarlet footnote. And a Mao portrait by Warhol over the mantelpiece is just the thing.

No wonder it is Elizabeth Bentley who was garishly marked as a "neurotic spinster" from the hot July day of her 1948 testimony forward, tattooed in memory with faintly lurid question marks. Look carefully, though, where the slander against Bentley originated: The very first malign expectoration against her shot from the mouth of NKVD agent Gregory Silvermaster himself (KGB cover name "Pal"). It was Silvermaster who brazenly dismissed Bentley's charges before the House Committee on Un-American Activities before serially invoking the Fifth Amendment against self-incrimination (including about his own basement). On August 4, 1948, the Soviet superspy said, "I can only conclude that she is a neurotic liar."[81]

It was just a short hop from neurotic "liar" to neurotic "spinster"[82] and back again, the constant being "neurotic." It was no coincidence, either, that Soviet agent and Ware group cell leader Lee Pressman additionally savaged the testimony of American patriot Whittaker Chambers as "the stale and lurid mouthings of a Republican exhibitionist."[83]

Then, thanks to the amplification of the echo chamber—from the Communist rag *The Daily Worker* to "respectable press" such as *The Milwaukee Journal, The New York Post,* and *The Washington Post* to the president—the Party line that it was all in their heads soon was all in our heads. *Pace* Orwell, if the mind was controllable, what then? Even when physical evidence—typewriters, rugs, *microfilm*—increasingly bore out Chambers's word, Communist Party lies vaporized into a dense haze of suspicion that obscured what should have been a diamond-clear line of sight to judgment: Hiss, Silvermaster, and the rest, *guilty.* Chambers, Bentley, *heroes of conscience.* But with a Communist-seared "liar" brand still smoking on Bentley's and Chambers's hides, the only guilty verdicts that endured were their own, the false verdicts that were upheld in the kangaroo court of elite opinion, the people with rattles and noisemakers, penthouses and publishing imprints, judge and jury with no more claim on fact and reason than the men who sent fourteen women and five men to their deaths for witchcraft in seventeenth-century Salem, and with the same zealotry.

Wait a minute. Wasn't it the anti-*Communists who were the big, bad witch hunters?*

Certainly, that's the message Americans have had drummed into their heads, Mao's-Little-Red-Book-style. The more literary text of choice in this case is, of course, Arthur Miller's *The Crucible.* Instead of violent Red Guard troops forcing us to live by it, our reeducators were high school teachers who merely assigned us to read it and *absorb its lessons.* (I had to read the thing in the eighth grade.) For two or three generations, anyway, Arthur Miller's dramatic re-rendering of congressional efforts to disclose extensive and clandestine Kremlin-directed assaults on our constitutional republic as the irrational and imaginary fetish of "repressed" and "Puritanical" "zealots" in Pilgrim hats was a classroom staple—Silvermaster's "neurotics" and "exhibitionists" elevated to the realm of theah-tuh. As a 2005 (post-Venona) collection of twentieth-century American drama puts it, "Miller wrote *The Crucible* in 1953 and it presents a clear parallel between the American anti-Communist paranoia of the period and the 1692 witch trials of Salem, exposing both to be maliciously motivated with ritualistic public denunciations of largely innocent people."[84]

Largely innocent? I'd like to plop the 650 damning pages of *Spies* right down in front of the editor that wrote that tripe. What is most breathtaking here, though, is the obdurate endurance of the glaring lie. In fact, a greater intellectual hoax than the Saleming of the Red hunters is beyond imagination. (Islam-is-peace is as great, but no greater.) Unchanged by the hard evidence, the deception continues, as impossible to claw back from the culture at large as a cloud.

This is telling. The great witnesses (Bentley, Chambers, J. B. Matthews, Louis Budenz . . .), the great investigators (Dies, McCarran, McCarthy . . .), took their stand to save America from Communist subversion. Whether they realized it—and, for the most part, how could they?—they also took their stand to save the essential base of reality itself: the importance of fact-based narrative; the primacy of "neutral truth"; morality's need for absolutes. All would dissipate rapidly in society at large following anti-Communism's demise in American culture. It was the ultimate defeat for the anti-Communist opposition, with their facts and conclusions, their witnesses and their affidavits, their investigations and their implications. This defeat cleared the field for the rise of brand-new waves of subversion: fungible facts, moral relativism, deconstructionism, and other explosive assaults on the rocks of civilizational equilibrium.

This was revolutionary struggle, raw and desperate. Unlike the discreetly private conspiracy to take Gareth Jones down back in the spring of 1933 in order to hide Soviet perfidy inside the Soviet Union—the very first Big Lie of the Terror Famine, as Conquest tells us—this was an all-out assault on the witnesses and investigators of Soviet perfidy *inside the United States.* When this battle was joined in our own backyard, the struggle against exposure took on climactic intensity. Whittaker Chambers explains why, and eloquently, in *Witness:*

> The simple fact is that when I took up my little sling and aimed at Communism, I also hit something else. What I hit was the forces of that great socialist revolution, which, in the name of liberalism, spasmodically, incompletely, somewhat formlessly, but always in the same direction, has been inching its ice cap over the nation for two decades . . . [This] is a statement of fact that need startle no one who voted for that revolution in whole or in part, and, consciously or unconsciously, a majority of the nation has so voted for years. It was the forces of that revolution that I struck at the point of its struggle for power.[85]

Did We, the People undergo a socialist revolution called "liberalism"? I would say yes, obviously—only it's not obvious at all. Chambers was right, but he not only struck at revolution generally, but also very specifically in the person of Alger Hiss, one of the secret Soviet assault's most celebrated agents. What electrified Chambers's case—or "the Case," as he calls it—with its epochal frenzy was that Chambers unexpectedly pulled the mask off this leading member of the Liberal Establishment to reveal the Communist conspirator underneath.[86] "For a decade, the Committee (first as the Dies Committee and later as the House Committee on Un-American Activities) had been trying to hack off the Gorgon head of Communist conspiracy, which it had never quite succeeded in locating," Chambers wrote, placing his testimony into historic context. "Now, almost casually, the snaky mass had been set down on the congressman's collective desk. It was terrifying. It petrified most of them."

It wasn't the hideous head alone that petrified them, but also its aroused and thoroughly vicious defenders, the ones who insisted the Gorgon was a pussycat, the ones who argued that the nightmare of alien conquest was a . . . "bugaboo." In that election year, Chambers observed, the "hostile clamor . . . battered the Committee into a state bordering on anxiety neurosis." A precarious state, in other words, in which the committee seriously considered abandoning the whole case. Which would have had catastrophic implications, Chambers believed. Had the committee's investigations (the ones Truman wanted the FBI to denounce as a "red herring") not gone forward, he writes,

> it is probable that the forces which for years had kept the Communist conspiracy in Government from public knowledge would have continued to be successful in concealing it. Alger Hiss would have remained at the head of the Carnegie Endowment, exerting great influence in public affairs through his position and ramified connections. With him, the whole secret Communist front would have stood more unassailable than ever because the shattered sally against it had ended in ridicule and rout. Elizabeth Bentley's charges would almost certainly have been buried in the debris.[87]

There is a certain irony to this statement. All the items on Chambers's list—the successful concealment of Communist conspiracy, the influence of at least Hiss's defenders in public affairs, the disappearance of Elizabeth Bentley's charges—came to pass more or less despite the fact that the committee took his case forward, despite the fact that Hiss was later convicted of perjury—the exception being that Alger Hiss did indeed lose his Carnegie presidency. He would rise, however, phoenix-style, as the Great Martyr of the Left. Chambers claimed victory too soon.

It's easy to see why. At the point he was writing, he was preparing his remarkable memoirs for prestigious Random House; Alger Hiss was serving a forty-four-month prison term for perjury related to his congressional testimony against Chambers; and Richard Nixon, Chambers's patron congressman, whom Chambers credits with steadying the resolve of the committee to continue with the Hiss-Chambers investigation, was somewhere on his meteoric rise from congressman to senator to vice president. If sweet, however, victory was short-lived. Like a submarine that got away, the Communist conspiracy resubmerged, at least in our consciousness, which is exactly where it counts; the subversive nature of Communism was reconceived as a "bugaboo" to shrug off; and the anti-Communists were subject to ridicule and rout once again and for always—and particularly Elizabeth Bentley, who, along with her charges, was definitely buried in the debris.

How did this happen? The answer has to do with another relic of the day, the Communist front, the infiltration mechanism deployed around the world beginning in the 1920s by which Communists, directed by Moscow, would advance, Trojan-horse-style, deep into any enemy's territory through intensive campaigns of deception and manipulation. Eugene Lyons quotes Nechayev, "one of the prophets of Russian Bolshevism," who provided the formula for manipulating "liberals of every shade" in his *Catechism of the Revolutionist*—yet another precursor to Alinsky's *Rules for Radicals:* "One may conspire with them in accordance with their program, making them believe that one follows blindly and at the same time one should take hold of them, get possession of their secrets, compromise them to the utmost, so that no avenue of escape may be left to them, and use them as instruments for stirring up disturbances.[88]

Deathly amoral stuff. In this very way, false front organizations *appear* to be self-governing and independent but are, as a Comintern resolution of 1926 explained, "in reality under communist leadership." Otto Kuusinen, a member of the Comintern secretariat, summed up the idea in strategic terms, also in 1926: "We must create a whole solar system of organizations and smaller communities around the Communist Party, so to speak, smaller organizations working actually under the influence of our Party."[89] Members didn't know, didn't have to know (although surely some did); they only had to follow.

By following the Party line—following the Silvermaster line on "neurotic" Bentley being a clear example—the Eastern Liberal Establishment did indeed function under Communist influence. By 1948, this was nothing new. It was the modus operandi of the scores of front organizations Martin Dies successfully exposed during his tenure as chairman of the House Committee on Un-American Activities. All of these groups and organizations were working under the influence of the Communist Party. In 1963, Martin Dies made the logical leap when he wrote, "By Kuusinen's definition, 'organizations working actually under the influence of the Communist Party,' there is no question that the New Deal functioned as a Communist front."[90]

I agree, but Dies is wrong on one point. Yes, the New Deal functioned as a Communist front; but there are certain to be a lot of questions about it, welling up and blasting off in sputtering indignation. Then there is the question of how

to break this to the busloads of American tourists who believe it is their patriotic duty to pay homage to FDR at his memorial. How to break it to them? How
to break it to those continuously forming blue-ribbon panels to elevate FDR to
the presidential pantheon one more time? How to break it to Doris Kearns
Goodwin? This sounds flip, but it's not. The problem of how to overturn more
than three-quarters of a century of grounded, anchored, riveted historical understanding is grave indeed.

Eugene Lyons made what may be a more accessible and palatable comparison to illustrate the workings of the New Deal bureaucracy when he explained
that it functioned as an unofficial Popular Front government. Establishing
"People's Front" or "Popular Front" governments had been the main purpose
of the Comintern in its "fabulous 'democratic' period" in the mid-1930s, Lyons
writes, tongue firmly in cheek. These weren't run-of-the-mill coalitions, of course.
The main characteristic, Lyons writes, was "the inclusion of the communists—
not so much as a domestic political element but frankly as agents and spokesmen of Soviet Russia." A sovereign domestic cabinet that included Moscow
representatives, in other words. This came about in France in the Leon Blum
government, and in Spain briefly, for example. In the United States, where
Communists were always a neglible demographic, a different vehicle took
shape, what Lyons called "an amazing unofficial Popular Front government—
unrecognized, unadmitted, independent of the Administration, yet operating
energetically within the New Deal framework." He continued, "It added up to
the most potent and ubiquitous influence in Washington, a half-clandestine
government-within-the-government, arrogantly open in some spots on some occasions but conspiratorial in essence . . . With every passing month, the penetration was deeper, the entanglement closer."[91] This is exactly the force that
William A. Wirt detected back at the very beginning. Even by 1941, Lyons
didn't know half of the half of it, with the worst of the penetration and entanglement still to take place, its existence to remain a state secret for half a
century.

Both Dies's and Lyons's formulations serve to identify the *implications* of the
infiltration of secret agents and spokesmen of Soviet Russia into our government institutions, the infiltration that the intelligence record now confirms. It's
not enough to play "Where's Waldo?" and end the game when some (not all!) of
the agents of infiltration have been identified and pinpointed; it's crucial to assess the impact of this secret army of occupation. This hasn't happened, certainly not on the national stage. Even Red hunters of the period got stuck on
identification as the endgame, says veteran intelligence officer Peter B. Niblo.
In his 2002 book *Influence,* Niblo points out the consequences of this narrow
approach:

The "he's a communist" scandal fogged real acts of espionage and treason carried out by Soviet intelligence assets—*agents of influence*—in high American office. If espionage was alleged, its objectives and targets were rarely made clear, confirmed, or admitted until years later. *Swept under the rug was the fact that Soviet agents of influence were making key decisions in Washington that affected the security of the American people,* smoothed the way for a Japanese attack at Pearl Harbor, and the disastrous division of Europe that spelled Cold War [emphasis added].[92]

For now, the compelling question is, How could their origins in Moscow have stayed swept under the rug? The answer has to do with a new gospel of falsehood, new commandments, new patterns of thinking, new modes of reaction. Emerging from the requirements of habitual secrecy and lies, this gospel inspired its followers, on an unprecedented scale, to decouple fact from implication, knowledge from conclusion, logic from judgment. In serving enemy ideology, they exonerated the guilty (example, Hiss), denied evidence (example, the Pumpkin Papers, which included microfilm), and flailed its source (example, Chambers). Doing so, consciously or not, bent them. It bent their brains, bent their thought processes—and, by unavoidable extension and necessary entanglement, bent ours, too, undermining the solidity and credibility and worth of absolutes. Facts and evidence no longer had the same heft they used to. Givens were taken, or had to be nailed down going out the door, which left gaping holes. Oaths, so help me God, were flouted with a demystifying, cheapening regularity. Two plus two might equal five, it might not.

I am not at all suggesting lying didn't exist before this struggle over exposure—why else would God have sent Moses down the mountain with the Ninth Commandment? Similarly, I am not suggesting that prevaricators, scoundrels, and dirty rats didn't lie early and often—why else would perjury be a felony throughout the Western world? However, I don't believe that in all of American history we had ever all of us had to bear witness, rubbing our eyes and shaking our heads, to lying on a scale this sweeping, this public, this officially elevated. The spectacle—the ordeal—was itself corrupting, initiating, or perhaps consolidating, a far more profound revolution than the nuts-and-bolts espionage efforts (stealing documents, influencing policy, etc.) of Hiss and the rest.

It was all destabilizing in a new way. After Alger Hiss—Phi Beta Kappa, Harvard Law School, White House, State Department, Carnegie Endowment—took an oath to tell the whole truth so help him God on August 5, 1948, before the House Committee on Un-American Activities, he proceeded to deny sweepingly and convincingly that he had ever known or even set eyes on Whittaker

Chambers. Chambers, closeted in his *Time* magazine office in New York City, received a panicky phone call from one of the committee's chief investigators in Washington.

"Are you sure," "In a voice in which I caught the unmistakable note of desperation," Chambers would write, he asked, "are you sure you are right about Alger Hiss?"

Of course, Chambers reassured him in the course of the jittery call.

"You couldn't have mistaken him for somebody else?"

"Of course, I haven't mistaken him," Chambers said. Later, Chambers wrote, "What stunned me as I stared at my desk, and was to puzzle me for some time to come, was a simple question: 'How did Alger Hiss, in the face of the facts that we both knew, and under the eyes of some 150 million people, suppose that he could possibly get away with it?' "[93]

It was a good question—if, that is, you were coming from an Enlightenment world of fixed laws, legal and moral, a world where objectivity was magnetic north, a world that was already a dying star. Chambers's years in the Communist underground notwithstanding, his question came from this fin-de-siècle Retroland. Hiss, meanwhile, was opening brave new territory where facts were juggling balls, truth was strategically expendable, and ideology and raw power set life's course. Deconstructionists would follow. They had to. A school of systematic thought had to emerge to reflect and enforce the pressures to abort the search for objective truth.

Such a search for objective truth had previously defined Knowledge at least since the ancient Greeks came along, and, as Keith Windschuttle tells it, sought to replace the mythologies other cultures used to affirm their "sense of self-worth and place in the cosmos" with something brand-new: the attempt "to record the truth about the past."[94] This became what Orwell described as "neutral fact," which, by his observation, ended in 1936 in Spain, and Koestler agreed. Today, the Greek example is forgotten, or dismissed as that of the deadest of white males, and mythologies of self-worth are back in vogue, underscored by the widely shared assumption that truth isn't "within the historian's grasp," as Windshuttle puts it. This is what our children are taught in school, perpetuating this mythology of mythologies. This means, perhaps, we might look back on Alger Hiss and see not just an epic *traitor* who committed *treason* but also a pioneer of a shamelsss future. Like an early performance artist, Hiss, sans NEA grant, smeared lies all over naked, defenseless, truth, successfully cutting us all off from the facts, from reality, from our history.

Yes, we are looking at another virtuoso performance—but whoever would have imagined Uncle Sam himself playing in support.

CHAPTER SEVEN

Not even high intelligence and a sensitive spirit are of any help once the facts of a situation are deduced from a political theory and not vice versa.

—ROBERT CONQUEST[1]

Since, as a consequence of the war called "necessary" to overthrow Hitler's despotism, another despotism was raised to a higher pitch of power, how can it be argued conclusively with reference to inescapable facts that the "end" justified the means employed to involve the United States in that war?

—CHARLES A. BEARD[2]

About Harry Hopkins.

I've thought long and hard about whether it is plausible to make this one man into the linchpin of an epoch, particularly given the permanent strategic infrastructure set in place by Soviet agents Harry Dexter White and Alger Hiss—not to mention the various accomplishments of hundreds more Soviet agents, not to mention the lasting impact of their willing, able, and unaffiliated (and even unconscious) accomplices. I've decided Hopkins merits special consideration due to his unique slot at the very pinnacle of the U.S. government, inside the White House—inside the White House family quarters, in fact. There, for three years and seven months, he was practically roommates with Roosevelt. " 'Just what does Harry Hopkins do?' is a constant question in Washington," *The New York Times* wrote in July 1942. Whatever it was, the paper noted, "Officials commonly say that a project of national or international importance has not been finally approved by remarking 'I haven't seen an H.H. on it.' "[3]

An "H.H." on it? Not an "H.L.H." on it?

I wish I could bend time to get this tidbit back to Maj. George Racey Jordan, just for the anecdotal support. Jordan was grilled to a carbon crisp over his recollection of the note he said he came across in one of those black suitcases and attributed to Harry Hopkins. He recalled it as having been signed "H.H."—not "H.L.H.," as cronies, including Hopkins papers editor Sidney Hyman, later swore Hopkins always signed off with when using initials.[4] Not that they would have accepted the rest of Jordan's story, even the fully corroborated parts, if he'd recalled the complete monogram. For the record, House investigators found memos signed "H.L.H.," "Harry," and "Harry L. Hopkins," but the only "H.H." the investigation came across was in a memo from Roosevelt *to* Hopkins. That said, investigators were denied permission to review Lend-Lease and other files in the archives and State Department.[5]

The point of the 1942 *Times* story was there was a time in Washington when the execution of American power *required* Harry Hopkins's stamp of approval. Without it, the record compellingly demonstrates, some of the best-laid plans *of Moscow* would never have come to pass.

How can I say such a thing? Remember George C. Marshall's shocking statement to his biographer in 1957: "Hopkins's job with the president was to represent the Russian interests. My job was to represent the American interests."

Whether controlling the pace and flow of negotiations in Moscow from Washington (Hopkins memo to Stettinius: "I would like to be in direct touch with Harriman and the Mission in Moscow and any replies to Harriman's telegrams I would like to have sent through me and signed by me. Will you please notify everybody over there about this, so there will be no possible hitch about it."[6]), blocking strategic communications to FDR (as when he openly discussed withholding cables from *Winston Churchill* and the U.S. ambassador in London lest they persuade FDR to offer air support to anti-Nazi, *anti-Soviet* Poles during the Warsaw Uprising in September 1944[7]), or assiduously inserting Stalin's strategic imperatives deep into U.S. policy (as with his furious lobbying for Stalin's "second front" in France, again contra Churchill[8]), Hopkins made the Russian interest the American interest. There is a reason—there is a record—that explains why Spymaster Akhmerov, as Gordievsky recalled, considered Hopkins, above Hiss, White, Currie, and the rest, "the most important of all Soviet wartime agents in the United States."[9]

Without this one unlikely human hot spot of Kremlin influence, without this sickly man who alternately haunted death's door and high-life's watering holes until finally succumbing in January 1946, without his artful domination of the thirty-second president, without his lockstep-loyal network of intragovernmental assistants he assembled to bypass constitutional checks and balances, World War II, the war that remade the world even as we know it today, would have taken an unrecognizably different course. In military terms—which are also human terms—the fighting would have likely ended much, much sooner, and much, much better, from the *American* point of view, not the Soviet point of view. In political terms—which are also human terms—a shorter war would have prevented the Soviet enslavement of half of Europe and beyond, which occurred due to the relative positions of Allied armies in Europe in May 1945.

In human terms, a shorter war would have meant *millions fewer casualties,* from the Nazi death houses to the battlefields; indeed, a shorter war would also have spared Central Europe's urban centers, which were flattened by Allied firebombing campaigns mainly in that final year of war, and particularly in those final months of fighting. The ultimate firebombing attack came at Dresden, where roughly one thousand British and U.S. heavy bombers dropped roughly four thousand tons of explosives and incendiary devices on the city center between February 13 and 15, 1945, less than three months before V-E Day on May 8, 1945. It is said, as the late historian John Keegan wrote, that this atrocious act was taken at the behest of Stalin.[10] In the past, I've defended the firebombing of Dresden on the basis of the mission's stated objectives and the Nazis' refusal to surrender, but it is with a heavy heart that I now believe it was "necessary" only to facilitate Soviet territorial gain. On an extremely low level, defending Dresden makes me just another dupe of the great Communist con. Was obliterating Dresden and some thirty thousand of its residents *to expedite the Soviet march on Berlin* in America's best interest? Of course not. It wasn't in humanity's best interest, either. Ironically, it was in the best interest of Dresden residents Victor and Eva Klemperer, who, having received Nazi orders to report for labor duty on the day before the firebombing campaign would begin, were able to escape near-certain death by the light of these raging flames of destruction.[11] Then again, if the war had been shorter, it all would have been unnecessary.

The duration and outcome of the war itself, then, become a potential case against Harry Hopkins as the bayonet point of Soviet influence penetrating the White House. With a shorter war, it seems unlikely the Soviet Union would have emerged as a superpower; certainly not a territorial behemoth with a new empire. This hypothesis makes Hopkins the most overlooked catalyst of the twentieth century. History may remember him as a bit player, but it's time to refocus posterity's attention.

At first glance, of course, our sight line is short, blocked by those shelves of history books that, incredibly, gloss over Hopkins's controversial role. It *is* incredible—seemingly a virtuoso feat of misdirection worthy of a master magician—but how did it happen? The very day after Hopkins's death in 1946, *The Los Angeles Times*'s editorial page took the occasion to score Hopkins's unelected powers and globe-trotting machinations for being "out of bounds by any constitutional concept" and urged the American people to ensure that "a Harry Hopkins in the White House does not recur."[12] At that moment, who would have imagined that "a Harry Hopkins in the White House" would, for most intents and purposes, be forgotten?

In light of Hopkins's posthumous disappearing act, it's not surprising to learn that FDR prized the skinny, bluff man for his discretion, as *The New Yorker* reported in a gushing, two-part 1943 profile. "He knows I keep my mouth shut," Hopkins said. Hopkins didn't much function in public; didn't go to an office even, doing most of his work from a card table in his White House office-bedroom—"his bed littered with papers, notes, memorandums and pamphlets," as we learn in Adm. William H. Standley's 1955 memoir, *Admiral Ambassador to Russia.* Standley was recounting a typically curious audience with Hopkins in December 1942 in which Standley sought to receive assurances that orders *already approved by the President himself* would go through to place Hopkins's Lend-Lease man in Moscow, Gen. Philip Faymonville, under Standley's authority. Which is what I meant earlier when I said there was a time in Washington when the execution of American power, including presidential power, required Harry Hopkins's approval.

Funny thing about Faymonville, who, at least until his Hopkins-secured promotion to general was known as the pro-Soviet "Red Colonel." Army intelligence had tagged him a serious security risk, even arranging his recall from Moscow in 1939—after which Roosevelt reacted by "publicly receiving Faymonville at the White House and going on a private fishing trip with him," as historian Dennis J. Dunn writes.[13]

Which is in itself curious.

Hopkins muscled Faymonville back into place over both War Department and State Department objections to become the administrator of Lend-Lease in Moscow in 1941. "You might as well get his papers ready," Hopkins bluntly told the army, "because he's going over."[14] As indeed he did.

We now know the intelligence against Faymonville was right all along; he wasn't just a security *risk,* he was a security disaster. Romerstein and Breindel discovered that in 1942 the NKVD "developed" Faymonville (Soviet lingo for "recruited") through an agent who acted as Faymonville's male lover. Standley, also in 1942, was rightfully suspicious of Faymonville, whom he regarded as a conduit of U.S. military information to the Soviets. The ambassador wanted him restricted. That's what Standley told Roosevelt over lunch with him and Hopkins on trays in the "president's private study." Standley describes Hopkins eating from a plate in his lap, "relaxed against the cushions as if deathly tired."

Roosevelt agreed to Standley's request, but nothing happened—that is, no orders were issued. So Standley went to see Hopkins at his card-table command post in the Lincoln Bedroom.

> "Hello, Admiral," he said, waving me to a seat without rising. I've never seen a man look so sick and still keep producing. And yet, I reflected, he has more power in the United States than anyone but the President and probably more influence and real power among the Western Allies than anyone but the President and Winston Churchill.
>
> "How are you, Harry?" I said as I seated myself.
>
> He ignored the question. "When are you returning to Moscow, Admiral?"
>
> "That depends on you, Harry."
>
> "How's that?"
>
> I grinned ruefully. "The President directed that orders be issued to General Faymonville to report to me for duty. I have been informed by Mr. Stettinius [Hopkins crony and titular Lend-Lease chief] that you are the only person in Washington who can issue those orders. When those orders have been issued, I will leave for Moscow."
>
> Harry leaned back and closed his eyes for a moment. "See Jim Burns tomorrow, Admiral. It will be arranged."[15]

Whatever was "arranged" didn't much change the chain of command in Moscow, where the Lend-Lease bureaucracy, as Dennis J. Dunn explains in *Caught Between Roosevelt and Stalin,* his indispensable study of the first five American ambassadors to Soviet Russia, functioned as "State Department, the War Department, and the ambassador and embassy in Moscow."[16] The "Hopkins Shop" was a government within a government, or an engine room within the ship of state as piloted by this very strange captain. His influence was boundless. Notes scribbled across a presidential cable in 1941, for example, tell us it was Hopkins who urged that the president "should personally deal with Stalin" after Hopkins's initial and, intriguingly, *private* meeting with Stalin— sans U.S. ambassador or any other American witnesses—in July 1941.

Was it Hopkins who fed FDR the line that he (FDR) and he only could deal with Stalin the man, as FDR unctuously and famously imparted it to Churchill?

Hopkins also jotted down, matter-of-fact imperiously, the following: that after he "spent the afternoon with Stimson and Marshall"—the secretary of war and the army chief of staff—"Stimson is obviously unhappy because he is not consulted about the strategy of the war, and I think he feels I could be more helpful in relating him and Marshall to the President."[17]

The linchpin in action.

Hopkins left behind voluminous files, which his personal assistant, Sidney Hyman, spent eight months "putting into order" before official biographer, Robert Sherwood, even arrived on the scene, swooping in from Hollywood where he'd just finished the Academy Award–winning screenplay of *The Best Years of Our Lives.*[18] It was these papers *as put in order by Hyman* that Sherwood drew from for the 971-page Hopkins biography, a work with unusual authority, one realizes, on seeing it referenced as a primary source in State Department records of the historic wartime conferences between Roosevelt, Churchill, and Stalin.

I underscore Hyman's stewardship of the papers because it makes me nervous. The reason goes back to the Hopkins uranium story, as experienced and boldly recounted by Maj. George Racey Jordan, for whose nearly unique witness of Hopkins committing treason on Moscow's behalf we should be eternally grateful. Hyman was a loud voice in the echo chamber attacking Jordan's testimony under oath before Congress in which Jordan, as we saw in chapter 5, declared that Harry Hopkins had in 1943 ordered him to expedite a shipment of ultrasensitive uranium to Moscow—off the books and on the Q.T. The Hyman tack was to insist that Hopkins, who died in 1946, couldn't have so ordered Jordan in 1943 because Hopkins didn't even know what uranium was at that time, and, further, didn't know about the Manhattan Project until after Hiroshima in 1945. It was *Newsweek* that reported Hyman's response to Jordan's testimony in December 1949:

Moreover, according to Sidney Hyman, FDR's confidant didn't have the faintest understanding of the Manhattan Project until he read about the A-bomb being dropped on Hiroshima. Hyman said, "He didn't know the difference between uranium and geranium." It wasn't until weeks later that Hopkins talked with several of the atomic scientists and learned about "the engineering feat of production."[19]

Hopkins didn't know the difference between uranium and geranium?

"I am burning up on that," Jordan told Congress in March 1950, three months after his first appearance. Jordan went on to cite the relevant passages as published *in the Hyman-aided Sherwood biography of Hopkins,* which lay out Hopkins's extremely intimate awareness of and central involvement in setting up and monitoring what became known as the Manhattan Project—awareness and involvement that also predated FDR's! According to the Sherwood biography, it was Vannevar Bush, the atomic project's overseeing scientist, who made Hopkins the intermediary between himself and Roosevelt, and it was Hopkins who helped Bush draft the letter initiating the research project for Roosevelt's signature on June 15, 1940. Later, Churchill would conduct "his correspondence on the atomic project with Hopkins rather than with the President,"

Sherwood notes, adding elsewhere, "Hopkins never lost his interest in the fission of uranium."[20]

Based on the record assembled by Hyman himself for Sherwood, we must conclude that Hopkins did indeed very much know the difference between uranium and geranium—knowledge that wasn't in any way controversial until Jordan, stubborn witness, popped up to report on what he knew of Hopkins's role in shipping that uranium to the Soviet Union during the time of the USSR's massive espionage plot, code-named "Enormous," to beg, borrow, and steal U.S. atomic technology as fast as it was being secretly invented. Additionally, when this same massive espionage plot first came under FBI surveillance *Hopkins warned the Soviets,* as I will explain below.

Why would Hyman lie in 1949, when the truth was published in the 1948 bestseller he himself helped prepare? My best guess is desperation. Jordan's bombshell—that Co-President Hopkins was potentially involved in the Soviet atomic operation—couldn't be allowed to develop into a respectable line of inquiry without turning into a press sensation that would crack open the Roosevelt White House. Hyman thus participated in the creation of another Big Lie, that surefire mechanism of thought control, which, as Conquest tells us, was originated by Stalin. Throw enough body blows at Jordan—uranium-geranium, a column by Drew Pearson seeding suspicion about Jordan's motives, a blatantly grotesque snapshot of Jordan in *Life* magazine (the photo editor should have been ashamed)—and Jordan goes down for the count, leaving Hopkins, the real perp, to readjust his hat, smooth his lapels, and walk on, posthumously speaking, absolved of all explosive charges. Thus, he could also be forgotten, because who really needs to remember a man who didn't know uranium from geranium?

Hopkins himself sometimes lamented the backstairs stealth of his career. In the August 1943 *New Yorker* profile, the magazine noted that Hopkins was "sometimes depressed by the thought that some of the history of this period will probably never be known to the public." *No one will ever know how smart I was?* This makes for an intriguing flicker of personal regret coming from someone whom official biographer Sherwood would document as a highly secretive person from childhood. "I can't ever make Harry out," his mother said. "He never tells me what he's *really* thinking." This isn't necessarily exceptional human behavior, but it would fit Hopkins's lifelong pattern. In meetings, he was notorious for arguing all sides of an argument without letting on which one he favored, a technique dependent on a high degree of sangfroid.

Sherwood also relates a particularly apt story from Hopkins's college days at Grinnell, where, by the way, this son of an Iowa harness maker was known as

"Dirty Harry" for lowdown moves on the basketball court. "As a senior at Grinnell [Hopkins] was approached by Sophomore leaders for advice on strategy and tactics in the annual Sophomore-Freshmen Class Battle. He gave it, freely. Then he was approached, quite independently, by Freshmen leaders for advice. He gave that, freely, too—telling the Freshmen how to counter 'possible' Sophomore strategy (which he had suggested). Neither side knew that Hopkins had master-minded both sides."[21]

Given Hopkins's White House role in influencing and also shaping "Sophomore" (U.S.) strategy on behalf of the "Freshmen" (USSR), and also deviously sharing that "Sophomore" (U.S.) strategy with the "Freshmen" (USSR), something we know from Venona, the parallels are uncanny, his early penchant for double-agenting chilling. We know this also from another Soviet source, the Mitrokhin archive, which tells us that "earlier in the year he [Hopkins] had privately warned the Soviet embassy in Washington that the FBI had bugged a secret meeting at which Zarubin (apparently identified by Hopkins only as a member of the embassy) had passed money to Steve Nelson, a leading member of the U.S. Communist underground."[22]

Let's leave aside the unsubstantiated parenthetical comment preemptively declaring Hopkins "apparently" guileless: We have just learned that Hopkins blew an ongoing FBI surveillance operation by revealing to the Soviet embassy that a Soviet official had been bugged delivering money to the American Communist underground. Never mind that this Soviet chain of activity was in flagrant violation of the 1933 terms of U.S. diplomatic recognition prohibiting espionage activities in this country. The footnote to the statement cites Mitrokhin's archive (vol. 6, ch. 12) and further notes, "Hopkins had been personally briefed by Hoover on Zarubin's visit to Nelson. Hoover would doubtless have been outraged had he known that Hopkins had informed the Soviet embassy."[23]

With good cause. Hoover's briefing came in the form of a "personal and confidential" letter to Hopkins, which the authors cite from Benson and Warner's book *VENONA*, where it is reproduced in full.

To unpack Andrew and Mitrokhin's statement and really shake out the wrinkles, we need to know, first, that Vasily Zarubin, who used the cover name Vasily Zubilin (that'll throw people off), was a Soviet Comintern agent, later identified as the top NKVD *rezident* in the United States. We need to know also that Hopkins knew that Zarubin was a Soviet Comintern agent, despite Andrew and Mitrokhin's parenthetical testament to Hopkins's "apparent" ignorance. *We know Hopkins knew this because J. Edgar Hoover, in the very letter Andrew and Mitrokhin cite, told Hopkins so.*

"Dear Harry," Hoover wrote in a letter marked "personal and confidential," stamped May 7, 1943—some weeks after George Racey Jordan claims to have gotten orders from Hopkins to expedite a uranium shipment to Moscow:

> Through a highly confidential and reliable source it has been determined that on April 10, 1943, a Russian who is an agent of the Communist International paid a sum of money to Steve Nelson, National Committeeman of the Communist Party, USA, at the latter's home in Oakland, California.
>
> The money was reportedly paid to Nelson for the purpose of placing Communist Party members and Comintern agents in industries engaged in secret war production for the United States Government so that information could be obtained for transmittal to the Soviet Union.
>
> The Russian agent of the Communist International has been identified as Vassili Zubilin, Third Secretary of the Embassy of the USSR.

Zarubin/Zubilin was the top Soviet intelligence officer in the United States, who, we would later find out, "supervised Soviet atomic espionage."[24] In fact, it was from this bugging of Nelson's home in Oakland, California, that the FBI learned about both the existence of the supersecret Manhattan Project and the Soviet espionage operation targeting it for the very first time.[25]

Hopkins's reaction to Hoover's revelation may be the most damning piece of evidence of all in the case against Harry Hopkins. When we read what Hoover told Hopkins in his confidential letter—that a Comintern agent posing as a senior Soviet diplomat in Washington was passing money to the American Communist underground to establish Comintern networks within the U.S. war industry to steal military secrets—and see Hopkins immediately turn around and tell the Soviet Embassy, where that same "diplomat" was posted, that the FBI was onto them, we have to realize we are looking at a traitor acting with Soviet, not American, interests at heart. I don't see any other plausible conclusion—and this traitor was the closest adviser of the president of the United States.

I must interject one additional detail that Romerstein and Breindel provide in their report on the Zarubin-Nelson link, as recorded by a young FBI agent named William Brannigan, who would go on to head the FBI's Soviet Counterintelligence Section. In the course of their conversation, Zarubin and Nelson also discussed the work of Gregory Kheifetz, NKVD San Francisco *rezident,* and his mistress, Louise Brantsen, a wealthy California Communist who hosted parties bringing agents together at her San Francisco home.

Kheifetz was the agent assigned by Moscow to raid UC Berkeley's Radiation

Laboratory, where work on the atomic bomb was being done.[26] George Racey Jordan mentioned Kheifetz in his 1950 testimony on the shipment of atomic materials—the cadmium rods, heavy water, uranium, and other atomic pile ingredients that went through the Lend-Lease hub under his supervision in Great Falls, Montana. Discussing a young Soviet sergeant Jordan believed was, in fact, a KGB minder sent to Great Falls to watch over the Soviet Lend-Lease chief at the base, Colonel Kotikov, Jordan mentioned that this particular sergeant took a lot of "mysterious" trips for a junior NCO.

Where would he go? "When he would apply to go to San Francisco, he would go to see Gregory Kheifetz," Jordan recalled.[27]

This detail may not *connect* another dot, but it does add a dot to enlarge the plane on which the Soviet conspiracy was taking place. As Kotikov was collecting the ingredients in his "Bomb Chemicals" folder, his minder was tripping off to San Francisco to see a senior NKVD officer overseeing atomic espionage in the United States. From Jordan we have testimony that Harry Hopkins telephoned to push uranium through Great Falls to Moscow in April 1943. From Mitrokhin's KGB archive we know that Hopkins tipped off the Soviets to the FBI's April 1943 surveillance of atomic espionage in San Francisco. From J. Edgar Hoover's May 1943 letter we know that Hopkins knew, at the very least, that he was tipping off the Soviets to FBI surveillance of a known Soviet agent seeking U.S. military secrets. In light of what Hopkins did upon receiving the Hoover letter, I don't see how Hopkins can conceivably be described as anything but a conscious and conscientious agent of the Soviet Union.

The Hoover letter goes on to note the existence of further evidence of cooperation between the CPUSA and the Comintern in such penetration operations, to offer details on Nelson's background, and to caution Hopkins about the confidential nature of the information "inasmuch as the investigation is continuing." Summing up, Hoover wrote, "Because of the relationship demonstrated in this investigation between the Communist Party, USA, the Communist International and the Soviet Government, I thought the President and you would be interested in these data."[28]

"The President and you." It wasn't just burbling magazine copy that promoted the Roosevelt-Hopkins co-presidency; it was for real. Sure enough, Hopkins was so very interested in Hoover's data he couldn't wait to tell . . . the Soviets. (Did he ever even tell Roosevelt? We don't know. Somehow, I doubt it.) The net effect of Hopkins's spilling the FBI's beans to the Soviets, then, was to make the Soviets—the "Freshmen"—more discreet in the future, more mindful of FBI eyes and ears. Just think: We wouldn't know about this act of treason if a retired KGB archivist named Mitrokhin hadn't bothered to copy, hide, and successfully smuggle his archives out of the former Soviet Union in 1992. Hopkins's guilt on this particularly damning count would have remained secret, probably forever.

Still, clues to Hopkins's Soviet allegiance were always in plain sight, however unremarkable they might sometimes have appeared amid the rosy-Red outlook of the day. Despite the pro-Soviet mood, however, it's hard to imagine even a casual *New Yorker* reader, diverted by single-malt Scotch ads and Broadway reviews, failing to pick up on Hopkins's abnormal partiality to Communist Russia on scanning his 1943 profile. It was a leading attribute. *The New Yorker* called him "next to Roosevelt, the country's first really influential appreciator of American friendship with Soviet Russia," described him as "an articulate propagandist for all-out aid to Russia," noted that "Hopkins still thinks the Russian front is the most important one," and quoted him as saying, "I had the Russian story for the President," "The political implications of extending Lend-Lease to Russia have never bothered me," and "I carried that [Soviet] banner around town, Marshall is fine with it."

Circa 1943, everybody, practically, was fine with it, or kept his mouth shut for fear of being labeled a dread "isolationist," or worse, "pro-Hitler." The only enemy in the world was Adolf Hitler and his ideology, Nazism, the U.S. government line went. Japan, too, but that was practically an afterthought. From Hollywood to Times Square, we heard that Stalin and his ideology, Communism, were A-OK, and that nothing short of alliance with him could vanquish the Nazis anyway.

Just for fun, invert reality and try this: *Hopkins was, next to Roosevelt, the country's first "really influential appreciator of Nazi Germany," he was an articulate "propagandist for all-out aid for Hitler," and he said, "I carried that Nazi banner around town, Marshall is fine with it."* The notion that the president's top adviser was pro-Nazi triggers revulsion, as, of course, it should—but why was it all right for him to carry the tear-, blood-, and sweat-drenched Soviet banner, which flew over the world's original concentration camps, the revival of execution without trial, state hostage-taking, the eradication of political parties, and more inhumanities? Why was it so easy to distract Americans with deceitful rhetoric, slick pictorials, and ironic cartoons? Anything to defeat the Nazi beast.

Even supporting another, already demonstrably worse (body count to body count) Communist beast?

When his *New Yorker* profile appeared, Hopkins had been living with "dressing-gown run of Roosevelt's floor in the White House" for over three years. The previous summer, Hopkins had gotten married in the president's second-storey oval study, immediately moving his bride into his Executive

Mansion digs. As a couple, the Hopkinses dined "with the President or Mrs. Roosevelt or both about five nights a week." Much more than a permanent houseguest with special perks ("The Hopkinses get setups for drinks by calling the White House pantry."), Hopkins was frenetically busy wielding formidable governmental, even presidential war powers.

Example: As chairman of the Munitions Assignment Board, Hopkins "presides over a group of British and American generals and admirals," *The New Yorker* wrote, describing a role that sounds decidedly commander-in-chiefish. This particular group, which met once a week during the war, determined which Allies received what American munitions—how many bombers should go to the USSR, for example. Hopkins, meanwhile, continued to supervise his handpicked Lend-Lease staff at home and abroad. Did I mention Hopkins was also chairman of something called the President's Soviet Protocol Committee? This panel, as described by *The New Yorker,* was set up "to assess adequate treatment of Soviet requests." In other words, to ram 'em through. As the Soviet Protocol Committee minutes of November 26, 1942, tell us, it worked like so: "This decision to act [i.e., supply the Soviets] without full information was made with some misgivings, but after due deliberation. Mr. Hopkins said that there was no reservation about the policy at the present time, but that the policy was constantly being brought up for rediscussion. *He proposed that no further consideration be given to these requests for rediscussion* (emphasis added).[29]

How Politburo-like.[30]

What did Roosevelt think about all of this? Coming to this project, let's say, as a citizen-historian trying to understand why history hasn't been adding up, I have been relieved to encounter continual reference to the inscrutability of FDR, even from close associates. In other words, it wasn't just unfamiliarity with the material that makes Roosevelt difficult to understand; he *was* difficult to understand. He liked stamps and sea stories and took a childlike delight in such things as having two "neighbors" from southern Dutchess County in his cabinet (Morgenthau and Forrestal).[31]

This was the simple side of the man, which either masked the sage or revealed the lightweight. Meanwhile, Roosevelt was always the steely politician, the man who brought forth on this continent a new collection of special interest groups, surely leading us away from political Eden by ignoring Madison's warning about factions in Federalist 10. This was the Machiavellian side of the man, which was above all power-driven. Unexpectedly, he appears also to have been largely nonideological—unprincipled, said his detractors. This may seem like a paradox given that FDR presided over the ideological transformation of the Democratic Party, which, pre–New Deal, was, like the GOP, more identified with traditions and personalities than with a specific and entrenched doctrine. As "dean of the Washington newsmen" Arthur Krock saw it, Roosevelt "didn't have much political philosophy," but ideology became a means to an end. Also according to Krock, it was under Harry Hopkins's tutelage that FDR came to regard the New Deal political alliance of labor and farmers as "the golden key to perpetuity of power, which proved to be true."[32]

There was, however, one point of ideology that Roosevelt does seem to have fervently embraced, which historian Dennis J. Dunn believes made him an ideologue after all. FDR, Dunn writes, seized on the theory of "convergence" as it applied to the United States and the USSR, the idea being that capitalism and Communism would take on enough characteristics of the other to "converge." Sounds very Zen and 1970s, but no. Convergence theory powered all manner of trade, social, scientific, and political byplay between the United States and the USSR from the start of relations up to and including that Nixon-Kissinger relic, détente.[33] Further, in their memoirs, sources as disparate as Roosevelt bête noire Rep. Martin Dies and Roosevelt ally Cardinal Spellman describe separate, private conversations with FDR in which the president expanded on the concept in 1940 and 1943, respectively.[34] Similarly, Averell Harriman underscored its importance in Roosevelt's thinking, as did Sumner Welles.[35]

Roosevelt's belief in convergence makes perfect sense. After all, the New Deal—in Martin Dies's apt formulation the classic "Communist front" organization secretly directed by Communists—expanded the powers and reach of the centralized state, becoming a gigantic, one-way "convergence" enterprise of its own. Not that we are taught to see it in such terms.

As Dunn explains it, the convergence theory "held that Soviet Russia and the United States were on convergent paths, where the United States was moving from laissez-faire capitalism to welfare state socialism and the Soviet Union was evolving from totalitarianism to social democracy." Having himself moved the United States from laissez-faire capitalism to welfare state socialism, FDR knew he was at least half right, but being half right doesn't validate the whole theory. That is, there's no "convergence" if only one side is doing all the converging; that's capitulation—and, going forward, appeasement. With the fervor of the true believer, the president set his political progress accordingly—and the nation's.

Dunn argues that it was this overriding belief in a common point of convergence that allowed Roosevelt to discount and overlook all violently contradictory evidence between here and there; in other words, the purely theoretical end justifies the concretely brutal means. Such means included millions killed and jailed to secure the Soviet regime at home, millions jailed and killed to secure the Soviet regime abroad, and every Big Lie, act of police-state repression, and flame of fear and terror generated in between.

Not only did FDR overlook the external evidence; FDR ignored the counsel of key experts at the State Department, which, at the time, was home, mirabile dictu, to an educated and experienced cadre of anti-Communists, or, better, Communist *realists*—yesteryear's "Islamophobes"—who would be neutralized and dispersed, *purged,* in two waves. The first wave was in 1937, when even the Russian research library at the State Department was broken up, the files on Communists, foreign and domestic, ordered destroyed.[36] The second wave was in 1943. Both purges took place under Soviet pressure and even direction as when in March 1943 Foreign Minister Litvinov, incredibly, handed over a list of American diplomats the Soviets wanted fired.[37] This list included the scholarly anti-Communist Loy Henderson, who would, as a direct result of Soviet pressure, be reposted *to Iraq* as a "guilt offering to Stalin from Roosevelt," as Martin Weil speculates. How else to atone for an adviser who committed *crimethink* multiple times by arguing, among other things, not only that the democracies could survive a Nazi conquest of the USSR, but also that, if the world were ever lucky enough to see the Communist tyranny fall, the United States should not recognize a Soviet government in exile?[38] Of course, the United States never presented the Soviet government with a similar list of grievances about Politburo hardliners who were antagonistic toward the United States. What vassal state would dare?

This question follows from earlier arguments that the vast and deep extent of Communist penetration, heretofore denied, had in fact reached a tipping point to become a de facto Communist occupation of the American center of power. Reading about the abrupt disappearance of tens of thousands of anti-subversive files from the Office of Naval Intelligence in 1944, and the wreckage of thousands of army G-2 counterintelligence records in a campaign of "dismemberment" in 1943–44 (at the behest of Harry Hopkins and the Secret Service, army officials told the FBI) brings to mind a new order sweeping in to clean out the old.[39] Indeed, under Roosevelt, the United States engaged in certain behaviors that we may recognize as those of the supplicant nation driven by undue concern, even fear, of annoying or angering its patron. An unnatural solicitude for an empire that was evil long before any American president dared mention it led the United States down a path of unreturned concession and unredeemable appeasement. Something else, too, was set in motion when the United States recognized the Soviet Union on November 16, 1933—eight months after Gareth Jones, then Malcolm Muggeridge, were "smacked down" for reporting to the wider world the facts of the Terror Famine; something else that came into the world as recognition was toasted with "quaffs of what was almost the last of Prohibition beer" in the wee hours of November 17.[40]

When Franklin Roosevelt finally extended "normal diplomatic relations" in exchange for a page of Soviet concessions signed by Foreign Minister Maxim Litvinov (who, Prohibition beer on his breath, then returned to the Soviet Embassy "all smiles . . . and said, 'Well, it's all in the bag; we have it'"[41]), the U.S. government found itself derailed onto a strange, new track through an unfamiliar, soon monotonous, land of endless apologetics. The crux of the U.S.-USSR agreement rested on a series of promises, accepted and signed by Litvinov, that listed very specifically what the Soviet Union would not do "in the United States, its territories or possessions": namely, it would not attempt to subvert or overthrow the U.S. system. The declaration "scrupulously" stated the USSR would refrain and restrain all persons and all organizations, under its direct or indirect control, from taking any act, overt or covert, aimed at the overthrow or preparation for the overthrow of the United States. It further specifically stipulated that the Soviet government would not form or support groups inside the United States—such as the Soviet-supported CPUSA and myriad "front groups," such as the Soviet-directed underground espionage networks Bentley and Chambers later broke with, such as the CPUSA-Comintern group on the West Coast that Harry Hopkins found out Hoover was bugging (and knowingly told the Soviets).[42] The agreement, in other words, was a bunch of lies, the first bunch of lies of many. To make it all stick, however, to keep this sorriest of bad bargains, to perpetuate the myth of U.S.-Soviet accord, *the United States had to pretend otherwise.* The United States had to retire to a new fantasy world of its own creation in which the Soviet Union was keeping its word, in which Soviet-directed and -financed espionage did not exist . . . in which Communists were *not* under every bed, in which even the act of looking was "Red-baiting" and anti-Communists were paranoid about "bugaboos." As our most respected and beloved leaders increasingly sought refuge in this world of pretend, they led the nation on a disastrous retreat from reality from which we have never, ever returned. In our retreat, we left morality behind, undefended.

Now, as far as we know, Harry Hopkins had nothing to do with this beginning. Then again, I have found that we don't know much about who did. "Four presidents and their six Secretaries of States for over a decade and a half held to this resolve" not to recognize the Soviet government, as Herbert Hoover, one of those four presidents, wrote in *Freedom Betrayed,* his posthumously published (2011) history of World War II. These American leaders understood that the Bolsheviks' seizure of the government by force, their reign of blood, their pledge to conspire against other governments, made the "mutual confidence" required for diplomatic relations impossible. However, Hoover doesn't explain the shift in thinking.[43] Indeed, who or what specifically inspired FDR to undertake this momentous decision is largely glossed over in the historical narrative in general, although we do know Soviet recognition was applauded by businessmen eager to buy their rope from Lenin. The interchanges that followed, the relations that evolved, were marked and warped by paradoxes we would later understand and explain as "Orwellian." Some of them Aleksandr Solzhenitsyn would bring to our attention some forty years later.

In his very first speech on his very first trip to the USA in 1975, the fifty-six-year-old Solzhenitsyn asked the question he had wanted to ask America most of his adult life. He set it up by comparing America's historic aversion to alliance with czarist Russia to Roosevelt's rush to recognize a far more repressive and infinitely more violent Bolshevik Russia in 1933. Pre-Revolutionary executions by the czarist government came to about seventeen per year, Solzhenitsyn said, while, as a point of comparison, the Spanish Inquisition at its height destroyed ten persons per month. In the revolutionary years of 1918 and 1919, he continued, the Cheka executed without trial more than a thousand per month. At the height of Stalin's terror in 1937–38, *tens of thousands* of people were shot per month. The author of *The Gulag Archipelago* put it all together like so:

> Here are the figures: seventeen a year, ten a month, more than one thousand a month, more than forty thousand a month! Thus, that which had made it difficult for the democratic West to form an alliance with pre-revolutionary Russia had, by 1941, grown to such an extent, yet still did not prevent the entire united democracies of the world—England, France, the United States, Canada, and other small countries—from entering into a military alliance with the Soviet Union. How is this to be explained? How can we understand it?[44]

Presidents Wilson, Harding, Coolidge, and Hoover all rejected relations with the Bolshevik regime. This would seem to mark these men as belonging to the earlier era of Albert Dreyfus, when, as Robert Conquest notes, "the conscience of the civilized world could be aroused by the false condemnation to imprisonment of a single French captain for a crime which had actually been committed, though not by him."[45] A generation or two later, the conscience of the civilized world couldn't be aroused, period, not by the false condemnation of one nor the false condemnation of thousands, tens of thousands, or hundreds of thousands, as Conquest explains. "The Soviet equivalent of the Dreyfus Case involved the execution of thousands of officers, from Marshals and Admirals down, on charges which were totally imaginary."[46] What happened to the "conscience of the civilized world"?

The West's decision to recognize the USSR—and its determination to keep recognizing it, no matter how much lying and acquiescence to betrayal that entailed—did more to transform us than any single act before or since. The profound diplomatic shift—part Faustian bargain, part moral lobotomy—didn't just invite the Soviet Union into the community of nations. To make room for the monster-regime, the United States had to surrender the terra firma of objective morality and reality-based judgment. No wonder, then, that tens of thousands of Dreyfus Cases in Russia meant nothing to the "conscience of the civilized world." *Implications* had already been officially sundered from *facts*.

To be sure, there was something new in the way recognition ever after reordered the priorities and actions of our republic, something that marked the beginning of a different kind of era. The fact is, the implications of normalizing relations with the thoroughly abnormal USSR didn't just reward and legitimize a regime of rampantly metasticizing criminality. Because the Communist regime was so openly and ideologically dedicated to our destruction, the act of recognition defied reason and the demands of self-preservation. Recognition and all that came with it, including alliance, would soon become *the enemy* of reason and self-preservation. In this way, as Dennis J. Dunn points out, we see a double standard in American foreign policy evolve, and, I would add, in American thinking more generally. It was here that we abandoned the lodestars of good and evil, the clarity of black and white. Closing our eyes, we dove head first into a weltering morass of exquisitely enervating and agonizing grays.

This is the journey that forced open our psyches to increasingly expansive experiments in moral relativism. Only a very few refused to go; only a very few saw the sin. There is something poignantly allegorical in Solzhenitsyn's recollection of being a young Red Army soldier flummoxed by what he and his comrades heard as Roosevelt's disastrous misreading of Stalin at around the time of the Tehran Conference. As they marched on the Elbe, he said, they hoped to "meet the Americans and tell them." He added, "Just before that happened I was taken off to prison and my meeting didn't take place." Just before that happened, just before he was going to tell his American compatriots the truth about Stalin, about the Soviet Union, the twenty-six-year-old was arrested by the NKVD for the most mildly derogatory statements about Stalin written in a letter. He was sentenced to a labor camp for eight years.

Solzhenitsyn would have been too late anyway. Having abandoned the Western moral tradition and Enlightenment logic as a precondition of the U.S.-USSR relationship, we already inhabited a brave new—and dangerous—realm. Wishful thinking was in. Evidence was out. Ideology was in. Facts were out. With an exchange of rustling paper at the White House, the revolution was here, the epicenter of American betrayal.

Two years before the NKVD arrested Solzhenitsyn somewhere in eastern Prussia, William C. Bullitt, the former and first U.S. ambassador to the

USSR, laid before his good friend Franklin Roosevelt a detailed prophesy contained in a letter of all that was about to happen to the world given the USA's current course of action—and that did happen. This letter, dated January 29, 1943, is surely one of the most remarkable documents to come out of World War II. Not too many years earlier, Bullitt had been a famed (notorious) Sovietophile who, as a forty-two-year-old assistant to the secretary of state, enthusiastically shepherded the 1933 negotiations leading to U.S. recognition of the USSR. His role was key: SOVIET PACT HELD BULLITT TRIUMPH, as one newspaper headlined it. His uncle Archdeacon James F. Bullitt's reaction to the pact was also front-page news: BULLITT'S UNCLE SAYS SOVIET DEAL DISGRACES UNITED STATES. Uncle Bullitt turns out to have been savvier than his nephew—"Russia will keep no promises with us," he correctly predicted—but William Bullitt's disillusionment was not long in coming.[47]

As ambassador *en poste,* Bullitt soon realized that every "pledge," "promise," and "assurance" that the United States had extracted from the Soviets—on war debt, on the treatment of American nationals and property in the USSR, on religious freedom, on subversion of the United States, and, of course, on revolution in the United States—in exchange for recognition wasn't worth the rags the paper was printed on. This was becoming patently clear to him by 1935 after Stalin convened the world's Communist parties, including the American Communist Party, in the Seventh World Congress of the Communist International. CPUSA leaders Earl Browder and William Foster took leading roles in the congress. This display directly violated Soviet pledges to refrain from directing subversive activities in the United States.[48]

It turns out that Bullitt, despite his (subsiding) Sovietophilia, was a fact-based, Enlightenment kind of guy after all. It seems he couldn't help himself, not while watching his pet theories about workers' paradise crack up against the facts. His cable to FDR on July 15, 1935, captures a mind in flux, no longer weighed down by delusion and wishful thinking. He has grasped the Communist mind. He doesn't advise Roosevelt to break relations, although he discusses it as a possible American response in the event that violations of the recognition agreement at the Comintern congress, still unfolding, turned out to be "not technical but gross and insulting." In that event, he wrote, he suspected FDR "will feel obliged to break relations."

Bullitt suspected wrong. He continued, "If we should not [break relations], the Soviet Government would be convinced that it could break its pledges with impunity and would feel free to direct actively the American communist movement."[49]

Would feel free? The Soviet government was already doing precisely that and more inside the United States, as Bullitt would later learn. This would have been a perfect moment to cast out the snake—simply "to treat Stalin like an adult," as a future ambassador, William H. Standley, would similarly advise the president in late 1942, "keep any promises we make to him, but insist that he keep his promises, too."[50]

It sounds so simple. It *was* so simple. However, it was rational, too, and reason had no place in this sick relationship. For those who tried to inject it there was only frustration.

Most people didn't. So it would be that in 1982, when Ronald Reagan asked his arms control advisory committee to conduct a review of Soviet compliance in twenty-five years of arms controls treaties, it was the first such concerted review ever. The answer to Reagan's question on Soviet compliance was that there was none. In his excellent 1988 study of the West's resolve to ignore the implications of Communist ideology in its relations with the USSR, *Why the Soviets Violate Arms Control Treaties,* Joseph D. Douglass Jr. takes note of this pattern of behavior adopted by the Western world: "The Soviet Union repeatedly violates treaties, and the rest of the world turns their heads and proceeds to enter into still more treaties, which the Soviets violate with impunity."[51]

Back at the beginning, back at the source, not even the accomplished Bullitt could stop it, although he did try. Days after his July 1935 letter to FDR about the Comintern Congress, he wrote a startlingly prophetic cable to Secretary of State Hull emphasizing the point that contrary to reports, beliefs, and desire (and of course disinformation, but he didn't mention that), there had been "no decrease in the determination of the Soviet Government to produce world revolution . . . If this basic postulate of the Soviet Government is understood, there is little or nothing in Soviet domestic or foreign policy that is not clear." As if to prove his own point, Bullitt proceeded to explain the Soviets' "heartiest hope" for war between Japan and the United States, which they would enter "after Japan had been thoroughly defeated . . . to acquire Manchuria and Sovietize China," and for war in Europe between Germany and France, which they would similarly exploit "to protect and consolidate any communist governments which may be set up as a result."[52]

That was written in July 1935. There was little or nothing in Soviet domestic or foreign policy that wasn't clear to Bullitt, but such clarity impinged on his relationship with Roosevelt, who preferred the view through rose-Red-colored glasses. While their friendship became strained, Bullitt would continue to press his case. In the extraordinary letter to FDR dated January 29, 1943, noted above, Bullitt warned Roosevelt what would happen if the president continued pursuing the policies of appeasement toward Stalin that formed the foundation of the American war strategy. Specifically, Bullitt pleaded with the president not to "permit our war to prevent Nazi domination of Europe to be turned into a war to establish Soviet domination of Europe." Fifteen thoughtful pages later,

Bullitt had accurately foretold that the Soviet Union would annex half of post-Hitler Europe, with the grotesque effect being that the United States had gone to war to replace one tyrant with an even bigger tyrant. George F. Kennan later tagged this letter as the earliest warning of the "effective division of Europe that would ensue if the war continued" under prevailing policy.[53] It was a policy based on what Bullitt called "the vice of wishful thinking" unsupported by any evidence.

Wishful thinking in the 1940s was no different from wishful thinking in the 1930s; it had become, however, the basis of an incessant propaganda campaign controlled through the absolute powers of the federal government in wartime. It was also promulgated and promoted by Communist-penetrated government agencies, such as the OWI.[54] The basic story, repeated over and over again, was that Stalin had changed, Stalin had no interest in territorial gains or world revolution, and Stalin was taking the Soviet Union in the direction of democracy and liberty. This was exactly the set of lies that military analyst Hanson Baldwin identified as "great mistakes of the war" in his 1949 book of the same name. What Bullitt understood early on, however, was that these lies were no "mistake." Instead—and this is crucial—they were exactly "the view being propagated by the Comintern." He elaborated, "It is the communist party line in Great Britain, the United States and all other countries where there are communist parties. It is the line of fellow travelers and many 'liberals.' Since Stalin personally sets the party line, it is what Stalin wants us to believe about him . . . The most careful search for factual evidence to support the thesis that Stalin is a changed man reveals none."[55]

The most careful search for evidence reveals none—but reveals Bullitt to have inhabited the universe of reason. Without supporting facts, there could be no conclusion to the contrary, and wishful thinking wasn't enough to base battle plans on—a lesson our leadership still hasn't learned, as we see in Iraq, Afghanistan, and elsewhere. Ideology was and is no substitute for reality. What despair, what frustration must have descended on Bullitt when he realized, in the course of a three-hour discussion with FDR about this January 29, 1943, letter, that the president, in response to his reasoned arguments, was regurgitating exactly this same Communist Party line.

"Bill, I don't dispute your facts, they are accurate," Bullitt quoted FDR as saying. "I don't dispute the logic of your reasoning. I just have a hunch that Stalin is not that kind of a man. Harry says he's not and that he doesn't want anything in the world but security for his country, and I think that if I give him everything I possibly can and ask nothing from him in return, *noblesse oblige,* he won't try to annex anything and will work with me for a world of democracy and peace."[56]

Translation: Bullitt's facts are accurate (just as Robert Conquest's facts would be thirty, forty years later). Bullitt's logic, too, is undisputable. It's just the *implications* of those facts and logic that FDR could not—*would not*—accept.

Yes, we're back to that, the same sundering of fact from implication that has plagued us since Soviet recognition. The same quarantine around knowledge, preventing "contamination" by conclusion. Instead, we see the insidious infiltration of emotion and ideology, action based on theory, and theory based on *propaganda.* Then there's the say-so of our old friend Harry Hopkins—a point most historians, Paul Kengor has noted, snip from the Bullitt quotation (the better to fit their existing view of the world). As a result of this juggernaut, Bullitt and other students of traditional reason became caught up in a new force field, a reverse Big Bang that froze rather than enlivened the building blocks of reason at the core of Western society. Black became white. Defeat became victory. Stalin worked for world peace. Elizabeth Bentley was a liar. By the time Orwell sat down in a lonely farmhouse in the Scottish Hebrides to write about far-off 1984, he was no longer operating in the realm of science fiction. Western society was already a theater of lies and paradox, driven by "the vice of wishful thinking," as Bullitt put it, conditioned and regulated according to an unprecedented, Soviet-directed, American-executed worldwide propaganda campaign.

Bullitt revealed this conversation with FDR in an article he wrote for *Life* magazine called "How We Won the War and Lost the Peace." It was August 1948. The following year, Orwell's instantly timeless vision of a world upside down came out, received as a fantasy about mind control and ideological domination. Bullitt's article reveals it all in momentous action, with "Harry," not incidentally, manning an important control lever.

In his letter to Roosevelt, Bullitt elaborated on the dangers of self-deception. "Wishful thinking has produced the following logic: Because the Red Army has fought magnificently, the Soviet Union is a democratic state which desires no annexation and is devoted to the Four Freedoms; because Stalingrad has been defended with superb heroism there is no O.G.P.U. (Secret Police)."[57]

This rang a bell. In his 1973 memoir *Witness to History, 1929–1969,* veteran diplomat Charles E. "Chip" Bohlen—a protégé of Harry Hopkins, by the way, whose 1953 appointment by Eisenhower to become U.S. ambassador to Moscow was unsuccessfully contested by Senate anti-Communists as a continuation of Rooseveltian appeasement policies[58]—noted the impact of Soviet propaganda in America. Bohlen was specifically referring to the efforts of "Party-line boys" to promote the Soviet Union in the heat of the war effort. With some people, he wrote, "these feelings were so strong you could hardly say it was cold in Russia without being accused of being anti-Soviet." Shortly after the Soviet victory at the Battle of Stalingrad, which was right about the time Bullitt wrote to FDR in January 1943, Bohlen recalled, "One night, at a party where the Russians were being lionized, John Russell, a young officer in the British Embassy whom I had known in Moscow, observed, 'There are people in town who think the defense of Stalingrad proves there is no GPU.' "[59]

This is Bullitt's anecdote exactly. Now, it's quite possible that Bullitt and Bohlen, colleagues from the U.S. Embassy in Moscow back when Bullitt was ambassador, were standing, cocktail to cocktail, hearing the same story at the same party. However, Victor Kravchenko reports encountering much the same argument in his American travels, and repetitiously so: the nonlogical progression that linked "Russia's tragically costly victories" with "the genius of Bolshevism" or even "the rightness of the regime." To Americans, Kravchenko wrote, "Hitler's offensive proved only that the beast was mighty, but Stalin's counter-offensive somehow confirmed the validity of Bolshevism."

As a Soviet official under near-constant supervision, Kravchenko said, "I could not speak up, could not defend my countrymen against the monstrous perversion of the facts. A thousand times I had to listen in frustrated silence while the Soviet dictatorship was being given full credit for the achievements of the Russian people."

He continued, "Someone somewhere had manipulated the surge of fellow-feeling for Russians for Stalin's benefit"—and not, as Kravchenko fervently wished, for the democratic aspirations of the Russian people. "Americans seemed intent on explaining everything in Stalin's favor, to the discredit of the democracies," he observed. He added, "An incredible thing seemed to have happened in the American mind: the Soviet dictatorship was fully identified with the Russian people. What the Communists had not yet succeeded in doing in their own country—as the purges and the millions of political prisoners indicate—*they had succeeded in doing in America!*" (emphasis added).[60]

This is a stunning assessment, testament to the successful penetration, infiltration, and subversion of key strategic territory: the American mind. As Kravchenko further ventured into discussions with Americans, he also came to believe that Russians, trained over the years to discount propaganda and read between the lines of the Soviet state-run press, had an advantage over Americans, who, confident of the freedoms protected by the First Amendment, accepted propaganda transmitted by correspondents, uncritical or censored, from Moscow. They also accepted the news as produced by Communist-penetrated U.S.-government organs such as Voice of America or the Office of War Information—state-run media, U.S.-style. "Every Kremlin lie or diplomatic twist thus . . . found readier credence here than at home," he observed. It was a remarkable flip that he described. Slave labor, famine, police dictatorship—"these were things of which everyone inside Russia was deeply conscious," he wrote.

There might be apologists or fatalists who shrugged them off, he continued, but "it would not occur to us to *deny* them." Americans, however, did both. Then, for Kravchenko, the light dawned: "The greatest Soviet triumph, it was borne in upon me, was in the domain of foreign propaganda."

The reaction to Kravchenko's defection provides a case in point. The logic behind Kravchenko's clean break from his past life was that Soviet Russia was a totalitarian monstrosity akin to Nazi Germany. (Once, FDR believed that—or, rather, delivered a speech saying so. "The Soviet Union is run by a dictatorship as absolute as any other dictatorship in the world," he said on February 10, 1940—three months before "H.H." moved in to stay.) Of course, to anyone with a stake, ideological, careerist, or misguided, in preserving the pro-Soviet status quo, this was unthinkable, unspeakable—and literally so. By this point, readers may not be shocked to learn that it was silence that largely greeted Kravchenko's sensational defection in March 1944, as noted by *Time* magazine: "Editorial comment was minimum and cautious. Most U.S. editors, mindful of the delicacy of U.S.-Soviet relations, of the gravity of the war, and of the 26-year-old difficulty in getting at the truth in any item dealing with Russia, did not want to stick out their necks."[61]

A neat rationale, euphemistically packaged. (Still, it is hard not to be grateful for the confessional note about "necks.") As seen in the spotty coverage of the 1932–33 Terror Famine a decade earlier, factors having zero to do with delicate U.S.-Soviet relations, war, or any supposed "difficulty" in getting at the truth about Russia had already turned an ostensibly free press into a school of turtles in the recoiled position. "A deaf-and-dumb reporter hermetically sealed in a hotel room could not have escaped knowledge of the essential facts," Eugene Lyons had written of his own and his colleagues' shameful Terror Famine whitewash.[62] This, the first Big Lie, as Conquest noted, was the Original Sin committed by a smallish fraternity. It was a precursor to the institutional Fall as marked by U.S. recognition of the USSR. We had lower depths to plumb: our own active collaboration in Big Lies, which wasn't evident until what is known as the Katyn Forest Massacre.

When in early April of 1943—one year before Kravchenko's defection—the mass graves of thousands of shot, bayoneted, and asphixiated Polish officers began to be uncovered beneath the pines in the forest of Katyn near Smolensk, Russia, by invading Nazi troops, all of the ghoulish evidence, the Nazis said, and triumphantly so, pointed to Soviet guilt.

Nazi propaganda, thundered Stalin. "German fascists" had executed the Polish officers, he told FDR in an aggressive rant on April 21, 1943, that excoriated their mutual ally, the Polish government in exile, for daring to call in the nonpartisan International Red Cross to investigate this crime against Polish humanity.

Then what happened? Before I write the answer, I want to introduce a hypothetical case for a moment. Imagine the plight of a people forced to repeat and live by a conqueror's lies—a familiar enough tableau from the past century. We shake our heads sadly, if also a little smugly, and shrug in empathic embarrassment that any nation should be reduced to such servility. But as the story of Katyn Forest Massacre tells us—or, rather, the story of the story of the Katyn Forest Massacre tells us—we must ask ourselves what difference there is between that hypothetical subject nation and our own. The Allied reaction to the Soviet massacre of twenty-two thousand Polish officers is what some would, did, and do call denial for the greater good. I have concluded it was our moral unraveling.

The simplest chronology follows.

On April 13, 1943, Radio Berlin broadcast news of the German discovery of thousands of corpses of Polish officers, who, the report said, had been executed by the NKVD when the Soviets held the territory in the spring of 1940. Was this "unscrupulous Nazi propaganda" designed to hide yet another *Nazi* atrocity, or did this appalling discovery explain why it was that Stalin told the Allies he was unable to locate thousands of Polish officers "missing" in Soviet-controlled territory for almost two years?[63]

On April 15, 1943, Radio Moscow countered that the Poles had died at the hands of "the German-Fascist hangmen in the summer of 1941." *Not until 1990, forty-seven years later, would the Soviet regime finally admit the truth: The Katyn Massacre was a Soviet crime.*

Also on April 15, 1943, the Polish government in exile in London asked the independent International Red Cross in Geneva to investigate the scene of this massive crime. It simultaneously underscored its unaltered antipathy for the Nazi regime. Poland, after all, had been invaded by Soviets and Nazis both in September 1939—another historical fact we "forget."

The Nazis also called in the Red Cross, desperately hoping to capitalize, kettle-calling-pot-black-style, on the evident butchery of the Soviets. The Swiss aid organization agreed to investigate, but only on the condition that all three interested parties—Germany, Poland, and the USSR—agreed. The USSR did no such thing, instead throwing fits that, like a crazy girlfriend, would turn its junior partners into desperate, placating suitors.

On April 19, the Soviet organ *Pravda* smeared the Poles as "Hitlerite lackeys" who would "go down in history as the helpmates of Cannibal Hitler."[64]

On April 23, Elmer Davis, famed journalist, radio personality, and chief of the Office of War Information, broadcast a report on Katyn parroting Soviet lies that Katyn was a Nazi crime, setting the line for U.S. government information agencies that wouldn't be broken *until 1951.*[65]

On April 24, Churchill cabled Stalin that he was thinking about "silencing those Polish papers in this country which attack the Soviet government."[66]

On April 25, Stalin thanked Churchill for his "interest in the matter" and announced he would be breaking relations with the Poles due to "public opinion in the Soviet Union"—hah—"which is extremely indignant at the ingratitude and treachery of the Polish government." Historian Laurence Rees comments, "It is worth noting the lengths to which Stalin now felt confident to take this device of protesting at being accused of a crime that he knew he had committed."[67]

On April 26, the USSR broke relations with the Polish government for its completely natural, understandable response to evidence indicating that the Soviets had decimated the Polish elite in cold blood.

On April 28, Winston Churchill cabled Stalin that he had told the Poles that there could be no fruitful relationship with the USSR "while they make charges of an insulting character against the Soviet Government and thus seem to countenance atrocious Nazi propaganda."[68]

On April 30, an ad hoc committee of experts invited by the Nazis from twelve European universities and neutral countries unanimously dated the time of the massacre to the spring of 1940 when the area was under Soviet control.[69]

Back in the States, Harry Hopkins privately beat back suspicion of the Soviets by accusing the Poles—who, at the time, had some eighty thousand troops fighting against the Axis powers—of falling under the influence of "large Polish landlords" who simply wanted to keep their estates out of Russian hands.[70]

As for FDR? After receiving a toxic blast of propaganda from Stalin about the Poles' "absolutely abnormal" and "vile slander" dated April 21, 1943, Roosevelt soothingly replied on April 26, "I can well understand your problem." The Poles made "a stupid mistake" in asking the International Red Cross to investigate. (Thankfully, somebody—I think it was supposed to have been Secretary of State Cordell Hull—got FDR to cross out the word "stupid" before the cable went out.)

On May 1, the Polish government in exile withdrew its request for the Red Cross investigation.

On May 5, FDR, apparently impressed for all the wrong reasons, effectively pledged fealty to the brute. He wrote a personal letter to Stalin, to be hand-delivered by professional sycophant and all-around boob Joseph Davies, proposing a tête-à-tête "between you and me." No staff—other than Harry Hopkins, natch—would be invited, plus an interpreter and a stenographer. Definitely no Winnie. It wasn't only that all was forgiven by FDR; all was ignored.

Not by everyone, though. By the third week of May, an Anglo-Irish diplomat named Owen O'Malley had completed a lengthy, careful, and logical analysis of

the Katyn case that began to circulate within the British government. It left little doubt that Katyn was a Soviet atrocity. More than that, this document attests
to the existential damage underlying the British and, by extension, American
cover-up of the atrocity. Historian Laurence Rees calls O'Malley's cri de coeur
"one of the most remarkable documents in the history of Anglo-Soviet relations."[71] I would go further still and call it one of the most remarkable documents
of the century, evoking Shakespeare and Plutarch in its narrative of quandary
foreshadowing tragedy. It is an expression and elucidation of the very mindset I
have been writing this book to try to understand.

O'Malley enters this roiling philosophical deep by acknowledging as a given
the constraints imposed by "our urgent need for cordial relations with the Soviet government." This, he continues in his report's concluding section, makes
us "appear to appraise the evidence with more hesitation and lenience than we
should do in forming a common sense judgment on events occurring in normal
times or in the ordinary course of our private lives."

This tells us that O'Malley's meticulous analysis of events, which precedes
this statement, is, in fact, restrained, and that in holding back "common" sense
he is also withholding "normal" judgment. *This emphasis on the purposeful suppression of "normal" reactions is key.* It characterizes the basis of the West's
abnormal relationship to Communism. O'Malley continues, "We have been
obliged to appear to distort the normal and healthy operation of our intellectual and moral judgments."

If I were writing an English paper on the O'Malley report, I would jump all
over the use of the passive voice—*we have been obliged*—as a means of denying
volition, avoiding responsibility. I understand O'Malley is referring to the policy of desperation set by British and American leaders to retain Soviet Russia as
an ally against Nazi Germany at all costs—a policy that was in all probability
the result of a brilliant Soviet influence operation. It had become unthinkable
that there was any way to victory that did not defer to Soviet whim, feelings,
and strategic advantage, but there was a shorter, life-and-treasure-saving route.
As Solzhenitsyn would later tell us, "World democracy could have defeated one
totalitarian regime after another, the German, and then the Soviet. Instead it
strengthened Soviet totalitarianism [and] helped bring into existence a third
totalitarianism, that of China."[72]

Tell me again who won World War II?

In flagging the repression of common sense and judgment he observed the
British and Americans engaged in to conform to the Soviet version of Katyn,
O'Malley also offers a glimpse into our new role as official promulgators of a
Big Lie. This is nothing less than the act of the moral vassal who, having bent to
the Soviet standard, has accepted and legitimized it. "Morals and ethics do not

exist [here] as we understand them," U.S. ambassador to Moscow Laurence Steinhardt wrote from Moscow in 1940.[73] This meant that Westerners raised on Judeo-Christian morals and ethics either had to reject Communism's nullification of them or embrace Communism's nullification of them. O'Malley's report demonstrates the extent to which the Communist interpretation had been embraced—internalized, even.

He continues, ticking off some of the unnatural acts that followed from such acquiescence. "We have been obliged to give undue prominence to the tactlessness or impulsiveness of Poles, to restrain the Poles from putting their case clearly before the public, to discourage an attempt by the public and the press to probe an ugly story to the bottom."

I am suddenly put in mind of more contemporary Western constraints imposed on a kind of latter-day Poland—Israel—in the face of our capitulations to Islam.

O'Malley goes on, "In general we have been obliged to deflect attention from possibilities which *in the ordinary affairs of life* would cry to high heaven for elucidation, and to withhold the full measure of solicitude, which, *in other circumstances,* would be shown to acquaintances situated as the Poles now are" (emphasis added).

Here we see plainly expressed a double moral standard. The Poles, meanwhile, at that moment fighting and dying in the North Africa Campaign, were much more than "acquaintances" and deserved far better than the callous cover-up O'Malley describes. What we see in Allied behavior as described by the fifty-seven-year-old career diplomat is nothing less than a Frankensteinian transformation of human nature as observed not just by a sharp eyewitness but also by a participating and aghast guinea pig. Normal, healthy common sense and judgment have been proscribed; O'Malley understands that what has supplanted them is a reflex mendacity shaped by unnatural and nerve-racking constrictions of morality and logic. Echoes of *Macbeth* follow: "We have in fact perforce used the good name of England like the murderers used the little conifers to cover up a massacre."

Then the pivot: "And in view of the immense importance of an appearance and of the heroic resistance of Russia to Germany, few will think that any other course would have been wise or right."

As abnormal, unhealthy, unordinary as this course was, no other course could possibly have been *wise or right.* Really?

O'Malley himself doesn't seem entirely convinced. He goes back to contemplating those "little conifers"—the trees the Soviets planted over the mass graves in the forest—and how they might grow. "This dislocation between our public attitude and our private feelings we may know to be deliberate and inevitable, but at the same time we may perhaps wonder whether, by representing to others something less than the whole truth as far as we know it, and something less than the probabilities so far as they seem to us probable, we are not incurring a risk of what—not to put a fine point on it—might darken our vision and take the edge off our moral sensibility."

Exquisite excruciations aside, the Big Lie about Katyn, born in Moscow, would grow in London and Washington. That "vision" O'Malley references was shot, that moral edge gone. Otherwise they—we—would not have even considered incurring more of what O'Malley calls "risk." The Katyn cover-up, then, was a grisly manifestation of our fallen state of mind. What O'Malley depicts is a Dorian Gray–style portrait of moral decrepitude on the one hand and Communist power and influence on the other. *We* were on *their* string.

The cold logic behind the realpolitik response to the O'Malley report by British foreign secretary Sir Alexander Cadogan is more confirmation of this subject status. Cadogan himself wanted to suppress the O'Malley report, stopping it from circulating further even within the British government. He writes, "I confess that, in cowardly fashion, I had rather turned my head away from that scene at Katyn—for fear of what I should find there . . . I think no one has pointed out that, on a purely moral plane, these are not news. How many thousands of its citizens has the Soviet Union butchered?" . . .

These thousands killed are not "news" any more than those other thousands—millions, actually—killed were "news." "They died on the very edge of Europe. And Europe didn't even notice it. The world didn't even notice it—six million persons!" So Solzhenitsyn exclaimed about the Terror Famine in 1975, and millions more had perished since, even before Hitler had liquidated his first million. What horrors these two monsters both were. Why was it wrong to think that? Cadogan's answer, the crime-family logic of the capo coming through in Oxbridge overtones, was that the deal with this Soviet devil had been struck long ago; stick to it.

He continued, falling back on the crutch of inevitability O'Malley had leaned on, "Quite clearly, for the moment, there is nothing to be done. Of course it would be only honest to circulate it [O'Malley's report]. But as we all know (all admit) that *the knowledge of this evidence cannot affect our course of action,* or policy, is there any advantage in exposing more individuals than necessary to the spiritual conflict that a reading of the document excites?"[74] (Emphasis added.)

Here is the template of moral abdication of the Western world. When knowledge and evidence "cannot affect" our course of action, knowledge and evidence become an unnecessary source of "spiritual conflict"—not a guide, not an inspiration for moral behavior, for logical action. From this same fount of expediency flows the fractured reaction to Conquest: *We accept your facts, old boy, just not your implications. Certainly not in such a way as to affect our course of action. After all, old bean, we are morally dead—captives of Communist ideology, or Communist blackmail at any rate, which means much the same thing in the end, what? Why "expose" others to the "spiritual conflict" this dashed old massacre might arouse when our collusion in silence is assured anyway? Now, we are all complicit.* From such chilling candor, from such civilized quarters, we get a glimpse into exactly how great terrors and blood purges are rationalized and thus enabled: Don't look; don't think; don't feel; no need to get excited; there's nothing to do about it anyway.

Unsatisfied, perhaps, Cadogan would carry this debate into the pages of his diary. On June 18, 1943—the decision to go ahead in 1944 with the Normandy invasion, Stalin's Second Front, having been recently made—he notes, "I pointed out that years before Katyn the Soviet Government had made a habit of butchering their own citizens by the 10,000s, and if we could fling ourselves into their arms in 1941, I don't know that Katyn makes our position more delicate."[75]

He was right. It didn't. So long as there was no reckoning, no return to standards that not so long ago made "normal" relations with the Soviet Union impossible (1918–33, in the U.S. case), Katyn did not make the Allied position "more delicate." It did, however, make it more intensively redolent of spoiled fish and, worse, made the Allies complicit for the first time in doing our concerted part to preserve and elaborate on a new Big Lie—*this one, to some transformational extent, of our own official making.* Katyn couldn't have lived on without Churchill and Roosevelt. It couldn't have breathed; couldn't have sustained itself. "When people renounce lies, they simply cease to exist. Like parasites, they can only survive when attached to a person," wrote Solzhenitsyn. The problem is—the problem always is—one lie begets another. Three decades later, Aleksandr Solzhenitsyn would express his puzzlement over how this predicament had come about. Remember his figures: seventeen a year, ten a month, more than a thousand a month, more than forty thousand a month. Thus, he said, "that which had made it difficult for the democratic West to form an alliance with pre-revolutionary Russia had, by 1941, grown to such an extent and still did not prevent the entire united democracy of the world . . . from entering into a military alliance with the Soviet Union."[76]

At Katyn, it still did not prevent those same united democracies from themselves entering into criminal conspiracy with the Soviet Union. Here is where we see the Communist triumph in the inversion of Western morality and logic to serve Communist ends—and not just military ends. There was that peacetime alliance in the offing, a cooperative reconstruction of the postwar world at that very moment under way, with work on it to begin soon at Nuremberg. Looking down the road, Cadogan wonders later in the same diary entry regarding Katyn, "How can we discuss with Russians German 'war criminals' when we have condoned this?"

The answer would lie in more lies for—as these novices told themselves if they were as sensitive as O'Malley, as knowing as Cadogan—some "greater" good. By the end of his Katyn report, O'Malley makes the extent of this sunken state appallingly clear even as he still has the ability to perceive it fully: "We ought, maybe, to ask ourselves how, consistently with the necessities of our relations with the Soviet government, the voice of our conscience is to be kept at concert pitch."

A good question with a bad answer. "Our relations" with the Soviet government could not under any circumstances be consistent with "conscience . . . at concert pitch." Our relations required muffling, the *piano* pedal, the snuffing out of morality itself. O'Malley knew that. He wrote, "It may be that the answer lies, for the moment, only in something that can be done inside our own hearts and minds where we are masters. Here at any rate we can make a compensatory contribution—a reaffirmation of our allegiance to truth and justice and compassion."

A reaffirmation of truth and justice inside our own hearts and minds. Where no one could possibly hear it. A mute pledge. A silent, private, and pointless protest that a subject, a slave, or a captive might seek succor in at the end of a humiliating, debilitating day of hard labor and deprivation. Indeed, O'Malley seems to echo the thoughts of the numbered *zek* in a labor camp north of the Arctic Circle, not the declaration to the British Foreign Office by a diplomat appointed by the king of England, a soon-to-be-titled, Harrow-and-Oxford-educated member of the ruling class complete with ancestral family home.

Only inside our hearts and minds are we masters, O'Malley writes. Outside in the world, the implication is, we are not masters. Outside where we function, act, and strive we are vassals, minions, tools. Whose tools? The master calling the shots. His name was Stalin, and he had long ago won the most important prize. What was it Kravchenko wrote? *Stalin's grip on the American mind, I realized, was almost as firm as his grip on the Russian mind.*[77] Ditto the minds of all the Allies.

To my knowledge, there exists no exploration into the psyche of moral slump on the American side; no reaction to O'Malley's report if it even circulated at the top. We do know that Churchill sent FDR a copy on August 10, 1943; we also know he recorded no reaction. FDR never even acknowledged reading or even receiving it, nor did he return it to Churchill when asked repeatedly.[78] The silent treatment was the classic mode of Roosevelt rejection. The man didn't say no; he just didn't say. Or did he never receive it? Did Hopkins intercept it? We don't know. Maybe FDR was just too busy reading another document dated August 10, 1943, likely handed to him by good ol' Harry. With the 1970 publication of the 1943 Quebec Conference papers, we learned this secret memorandum was authored by Gen. James "Russian interests come first, last and always"[79] Burns, a mainstay of Soviet Lend-Lease and "the Hopkins Shop," whom we see serving as Hopkins's flunky when Admiral Stanley asked Hopkins to approve a presidential order in chapter 6. Who knows? Maybe Hopkins wrote it himself. Russia, the memo says, "must be given every assistance and every effort must be made to gain her friendship. Likewise, since without question she will dominate Europe on the defeat of the Axis, it is even more essential to develop and maintain the most friendly relations with Russia."[80]

Without question? The fix was in, again.

Once again, it didn't have to be this way. On August 11, 1943, John C. Wiley, a Soviet expert in the OSS, wrote a lengthy letter to FDR, a Bullitt-like blast, warning the president of Soviet designs on Eastern and Central Europe and explaining how not to be "maneuvered into aiding and abetting the rape of a large part of Europe." Wiley recommended the expeditious setup of a second front, "but in the Balkans where it could best influence the course of the war, diplomatic relations with the Kremlin, and the peace to come. True, a Balkan front is difficult . . . but if it is merely difficult and not impossible, we must by all means set up the Balkan front. An invasion of France and the Lowlands would give us no political authority in central and eastern Europe. Only a successful Anglo-American invasion of southeastern Europe can give us a real voice in the eventual peace settlement."[81]

It was a busy mailbag that August. A few days before Wiley wrote his letter to the president, on August 7, 1943, the director of the FBI received an anonymous letter written in Russian that identified leading KGB officers operating under diplomatic cover from Canada and the United States to Mexico. The identifications all proved to be accurate. The letter also correctly ID'd Zubilin/Zarubin as the chief KGB officer in the United States, just as it also correctly claimed he had participated in the Katyn Forest Massacre, at the time, of course, officially attributed to Germany.[82] We already know without doubt that Co-President Hopkins knew Zubilin/Zarubin was a Soviet intelligence officer seeking U.S. military secrets. Did he also know he was a mass murderer?

I keep looking through Robert Sherwood's authoritative two volumes about Hopkins, circa 1939–45, but I can't find anything written about the Katyn Forest Massacre and the ensuing diplomatic blow-up (Stalin) and fire snuffing (Churchill and Roosevelt) among the Allies. As for the 1987 McJimsey biography, completed with access to additional papers held by Hopkins's children and from elsewhere, Katyn gets one crummy paragraph. Hopkins's reaction, meanwhile, gets one sentence (as distilled from a Joseph Davies diary entry):

"Angered by this complication, Hopkins dismissed the Poles as troublemakers influenced by 'large Polish landlords' who wanted to make sure their estates were not lost to the Russians."[83] Via Venona we learn that Zarubin/Zubilin— warned thanks to Hopkins's passing FBI intelligence to the Soviet Embassy in May 1943—was also a key operative in the mass murder of the Poles at Katyn, a chilling revelation that brings not just the proverbial elephant but the real-life evil empire into the room.

Thankfully, we do have at least one American's very different response to the same appalling Katyn situation: that of George H. Earle. Earle—American blueblood, Harvard dropout, lawyer, sugar magnate, diplomat, polo player, dog breeder—was what is known in swashbuckling terms as a man of action. He fought Pancho Villa with Pershing, enlisted in World War I, winning the Navy Cross commanding a submarine chaser (his own private yacht), and served as a New Deal governor of Pennsylvania. He also insulted Hitler to his face ("I have nothing against the Germans, I just don't like you"[84]) and beaned a Nazi officer in a Bulgarian café with a champagne bottle when said Nazi objected too vociferously to Earle's song request ("Tipperary"[85]). Even George H. Earle was unable to break the Katyn moral paralysis, but he tried.

Earle became a special representative of FDR abroad, returning to Washington in May 1944. He brought with him a dossier of photos and affidavits he had gathered in Europe that implicated the Soviets in the Katyn atrocity. Testifying in 1952 before a select congressional committee called to investigate Katyn and its cover-up, Earle described arriving with his Katyn dossier at Union Station, where he was met by an old friend, Joe Levy of *The New York Times*. Levy, Earle testified, told Earle that bringing an anti-Soviet report on Katyn to FDR would be a career ender. As Earle told Congress, Levy said, "George, you don't know what you are going to over there. Harry Hopkins has complete domination over the President and the whole atmosphere over there is 'pink.' "[86]

"Pink," by the way, was cute-speak for pro-Communist and pro-Soviet, but a "pink" atmosphere was toxic to truth tellers, particularly to their careers. Earle didn't care. Like Whittaker Chambers bearing witness for the first time in September 1939, like Solzhenitsyn still fighting his way toward the American line on the eastern front, like Major Jordan knocking on Washington doors in January of that same year to alert the authorities to his Lend-Lease suspicions, like Kravchenko, who had just defected in April and was now in hiding, Earle just wanted to get his evidence before the president. When he did, he went over the photos with Roosevelt with a magnifying glass. He took him through the affidivits he had from Bulgarian Red Cross and White Russian sources.

Roosevelt wasn't buying. FDR waved off every piece of evidence. As Earle later told Congress, "He said, 'George, this is entirely German propaganda and a German plot. I am absolutely convinced the Russians did not do this.'" Earle replied by telling the president he completely disagreed. "Mr. President, I think this evidence overwhelming."[87]

Earle, like Bullitt and Wiley before him, went on to offer FDR an appraisal of Soviet intentions to seize swaths of Europe. As Earle testified, he told the president that the Russian menace was actually greater than the German menace.

"I said, 'Mr. President, I am very much worried about this Russian situation. I feel that they are a great menace, and I feel that they have done their best to deceive the American people about this Katyn massacre, and, also, primarily and most important of all, by this dreadful book of Joe Davies, *Mission to Moscow,* which made Stalin out [as] a benign Santa Claus. We never recovered from that. It made such an impression on the American people.'"[88]

Earle probably didn't realize the extent to which both versions of *Mission to Moscow,* the 1941 book and the 1943 Warner Bros. movie, were in a very real sense White House creations, as described earlier. "This will last," FDR had written in his own copy. So it did, at least in the Roosevelt White House.

Earle's audience with FDR came to an end. "I felt pretty hopeless after that," Earle said. "In the anteroom there I met Secretary [James] Forrestal of the Navy and talked to him about it and he said: 'My God, I think this is dreadful. We were all alone over here. Russia can do no wrong. It is perfectly dreadful.' He said: 'They just simply are blind to the whole situation.'" Forrestal asked Earle to come over and talk some more about this dire situation at the White House but Earle never did, much, as he told Congress, to his later regret.[89] Forrestal committed suicide in 1949.

What was it Earle's pal said about the White House atmosphere being "pink"? Airless, too, its doors hermetically sealed against facts, its shades down to block evidence that might undermine an ideologically correct state of being. Earle never did manage to bust through. Finally, almost a year later, he had had it. With major operations over and the war wrapping up, Earle would try to see FDR one more time, be rebuffed by an aide at the White House door, and later send a message to FDR. He sent it in a letter to FDR's daughter, Anna Boettiger, not to FDR, because, as he told Congress, he was afraid, with Roosevelt secretary Steve Early away, it might not get to Roosevelt otherwise.

No one questioned Earle on what he meant by that, but I note that elsewhere in Earle's evidence he specifically stated that all of his dispatches went to Roosevelt directly *"or through Harry Hopkins."*[90] We already know that Hopkins openly discussed withholding from FDR cablegrams even from Winston Churchill if they crossed his policy recommendations.[91] Was interference from Hopkins (then at the Mayo Clinic) or others something Earle was aware or suspicious of?

In his letter of March 21, 1945, Earle told Anna he had been "brushed off" by the White House due to his "anti-Russian views," which constituted, as he put it, "[telling] your father the truth about conditions in Russia and in countries occupied by Russia." Earle went on to make a proposition. Unless the president objects, he wrote,

> I want to present the following to the members of Congress and to the American people . . . I shall point out why Russia today is a far greater menace than Germany ever was, because of its manpower, natural resources, prospect of Bolshevizing Europe, including Germany, and because of its millions of fifth columnists. I shall show how Russia twenty-five years after its Revolution is exactly the same Red Terror it was then, of its 15 million people in concentration camps, of its treatment of the Jews and of Labor. I shall prove how Stalin deliberately started this war with his pact of friendship with Hitler so that the capitalistic nations would destroy each other.[92]

By this time, as Earle later pointed out to Congress, the major fighting in Europe was over; the expediencies of military alliance no longer existed. On the other hand, the political fight FDR—or, conceivably, his advisers—waged on behalf of the USSR had actually intensified. In a letter dated March 24, 1945, FDR wrote:[93]

> Dear George:
>
> I have read your letter of March twenty-first to my daughter Anna and I have noted with concern your plan to publicize your unfavorable opinion of one of our allies at the very time when such a publication from a former emissary of mine might do irreparable harm to our war effort. As you say you have held important positions of trust under your government. To publish information obtained in those positions without proper authority would be all the greater betrayal. You say you will publish unless you are told before that I do not wish you to do so. I not only do not wish it, but *I specifically forbid you to publish any information or opinion about an ally that you may have acquired while in office or in the service of the United States Navy.*
>
> I am sorry that pressure of affairs prevented me from seeing you on Monday. I value our old association and I hope that time and circumstance may some day permit a renewal of our good understanding. [Emphasis added.]

So ordered, Earle asked to be released from active service. He got his answer a few days later, as Laurence Rees reports, while sitting in a boat, fishing in a remote Maryland lake. "Suddenly he looked up and saw another boat coming toward him. On board were two FBI agents. They came alongside and said: 'Mr. Earle, we have a letter for you.' It contained the news that—with immediate effect—Earle had been appointed head of the Samoan Defense Group."[94] Samoa is a whole lot better than Siberia, but the effect—silencing political opposition—was similar.

I know I promised a simple chronology, but it turns out there is nothing simple about these tangled timelines. Almost no sooner had Earle been dispatched to the South Pacific than another Katyn report, like a corpse washing up on the tide, arrived in Washington. It was shortly after V-E Day, May 8, 1945. This one came in the person of Lt. Col. John Van Vliet, a fourth-generation West Pointer who had been captured by German forces while fighting in North Africa. Van Vliet was among a group of several American and British officers the Germans had taken to witness the exhumation of the mass graves at Katyn, to examine the evidence therein that proved that the atrocity was Soviet, not Nazi. Upon liberation from a POW camp south of Berlin, ironically by the Red Army, Van Vliet made his way to American lines and home to the States as quickly as possible so he could report on what he had seen. As Van Vliet would tell Congress in 1952, he arrived at Katyn in April 1943 predisposed to disbelieve any German version of events. Evidence of Soviet guilt, however, was overwhelming. For example, the dead reserve officers were wearing heavy winter clothes (while the Soviets claimed a German slaughter had taken place in August), which looked new, as did their leather boots. To Van Vliet, dressed in his own shabby uniform, this seemed to contradict the claim that the Poles had been prisoners for three years when, according to the Soviet version of events, they were supposedly killed. The newspapers, notebooks, and diaries that came out of the graves, too, were compelling circumstantial evidence; none was dated past the spring of 1940.

What Van Vliet wanted to bring home ASAP were the facts on the ground; the indicators of Soviet perfidy; the solid foundation of understanding on which to base our judgments and future course of action; a place from which to see reality itself. Of course, Katyn was just another installment in the horrific Soviet story of blood, deception, and conquest. The circumstances and details were different, but it was the same story Bullitt told FDR in January 1943; the same story George Racey Jordan tried to tell in January 1944; the same story Kravchenko alerted the American public to on defecting in March 1944. It was what Solzhenitsyn as a Red Army captain wanted to warn U.S. troops about in 1945; what made Whittaker Chambers offer government officials secrets about the Soviet conspiracy back in September 1939; what Eugene Lyons came clean about in the late 1930s; what Martin Dies did so much heroic work to uncover, piece by piece, on establishing the House Committee on Un-American Activities in 1938; what young Gareth Jones told the world about in 1933, only to be tackled by the emperor's courtiers. Like his predecessors, Van Vliet probably believed it was simply the facts that were missing; that when he corrected the figuring, the whole equation would suddenly come right. What none of these men understood, at least at first, was that the facts, their implications, the truth, and reality itself were all anathema in Uncle Sam's Communist-influenced, Communist-occupied corridors of power.

Imagine the haste with which Lt. Col. John Van Vliet strode those same corridors in the spanking-new Pentagon to get to the office of army intelligence (G-2) chief Gen. Clayton Bissell on Tuesday, May 22, 1945. Looking thin, tense, and tired (Bissell's words), Van Vliet proceeded to dictate his vivid recollections in what became known as the Van Vliet Report on Katyn. It made a cogent, convincing case for Soviet guilt. Van Vliet initialed it; Bissell read it, tagged it TOP SECRET. As Van Vliet would write in 1950, the general "then dictated the letter directing me to silence, and had me sign a copy of it in his presence. He explained to me the importance of my remaining silent, gave me my copy of the letter and thanked me."[95]

The importance of remaining silent.

Why?

That's what Congress wanted to know starting in late 1949, when its investigation into the cover-up of the Katyn Massacre began after the appearance earlier that year of two compelling articles in *The New York Herald Tribune* by the tenacious journalist and historian Julius Epstein. Epstein's research debunked the U.S.-USSR story that the Katyn Massacre was a Nazi atrocity—the version of events still disseminated by the U.S. government until 1950 when, inspired by Epstein's research, Congress, specifically Rep. George A. Dondero of Michigan, began demanding a reckoning.[96] Congress also wanted to know what in tarnation had become of the Van Vliet Report, the key eyewitness account in Katyn history whose existence Epstein had learned about. The army and the State Department just couldn't find it anywhere. In fact, the Van Vliet Report—get ready for this—had vanished from government archives.

It seems that Owen O'Malley's "darkened vision" of cover-up in the picturesque form of "little conifers" had lived on even after the overriding rationale—winning the war against Nazi Germany at all costs, even an alliance with the devil—was no more. When Van Vliet made his report, Nazi Germany was no more, but we were still kicking dirt over evidence of Soviet murder.

Why?

This time, it was for the sake of the "peace."[97]

The report of the select committee to investigate Katyn elaborated on this mindset: "General Bissell himself admitted to the [Madden] committee that had the Van Vliet report been publicized in 1945, when agreements for creating a United Nations organization reached at Yalta were being carried out in San Francisco, Soviet Russia might never have taken a seat in this international organization."[98]

The timelines overlap. A couple of days before newly liberated Van Vliet told his story to army intelligence, *The New York Times* reported NEW SECURITY CHARTER SEEMS TO BE ASSURED.[99] The day before Van Vliet showed up in General Bissell's office, the UN story of the day was SAN FRANCISCO OUTLOOK: HOPE OF BANNING WAR STIRS WORLD DESPITE HISTORY'S SOMBER TEACHING.[100] It was as if General Bissell believed he was saving the world by creating an alternate universe: deep-sixing the Van Vliet report with a TOP SECRET stamp to keep reality at bay. This rationale we now know as "politicizing the intelligence." It means editing the facts—omitting the facts—to fit an ideology. The belief. The dream. The hallucination. That damn "existing" view of the world.

This all very much "dismayed" the Madden Committee, which chastised Bissell for "considering political significance of the Van Vliet document, which should have been treated objectively from a strictly Military Intelligence standpoint."

Treated objectively? An indictment of the Soviet Union? Communism? By Uncle Joe's vassals? As Bissell's explanation demonstrates, the interests of the Soviet enterprise dominated the thinking of the United States establishment, even the chief of army intelligence. Bissell stated, "I saw in it [Van Vliet's report] great possibilities of embarrassment; so I classified it the way I have told you, and I think I had no alternative."[101]

Sure, General. Far better for the national soul, for the well-being of this nation and others, for the peace, for the future, for the sacrifice of the dead, to suppress the facts of Katyn—to save the Soviet Union from embarrassment. The Katyn coverup was another stake through the body of moral teachings once upheld in the Judeo-Christian world as guiding principles. It was a foundation of the laughably named United Nations, formed from the fractured basis of destabilizing falsehood and moral compromise.

Forty years later, Jeane J. Kirkpatrick would make a similar point when she offered an overview of American postwar foreign policy in a 1985 *Commentary* magazine symposium.[102] The entire concept of the UN, she wrote, "was based from the outset on falsification." This began, she continued, with the basic fact that the USSR was not, as the UN Charter assumed of all members, a democracy with democratic values. "Founding the UN required denying and falsifying the nature of the Soviet Union," she wrote. "Optimism about the new era of peace and the United Nations was maintained only by denial," and it was falsehood-based "denial and fantasy," Kirkpatrick observed, that became "permanent features of the postwar world."

Yes, but denial and fantasy were already permanent features of the world *before* the war. In fact, it's difficult to imagine circumstances under which the UN could have or would have been founded if such denial and fantasy were not already regnant. America's official and trumpeted acquiescence to the UN principles of world government, then, came at the end of a long moral slump that began with Soviet recognition in 1933, that continued with wartime alliance in 1941, that accelerated with the cover-up of Katyn in 1943 and beyond. We had long fallen in behind the evil emperor, surrendering a strategic swath of moral sovereignty that would never be reclaimed so long as we clung to the edges of his bloody train.

We may chide the Soviets for repressing the truth about Katyn until 1989, but for an unbelievable eight crucial years, U.S. government organs (Office of War Information, Voice of America, etc.) parroted this same Soviet disinformation. Even as late as 1978, an anniversary report on Katyn from Voice of America's correspondent in Poland was edited in Washington to remove mention of "Soviet" guilt.[103] Such patterns of censorship and, worse, self-censorship do things to people; do things to our vision and grasp of the truth, our respect for facts, our reliance on judgment. The less respect we accord facts, the less secure we can be in our judgment; and the more that mystery holes filled with lies begin to pock the record. So full of holes is our record that trying to find a way back to the facts as scrambled by con artists and partly reassembled by patient scholars is like traveling blind with a half-torn map across a land of booby traps, a hostile terrain where landmarks—the most crucial official documents—have been ransacked or destroyed altogether.

Where do we find our bearings after learning that army intelligence during this period functioned as an adjunct of the NKVD in disposing of the Van Vliet report? After learning, as Congress reported, that "there was a pool of pro-Soviet civilian employees and some military" in army intelligence who apologized for "almost everything that the Soviet Union did"? That this same pool exerted "tremendous efforts to suppress anti-Soviet reports"? That it ensured that officers "too critical of the Soviets were by-passed" for promotion? So testified three high-ranking army intelligence officers whom the committee investigating Katyn heard in executive session.[104]

Their full testimony should be part of the open record now. However, as M. Stanton Evans reports (uh-oh), "unfortunately for the historical record . . . the transcript of the executive hearing itself has vanished from the National Archives."[105]

Vanished.

What more could the NKVD have done to subvert and twist our record, except for maybe killing Van Vliet himself? That didn't happen, of course, although maybe the "of course" is a bit smug. Maybe Van Vliet was lucky. Or maybe an American uniform provided sufficient protection.

Not so lucky was Ivan Krivosertsov, a Russian peasant who spent his boyhood near the woods at Katyn, who knew of a time when it was a place to gather firewood, mushrooms, and berries.[106] Then came the Russian Revolution and then came the secret police: first the Cheka, then the OGPU, then the NKVD, then the NKGB seized the secluded area, perfect for summary executions. Never were there so many executions as there were in that spring of 1940. Krivosertsov knew that, too. Krivosertsov saw the prison trains arriving, the Polish officers inside arriving, then departing in "black ravens"—prison cars— with NKVD escorts. He heard the talk of a black raven driver, a lorry driver, a relative: The NKVD were shooting the Polish officers in the woods. Later, he saw the graves himself, and a small wooden cross. In the spring of 1943, Krivosertsov was the person who first showed these mass graves to incoming German troops, after which he worked for three months digging them up. Later in the war, when the Germans retreated, the peasant retreated with them. He worked in a railway yard in Berlin after that, at least until the Red Army arrived. Krivosertsov watched, furtively, as American and British troops fraternized with the Red Army. This perturbed him. Like the brilliant Solzhenitsyn, the uneducated peasant thought the Americans and British should learn the true nature of their Soviet "ally." He made it his business to try to tell them what he knew of the horrific slaughter in the woods at Katyn. He had a terrible time making himself understood; an American military policeman almost did the peasant the "favor" of returning him to Soviet custody. Finally, Krivosertsov made his way to a Polish DP (displaced persons) camp in western Germany.

So it was that on May 31, 1945, nine days after Van Vliet made his top secret statement in Washington, D.C., and was ordered into silence, Krivosertsov made his statement about Katyn to a Polish chaplain. That statement would be entered into the 1952 congressional records of the Katyn cover-up investigation.

Ivan would make it to England, where he lived and worked quietly under a new name. Kept to himself mainly, although he made a new Russian friend, or so the story goes. One day in 1947, Ivan didn't show up for work. No one knew where he was until he was finally found outside London far from his place of work in an empty shed near an abandoned orchard, hanged. The authorities said it was suicide, but they said very little.[107]

It was second nature by then.

CHAPTER EIGHT

Sure, we saw no forced labor. When we approached anything that looked like it, we closed our eyes tight and kept them closed. We weren't going to lie about it.

—JIMMY ABBE, AMERICAN PHOTOGRAPHER, 1933[1]

I assure you that, if I see something which I don't like, or which, if revealed in the United States might create an unfavorable impression, I will keep quiet about it. The greatest desire of my life is to improve Soviet-American relations.

—WENDELL WILLKIE[2]

Up to thirty books on the Gulag were published in Europe before mine and hardly one of them was even noticed.

—ALEKSANDR SOLZHENITSYN[3]

There is no coming to terms with Communism's battle against the Free World without also coming to terms with the simultaneous battle waged between the David-forces of exposure and the Goliath-forces of concealment. It is in David's unhappy story of betrayal and defeat where I have come closest to the answers to the questions that became a driver for this book: why Soviet crime never made a dent in public consciousness; and why the Soviet fall wasn't cause for widespread affirmation.

In turning these questions over, I keep coming back to that first speech Solzhenitsyn gave in the USA on June 30, 1975. I find that it contains a set of clues to all of the mysteries that relate to that undetected crime I began setting up some chapters ago. In 1975, Solzhenitsyn, like the witnesses and investigators who came before him and also after—Jones and Muggeridge and Lyons and Utley and Valtin and Krivitsky and Dies and Bricker and Bullitt and Earle and Van Vliet and Kravchenko and Bentley and Chambers and Jordan and McCarthy and Epstein and Conquest and Bukovsky and others—still seemed to operate under the assumption that principles of logic were universal, that adherence to them, that trust in them, was the distinguishing basis of the non-Communist world as he (and all the others, once) thought they knew it.[4] It was a world, they all seemed to believe, in which ideology did not trump all, in which ideology had not infected all; certainly in which Communists, fellow travelers, their dupes, and innocents had not penetrated and occupied all. According to the old set of rules—rules that were permanently upended in what may be best understood as the Red Plot Against Conclusions—the logical presentation of hard facts would spur debate, understanding, decision, and action, and in the nick of time to avert disaster. In Solzhenitsyn's maiden American speech, it seems clear that he still believed that the truth, which he, with his special knowledge and unique stature, could marshal, would serve as the essential catalyst in a most salutary and restorative chain reaction.

It was so simple. Recall Solzhenitsyn's string of figures that encapsulated America's post-1933 capitulations to totalitarian Communism: seventeen a year, ten a month, one thousand a month, forty thousand a month.[5] Surely, the *implications* of this number set were obvious: The United States must halt its immoral and submissive accommodations and take action to reorder a moral universe long ago knocked off its axis of principle. Let the historians worry about *why* it went out of whack, Solzhenitsyn also said. He was here to present the facts that would, in their effect, put everything right.

Little wonder the Soviet regime considered Solzhenitsyn dangerous. His novels and other works, beginning in 1962 with *One Day in the Life of Ivan Denisovich,* were narratives of searing revelation. As Solzhenitsyn himself would later write, "The Soviet regime could certainly have been breached only by literature."[6] Indeed, the Soviet regime expended much energy and resources on shoring up this breach, as the voluminous KGB record on meetings and deliberations about Solzhenitsyn shows. Declassified by Boris Yeltsin in 1992 and published in Russian the next year (in English in 1995), this long, weird dossier of secret Soviet government documents, including minutes from Politburo sessions and Central Committee meetings, memos, reports, letters, bugged conversations, and interrogation records, unfolds like an anti-literature of its own,[7] showing how it was that a writer, a novelist, a single man without an army or any power, became the nemesis of the mail-fisted dictatorship, all for the ultimate anti-Soviet "crime": exposure.

Yes, exposure is exactly the same "crime" that Lyons and Chambers and Matthews and Bentley and Jordan and McCarthy and all the rest committed in speaking out about the sinister workings of that same mail-fisted dictatorship *here*. Rather than elevate these heroes to liberty's pantheon, however, we salute the hardened agents of Stalin for invoking the Fifth Amendment against self-incrimination *to this day*. In fact, what was "taking the Fifth," as so many Communists did before Congress, but a tactic to protect Moscow's conspiracy to destroy this country and control the world?

Rather than applaud the truth tellers' courage to break ranks with this conspiracy and bear witness, however, we regard as shameful their acts of exposure. But what was "naming names" but stripping American traitors of their conspiratorial anonymity that made it possible for them to serve a malign, foreign dictatorship?

These are the questions that celebrated Broadway and Hollywood director Elia Kazan asked himself before he finally decided to testify frankly and fully, including "naming names," in front of the House Committee on Un-American Activities in 1952, seventeen years after leaving the Communist Party. "Wasn't what I'd been defending up until now a conspiracy working for another country?" he wrote in his 1988 memoir, *Elia Kazan: A Life.*

"Hadn't I watched my "comrades" staggering through political switch after political switch by instructions not written in this country?

"Was the question really what the 'comrades' said it was, the right to think what you will and say what you believe? Or did it have to do with acts, allegiances, and secret programs?[8]

The answer Kazan came to was this: "I believed that this committee, which everyone scorned—and I had plenty against them, too—had a proper duty. I wanted to help break open the secrecy . . . There was no way I could go along with their [the Communists'] crap that the CP was nothing but another political party, like the Republicans and the Democrats. I knew very well what it was, a thoroughly organized worldwide conspiracy."[9]

That "crap"—that the Communist Party was just like any other political party—became the crown jewel of that thoroughly organized worldwide conspiracy, the precious if false cover story that had to be polished and displayed at any and all costs. Not that this fakery was always believed. In certain quarters, it was always recognized for what it was ("crap"), going back to the early days when, as historian Paul Kengor notes in *Dupes,* CPUSA leaders were "surprisingly open about publishing Moscow's instructions to them."[10] As we've seen, twenty-five years after its 1919 founding, the fact that the CPUSA, its underground offshoots and fronts made up a Kremlin fifth column in the USA had become an issue in the 1944 presidential campaign when GOP vice presidential candidate Ohio governor John Bricker raised it; in 1950, CPUSA claims of kinship with all other American political parties, past and present, was eruditely debunked by Supreme Court Justice Robert H. Jackson in an opinion.[11] Still the "crap" kept on coming back. It never went away. Proofs of American Communist subservience to Moscow remained mainly and elusively circumstantial. At some tipping point, probably after the destruction of Joe McCarthy, the "crap" became consensus, sometimes uneasily regarded or even quietly rejected consensus, but consensus nonetheless. It was an honest-to-goodness "Party" line: There was no "conspiracy" overseen and funded by Moscow to overthrow the USA. American Communists were just a bunch of harmless, idealistic, and homespun "progressives." Freedom of conscience, and all that. Of course, they deserved to be left alone in peace and privacy (and secrecy). *Have you left no sense of decency?*

Director Edward Dmytryk, the one charter member of the Hollywood Ten who later broke Communist ranks to testify before Congress as a "friendly" witness, analyzed this breathtaking scam in his 1996 memoir, *Odd Man Out:* "What thousands of confused liberals have believed . . . was that one must allow a seditious Party to destroy one's country rather than expose the men and women who *are* the Party. In other words, naming names is a greater crime than subversion. That's what I call the 'Mafia Syndrome' and I find no shame or indignity in rejecting it."[12]

Naming names is a greater crime than subversion. In this mantra, confused or not, lies one of the greatest Big Lies the Goliath-forces of concealment put over: the inversion of morality. When unmasking the nation's secret enemies became a greater crime than their secret war on the nation, they won. This was not only the belief of "confused liberals" once upon a time, it remains the essence of consensus today, particularly as the whole era further recedes from memory. By now, we have only the most basic, key-word associations.

Taking the Fifth: freedom of conscience, as American as apple pie.

Naming names: what stool pigeons do; a crime.

Actually, working incognito on behalf of a murderous dictatorship of thugs to subvert the U.S. Constitution and advance totalitarianism is the only crime here—just not according to the Communist paradigm Americans learned to accept, no questions asked. Thus, the Kazans and Dmytryks and other "friendly" witnesses remain "traitors" in the fuzzy lens of dimming memory. No one thinks to sharpen the focus by asking, "traitors" to what? The answer, of course, is traitors to the evil empire.

Thus, our true heroes were branded with the twentieth century's scarlet letter—*A* for anti-Communist. There was no bricks-and-mortar Gulag for them; their punishment was social, professional, and also political, what Eugene Lyons called "a species of intellectual ostracism" that was "the price of rebellion."[13] But it was forever. On the occasion of Kazan receiving a lifetime achievement Oscar in 1999, half a century after he identified for Congress eight Communist agents serving Stalin, the biggest butcher the world has seen (next to Mao)—sixty-seven years after the Terror Famine, sixty years after the blood purges, fifty-nine years after the Katyn Forest Massacre, fifty-two years after forced repatriation and servitude and death of two million in Europe (and Katyn witness Ivan Krivosertsov's murder), fifty-one years after Victor Kravchenko proved the crimes of the Soviet system in a Paris courtroom, forty-three years after Hungary, thirty-one years after Prague and the documented revelations of Robert Conquest's *The Great Terror,* twenty-five years after the publication of *The Gulag Archipelago,* seventeen years after martial law came to Solidarity-inspired Poland, sixteen years after the shootdown of KAL Flight 007, nine years after the fall of the Berlin Wall, six years after Yelstin admitted the USSR was responsible for Katyn and partly opened the archives (before Putin sealed them again)—the surviving Stalinist remnant in Hollywood rallied to fresh applause to protest "Kazan's betrayal." Talk about retarded.

"Judas," we were supposed to hiss at the eighty-nine-year-old director; *"rat,"* we were supposed to spit. Indeed, the cover of *The Village Voice* marking Kazan's Academy honors depicted a sweaty Kazan grasping a rat-shaped Oscar. The putatively mainstream *New York Times* carried a column by Maureen Dowd, who castigated Kazan's efforts to unmask the secret agents of totalitarianism as "scuzzy" and lionized one such agent, Communist-blacklisted screenwriter Bernard Gordon, eighty-one, who co-organized the anti-Kazan protests with former Communist-blacklisted screenwriter Abe Polonsky. "We must protest everything Citizen Kazan stood for," said Gordon, giving off an odd whiff of Robespierre. Polonsky, eighty-eight, went on to say, "I'll be watching . . . hoping someone shoots him."[14]

Such nice people.

Brimming with bile, the extremely Old Left still hated Kazan for having gotten away with his "apostasy." Had he, though? When Kazan died at age ninety-four in 2003, his lionizing obituaries were also studded with pointed rebuke. A trailblazing director, a theatrical and screen giant, yes; but he "named names," he "angered" people, and "his decision to inform on others" prompted "many in the arts" to "excoriate him for decades."

"Inform" on *"others"?* Note the verb of darkness and the innocent noun. Kazan decided to break silence on a treasonous cabal operating under Stalin's orders. Should he have been "excoriated for decades" for that? Not unless his book of deeds was written from the point of view of the Politburo. *But so it was.* That's the point. As Kravchenko understood long ago, Moscow's subversion of the American mind—the winning strategy of the Goliath-forces of concealment—was its greatest success.

When Solzhenitsyn, preceded by Part One of his magnus opus, *The Gulag Archipelago,* was ejected into the West, he presented this same set of Communist conspirators and fellow travelers with a new version of an old problem: how, in the face of his formidable witness, to maintain the pretense that the

USSR was not a moral monstrosity that had destroyed and enslaved and broken millions of people. It's not at all the case that Solzhenitsyn was the first emissary of this grimmest reality. Memoirs and scholarship of the Gulag filled Western bookshelves for decades preceding his works. As early as 1949, for example, a *New York Times* reviewer could describe *Soviet Gold,* Vladimir Petrov's testament of his six years as a slave laboring among the *dokhodyagas* of Kolyma ("prisoners who have been reduced to the lowest level of physical and moral degradation") as "another addition to the already extensive list of memoirs by former prisoners of slave labor camps."[15]

I, for one, certainly didn't realize there existed any such "already extensive list" in 1949, but so there did. Not just a list, either. In 1951, a book called *The Soviet Slave Empire* by Albert Konrad Herling was said by *The New York Times* to have earned a special place in the "whole library [that] has already been written on the subject." *The whole library that's already been written on the subject?* That the Gulag wasn't news will come as news to many readers. It also deepens the mystery about our numbness toward Soviet crime. After all, if a decent Gulag library in 1951 was anchored by the seminal 1947 book *Forced Labor in Soviet Russia* by David J. Dallin and Boris I. Nikolaevsky,[16] in which the authors demonstrate that ten million to fifteen million slaves were at that time powering the Soviet economy, why did we still need to wait two and three decades for the findings of Conquest, the life story of Solzhenitsyn, the suffering of Sahkarov? That said, looking back it turns out the Dallin-Nikolaevsky book was quite influential. Not only were the authors famously and fatuously denounced at the UN in 1947 by the ubiquitous and terrible Andrei Vyshinsky, then Soviet deputy foreign minister (we last saw him fixing the docket at Nuremberg to exclude Soviet war crimes), as "complete idiots or gangsters," for their thoroughly corroborated research into Gulag suffering, but in 1960, the conservative quarterly *Modern Age* credited the book with creating a public furor that made forced labor "a liability in the propaganda wars" for the USSR, which, after all, claimed to be "a regime representing the workers of the world." As a result, *Modern Age* wrote, Kremlin leaders "whittled down" the institution of Soviet slavery. *Modern Age* summed up, "It is not too much to say that thousands of people owe their freedom to events set in motion by this book."[17]

Solzhenitsyn himself may well have been among them. A quarter century later, he would hit us on the head with that 1,800-page trilogy of his. To be sure, he wasn't your average anti-Communist émigré. An international celebrity before he crossed Andropov's KGB, the celebrated novelist was a darling of "thaw." He offered Khrushchev-approved "proof" that Stalin's regime, retroactively in bad odor after some of the nasty bits about it had seeped into Western consciousness, had been an Communist aberration—a tiny band of extremists, you might say, who had hijacked a great political philosophy. However, the author's renewed persecution and suppression by the post-"thaw" Communist police state under Breshnev, symbolizing the persecution of so many others, threatened the high gloss of 1970s "normalcy" that made "friendship," "détente," "parity," "world peace," and, of course, "moral equivalence" possible; and, more than possible, so alluring to the West. "We're all the same, you know," as the le Carré darling said. Solzhenitsyn bore witness to the falsehood of this popular conceit. In fact, the more indelibly Solzhenitsyn engraved the reality of the Communist police-cum-slave state on the West's radar screen, the more jeopardized was the whole moral equivalence brand, which, as we've seen, had its tragic origins in recognition back in November 1933. The more Solzhenitsyn laid waste to the West's record of Soviet appeasement, the more garish and lurid the political spectrum of Poltiburo-red to Roosevelt-pink appeared.

This explains why the elite Western embrace of Solzhenitsyn was always cold and stiff. Arm's-length was the only way to keep Solzhenitsyn's blacks and whites from getting all over those gorgeous le Carréllian grays. The irony is rich: What we learned about the Holocaust made us excoriate the German people for turning a blind eye to Nazi camps for the twelve years their country was a National Socialist police state; what we *refused* to learn about rolling Soviet holocausts made us *congratulate* ourselves for turning a blind eye to Soviet camps for the forty, fifty years we so often apologized for and enabled the Communist police state. Nothing had changed since the 1930s, when Eugene Lyons observed that "people defended executions and concentration camps in Russia and went purple denouncing the same phenomena in Germany."[18]

Solzhenitsyn threatened this impossible balance. "No other regime on earth," he wrote in *The Gulag Archipelago,* "could compare with [the Soviet Union] either in the number of those it had done to death, in hardness, in the range of its ambitions, or in its thorough-going and unmitigated totalitarianism—no, not even the regime of its pupil Hitler, which at that time blinded Western eyes to all."[19]

Maybe it was for this particularly apt equivalence—Soviet-Nazi, not US-USSR—that Solzhenitsyn became one of KGB Chairman Yuri Andropov's "personal obsessions," as Andrew and Mitrokhin write, and *also a thorn in the underside of the West.*

Ah so. The forces of concealment, East and West, had a common enemy in the forces of exposure, East and West.

Soviet-Nazi equivalence was the equivalence, so patent as to be obvious, that dared not breathe its name.[20] It called too much attention to the sordidly symbiotic liaisons between the "enlightened" Left and the Stalinist Left. Given a shared discomfort, then, it might be said that Andropov did Western elites a favor when he expelled Solzhenitsyn from the USSR in 1974. Somehow, the KGB boss sensed that taking away Soviet citizenship and forcing freedom onto the Nobel-Prize-winner would ultimately diminish the writer's voice and shrink his image as The Man against The Regime. At the very least, life in the West would wear away the imposing mantle of suffering witness that endowed the author with his rare sanctity. Outside the Soviet Union, speaking and writing in uncensored opposition to the Communist system would no longer carry the same risk, nor exemplify the same courage. It might even invite a new, critical scrutiny. What sounded brave and soulful in dreary Moscow might sound shrill and repetitive and, worse, *anti-Communist* in storybook Switzerland, which is where the author first took refuge.

Andropov, meanwhile, didn't trust exile alone to neutralize Moscow's Solzhenitsyn problem. He also directed the KGB to execute a "multifaceted plan" to destabilize and discredit Solzhenitysn and his family in the West.[21] It was, Andrew and Mitrokhin write, "a plan striking for the enormous priority and resources devoted to it."[22] Solzhenitsyn's Swiss ménage, for example, was penetrated by a band of Soviet agents posing as Prague Spring dissidents up to and including the Czech translator of *Gulag*.

Even more disturbing, though, is that KGB "active measures" were probably unnecessary to undermine Solzhenitsyn in the Free World. He, his family, and his gravitas arrived in the West during the high days of détente. Never mind that détente was always a ruse, a sham, as Brezhnev himself declared in a secret 1973 speech to Communist Party leaders in Prague, to enable the Soviets to keep their diplomatic togs on while building military strength and, importantly, terror networks. Never mind that British intelligence passed along Brezhnev's secret, between-us-Communists declarations to this effect to American officials (and someone leaked a version to *The New York Times*). Never mind that the British considered the Soviet dictator's admission of the tactical sham of détente to be "dynamite, comparable in importance" to Khrushchev's secret 1956 speech admitting (some of) the crimes of Stalin.[23] Notice how it is that we all of us know from Our Narrative about the Khrushchev secret speech; the Brezhnev secret speech, however, remains almost entirely obscure. Emphasis on the former moved the Soviet program forward; emphasis on the latter would surely have set it back.

"The [Brezhnev] report was as welcome as a dose of chicken pox as far as Henry was concerned," an unnamed source told *The Boston Globe* in 1977.[24] "Henry" would be Henry Kissinger, of course, high priest and night nurse of détente in the West. He managed to innoculate his White House team against the Brezhnev speech. Or, in other words, he convinced others to discount the *implications* of the report, which directly threatened détente, rapprochement, "arms control," "summits"—exactly where the 1970s were at, or at least supposed to be. (Chalk another one up for the Goliath-forces.) The 1970s were also all about Soviet expansionism into the Third World, sensational kidnappings, bank heists, airport shootings, strings of hijackings linked to the rise of international terrorism, but never mind. So what if this organized unrest initiated a new age of Islamic jihad that flourishes three decades later?

We may forget, but throughout the 1970s and beyond, Red terrorists from Europe and the Islamic world struck at civilian targets from Italy to Sweden to Japan to Israel. Not that we ever thought of that world as Islamic; it was always described as "Arab." Often directed by Cubans, Arabs, and Czechs, these forces were clandestinely bankrolled, trained, and supported by Moscow to destabilize the West. Such were the findings of Claire Sterling published in *The Terror Network,* the groundbreaking 1981 book that became a bible to the Cold Warriors of the incoming Reagan administration due to its exposé of the Soviet-sponsored international network of Communist and, again, less noticed at the time, *Muslim* terrorists. "In effect, the Soviet Union had simply laid a loaded gun on the table, leaving others to get on with it," Sterling wrote, summing up the Soviet modus operandi as evil clockmaker of international terrorism.[25]

Once again, the response of Western leaders to this Soviet assault on Western society was an "official flight from reality," as Sterling put it. She describes what was by then the familiar mode of Western behavior: a mass avoidance of all the densely accumulating evidence that led to the conclusion that the Soviet Union was the culprit behind the chaos and terror. This led to a group hug around delusion. This phenomenon is familiar to Robert Conquest, who has observed the Western impulse to avoid judgment on Soviet crime through undue "concentration on reputable, or reputable-sounding phenomena." This leads, he writes, to "an attempt to tame the data or, perhaps more correctly, a mental or psychological bent towards blocking the real essentials, the real meaning."[26]

Why? Why would anyone want to block the real meaning of anything? In the cases where facts are discarded for their gross incompatibility with principles of ideology, it comes down to a panicky impulse to avoid scrapping the ideology, especially if doing so necessitates the unpleasant exertions of self-defense. Surely, this defines a kind of mental cowardice, perhaps a new kind. The new Big Lie that arose in the 1970s was to save not only the Soviet conspiracy but also Western face. This led to the delusion that there was no such thing as Moscow-directed terrorism. Rapprochement was the answer; it sounded nice in French, and it was protected by a fresh onslaught of *dezinformatsiya* from the West as much as the East.

Solzhenitsyn's voice threatened the whole, phony, passing parade. What could official Washington do but look the other way when he arrived in 1975? It was the old ostrich routine: closed doors at the Ford White House; something about the president's "scheduling difficulties." If the 1973 British intel report debunking détente had given Kissinger chicken pox, it's easy to imagine him breaking out in hives at the approach of the Russian author two years later. Naturally, as Dr. K later put it at a press conference called to explain the Solzhenitsyn snub, he personally had "enormous respect and admiration" for Solzhenitsyn. Why, Kissinger continued, Solzhenitsyn's work "is one of the few unclassified documents I have been reading" (and everyone knew what an admirably, enviably busy man he was). "This country can well afford to listen" to Solzhenitsyn's views, he continued, "without worrying about what effect it will have on the foreign policy interests of the United States."

Of course, there was a "but."

Busy Kissinger could make time to read Solzhenitsyn, Americans could "well afford" to listen to him, but . . . senior White House officials couldn't meet with him. In that German-inflected monotone Kissinger explained, "From the point of view of foreign policy the symbolic effect of that can be disadvantageous—which has nothing to do with a respect either for the man or for his message."[27]

Why does this sound so familiar?

We respect the man and his message; just not their symbolic effect on foreign policy. Why, show Solzhenitsyn the respect he deserves and the Soviets might think we actually believe their regime and its totalitarian system are from hell.

Up and down, it was the old story. Facts, sure; but conclusions? *Nyet.* The evils of the system; yes. The system is evil, no. There was that wedge again. Claire Sterling, busy tracking KGB activity through the 1970s terror decade, stumbled into it and reported in her book, incredulously, about the repeated failures, or refusals, of Western officials to assess glaring evidence of Soviet culpability, Soviet strategy, Soviet aggression. It was denial—concealment—of the Terror Famine, the show trials, the blood purges, Katyn Forest, and so much more, all over again. Only this time, denial didn't suppress the facts about barbarous attacks on the captive peoples of the evil empire, but rather about barbarous attacks *against our own people in our own Western societies.* We had hit new lows—again.

Shockingly enough, Sterling herself, the Cassandra of Soviet terror-crime, was subject to this same syndrome of denial. In her foreword, as she prepares to introduce readers to the Moscow-supported networks of Marxist-Leninist revolutionary terror gangs united by their effort to destroy lives, property, peace, and freedom in the non-Communist West, Sterling strikes a note of preemptive apology for the truths she has uncovered. "It would have been easier," she begins, to write about right-wing terrorists—"always a virtuous point."

She continues, "Writing about left-wing Red terrorists did not make me feel virtuous: it saddened me. Few of us, in my generation or my children's, can easily shake off the belief that the Left is always and necessarily Good."[28]

Et tu, Claire?

Sterling's comment is testament to the awesome powers of "the belief" in the Big G-Goodness of the "Left," the political, cultural catchall term we use to encompass all abstractions and ideologies of the revolutionaries and "reformers" who were, and are, naive or egotistical or zealous or power-mad enough to force utopian transformation on the rest of us by government fiat, by mandatory "inclusiveness," by police-backed diktat. The Left is all and only about social harmony by command performance. We can chalk up at least one hundred million murders to its most successful alumni, as tallied by *The Black Book of Communism,* but the animating spirit of "the Left" still retains its glow, its catechisms archaic but basically unchanged, the faith long having become a hardwired reflex:

Left, Good; Right, Bad.

"The people," good; We, the People, "imperialist."

Individuals (especially businessmen), greedy.

Hollywood Blacklist, bad.

Hollywood Ten, martyrs (except "squealer" Dmytryk).

Elia Kazan, Judas.

Communists: persecuted freethinkers. *Have you left no sense of decency?*

McCarthyism: repression.

Mao, expensive decorative art.

Che Guevara, fashion statement.

Ho Chi Minh, agrarian.

Mommy, who's Ho Chi Minh, and what's an agrarian?

Scratch Ho. The signposts recede from view, but the direction is fixed, which is why "evil empire" still triggers that patronizing chortle to make Pavlov proud and earn his dog a cookie. *How Neanderthal can you get?* says the roll of the eyes. No answer is necessary because our minds have been battened down against logic and morality both. *Seventeen a year, ten a month, a thousand a month, forty thousand a month . . .* Solzhenitsyn's moral calculus, like Conquest's compendia of Communist slaughter, or Bentley's eyewitness evidence of Communist treason, or Bukovsky's "détente" nightmare in psychiatric hospitals and prisons, remains beyond our ken and comprehension, much like Solzhenitsyn himself, who was virtually locked out of the White House in the summer of 1975. Twenty-four years later, Elia Kazan had to be sneaked into a side door to receive his special Oscar to avoid pro-Communist (pro-hundred-million-killed?) protesters in front of a Los Angeles theater. In the meantime, Solzhenitsyn never really got *inside* with his story, the one he always wanted to tell us Americans.

The historical trigger for him was a toast Franklin Roosevelt made to Winston Churchill and Joseph Stalin in late 1943 at the Tehran Conference, the first of two utterly disastrous wartime meetings (unless you were Stalin) of the so-called Big Three in which the Soviet Union presented its measurements for the "Iron Curtain," and Britain and the United States helped him hang it.

You want some more Poland? Help yourself. The Baltics? Why not? Those two million anti-Bolsheviks in Western Europe? You're right, Uncle Joe; they should be shot! To the Gulag with them. Here, let us help . . .

That was still to unfold when Captain Solzhenitsyn, probably glued to a radio in a cold encampment somewhere in Europe's east, got stuck on a point of principle. As he recalled it, the American president's Tehran toast went like this: "I do not doubt that the three of us"—meaning the "Big Three," Roosevelt, Churchill and Stalin—"are leading our peoples in accordance with their desires and their aims." Solzhenitsyn and his comrades were aghast. How could FDR say such a thing—that Stalin, the blood-drenched dictator of fear, was fulfilling the Russian people's "desires and aims"? Did Roosevelt believe this? As Solzhenitsyn said in his 1975 address, "How can this be understood? Let the historians worry about that. At the time, we listened and were astonished. We thought, 'When we reach Europe, we will meet the Americans and we will tell them.' "[29]

How poignant. These Red Army Rover Boys actually seemed to believe: We will meet the Americans and we will tell them . . . *and everything will be all right.* This wasn't naïveté, exactly. It was just the regular old way of thinking, of assessing what Orwell called "neutral fact," of analyzing the situation and judging it. In essence, Solzhenitsyn believed two plus two does indeed equal four, not five; this, however, contradicted the ideological order.[30] It was the same honest impetus of logic that drove an older and more seasoned apparatchik such as Victor Kravchenko to defect and fire his salvo in *The New York Times* against the Soviet regime in April 1944 and, later, to go to court to prove his claims (and win!) in Paris in 1949; it was what inspired World War I veteran and businessman Maj. George Racey Jordan to request leave from his Montana airfield to knock on government doors in Washington in January 1944 to tell somebody with clout somewhere that something fishy was going on with Lend-Lease. It was what impelled American aristocrat William C. Bullitt into the Oval Office to plead with FDR to start facing those same facts in early 1943; and it was what would move ex-POW Maj. John Van Vliet to jump the line home from the war's end to tell what he had eyewitnessed at Katyn. The same goes for frightened, defenseless Ivan Krivosertsov, who would make his way on foot from Soviet-occupied Bremen to the Western Zone during that first summer after the war in Europe, driven to tell what he had seen America's bosom "ally" do to thousands of Polish officers in those dark woods, terrified he would be murdered by the NKVD first. So it went for all the others, all of whom believed they possessed the clinching, cinching evidence necessary to show, to prove, that a contest between deceived good and deceptive evil was taking place. Just tell the truth, they thought—about the lies, the crimes, the secret plots—and the all-out war against morality, truth, and liberty would be exposed and thwarted.

This was our army of Davids, fighting for exposure. Common sense, common decency, *natural reflexes*, they assumed, would take care of everything else. I italicize "natural reflexes" because the surprise and irony is that there weren't any—or, rather, that they had been reconditioned to respond to new and very different stimuli.

Solzhenitsyn, of course, never made it to the Elbe. On February 9, 1945, three months shy of Germany's unconditional surrender, he was arrested by the NKVD in eastern Prussia for the "crime" of "criticizing" Stalin in a personal letter. (He had told a joke.) He was sentenced to eight years in the Gulag. "At that time this was considered a mild sentence," Solzhenitsyn would write, matter-of-fact.[31] Two days later, on February 11, 1945, millions of people living in Europe's East and two million more scattered by war throughout Europe's West were also convicted and much more severely sentenced to life, and, in many cases, death. They had been secretly condemned to Stalin's custody at Yalta by Allied agreement on the Soviet occupation of Eastern Europe, which we mostly know about, and Soviet "repatriation," which we mostly don't.

In contemporary terms, "repatriation" was a policy of reverse "ethnic cleansing" that scrubbed Western Europe of displaced or captured Russians and other nationals claimed by the Soviet regime. Who did the scrubbing? The sick-making fact is, *British and American troops.*[32] Between two and, possibly, as many as four million people were thus transferred, often forcibly, with many hundreds of thousands of these unfortunates becoming slave laborers in the Gulag.[33] Which presents us with a truly fearful symmetry: Just as Soviet occupiers couldn't have reached Eastern Europe without American Lend-Lease trucks, millions of Soviet refugees couldn't have ended up in the Gulag without British and U.S. soldiers.

Here was a harrowing new development in our self-destructive relationship with Communist Russia. Having swallowed any number of Big Lies about Soviet atrocities (Terror Famine and on) to maintain sunny relations with the USSR, having perpetrated a Big Lie ourselves about a Soviet atrocity (Katyn) to continue to fight on as supposedly like-minded allies, the Western Allies went further still: We became *accessories* to a Soviet atrocity—a war crime and crime against humanity.

How did this happen? There are many factors to consider. With unseemly enthusiasm, the British took the lead on the repatriation issue and we followed, despite the moral consternation of U.S. diplomats such as Joseph Grew, who, as acting secretary of state, balked at the policy. Again, the fix was in. Historian Nikolai Tolstoy writes that "negotiations at Yalta on the issue appear to have been handled chiefly by Alger Hiss, the inexperienced Secretary of State, Edward Stettinius, being ill-equipped to conduct them."[34] Correction: the inexperienced secretary of state, Edward Stettinius, being *"the loyal protégé" of agent of Soviet influence Harry Hopkins and therefore you bet* "ill-equipped" to conduct them. Meanwhile, as State Department official J. Anthony Panuch would later testify under oath before Congress, Hiss exerted "Svengali-like influence over the mental processes of Junior Stettinius."[35]

So if Soviet spy Hiss presided over the repatriation issue, who presided over Hiss? In his 1994 memoir, Soviet spymaster Pavel Sudoplatov, whose duty it was to prepare psychological profiles of the members of the American delegation at Yalta, wrote, "I had the feeling that Hiss was acting under the instructions of Hopkins."[36]

Creepy feeling, no? Hiss would journey from Yalta to Moscow, where, Venona tells us, he would be secretly decorated by a grateful Soviet government.[37] Was he regaled with Soviet testimonials about how he had fended off an existential threat to Mother Russia even as Solzhenitsyn was at the very same time beginning his prison sentence for anti-Soviet behavior? Hiss, after all, had helped ensure the destruction of the anti-Bolshevik masses in free Europe, many hundreds of thousands of whom had actually taken up arms against the Communist dictatorship by serving in the German army. Some were German-captured slave laborers; others wanted to fight the Communist dictatorship under any flag. Indeed, according to Julius Epstein, who broke this story wide open in 1973—Epstein himself a refugee from Nazism whose trailblazing 1949 research triggered Congress's inquiry into the cover-up of Katyn[38]—it was the 850,000-strong army of Gen. Andrei Andreyevich Vlasov, having "gone over to the other side to save their country from Stalin" and having later surrendered to U.S. forces in German uniform, that "formed the core of those forcibly repatriated between 1944 and 1947."[39]

In effect, then, we helped Stalin liquidate a potentially history-changing, anti-Communist rebellion before it could begin?

Yes. Once again, the implications are stunning, even overwhelming, particularly given the enumerated toll of suffering and death that blackens this unreckoned stretch of Allied history. Now an obsolete road long overgrown and forgotten, *Uncle Sam and John Bull once traveled it together to betray an anti-Communist Russian army of nearly one million soldiers to death and to the Gulag.* It was "truly the last secret, or one of the last, of the Second World War," Solzhenitsyn wrote of repatriation in 1973 when Julius Epstein's research into "Operation Keelhaul," the U.S. Army code name for the forced repatriation of Soviet POWs and displaced persons, first became public. (Notice how Solzhenitsyn hedged his bets—"or one of the last." This was wise, as it turns out.) He continued, "Having often encountered these people in camps, I was unable to believe for a whole quarter-century that the public in the West knew *nothing* of this action of the Western governments, of this massive handing over of ordinary Russian people to retribution and death."[40]

"This massive handing over" of millions of refugees from the USSR, from generals of armies to intellectuals, Cossacks, kulaks, teachers, peasants, and workers, men, women, and children, took place practically within earshot of the gavels of the Nuremberg Trials, then in session. Occasionally, the deportations made the papers at the time, piecemeal, to be sure, and without a sense of their scope. At least something about them was reported nonetheless, and in the prominent pages of *The New York Times:*

DACHAU—Ten renegade Russian soldiers, in a frenzy of terror over their impending repatriation to the homeland, committed suicide today during a riot in the Dachau prison camp . . .

Twenty-one others were hospitalized, suffering from deep gashes that they inflicted on themselves, apparently with razor blades . . . Many suffered cracked heads from the nightsticks wielded by some 500 American and Polish guards [January 20, 1946].

ROME—Many thousands of persons hostile to the present regime in the Soviet Union are being forcibly sent there by Americans and the British under the Yalta Agreement, Eugene Cardinal Tisserant asserted today, and he said the Catholic Church constantly received appeals from "displaced persons" terrified of being sent back to territory now controlled by Russia . . .

The Cardinal gave the writer the permission to quote him, saying "It will compromise me, but the world must know of these things. [March 5, 1946]"

The world must know of these things . . .
We will meet the Americans and we will tell them . . .

The world—the Americans—didn't care. Just like the admiral who had to check with his imam back at the beginning of the book. It wasn't knowledge or information that anyone needed, or wanted, to judge for himself. The facts could all be neutralized in an ideological interpretation.

Following the appearance of the Dachau story, Gen. A. Deniken, the elderly former commanding general of the White Russian armies (1917–20), which were supported by the USA, not incidentally, in our completely forgotten first war against the brand-new Bolshevik regime, wrote an extraordinary letter to Gen. Dwight D. Eisenhower, the commanding general of the European theater. The Russian general wanted to explain to this modern Colossus why it was that his countrymen "prefer death to repatriation to the Soviets." The letter, dated January 31, 1946, was also a plea for their lives. "Presuming that you are not fully acquainted with the true story concerning these people," Deniken described the extenuating circumstances that led these men to serve in Nazi Germany's army, none of which, he asserted, had to do with "Germanophilism" ("they hated the Germans," he wrote). He described the harrowing experiences of Red Army soldiers captured by Nazis—the exhaustion, the cattle cars, the bayonets, the cold, the death toll; their starvation and bestial treatment as Nazi-certified *untermenschen;* their decisions to accept rations and freedom as conscripts in the German army; their desire to "join the ranks of the Anglo-American armies."

Now, he continued, they knew exactly what awaited them in "Soviet paradise." He wrote:

No wonder on being assembled in Dachau they sought immediate death— cutting their throats with small razor blades, suffering unimaginable agonies and tortures, setting fire to the barracks, discarding their clothing to burn quickly, baring their chests to American bayonets and bowing their heads to American clubs—all this not to get into Soviet prisons.

I can imagine the feelings of the American officers and soldiers who participated in such executions.

General, there are the provisions and the paragraphs of the "Yalta Treaty," but, there are also traditions of free and democratic people—"the right of asylum"—there are military ethics, which prohibit the use of violence even on the defeated enemy, and, finally, there exist the Christian morals which call for justice and pity.[41]

No soap. Not only did Eisenhower not yield, he didn't reply. Not personally, anyhow. Perhaps, in Conquest's words, it would have broken his "concentration on reputable, or reputable-sounding phenomena," and ruined his attempts "to tame the data." His chief aide answered the Deniken letter on February 18, 1946, with a flat statement denying repatriation was forcible except under certain circumstances—all of which happened to apply to the Russians.

Thus, at least two million people were "repatriated." And We, the People knew nothing or little of it until 1973 when Julius Epstein, an indefatigable truth teller, told this supposedly "last secret." Who was listening then? What do we as a people know of it now?

> American and British soldiers shed tears as they carried out the orders to club and blackjack prisoners into insensibility, hold them down at bayonet point, bind the cut arteries with which they had attempted to commit suicide rather than be returned to Stalin's "justice," shoot their feet so that they could not run, toss maimed and mangled bodies back into trucks after beating them into unconsciousness, or drugging them into insensibility.[42]

Still nothing.

When Epstein's book on the subject, *Operation Keelhaul: The Story of Forced Repatriation*—the product of twenty years of research, of painstakingly prying the release of repatriation documents from the U.S. government—came out in 1973 (unforgivably, no review in *The New York Times*), he could report that there had been at least some public debate in the 1950s on Britain's prominent role in this crime against humanity. Government ministers, including Winston Churchill, then prime minister, were publicly quizzed in Parliament about the operation. "In the United States," Epstein noted, "not one of the surviving high officials responsible for Operation Keelhaul has yet been asked any questions in the Congress." With the exception of the testimony of a few witnesses, including Epstein, who came before Congress in 1956, "the Congress and the American people have never been officially informed about the basic facts concerning Operation Keelhaul, past and present."[43]

To my knowledge, the same holds true four decades later. In this way, this suppressed history of repatriation has reverted to the status of academic curiosity, a line of exotic research with no relevance or impact on us as a nation or on our history. In this way, we lose, for example, the impact of the American betrayal of Vlasov, all the worse since "the Vlasov soldiers surrendered to the British and Americans after they had been expressly invited . . . and after they had received solemn promises that they would not be returned to the Soviets against their will."[44] Epstein explained the deeper implications: "The Vlasov people wanted to fight Stalin and Stalinism—a regime certainly not better than Hitler's Nazi regime—but were condemned by the West for one reason only: that we were allied with Stalin's terror regime."[45]

We had gone over to the devil. Our corruption was complete.

Vlasov's Prague Manifesto of November 14, 1944, could stand next to our own founding documents, but we rejected him and it.

Vlasov wrote, *"There is no worse crime than the one Stalin commits, of destroying countries and suppressing the peoples who strive to preserve the land of their forefathers and build their happiness by their own labor."*

These were the words of the people who gave the lie to the myth—which was by then part of our own belief—that the USSR was a natural ally of democracy and freedom. They had to be destroyed for that.

Vlasov continued, *"The Bolsheviks robbed the peoples of freedom of speech, freedom of political convictions, their personal liberties, free choice of domiciles and travel, freedom of profession, and the opportunity for everyone to take his place in society in accordance with his capabilities. They replaced these freedoms with terror, party privileges, and arbitrariness toward the individual."*[46]

We helped destroy them.

Or: *So, we helped destroy them.*

Who was pulling the strings?

Or: *Who from Communist-occupied Washington was pulling the strings?*

Are such questions unfair? As in, Have I left no sense of decency? Or are they logical, even bloody obvious? Decades later, they remained unanswered, unasked, Epstein's magnificent contribution to the historical record virtually ignored.

One year after Epstein's book came out to little if any mainstream acclaim, a Russian writer—not an army of "Russian outlaws wearing German uniforms," as *The Saturday Evening Post* described the Vlasov forces (which, in fact, liberated Prague from the SS[47])—suddenly appeared in the West to give the lie to this same tedious, overriding myth of Soviet democracy and freedom. This unarmed literary celebrity couldn't be destroyed. His fame was too great, his eyes, the lines on his face, his beard, too familiar. Could he perhaps destroy himself?

It was as a Nobel Prize winner, an international bestseller, and a Gulag-state exile that the Russian author returned in his 1975 speech in Washington, D.C., to the same theme that had driven them all as young men: "But now, after great delay, the same hand has thrown me out of the country and here I am. After a delay of thirty years, my Elbe is here, today. I have come to tell you, as a friend of the United States, what, as friends, we wanted to tell you then."[48]

"My Elbe is here, today." *Now, at last, I cross this final frontier, I break this last barrier, I reclaim my opportunity, stolen so long ago, to bring you, Americans, Good Guys and last, best hopes, the facts you need, the facts you are missing . . . obviously . . . because otherwise (subtext) why would you behave so weakly, so irrationally, so immorally?*

What doesn't seem to have been evident to the great sage was the extent to which we Americans had already closed ourselves, or, *pace* Communist infiltration—and we "only knew the half of it"—the extent to which we had already *been closed* to the calculations, political and moral, he finally had the opportunity to lay before us. In other words, Solzhenitsyn's Elbe might well have been "here, today" in 1975, but there just weren't very many of us left on the riverbank to greet him.

Nor would there have been in 1945. Surprisingly, it is to World War II where we must direct our attention, searching for our missing gaps. We must fill in what's missing from this period even if it is inevitable that what makes us whole also breaks our hearts. As a cultural bulwark, a great wall of history dividing a traditional past from a postmodern present, World War II has long represented a break in the human experience practically as significant as A.D. and B.C. Looking back, the burnished image of the USA, circa 1945, stands out, an admirably simple engine of moral clarity that powered an epic, black-and-white fight against unmitigated evil—Nazi Evil. This, as we have long been taught, was the singular evil in the world (at least until we diagnosed our own postwar conditions of chronic "isms" and "phobias"). As our history books tell us, it was the existential threat of Nazi Germany that spurred finest-hour America into action, driving the aw-shucks avenger to smite evil into rubble and make rubble into new cities. Wasn't Roosevelt, as the accepted lore would have it, devilishly clever to figure out so many cunning tricks to get a legally neutral country like the USA into the fight? He had even made neutrality a plank of his presidential campaign in 1940, lying through his teeth clenched around that cigarette holder the whole time. Wasn't that . . . *wonderful?*

I hope at this point it's needless to say that the view through these red-white-and-blue-colored glasses completely camouflages the hammer-and-sickle that was growing like a catastrophic cancer in the shadow of the swastika. This was the dark vision we were denied by our Communist-occupied government; the core historical plot we were waved off even as we, as a nation, enabled its advance, our blinkered outlook set by the propaganda the Communist-penetrated U.S. government created, controlled, and disseminated. "We became victims of our own propaganda," as Hanson Baldwin put it, and he didn't know the half of it. It wasn't just "the cloak of his popularity" that Roosevelt cast over Stalin by recognizing the Soviet Union, as *Time* magazine put it as early as 1934.[49] It was the systematic censorship and suppression by the U.S.

government, from Roosevelt on down, of all critical truths about the Soviet Union. This meant the systematic censorship and suppression of the truth tellers beginning with old Dr. Wirt. It meant Goliath's total war against David.

"I have noted with concern your plan to publicize your unfavorable opinion of one of our allies," FDR replied to a query from his erstwhile political ally and European emissary, former Pennsylvania governor George Earle, whom we've met earlier. The date was March 22, 1945. "I do not wish you to do so. Not only do I not wish it, I specifically forbid you."

Just to make sure, Roosevelt ordered Earle *to Samoa* for the duration.

A few days after Roosevelt's letter went out, Army Chief of Staff George C. Marshall issued the following order: "Censor all stories, delete criticism Russian treatment." With this March 26, 1945, order, Marshall silenced returning American POWs whose great misfortune it was to have been "liberated" by a hostile, abusive Red Army. Of course, these ex-POWs were the lucky GIs who actually came home from Soviet custody; *as many as twenty thousand U.S. POWs did not,* a hidden moral stain expanded on below.

The concerted, institutional effort to conceal Soviet crime could become absurd at times. After British POW James Allan fled German captivity in 1940 for, he thought, the relative safety of internment in then-neutral Russia, he sustained so much in the way of beatings, brutal interrogations, and solitary confinement at the hands of his Soviet captors that, following his release, he was awarded the Distinguished Conduct Medal, second only to the Victoria Cross. His medal, however, came with *no citation,* no written record—which, of course, is customary—of the conditions under which he distinguished himself. Allan's ordeal at our ally's hands was officially null and void. This is especially nettlesome given that his story was well known to the highest British and also American officials. The first boat available to take Allan home from the USSR happened to be carrying British and American dignitaries from the first Lend-Lease conference in Moscow in October 1941, the one that Harry Hopkins was controlling from his White House bedroom, as noted earlier. Allan, having just been released from the bowels of the Lubyanka, wasn't "well enough to climb into a hammock" or even drink a glass of whisky, but he was able to tell his whole story to many of his powerful shipmates: first to the captain, then again to Lord Beaverbrook (pro-Soviet British minister of war production), to Lord Ismay (Churchill's chief staff officer and military adviser), and later to Averell Harriman (Hopkins's Lend-Lease man in London).[50]

"Goodness gracious, call off the agreement with these monsters to whom we have just pledged $1 billion and enough Dodge trucks to occupy eastern and central Europe," they all didn't say in one voice.

They said nothing, of course, and neither did Allan, whose personal account, *prohibited from publication* until 1947—two years after the war ended—"lay in a cupboard at his home in Yorkshire." His book, which is titled *No Citation,* ends with his return to England, where he boards a train to his home. A railway officer he met on the train "obviously was very reluctant to believe my story," Allan wrote.

Incredulous is probably more like it. After all, the railway officer had no context, no officially, widely acknowledged body of facts into which Allan's story could fit. Reading such accounts makes it clear that even had Aleksandr Solzhenitsyn evaded arrest and made contact with Americans on the western bank of the Elbe—their drive to Berlin and points east, not at all incidentally, having been abruptly halted by Washington to allow the Red Army into Central and Eastern Europe[51]—it is highly unlikely anyone would have regarded him as a modern-day Paul Revere.

I can almost prove it. On March 22, 1945, a month after Solzhenitsyn's arrest and the conclusion of the Yalta Conference, the British ship *Arawa* set sail from Italy on one of the earlier voyages of repatriation (1944–47). It was commanded by a Russian-speaking British officer, Capt. Denis Hills, and carried 1,657 Turkomans, Muslims, Soviet citizens, many of whom had volunteered for the German army to fight Communist rule. They and their multiethnic brothers-in-German-arms from the USSR were "a constant reminder," Nikolai Tolstoy writes, "of the fact that the USSR alone of all the Allies had provided the enemy with thousands of recruits."[52]

Again, how could that be? Hadn't these Third Reich recruits heard OWI broadcasts exonerating the Soviets of guilt for the Katyn Forest Massacre, as read on air in the soothing voice of OWI's Elmer Davis himself?[53] Hadn't they pored over the Siberia pictorial in the December 1944 issue of *National Geographic* magazine (photos and text by Stalinist toady Owen Lattimore[54]), phony smiles and all, which even included happy snaps of Vice President Henry Wallace's trip to Kolyma, the ultimate Gulag hell where hundreds of thousands of people perished (and where NKVD authorities had gone so far as to dismantle guard towers and stock empty stores for the visitors' benefit)?[55] Hadn't they heard, as Harry Hopkins himself said, that Stalin just "was not that kind" of man? Seen Hollywood's 1943 agitprop classic, *Mission to Moscow?* Poor, pre-defection Kravchenko might have cut his clenched palms with his fingernails during a screening of this Hollywood Hallmark card to Stalin's show trials, but, as Hopkins said, he was a "deserter."[56]

Then again, so were these Turkomans, among the first of many hundreds of thousands of people to be carted to Soviet captivity, courtesy of the U.S. and the U.K.

Wait a minute, says the American brain, its brimming repository of "Good

War" nostalgia sloshing over its synapses. This is unbelievable, nonbelievable, as wildy out of place as poisonous toadstools in a fresh turf lawn.

That lawn, those toadstools, symbolize the triumph of concealment: Facts have become something to uproot, weed out from the "existing view of the world." One British veteran of a forced repatriation mission interviewed in 1990 explained that he hadn't spoken a word about his experiences at Bergen-Belsen (yes, that Bergen-Belsen) since 1946. He claimed that after British troops, himself among them, handed over a convoy of Soviet-claimed returnees previously housed at the ex-Nazi concentration camp, Soviet troops fired on the unarmed prisoners before British troops were out of earshot. The vet simply stopped telling the story, Nigel Cawthorne reported in *The Iron Cage,* because "no one would believe him."[57]

No one would, could, or wanted to believe him. That's what happened on the *Arawa*. Tolstoy writes, "Several men approached the Russian-speaking Captain Hills with an air of distress, asking what was happening. They seemed anxious about the reception awaiting them."

It is not the Turkomans' fears so much as Hills's reaction to them that is crucial to reckon with. "Hills himself dismissed their fears with incredulity; *everything he had read or heard in the past four years* led him to picture Soviet Russia as governed by men devoted to overthrowing tyranny and establishing the Four Freedoms" (emphasis added).[58]

No, everything he had read or heard in the past four years had made him bulletproof against reality. In Captain Hills we find the poster child of the age. Just like the Brits who disbelieved the war stories of forced repatriation or Soviet prison camps, Hills had been stripped of his mental tools, the building blocks on which to base any understanding of what these Turkomans were trying to tell him. He had been conditioned by Soviet propaganda *as recreated and disseminated by the Free World.* Does that state of controlled information not define an occupied territory? This was the same mindset that shocked Victor Kravchenko. "The greatest Soviet triumph, it was borne in upon me, was in the domain of foreign propaganda," Kravchenko wrote in *I Chose Freedom.* The American reflex to Soviet reality was either incredulity or "cocksure denials."[59]

Solzhenitsyn would have had no better luck if he'd made it to the Elbe. His story, too, would have arrived like a square peg on a board of round holes. *What was he talking about? Let's not find out because then we would have to do something about it.* On first reading the Tolstoy repatriation book a decade or more ago, I recall thinking that even as the evidence was compelling, it didn't fit in with what I "knew" about the Allied war. I had no awareness of the spiraling moral descent that led to this ultimate Western war crime. Without such awareness, what Tolstoy describes remains somewhat inexplicable. So, as history, it remains set apart. Just like the intelligence history that remains separate from general historians' "existing view of the world," so, too, does the history of forced repatriation. Let these things into our flow of knowledge and the mainstream is forever changed. That's why the bubble of denial must be protected at all costs. This explains why when Ronald Reagan came along and invoked, quite mildly, the "evil empire," the whole world popped.

Tap-tap, goes the magician's wand. Stop looking. There's nothing here, anyway. Move along, back to what's "real": outrage over "McCarthyism"; snorts over *Dr. Strangelove;* scorn for the "Red Scare" (scare quotes required), gnashing teeth over the Hollywood Blacklist, the Vietnam War, Kent State, American imperialists, male chauvinist pigs, Fundamentalist Christians, Rush Limbaugh, Islamophobia, and always back to "McCarthyism." In this alternate reality, it is the Neanderthals, the Red-under-every-bed nutcases, the anti-Communists, who rear their ugly, ugly, buzz-cut heads and five o'clock shadows and *ruin everything.* Make love, not war.

Which is kind of where Solzhenitsyn came in.

In that 1975 speech, he challenged us to rise to a "moral level" and admit—confess—the following: "In 1933 and in 1941 your leaders and the whole Western world made an unprincipled deal with totalitarianism."

Did anyone in the hall know what he was talking about? "Uncle Joe"? The "Good War" that defeated Adolf Hitler? No context.

He kept talking. "We will have to pay for this; someday it will come back to haunt us. For thirty years we have been paying for it. And we're going to pay for it in an even worse way in the future."[60]

What deal? What payment? How could there be anything unprincipled about defeating Nazism? Book sales, hype, and laurel wreaths notwithstanding, Solzhenitsyn's warning clashed with and was repelled by impervious consensus. No one knew the half of it, naturally. Well, some people did. Still, from this very first moment, people may have applauded, but Solzhenitsyn failed to make much headway. Indeed, he progressively lost steam. It wasn't long before secular, self-indulgent elites would find it easy to dismiss the writer for his religiosity, his Russian nationalism, or his antipathy for popular culture. It was the holes in our own understanding, holes of our own making, that swallowed up the substance of his simple message, the point he embodied as living proof, literally, of the evils of Communism. It was more complicated than that, though. As an ex-*zek* from the Gulag, as totalitarianism's witness, Solzhenitsyn also personified an indictment of *American* appeasement, collusion, and complicity with those evils, and, as Kissinger put it in his gruff monotone, "the symbolic effect of that can be disadvantageous."

You can say that again. Famously, Solzhenitsyn would take refuge inside fifty fenced-and-barbed-wired acres in Cavendish, Vermont, where he lived as a recluse for nearly twenty years before returning to post-Soviet Russia—his exile self-imposed, of course. It was a refuge from both KGB harassment and, I am guessing, Western rejection. *Solzhenitsyn didn't understand America,* it was said, even, or should I say especially, after he died at age eighty-nine in 2008. I think it's just as much the case that America didn't understand—*couldn't* understand— Solzhenitsyn. We grew angry with him, impatient, anyway, particularly after his famous 1978 Harvard commencement address.

A surreal coda to this hotly debated address would follow in Moscow, as described by Andrew and Mitrokhin, when a large, even unprecedented group of senior Kremlin and KGB officials came together to assess the impact of Solzhenitsyn's critique of the West delivered at one of its most hallowed but also hollow citadels. Together, these murderers and gangsters sat through a Kremlin screening of the Solzhenitsyn commencement address—that "measure of bitter truth" the writer doled out to America's best and brightest and their doting parents, a highly privileged group of Americans lightly moistened by a June drizzle over Harvard Yard. Hard-bitten Party leaders and senior KGB spies watched the Hated One denounce the silence and inertia of Western collusion with Communism, the moral poverty of materialism, the spiritual wasteland of freedom without purpose. No doubt they also sat through an apparatchik's report on the opprobrium from the U.S. media that, in response, had come down on the head of the former Soviet dissident—now, in effect, practically a Western dissident as well.

What next? Would a new round of "active measures" be in order—some new vector of *dezinformatsiya?* Another insertion of spies masquerading as dissidents into the S. household?

No. This time, according to Mitrokhin's notes, the Soviets decided Solzhenitsyn had really done it—to himself. His critique "had alienated his American listeners" and "could not fail to have a negative effect on his authority in the eyes of the West and his continued use in anti-Soviet propaganda."

So, to conclude, Comrades: "The meeting of KGB and Party notables agreed that no active measures were required to counter the Harvard Address. Solzhenitsyn had discredited himself."[61]

Solzhenitsyn was neutralized, finally. Or is it that we were neutralized— again? I'm still stuck on those dates he had brought to our attention a few years earlier: 1933 and 1941. Diplomatic recognition of the USSR and military alliance with the USSR. On November 7, 1933, we feted the wrong passenger debarking from the *Berengaria*. All eyes were on Maxim Litvinov, who in nine days would, as noted in chapter 7, return to the Soviet embassy a few blocks from the White House with a signed agreement on recognition and announce, "It's in the bag." In *The Forsaken*, Tim Tzouliadis relates that also disembarking from the *Berengaria*, but from steerage class, was a "fugitive American trade unionist" named Fred Beal, who had escaped from the Soviet Union—already a prison—under a false identity. Employed by the Communist Party to work with Americans in Kharkov at a tractor plant, Beal had made a couple of unauthorized field trips outside the city into Terror Famine territory, seeing, feeling, and smelling the horror of the painful deaths of millions by state-engineered starvation. His testimony, like that of so many others, would be virtually ignored. Tzouliadis writes, "On his return to America, for all of his radical contacts, Fred Beal could find only one newspaper willing to print his account of the famine that had claimed an estimated five million lives. The socialist *Jewish Daily Forward* of New York published his testimony in Yiddish."[62] No one on the Left wanted to hear about the Terror Famine. They didn't want to hear about it from a "fugitive trade unionist" such as Beal; they hadn't wanted to hear it earlier in the year from a disillusioned British Socialist like Muggeridge, a Welsh freelancer like Jones, Ukrainians of any stripe. They hewed to the Soviet line as laid down by Litvinov, who, in response to a famine query from U.S. Rep. Herman Kopplemann, a freshman Democrat from Connecticut swept into office with Roosevelt, answered thus:

"Thank you for drawing my attention to the Ukrainian pamphlet. There is any amount of such pamphlets full of lies circulated by the counter-revolutionary organizations abroad who specialize in work of this kind. There is nothing left for them to do but spread false information and forge documents."

We find this Litvinov letter of January 3, 1934, excerpted in *The Congressional Record*, but for much of the preceding year leading up to diplomatic recognition in November of 1933, as Conquest made palpably clear, the truth was "widely available" in the West, with "full or adequate reports" appearing in "scores" of papers.[63] The subject didn't even merit a mention in U.S.-USSR negotiations over recognition, however. This means that ignoring or even tolerating the millions killed by the state-engineered Terror Famine was in fact a prerequisite to recognition—that "unprincipled" deal with totalitarianism, as Solzhenitsyn almost lightly called it. This makes recognition a political sin of epic, also biblical, proportions. Dennis J. Dunn agrees with historian David Mayers, who has argued that the failure of the U.S. government under Roosevelt to reckon with the profound crime of the Terror Famine in negotiations over recognition made it—us—"a passive accomplice to Stalin in the Ukraine."[64] I agree. Which makes 1933 the year of America's Fall.

Martin Weil cites a diary entry of the time expressing similar concern. It was written by Ella Phillips, wife of Undersecretary of State William Phillips, who opposed recognition. "We are only following the majority of other 'Christian' countries," she wrote, "but in so doing I feel we have lost our moral standing . . . It is sad and demoralizing when we lose our honor for expediency."

Weil continues, "Joseph Grew in Tokyo echoes Mrs. Phillips' reservations. Recognition constituted a 'serious sacrifice of principle and letting down of standards.' The United States, he insisted, should never 'palliate by recognition the things Soviet Russia has done and the things it stands for.' "[65]

Alas, that is exactly the impact of the U.S. recognition: to "palliate" the colossal crimes of Soviet Russia, most of which, incredibly, still lay ahead, and all that the evil empire stood for. Indeed, in the unjustifiable act of recognition itself, the answers to my questions begin to take shape. Having thrown the cover of normalcy over the USSR, despite its colossal crimes, despite its revolutionary and repressive collectivism, we became complicit in and transformed by both.

And 1941? This was the year of American military alliance with the USSR, a relationship that quickly morphed into an unseemly episode of something akin to fealty to the USSR, certainly in Communist-occupied Washington, a subservient, worker-queen relationship that would have the effect of entrenching and extending Communist dominion in the world. I think of 1941 as the Second Chance Not Taken. On a course of "convergence" set by FDR eight years earlier, the American people were now harnessed to power Communism forward across the continents, from Berlin to Peking and beyond.

It didn't have to be this way. Just for a moment, indulge in a diplomatic daydream based on a State Department memo Martin Weil fished from the archives for his history of the foreign service, *A Pretty Good Club*. The memo was written in 1941, during that last summer before America entered the war. I like to think it was a beautiful Washington day, long after the cherry blossoms, of course, but still in the thick of roses and clematis, before Washington's springtime green overblooms itself into swampy summer. It's a good bet State Department office windows were open in those pre-air-conditioning days. Maybe a passerby heard the percussive beats of a manual typewriter as Loy Henderson, a resolutely anti-Communist Foreign Service officer, tapped out a plan for the United States in the increasingly likely, even expected event that Hitler's Germany attacked Stalin's Russia somewhere along a line of battle four or five thousand miles away from Foggy Bottom—as indeed the Germans would do in launching "Barbarossa" the very next day. It was June 21, 1941.

The correct American response, according to the man at the typewriter, was to do very, very little. After Nazi Germany attacked Communist Russia, Henderson wrote, the United States should merely relax restrictions on exports to the Russians, while securing a quid pro quo for further assistance. In other words, there should be nothing automatic or unlimited about expanding Bribe-Give, I mean, Lend-Lease, to bulk up the Communist regime. Pay as you go, maybe; or exchange service for service. Weil sums up: "Finally, should the Soviet regime fall, Henderson argued, we should refuse to recognize a Communist government-in-exile, leaving the path clear for establishment of a non-Communist government in Russia after the war."[66]

Finally, should the Soviet regime fall . . . the sky won't fall, too. This is a cloud-parting concept, revealing beacons of a never-before-glimpsed light. *Finally, should the Soviet regime fall . . . we should let it. Finally, should the Soviet regime fall . . . an anti-Communist government could take its place after the war.*

At least at the U.S. State Department, there was life after Stalin, contingency plans after Communist Russia—but this, circa 1941, was subversive talk. A Soviet collapse was not a point of open debate at the time or since. The linch-pin of U.S. military alliance in 1941 was the sacredness of the survival of Soviet Russia.

Washington wasn't Communist occupied for nothing.

Henderson went further, in Weill's paraphrase, urging the U.S. government to declare, "Russia does not fight for the same ideals as the United States."

Such common sense would have, could have, quite literally, changed the world, but to say that the Roosevelt administration took the opposite tack is to miss the point. In declaring, as it did, that Russia fought for the same ideals as the United States, the Roosevelt administration wasn't merely lacking common sense. *The Roosevelt administration was lying.* For example, FDR himself went before the press on September 30, 1941, insisting there was freedom of religion in the USSR. "The claim that Stalin's Russia allowed religious freedom was the first step in a massive pro-Soviet campaign that the White House coordinated for the duration of the war," Dennis J. Dunn writes. Dunn argues that as a believer in "convergence," FDR probably believed the Soviets would change[67]—and probably, I would add, because "Harry" told him so. Nonetheless, it was still a Big Lie, made in the USA, and it confused an already mixed-up populace.

Soon after Nazi Germany and Soviet Russia were at war with each other, William C. Bullitt was troubled enough to inform FDR on July 1, 1941, that "public opinion is now befuddled" by a belief that "Communists have become the friends of democracy." Bullitt suggested the president use his very next press conference to disabuse us all and point out "that Communists in the United States are just as dangerous enemies as ever, and should not be allowed to crawl into our productive mechanism in order later to wreck it when they get new orders from somewhere abroad."[68]

That'll be the day. As described earlier, under Lend-Lease and other government efforts, Communists were in fact invited into our productive and propaganda and military and other mechanisms (and even warned, by Co-President Harry Hopkins, when they got too close for FBI comfort). As for seeking the end of the Communist regime, on the contrary, the Roosevelt administration threw itself into shoring up the USSR at any cost—including, say, the twenty-three out of thirty-four ships lost on just one Lend-Lease supply voyage in July 1942, or, say, the 151,000 troops left unsupplied on the Philippines, or, say, the British colony of Singapore, which was left without air cover in order to satisfy Stalin's needs. If that weren't enough, by mid-1943, as we've seen, the White House, *having been presented with a "list of officials who were supposedly undermining American relations with Russia" by Soviet foreign minister Maxim Litvinov,* resumed the purge of anti-Communist Foreign Service officers begun in 1937. The first round, quite possibly at the behest of but at least with the support of Eleanor Roosevelt and our friend Harry Hopkins, according to Weil,[69] abolished the Division of Eastern European Affairs—too anti-Communist—and sent its chief, Robert Kelley, a true scholar of Russian foreign relations who had opposed Soviet recognition, off to Turkey (naturally?) to finish his career. This so-called New Deal reorganization of the State Department also called for the destruction of "the best Soviet library in the United States," as Loy Henderson called it.

Well, not *destruction,* at least not in the crudest sense of the word. In his memoir, George Kennan elaborated: "The beautiful library was to be turned over to the Library of Congress, to be dispersed there by file numbers among its other vast holdings and thus cease to exist as a library."[70] Kelley's lieutenant, Raymond Murphy, Weil writes, was "ordered to destroy his dossiers on communists, foreign and domestic." Murphy managed to save a considerable portion, Weil tells us in a footnote, later turning them over to the CIA.[71]

All of which is incredible, but commonplace for the Roosevelt years. It is also commonplace in the Obama years, during which both the Justice Department and the Pentagon have overseen methodical purges of "anti-Islamic" educational materials from security and military files and training courses.[72]

A half century before M. Stanton Evans began stumbling across the sinkholes and crevasses in our archives where national records once existed, Rep. Martin Dies discovered that the government's archive of Communist records and correspondence had similarly been destroyed. Dies wrote, "I was informed, confidentially, by a man well placed in the Department of Justice, that they were destroyed after it was learned that the Dies Committee was determined to conduct a full-scale investigation of Communism." Since the Dies Committee was up and running by 1938, the sacking of the State Department library took place in the same general time frame. (What do you know, it was Harry Hopkins, along with the attorney general, who turned down Dies's request for assistance from Roosevelt to help furnish the nascent committee with a staff of lawyers, investigators, and stenographers.[73]) Imagine, had the CPUSA records been saved, how many formerly card-carrying Communists would have been cheated of their grandstanding moment taking the Fifth. Of course, as Dies also pointed out, the CPUSA stopped issuing cards after his committee opened shop.[74]

But I digress.

Following the second great State Department purge in 1943, Loy Henderson, author of the June 1941 fantasy memo, was sent to Iraq, Raymond Murphy was also taken out of the Soviet loop, and another anti-Communist Foreign Service officer, Ray Atherton, was made ambassador to Canada. Henderson was "completely removed from the sphere of Russian affairs during the war period, for advocating a strong line vis a vis the Soviets."[75]

In 1942, between Purges No. 1 and No. 2, Murphy wrote a memo to Henderson: "Current communist tactics [are] to force from government service any public official who will not go along with what they conceive to be the best interests of the Soviet Union and the Communist Party of the United States."[76] Guess what? "Current Communist tactics" worked. Because the American way and the Soviet system were diametrically opposed, FDR had to lie to present common ground to the American people. In order to make his Big Lies stick, he also had to remove the people who knew better. Literally. On a larger and more punitive scale, Kravchenko discussed this same process in action.[77] Easier to converge that way.

That doesn't mean we got away with anything, not really. The reckoning Solzhenitsyn urged upon us so many decades ago remains relevant. That's because from the beginning, one Big Lie has begotten another Big Lie, and maintaining them *to this day,* moving them through the air in perpetuity like a juggler's balls, makes us all Big Liars.

With this in mind, it is instructive to go back to the double standard in U.S. foreign policy that historian Dennis J. Dunn pegs specifically to FDR's embrace of "convergence" theory, the theory that held that the Soviet Union and the United States, would meet, ideologically and operationally speaking, roughly halfway, and any concessions, moral and other, were a price worth paying. I think Dunn's right. The perpetually blinded eye, the unstinting apologetics, the customary capitulations, the nullifications of promises, devalued contracts, pointless treaties, and empty words—all of this transformed the conduct of U.S. foreign affairs, and the American citizens charged with conducting them, as well as the people who voted for them. It went farther than that, and deeper, too, especially as our institutions—political, media, entertainment, academia, religious, philanthropic—were targeted and also infiltrated by this Communist army of occupation. The double standard in foreign policy Dunn seized on became double, triple, innumerable standards all around us. It wasn't long before we labeled the resulting morass "moral relativism" and wondered, genuinely, sincerely, brows furrowed, stumped, where it all could possibly have come from.

This is where it came from: the chain of Big Lies to which we hitched ourselves, tied ourselves, the noose constricting with each new lie. Our history necessarily became one of suppression, while desperation colored our relations with the USSR, all because *we had things to hide, too.*

Take the two million miserable "repatriated" victims. Fact. The implication? The Gulag Archipelago was not just a monument to Communist crime. It was also a repository of *Western* guilt, a locked pit of our own complicity, where the secrets of our weakness stay well hidden—and I haven't even covered the half of it.

What did we get in exchange? The myth of the "Good War," the notion of "American exceptionalism." These are only slogans. In the treaties and alliances between putative land of liberty and dead-to-rights Communist totalitarianism, the United States exchanged foundational principles and guiding ideals for . . . nothing. Empty words. False promises. Vain, destructive dreams. As truth—eyewitness reality itself—lost its authority, its pride of place, even its relevance, a vacuum appeared. In this vacuum, facts are weightless, conclusions disappear, judgment becomes a relative thing, and implications founder in emotionalism and ritual. Reckonings are put off, indefinitely, no matter how many millions of corpses demand them. Not that there's anything figurative about corpses. In our brave new world, however, the impartial authority of evidence, whether observed by a Jones or Jordan, amassed by a Conquest or Epstein, or lived by a Solzhenitsyn, stacks up in heaps, unclaimed, unwanted, like so many deliveries on the porch of a vacant house.

What are we supposed to do with them?

This is the question that stumps even our very best scholars. For example, in the landmark espionage work *The Haunted Wood,* the authors make plain that "the truth is that a large number of American agents and sources . . . carried on espionage for Soviet operatives throughout the New Deal and war years."

Check.

Yes, they continue, these same agents turned over the most sensitive secrets to Soviet intelligence, including secrets related to building an atomic bomb.

Check.

Additionally, the authors add, they themselves didn't even draw on all of the evidence they collected.

In other words, *they only told us the half of it.*

However, in their concluding words, the authors seem not to flinch, exactly, but to take a modest turn. In their telling, the civilizational subversion and national theft boils down to something ultimately personal, something that happened to *the agents*. "In the end, the enduring legacy of those Americans who sacrificed country for cause is one of the inglorious constancy to a cruel and discredited faith."[78]

Inglorious constancy? That's it? This was the Red Plot Against America—against the whole world—not the Red Plot Against a Few Agents. The sorrows or disappointments, maudlin or genuine, of a web of traitors are trivial next to the tragedies these traitors inflicted on humanity itself. But that's too much for us, too all-consuming. Better to recoil, withdraw, look within or away.

Enough.

The scene of the crime is on the next page.

CHAPTER NINE

In this last of meeting places
We grope together
And avoid speech
Gathered on this beach of the tumid river

Sightless unless
The eyes reappear . . .

—T. S. ELIOT, "THE HOLLOW MEN"

I'm not going to pretend I can parse T. S. Eliot—who can?—but it somehow seems right to assemble on Eliot's beach in "The Hollow Men" to view the scene of the crime, even though Eliot takes us to a beach beside a "tumid river," not the English Channel.

Sightless unless the eyes reappear. Or, sightless unless the last eight chapters were a blur. Sightless unless we finally try to see all the implications of a toxic record, large chunks of which are now before us, and put an end to the fumbling so we no longer "grope together and avoid speech." Now, much too late, we must see into the darkest craters in our past and zero in on the shape-shifting extent to which Stalin, through his infiltration and occupation of our power centers by a well-placed army of agents, fellow travelers, and dupes, prodded and coaxed along Allied strategy *throughout World War II* to further the entrenchment and expansion of the evil empire. The greatest, undetected, unpunished, unimagined crime ever. Which is why I thought to begin this chapter at Eliot's uneasy, if not portentous, meeting place on a beach.

The scene of the crime.

What if D-day were a Soviet plot?

Naturally, it sounds preposterous, and for at least two reasons. One, simply, because it *is* preposterous—completely contrary to common sense. However, the other reason might well be due to our ingrained habit of rejecting not just implications but even questions raised by facts that disturb our existing view of the world—the conditioned response. We reject input along these lines of inquiry just as our bodies reject the transplant of essential organs. The anguished furor over the inclusion of Stalin's bust among Allied leaders at the National D-day Memorial in Bedford, Virginia, in 2010 captures this autonomic reflex in action.[1] The fact is, Stalin was an Allied leader, and, as such, historically speaking, *belongs* with busts of Churchill, FDR, Truman, and Chiang Kai-shek. Beyond that, however, the historical record shows that Stalin was, arguably, *the primary booster of the invasion of northern France* that the memorial commemorates; without doubt, he was its leading non-American booster. Another fact is, Harry Hopkins, Roosevelt's precious friend and Stalin's precious asset, was also, arguably, the primary non-Russian booster of the extremely contentious decision to stage the main Allied assault on northern France (Stalin's choice) rather than on southern Europe (Churchill's choice). Given what the long-hidden record now reveals about ongoing Soviet influence operations against the Allies, it is an ostrichlike exertion not to attempt to see whether these two facts are connected. While the heroism, sacrifice, and achievement of all Allied forces in Normandy stand undimmed, a most disconcerting question necessarily arises: To what end—ours, or Stalin's?

It's impossible to overestimate the centrality of D-day in Americans' sense of ourselves, in our understanding of our role in the world, in a national nostalgia for a made-in-USA goodness that stands, guardian of our consciousness, in perpetual contrast to that worst evil—Nazi Evil. As a tourist in Europe in recent years, I have found myself reflexively aquiver with pride, empathy, and upset on coming across the unexpectedly familiar names of the towns in northern Europe marking the arc of war from France to Germany—from Bastogne to Malmedy to Monschau. Due to the triumphs and tragedies that long ago played out in or around these many towns—mainly American and British triumphs and tragedies—I discovered surprisingly proprietary feelings for the area. My European friends, meanwhile, draw on no such reserves of glory. That is, these were not Belgian or Dutch or other European battles; they were American and English, mainly, and they were German. The native peoples, French, Belgian, Dutch, and so on, were occupied; persecuted; conscripted; hungry. Theirs is mainly the lore of subjugation and collaboration, resistance and deprivation, the will to survive, and, eventually, the relief of liberation. Even the latter, however, wasn't the climactic ending for them that it was for tens of thousands of American civilian-soldiers, my own father among them.

It could be that I feel the stab of my own theory a little more sharply as the daughter of a late veteran of the Normandy campaign. June 8, 1944—D-day plus two—was the day my dad walked ashore onto a secured Omaha Beach, a twenty-year-old GI from Brooklyn on "the Continent," you might say, along with thousands of other very young American men, for the first time. As a member of the 102nd Cavalry Reconnaissance Squadron in Gen. Omar Bradley's 2nd Army, Pvt. Elliot West's shooting war would begin amid the French *bocage* at the Battle of St. Lô. Some of the shrapnel he took there in high summer became part of him forever, as did the war itself. He didn't much mention it, not to me, until his seventies when he was writing what would be his final novel, an unfinished saga beginning in the cauldron of 1930s revolt and revolution that exploded into world war in the 1940s (his war) and continued to roil in struggles, cold and hot, and in revolution, open and clandestine, up until the 1960s (his political war as a conservative writer in Hollywood), by which time his book's hero, a veteran of it all, becomes a professor at Berkeley *(and boy, what happens then . . .).*

Not a day passed, he later said, without some fleeting thought of his youth at war. Even so, with everything he knew, had done and seen, and would read, including Nikolai Tolstoy's *The Secret Betrayal,* whose research would inspire a novel of the forced repatriation—Soviet cleansing—of two million (rejected, as noted earlier, by Cass Canfield–like publishers as anti-Communist, antidétente "axe-grinding"), I don't think he ever came to think of this particular theory. I wonder what he would say.

A clear, tangible record exists attesting to Hopkins's shepherding role in the decision to implement the cross-Channel invasion into northern France on June 6, 1944, the so-called second front, which we know and regularly commemorate as D-day. It shows up in his comings and goings as Roosevelt's special emissary of the "second front"; it is less noticeable in official State Department wartime conference minutes, where his is a supporting role; it is very clear in Sherwood's official biography, and, sometimes, most vividly of all, it comes into sharp focus from the unique vantage point of key witnesses to these same events who later set down their recollections in memoirs. These witnesses, by the way, sometimes seem as nonplussed or perplexed by Hopkins's behavior as I am.

First, the obvious question, defensively. *What could possibly be wrong with Harry Hopkins, or anyone else for that matter, pushing D-day in the first place?*

I believe Hopkins's role in the Allied decision to invade Normandy could very well be the ultimate influence operation of World War II, not only setting the European chessboard that became battle lines in what we know as the Cold War, but also enlarging the evil empire itself.

But isn't D-day everything that was ever good about America wrapped into one hallowed date?

Not if you look at it this way: *R*einvading Europe through both northern France (OVERLORD) and, often forgotten, southern France (ANVIL), rather than pressing on from the already established Allied front and bases in Italy, and expanding operations from the Adriatic and Aegean Seas into south central Europe, as Churchill repeatedly and quite desperately proposed, left Eastern and Central Europe wide open to millions of Red Army troops. Unopposed, unchecked, these Red Army troops would ride their Lend-Lease fleets of Jeeps and Dodges deep into a Europe that was being ethnically cleansed of millions of anti-Bolsheviks by U.S. and British troops.

All hail the true victor of World War II, a totalitarian regime with a freshly conquered empire. Russian historian Viktor Suvorov crystallizes this jaw-dropper of a paradox in his 2008 book, *The Chief Culprit: Stalin's Grand Design to Start World War II:* "The world hated Hitler, and commiserated with Stalin. Hitler conquered half of Europe, and the rest of the world declared war against him. Stalin conquered half of Europe, and the world sent him greetings."[2]

What Suvorov describes is a world sick with fever. This was the contagion of Communism, a practically biological kind of warfare at a certain point in its psychological operations—its Big Lies, its *dezinformatsiya,* its deception, influence, guile, appeal, and heretofore unimagined predations and pressures. It was the age-old fever of masses, its lineage in the hysterics of Tulipmania and the zealotry of witch hunts, born gigantically anew in the enlarging scope of media, surveillance, and ease of movement in the twentieth century. "You could hardly say it was cold in Russia without being accused of being anti-Soviet," Charles Bohlen had written, conveying the premature "political correctness" of the Washington cocktail circuit during the war.[3] No wonder things turned topsy-turvy, as Suvorov describes:

> To ensure that Hitler could not hold on to the conquered European countries, the West sank German ships, bombed German cities, and then landed a massive and powerful army on the European continent. To enable Stalin to conquer and hold on to the other half of Europe, the West gave Stalin hundreds of warships, thousands of war planes and tanks, hundreds of thousands of the world's best war vehicles, and millions of tons of its best fuel, ammunition, and supplies.[4]

Curious. Sickening, too. For what Suvorov is describing is a Big Lie we know as "the Good War." It is a particularly stubborn narrative, as Suvorov himself discovered when he first defected in 1978, primarily, he said, to publish evidence of his groundbreaking theory that, far from being duped by Hitler, Stalin had supported and wooed Hitler as part of his own long-range strategy of Communist conquest; further, that history concealed Stalin's responsibility for starting World War II. "It quickly became apparent that the Western academic community was as reluctant as the Communist apparatus to accept my new interpretation as the cause of World War II," he wrote in the introduction to *The Chief Culprit.* "Instead of confronting my arguments the way the Soviets did, my Western opponents chose a different kind of confrontation—silence."[5]

Why? Maybe because even to entertain such a theory requires exploratory probing of the double standard that still exists regarding Hitler (enemy) and Stalin (ally) and "the Good War." The term itself, quotation marks and all, comes from the 1984 book by the same title written by that lovable Lefty Studs Terkel. The book is called *The Good War,* Amazon explains, "because, in the words of one soldier, 'to see fascism defeated, nothing better could have happened to a human being.'" No word on what emotion said soldier-cum-human-being felt on seeing Communism triumph. In all likelihood, he didn't notice.

Some people did, however. All-American, all-anti-Communist Martin Dies opens his 1963 memoir with this statement: "We lost World War II. It was not the brave men who offered and gave their lives who lost it for us; it was the politicians. Politics betrayed the 1,076,245 casualties of World War II, and the 157,530 casualties of the Korean War. Now we are losing the mis-called 'cold war.'"[6]

This completely confounded me at first. Of course, for all Martin Dies did know—and for all the nation knows because he personally investigated and exposed it—even he didn't know the half of it. It was the secret Communist occupiers and the politicians—sometimes one and the same—who lost World War II for us, and won it for the USSR.

"We celebrated a victory when in reality we had not won the war," Gen. Mark Clark, commander of Allied forces in Italy, writes in the final pages of his 1950 memoir, *Calculated Risk.*[7] After reading Clark's hair-raising account of an army decimated and a front stymied by the decision to reinvade Europe via northern and southern France, I understood where he was coming from. In fact, it may have been Clark's book more than any other that suddenly convinced me something was very wrong with history as we know it.

More research yielded more chords of ambivalence and unease. Gen. Albert C. Wedemeyer called the concluding chapters of his memoir "The War Nobody Won," parts 1 and 2.[8] As noted earlier, William C. Bullitt published an early appraisal of the defeat the United States had suffered in *Life* magazine titled "How We Won the War and Lost the Peace."[9] A new trope emerged, dividing victory into two parts, military and political. This split-screen vision allowed the United States to claim a clean military victory, as if "political" victory—the Soviet military occupation of half of Europe—were beside the point and somehow actually beneath our concern. Dwight D. Eisenhower famously seized on this dichotomy as something of a virtue in his 1948 war memoir, *Crusade in Europe.*[10] Such semantic gamesmanship held the field for a time; at some point, however, the position eroded, and from the rubble a supreme, unalloyed American victory rose up, a concept pure and simple, a continuous loop of razzle-dazzle, didactically enforced to this day in grainy but authoritative black and white on the History Channel. Indeed, when it comes to World War II what endures is a rather bizarre emphasis on "pure." But come now—we didn't even save the Jews.[11]

During the war and in its aftermath, the obvious parallels between Dictator Hitler and Dictators Lenin and Stalin were obscured by a new zealotry, a new orthodoxy. A Dies or a Bullitt, a Taft or a Hoover, a Kravchenko, a Krivitsky, a Valtin could speak up and point out that these two emperors of blood wore the *same* clothes, but in response Stalin's courtiers by the score would turn on them and boo, yelling the magic word that turned dissenters into toads: *"Red-baiter!"* Then, suddenly, where once two emperors of blood had threatened each other in mortal combat, there was only one, bigger and more powerful than before, who threatened the world. After four years of "total" war in Europe—ensured by the disastrous Allied policy of "unconditional surrender"—there were no more natural rivals to hem the Communist regime in at the sides.

There was only us, from across the oceans. As first runner-up in the war, our main prize was the "Good War" legacy, wrapped in patriotic bunting, dressing up—disguising—our radical commitment to world governance and global economy that marked the postwar era of "interdependence," which Lend-Lease kicked off back in 1941. This was, after all, the Kremlin dream, the Communist grail. Now it was real, its headquarters rising in concrete and steel over Turtle Bay in New York City, brought into existence by a bevy of Soviet agents lodged deep in the vitals of the United States and other Western governments. No kidding. Think about what Hopkins, Hiss, and White actually *accomplished.* Gregor Dallas observes:

> Thus the world found itself in 1945 at the conclusion of catastrophe with a whole series of international institutions—ranging from commercial agreements, to exchange rates, to war credits and loans, to the administration of territories without governments, to an ambulating world without citizenship, to the United Nations itself—which had been imposed by the United States. *But even more important was the fact that all the "charters" and constitutions of these world institutions had been composed by America's leading Soviet agents* [emphasis added].[12]

And we call it the "American Century."

If we can believe the road to hell is strewn with good intentions, can we believe the road to Soviet-occupied Berlin, the Eastern Bloc, world government, and global economy is, too?

Not now. Not anymore. Not if we have incorporated the implications of Soviet penetration. Not if we have finally accepted that the U.S. government was riddled with Red agents, separate and overlapping groups and cells and nests and vipers of them actively enabling, assisting, extending, implementing, blessing Soviet strategy. *In the White House. In the State Department. In Hollywood.*

I find myself uconsciously repeating the series of subheads from that used book I picked up long ago, those banners across the red, white, and black cover of Robert Stripling's 1949 account of his tenure at the Un-American Activities Committee, *The Red Plot Against America.* Back then, they looked like late-night studio-audience bait, punch-line prompts of hooting laughter over cartoon thought bubbles indicating that Stripling and his boss and anyone who bought this book was a raving right-wing lunatic. I don't hear the laughter as much anymore, immersion in the material having overcome my own conditioning. It's just not so "dirty rotten Commie" funny anymore, not if any of my argument is sticking.

But D-day?

Some background. After Nazi Germany invaded Soviet Russia on June 22, 1941,[13] the call-to-arms against the Axis Powers (Italy, Germany, and Japan) was for an Anglo-American "second front" in Europe. The idea was to draw German forces away from the beleaguered Russian front, the putative "first" front.

It sounds good, but it was always a numerically incorrect equation. After all, *Poland* in September 1939, not the USSR in June 1941, was the "first front" in Europe after its invasion by Germany and, of course, the USSR. (China was the "first front" in the Far East after Japan invaded in 1937; China's subsequent calls for the *USSR* to launch a "second front" on China's behalf against Japan failed to make a dent.[14]) Meanwhile, no matter how many fronts Anglo-American forces opened and fought on, to Stalin they were all so much *nare-zanno pecheni*—chopped liver. So was the fact that after December 7, 1941, both the United States and Britain were simultaneously at war on two fronts while their Soviet "ally" remained resolutely at peace with Japan[15] (until one fateful, land-grabbing week in August 1945).

If Russia entered the war against Japan, General MacArthur cabled the War Department from the besieged Philippines shortly after the attack on Pearl Harbor, a "golden opportunity" would arise for a "master stroke" against Nippon.[16]

The absolute, dead-last thing the Soviet Union wanted to do was enter the war against Nippon. Winston Churchill may have had to be practically restrained from declaring war on Japan on hearing a radio news flash about Pearl Harbor (before receiving official confirmation[17]); Stalin, on the other hand, not only knew about Japanese plans to attack the United States months in advance, but there is ample, recently developed evidence that the Soviets were themselves extensively involved in instigating the attack on the United States in the first place.[18] (There is also evidence suggesting the USSR became aware of the Pearl Harbor attack before it began.[19]) Indeed, Pearl Harbor may well represent the culmination of the most successful and complex KGB influence operations ever, coordinated simultaneously on two continents through Communist cells that penetrated leadership circles in both Tokyo and Washington, both "working in mid-1941 to avert a Japanese invasion of the Soviet Union," as Jerrold and Leona Schecter report in *Sacred Secrets: How Soviet Intelligence Operations Changed American History.*[20]

In Tokyo, as M. Stanton Evans explains, Kremlin ace Richard Sorge directed an espionage network (including members of the later-notorious, later-investigated pro-Soviet think tank, the Institute of Pacific Relations) that penetrated the Tokyo power structure, pushing it to strike not north at the USSR but south at British, Dutch, or American interests.

In Washington, the Soviet goal was to avert an American modus vivendi with Japan, the painstaking work of such distinguished diplomats as U.S. ambassador to Tokyo, Joseph Grew. The work of Grew and others was vociferously opposed by such well-placed Soviet agents as Lauchlin Currie, who were able to influence the United States to provoke a Japanese attack on itself. The shocking details about how this all came about, the Schecters tell us, didn't emerge until 1995 when former Kremlin agent Vitaly Pavlov published in Russia an article, and, in 1996, a book recounting his role in Operation Snow.[21]

Never heard of Operation Snow? The intelligence history community may still disagree about its ultimate impact—"influence" being an intangible thing—but they agree that the plot, as revealed by Pavlov, its Russian controller, was conceived in Moscow, conveyed to Washington, and imparted to Harry Dexter White. Dutifully, White managed to insert Soviet language calculated to bring Japan and the United States to war into the U.S. diplomatic cable flow. It worked.

My point is, if it was possible for well-placed Communist agents to serve Soviet ends by apparently bringing nations to a specific point of battle in the Pacific, why wouldn't well-placed agents try to do the same thing in Europe? Certainly, the line of inquiry is worth a sufficiently cynical examination.

We can pick up on the "second front" as it was first presented to the British by Harry Hopkins and George C. Marshall in London in mid-April 1942. See if there doesn't seem to be something odd about these Americans' instincts from the start—something wrong with this picture, at least as newspaperman Chesly Manly frames it in his pointedly concise account: "In London on the night of April 14, five days after the abandoned American and Filipino forces on the Bataan Peninsula had been overwhelmed by the Japanese, and three weeks before the defenders of Corregidor were to meet the same fate, the decision was made to aid Communist Russia by invading Germany through France."[22]

Disconcerting, no? The proposed plan of attack, which was to begin in the fall of 1942 (no later than the spring of 1943, they said) was initially code-named ROUNDUP, later OVERLORD. It won extremely tentative British assent, although, in fact, nothing was really settled. As Hanson Baldwin almost lyrically described it, this was just the beginning of a "dispute that roared on down the roads of time, exploding now and again at conferences—never settled, always recurrent."[23]

It is hard not to be struck by the fact that even as Hopkins and Marshall pressed for an invasion of northern France ASAP, thousands of captured Americans and Filipinos were at that moment struggling for their lives on the infamous Bataan Death March, or hanging on at Corregidor. Meanwhile, the Philippine nation itself, to which the United States had pledged protection, was under cruel Japanese dominion. Military losses were heavy: Ten thousand American and Filipino troops were killed at Bataan; twenty thousand were wounded. Added to the three thousand killed at Pearl Harbor, there was already much American blood on Tokyo's hands.

Washington—Roosevelt, Marshall, Hopkins—didn't seem to care, not really. All Hopkins and Marshall could think of, talk about, was a "second front" in northern France. That was true from the start, even before Bataan fell, back when MacArthur still had bulldozers working around the clock, carving out four airstrips in the central Phillipines and nine on Mindanao because the general believed, *really believed,* U.S. ships would be full-steaming ahead to bring him supplies, reinforcements, *war planes.* It wouldn't have taken all that much to turn things around. William Manchester writes that in those first days of war Gen. Hap Arnold "told an RAF commander that if eighty B-17s and two hundred P-40s could get to the islands, he believed 'we could regain superiority of the air in the theater.'" Later, MacArthur would beg Washington for "just three planes so I can see. You can't fight them if you can't see them. I am now blind."[24] They never came. Nothing did.

Why didn't the United States make the effort to get through to the islands? To be sure, Manchester writes, MacArthur and Philippines president Manuel Quezon "were given every assurance that immediate relief was on the way"— including a late-January/early-February 1942 cable of particularly outrageous lies from Roosevelt to Quezon: *"A continuous stream of fighter and pursuit planes is traversing the Pacific."*[25] Well, why weren't they? Why wasn't supplying Americans in the Philippines taking precedence over supplying Russians in Europe? No risk was small enough, apparently, to supply MacArthur; no cost was too large, demonstrably, to supply Stalin.[26] Why? The answer was the American policy of what might as well be called Russia First.

The Russia First policy evolved over 1941, the year in which Congress ceded those superpowers to FDR in the Lend-Lease bill—arguably, the most Soviet-ized piece of American legislation ever (Hammer to Hopkins to White). Lend-Lease, of course, empowered FDR, "notwithstanding the provisions of any other law," to aid and supply "the government of any country whose defense the President deems vital to the defense of the United States."[27] Aside from the fact that the bill decoupled presidential powers from all checks and balances, there was no mention of any specific country to receive aid—just "any countries." That's because in 1941, aid to the USSR was still "the big sticking-point" in Lend-Lease debate, as Sherwood put it—"what the isolationists feared the most." In the atmosphere of the day, if the "isolationists" feared it, it was a virtuous idea.

Sherwood continued, "Even those who grudgingly conceded that perhaps Britain might be deserving of some charity were horrified at the thought that American taxpayers might be called upon to pay for supplies for the Red Army."

Maybe these political opponents of the Roosevelt White House weren't so thoroughly "isolationist" as they were thoroughly anti-Communist, but that aside: What lover of liberty wouldn't balk at supporting liberty's mortal enemy? That was the rub, but it was no obstacle to the dirty-pool players in power, who "confidentially" signed their first aid agreements with the USSR at the Moscow Conference in early October 1941 ($1 billion in no-interest aid). They didn't confess to this flow of "Soviet" aid because a majority of the American people, still not completely conditioned otherwise, didn't want to support the Bolshevik Police State—no, not even after Roosevelt's Communism-is-freedom-of-religion offensive during which he bald-faced-lied that there was in the USSR "freedom of conscience, freedom of religion" along the lines of "what the rule is in this country." The President even cited "Article 124 of the Constitution of Russia" to prove his bogus point—an unfortunate reference to the so-called Stalin Constitution of 1936, two-thirds of whose drafters, as Eugene Lyons picquantly pointed out in *The Red Decade,* had already been "liquidated."[28]

Roosevelt's remarks didn't go over well. Probably better not to have said anything at all. Indeed, as late as October 30, 1941, the day Roosevelt cabled Stalin his approval of aid to the USSR, McJimsey tells us, "Hopkins warned the War Department that the names Lend Lease and Russia should not be used in the same communication by 'anybody, anywhere, at any time.' "[29] Sherwood put (spun) it this way: "It is an indication of Roosevelt's concern for public opinion that he did not formally include the Soviet Union among the recipients of Lend Lease until November 7" (which happened to be the twenty-fourth anniversary of the Bolshevik Revolution).[30] It was that explosive, or so Roosevelt thought.

Doesn't sound like "*concern* for public opinion" so much as fear of it—fear that exposure would disrupt a secret plan.

After the United States was attacked at Pearl Harbor, however, something was different. Or was for a very short time. Initially, military officials "imposed an embargo on all lend-lease shipments, called back ships just underway to England and Russia, and hastily unloaded aircraft, guns, and ammunition for reshipment to Hawaii and the Philippines." *Naturally.* That is, this was the natural, patriotic reaction. It lasted all of twenty-four hours before being reversed from the top.[31] Meanwhile, on the other side of the pond, the British assumed, also naturally and patriotically in an empathetic sort of way, that Japan's attack on the United States would recalibrate the overall Allied war strategy. It didn't. I don't know at what point this paradox became clear to the British in those initial post-Pearl meetings in December 1941 with their American counterparts during the First Washington Conference, which is known as Arcadia. Sherwood noticed it, writing, "When the British gathered for the Arcadia Conference they suspected that extraordinary events in the Pacific might well have produced a reversal of strategic thinking in Washington and they would be met with plans for an all-out American effort against Japan."

They suspected wrong. Cooler heads prevailed. Or was that *Soviet-influenced* heads prevailed? It's hard to say—but harder not to wonder.

Sherwood continued, noting, "Certainly, the isolationist press was clamoring, at the time and continued to do so, for just that policy."[32]

Let them clamor, boys; it's only the "isolationist press"—kind of like today's Tea Party with typewriters only worse. Later, when Hopkins and Marshall sat down with the British on April 14, 1942, just after the surrender of Bataan and shortly before the surrender of Corregidor, the paradox must have been, if anything, even more striking.

Sherwood noticed it, too. These talks with the British chiefs, Sherwood wrote, "produced the contradictory circumstance of the American representatives constantly sticking to the main topic of the war against Germany while the British representatives were repeatedly bringing up reminders of the war against Japan." Hopkins tried to explain. "When it came his [Hopkins's] turn to speak he started out by saying that there was no question of doubt that American public opinion was generally in favour of an all-out effort against Japan."

Hopkins bows to the validity of the opposing argument—a favorite opening gambit of his. Sherwood's account of Hopkins's pitch continued: "However, Hopkins said, the President and the American military leaders and the American people were all agreed on one point: *'Our men must fight!'* " (Emphasis in original.)

Vigorous non sequitur to throw off listeners—another Hopkins hallmark. That is, weren't our men fighting—and dying—in the Philippines? Hopkins, however, was on a roll.

"Obviously, Western Europe was the one place where the enemy could be fought most quickly and most decisively. . . . Hopkins said the Americans did not want their men to be sent across oceans merely for purposes of sightseeing: they wanted to engage the enemy and finish the war."

Who, pray tell, was sightseeing on Corregidor, where in three weeks' time General Cartwright would surrender himself and his forces to the Japanese? It sounds to me as if Hopkins was unprepared to argue the case and said whatever it was that came to mind, *con brio*. He had only one point to get across to the British, and one point only. Sherwood wrote, "Hopkins said very positively that once this decision was taken to go ahead with the trans-Channel Operation it could not be reversed."[33]

The decision could not be reversed *for any reason*? Any reason at all? Did he mean that? He sure did. This became evident just a couple of months later after the unexpected and catastrophic defeat of the British Army at Tobruk in Libya. Under scrutiny today, Hopkins's and Marshall's tag-team reluctance to revamp Allied policy to take into account this new contingency in June 1942 looks nothing if not rigidly . . . Stalinist.[34]

You don't believe me? Tobruk falls. Churchill, in Washington for the Second Washington Conference, is devastated. The Russian line is holding, by the way, at this moment of British collapse. Does it really make sense to ignore a massive Allied defeat in Africa? On June 20, 1942, the fateful day of the fall of Tobruk, in Sherwood's words, Hopkins and Marshall both "vigorously opposed" any new operation in North Africa. Why? It would delay the "second front."

But . . . a North African front would be a "second front."

Nope. Only northern France counted as Front No. 2.

Rather amazingly, it is Stalin's opportunistic branding of the "second front" that historians use to this day to describe the invasion of Normandy. Not only is the concept arithmetically wrong, it also fails utterly to indicate that "second front" meant specifically "French front." Our use of Stalin's lingo makes no sense now, and never did. For example, long before D-day, British and American forces massed to invade North Africa in November 1942—truly the "second" front from the Soviet's numerical starting point. The preemptive word from the Russkies was "not good enough." October 27, 1942:

WASHINGTON (U.P.)—A highly reliable informant who has first-hand information of events in the Soviet Union said tonight the Russian people would not regard even a major Allied success in North Africa as the answer to their desire for the opening of a second front.[35]

Apparently, FDR didn't get the message. He greeted the November 7, 1942, invasion of North Africa by over one hundred thousand Allied troops as "effective second front assistance to our heroic allies in Russia."[36]

Nyet on your life, Stalin replied in a follow-up story on November 8, 1942. STALIN STILL INSISTING ON THAT SECOND FRONT...BELITTLES FIGHTING IN AFRICA.[37]

By the following week, the dictator had softened his critique some, damning with faint praise the Americans and British as "first-rate organizers" who had created both "the conditions for putting Italy out of commission" and "the *prerequisites for establishing a second front* in Europe nearer to Germany's vital centers" (emphasis added).[38]

Stalin had mentioned Italy. In our own Normandy-focused perspective on the war, we tend to overlook the role of Mussolini's Italy in the Axis, and, later, after Italy's grossly underplayed surrender in September 1943, to ignore the Allied front against formidable German armies in Italy.

What's more, we always did. U.S. Rep. Clare Boothe Luce made a trip to Italy's front lines in 1944 and wrote an article for her husband's *Life* magazine called "The Forgotten Front." How do you forget a front? Maybe the Communist-riddled Office of War Information, which, of course, controlled war information, could have answered that question. Since the Italian front wasn't Stalin's "second front," it wasn't news to good Communists. In fact, Italy was *bad* news to good Communists. Which has something to do with the fact that the Italian front barely figured for the rest of us. The resulting historical blank ill serves the 124,917 casualties suffered by the U.S. 5th Army under Gen. Mark W. Clark. That includes 20,889 dead, 84,389 wounded in action, and 20,139 missing in action, all incurred in Italy *before D-day*—by the date of the Allied liberation of Rome, June 4, 1944.[39]

The allied liberation of Rome: There's a milestone that doesn't resonate. Doesn't inspire TV specials; doesn't draw Gen X officials to express their gratitude to dwindling gatherings of elderly veterans, either. Famously, infamously, Stalin would emphatically nix an Allied breakout from Italy into Austria and Germany from *bases already hard won or soon to be hard won in Italy,* or any invasion of any kind into the nearby Balkans from the Adriatic or the Aegean Seas. This decision, by the way, for Stalin, was worth the whole trip to the Tehran Conference, Stalin's first "Big Three" powwow with Roosevelt and Churchill in the Iranian capital in November–December 1943. Famously, infamously, Roosevelt sided with Stalin at Tehran. Churchill was beside himself.[40]

"If there was any supreme peak in Roosevelt's career, I believe it might well be fixed at this moment, at the end of the Tehran conference," Sherwood wrote. *"It certainly represented the peak for Harry Hopkins"* (emphasis added).[41]

Hopkins's protégé Charles Bohlen, who served at Tehran as a Russian translator for the Americans, saw things a little differently.[42] At Tehran, Bohlen wrote in his 1973 memoir, the show was Hopkins's alone. "Roosevelt was relying more and more on Hopkins, virtually to the exclusion of others. *At Tehran, Hopkins' influence was paramount"* (emphasis added).[43]

Harry was such a popular fellow, too. "When Stalin saw him [Hopkins] enter the conference room" at Tehran, Averell Harriman recalled in 1981, "he got up, walked across the room and shook hands with him. I never saw him do that to anybody, not even Roosevelt. He was the only man I ever saw Stalin show personal emotion for."[44]

The decision to abandon Italy as an expanding, leading front at the end of 1943 made very little sense—unless, cynically, the true objective was to ensure that Central and Eastern Europe remained open for Soviet invasion. Then again, maybe that's putting things too crudely, too harshly. Let me rephrase: The advantages to enlarging upon Anglo-American gains in Italy were obvious. There was no good strategic objective to be served by virtually abandoning this theater. Not because I say so. The top U.S. commander of strategic bombing in Europe, Gen. Carl Spaatz, said so, too. Capt. Harry C. Butcher recounted Spaatz's views as expressed to Harry Hopkins on November 23, 1943, in the run-up to the Cairo Conference.

> Spaatz didn't think OVERLORD was necessary or desirable. He said it would be a much better investment to build up forces in Italy to push the Germans across the Po, taking and using airfields as we come to them, thus shortening the bombing run into Germany. He foresaw the possibility of getting the ground forces into Austria and Vienna, where additional fields would afford shuttle service for bombing attack against the heart of German industry, which has moved into this heretofore practically safe area. Hopkins seemed impressed.[45]

Hopkins seemed impressed, or . . . was Mr. Poker Face about to have a cow?

More significantly, the top U.S. commander of ground forces in Europe, Gen. Dwight D. Eisenhower, agreed with this same assessment—at least he agreed with it before he was made top U.S. commander of ground forces in Europe. On November 26, 1943, at the Cairo Conference, which immediately preceded the Tehran Conference, Ike told a beribboned, bemedaled gathering of the American and British brass how vital Italy and southern Europe were to the war. Quote:

"Italy was the correct place in which to deploy our main forces and the objective should be the Valley of the Po. *In no other area could we so well threaten the whole German structure including France, the Balkans and the Reich itself.* Here also our air would be closer to vital objectives in Germany" (emphasis added).

Italy was the correct place to deploy? *In no other area* could we so well threaten "the whole German structure"? Ike wasn't disavowing OVERLORD— neither would Churchill, for that matter—but he sure sounded gung ho for the Churchillian option, right down to Aegean action.

"The next best method of harrying the enemy," Eisenhower continued, "was to undertake operations in the Aegean . . . From here the Balkans could be kept aflame, Ploesti would be threatened and the Dardanelles might be opened."[46]

At this point in my reading of the State Department record, I reached for my copy of *Crusade in Europe,* Eisenhower's 1948 war memoir, to seek some elaboration, some indication of how Ike's extremely heterodox vision— heterodox to Hopkins and Marshall (and Stalin), that is—had gone over. Did Marshall chew him out, as he did Gen. Ira Eaker, who similarly boosted Adriatic operations, for having been "too damned long with the British"?[47] Did Harry Hopkins have conniptions over Ike's Italian/Balkan campaign just as he did over Churchill's?[48] We don't know. Eisenhower doesn't mention his enthusiastic advocacy of military measures in line with Churchill's preferred strategy in his memoir. Anywhere.

Strange, no? Not only is it not to be found. Ike goes further still in his book, describing his position as having been for OVERLORD first, always, and practically exclusively, imagining only the most modest objectives for Allied forces in the Mediterranean. As he put it in 1948, "My own recommendation, then as always, was that no operation should be undertaken in the Mediterranean except as a directly supporting move for the Channel attack and that our planned redeployment [out of Italy] should proceed with all possible speed."[49]

That's funny, since didn't he say in 1943 there was no better place than Italy from which to "threaten the whole German structure, including France, the Balkans and the Reich itself"?

Yes.

Of course, no one would be able to see that in black and white until 1961, when the State Department finally published the 1943 Cairo Conference records. Still, you didn't need to be a military genius to know what would happen if the Allies abandoned southern Europe as a priority. All you needed was a map to see that the conquering Red Army would roll into the resulting vacuum on Dodge trucks, right up to and including Berlin. (Even so, it almost didn't come off until Eisenhower halted U.S. forces before they could liberate Berlin, Prague, and Vienna.[50] That was odd, too.) The same map told you that so long as Anglo-American armies were on the march from Italy, there would be no vacuum.

In fact, a map was exactly what a *New York Times* correspondent used on September 12, 1943, after *nearly two hundred thousand Anglo-American forces poured into mainland Italy* at Salerno from Allied-liberated Sicily to assess the war ahead.

The invasion of Italy, by the way, didn't count as Stalin's "second front," either.

The *Times* piece remains striking for both its clarity about the map still in play, and for its naïveté about Stalin's designs on that same map. In fact, the piece still glistens with the kind of dewy innocence (ignorance) that was no match for the ideological imperatives of the Communist world revolution in progress. (Today, such ignorance is no match for forces laying the groundwork for an Islamic caliphate.)

The gist of the article by *Times* Russia correspondent Edwin L. James was as follows. The distance between the toe of Italy and the southern border of Germany was roughly the same as the distance between the Dnieper River on Russia's western edge and the eastern border of Germany, as James pointed out. This meant that, should Hitler's Germany collapse, no longer was the Soviet army the only army anywhere near the German frontier. With the likely opening of a major Allied front in Italy, James continued (foreknowledge of Stalin's anti-Italy gambit to come at Tehran, which decimated that Allied front in Italy, was beyond his psychic powers), "the British and Americans are in a position to get to Germany just as rapidly as are the Russians." As a result, he declared, there was no longer reason for concern among "those addicted especially to worry about the Moscow government's role in post-war affairs"—no longer reason to worry that in the event the Red Army occupied Germany, "Moscow would gain control of Czechoslovakia, Yugoslavia and France."

And they lived happily ever after . . .

Unless, of course, the British and Americans were to gut their armies in Italy to reinvade the continent from northern France.

James writes, "The point is that the political implications of the Russians having the only army ready to march into a deflated Nazi Reich no longer exist. So far as geographical considerations go, Americans, British and Russians all have a chance."[51]

If Stalin was reading along, he probably burst a *krovenosnyi sosud*. Not that he had much to worry about. Roosevelt, we know for a documented fact, by this time already regarded the Soviet conquest of half of Europe as a fait accompli. We know this because Cardinal Spellman, after spending ninety minutes with Roosevelt on September 3, 1943, nine days before James's story ran in the newspaper, typed up an aide-mémoire of an extremely disturbing conversation in which Roosevelt said exactly that. (I first read about Spellman's conversation in Martin Dies's memoir, where Dies notes that FDR made similar remarks to him as early as 1940.) "The European people will simply have to endure the Russian domination in the hope that in ten or twenty years they will be able to live well with the Russians," Spellman recounted FDR saying at this pre-Tehran, pre-Yalta moment. Finland, Estonia, Lithuania, Latvia, Bessarabia, the eastern half of Poland, Czecho-Slovakia, Austria, Hungary, Croatia, Germany—FDR conceded *all* to Communist regimes or Soviet protection! What is most weird and most disturbing about Roosevelt's obdurate fatalism is that the entire Red Army at this time was *still inside the USSR*.

Spellman's notes continued, "Finally, he hopes, the Russians will get 40% of the Capitalist regime, the capitalists will retain only 60% of their system, and so an understanding will be possible."[52] Convergence again. Convergence would rule, and neatly so.

Poor inkstained wretch James, meanwhile, had no idea the fix was in—in the president's mind, anyway, which is where it really counts. Relying on precepts of pure Western logic, not muscular Marxist-Leninist strategy, the *Times*man inserted the $64,000 question into his September 12, 1943, article: "What is there Stalin could gain from an Allied front in France which he could not gain from an Allied front in Italy, or another one in the Balkans?"

The answer to James's question, of course, was nothing—if, that is, Stalin's objective was the speedy defeat of Germany. But it wasn't. It never was. On the contrary, as Russian historian Viktor Suvorov argues, Stalin wanted war to last as long as possible in order to exhaust both Germany and its Anglo-American opponents. Stalin was fighting to expand the Communist Empire. He wanted open-ended war to do so. He had been wanting such a war since the Spanish Civil War, back when his intelligence commissars failed to drag the Allied powers into it (and were shot for their failure), as Suvorov also argues. As his joined-at-the-hearts-and-minds ally, then, so, too—sometimes nefariously, mostly unconsciously—were we then fighting to expand the Communist Empire. Hardly anyone noticed, though.

*Times*man James continued, bubbling over with good sense, "Any time or any place where German forces are engaged by the Americans and the British represents good luck for Stalin. That is true because Hitler's strength is taxed just as much by fighting to the south as it would be fighting to the west."

He was right, but such Anglo-American "fighting in the south" wasn't in Stalin's interest. Anglo-American " "fighting in the west" was. That's because taxing Hitler's strength alone wasn't the issue, couldn't be the issue, not if Stalin were to succeed in his territorial designs. It was these divergent war aims that were at the crux of the tension and division among the "Big Three" Allies: namely, whether World War II was for simply defeating Hitler or for "Saving Marshal Stalin." In terms of logic, in terms of strategy, certainly in terms of political reality, there is a strong argument to be made that to have withdrawn from the European continent to reinvade the European continent was crazy.[53] It made no sense to Churchill; it made no sense to Gen. Mark W. Clark, the commander of the U.S. 5th Army in Italy, who had to watch, horrified, as his battle-tested forces were broken up and removed from the field while his equipment, landing craft, in particular, was taken from service.

Typical is this entry from Clark's eye-opening memoir *Calculated Risk*: "In the latter half of December [1943], however, our problems increased, partly as a result of the intensifying preparations for the invasion of France, which limited replacements for battle-worn units in Italy, and cut down on reinforcements."[54]

What remained to Clark in terms of men and matériel had to be stretched ever thinner, ever wearier, all according to the Tehran agreement between Roosevelt and Stalin (with Churchill dragging his feet) to shift the center of Allied operations to France—famously, to northern France (OVERLORD), and, less well known, also to southern France (ANVIL). Last-straw-like, it was the logistical demands of the invasion of Southern France, ANVIL (later known as DRAGOON), that put an end to Churchill's Italian-Balkan-Aegean dreams. We also find that ANVIL put an end to the life of Antoine de Saint-Exupéry, "Saint-Ex," the great French aviator and author of *Night Flight; Wind, Sand and Stars;* and the still widely read fable *The Little Prince*. His plane went down flying a lonely reconnaissance mission over southern France a few days before the controversial battle began. Saint-Exupéry was forty-four.[55]

Clark makes note in his memoir of the fact that since it was his own army being destroyed by some nightmarish strategic design, his dismay might be seen as prejudiced. Indeed, there was a military argument to be made to refocus on France. In *Wedemeyer Reports!* Gen. Albert C. Wedemeyer, one of the early planners of the invasion of France, makes a compelling military counterargument against Churchill's and Clark's "soft underbelly" strategy. Essentially, when he looked at the map, Wedemeyer didn't see the requisite harbors through which a massive Italian-Balkan operation could be supplied as it made its way through almost practically impassable terrain. To be sure, this military debate remains open-ended.

Still, it's important to note, as Clark does, that the disappearance of Allied men and matériel from Italy seemed completely incomprehensible to another professional military man, Field Marshal Albert Kesselring, top commander of German forces in Italy. Clark writes that Kesselring's intelligence section "was completely mystified in coming weeks when our great forward drive failed to take full advantage of its chance to destroy the beaten and disorganized German Army in Italy."

Clark continued, "It was some time before the Germans understood what had happened to the American troops in Italy; for weeks the Counterintelligence Corps, under the able direction of Lieutenant Colonel Stephen J. Spingarn, was catching enemy agents who had *orders to find out 'where in hell' were various Allied divisions that were being sent to France*" (emphasis added).[56] Historian Dennis J. Dunn offers a crystallizing description of the seemingly incomprehensible Great Switcheroo in progress. "It is paradoxical that the Americans were insisting on a withdrawal from the Continent in order to reinvade the Continent from another angle."[57]

Paradoxical?

Whiz through the chronology and see if it still seems paradoxical. Was it merely paradoxical back in May 1942, when, according to *Soviet* records, Harry Hopkins privately coached Foreign Minister Molotov on what to say to FDR to overcome U.S. military arguments against a "second front" in France in May 1942?[58] Whatever Molotov or Hopkins said, it worked. Roosevelt agreed. Then again, maybe FDR was just plain tuckered out by the six days Molotov spent talking about the "second front"—nonstop, according to columnist Anne O'Hare McCormick, who wrote that "at least nine-tenths of his conversations with the President, Mr. Hopkins, and the military leaders and officials" were about a "second front" in "the west" of Europe."[59]

Only shocking British reverses on June 21, 1942, interrupted Allied plans for such an assault that same year, or soon thereafter. Instead, a new, numberless front—the X-front?—opened in November 1942 in North Africa. It would become the base from which Anglo-American armies would fight, really by accident, into southern Europe via a series of other nonsecond fronts in Tunisia, Sicily, and Italy.

"I feel damn depressed," Hopkins would scrawl on a piece of Downing Street notepaper on July 22, 1942, probably for Marshall's eyes,[60] when on a follow-up London trip they were unable to recommit Churchill to the notion of a "second front" in northern France in 1942.

Why? Why "damn depressed"? Why did it upset Hopkins so much when his own boss, the president of the United States, wasn't fazed by the unexpected but quite logical shift to Mediterranean operations?

In this case, FDR acted with unusual decisiveness to order the invasion of

North Africa. "This was one of the very few major military decisions of the war that Roosevelt made entirely on his own and over the protests of his highest-ranking advisers"—Hopkins and Marshall, no doubt—Sherwood noted. Given the German advance on the Middle East, it appears to have made sound military sense to refocus Allied efforts on North Africa, and later Sicily, and eventually Italy, and so the Allies did. Which is why Sherwood's next observation is disconcerting: "It is evident that even after Hopkins, Marshall, and King returned from London on July 27 [1942] there were further attempts to change the President's mind about the North Africa operations."[61]

Why? Imagine, again with the revisionist eye: The president of the United States and the prime minister of Great Britain are in accord on a joint operation to counter a staggering, wholly unexpected British defeat in North Africa, and yet "further attempts," *which happen to be simpatico with Stalin's oft-stated wishes,* continue to be made in Washington, likely by Hopkins and Marshall, to deep-six the U.S.-British strategy in favor of the Soviet one.

Is it just me, or, given everything else, does this seem sinister?

Meanwhile, the clamor for Stalin's "second front" never stopped. "So often was this demand repeated by Soviet diplomats in Washington," the Schecters write, "that even officials who knew not a word of Russian could repeat the mantra *vtoroi front,* second front."[62] During his carefully guided tour of the USSR in 1941, Wendell Willkie got to speak with an apparently genuine man of the people working his lathe in an aircraft factory. "What part is that?" he said to the man.

"Quick as a flash, he shot back his own question, in English with a heavy Russian accent, 'What about the Second Front?' "[63]

"This talk about a 'second front' is getting annoying," a letter to the editor dated February 23, 1943, begins. Listing assorted theaters of war including China, the South Pacific, Burma, and North Africa, the writer concludes "that when people talk about a second front what they mean is *a ninth front*" (Emphasis added).[64]

SOVIET RENEWS CRY FOR SECOND FRONT, the *New York Times* headline of March 12, 1943, said. So, predictably, did Communist Parties in London and New York. CALL FOR SECOND FRONT: LONDONERS AT COMMUNIST-SPONSORED MEETING URGE ACTION, another headline said on March 15, 1943. SECOND FRONT STRESSED BY AMTER, another headline said on March 27, 1943 (Israel Amter being the chairman of the New York State Communist Party). Behold the international echo chamber in action.

On June 23, 1943, finally, a little pushback: "SECOND FRONT LAG IS DENIED BY KNOX (Frank Knox was Secretary of the Navy). The story concluded, "Diplomatic circles were cautious of direct comment on the Soviet demand for a second front, but it was pointed out unofficially that it was considered interesting that the Soviet Union was going to such pains to make its position clear."[65]

"Interesting" is one word for it.

Hopkins, too, kept up the pressure behind the scenes. In May 1943, when Churchill again visited Washington, this time to try to persuade the president to follow up on Allied victories in North Africa by pressing on into southern Europe, Hopkins bragged to Lord Moran, Churchill's physician and biographer, that "Marshall was at the president's elbow to keep in his mind the high urgency of a second front." Again—"second front" meaning specifically the invasion of northern France.

The Americans had "done some very hard thinking" since "those disasters of a year ago," Hopkins told Moran—referring, it seems, to the disruption of "second front" plans by the British defeat at Tobruk—but Hopkins, as he put it to the doctor, was now getting "results."

Results?

The results, according to Hopkins, were very satisfactory. The president could now be safely left alone with the prime minister.[66]

Hopkins had erected a siege wall around FDR *against Winston Churchill*.

On July 11, 1943, *The New York Times* reported that here it was, finally (again): Stalin's "second front." Sicily. If the invasion of North Africa didn't count, surely the invasion of Sicily did. In a story headlined ZERO HOUR, the "newspaper of record" declared, "At 3 o'clock yesterday morning, the Battle of Europe began. The Second Front was opened. The moment which the Allied world has long awaited came with dramatic suddenness in the dead hours of a moonlit Mediterranean night."

Good stuff.

"From North Africa to Sicily moved thousands of Allied troops that have for months been in training for the initial assault on the fortress Hitler has made of a continent."[67]

Ring the obsolete church bells in the godless Kremlin?

Not so fast. Yes, the people of Moscow "joyously welcomed" news of Sicily's invasion, the AP deadpanned, but, "they were saying," the AP continued, quoting unnamed masses: " 'It is not the second front.' "[68]

Before you knew it, SECOND FRONT CALL RENEWED, *The New York Times* reported on July 29, 1943.

The king of Italy fired Mussolini that same day, as Anglo-American bombers continued to firebomb the German city of Hamburg in a week-long assault that killed forty thousand people.

RUSSIA STILL ASKS FOR SECOND FRONT; SICILIAN CAMPAIGN CONSIDERED FINE

BUT NOT A SUBSTITUTE FOR MAJOR OPERATION, the *Times* headline said on August 11, 1943.

Just for the record, at the peak of this operation, there were *nearly half a million Allied forces* deployed in that "fine but not major" Sicilian campaign. The following week, Churchill and Roosevelt would meet at the first Quebec Conference, where Churchill would pass FDR the O'Malley report on Katyn. Hopkins would bring along a paper by Lend-Lease Moscow gun General Burns that simultaneously declared and apologized for the Soviet domination of Europe—again, even as the Red Army was still inside Russia. As we've seen earlier, Roosevelt would never react to the O'Malley report (nor return it to Churchill); but he seems to have internalized the Burns report, as Cardinal Spellman's aide-mémoire of September 3, 1943, attests.

In early September 1943, Italy surrendered.

RUSSIANS RESUME SECOND FRONT PLEA, the paper reported on September 22, 1943.

On October 7, 1943, Churchill cabled Roosevelt to request troops for an assault on the island of Rhodes before the Germans could dig in.

Nothing.

The prime minister then followed up with a phone call to the White House.

Hopkins biographer McJimsey writes, "Roosevelt was out of town, so Hopkins, who had read the cable, tried to let Churchill know gently that his request would most certainly be rejected, as indeed it was."[69] Funny how Hopkins was always right.

Perhaps the most amazing thing about the relentless, unceasing clamor for a "second front" was the fact that by the end of November 1943, when Roosevelt arrived at the Cairo Conference with Churchill and Chiang Kai-shek that preceded the Tehran Conference with Churchill and Stalin, Roosevelt himself still wasn't entirely convinced (brainwashed?) that there weren't benefits to Churchill's proposed operations in southern Europe. Such talk filled Hopkins with "sneers and jibes," as Lord Moran observed on November 25, 1943.

"What I find so shocking," Moran wrote, just as the fateful Tehran Conference was about to begin, "is that to the Americans the P.M. is the villain of the piece; they are far more skeptical of him than they are of Stalin."[70]

You don't have to be an Anglophile to be aghast, to question Hopkins's motivations, to marvel at the respect and camaraderie he had for Stalin, a Hitlerian clone who ruled with blood, over Churchill, a democratically elected leader of a nation of laws. "Shocking," as Moran wrote, is one word for it. Upsetting, senseless, and nuts are good alternatives. But if one has consciousness of

Hopkins's perfidy as a Soviet asset, the fitting words are treacherous and dis-loyal to the United States of America.

Indeed, it is at Cairo-Tehran where we see Hopkins's own agenda dramati-cally diverging from FDR's, who still remained agnostic, if not even noticeably receptive to the secondary operations in southern Europe that Churchill still advocated—operations that could likely have forestalled a Soviet empire in Eu-rope and everything that followed from it. After a combined chiefs meeting in Cairo on a plan of campaign to present to Stalin at Tehran, Moran recalled:

> According to Harry, Winston hardly stopped talking, and most of it was about
> "his bloody Italian war." Harry went on in his dry, aggressive way:
>
> "Winston said he was a hundred per cent for OVERLORD. But it was very
> important to capture Rome, and then we ought to take Rhodes.
>
> Harry made it clear that if the P.M. takes this line at Tehran and tries again
> to postpone OVERLORD the Americans will support the Russians. . . .
>
> "Sure, we are preparing for battle at Tehran. You will find us lining up with
> the Russians," he threatened.[71]

It was during the Cairo and Tehran conferences that it became clear, even in Churchill's mind, that Stalin's favored front in France and his own favored front in southern Europe were not mutually exclusive. This must have alarmed Stalin, as the record from Tehran seems to show. When Churchill discussed the virtues of his southern European campaign as an operation completely inde-pendent of Overlord, it's worth noting Stalin asked for this clarification.

From the State Department minutes:

> MARSHAL STALIN inquired if the 35 Divisions which he understood were
> earmarked for OVERLORD would be affected in any way by the continuation
> of the operations in Italy.
>
> THE PRIME MINISTER replied that they would not, since entirely sepa-
> rate Divisions were being used in the Italian Theater.[72]

Say good-bye to "entirely separate Divisions" in the Italian theater. The next time Stalin took the floor it was to question the wisdom of "dispersing allied forces" in too many theaters of operation, Turkey, the Adriatic, southern France. He had a much, much, *much* better idea.

"He said he thought it would be better to take OVERLORD as the basis for all 1944 operations; that after the capture of Rome the troops thus relieved might be sent to Southern France, and in conjunction with forces operating from Corsica might eventually meet in France the main force for OVERLORD from the north."[73]

This is an important moment. Not only is Stalin pushing to bottle up Anglo-American forces in France, it was the removal of these same forces from Italy to *southern* France that ultimately gutted and broke the Allied campaign in Italy—a campaign already weakened but still not paralyzed by the demands for men and matériel to be taken from the Italian front for the Normandy invasion. This—"the weakening of the campaign in Italy in order to invade southern France instead of pushing on into the Balkans"—writes Gen. Mark Clark, "was one of the outstanding political mistakes of the war."

Outstanding, for sure, but if it was Soviet strategy carried out through Soviet persuasion, influence, and an agent of influence, it didn't happen by mistake.

Noting that Stalin was one of the strongest boosters of the invasion of southern France "to keep us out of the Balkans," Clark continued, "if we switched our strength from Italy to France, it was obvious to Stalin, or to anyone else, that we would be turning away from central Europe. From France, the only way we could get to the Balkans was through Switzerland. *In other words, ANVIL led into a dead-end street*" (emphasis added).

So much history has been thrown out to craft the World War II fairy tale we have lived on; Clark's deduction, "obvious," he thought, but nonetheless wholly unimagined by those of us long used to another story, rips the tinsel off the tree. ANVIL led into a dead-end street? How did we end up there? Were we lured into it by Stalin? Did Harry Hopkins's influence make the difference?

Clark doesn't know; doesn't think that way. Who would? Who could? Who knew the half of it in 1950 when his memoir appeared? Clark points out, however, that it was "generally understood Roosevelt toyed with the notion [of the Adriatic operation] for a while," he wrote, "but was not encouraged by Harry Hopkins."[74]

"Not encouraged" is putting it mildly. Sherwood, in his account of the first meeting of the Big Three at Tehran on November 28, 1943, captures Hopkins's intense frustration in the conference room, this time not at Churchill, *but at Roosevelt*. "Roosevelt surprised and disturbed Hopkins by mentioning the possibility of an operation across the Adriatic for a drive, aided by Tito's partisans, north-eastward into Roumania to effect a junction with the Red Army advancing southward from the region of Odessa."[75]

President Roosevelt "surprised and disturbed Hopkins"—for not agreeing with him, eh? This is rich, particularly in light of how, once upon a time, Hopkins, buffing his reputation as FDR's reliable yes-man, assured the Senate that in matters of policy, he always "would go along with the President." Hopkins further stated, "If the President this afternoon decided to develop another issue which fitted into his political philosophy, and he wanted me to get into action, it would take me about five minutes to get in there and fight."[76]

So long as it didn't go against Hopkins's own political philosophy, Hopkins maybe meant to say. Meanwhile, back in the Tehran conference room, "Hopkins thereupon scribbled a note to [chief of staff] Admiral King: 'Who's promoting that Adriatic business that the president continually returns to?' "[77]

As Chesly Manly observed, "Hopkins was virtually accusing the Commander-in-Chief of insubordination."[78] An acerbic comment, but not an exaggerated one. FDR's volition aside, Hopkins was the enforcer here. The next day (November 29, 1943), Sherwood writes, "Churchill made one final and, one must say, gallant attempt on behalf of Rhodes and Turkey as strategic points."[79] It didn't go very far, but it bugged Hopkins, clearly. He must have been seething all day long, all through dinner—Stalin's treat, by the way, a lavish banquet infamous for the Soviet dictator's nonstop needling of Churchill. After it was all over, Hopkins paid a late-night call to Churchill at the British Embassy. In Charles Bohlen's account, he writes that Hopkins told the prime minister that "he was fighting a losing battle to try to delay the invasion of France."

Says which man's army? The question doesn't seem to have come up. Hopkins, via Bohlen, continued, "The view of the United States about the importance of an assault across the Channel had been firmly fixed for many months, Hopkins said, and the Soviet view was equally adamant. There was really little Churchill could do, *Hopkins emphasized, in advising the Prime Minister to yield with grace*" (emphasis added).

It's time to vent: Who was Harry Hopkins to advise the prime minister of England to "yield," with grace or otherwise? Was he just a heartland Napoleon, or was this the KGB's "Agent 19" speaking? Notably, there is no mention of this visit in Sherwood, in State Department records, in Churchill's own accounts, in McJimsey's biography of Hopkins, in Moran's biography of Churchill, or in any other record I have come across. Just Bohlen's. Maybe Hopkins hoped it would remain a secret, too.

Bohlen continued, "It is still not clear whether Hopkins acted under Roosevelt's instructions in going to Churchill. I was not privy to Hopkins's talks with Roosevelt or with Harriman. *But at that time, Roosevelt was relying more and more on Hopkins, virtually to the exclusion of others. At Tehran, Hopkins' influence was paramount*" (emphasis added).[80]

What Bohlen seems to be saying is it almost didn't matter whether Franklin sent Harry to Winston to tell him to lay off. What Harry said went—and "virtually to the exclusion of others." Personally, I don't believe Hopkins was in this case acting under FDR's instruction. There is no evidence that FDR felt inhibited about expressing himself to his British counterpart.

Nonetheless, the next morning, Tuesday, November 30, 1943, the Anglo-American combined chiefs met and agreed to launch OVERLORD in May 1944, to invade southern France "on as big a scale as landing craft permit"—sucking Italy dry—and to cap operations in Italy. Any decisions about Aegean operations were deferred.[81] In other words, it was the end of Aegean operations. At the luncheon that followed, Stalin was most pleased. Roosevelt, too. Churchill was beside himself.[82]

Days later, ill, manic, exhausted, a sixty-eight-year-old Winston Churchill insisted on planning a trek to Italy to visit "Alex," Gen. Harold Alexander, commander of Allied forces in Italy. This drew a medical rebuke from his physician. "I told him it was madness to set off on a journey when he was under the weather like this," Moran recalled. "At that he lost his temper. 'You don't understand. You know nothing about these things. I am not going to see Alex for fun. He may be our last hope. We've got to do something with these bloody Russians.'"

At the time, Moran put this episode down to Churchill's "cussedness." Writing in his memoirs published more than twenty years later, Moran continued, "But now I wonder if whether it was the first indication that Winston had arrived at the conclusion that if he wanted to help the countries of Eastern Europe he must get there before the Red Army."[83] It was probably already too late. Soon it would be past the "the eleventh hour," in Wedemeyer's eyes. In the last stage of the war, the American general wrote, Churchill didn't have a chance at saving anything. "The American chiefs were running the show" under orders from Roosevelt, later Truman, to "smash Germany's armed forces and adhere to the agreements made with Stalin even though he had already broken them in Poland."[84]

The great Churchill had been marginalized.

Is it possible that in marginalizing Winston Churchill, defusing the threat to the Soviet Union posed by an Allied advance on Germany from central Europe, Hopkins had executed the biggest influence operation of his career? Conversely, did Winston Churchill, finding himself odd man out, ever wonder whether he had stepped into a vortex of secret forces beyond his ken and control? These are questions to ponder on the sands of Omaha, Juno, and Sword, quite possibly the mechanism of the greatest influence operation ever. There is a case to be made that Hopkins himself saw this coup as Mission Accomplished. After Tehran, Hopkins returned to Washington to a new life, a new routine, moving out of the White House and into a home in Georgetown with his wife, Louise, and daughter Diana. It seems hard to believe Hopkins would have let himself be maneuvered out of those White House digs if he still had real reason to be there; on the other hand, I've read reports indicating there was friction in the blended ménage of Hopkinses and Roosevelts, which may have prompted the move. There's just not much record to go on here.

The subject almost becomes moot when, just a few weeks later, on New Year's Day 1944, while "having a fine time with friends," as Sherwood tells us, Hopkins "seemed to droop" and had to go to bed. His collapse was no passing thing. Hospitalized first at the Naval Hospital, then at the Mayo Clinic for another "severe" operation, Hopkins would convalesce in White Sulfur Springs for months. All told, Harry Hopkins was away for seven months before returning to Washington on the Fourth of July 1944.

Not to worry. There was plenty of damage left in Hopkins. Still, committing the crime of the century takes a lot out of a man.

CHAPTER **TEN**

The irony of it all is that the Soviet empire is largely one of our own creation.

—GEN. ALBERT C. WEDEMEYER[1]

I can hear the carping: *But the USSR was our ally against Hitler.*

No. The USSR was *not* our ally. It was our secret master-manipulator. We were secretly master-manipulated, not into defeating the Nazis, who, but for the de facto Soviet occupation of Washington, I now am persuaded could have been eliminated in *1943,* but rather into decimating, obliterating, Germany, Soviet Russia's natural barrier against expansion into its European empire. Japan, very much too, for that matter, in the East.[2]

Of course, D-day was in 1944. I am about to describe *another* crime of the century, further establishing World War II as the War for Soviet Aggrandizement and Communist Expansion. And somehow, the "Boogie Woogie Bugle Boy of Company B" never sounds the same again.

To see how this could be we have to return to the first half of 1943, a busy time, particularly for Harry Hopkins. This is when we know from secret documents written by Soviet agents and gleaned from Soviet archives that "Assistant President" Hopkins twice covertly passed vital secrets to the Soviets. Both incidents took place around the time that evidence of Soviet guilt for the Katyn Massacre was being uncovered, then covered up again, even as Stalin was breaking relations with the Polish government in exile over Polish calls for an independent investigation into the massacre. (Not this rift among the Allies and not the Katyn Massacre itself are even mentioned in Sherwood's "official" Hopkins biography.) These same acts of espionage by Hopkins—which, again, we only know about from chance Soviet sources (Mitrokhin's archive and Venona interceptions)—were taking place in the same spring that the president's top adviser called up Major Jordan to ask him to speed a shipment of uranium along to Moscow on the Q.T. Jordan remains the only American to step forward as a witness to testify to Hopkins's perfidy.

It was also in this same spring of 1943 that Dr. Josef Mengele joined the staff at Auschwitz and began to conduct experiments on prisoners.

Why mention this? It's important to fill in the timeline of civilization's destruction, to indicate what horrors had already been unleashed upon the world, and what horrors had not yet been unleashed upon the world—*and might never have been.*

The spring of 1943 was also, to draw a bright new strand into the loom, when German chief of intelligence Adm. Wilhelm Canaris telephoned George H. Earle, former governor of Pennsylvania and special emissary of FDR (whom we met in chapter 7), now in Istanbul, to inquire what might have come of *the peace feelers the Abwehr director had two months earlier clandestinely extended in person to Earle to present to President Roosevelt.*

We are now entering more Lost Narrative, and I am wondering if even the notion that Canaris, a high official in the Third Reich, secretly aided British intelligence, let alone freelanced peace negotiations with Americans (and the British), can ever penetrate the obdurate wall sheltering hoary consensus. It's just that hard to take: Nazi intelligence chief as Good Guy?

In this attempt to rough out a new narrative that more accurately reflects events than the ideologically censored version we are familiar with, there is the risk of oversimplification. At this point, though, the far greater risk is overcomplication. These historical concepts are basic, and they underlie a national scandal. There existed many German anti-Nazis, even many high-ranking ones such as Canaris, who wanted to end World War II early; that's the basic concept. The chapter ahead tells how we ignored them and *why*, which is the national scandal: Our best interests, once again, were subverted for Soviet ends.

There is a fleeting reference to "the amazing anti-Nazi resistance movement" in Germany in Chesly Manly's *The Twenty-Year Revolution.* He mentions in passing Allen Dulles's 1947 account, *Germany's Underground,* a book Dulles wrote about his personal wartime experience as our OSS man in Switzerland. In this slim book, Dulles recounts his extensive secret contacts with members of the anti-Nazi underground, which he kept OSS headquarters in Washington duly apprised of. Like a foreign correspondent whose newspaper never printed his reports, Dulles got nowhere with his work. The German anti-Nazi underground, Dulles makes clear, was the only anti-Nazi underground that wasn't supported by the United States.[3]

The reason is shocking and goes to the heart of the national scandal: This German underground movement was resolutely and operationally anti-Communist just as much as it was anti-Nazi. In Communist-occupied Washington—and London, too—this particular wing of the anti-Hitler resistance was viewed as the enemy just as much as Hitler was. Allen Dulles, future CIA chief, doesn't paint the problem in the same bold strokes I have chosen, but I think he makes it plain:

> The plotters . . . were told clearly and repeatedly that we had made common cause with Russia in the determination to continue together to a complete and united victory . . . [4]
>
> A majority of the conspirators favored England and the United States and some even hoped that after they had removed Hitler they might be able to surrender to the West and continue the war against the Soviets. *This was known in Washington and London and was one of the reasons they received no encouragement from the United States and Britain* [emphasis added].[5]

In other words, anti-Nazis who were also anti-Communist need not apply. This meant common cause with the Communist regime superseded all, *even German surrender.* It was a brilliant strategy—from Stalin's point of view. A post-Hitler government in Germany that was both anti-Nazi and anti-Communist would have blocked Communist expansion into eastern and central Europe. The conspirators' general idea was to surrender German forces to Anglo-American armies on the single condition that German forces then be permitted, with undetermined Allied support, to redeploy to fend off a Soviet invasion of Europe and Germany in the east. In one of his many cables home about the German underground, Dulles elaborated:

> The principal motive for their action is the ardent desire to prevent Central Europe from coming ideologically and factually under the control of Russia. They are convinced that in such event Christian culture and democracy and all that goes with it would disappear in Europe and that the present dictatorship of the Nazis would be exchanged for a new dictatorship.[6]

Their worst fears would start to come true with the Soviet invasion that rolled all the way to Berlin, as Khrushchev later pointed out in a burst of candor, on half a million trucks and jeeps made in the USA.

Clearly, they must be stopped, was the Washington mantra.

They didn't however, mean the Red Army.

During the Nuremberg Trials in March 1946, the scope of this, yes, "amazing anti-Nazi German resistance movement" became briefly visible to the American public in a *New York Times* story, whose headline underscores the point Dulles would make in his book: FULL STORY OF ANTI-HITLER PLOT SHOWS THAT ALLIES REFUSED TO ASSIST.[7]

It's notable that the Allies' refusal to assist shares primacy with the full story of the anti-Hitler plot. This Allied failure was that newsworthy, although the *Times* doesn't probe too far. The intricacies of this mystery quickly receded from press attention, which, naturally, had riveted itself on the overwhelming revelations of Nazi evil. I say "naturally," but I have to wonder, too, if there were any flickers of wonderment over the apparent fact that the Allies might have been able to prevent some of that evil by assisting the anti-Hitler plotters—a story almost too terrible to contemplate.

Probably not, given the universal belief in the rock of the wartime alliance, even as it was already cracking up. For the record, the *Times*'s explanation for the snub was EDEN SAW THREAT TO SOVIET AMITY, as the subhead put it (referring to British foreign minister Anthony Eden). What is not explained is why maintaining "Soviet amity" was valued more highly than bringing the war to a swift end. It is almost as if there were no need for such an explanation. Reporter (and nephew of the *Times*'s owner) C. L. Sulzberger manages to convey a certain empathy for that amity: for example, the senior plotters were "morbidly suspicious of the Russians"; one of their great failures, he wrote, was not to reach out, as we would say today, to German Socialists and Communists "who always suspected the conservative tinge of the *putschists*." More important to realize, however, is it wasn't just Eden who balked at helping this resistance. There were many, many others.

It is Eden, however, who is singled out in this particular story for having refused to take action as early as 1942 on being passed a list of the chief German plotters originating with the Rev. Dietrich Bonhoeffer "on the ground that it might make the Soviet Union suspicious." Suspicious of what—the overthrow of Hitler?

That same year, 1942, Nazi Germany's intelligence chief Canaris made contact with Sir Stewart Graham Menzies, Britain's intelligence chief. From Menzies's obituary in 1968: "It is said that had it not been for the Foreign Office's fear of offending Russia that he might have established direct contact with the admiral [Canaris] in 1942 on the removal of Hitler as a means of shortening the war."[8]

How did that "fear of offending Russia" or raising Russian suspicions become the leading driver of Allied war strategy? Even Dulles only knew the half of it—and only his Swiss slice of the German anti-Nazi effort. That is, his book doesn't include the simultaneous experiences of other Allied agents and emissaries, George H. Earle included. Still, what he reveals is a sufficiently dedicated if often hapless and unlucky network to behold as a promise of what might have been, what likely would have been, *were it not for the Communist occupation of Washington*.

Dulles writes:

As the conspiracy developed two leading figures emerged: Colonel General Ludwig Beck, Chief of Staff of the German army until the summer of 1938, and Carl Friederich Goerderler, a onetime mayor of Leipzig. Closely associated with them were the former German Ambassador at Rome, Ulrich von Hassell, and Johannes Popitz, the Prussian Finance Minister who had served under the Nazis and then turned against them. Among the most important military conspirators were Colonel General Kurt von Hammerstein, Commander in Chief of the German Army from 1930–1934; General (later Field Marshal) Erwin von Witzleben . . .

Beck, Goerderler, von Hassell, Popitz, von Hammerstein, von Witzleben . . . . Reciting these German names in an anti-Hitler context is almost like learning a new foreign language.

. . . General Eduard Wagner, Quartermaster General; General Georg Thomas, head of the economic division of the planning staff of the army; Major General Hans Oster, chief assistant to Admiral Canaris, head of the Abwehr; and General Friederich Olbricht, and Colonel Claus von Stauffenberg, who had key positions in the Replacement Army (often called the Home Army).[9]

Dulles additionally lists two labor leaders, Wilhelm Leuschner and Julius Leber, and refers to the Kreisau Circle, a key group of conspirators drawn from the church, labor, business, and government and centered about Helmuth von Moltke.

Only two among all of these men named above died from natural causes. The rest were executed by the Nazis or committed suicide first.

That certainly doesn't fit the existing view. In fact, the average American reading Dulles's list would probably only recognize the name of von Stauffenberg, and mainly thanks, improbably enough, to Tom Cruise, who, by chance, decided to interrupt his string of outlandish action pictures to chronicle von Stauffenberg's failed attempt to assassinate and lead a coup against Hitler in the 2008 movie *Valkyrie*. This July 20, 1944, episode marked the tragic climax of a star-crossed, long, and, by the Allies, unsupported German conspiracy against Hitler. Still, the very concept of such a conspiracy is probably fantastic to most Americans, who have remained largely bereft of the facts all these years.

This resistance movement was real, all right, even if officially ignored. On May 10, 1945, just a few days after the unconditional surrender of Nazi Germany, General Eisenhower saluted Europe's resistance forces, singling out anti-Nazis in France, Belgium, the Netherlands, Denmark, and Norway.[10] You fought on, he said, addressing them in a speech carried on the BBC, "regardless

of the disappointments you suffered and of the danger you have undergone."
Missing from the list was Germany, where thousands of bona fide anti-Nazis
had been executed.[11] It so happened that only a few weeks before Eisenhower
spoke, Admiral Canaris himself had been hanged at Flossenburg concentration
camp for conspiring against Hitler—hanged twice, a witness later told a court
hearing evidence against the SS guards who executed him and four other members of the July 20, 1944, conspiracy, "once to show him what death 'tasted
like.' "[12]

That doesn't fit our "existing view," either. Nor does the fact that the Chabad
Lubavitcher, a center of the Hasidic Orthodox Jewish community, in 2009 requested that Yad Vashem's Holocaust Memorial recognize Adm. Wilhelm Canaris as a righteous gentile for saving five hundred Jews from the Warsaw
Ghetto.[13] It's literally incomprehensible to a society shaped in some large part
by vast armies of Nazi villains sweeping across pop culture (their understudies
either CIA or corporate villains), ranging far beyond the time and bounds of
the twelve-year Third Reich—and with never a commissar, Gulag guard, or
show trial judge in sight. This may explain the jolt of uneasy recognition that
comes from reading in *The Captive Mind,* Czeslaw Milosz's famous study of
Communist totalitarian thinking, the reasons the Soviets encouraged a singular
literary focus on the crimes of Hitler's Germany. "Concentrating the readers'
attention upon German atrocities channeled their hatred into a single direction
and so contributed to the 'psychological preparation' of the country," Milosz
wrote.[14] Milosz was talking about Sovietized Poland, circa 1951; what he describes, however, fits a stream of Hollywood movies for over half a century—
one proximate cause of our numbness when it comes to Soviet crime and all
that. What does it tell us, though, about the "psychological preparation" of our
own country? I believe Cruise's movie about the heroic German military underground, meanwhile, was an anomalous American *first.*

Surely, this marks another triumph of the forces of concealment, but to what
end? British journalist Ian Colvin, author of a remarkable, consensus-shattering
biography of Admiral Canaris, offers some clues. Colvin's 1951 book for the
first time made the case that not only was Canaris among the anti-Hitler plotters, but he was actually working as best he could under ridiculously dangerous
circumstances during the war on behalf of British intelligence.[15] Among his
accomplishments, Colvin maintains that Canaris thwarted the assassination of
Churchill, prevented Spain from joining the war, provided German troop
movement information to the British, and withheld key intelligence from Hitler, all the while protecting the anti-Hitler plotters on his staff. It is this last ac-
complishment that may be most significant, revealing a hidden stratum of war

history. In other words, Canaris was not just a singular man; he symbolized a singular movement. The book, Colvin wrote, contains "the disturbing assertion that the Chief of German Intelligence and a great number of his staff were in secret sympathy with the Allies before and during the War. Furthermore, that this movement of sympathy was known to the British Foreign Office, but either not sufficiently fostered to be useful, or neglected."[16]

Let me count the ways.

In his 1958 memoir, *Wedemeyer Reports!*, General Wedemeyer picks up on George H. Earle's series of secret negotiations with the German underground, which began with Canaris. Notably enough, these negotiations, which Earle didn't bring to public attention until 1958, came as news to Wedemeyer, too, even though Wedemeyer was himself a key military strategist of World War II. What's more important, Wedemeyer agreed with Earle's contention that such a U.S.-German deal might have ended the war in Europe in 1943. What a staggering concept. "Countless lives would have been saved," Wedemeyer writes, "and, of greatest importance, the Allies would not have supplanted one dangerous ideology for another."[17]

Before entertaining the implications here, there is an unexpectedly surreal aspect to this breathtaking meeting of the minds, Wedemeyer's and Earle's, which is worth mentioning because it sheds light on the tenor of their time. Wedemeyer first read about Earle's 1943 negotiations not in a briefing paper, not in State Department records, not in a diplomat's memoir, not in a newspaper of record. He read about them in the pages of a supermarket-style tabloid— *Confidential* magazine, a short-lived *National Inquirer*-style scandal sheet.

It's hard to imagine that Earle set his sights on publishing this formidable story in *Confidential.* This suggests that the journals and papers of the day were unimpressed by Earle's yarn, weren't interested in publishing a history-changing account by a former governor and Roosevelt envoy about his secret peace talks with the head of German intelligence, who was later executed by Hitler. They weren't even moved by their own professional responsibility to preserve a historic, behind-the-scenes memoir of what was, let alone what might have been. Earle was also, by that time, notably anti-Communist. Was that part of the "problem"? Amazingly, I was able to locate a well-preserved copy of the August 1958 edition of *Confidential* on eBay for about ten bucks. I couldn't wait for it to arrive, and then there it was.

Cover-story headline: F.D.R.'S TRAGIC MISTAKE! by "George H. Earle, Former Governor of Pennsylvania." There is a page-filling shot of FDR's face, tip-top jaunty style, cigarette holder at attention. A list of secondary stories gracing the cover includes:

"The Clinic for Female Frigidity"

"20 Minutes to Live—a Death House Diary"

"A Cure for Excess Hair . . . Now Science Has the Answer"

The more I read over these titles, the more I wondered how many times Earle was turned down by more "respected" publications. Oh well. Three cheers for the rag that saved the story for the republic, *Confidential,* which lived up to its motto: *"Tells the facts and names the names."* Then again, maybe Earle wanted to get his story past the elites to the general public.

According to Earle's account, he sent Canaris's initial query regarding a negotiated peace to the White House via diplomatic pouch in early 1943.

Who wants to bet it was Harry Hopkins on the other end opening up the pouch?

No bet. I already know the answer. Just before Earle departed the United States to become FDR's special emissary in Istanbul (officially, naval attaché), he wrote the following letter on December 19, 1942, from New York City on Ritz-Carlton stationery.

Dear Harry:

If you don't mind I'm going to report to you direct my activities. I like the way your mind works and I know you will sort out what you think of importance enough for the President.[18]

Maybe Harry thought George meant "throw out."

As I examined this letter, which I came across in a miscellaneous folder of Hopkins correspondence at Georgetown University Library, I found something puppy-doggedly disingenuous about Earle coming through his round, bold handwriting on the page. The letter, by the way, probably wasn't where it belonged, and thank goodness.

The single designated file of Earle-Hopkins correspondence, I discovered, is specified by label to span June, 3, 1943 to November 22, 1944. There is no file in the Hopkins collection for any earlier Earle correspondence—no epistolary record from the time in January 1943 when Earle arrived in Istanbul and shortly thereafter came into contact with anti-Hitler Germans, including Abwehr chief Canaris and German ambassador to Turkey Franz von Papen, and, as we know from Earle's account, wrote Hopkins and Roosevelt all about it. Where did these letters go? Had the record been cleaned out? Had I stumbled across my own black hole of antiknowledge?

The one Earle file—Folder 6—was, according to its description in the Index, supposed to contain: "correspondence from George Earle, in a folder marked "Sydney Hyman,"[19] compiled by Sherwood in his book on Hopkins. Folder contents have been maintained in their provenance prior to arrival at Georgetown University."

Really?

The only clue I could find to explain what appears to be a grievous hole in the record is a single typed sentence on the final sheet of this file: "Previous correspondence to and from Lt. Comndr. George Earle was packed and sent to Mr. Hopkins' home November 22, 1944 for his use."

"His use"? "Was packed"? What for? By whom? Then what happened? There are no answers to these questions. (A librarian looked at me helplessly.) Someone gutted the historical record, and we are left to our own devices—to collect and piece together the fragments of this shocking, shaming history that this same someone, it seems, very much didn't want anyone to find out about.

So here goes.

Without undertaking a history of the anti-Nazi Germans, suffice it to say we see significant contact with the British by 1938. By 1942, Canaris had a plan before British intelligence that was under serious consideration but, of course, went nowhere.[20]

Earle tells us Canaris came to see him in Istanbul early in 1943 following Roosevelt's stunning announcement of an Allied policy of "unconditional surrender" on January 24, 1943, the final day of the Casablanca Conference with Churchill. Did FDR really mean what he said? Canaris wanted to know. Was there anything more to talk about? Earle reported the incident "faithfully" to FDR, he wrote fifteen years later in *Confidential*. His dispatch went off by plane in the next diplomatic pouch. "I waited patiently for his reply," Earle wrote.

Yes, to keep our story threads straight, these German-American peace feelers began probing at about the same time former U.S. ambassador to the USSR William C. Bullitt presented FDR with his prophetic blueprint of what the postwar world would look like if Anglo-American appeasement of Stalin didn't stop.

Perhaps ironically, also at this same time, on February 1, 1943, army intelligence finally decided to open the canvas bags of encoded Soviet messages that had been accumulating since 1939, when telegraph companies were ordered to turn over copies of cable traffic between Soviet missions in the United States and Moscow after the signing of the Nazi-Soviet Pact. This would become the Venona project, and according to the Schecters, the idea was to read Soviet cables to better understand Soviet thinking and thus be better allies. No kidding. No one seemed to have had an inkling that U.S. codebreakers would, in reading or partly reading a reported 2,900 messages out of an estimated two million, uncover a giant complex of American traitors at work for the Soviet Union.[21]

Stalin, meanwhile, continued hectoring Roosevelt on an array of supposed Anglo-American inadequacies. Bullitt's prophecy aside, Roosevelt continued to appease and placate Stalin.

Roosevelt to Stalin, February 22, 1943: "I regret equally with you that the Allied effort in North Africa did not proceed in accordance with the schedule which was interrupted by unexpectedly heavy rains . . . I fully realize the adverse effect . . . I am taking every possible step . . . I can assure you we are making maximum effort . . . I understand the importance of military effort on the Continent of Europe at the earliest practicable date in order to reduce Axis resistance to your heroic army."

About that army: "On behalf of the people of the United States," FDR wrote in a second cable to Stalin on February 22, 1943, "I want to express to the Red Army, on its twenty-fifth anniversary, our profound admiration for its magnificent achievements unsurpassed in all history."[22]

Slurp, slurp. Little wonder, then, really, that on March 4, 1943, Maxim Litvinov, the Soviet ambassador, felt emboldened enough to visit Undersecretary of State Sumner Welles at his office, where Litvinov "left him with a list of officials who supposedly were undermining American relations with Russia"— and who would be purged, American-style, by June 1943, as noted earlier.[23] Little wonder, too, that after Standley, the U.S. ambassador to Moscow, talked turkey to the press in Moscow on March 8, 1943, about Soviet efforts to deny Lend-Lease contributions to the USSR, the White House set about replacing him.[24] Meanwhile, Moscow was at this same moment trolling the USA and Canada for uranium.

Back to Earle.

"One morning in March," Earle wrote, the phone rang and he recognized the voice of Canaris.

"I'm the gentleman who called on you unannounced two months ago. Has there been any progress in the matter we discussed?"

"No," Earle said. "No progress."

"I am very sorry," Canaris replied and hung up.[25] The German spychief would try again to reach Churchill that year, traveling blindfolded to the Paris convent that, amazingly, served as British intelligence headquarters in Nazi-occupied France. Earle never heard from him again. He would, however, hear much more from Canaris's fellow conspirators.[26]

On April 3, 1943, ten days before the Katyn Forest Massacre became known to the world, NKVD officer Elizabeth Zarubina met for the first time with Franz L. Neumann, a brand-new KGB recruit on the German desk at the OSS in Washington.[27]

With so much Soviet espionage activity going on, why is this particular meeting significant?

Neumann, a leading light of the so-called Frankfurt School—poison-gas incubator of such noxious theories as "cultural Marxism," "political correctness" and "critical theory"—was already passing secret documents to his Soviet masters. Soon he would also be writing top secret memos for U.S. intelligence *analyzing the potential of anti-Nazi groups in Germany*. Guess what? Neumann tended to see more promise in German "workers" (read: Communists) than in German "conservatives" (anti-Communists), as he explained in memos to American intelligence. For example, later on, after von Stauffenberg's failed coup and attempt on Hitler's life in July 1944, Neumann assessed the anti-Nazi plotters thus: "The group represented nothing more than bankrupt generals, nationalist intellectuals, and (possibly) nationalist Social Democrats and civil servants."[28]

"Bankrupt" generals aside, "nationalist" was a buzzword as bad as "isolationist." Nevertheless, such was the word from what was, in effect, Neumann's NKVD desk at the OSS—no doubt to the satisfaction of his NKVD controller Zarubina, also the wife of KGB spychief and "diplomat" Zarubin/Zubilin, whose own espionage activities, of course, would prompt Harry Hopkins to inform the Soviet Embassy that the FBI was listening in. Quite a tightly wrapped cluster of Soviet interests, no? I'm not exactly suggesting a harmonic convergence; for one thing, the discipline of Communist cells often ensured an amazing degree of anonymity among agents. At the top of the OSS, for example, Duncan Lee, Wild Bill Donovan's aide *and KGB source,* had no idea that his old friend and OSS employee Donald Wheeler was also working for the KGB— and was probably the KGB's "most productive source," according to Haynes, Klehr, and Vassiliev.[29] That said, it doesn't seem unreasonable to note the overlap in purpose, task, and mission across so few degrees of separation.

Neumann, after all, was a Red pea in a pod along with his more enduringly famous OSS colleague and Frankfurt School cofounder Herbert Marcuse—yet another German-born Marxist analyzing top secret American intelligence for the OSS. (Yes, your hair should be standing on end.) Was Marcuse an NKVD agent, too? His relationship with Soviet intelligence remains unconfirmed. "Re Herbert Marcuse: We have taken an interest in him in connection with his work for the cabin," a KGB document of this same vintage (January 1943) reports. "Cabin" means OSS.[30] The KGB report noted that Marcuse was a "close friend" of Neumann's—Marcuse would marry Neumann's widow in 1954— and he was "very close" to Communist Party members back in Germany. Twenty years later Marcuse would also be very close to the 1960s antiwar movement.

No, I don't digress. It's all of a scary piece. It is revelations such as these that must come together in a new, Communist-conscious, American narrative of World War II and the world, our world, that formed in the war's aftermath. Without it, we remain ill equipped to understand ourselves or our world. It turns out the war narrative does not begin on December 7, 1941, "a day which will live in infamy," and end on August 14, 1945, after the United States dropped atomic bombs on Hiroshima and Nagasaki, soon to be sealed with Alfred Eisenstaedt's photograph of the ultimate kiss in Times Square.

My new war narrative is different. It burns more quietly inside beige government offices and impersonal conference rooms, where, in sunlight and shadow striated by the wooden slats of midcentury venetian blinds, Alger Hiss, Virginius Frank Coe, Lawrence Duggan, Julian Wadleigh, Harold Glasser, and Lauchlin Currie—all confirmed Soviet agents—made their "contributions" to Postwar Foreign Policy Preparation.[31] It goes on even inside busy downtown restaurants such as the venerable Old Ebbitt Grill, where, in the spring of 1941, KGB agent Harry Dexter White received his "Operation Snow" espionage orders from Vitaly Pavlov, right across the street from White's office at the Treasury Department. White, as we have seen, was told to insert certain demands into the State Department's cable flow to Tokyo, specific language crafted in Moscow purposefully to bring the United States and Japan to war by the end of 1941. Which he did, and which it did.

This new war narrative takes place also inside the Justice Department and around Capitol Hill, where, in late June 1941, as Robert Stripling wrote in his memoir, the acting attorney general informed Rep. Martin Dies that "after discussing the question with the President and Secretary Hull," he was denying permission to the House Committee on Un-American Activities to hold hearings on Japanese spying on the Pacific Coast and in Hawaii.

Why?

Stripling, of course, knew nothing of Operation Snow, *at that very moment in progress,* but his sense of the impact that hearings on Japanese espionage activity could have had makes it clear that their cancellation for whatever reason furthered the Soviet plot to push Japan and the United States to war.

"For the remainder of my life," Stripling wrote in 1949, "I will always believe that our disclosures would have aroused enough alarm among our people to have caused the Japanese to abandon their planned attack on Pearl Harbor."[32]

The forces of exposure were thwarted again. Lighting up Japan's dark designs on American territory would have rung an alarm for Americans, quite likely resulting in hasty Japanese recalculations (retreat). That wasn't in the master plan—in Moscow's master plan. As Peter Niblo writes in *Influence,* "Moscow, of course, urgently needed the Pearl Harbor attack to succeed."[33]

Could the Justice decision, the result of consultations with the White House (input from Hopkins? input from Currie?) and the State Department (input from Hiss? advice from IPR?) have been cobbled together in concert with, under pressure from, due to indirect influence of the force field emanating from Operation Snow?

I don't know the answer, but the record shows that whatever Moscow "urgently needed," Moscow usually got. They needed a weapons and matériel lifeline, and they got Lend-Lease, which, as we've seen, came together after a successful triple play of Stalin's influence team—Hammer to Hopkins to White. They needed the Japanese to drive south in the Pacific, away from Soviet interests, and they got, among other things elaborated on by Peter Niblo and others, Operation Snow, which helped precipitate Pearl Harbor. They needed that "second front," but only in northern France to keep Anglo-American forces from landing in southern Europe, and they got OVERLORD and ANVIL, thanks, in some significant measure, to the labors of Harry Hopkins. They needed to neutralize the anti-Nazi, anti-Communist opposition in Germany to facilitate their expansion into eastern and central Europe, and they got that, too. Who helped that along? Hopkins, likely, standing over the diplomatic pouch—but this, as we'll see, was a group effort.

What else did Moscow urgently need?

The destruction of Germany. That would be laid out in the Morgenthau Plan of 1944, another Harry Dexter White Special. Meanwhile, though, is it possible that Roosevelt's policy of "unconditional surrender"—which virtually guaranteed the destruction of Germany—was in any part the creation of yet another influence operation?

"Unconditional surrender" is usually portrayed as having sprung whole and spontaneously from Roosevelt's lips—much, as we've seen, as Lend-Lease is usually (and inaccurately) portrayed. According to sources such as Roosevelt's son Elliott, FDR himself established the unconditional surrender policy on the spur of the moment: "The thought popped into my mind . . . and the next thing I knew I had said it."[34] This was not at all the case, as even Sherwood points out, and much later (a generation later[35]), State Department records of the January 1943 Casablanca Conference make clear. Such gratuitous myth-making, such a gratuitous *lie,* is strange in and of itself.

Actually, the entire official record, such as it is, is strange. A footnote in the State Department Casablanca Conference records describes this controversial surrender policy as having been the brainchild of one of those quasi-official State Department–cum–Council on Foreign Relations panels (that'll raise some hackles[36]) that sprang up right before the war, with Roosevelt being informally briefed at some point after May 1942 and before January 1943. So much for the spontaneity myth. The State Department, meanwhile, certainly wasn't behind it, or even in the loop, but what else is new?

Immediately preceding the Casablanca Conference on January 7, 1943, State Department minutes tell us, Roosevelt brought up unconditional surrender with his U.S. military chiefs as a fait accompli to raise with Churchill—who knew nothing about it at this point—to discuss "the advisability of informing Mr. Stalin" of their intentions.[37] More pins in the spontaneity bubble. On January 24, 1943, announcement day in Casablanca, Sherwood reports, Roosevelt spoke on background (not for quotation) to reporters from several pages of notes that had been "carefully prepared in advance." While we don't have a record of what was said, what Sherwood calls "notes" sounds more like polished text. Knowing how closely Hopkins worked with Roosevelt, it's reasonable to assume Hopkins prepared or at least edited the written statement.

Quite notably, however, the very first use of the phrase "unconditional surrender" at Casablanca was by Harry Hopkins himself.[38] In a January 23, 1943, meeting, one day ahead of the president's sensational announcement, Hopkins told the grand vizier of Morocco, "The war will be pursued until Germany, Italy, and Japan agree to unconditional surrender."

Those were his very words. Clearly, Harry Hopkins was at least on board with the policy; we don't know whether he was driving it, but we have to wonder. I'm taking these pains to describe this policy and the means by which it became Allied doctrine, however, because unconditional surrender may well be what cemented our ultimate defeat . . .

Is that too harsh a formulation? Let me rephrase . . . because unconditional surrender may well be the policy that ensured Soviet dominion over half of Europe. It was also, as Ian Colvin noted in the preface to a 1957 edition of his Canaris biography, a "pivotal point" in the tragedy of the German underground.

"Unconditional surrender" would set the strategy of "total war" (Allied) as the only appropriate response to "total guilt" (German). Such a strategy presumed, indeed, drew inspiration from, a belief in the unwavering, monolithic German support for Nazism and Hitler, which the very existence of a significant anti-Nazi German resistance movement belied. For the sake of the policy then, the significant anti-Nazi German resistance movement had to be denied, shut out. Otherwise, "total war," and the total destruction it required, wasn't justified. Otherwise, I say, Stalin wouldn't win.

General Wedemeyer devotes an entire chapter of his memoir to making the devastating strategic case against unconditional surrender. The general did not mince words: "We annulled the prospect of winning a real victory by the Casablanca call for unconditional surrender," he wrote.[39]

Why?

"Our demand for unconditional surrender naturally increased the enemy's will to resist and forced even Hitler's worst enemies to continue fighting to save their country."[40] (This "will to resist" would only intensify with the September 1944 leak of the Morgenthau Plan for the "pastoralization" of Germany, noted below.)

Many leading Allied officials shared Wedemeyer's concern about the unifying, animating effect FDR's declaration would have on Germany, fearing it would prolong the fighting, ensuring that it would be all last-ditch and to the bitter end.[41] On the other side, too, the view was the same. In the book *The German Generals Talk,* Lidell Hart writes, "All to whom I talked dwelt on the effect of 'unconditional surrender' policy on prolonging the war. They told me that but for this they—and their troops, the factor that was more important—would have been ready to surrender sooner, separately or collectively."[42]

Wedemeyer elaborated, "We failed to realize that unconditional surrender and the annihilation of German power would result in a tremendous vacuum in Central Europe into which the Communist power and ideas would flow."

About that vacuum in Central Europe: Is it the case that "we" simply "failed" to realize that a vacuum would emerge? Or had enough of us instead bought the Moscow line that Stalin wanted "nothing more than security for his country," as Roosevelt, invoking Harry Hopkins, told William Bullitt at this same fateful moment? What about those among us in positions of power who had already decided that Stalin in Europe would be a good thing?

Remember Hanson Baldwin's Numero Uno "great mistake of the war": the belief "that the Politburo had abandoned . . . its policy of world Communist revolution and was honestly interested in the maintenance of friendly relations with capitalist governments."

Where did that belief—propaganda—come from?

Wedemeyer explains, "We poisoned ourselves with our own propaganda and let the Communist serpent we took to our bosom envenom our minds and distort our ideals." Baldwin is more matter-of-fact. "We became victims of our own propaganda," he wrote. "Russian aims were good and noble. Communism had changed its spots."

We were victims, all right, but not of "our own" propaganda; it was *their* propaganda. It was propaganda conceived in Moscow and disseminated by bona fide Kremlin agents, mouthpieces and organizers of Communist parties, fellow travelers, and many, many dupes ("liberals," "all the best people," opinion makers, etc.). Our message wasn't our own anymore because our perception of reality itself had been subverted, and by brilliant, lucky, spontaneous, concerted, fateful, inexorable design.

Sometimes this was subtle stuff; often it was as stark as a censor's black marker. Some of the more shocking confirmation comes from an illuminating 2010 book called *Hollywood's War with Poland, 1939–1945* by M. B. B. Biskupski. A victim of Soviet aggression since the Nazi-Soviet Pact was consummated in the Nazi-Soviet invasion of Poland in 1939, Poland, Biskupski documents, was consistently denigrated in Hollywood's effort to boost the Allied war effort—an effort overseen by Communists and fellow travelers in the chock-full-of-Commies Office of War Information and its similarly "progressive" spin-off, the Bureau of Motion Pictures. Often, this was by sin of omission. What Biskupski calls "the occupation subgenre" of the Hollywood war movie, for example, was invariably set in Britain, France, or Norway; never Poland. Biskupski also explains how Victor Laszlo, the Czech resistance hero in *Casablanca,* co-written by noted Hollywood Lefty (Stalinist) Howard Koch, one of the "unfriendly nineteen" later called before Congress, could never have been a Polish national in pro-Soviet Hollywood. Indeed, among the multinational refugees crowding Rick's Café Americain there are Austrians, Germans, Russians, Czechs, French, Norwegians, even Bulgarians—but no Poles. Nor is Poland mentioned in a Nazi character's listing of underground movements, despite being home to Europe's largest.[43] There were sins of commission, too. Drawing from a memorandum in the BMP files, Biskupski describes how the U.S. government baldly called for pro-Soviet propaganda to be inserted directly into the 1944 MGM movie *Song of Russia:* namely, that the movie script explain the Hitler-Stalin Pact as "only an expedient," and the Soviet invasions of Finland and Poland as "defensive gestures." These same "expedient" and "defensive" measures, by the way, would constitute German, *but not Soviet, war crimes,* at the Nuremberg Trials.

There's more. Not only was the United States government directing MGM, a private movie studio, to disseminate Soviet propaganda, the BMP chief, an American public servant, "sent the MGM script to the first secretary of the Russian embassy in Washington, Vladimir Bazykin, who offered specific wording" *to bring the script into conformity with the Kremlin line.* Such wording was indeed specific. According to Biskupski, "In the inserted dialogue, the character who suggests the Hitler-Stalin pact revealed cooperation between the Soviets and the Germans is shown to be wrong and is embarrassed by his fatuity."[44]

Soviet agitprop. It was everywhere. Stanislaw Mikolajczyk, prime minister of the Polish government in exile, felt compelled to lodge a complaint with the State Department about American broadcasts into wartime Poland by the Red-riddled OWI, because, he wrote, the U.S. government's "pro-Soviet propaganda duplicated the broadcasts sent from Moscow." Indeed, these American broadcasts, Mikolajczyk continued, *"might well have emanated from Moscow"* (emphasis added).[45]

Basically, they did.

So I have to wonder: Why not unconditional surrender, too? Given how many U.S. war policies and strategies may be traced back to Moscow and its minions, it seems worth considering. Another example: One of the great moments in Soviet Deception History took place when FDR magnanimously (he thought) handed off an OSS document on Yugoslavia, "lyrical in its praise of Tito," as M. Stanton Evans notes, to Stalin himself at Tehran—except that the document in question was in fact Soviet disinformation as prepared by a KGB contact in the OSS for American consumption. It was designed to build support for the Communist leader Tito and undermine support for the anti-Nazi, anti-Communist leader, Draja Mihailovich. Which it did. After an intense Soviet disinformation campaign, spearheaded by KGB agent James Kluggman from his Cairo perch in British intelligence, the Allies were persuaded to drop all support of Mihailovich and support Tito, who would establish a Communist despotism, hunt down Mihailovich, put him on (show) trial, and execute him.[46]

With this complex of deception operations under way in mind, I went back to the State Department footnote on the mysterious origins of unconditional surrender policy.

In tiny print it says that the policy was first affirmed on May 6, 1942—the day of the surrender of Corregidor—and "reaffirmed" on May 20, 1942. To wit: "The Subcommittee on Security Problems of the Advisory Committee on Post-War Foreign Policy at its third meeting on May 6, 1942 began a consideration of armistice and unconditional surrender. According to the minutes of the subcommittee . . . quick agreement on the matter was reached."

"Quick agreement" on such a weighty issue with so many opponents in the military and diplomatic establishment seems a tad hasty, but the minutes continue: "The subcommittee agreed to begin its discussion . . . *with the assumption* that unconditional surrender would be exacted from the principal defeated states." (emphasis added).

Then, "The Subcommittee reaffirmed its support for unconditional surrender at its fourth meeting on May 20, 1942." From the minutes: "There was considerable discussion of whether an unconditional surrender, rather than an armistice, must be exacted of the principal enemy states."

A squabble?

"It was held that, while unconditional surrender would undoubtedly be preferable if the military situation permitted, study should also be given to possible conditions of an armistice and possible conditions of a negotiated peace."

The footnote goes on to note that the president was "informally apprised" of the subcommittee's views by its head, Norman L. Davis, a well known diplomat and disarmament advocate.

It seems clear that there still existed a divide on the issue. So, which officials might have been on the side of "quick agreement"? Here are some guesses, culled from the roster of the subcommittee's parent Advisory Committee:

> Lauchlin Currie
> Laurence Duggan
> Alger Hiss
> Julian Wadleigh[47]
> Harry Dexter White.[48]

Yes, that is a partial roll call of the KGB all-stars in Washington.

Also working in and around this same key advisory committee were other spies: Virginius Frank Coe and Harold Glasser. We might also note the presence on the committee of White House aide David K. Niles, not only for his own Communist connections, but because "he spoke in a sense for Harry Hopkins in accord with the wishes of the President," as the State Department record states.[49] Did they influence the subcommittee debate on unconditional surrender? It is difficult to say, given the anonymous bureaucracy in which such momentous policy was made.

Secretary of State Hull, meanwhile, had absolutely no clue as to when or how unconditional surrender became U.S. policy. In his memoir-discussion of unconditional surrender, Hull offers a sad little tag line to the disconnection between his office and policy making. "Originally, this principle had not formed part of the State Department's thinking. We were as much surprised as Mr. Churchill . . . In our postwar planning discussion in the State Department, which had begun more than three years prior to the Casablanca Conference, we had not embraced the idea of unconditional surrender."[50] No, "we" had not— but that subcommittee of an advisory committee under "our" aegis had. The forty-seventh and longest-serving secretary of state wouldn't get the message until after it was out of Roosevelt's mouth.

Hopkins biographer George McJimsey argues that Roosevelt was determined to make the announcement about unconditional surrender at Casablanca because he saw the "doctrine as an approach to Stalin . . . a device—along with Lend Lease aid and the promise of a second front—for convincing Stalin of his good will."[51] In other words, it served as a blandishment first, not for speeding the end of the war but for enhancing the U.S.-USSR relationship— increasingly the American priority. As such, then, it seems that the unconditional surrender policy itself had to be protected from everything, including, it seems, *the end of the war,* particularly an end to the war that was "premature"—in other words, before the Soviet Union's enemy Germany was destroyed and, presumably, its own army was in place. To repeat, the anti-Nazi, anti-Communist resistance never had a chance because we wanted a relationship with the USSR more than we wanted to end the war.

Thus, we took all precautions. When Louis Lochner, for many years the AP bureau chief in Berlin, attempted to file a story on the activities of anti-Nazi Germans operating out of France in October 1944, U.S. military censors blocked the story. Why? "The government official in charge of censorship was forthcoming enough to confide to Lochner that there was a personal directive from the president of the United States 'in his capacity of commander in chief forbidding all mention of the German resistance,'" writes Klaus P. Fischer in his 2011 book, *Hitler and America.* Drawing from Lochner's 1956 memoir *Always the Unexpected,* Fischer quotes Lochner's explanation for this seemingly inexplicable and outrageous censorship: "Stories of the existence of a resistance movement did not fit into the concept of Unconditional Surrender!"

Exactly—and this was precisely what Ian Colvin was writing about in 1951. Meanwhile, who benefited most from the concept? Stalin. Lochner continued, "My belief that President Roosevelt was determined to establish the guilt of the entire German people, and not only the Nazi regime for bringing on World War II, had already received confirmation in the summer of 1942."[52]

Turns out, Lochner knew Roosevelt personally, and both men had a mutual friend in Prince Louis Ferdinand of Prussia. Lochner had been in contact with the anti-Hitler opposition in Germany since 1939. In November 1941, German anti-Nazis asked Lochner, heading home on leave, to contact the president on their behalf, to ask Roosevelt to speak out about what form of government he would like to see take shape in post-Hitler Germany, and to provide the president with secret radio codes so that Americans and German anti-Nazis could communicate directly with each other. So writes Peter Hoffman in *The History of the German Resistance, 1933–1945,* which first appeared in Germany in 1969, drawing from the 1955 German edition of Lochner's memoir, certain details of which Hoffman says are not in the English version.

Lochner was interned by the Nazi regime at the outbreak of the war in December 1941 and didn't reach Washington until the summer of 1942. This would have been shortly after "unconditional surrender" was affirmed and reaffirmed by the president's postwar advisory council subcommittee, and shortly after Roosevelt had promised a "second front" to Soviet minister Molotov. Lochner immediately informed the White House that he had personal and confidential messages for the president from the prince "and secret information on resistance groups in Germany that he might not confide to anyone else."

No answer. No interest.

Lochner's attempts at gaining an audience in June 1942 failed. Lochner followed up with a letter and received no reply. Finally, he was informed by the White House through the AP bureau in Washington, Hoffman writes, that "there was no desire to receive his information and he was requested to refrain from further efforts to transmit it." It was a terse response, Fischer adds, quoting Lochner, to the effect that his persistence was "most embarrassing."

Most embarrassing? To whom? Who wrote that terse response? I have not been able to learn the answers to these questions, but Hoffman reveals an important piece of the puzzle in a footnote. Lochner's final attempt to reach Roosevelt on June 19, 1942, was in a letter addressed to a trusted presidential aide. That aide was *Lauchlin Currie.*[53]

If this were a movie, forks of lightning would crack and light a black sky over the White House. I don't think we actually can say the buck stopped there, at Soviet agent Currie's desk, but it looks as if this gesture from the anti-Nazi German resistance did. Such "good Germans" might have spoiled the chances for both unconditional surrender, recently "reaffirmed" in May 1942, and, of course, Stalin's "second front," the subject of Molotov's secret discussions with Hopkins, also in May 1942. Given the stunning Axis victory at Tobruk on June 21, this White House brush-off of anti-Nazi German resistance hardly seems to be in the Allies' best interests—only in Stalin's best interests.

"This means war to the end, the destruction of Germany as a military power, and the emergence of Russia as the dominating force in Europe," Abwehr chief Wilhelm Canaris had told George Earle in his Istanbul hotel room following the conclusion of what Roosevelt himself called "the unconditional surrender conference" in January 1943.[54] What Canaris didn't think to ask was whether Roosevelt actually objected to such a ghastly outcome. I think it's fair to say Roosevelt did not so object; indeed, he seems to have looked forward to it.

The next approach to Earle, also in that spring of 1943, came from Baron Kurt von Lersner, a German aristocrat of Jewish extraction who lived in virtual exile in Turkey. He, too, had a proposal for the Allies. Earle wrote, "According to Lersner—and I could not doubt him; he had placed his life in my hands—some of the highest officials in Germany, Papen included, loved their country but hated Hitler. They wanted to end the war before he bled Germany of all her youth, all her strength and resources. At the same time, they were deeply concerned about Russia's growing might and power."

Unbeknownst to Earle, fostering "Russia's growing might and power" seemed to have become the purpose of our war. Earle wrote, "What Lersner wanted to know was this: If they delivered the German Army to the Allies, could they then count on Allied cooperation in keeping Russian troops out of Germany and her buffer states to the east?"

Earle sent off another dispatch to FDR at the White House marked "Urgent." Again, Earle received no reply. "I pressed the matter with every ounce of my persuasion and judgment," Earle wrote, "but I sensed the old trouble. Lersner's call for an overt stand against Communist expansion distressed Roosevelt."[55]

It *really* distressed Hopkins. It's even possible Harry Hopkins made the decision to ignore Earle's offers from the German underground himself. Or, if Hopkins brought FDR into his deliberations, he certainly managed to convince him to ignore Canaris. Hopkins's star was easily that high.

"All that summer Lersner asked and pleaded for encouragement," Earle wrote. "I had nothing for him from the White House. There was nothing to say."

Earle wrote that his German contacts came back to him with another more specific plan, laying out the involvement of Field Marshal Ludwig Beck; Count Wolf Heinrich von Helldorf, chief of police of Berlin; Prince Gottfried Bismarck, a Potsdam official and grandson of the "Iron Chancellor"; and a well-known cavalry officer, Freiherr von Boeselager. Again, the plan was to stage a coup, turn over Hitler and his top henchmen to the Allies, and bring about Germany's "unconditional surrender, with one condition": The Russians were not to be allowed into Central Europe, including Germany or territory at that time controlled by Germany.

Earle sent this dispatch off with high hopes, he wrote. Maybe it was the specificity of the plan, but Earle really got into the spirit of it this time. "Papen had a plane standing by. When the president's word came through, Earle wrote, he, Earle, would drive out to the airport in his lieutenant commander's uniform and fly to Berlin. "I felt this way: I might not come back," Earle wrote. "If I didn't I wanted to go out in an American uniform." Earle even wrote farewell letters. They sat. He sat. Days, weeks passed. Lersner kept checking in.

Earle doesn't specify how much time went by, but finally an answer from the president came through. It was stiff and impersonal. "All such applications for a negotiated peace should be referred to the Supreme Allied Commander, General Eisenhower," Roosevelt wrote. The reference to Eisenhower's rank dates the reply to after Eisenhower was promoted in December 1943. Earle explains, "In diplomatic language, this was the final runaround. Even if we did get to Eisenhower, the matter would be referred back to Roosevelt for a decision. The President's answer was therefore a clear indication of his complete disinterest in this plan to end the war. I couldn't explain to Lersner. I didn't even try."[56]

* * *

Now, the question: What if Lochner's query had been received with natural interest and acted on in mid-1942? What if the U.S. government had initiated contact with the anti-Hitler opposition at that point and supported a successful coup against Hitler in Germany? Or, what if six months later, Canaris, Hitler's secret opponent, had been encouraged to produce the defection of the German army and negotiate its surrender to the Allies? What if one of the subsequent, serious attempts that other opponents of Hitler made through various Anglo-American emissaries in 1942, 1943, and 1944 had been able to overthrow the Führer, close down the concentration camps, abort the Final Solution, thwart Soviet conquests in Europe and Asia, call off every battle from Monte Cassino to D-day to the Warsaw Uprising to the Battle of the Bulge, avoid the destruction of city centers from Hamburg to Dresden, and save the lives of millions and millions and millions of people in between?

The scale of suffering that might have been averted, and, equally as important for the psyche of civilization, *might never have been imagined,* is too vast and deep to grasp, too massively crushing to entertain, like a black hole from space in your living room, but there it is: World War II could have ended years earlier had Communists working for Moscow not dominated Washington, quashing every anti-Nazi, anti-Communist attempt, beginning in late 1942, throughout 1943 and 1944, to make common cause with Anglo-American representatives. Their main condition, Allied support on keeping Russian troops out of central and eastern Europe, was an instant deal breaker, the red line—no, the anti-Red line—neither the Communist-occupied British government nor the Communist-occupied American government would dare to cross. Sure, we would spend the next forty years trying to keep Communism from spreading westward, but at more propitious moments to save central and eastern Europe, we wouldn't, couldn't even consider trying.

Later, the impact of unconditional surrender would be magnified by the September 1944 leak of the Morgenthau Plan, the Roosevelt White House plan—Harry Dexter White's plan—to "pastoralize" and "de-industrialize" and "dismember" Germany (i.e., destroy all science, industry, and technology in Germany, just for starters).[57] If "unconditional surrender" poured the oil to re-ignite German fires in 1943, the Morgenthau Plan was high-octane propaganda for the Nazis to work with in 1944 until the bitter end. "Almost overnight the morale of the German people seems wholly changed," said GOP presidential candidate Gov. Thomas E. Dewey on October 18, 1944, during Roosevelt's fourth and final campaign. "Now they are fighting with a frenzy of despair." Roosevelt's own son-in-law, Lt. Col. John Boettiger, estimated that the Morgenthau Plan was "worth thirty division to the Germans." General Marshall, too, would complain to Morgenthau that the plan appeared to have stiffened

German resistance. Gen. Omar Bradley talked about "the near-miraculous re-vitalization of the German Army in October" 1944—after news of the plan had leaked.[58] In his autobiographical account of World War II, former CIA director William Casey confirmed that fear of Germany being turned into a "potato patch" was driving German forces, as "captured letters from front-line troops showed." John Dietrich, who gathered these and more observations of the plan's war-prolonging impact in his devastating 2002 book, *The Morgenthau Plan: Soviet Influence on American Postwar Policy,* writes: "There is no way of calculating the number of American servicemen who lost their lives as a result of this policy."[59] It's quite possible, he continues, that Hitler was able to use German fear of the plan to mount his final major offensive in the West in the Ardennes.

That hits home. I mentioned earlier that my dad was wounded at St. Lô in July 1944. After a quick fix in a British hospital and an odyssey across northern Europe (he probably would have been arrested for being AWOL if he hadn't been heading toward the front) to rejoin his unit (practically all replacements, he discovered), he found himself outside the German border town of Monschau in the northern Ardennes, a beautiful wooded area that spans westernmost Germany and Belgium. It was fall. I doubt he got inside the town itself, because I think he would have mentioned how storybook-exquisite it is, as I got to see one recent June. By the time my dad arrived in the forest, it was getting cold, and he was still wearing the lightweight uniform that suited summer in Nor-mandy. Not too surprisingly, he became sick—coughs, chills, hot-potato fever. I think it was the high temperature that triggered his hospital leave as fall be-came winter 1944. If his fever hadn't shot up one night, bivouacked under icy moonlight in a snowy, Grimms' Fairy Tale forest on the leading edge of the American line, it's no stretch to say I wouldn't be writing these words. That's because days later, shortly after he had safely made it to sick bay somewhere behind the front lines, German forces launched their unexpected, last-ditch offensive through the Ardennes, the epic fighting best known to us as the Battle of the Bulge. In all, nineteen thousand Americans were *killed* before it was all over in late January 1945, making this battle the costliest battle for the United States in the whole war.

According to this new way of looking at the war, of course, the Battle of the Bulge, which, like Normandy, happens to bookend my dad's personal fight to liberate Europe from the Nazis—or, rather, his personal fight to liberate Eu-rope *for the Soviets*—never should have taken place. It never would have taken place if it hadn't been for the Communist occupation of Washington. Without that, this most destructive of all wars would likely have ended before it became most destructive.

As for my dad—who, as an eighteen-year-old at Erasmus High School in Brooklyn had parlayed my grandpa's job as a Loews-MGM movie theater manager into a job as a script boy at MGM—he might never have had to leave the lot in Culver City for basic training in 1943, certainly would have gotten no further than Fort Riley, and, I have no doubt, like tens of thousands of other young American men, would have been frustrated at not having seen any military action in the course of a life that, I also have no doubt, would have taken some different track.

As would have the whole world. Had the war ended two incalculably costly years earlier, we all would inhabit a different place, physically and mentally. At the end of 1942, the great war reporter Ernie Pyle described the fighting men he was living alongside in North Africa, specifically the transformation that had changed these first American troops in combat in Europe from homesick young men into soldiers whose "days become full of war instead of American days simply transplanted to Africa." Pyle continued, poignantly and presciently offering his American readers insights into a transformation of greater proportions.

> Our men can't make this change from normal civilians into warriors and remain the same people. Even if they were away from you this long under normal circumstances, the mere process of maturing would change them, and they would not come home just as you knew them. Add to that the abnormal world they have been plunged into, the new philosophies they have had to assume or perish inwardly, the horrors and delights and strange wonderful things they have experienced, and they are bound to be different people from those you sent away.

It wasn't only that they were rougher, Pyle wrote, or that their language had changed from "mere profanity to obscenity," or that they missed women and showed the absence of "the gentling effect of femininity." Pyle saw something else: "Our men have less regard for property than you have raised them to have." An unexpected observation. He continued:

> Money value means nothing to them, either personally or in the aggregate; they are fundamentally generous, with strangers and with each other. They give or throw away their own money, and it is natural that they are even less thoughtful of bulk property than of their own hard-earned possessions.
>
> It is often necessary to abandon equipment they can't take with them; the urgency of war prohibits normal caution in the handling of vehicles and supplies. One of the most striking things to me about war is the appalling waste that is necessary. At the front there just isn't time to be economical. Also, in war

areas where things are scarce and red tape still rears its delaying head, a man learns to get what he needs simply by "requisitioning." It isn't stealing, it's the only way to acquire certain things. The stress of war puts old virtues in a changed light.[60]

What Pyle describes is a new man in the making, his personality augmented and changed by the state. He is also describing the personality of the new state as augmented and changed by the war, the war driven on and on, past Dooms-day. Maybe I'm reading too much into Pyle's observations, but they put me in mind of all the big-government "wars" to come in which "big spending" on "government programs"—appalling waste and the old virtues in a changed light—would mark the postwar era of prosperity. And they put me in mind, too, of Harry Hopkins, who certainly would have approved of this new man and this new state—both, in significant ways, of his own creation:

> I believe people are poor in the main because we don't know how to distribute the wealth properly. I've got away from the notions I once had about a socialist state. I think it can be done under a capitalist economy. WPA showed that. Twenty-five million got their income under that. I think that after this war, if you run up a debt of two hundred billion dollars, the country can stand it . . . We must get the right relationship between government and private enterprise. The government is in this thing and in it for good.[61]

Who's "we"? Not the people. Can't you just hear Harry upstairs at the White House, mixing up a sundown shaker of martinis, on a roll to FDR as they talk about how "we" can get this relationship between government and business right? "Convergence"—a nice name for the fascism Hopkins described—here "we" come. Less than the war to make the world safe for de-mocracy (as if), World War II was the war to grease the skids for continued centralized state power everywhere—removing all obstacles, emotional, philo-sophical and, of course, physical.

Germany was just another such obstacle.

From testimony before the Senate subcommittee investigating interlocking subversion in government departments, May 29, 1952:

> SENATOR EASTLAND: *Do you know who drew up that plan [the Morgenthau Plan]?*
>
> MISS BENTLEY: *Due to Mr. White's influence, to push the devastation of Germany, because that was what the Russians wanted.*

SENATOR FERGUSON: *That was what the Communists wanted?*

MISS BENTLEY: *Definitely Moscow wanted them completely razed because then they would be of no help to the allies.*

MR. MORRIS: *You say that Harry Dexter White worked on that?*

MISS BENTLEY: *And on our instructions he pushed hard . . .* [62]

SENATOR EASTLAND: *What you say is that it was a Communist plot to destroy Germany and weaken her to where she could not help us?*

MISS BENTLEY: *That is correct. She could no longer be a barrier to protect the western world.*[63]

Neither, it seems, could we—an increasingly painful realization. In the summer of 1943, Count Helmuth James von Moltke, an associate of Canaris, a member of the Kreisau Circle, would take the trip to Istanbul, to visit not George H. Earle but members of the OSS. According to Douglas Waller's 2011 Donovan biography, Moltke was prepared to accept "unequivocal military defeat and occupation of Germany." However, Waller continues, pitch-perfect in sounding the anti-anti-Communist note of the times *even in 2011,* Moltke's plan "was Russophobic." His plan, like the others we've seen, provided for the overthrow of Hitler and the establishment of a provisional anti-Nazi government. The German army would withdraw its forces from the West and "hold the Red Army at the Tilsit-to-Lemberg line in Poland."[64]

How *Russophobic* to want to prevent the Red Army from entering Lithuania and Romania and Hungary and Czechoslovakia and Germany and the rest, bringing secret police and devastation with it. No, Moltke's plan was *Russorealistic:* a plan to defend liberty in Europe, to save millions from Soviet servitude. Which is why it got nowhere in Russo*phillic* Washington. Moltke returned to Berlin, where he was arrested by the Gestapo and executed in January 1945.

More plans took shape, took flight, and were shot down. No one wanted Hitler's head in exchange for Allied help to fend off Russian conquest. No dice. *Mustn't offend the Russians.*[65] F. W. Winterbotham, chief of air intelligence for MI6, wrote in his memoir, *Secret and Personal,* that he personally approved of such a plan from Canaris as early as 1942. "It would certainly not have pleased Stalin," Winterbotham wrote in 1969, "but why we should fall over backwards to appease those who were, and are, pledged to destroy our way of life, I shall never understand."[66]

Never? Maybe now we can understand that a point of secret penetration and subversion had been passed beyond which appeasement was a fundamental principle. I wonder if Winterbotham, a top intelligence official and author of *The Ultra Secret,* the first popular account of how the Allies broke the German code, would now agree. He died in 1990—pre-Venona and all that—but I wish I could ask him now, with all the evidence that has been amassed, whether we are looking back on something that still defies understanding, as he wrote in 1969, or whether it was something as obvious as it was evil: a successful Soviet influence operation to thwart a separate peace with anti-Nazi Germans in order to enable Communist expansion into Europe. I wonder if he or any of the others would now agree that due to Communist penetration in the West, the savage in Berlin remained in power long enough to ruin our world and humanity itself; that under Communist influence, not "offending Russia" became a higher priority than removing Hitler from power; that having created the Soviet Empire by supplying and "cooperating" with it, we would spend the rest of the century imperiled by it; that we remain forever changed by it. I wonder, too, if deep and unbearable understanding came long ago to such men in the know—to British spymaster Menzies, for example, whose obituary noted that "he turned down all invitations to write and be interviewed after he retired in 1951."[67] That was the year Colvin's Canaris biography first came out. Probably a coincidence.

Later in this same all-important year of 1943, in October, one month before the fateful Tehran Conference, the first meeting of the "Big Three," a young American OSS agent working for *Reader's Digest* initiated contact with Franz von Papen, the German ambassador to Turkey and, by this point, hardened if not cynical veteran of anti-Nazi Allied intrigue. A devout Catholic, von Papen had also been in talks with Vatican representatives regarding a separate peace between Germany and the British and Americans—much to Moscow's consternation, as a matter of fact. In his 1994 memoir, Soviet spymaster Pavel Sudoplatov explained why, matter-of-fact: "Such an accord would limit Communist influence in Europe."

The logic and the implications of anti-Nazi German resistance were as obvious then as they are ignored today. Sudoplatov continued, "Stalin was so furious he ordered von Papen be assassinated, since he was the key figure around whom the Americans and the British would build an alternative government to Hitler if they signed a separate peace." The Bulgarian assassin "botched the job," he continued, adding, "We also had reports, without details, of a direct American approach to von Papen in Istanbul."[68]

I don't know if Sudoplatov was referring to Earle or someone else, but Theodore A. Morde also made such an approach. Morde's October 1943 plan was nothing new. It stipulated the overthrow of Hitler and the Nazi regime. It called for the formation of a provisional government to be overseen by von

Papen in exchange for yet-to-be-determined American assistance against the Red Army. Morde wrote lengthy OSS memos about his two conversations with von Papen, which also conveyed von Papen's emphatic belief that the Anglo-American unconditional surrender policy (Stalin never publicly signed on to it and, indeed, undercut his own "Allies" by promising a separate kind of peace to the German people through a Communist front known as the Free Germany Committee) was having a negative effect on anti-Nazi activity.[69] Von Papen was similarly convinced that Anglo-American firebombing raids on German cities were "doing more to spread Communism in Germany than anything else." Von Papen railed against the devastation of such cities as Hamburg, where, in the last week of July in 1943, for example, Anglo-American raids had killed forty thousand people in Operation Gomorrah. Morde conveyed von Papen's plaint:

> He begged that we stop this horrible bombing, that it was not necessary for us to win the war, that our leaders should realize that they were doing more harm than good. He went on, temporarily losing control of his feelings, and said that German people were not behind the Nazis, that they were beginning to feel that the Allies must be even worse than the Nazis, if they continued this ruthless bombing.[70]

"And his cities, one by one, will be destroyed by Allied air forces."
This line, with its practically biblical cadence, echoes through my mind. It comes from Harry Hopkins's landmark speech to a crowd of thousands at the Russia Aid Rally at Madison Square Garden of June 22, 1942. I wonder: Is it remarkable that Hopkins promised that German cities would be destroyed, one by one, in mid-1942, a point still so early in the American war? To be sure, it was natural to hail and wish for and fight for the decisive defeat of Nazi Germany—but the destruction of all German cities, one by one? Does that come under the rubric of acceptable rhetorical flourish, or was he possibly tele-graphing Communist strategy to destroy Germany? I honestly don't know. Given the facts we know about the Soviet strategy to destroy Germany, it sounds suspect.

It was at about the time of this speech that unconditional surrender was be-ing, in effect, rammed through U.S. government channels (May 1942), just as the big press for Stalin's "second front" was also under way. The basic elements of total war were falling into place, and nothing, seemingly, could stop it now—*even serious proposals to end the war.* This was not an American necessity. This was a Soviet design.

It was also in the spring of 1942 that Undersecretary of State Adolf Berle came up with a plan he thought might accelerate the collapse of the Nazi regime. Berle had been eavesdropping on secret German communications via the MAGIC decoding program and had become aware of cautious peace feelers in the German camp early in 1942. To help this movement along, he planned to publish a secret German cable that revealed the precariousness of Germany's internal situation. So sensational was this secret German document, Berle believed, he expected its release to undermine Germany's morale, thus making the Nazi regime come crashing down, thus saving "half a million" people's lives, he estimated, thus averting the possible use of chemical or biological weapons, and thus preventing, as he put it, the Russians "from advancing into Germany."[71]

Enter Robert Sherwood. It's quite fascinating suddenly to see the role Hopkins's biographer played when Berle consulted the literary light, who was also a keeper of wartime information on various government panels including OWI, which he headed with Katyn Soviet apologist Elmer Davis. Berle brought Sherwood his plan to expose this secret German communiqué, a frank inside appraisal of Nazi weakness. Sherwood then assembled a small intelligence group to consider Berle's plan—Edmund Taylor, Wallace Deuel, and James P. Warburg, the latter, by the way, a scion of a famous German-Jewish banking family whose father, Paul M. Warburg, founded the Federal Reserve banking system in 1913. James Warburg is best remembered as an outspoken proponent of world government "whether we like it or not," as he put it to the Senate in 1950, and, as a cofounder of the Institute for Policy Studies, a crypto-Marxist think tank, in 1963.

According to Christof Mauch, who reported the Berle-Sherwood conversations in his 2002 book *The Shadow War Against Hitler,* Sherwood's little group (cabal?) "feared that the action"—the exposure of Nazi weakness—"would have a negative effect on the home fronts in the U.S. and England, possibly 're-ducing public pressure for the opening of a second front in Western Europe.' "[72]

There are different ways to interpret this objection in April 1942. The most benign is that the Sherwood group feared news of Nazi vulnerabilities would only undermine "public pressure" for the "second front," *while simultaneously doing nothing to hasten Nazi collapse.* That's possible, although not stated.

Berle's feeling, meanwhile, was, as Mauch reported, that "the American people would fight harder" if they believed victory was assured, and, if the Nazi regime did suffer as a result of exposure, would have to fight less. Win-win, no?

Maybe not for devotees of world government, however. Maybe they feared that if Berle was right, the war would end too soon, before the so-called creative destruction they yearned for could take place.

Maybe such sentiments remained in the unconscious; maybe such sentiments didn't exist. This is pure speculation on my part. Still, it seems important to try to weigh the arguments that were taking place in wartime Washington when it appeared that the drive for Nazi collapse was taking a backseat to Stalin's wishes for the "second front," and even to the spread of Communist revolution or some more seemingly palatable "socialist" variant. Soviet foreign minister Molotov would be making his historic trip to Washington in just a few weeks' time to push the "second front" in northern France in earnest (with benefit of Harry Hopkins's secret advice). To hypothesize further, premature Nazi collapse would spoil all of these best-laid Communist plans.

Meanwhile, one document is missing from the archive. In his footnote, Christof Mauch reports that the intercepted German document Berle had such high hopes for, likely procured through the top secret MAGIC program, *"cannot be found in the OSS files."*[73] It's as if someone, something, some force, some agent or agents, set out on a reverse scavenger hunt equipped with razor blades and torches to give our past a lobotomy. However, one thing they—whoever "they" are—could never do while ransacking our past was change the map. The logic of the map is ours to this day, the key to the secret struggle. Theodore Morde recounted how his first meeting with von Papen in October 1943 ended:

> As we were about to shake hands and part, [von Papen] again took my arm and pulled me over to a large map on the wall. "Look at that great space," he said, indicating Russia. "Think what industrial havoc they can do, and what they can do to all Europe."[74]

Morde solemnly promised von Papen he would only divulge the details of their discussions to Roosevelt himself. He never got past "Pa" Watson, a.k.a. Gen. Edwin M. Watson, Roosevelt's secretary. Watson shunted Morde over to Robert Sherwood, whom Morde had worked for in a couple of capacities (which might well explain why Morde hadn't gone to see Sherwood first), including at OWI.

Sherwood listened to Morde's story. He wasn't unimpressed by Morde's work. In fact, he was beside himself, livid over what he described as Morde's "dangerous activities." In a memo to FDR on October 26, 1943, Sherwood described Morde's account of his talks with von Papen as "amazing"—but not, it should be emphasized, in a good way. Sherwood didn't just veto the Morde plan; he proposed that the U.S. government ground Morde. Literally—"I am going to make a full report of this to the Acting Secretary of State with the suggestion that Morde *should not again be given a passport to leave this country.*" (emphasis added).[75]

Why? Because Morde might actually succeed at bringing about the overthrow of Hitler and a bulwark against Stalin?

Impossible to say. Sherwood's memo then descends into an attack against

Reader's Digest ("the really important part of the whole story lies in the activities abroad of the *Reader's Digest . . ."*). Morde, a *Digest* writer, had told Sherwood about *Digest* plans to expand its free circulation among troops serving abroad in North Africa, Sicily, and Italy.

What could possibly be wrong with that?

Everything.

According to Sherwood, "As you know, *Reader's Digest* has become more and more bitter and partisan in its attacks on this Administration. In its worldwide circulation *it is, in effect, undoing the work that my outfit is constantly trying to do overseas.*"[76]

Reader's Digest? It's hard to imagine the *Digest,* so solid and soothing that it once appeared in every dentist's waiting room in America, as an attack organization sabotaging the U.S. war effort during World War II. Then again, the *Digest* was always resolutely anti-Communist, and the Roosevelt administration was always resolutely not.

I went back to the archives. While reviewing *Digest* back issues, I actually found plenty of pro-Soviet material in 1943—Maurice Hindus, for example, a giant of Soviet apologetics, published a piece in April 1943 called "The Price Russia Is Paying." Then I came to the lead story in the July 1943 edition. Its title is "To Collaborate Successfully—We Must Face the Facts About Russia," by Max Eastman. An ex-Socialist of note—Eastman had the distinction of having raised the money to send John Reed to see the Russian Revolution and was the first publisher of what became Reed's *Ten Days That Shook the World*—Eastman knew whereof he spoke.

An excerpt:

That Stalin is an absolute dictator is the simple truth. And it is so important a truth that I am not going to leave it in my own words.

The Soviet Union, as everybody knows that has the courage to face the facts, is a dictatorship as absolute as any other dictatorship in the world.

That statement, made by Franklin D. Roosevelt, February 11, 1940, is as true today as it was then.

Another:

"Don't say a word against Stalin or he won't accept our tanks!" seems to be the attitude of some of those who are giving away the national treasure so avidly.

This is an attitude of spirit which I find diplomatically foolhardy, morbidly disgraceful and dangerous to the survival of democratic institutions within this country.

Another:

Those eager to be fooled about Russia make eloquent pleas for Stalin's "good faith." But Bolsheviks do not believe *even theoretically* in good faith.

One more:

People who do not instinctively distinguish between what is true about Russia and what Communists and their fellow travelers want us to believe are not to be relied on in this day of democratic crisis.

Burn. Little wonder Sherwood was steamed. Eastman refuted every syllable of the U.S. government's pro-Red propaganda. Three days after Sherwood wrote his memo to FDR about Morde and *Reader's Digest*, OSS chief Wild Bill Donovan also sent a memo to FDR about what he called the Morde-Papen plan. Contrary to Sherwood, however, Donovan argued that the plan was quite promising. In fact, as he told Roosevelt, Gen. Patrick Hurley, Roosevelt's personal representative in Cairo, and Colonel Geunther, head of OSS in the Middle East, the only two people apprised of the plan and sworn to secrecy, both considered the Morde-Papen plan "feasible." As Donovan put it (rather unctuously) to FDR, it was "an idea that your skill and imagination could develop."[77]

That was on October 29, 1943.

On November 10, 1943, FDR gave his approval to the plan—the plan to deny Theodore A. Morde a U.S. passport.

It was a little like trying to put the genie back in the bottle, but it worked. Through silence, sabotage, and secrecy, through the natural attrition and disaffection of those very few in the know, the most promising lifelines out of the war were cut, the death warrants of millions were carried out, and a rich and vital vein of history was lost. It all vanished—the whole frustrating, daring, tragic history of this hapless, unwanted resistance. As if it never happened. Russia *über alles.*

More than two decades later, seventy-eight-year-old Francis Biddle, Roosevelt's attorney general during World War II, received an anonymous letter in the mail. The former Nuremberg judge was sufficiently intrigued by it to inform Gilbert Harrison, then editor of *The New Republic.*

August 28, 1966
Dear Gil:

I received anonymously the other day from Los Angeles a copy of an extraordinary statement to the effect that former Governor Earl [*sic*] of Pennsylvania was approached by Admiral Canaris, head of Hitler's secret service.

One nearly complete genocide, two large wars, and many revolutions later—all potentially avertable had the Allies and anti-Nazi Germans succeeded in ending World War II in 1942 or 1943 or even 1944—and an anonymous letter finally breaks the story of Canaris-Earle talks to Biddle, who served four years on Roosevelt's wartime cabinet. The news was "extraordinary," fantastic. Biddle's letter continues.

Earle was presented an offer to be sent to F.D.R. backed by the German General Staff stating that they would get rid of Hitler and "his crew" and surrender to the allies on condition that they be permitted to turn their entire forces against Russia and wipe out the threat of Communism.

This strange communication is signed the Committee on Patriotism.

Perhaps you could run it down. It would be worth an article . . . [78]

Worth an article?
Worth a world.

CHAPTER ELEVEN

When the politicians are silent, there is a reason.

—JOSEPH D. DOUGLASS JR.[1]

O n June 16, 1992, President George Bush and Russian president Boris Yeltsen held a joint press conference.

Q: Mr. President, do you think there are any POW's in the Soviet Union, Americans? This to President Bush first and then Yeltsin.

PRESIDENT YELTSIN: It is possible.

Q: Are they alive?

PRESIDENT YELTSIN: An investigating commission is working, led by Mr. Volkogonov. Many things have been revealed after the examination of the archives of the KGB and the Central Committee of the Communist Party. But that work is continuing both in the archives and in the places where the POW's were. We shall try to investigate each individual case. And all the information will be, of course, handed over to the American side. The initial information has been handed over to the Senate.

Q: Would you expect more information this week?

PRESIDENT BUSH: Let me just thank President Yeltsin for this because this is a matter of grave concern to the American people. He has made these observations, pledged full cooperation and support. I think this really expresses as well as anything else this new era that we were both talking about on the lawn. And I have every confidence that if what he says here is true, that they will get to the bottom of it. And if any single American is unaccounted for, they will go the extra mile to see that that person is accounted for. And I think that's what the American people need to know. I think that's what President Yeltsin has clearly pledged to do. So we are grateful to him for that.

Q: Does it come as a complete surprise to you, Mr. President?

PRESIDENT BUSH: Yes, it comes as a—

Q: You had no idea?

PRESIDENT BUSH: Thank you all very much.[2]

In other words, *Shut up, Boris; there is a reason.*

In 1992, that was the message to the president of Russia from the entire administration of George H. W. Bush—from the envoy to the new U.S.-Russian POW commission (Malcolm Toon) to the national security adviser (Brent Scowcroft) to the commander in chief himself. Not that it was easy to quash the irrepressible Yeltsin. During that visit to Washington two decades ago, Yeltsin would repeatedly use the dog-and-pony showcase of the Washington minisummit to break this mind-bending, history-kinking story, exponentially more newsworthy because of its source: The first president of new Russia was himself declaring that the old Soviet slave labor camp system held some indeterminate number of American prisoners of war dating back as far as World War II.

You had no idea, President Bush? Really? What about your predecessors, from President Reagan all the way back to President Roosevelt? This dark stain of a national scandal goes back further still if we count dozens, if not scores, of doughboys whom the spanking-new, blood-Red regime kept captive after World War I. Not that either Uncle Sam or the new Soviet government publicly admitted this at the time of the American Expeditionary Force's return from newly Bolshevized Russia. It was a short, invigorating blast of exposure from *The New York Times* that enlivened the issue, a story on April 18, 1921, reporting that "the Soviet government is holding Americans" hostage to recognition or commerce from the United States. Later that same year, on receiving a Soviet appeal for famine relief and medical supplies, President Harding responded with *conditions*—mirabile dictu—for any American aid as laid out in what is known as the Riga Agreement. "The sine qua non of any assistance on the part of the American aid," the 1921 agreement said, was the release of "all Americans detained in Russia." Such aid would be suspended or terminated "in case of failure on the part of the Soviet Authorities to fully comply with this primary condition."

Over one hundred American men were freed from Soviet dungeons.

Atta boy, President Harding. So why didn't basic reciprocity thus become the basis of U.S.-USSR relations until 1991 when the regime ended? The many reasons, all of them bad, describe the most duplicitous American crime of all of the American Century.

Notably, as Herbert Hoover later wrote in his autobiography, the United States in 1921 had only been expecting twenty men to emerge from Communist captivity.[3] After one hundred were set free, were there still more remaining? Refugees fleeing Red Russia throughout the 1920s said that there were. In November 1930, a Latvian American named Alexander Grube filed an affidavit swearing he had seen four American officers and fifteen American soldiers in Lubyanka Prison in 1927 and, later, "many" more in the Solovetsky Islands slave labor camp—among the very first slave labor "concentration camps," incidentally, inaugurated and named by Lenin, in what would become the sprawling Gulag Archipelago.[4] U.S. government officials tentatively were able to match two names Grube recalled with missing American soldiers whom the U.S. government had presumed dead (killed in action, body not recovered, or KIA-BNR).[5]

Then what? Not much. The fate of Americans-in-irons didn't concern Uncle Sam in his giddy run-up to Soviet recognition in 1933, twirling streamers of paper promises *(agreed: the Soviet Union will not attempt to overthrow the United States . . .),* eyes sparkling from those remaining draughts of Prohibition beer. Nor, of course, did the Soviet-engineered starvation of those "dung-colored" victims of the Terror Famine, either—"six million persons," as Solzhenitsyn would put it, who "died on the edge of Europe [and] the world didn't even notice it."[6] This was a purely corrupt and corrupting relationship from the start—for America the duped, that is—built on equal parts self-delusion and a gradually increasing, then quickly accelerating complicity. The longer this relationship continued, the more there was to hide.

When, as Tim Tzouliadis documents in his seal-of-secrecy-breaking book *The Forsaken: An American Tragedy in Stalin's Russia* (2008), American citizens by the hundreds joined what remnant of forgotten American soldiers remained in the burgeoning Gulag, they, too, became threats to the nascent conspiracy of silence. At least *two thousand* of these Great Depression émigrés and their children, lured by the promise of jobs and dreams of "workers' paradise," would be incarcerated in the Gulag never to return to the USA—never to be publicly acknowledged, let alone reclaimed by their government.

We never knew it—not as a people, that is. Individual Americans knew it all too well, as a tear-stained literature of desperate pleas from bereft family members to the State Department attests. Ignorant and deceived, the rest of us were expected to welcome the USSR into the "community of nations," work extra hard to provide the Communist regime with U.S. taxpayer-funded assistance, and engage in robust trade with the murderers and jailers of millions of innocent people—even including some of our own.

This was a secret from the start. Like a battered spouse determined to project an aura of normalcy, the United States government hushed up these dire Soviet assaults against our fellow citizens, whose treatment "would be little different if our country were in a state of war with the Soviet Union," George

Kennan wrote to Truman's new secretary of state, James Byrnes.[7] The date Kennan was writing was November 14, 1945. Amazingly, on that very same date, Assistant Secretary of State Dean Acheson was addressing the National Council of American-Soviet Friendship—later unmasked as a flagrant Communist front organization.[8] Acheson was pronouncing the U.S. government to be in sync with Uncle Joe: "To have friendly governments along her borders is essential both for the security of the Soviet Union and the peace of the world."[9] "Friendly" to the Soviet Union, of course, meant unfriendly to the Free World. It also meant Communist dictatorships for the "friendly"-governed peoples.

This chance pairing demonstrates the synchronity of the double game— Kennan's honesty on the inside that was restricted to a pained few; Acheson's propaganda on the outside, broadcast for happy public consumption. World War II was over, Acheson was preaching appeasement to the comrades in New York City, and Kennan was telling it straight, if officially sotto voce, to the secretary of state. These U.S. citizens in jeopardy, Kennan continued, his memo attached to the latest report detailing some of the desperate cases of Americans who'd been duped by Soviet tricks into surrendering their passports, were "mostly little people" who, the Soviets believed, won't "normally be able to make their voices heard."

Not through the megaphone of a Dean Acheson, to be sure.

Kennan continued, "Banking on this, [the Soviets] feel that they can safely continue to follow their policy of unconcealed arrogance and hostility in this obscure field of inter-governmental relations so important to them and—as they imagine—so unimportant to us."[10]

Kennan might well have been writing about the plight of hundreds, *thousands* of GIs—World War II officers and enlisted men, survivors of tank battles, airplane crashes, torpedoed ships, and then German prison camps—at that very moment in history looking around at the watchtowers and barbed wire of the Gulag and wondering when the hell Uncle Sam would get them out.

The answer was never.

This is another crime we don't recognize as our own—or even recognize, period, which is why Yeltsin's news came to us over the airwaves in 1992 as something streaming in from outer space.

To get our bearings, let's pick up the paper trail on March 3, 1945. One day earlier, Roosevelt, just back from his fourteen-thousand-mile round-trip voyage to and from the Yalta Conference, addressed Congress about the fateful Yalta Agreement, "ad libbing a great deal of it," according to Sherwood, and quite controversially withholding at least one known key point from the public regarding proposed voting procedure at the in-the-works United Nations.[11] This,

Sherwood reports, gave rise to "speculation as to whether there were other secret agreements as yet unrevealed."[12]

How far have we come since Yalta? What Congress, what people, what
press, expects any president or any other government official, from James Baker
to Hillary Clinton, to reveal the contents of international talks and agreements to us lowly citizens? None, as far as I can tell. We fully accept such non-
constitutional notions of "executive privilege," and we assume that officials have
and should have many, many secrets from us, and even have access to and use of
our own most private information.

This wasn't yet the American personality in 1945 when Roosevelt's sheen
began to dim. Sherwood strikes a gloomy tone: "After this speech, disillusionment began to set in." Maybe it was the as-yet-unnamed Iron Curtain crashing
down, first and swiftly, over Romania (Communist coup by March 6, 1945), and
then again, slightly more gradually, over Poland. Soon, the rising babble about
the dawn of "world peace" through the establishment of the "United Nations"
organization would become so distractingly loud that anyone shouting that
none of the emperors wore any clothes would have been drowned out. The pro-
cessional continued.

Roosevelt himself was a little riled, though. On March 3, 1945, under prodding from both our top diplomat in Moscow, Ambassador Averell Harriman
(long frustrated by "Soviet refusals and evasions" on the American prisoners issue[13]), and our top military man in Moscow, Gen. John R. Deane (also frustrated after months of Soviet stonewalling and reverses), FDR cabled Stalin to
request "urgently" that provision be made for ten American rescue crews to
move in and out of Soviet-captured territories to evacuate liberated American
prisoners of war, many of whom urgently required medical attention. Roosevelt
underscored this request as being "of the greatest importance not only for humanitarian reasons but also by reason of the intense interest of the American
public in the welfare of our ex-prisoners of war and stranded aircraft crews."[14]

As far as Roosevelt communiqués to Stalin went, this counts as pulling out
all the stops.

On March 5, 1945, Stalin replied: *Nyet.*

Then the Soviet dictator laid down the newest Big Lie: *There were no
American ex-prisoners in the Red zone.* (The Soviets would tell the British the
same thing about some twenty thousand to thirty thousand British ex-
prisoners.[15]) "On the territory of Poland and in other places liberated by the
Red Army, there are no groups of American prisoners of war," Stalin cabled to
FDR. "In view of this . . . there is no necessity to carry on flights of American
planes from Poltava [Ukraine] to the territory of Poland on matters of American prisoners of war."[16]

It is painful to say, but this Big Lie, like so many others that preceded and followed it, would soon attain the status of dry fact within the U.S. government and be incorporated into government statements, news reports, and the historical record—*and stay there.*

Not yet, though, not right away. Harriman, for one, personally knew Stalin was lying. He knew this after three-quarters of a year of fruitless prisoner negotiations with Soviet officials; he knew the truth straight from American ex-POWS he was now meeting in Moscow, Americans who had made their arduous way into Russia after roughing it for hundreds if not thousands of miles from their points of liberation from German custody. He had heard eyewitness accounts of some two hundred Americans left behind at Szubin when the Germans cleared out, and thirty or so more in a Russian hospital at Wegheim; the ex-POWs spoke of the life-saving hospitality of Polish peasants along the way, of the indifference, at best, shown them by the Red Army. A Polish report came out estimating one thousand Americans scattered across Polish cities.[17]

On March 6, 1946, despite any number of "protests" lodged by Harriman and his British counterpart in Moscow threatening "full consultation" among the three Allies—not exactly a big stick—the Soviets brought off that Communist coup in Romania, running amok through the Yalta agreements on political self-determination. Poland would be next.[18]

Vigorously disputing Stalin's account of the POW situation, Harriman cabled FDR on March 8, 1945:

Since the Yalta Conference [which concluded on February 11, 1945], General Deane and I have been in constant efforts to get the Soviets to carry out their [POW] agreement in full. We have been baffled by promises which have not been fulfilled.[19]

"Baffled" by unfulfilled promises? Hadn't Harriman been paying attention for lo, these last ten years—or just lo, these last ten days—of Moscow's unfulfilled promises? Or, alternately, was Harriman belatedly coming to realize that Big Boss didn't care a snap for the little concerns of Junior Partner?

Maybe. He continued:

I am outraged that the Soviet Government has declined to carry out the agreement signed at Yalta . . . namely that our contact officers be permitted to go immediately to points of where our prisoners are first collected, to evaluate our prisoners, particularly the sick, in our own airplanes, or to send supplies . . .

Baffled and outraged, then, Harriman called the Soviet bluff:

For the past ten days the Soviets have made the same statements that Stalin has
made to you [FDR], namely that all prisoners are in Odessa or entrained thereto,
whereas I have positive proof that this was not repeat not true on February 26,
the date on which the statement was first made . . .

  Our information received from our liberated prisoners indicate that there
have been four or five thousand officers and enlisted men freed . . . There appear to be hundreds of our prisoners wandering about Poland trying to locate
American contact officers for protection.[20]

For protection . . . from whom? The answer is our Soviet "ally," who, now
having launched Romania as a satellite, was preparing to impose a Communist
government in Poland. On March 11, 1945, FDR would cable Harriman, "It is
obvious that the Russians have installed a minority government of their own
choosing, but . . . Rumania is not a good place for a test case."[21]

What was a good test case? Poland? The safe return of our own men? Such
questions remained known only to a tiny handful of people dominated by an
authoritarian White House, which was dominated by an authoritarian man
even more brainwashed than Captain Hill, soon to set sail on the *Arawa*.[22]

Receiving no immediate White House response, Harriman appealed to Secretary of State Stettinius—a most sturdy Hopkins tool, as we've seen. Then
again, so was Harriman to the extent that his own rise to top government posts
had depended in crucial ways on a boost from the good old co-president. The
POW situation, however, galled him, at least for a while.

On March 14, 1945, Harriman cabled the whole sorry story to the secretary
of state. He detailed Soviet obstruction of U.S. evacuation and medical teams
waiting to enter Soviet-captured territory; the "serious hardships" of sick and
wounded American GIs after years of war and privation in German prison
camps; and obvious Soviet evasions of responsibility, as when Foreign Minister
Molotov tried to blame the (Soviet-controlled) Polish Provisional Government
for the pure-Moscow snafu.

Then Harriman suggested something novel and sensible. In the event that a
follow-up cable from Roosevelt failed to move Stalin, the administration should
consider "retaliatory measures." What a concept. Harriman suggested restrict-
ing the movement of Soviet contact officers riffling through Displaced Persons
camps in the Western zone for hapless returnees (there were over 150 Soviets at
Eisenhower's own headquarters where a special section of the staff was designated to assist them; Americans and British had no equivalent setup with the
Red Army), or perhaps halting further consideration of "non-military" Lend-

Lease material (Stalin was angling for another big "loan"). Harriman also recommended something even more effective—something for the ages. Harriman tentatively suggested "that consideration be given to allowing our prisoners of war en route to Naples to give stories to the newspapers of the hardships they have been subjected to" in the Soviet zone.

This was what was lacking, and this was what was needed. At any point, exposure, loud and clear, could have changed the U.S.-USSR dynamic in every way. It was the reality that We, the People were almost always, always deprived of in order to drive the Soviet conspiracy of Western silence forward, fueled by acquiescence, accommodation, participation and incorporation of all the Big Lies going back to the very first, the Terror Famine.

Dream on.

Still, in his way, Harriman soldiered on, suggesting that the War Department be enlisted to elaborate on the Yalta provisions on ex-prisoners that the Soviet government was failing to live up to "according to any reasonable interpretation." Last, Harriman signed off with a specific request to the secretary of state from General Deane: namely, that Chief of Staff General Marshall (another Hopkins crony, of course) be informed of the contents of this cable.[23]

This is an important bit to remember, given Marshall's action twelve days later (below).

On March 16, 1945, Churchill weighed in from London with similar concerns. "At present all entry into Poland is barred to our representatives. An impenetrable veil has been drawn across the scene," he cabled FDR, summoning a metaphor that would harden into his famous "Iron Curtain" speech almost one year later to the day on March 5, 1946, in Fulton, Missouri.

The prime minister continued, "This extends even to the liaison officers, British and American, who were to help in bringing our rescued prisoners of war . . . There is no doubt in my mind that the Soviets fear much our seeing what is going on in Poland."[24] Churchill's behind-the-scenes worries notwithstanding, official Allied silence left the public in oblivion regarding Soviet obstructionism on even this basic humanitarian effort. The conspiracy lived on.

The next day, on March 17, 1945, Roosevelt again cabled Stalin about the POW issue, dropping the noblesse oblige routine for the moment.

> I have information that I consider positive and reliable that there are a very considerable number of sick and injured Americans in hospitals in Poland and also numbers of liberated U.S. prisoners in good health who are awaiting [evacuation] or are at large in small groups that have not yet made contact with Soviet authorities.
>
> Frankly I cannot in all frankness understand your reluctance to permit

American contact officers . . . to assist their own people in this matter. *This Government has done everything to meet each of your requests. I now request you to meet mine in this particular matter* [emphasis added].[25]

Had the bubble popped? Had Roosevelt—or whoever was writing cables for the precipitously declining president—finally glimpsed the "real" Stalin sans Harry Hopkins's spin?[26] Stalin wasn't behaving according to conventions he had never shared and by rules he had never followed, and, by golly, Roosevelt "frankly . . . in all frankness" couldn't understand it. It is ironic to note that it is as a last resort that the president finally broached a mode of intercourse that should have governed all dealings between the United States and the USSR from the start: reciprocity. In return for requests already and continually (and in the future) met, FDR was saying, Stalin should "frankly and in all frankness" meet FDR's one paltry request—but it was only a request. FDR didn't back it up with even Harriman's minimal conditions. FDR "did pass on the War Department for reciprocal limitations on Soviet officers in France" at least, as Harriman wrote in his memoir. "But nothing more was done."[27]

Nothing more was said, either. This cable was FDR's last word to Stalin on the subject.

Just to coordinate timelines, it's worth noting that a few days later, on March 21, 1945, George H. Earle wrote his Bullittlike letter to FDR, this time in care of the president's daughter and companion Anna Boettiger. As noted in chapter 7, Earle was seeking the presidential permission to warn the American people that now, with Allied forces having all but defeated Nazi Germany, a new, more dangerous totalitarian enemy stood in the offing: the USSR.

On March 22, 1945, the *Arawa* set sail under Captain Hills, departing from Italy for Odessa (Odessa in southern Russia being the sole extraction point Stalin opened, contrary to original agreement, no doubt to keep Allied extraction teams from seeing the brutal Sovietization of Poland[28]). Unbeknownst to the prototypically brainwashed Hills—truly, the New Soviet Man—he was carrying a load of slaves for the Gulag. Hills would soon know better.[29]

Would Roosevelt? The man remains a mystery in so many, many ways, but I doubt the light ever penetrated, ever could penetrate, what Sherwood called that "heavily forested interior." He remained America's Dupe Number One to the end. Of course, what does that say about we who worship the man as a veritable demigod?

Also on March 22, 1945, Stalin turned down Roosevelt's final request to extract our men from the Red zone. "In reality on the territory of Poland . . . there were only 17 sick Americans," Stalin lied, and "very soon they (17 persons) will be taken to Odessa by planes."[30]

He concluded by rapping Roosevelt for alleged U.S. mistreatment of Russian POWs—in contrast, of course, to Russian treatment of Americans in Russian custody. This was a common Soviet feint, the kind of gratuitous attack General Deane wrote of frequently coming under in prisoner negotiations with the Soviets "when they fully realized the insecurity of their attack."[31] Anything to return us to the defensive—a tactic we fell for (or were pushed) time again.

On March 24, 1945, that letter mentioned earlier would go out to George Earle over FDR's signature that "specifically forbid" the former Pennsylvania governor, erstwhile New Deal ally, and wartime envoy, to assorted European capitals to publish any fact that put the Soviet Union in a bad light, even as such facts were pouring in on everyone's heads. "Dear George," the president wrote—or, rather, the letter that would go out over the president's signature read. I blur the line here because adding to the nation's secret peril was the worsening health of the already weak and sickly commander in chief. Even a year earlier, bad health was limiting Roosevelt to "no more than two to four hours a day" of what historian Michael Beschloss describes in his book *The Conquerors* (2002) as "intense public business"—as opposed to ribbon-cuttings, perhaps.[32] By this point in March of 1945, according to the latent witness of all of the government officials-cum-diarists around him, Roosevelt was in an easily distracted, meandering, sometimes childish frame of mind. State Department official James Dunn later recalled observing the president at this time as he looked at a cable about Poland—from Churchill perhaps. "He was seeing the paper, but not reading it . . . picking out something to show he was alert," Dunn told historian Martin Weil.[33] "He was in no shape to do anything." Churchill would later write about this post-Yalta period, "In my long telegrams I thought I was talking to my trusted friend and colleague as I had done all these years. I was no longer being fully heard by him . . . various hands drafted in combination the answers that were sent in his name."[34]

The record doesn't name these "various hands." For once, Harry Hopkins, ensconced at the Mayo Clinic since February 27, 1945 (he wouldn't return to Washington until April 13, 1945, the day after Roosevelt died), could be off the hook. According to the chronicle of FDR's last weeks put together by Beschloss, it was a small group of aides and cabinet secretaries who met and supped with Roosevelt now. Among them were Treasury Secretary Henry Morgenthau, puppet of Soviet agent Harry Dexter White; War Secretary Henry Stimson, who, approaching age seventy-seven, was no spring chicken himself; James Dunn (mentioned above); and the president's daughter Anna Boettiger and her husband, John, both of whom pop up "riding shotgun" for her father in meetings. Maybe that's not all the Boetiggers were doing. Beschloss writes:

She [Anna] told Joseph Daniels, an old family friend who had become Roosevelt's press secretary, that her father's "increasing incapacity" frightened her.

Anna was contemplating some kind of "regency," so Daniels recalled, with her and Boettiger in "dynastic positions," shielding the President from people who might annoy him and wear down his health. As he understood it, Anna aspired to be another Edith Bolling Wilson, who had acted as President-in-fact, protecting her invalid husband. "It scared the pants off of me."[35]

Indeed. Besides giving us a glimpse of perhaps hereditary meglomania, what is also notable here is that for however many weeks or months (years?) Roosevelt's impairment cut into presidential capacities, his policies continued without an evident shift or even blip. Chalk one up for the useful fools and the Moscow occupation: Whoever's "various hands" were at the helm of decision making, they might as well have been Roosevelt's. Then again, maybe they were.

Back again one more time to FDR's letter to Earle of March 24, 1945. "I have read your letter of March 21st to my daughter Anna and I have noted with concern your unfavorable opinion of one of our allies at the very time when such a publication from a former emissary of mine might do irreparable harm to our war effort."

Really? Or was that harm to the *Soviet* war effort? The Roosevelt administration, penetrated, fooled, subverted, in effect hijacked, by Soviet agents, as a matter of national policy, mixed them up, much to the world's deep, vast suffering. This "sell-out" to Stalin, as critics tagged it (and they didn't know the half of it), would become a bone of sharpest and most vociferous contention that the conspirators of silence on the Left, in the Democratic Party, and among the Washington elites would bury for as long as possible, desperately throwing mud over it and anyone who wanted to let the sun shine in. Why? As G. Bernard Noble, chief of the Division of Historical Policy Research at the State Department, wrote to Secretary of State Dean Acheson in 1950, the publication of the Yalta papers, for example, would "embarrass" too many people and, in the acid paraphrase of Bryton Barron, fired Yalta archivist and author of *Inside the State Department,* "lead to demands for publication of the minutes of other conferences."[36]

More exposure, and we can't have that.

Witness the long, tough slog by scholars, lawyers, and the Republican Party in the 1950s to compel the State Department to publish the diplomatic papers of the twelve conferences of World War II. By an agreement reached between the Senate and the State Department, the "Big Three" conferences, Tehran, Yalta, and Potsdam, were supposed to be published by 1955—already a decade or more after they took place. By 1956, as Barron notes, only a heavily edited version of Yalta had been released, and only after a Soviet-style (Soviet-inspired?) disinformation campaign promoted the notion that the crucial role Alger Hiss played at Yalta was, au contraire, "largely that of a notetaker." (The fact that numerous papers and activities of Hiss at Yalta *are not listed in the index* of the Yalta papers helped put that one over, as Barron noted in his book.) Hopkins's role, too, is downplayed by an introductory note that calls him "too ill to participate fully." As Barron notes, this assertion was "quite misleading," as a tally of Hopkins's attendance at meetings tells us, as does reading "some of the chits he exchanged with the President."[37]

Do I digress again? No, this is another crucial fact in the history of suppression of history. *Our history.*

Whether Roosevelt himself actually wrote that letter to George Earle in the early spring of 1945 is one of history's less significant mysteries; still, it so happens that also on March 24, 1945, Robert Sherwood was at the White House. He writes that he "went to see the President in his office and then walked over with him to the White House proper, where we had lunch with Anna Boettiger on the sun porch on the roof above the South Portico."[38]

Lunch with the "regent" wannabe and the Hollywood-Broadway information officer—how nice. Hard to imagine Earle's pesky letter of March 21, 1945, didn't come up. I wonder also if Harriman's latest POW cable, of March 24, 1945, came up; who knows?

Harriman was again writing FDR to contradict Stalin's "statement that our liberated prisoners are in Soviet camps under good conditions." On top of continued hardship, untended illness and everything else, he continued, "Red Army soldiers have taken wrist watches, clothing and other articles at the point of a gun."[39]

Roosevelt didn't want to hear any more about it. On March 26, 1945, he cabled Harriman to end the conversation. "It does not appear appropriate for me to send another message now to Stalin . . . There may be some prospect of results . . . at a later date."[40]

"Appropriate" was an odd word to use. American men, sick and wounded, hungry, too, were stranded on the war-torn roads of Europe where Roosevelt had sent them, where, further, they were being preyed upon by Russian thugs and prevented from coming home—but it wasn't "appropriate" for their commander in chief to send another crummy cable about this unconscionable outrage to the Soviet dictator, whose army, whose population, whose *nomenklatura,* not incidentally, were still being fully kitted out by the magnanimous American taxpayer via Lend-Lease. Indeed, it was at this point that Stalin was angling for another Lend-Lease installment worth hundreds of millions of dollars. I can't say I've ever known a reason to be nostalgic for President Harding, but dusting off his 1921 policy on Bolshevik aid and addressing it to Stalin would have done wonders—for our men for sure, but also for the entire world:

"The sine qua non of any assistance on the part of the American aid," the 1921 agreement said, was the release of "all Americans detained in Russia." Such aid would be suspended or terminated "in case of failure on the part of the Soviet Authorities to fully comply with this primary condition."

But no. Something had happened in the intervening quarter century: Communist occupation of too much of Washington, and too much of the American psyche.

Also on March 26, 1945, while Roosevelt was terminating his conversation with Harriman about the Soviet maltreatment of our men, General Marshall, almost assuredly briefed on the POW situation (as Harriman had specifically requested that he be twelve days earlier), was doing his bit to make sure no more such talk even began. Marshall issued guidelines on the censorship of American ex-prisoners heading for home from the Soviet zone. It was fine for the men to talk to the press, Marshall said, with sensitivity to intelligence concerns ("Individual interviews authorized provided personnel briefed beforehand against disclosure [of] camp intelligence activities, evasions and escape briefings, equipment"), but nix on anything negative about the Soviets. Or, as the order tersely put it, "Censor all stories, delete criticism Russian treatment."

The lockdown doesn't stop. The scene shifts to that remote lake in Maryland, where George Earle, perhaps licking his wounds suffered at the hands of his hero, was getting in his last fishing before being summarily dispatched to Samoa.[41] Roosevelt—or whoever was running the White House in these final weeks of the president's life—wasn't taking any chances on Earle's conscience and the risk of exposure he posed to the conspiracy. Silence was essential.

That's because truth itself had become incriminating. This is why so many truth tellers found themselves marginalized, put as far out to pasture as possible—and maybe the moon wasn't far enough. A year before Earle was ordered 7,000 miles from Washington, FDR tried to send William Bullitt to a diplomatic oasis in Saudi Arabia, 6,750 miles away. Not too unexpectedly, Bullitt, turned down by the U.S. Army, chose to fight out the rest of the war with the Free French instead. Another political exile was the anti-Communist Loy Henderson, who in State Department Purge No. 2 in 1943 was blasted off 6,200 miles away to Baghdad for the duration. State Department Purge No. 1 in 1937 had sent Robert Kelley, staunch opponent of recognition, off to Turkey, 5,200 miles away. Ray Atherton got off easy with a post in nearby Canada, only 566 miles away.

Nevertheless, truth will out (what we do with it is another matter). On May

10, 1945, the FBI, still coming up to speed on myriad Communist conspiracies in Washington, extensively reinterviewed Whittaker Chambers. That helped fill in some gaps. So did interviewing former CPUSA leader Louis Budenz in August 1945. So did the defection of Soviet agent Igor Gouzenko in Canada in September 1945. So did the climactic advent of Elizabeth Bentley, who, in November 1945, walked into an FBI office in Connecticut with a wild tale of Moscow-directed subversion and occupation that tied everything together.[42]

What about George Kennan? To return to the diplomat's concerns, also in November 1945, about hostile Soviet treatment of American citizens inside the USSR, it's worth noting he proposed the solution of exposure, albeit tentatively. He wrote, "If we were to find means"—it's called a press conference—"to state frankly to the American public what the situation is with which we are faced in this respect . . . I should recommend that this particular compartment of Russian-American relations, which has long remained in the dark . . . be given its airing and illumination."[43]

Airing and illumination? What in fact transpired was strangulation and blackout. Like Major Van Vliet's Katyn Forest Massacre report dictated six months earlier at the Pentagon on May 22, 1945, Kennan's cable, too, was filed away. (Unlike the Van Vliet report, however, Kennan's cable didn't vanish altogether.) Like Van Vliet himself, Kennan and his fellow diplomats (including Earle and Bullitt, come to think of it) remained unwilling to break their silence without their superiors' approval.

We were just following orders?

A few months after Kennan wrote this "airing and illumination" cable, he would compose its metaphorical antithesis: a longer and far more famous cable laying out the policy of American "containment" of the Soviet Union. At age forty-one, Kennan was a celebrated Cold War strategist, and, as Tzouliadis writes, "his earlier plea on behalf of the Americans trapped in the Soviet Union . . . was soon forgotten, even by its author."[44]

Of course! Far from "airing and illumination," the solution Kennan now proposed to the Communist problem—all Communist problems—was to "contain" everything. This was the perfect metaphor for what was already going on—"containing" secrets, putting them in boxes, sealing the boxes up, stowing them in the national attic in order to separate society from any contamination coming from the truth—or the truth tellers, for that matter, who were similarly "contained." Sometimes it was as easy as stamping a document TOP SECRET and "losing" it—no one will ever know! Other times containment was served by censorship.

A signal example of this came one week before the European war's end when military censors prevented the Associated Press's Wes Gallagher from reporting that American and British armies, sweeping across northern Europe into Germany, "could have easily taken Berlin before the Russians did so in May 1945 but for some reason were not allowed to do so." (The same thing went for Vienna, and Prague.[45])

So wrote the distinguished journalist and longtime AP executive Kent Cooper in his book *The Right to Know: An Exposition of the Evils of News Suppression and Propaganda* (1956), a provocative look at the first half of the twentieth century as a series of disasters stemming from government manipulation and censorship of the news. This particular act of censorship, Cooper argued, was not a matter of military security. It was political censorship, pure and simple, and thus a violation of the policies that were supposed to govern press coverage of the war. The consequences, Cooper argued, were dire:

If Gallagher's story had been published the day it was written, it is not probable that the American people would have blandly accepted the idea that the West should step aside in Russia's favor without at least a guaranteed corridor reaching to Berlin.[46]

Once upon a time, the absence of such a "corridor" to divided Berlin through a hundred miles of Soviet-controlled "East Germany"—all forgotten features of Cold War history at this point—brought U.S.-USSR relations almost to a boiling point and led to the Soviet blockade of Berlin and the 1948 airlift. The failure to secure a corridor was a blunder widely blamed on U.S. diplomat John G. Winant, who, according to the AP's Wes Gallagher (again), had flatly refused to negotiate a ground route to divided Berlin for fear of arousing "mistrust" in the Russians. Winant committed suicide in November 1947, having become "deeply affected," writes Cooper, by the rising tensions of the Cold War.[47]

The consensus was to pin the blame on Winant. Hanson Baldwin, however, became convinced that the blame for Berlin lay not on the shoulders of a dead man but rather in the corridors of power in Washington—in the White House and the State and War Departments. Winant, he wrote, "was an agent [of policy] rather than a formulator." When our military negotiators—Eisenhower and Gen. Lucius D. Clay—finally took up the matter of Berlin and access to Berlin after Winant's tenure, they were negotiating, Baldwin argues, "against the background of a psychological delusion, then so prevalent in our government, that the Russians were our political as well as military 'buddies,' and that we could 'get along' with Stalin."[48] That ship of fools sailed on, just like the *Arawa*.

Cooper makes the convincing case that informing the American people, rather than censoring these vital facts, would have triggered widespread public outcry and the kind of debate essential to the functioning of a democratic republic. Cooper believed such debate "surely would have brought about . . . modification of the pro-Russian policy." He was probably right. It's difficult to imagine Americans opening the morning paper at the butterless breakfast table where Johnny's chair had been empty for several years and reading about how U.S. and British troops appeared to have been ordered to cool their heels along the Elbe (near Berlin), the Mulde (Prague), and the Enns (Vienna) so the Russians could go marching in, and then simply turning the page.

Hence (it seems), no such information was passed by military censors to the American people, and no such public debate ever took place. This was a turning point. The U.S. government had clearly seized control of political news, of political facts, to use as weapons of political policy—and, in effect, weapons of Soviet political policy. It gets worse. An even cruder, emptier example of this manipulation was the embargo placed at the behest of the Allied leaders, Stalin, Truman, and Churchill (dragging his heels), on the news of the surrender of Nazi Germany in France on May 7, 1945, *until the Russians could rig up their own surrender ceremony in Berlin on May 8, 1945.* This stupendous act of appeasement, blanked out of national memory, was thankfully circumvented by a wise and bold AP reporter named Edward Kennedy, who believed the news of Germany's surrender "belonged to the Allied peoples," as he later wrote, and not to the Soviet propaganda department. Kennedy created a giant controversy for refusing to go along with this blatant *political censorship.* On learning that Allied military headquarters (SHAEF) had already authorized German radio to broadcast the news of the May 7 surrender, Kennedy filed his story regardless of the embargo, regardless of the Soviet plan. As Kennedy explained his decision (which cost him his job with the AP) in an *Atlantic Monthly* essay in 1948, "Truman and Churchill—the latter reluctantly and only on pressure from Washington—agreed to hold up the news, which belonged to the Allied peoples, until the time of the Berlin meeting . . . The Russian action was quite in line with the Soviet conception of the press for propaganda, and nothing to get excited about; *the fault was ours for falling for it*" (emphasis added).[49]

Of course, according to this new way of looking at our history, we fell for it because we were pushed, both from the outside and, more important, from the inside. As a result, Americans at large were left to try to make half-sense of the partial truths doled out by our leaders. Later, Cooper notes, a smaller, book-reading audience would sort through the many war memoirs written by military and political figures, Churchill's most famous among them, containing "laments" over their authors' having been "pushed around by the insatiable Russians." Cooper—the man who coined the phrase "the right to know"— comments acerbically:

Not one of them, however, has expressed any realization of how different it all might have been had they disclosed what they later so dolefully put in their memoirs to excuse their actions. The fact that they so needlessly conducted all political matters in secret and kept them so under protection of war censorship should be the basis of remonstrance from a democratic people.[50]

Should be. But we were, the whole lot of us, with precious few exceptions, a nation of Captain Hillses, a nation of Roosevelts, a nation of Hisses, a nation of Kennans, a nation manipulated, inured, numbed, cushioned, silenced— continually protected from the sharpest of timely revelations, continually told to be afraid of them. We were impervious to the cries of the most plaintive Cassandras, who themselves were often pressured or consigned to mumble into their memoirs or grumble off to Samoa. Only the most principled, the most shrill, the most desperate, or the most stubborn were constitutionally (in the personal sense) able to rise above the overwhelming buzz and static. It was on this level where the battle royal really began, pitting the lone truth-teller against the forces of suppression, in a political and informational landscape that had been denuded of all vital context. This reality vacuum, this echo chamber of lies, was both created and preserved by what Cooper quite intriguingly paints as *autocrats in charge of both governments* (U.S. and USSR). "Clothed with autocratic powers," he writes, "individuals in charge of both governments demonstrated how political censorship had helped Russia to win the war and the peace while England and America helped Russia win the war but lost the peace."

Of course, writing in 1956, Cooper didn't know the half of it and all that, but this seasoned newsman was acutely, if not uniquely, perceptive in observing the role U.S.-USSR censorship jointly played in Soviet triumph and Western defeat. As he put it, "History records that this occurred because both governments proceeded secretly, just as if they were in a private venture."[51]

Still, inconvenient facts could slip through. Five days after V-E Day, the AP filed a startling news report from SHAEF: "Nearly half of the estimated 200,000 British and 76,000 American prisoners of war still in Germany are believed to be within the Russian zone of occupation and Supreme Headquarters has twice requested a meeting or an arrangement to arrange their return."[52]

Not two months earlier, as we've seen, Stalin had belligerently insisted to the now-deceased FDR that there were only seventeen Americans left in the Red zone, and that these last few American boys were safely en route to Odessa.

Behind the scenes, on May 19, 1945, Supreme Commander Eisenhower himself signed a cable stating, "Numbers of US prisoners estimated in Russian control 25,000."

On May 22, 1945, ten days after the AP report, delegations from the Soviet and American armies met in Halle, France, to settle the POW matter. It was a meeting between a massive, guns-bristling, Soviet delegation and a much smaller and more modest American delegation. The problem they came together to discuss sounds simple, but the Soviets made it anything but. Maj. Gen. R. W. Barker documented these meetings in a memo that describes the emergence of ghastly, heart-stopping complications: Americans in Soviet custody were "in effect being held hostage"; "we may find a reluctance to return them all"; and they might not come home for an "appreciable time to come." The realization that they might never come home at all begins to break, dimly, like an execution-day dawn.[53]

Another jolt of synchronicity: May 22, 1945, is the date on which ex-POW Major Van Vliet made it to the Pentagon to blow the lid off Soviet guilt at Katyn Forest for the benefit of U.S. military intelligence (G-2)—or so Van Vliet thought. His efforts, of course, as we saw in chapter 7, turned out to be only for the dead file. What we see on this day is an overlap of events that becomes difficult to explain without almost believing America's stars were in misalignment: Just as Major Van Vliet in Washington was trying to unmask the murderers of twenty-two thousand executed Poles in the forest of Smolensk, Russia, General Barker in Germany was staring into the faces of those same murderers, trying to pry as many as twenty thousand live GI Joes from their clutches. Both attempts would be unsuccessful.

Other vectors sped into the global morass. On May 23, 1945, Harry Hopkins, having been roused from his sickbed (literally) in his natty Georgetown home a week earlier, took off from Washington for one final mission to Moscow. Accompanied by Mrs. Hopkins, Harriman, and Charles Bohlen—all Hopkins's personal picks—he was sent by President Truman as a matter of some desperation to try to smooth out the unseemly rupture between the White House and the Kremlin that had broken into the open since the war's end. At the same time, Truman dispatched Joseph Davies—that self-aggrandizing boob (at best)!—to inform Churchill that the United States would continue in the Rooseveltian tradition of appeasing Stalin. In so many words.

This is the period most historians regard as "the Creation" of the epic hostilities known as the Cold War, but I see it more as a continuation of hostility suddenly brought to light in part by President Truman's awkward, unschooled, and almost bumptious efforts to retrench (good instinct)—soon to be tamped down by those "better angels" of ours, Hopkins and Davies—in response to Stalin's jackbooting through territories and over peoples he now, thanks to us, possessed (good strategy—for Moscow). Churchill, at this disastrous point, appears to have felt increasingly used and abused by the bloody, costly charade of the Uncle Joe Alliance, especially with the Soviets "clamping down" what he was now seeing as a "steel curtain" over Red Army–captured lands. That's what the British prime minister made known to Davies when the envoy visited him at Checkers to sound him out on the idea from Washington that Truman's next parley with Stalin would be a Big Two, not Three.

The thousands of British and American men still in Soviet custody don't appear in the record of the conversation.

Churchill's criticism of the Communist regime, however, triggered a most extraordinary harangue—sorry, "expression of my personal views"—from Davies, which lasted into the wee hours of the morning (the 11:00 P.M. meeting on May 26, 1945, didn't break until 4:30 A.M.). Reading the State Department record, it is hard to imagine a more hysterical dressing-down of a head of state committed to official papers.

What was it all about? Essentially, Davies was "shocked beyond words," "staggered," and "found it difficult to bring [himself] to believe he'd heard right" when Churchill vociferously criticized the police states the Soviets were setting up in Europe. Davies, in effect, was telling the Prime to shut up. He seemed petrified that Churchill's feelings might become public knowledge. Davies feared that Soviet suspicions of hostility in the West "would harden into action if they knew of this [Churchill's] attitude." Indeed, in Davies World, Churchill's attitude, if known to the Soviets, "would be more than sufficient explanation for their actions in Europe" since war's end. In the mind of the über-apologist, it was Churchill's attitude, *not Soviet actions,* that posed the threat to so-called unity. As Davies put it, "It was not the facts, so much as the interpretation of the facts, which might have a destructive effect."[54]

What was that again?

It's not your facts, Prime Minister, it's just your interpretation of the facts.

Meanwhile, back in Moscow, Hopkins's role was a little different. In the course of six ministerial sessions and a private tête-à-tête with Stalin, Hopkins was there, in sum, to convince Stalin to ensure that "the facts" added up to the best possible "interpretation." Pro-Soviet Poland? No problem. Pro-Soviet border nations? Fine with us. In fact, the United States *wanted* to see "friendly countries all along the Soviet borders," Hopkins told Stalin.

Good-bye, national self-determination. Hello, Eastern Bloc.

The problem wasn't Poland, per se, Hopkins assured Stalin. "We had no special interests in Poland and no special desire to any particular government."

Hello, Sovietized Poland.

The problem, Hopkins explained, was U.S. "public opinion." I guess military censorship was starting to wear a little thin in the States. Apparently, just as Churchill had to be encouraged not to provoke any undue outcry by criticizing Sovietization, Stalin had to do his bit, too, *by making Sovietization less glaringly objectionable.* As Hopkins put it, "He hoped that the Marshal would put his mind to the task of thinking up what diplomatic measures could be used to settle this question, keeping in mind the feeling of the American people."[55]

To better fool them, right? When the Soviets arrested and incarcerated sixteen Polish underground leaders, all members of the four main Polish political parties, who had been invited by Moscow into Moscow to discuss the formation of a new government according to the Yalta Agreement, it was as if a toxic eddy threatened the whirl of events, tainting the flow of great news of victory and "world peace," at least a little. In his private meeting with Stalin, which Hopkins himself wrote up as a top secret memorandum, Hopkins pressed this issue—not as an injustice, not as outrage—as a *public relations problem.* He took great pains to explain to Stalin this incident's "unfavorable effect in America" and the political danger it posed to Truman's abilities to continue Rooseveltian policy if, as a result, he was unable "to carry American public opinion with him." This is why, Hopkins said, "it was in the interest of good Russian-American relations . . . to release these prisoners."[56]

Not in the interest of right and wrong, fair play, or humanitarianism, mind you, and not because these men were citizens not of the USSR but of an allegedly sovereign Poland, but in the interest of how it all played around the American watercooler. Think: If sixteen Polish prisoners of the USSR threatened to wake the sleeping giant (us), just imagine what would have happened if we had learned about the Soviet imprisonment of tens of thousands of American and British soldiers.[57]

That remained secret—it had to—a document trail to nowhere, as the Senate Foreign Relations Committee minority staff discovered on recreating it from government files in 1991. This final betrayal can be reduced to several pertinent documents, all created at the end of this same victorious—or is that "victorious"? (cue laugh track)—month of May 1945.

There is the May 30, 1945, Kenner Memorandum, named for Gen. Albert Kenner, Eisenhower's surgeon general at SHAEF headquarters. This memo states that twenty thousand Americans remained under Red Army control. It also states that twenty thousand British remained under Red Army control as well, not to mention literally hundreds of thousands of other nationals.[58]

There is the May 31, 1945, top secret letter from General Deane to a Russian general, General Slavin, assistant chief of the Red Army in Moscow, the staff officer Deane had been dealing with on and off for almost a year by this time. This document states that the number of American prisoners believed to be in Russian custody is 15,597.[59]

The Senate report continues, logically, noting that it is "therefore difficult to reconcile these facts" with a third document, a cable signed by Eisenhower on June 1, 1945, which reads, "It is now estimated that only small numbers of U.S. prisoners of war still remain in Russian hands."[60]

"Now"? Since when? Since the memos written twenty-four and forty-eight hours earlier? Fifteen, twenty, forty thousand men were now in the West, just like that? No. There is a gaping, deeply dispiriting chasm between these two conflicting sets of documents. Did Eisenhower recognize this abyss? We don't know for sure. The subject isn't even addressed in biographies written since the Senate disclosures, up to and including Jean Edward Smith's 2012 Ike biography, which weighs in at 950 pages.[61] What we do know is this, as the Senate report states concretely: "Given the contents of Major General Deane's TOP SECRET letter, and given the contents of the Kenner memorandum, the Eisenhower cable of June 1 appears to be an attempt to gloss over a serious problem."[62]

A serious problem of exposure, that is.

Americans were never supposed to know. This darkest secret didn't enter our history books, our movies, our lore. It remained another unseen void, another intensification of the black hole of antiknowledge. Such omissions help explain many things, including the riddle of why Soviet crime never stuck, maybe even why the fall of the Wall rang so few lasting bells of victory. Uncle Sam has been part of, or was made into part of, the Russian Bear's cover-up for too long, all to maintain the fiction, the lie, of relations with the Soviet Union. Sometimes we called it the anti-Fascist alliance, sometimes we called it peaceful coexistence, sometimes we called it détente. Whatever name was in vogue, each described a chain of Big Lies that lashed us together. No wonder Ronald Reagan's onetime use of that mild, storybook phrase "evil empire" sparked such outrage. The fortieth president, who came from outside this secret circle, was breaking omertà, flouting the Washington-Moscow Establishment. *This Establishment wears no clothes.* When such a large sector of that Establishment went down at the end of 1991, it wasn't just open Leftists and diehard Communists in the West who didn't feel like throwing a party because the wicked witch seemed to be dead. The better part of a century of silence had made all Western democracies complicit in the successive reigns of terror and entrenched regimes of tyranny. They would have remained complicit in silence, I do believe, forever, if the Soviet Union hadn't begun to crack apart, its secrets—our secrets—spilling out at the seams.

Remember, the Venona cables were not released until *after* the Soviet archives began to open.

Due to the West's conspiratorial record of denial, then, there was great ambivalence in the demise of the conspiracy's leader. There must have been great unease, too, about what might come out next, what Boris Yeltsin might say next, what document might pop out of the archive next—what would happen if by some miracle there would be no more secrets anymore. It was probably enough to give those senior Washington muckety-mucks cold sweats. Suspense: Would the great Soviet dissident Vladimir Bukovsky convince Yeltsin to inaugurate a Nuremberg-like trial of the Communist system? *I hope not, they said, ensconced in all of the best addresses of the West.* For these lifelong conspirators the end was nothing to celebrate. It was something to prevent.

Revelation and exposure, in other words, are not for VIPs. Whether it was the truth about Communist penetration at home or Communist perfidy abroad, those whom we might now think of as the "unindicted coconspirators" out there, high and low, had to do everything they could to suppress all. No wonder, as Bukovsky is quoted as recounting many pages ago, Yeltsin said no to a legal reckoning on the crimes of Communism due to "the enormous pressure he felt from the West not to have such a trial."[63] Who knows? Maybe it was under similar Western pressure that Yeltsin sealed Stalin's archives for forty years.[64] Me, I'll try to hang on if only to see if there's anything about Harry Hopkins in the files—although who would be surprised to learn any evidence was burned long ago? Meanwhile, who knows what else might be in the American Venona archives? The government line is always to keep a lid on it.

Eisenhower's June 1, 1945, cable only echoed that same government line. On the very day Ike was talking about receiving "only small numbers" of prisoners, the War Department announced that "substantially all" American soldiers taken prisoner in Europe were accounted for. End of exposure. Just like that. According to a brief *New York Times* report, Undersecretary Robert Patterson put a damper on lingering hopes that men who had been carried on the rolls as missing in action (MIA) for the duration might still be discovered as POWs. Patterson said, "This means that it is not expected that many of those who are still being carried as missing in action will appear later as having been prisoners of war."[65]

"In other words," the Senate report states—as though we need other words, but, OK, go ahead, give it to us straight—"on June 1, 1945, the U.S. government's public position was that most American GIs taken prisoner have come home and been repatriated, even though the classified cable traffic for the previous fortnight was reporting between 15,000 and 20,000 still held."[66]

What happened? The Senate report goes on to assemble the relevant record of subsequent statements, memos, tallies and the like to arrive at its bottom line: between 12,500 and 20,000 U.S. servicemen were left behind after World

War II, their lost lives locked away from view by the gates of the Gulag itself—but also and even primarily by American acquiescence, American silence. Our own men were "contained" along with everything—and I mean *everything*—else.

I can't think of anything that puts a more American face on this uniquely twentieth-century record of perfidy than the betrayal of our own fighting fathers, brothers, husbands, and sons, Americans of successive generations beginning back before the so-called Greatest Generation, all the way up to the baby boomers. Along with their long-suffering families, they would become the uniquely American sacrifice to the conspiracy of silence that improbably held the Free World and the Un-Free World together, partners in crime, over the course of the twentieth century. Sacrifices, all, to American betrayal.

What men? said Hanoi, Peking, Pyongyang, Moscow.

What men? said London, Washington.

Call and echo.

What kulaks starving by the million? What purges by the ten thousand? What massacres here, there, and everywhere? What forced repatriation and liquidation of millions? What slavery of more millions? What Gulag Archipelago? What strategic deception? What subversion? What Communist conspiracy? What espionage? What Hungary? What tanks? What Prague? What Red Terror network? What Soviet-inspired Western drug epidemic? What evil empire?

What men?

The president of Russia "misspoke," said the Bush administration, after Yeltsin was safely out of the country. This, British historian and author Nigel Cawthorne observed, was coming "as close as you can come to calling the head of a foreign power a liar without starting a war."[67]

War, shmar. As far as Washington was concerned, the overriding goal was to save the conspiracy—a far more difficult task with that gonzo Russian president having gone over to the Other Side . . .

What am I saying?

Let me rework that startling idea—that Yeltsin, in speaking about American POWs quite possibly still alive in Soviet captivity, had become the enemy to the Washington Establishment—and see if it still makes sense. In breaking with the Soviet past, Yeltsin was breaking silence, too, a silence that Washington—in one sense, the last conspirator standing—wanted to preserve above all. This indeed turned Yeltsin at that moment into a threat, a whistle-blower, *a turncoat,* who required neutralization, marginalization, the laugh-track treatment, something, anything, to shut him down via disinformation. Even Soviet Lite would do. Nothing extreme. Yeltsin's own "erratic" behavior, plus the overwhelming, all-consuming nature of the task before any mortal assuming leadership of the toxic waste dump known as the former USSR, would do the rest. The man was a drunk, they said (untrustworthy); the transcript translation was incorrect (it wasn't); he "misunderstood" the information that was "given to him" (incompetent). He meant well, of course, but he *"misspoke."* Anything to knock out the bomb thrower.

OK. The idea still makes sense. At this point in time, Yeltsin had become one them—I mean, *one of us.*

Because ultimately, the villain is "them." By "them," I mean anyone who preserves the Big Lie, any Big Lie. We are back to the *Invasion of the Body Snatchers* trope, the almost science-fictional subversion of the crisp-looking admirals and benevolent preschool principals whom we started with many pages ago. Presidential envoys, too. "It's clear to me that he misspoke, because we have found nobody here that will tell us that Mr. Yeltsin's information was correct," said Malcolm Toon on June 27, 1992.

"Here," of course, was Belly of the Beast Land—Moscow, where Toon heard only sympathetic echoes to his crazy-Yeltsin lament.

The New York Times's Serge Schmemann picked up on the same cry: "Mr. Toon's conclusion that Mr. Yeltsin misspoke supported previous responses from Moscow, Hanoi and Washington, where baffled officials insisted that no evidence had been found to support his assertion."[68]

What they all wanted was to cram this particular genie, with all of his dog tags, medals, and stars, back into the bottle. Would Americans sit up and notice the scant facts and massive implications coming from the "erratic" Yeltsin, or return to hypnotic static? If there was more to it than fiction, Boris Yeltsin was promising a real-life cliff-hanger. "Some of them were transferred to the former Soviet Union and were kept in labor camps," Yeltsin said in a television interview on the eve of his June 1992 visit. "We don't have complete data and can only surmise that some of them may still be alive. That is why our investigations are continuing. Some of them may have ended up in psychiatric asylums."

I hope it's clear by now that the answers to these questions don't lie only in the police state of Stalin, Khrushchev, Brezhnev, Andropov, Chernenko, Gorbachev, Yeltsin, and Putin. Sure, these police-state chiefs kept their police-state secrets, but we kept secrets, too. After World War II's end, for example, there were the Wringer files, secret U.S. Air Force reports compiled between 1947 and 1956 from interviews with roughly 300,000 former German and Japanese prisoners of war returning from Soviet camps, where a significant number of these ex-prisoners had been detained with American servicemen. At random, Tim Tzouliadis notes firsthand accounts from declassified Wringer archives describing a U.S. Army major in Vorkuta, about a hundred kilometers north of the Arctic Circle, a Fredericksburg, Virginia, pilot, who spoke broken German with an American accent and whose gold teeth were removed by a camp dentist. In 1948, a broken-down German serviceman attested to the presence of six American intelligence officers incarcerated in a "silence camp" in the South Ural Mountains where prisoners of all nationalities were forced to work in mercury mines. "None of the prisoners are supposed to be discharged and they are not authorized any connection with the outside world," the German said. "Mortality is very high."[69]

What about the death of hope? In 1954, a German officer reported that he had shared a cell in a Soviet prison near Moskva in 1949 with an American pilot—"30–35 years old, 1.8 meters tall, slim, sportsmanlike figure, normally full black hair yet shaved in prison"—and nineteen other German officers. "He was self-confident and expressed to his cellmates on several occasion the conviction that . . . his imprisonment would not last long as the American Government in the USA would intervene on their behalf."[70]

Sure, bub.

When we meet the Americans we will tell them . . . and absolutely nothing at all will ever happen.

Tzouliadis notes also the account of a "Major Thompson" from San Antonio, Texas, captured in 1944 when his plane went down and sentenced to twenty-five years for espionage. It was 1991—thirty-six years later—before his daughter learned for the first time that a German repatriate had told U.S. authorities about her dad in 1955, that he had been imprisoned at Budenskaya prison near Moscow and later in Tayshet labor camp. Not only was Thompson's daughter "overwhelmed," as the Senate report notes, picking up her story; she also wanted to know why her family had never been told by the United States government that Major Thompson, declared killed in action, body not recovered in 1944, had been seen alive and well enough in the Soviet Gulag in 1955.[71]

By 1992, when Yeltsin began broadcasting his own do-it-yourself headlines to the media, research into the plight of thousands of American soldiers in the slave-camp network in the USSR especially since 1945 had begun breaking into the public square. The story of "men left behind" after Vietnam had earlier entered pop consciousness but gone no further. Independent researchers John M. G. Brown, Jim Sanders, Mark Sauter, and others had been putting two and two hundred and two thousand and *twenty thousand* together to discover the scope of a scandal in which Uncle Sam is revealed to have regularly and knowingly sacrificed his own living sons to the bloodlust of Soviet Russia and its Red acolytes. Leaving men behind was not just a fantastical Hollywood premise; it was a secret ritual that marked the shameful aftermath of every losing American conflict with Communism—i.e., every American conflict with Communism. In 2002 Joseph D. Douglass Jr. would put these stories together powerfully in his book *Betrayed,* concluding that as many as twenty thousand American POWs were forsaken to Communist control after World War II, five thousand to eight thousand after Korea, one thousand throughout the rest of the Cold War, and two thousand at the end of the Vietnam War.[72] Incendiary though it is, the story never spread like wildfire. It is a scandal to report that in May 1991, one year before Yeltsin's trip to Washington, the landmark report by the Republican minority staff of the Senate Foreign Relations Committee (which I've been quoting in this chapter) on this unknown history of American men abandoned by the U.S. government came out, stopping no presses. Despite its solid documentation, concise form, and, as British historian Nigel Cawthorne would underscore, "august source," the report failed to generate much in the way of headlines, let alone Yeltsin-sized headlines. Not even the most shocking claim—possibly twenty thousand American enlisted men and officers, former prisoners of war in Germany, ceded to the Soviets in "the Good War"—moved the media. The report did, however, help kick-start the Senate into creating the U.S. Senate Select Committee on POW/MIA Affairs.

What did that do? Since the U.S. government was more interested in preserving the secrecy than doing public penance, or even saving fellow citizens who might actually have been living, not much. Looking back on the committee's record, journalist Sydney Schanberg wrote in 1994 that the committee had been dominated by a faction led by Senator John Kerry (D-MA) that "wanted to appear to be probing the prisoner issue energetically, but in fact never rocked official Washington's boat." He continued, "Nor did they lay open the 20 years of secrecy and untruths."[73]

In 2010, Schanberg speculated on the impact of opening the secret archives on POW/MIA history in *The American Conservative.*

> My guess would be that hell could break loose. Some people might go to jail for violating the public trust and their oaths of office. There's no statute of limitations on crimes like murder, and most of those abandoned prisoners are probably no longer alive. Those who began and continued the cover-up were surely accomplices in their deaths. At the very least, laws affecting the military would be rewritten. And the reputations of the people who played the largest roles would crumble all over the country—people such as Henry Kissinger, John McCain, John Kerry, and Dick Cheney, plus many others including Pentagon chiefs, national security advisers, secretaries of state, intelligence chiefs, and so on. Since this is probably all a daydream, may I say that perhaps it could be a cleansing of the temple—for a while at least, human nature being what it is.[74]

This, of course, assumes that we as a people would and even could react to the release of (more) documents confirming that Uncle Sam knowingly abandoned thousands of American servicemen to Communist servitude and medical experimentation over the course of the twentieth century,[75] in the way, for example, that our precious freethinkers, from Sydney Schanberg on the Left to Joseph Douglass on the Right, reacted after embarking on their own courses of independent study. Is it a reliable assumption? Doubtless, the kind of confirmation the archives hold (unless they've been scrubbed) would convince some of the people, but what is evidence, what are facts, to the postmodern mind? Things to manipulate. Things to cast out of the "existing view of the world." Our brains washed clean of context, we have been conditioned to laugh at morals and absolutes. We can't see straight. We have been communized. "Not even high intelligence and a sensitive spirit are of any help once the facts of a situation are deduced from a political theory, rather than vice versa," as Conquest wrote.

Thus, the ship of state secrets sails on. It always does. It was all but out of sight by 2005, well over a decade since the first President Bush practically gagged Boris Yeltsin in the Rose Garden, when the Pentagon commission charged with investigating whether American POWs were incarcerated in the Soviet Union finally announced that yes, Americans, including U.S. servicemen, were imprisoned in the Communist slave labor camps of the Gulag Archipelago. "We have multiple lists of American servicemen missing and, of course, they are arranged by conflict," the commission's executive secretary, Norman Kass, told CNN in 2005. "We have lists from World War II, from the Korean War, the Vietnam War and the various casualties during the Cold War." The hedging continued, however, with a bottom line that remained unofficial. "I personally would be comfortable saying that the number is in the hundreds," Kass said, somewhat anticlimactically.[76]

Sigh. To call "hundreds" a conservative estimate creates more gross understatement, but I suppose the main point to seize upon is that the U.S. government in 2005 officially admitted that American servicemen, going back to World War II, have been captives of the Gulag Archipelago.

What then? Did President George W. Bush take up the black banner of the POW/MIA cause and tell the American people what had happened? Did President Obama? Of course not. The ship of state secrets continued to sail on, course unchanged, port of reckoning circumvented. The story created no wake, as if everything were still invisible. Sydney Schanberg, having devoted a significant portion of his writing career to reporting on the POW/MIA issue, offered a revealing testament in his 2010 *American Conservative* article:

In recent years, I have offered my POW stories to a long list of editors of leading newspapers, magazines, and significant websites that do original reporting. And when they decline my offerings, I have urged them to do their own POW investigation with their own staff under their own supervision. The list of these news organizations includes the *New York Times,* the *Washington Post,* the *Los Angeles Times, New York* magazine, *The Atlantic, The New Yorker, Harper's, Rolling Stone, Mother Jones, Vanity Fair, Salon, Slate, Talking Points Memo, ProPublica, Politico,* and others. To my knowledge, none have attempted or produced a piece.

It is almost eerie to read a letter to the editor of *The Washington Post* that John M. G. Brown wrote twenty years earlier:

> All major circulation U.S. publications I have contacted, with the exception of the VFW magazine, have declined to publish documentable facts of the history of U.S. prisoners of war held by Communist nations. These publications have apparently declined to even investigate the matter seriously.[77]

"So what?" the cold, toneless voice of political calculation says. These men are almost assuredly dead. What could it possibly matter now?

The following memoir, testimony of a late-twentieth-century interview by investigators tracing the cold trails of lost men, may help us formulate the appropriately human rejoinder.[78] It is an [anonymous] eyewitness account by a former Gulag prisoner, a Soviet national released into "internal exile." It turns out that while the Communists could rob this man of his free will to live as he chose, they couldn't rob him of his free will to remember. Recounting scenes from his mind's eye—places, names, numbers of people, what they were doing, where they were going—he unveils a capacious expanse of memory defiled by the evil of others, and it is haunting.

> But then, in Udereya, my sad experience showed that the "flow" of Americans from the prisoner of war camps in Germany and in the Far East, and now from Korea, was proceeding at a robust pace, filling in the bottomless hell of the Gulag.

> I haven't even had a chance to discuss Korea.

> I first met these people in Peveka . . . There . . . four Americans, specialists in automation systems, were being detained. They were sent there from the mining

camps of the Northwestern Directorate of Sevvostlag to delve into the function-
ality of mobile electrical power stations that reached Chaunskaya Guba under
the Lend Lease program.

The Lend-Lease program—again. All that American booty pirated by
Harry Hopkins for Mother Russia. And what a terrible taunt to our men to have
had to tune up good ol' American equipment in the desolate Arctic reaches of
the Gulag. I wonder whether the "mobile electrical power station" referenced
above is the same thing as a "complete Mobile Depot unit"? I haven't been able
to find out. I wonder because on the other side of the Bering Straits and a universe away, on inspecting the Alaska stop in the Lend-Lease pipeline, George
Racey Jordan wrote of coming across such supplies awaiting transport to the
USSR. He wrote: "We saw many generators, complete Mobile Depot units,
complete instrument shops in crates, unwrapped tires of different sizes, and
thousands of boxes of aircraft parts buried so deep in snow that it was difficult
to tell if we were scraping the true bottom."[79]

On one side of the Arctic Ocean, a mobile power station was something we
couldn't ship fast enough to Russia. On the other side of the Arctic Ocean, it
became a mechanical snare to enslave Americans forever.

The source's recollections don't stop:

> Later, at the very beginning of the navigation in the Sea of Okhotsk, I met still
> another group of Americans in the summer of 1948, at the Magadan transfer
> point in the Bay of Negaev.

Sea of Okhotsk. Magadan. Bay of Negaev. These unfamiliar words on a
page fail to inspire the gray-white terror of the Arctic seascape and landscape,
the icy storms of the endless winter that make the seas impassable, broken by
those few, hot, muggy weeks of summer that make the land unbearable. A few
summers earlier, Vice President Henry Wallace visited Magadan, a city on permafrost built entirely by Gulag labor in the Kolyma region. It was a dolled-up
and de-watchtowered Magadan Wallace saw, where NKVD officers masquer-
aded as stalwart workers, pretty office girls dressed up as swineherds, and the
real workers, the slaves, far from stalwart, far from pretty, were confined to
barracks for three days—the only delicious days of inactivity the prisoners ever
got, as the great Gulag witness Elinor Lipper wrote in her bitingly, even un-
bearably, vivid memoir *Eleven Years in Soviet Prison Camps* in 1951. Wallace, of
course, was charmed.

Not so this group of Americans as they came ashore at the Magadan transfer
in the Bay of Negaev.

There were 14 of them and they had just been taken from the holds of a ship transporting slaves: helpless, enfeebled by a week-and-a-half's worth of tossing on the seas, hunger, exhaustion, and desperation. I cannot single out any one of them. They all appeared uniformly lifeless and faceless . . . They said they served with the navy somewhere out at sea. They were seized by the Japanese in 1943. They were detained in camps . . . then in Manchuria, outside of Harbin, where they were duped by Soviet "liberators." There was very little opportunity to communicate with them.

Very little opportunity then or ever. Fourteen Americans, young men still, one or two maybe still in possession of a token of home, a faded snapshot of a girl in a pocket, a pressed letter, now almost molded to his person, that Mom or Dad, worried, loving, had dropped in the corner mailbox near the house with the swing on the porch where he had grown up . . . *before*. Before the draft notice, before the navy, before the Japanese, before the Russians, before the bowels of a slave ship, a Gulag ship—very possibly an American ship, another lavish gift of Lend-Lease—and whatever lay ahead.[80]

It came quickly, the source said. One night they were taken off into the depths of Kolyma, into the bottomless abyss of its vastness.

The question before us now becomes more pointed. Do we leave our countrymen to this bottomless abyss of Kolyma's vastness? Or do we restore to our collective memory some trace of these lives seized, taken over, and destroyed by the aggressive evil Communist system and forsaken, erased, and denied by weak and corrupt American officials? So long as the silence remains unbroken, so long as our national understanding remains incomplete, their betrayal is forever. Glorified as fallen sacrifices to "the Good War," they paid the ultimate price to the conspiracy against truth and morality that coincides with the dawn of the "American Century." Until we reclaim them, their memories, and all of the other victims—not by the baker's dozen, not by the hundreds, not by the thousands, but *by the millions*—we remain prisoners, too, of a giant, acid-rinsed blankness, our own self-censored experience with lies that has made us what we are today. Victims of American betrayal.

CHAPTER TWELVE

We can see that all elements of the socialist ideal—the abolition of private property, family, hierarchies, the hostility toward religion—could be regarded as manifestations of one basic principle: the suppression of individuality . . . the destruction of individuality, or, at least, its suppression to a point where it would cease to be a social force.

—IGOR SHAFAREVICH[1]

The ultimate objective of the new policy is not to learn more secrets about the adversary, and not even to teach the masses in the West in the spirit of Marxism-Leninist ideology, but to slowly replace the free-market capitalist society, with its individual freedoms in economic and socio-political spheres of life, with a carbon copy of the "most progressive" system, and eventually merge into one world-wide system ruled by a benevolent bureaucracy which they call Socialism (or Communism, as the final and supreme stage of this "progress").

To effect this change, it is much easier . . . to change the perceptions of reality, attitudes, patterns of behavior and to create wide-spread demands and expectations, leading ultimately to the acceptance of totalitarianism.

—TOMAS SCHUMAN (A.K.A. YURI BESMENOV)[2]

There was a moment of silence while this, as it turned out, all too exact prophesy sank in, and then the previous conversation resumed.

—HIPPOLYTE TAINE AS RELATED BY MALCOLM MUGGERIDGE[3]

The funny thing about this book—if there is a funny thing about this book—is that in setting out to explore the breaches in those bastions of tradition (assumed to be manned by conservatives) that became apparent as the Western world struggled with an expanding, flexing, and combusting Islam, I expected to focus mainly on the disconnect between facts and conclusions about Islam—not Communism. Communism, it seemed, was an erstwhile threat, supposedly vanquished decades ago. Then the past eleven chapters took shape.

Meanwhile, I continued to write my syndicated newspaper column, amass-
ing a body of work supplemented by blog essays, which, since 9/11, amounts to
an almost uninterrupted chronicle of Islam's fearsome impact on the Western
mind—the place where denial and delusion insert themselves between fact and
conclusion. I have tracked this phenomenon through the culture, where sharia
norms (Islamic law) are increasingly deferred to (to avert violence), in politics,
where liberty shrinks to maintain an increasingly sharia-compliant order (to
avert violence), and in the military, where sharia-based demands for "respect"
(submission) drive military strategy, also to avert violence. It wasn't very long
after 9/11 that it became apparent that, like true *dhimmi,* we were "submitting"
to Islam's cult of supremacy as a by-product of our own cultural devolution into
childishness by choice.[4]

Of course, first I had to learn what *dhimmi* were. The Arabic term refers to
Christians and Jews, who, conquered by Islam, live suppressed and diminished
lives according to the strictures of sharia. These laws enforce the Koranic command that *dhimmi* "feel themselves subdued" (sura 9:29). The miserable history
of the *dhimmi* is the single most relevant aspect of Islam to anyone who is not
Muslim. Why? Even in those parts of the world culturally and religiously separate from Islam, the paradigm of the *dhimmi* not only defines Islamic attitudes
toward "infidels," it also prefigures the "infidel" response to Islam.

This relationship turns on what may be the oldest mind game in history. As
populations come under the pressure of Islamic immigration—a "phenomenon
of conquest through immigration called *al-Hijra,*" as the Netherlands' Geert
Wilders puts it[5]—they also come under the pressure of Islamic grievances and
demands, always accompanied by the threat or reality of violence.[6] This consti-
tutes a period of previolent jihad (broken by outbursts of violence), in which
passive-aggressive Islam is able to trigger in non-Islamic populations the apology reflex, the accommodation reflex, the appeasement reflex, and finally the
roll-over-and-play-dead reflex, all of which permit Islam's advance. Full-blown
violent jihad ensues as necessary. Whether official *dhimmi* status follows, what
historian Bat Ye'or calls "dhimmitude" deepens, as when, for example, a university in Britain—through whose unsurpassed literary tradition run veritable
rivers of mead, ale, and whisky—considers closing campus bars due to the minority Muslim view of alcohol as "immoral."[7] This dhimmitude, Bat Ye'or discovered, is a cultural, mental, and spiritual condition visible in all nations and
peoples contending with Islam through history, recognizable by markers of
supplication, self-abnegation, and, most tellingly, fear—and, most relevantly,
silence. Again, such dhimmitude can (and does) mark societies that are ostensibly non-Islamic.

Or is that pre-Islamic?

I was lucky to learn about dhimmitude early in this latest cycle of global jihad. My education began when, along with a Koran, I picked up a copy of Ibn
Warraq's essential *Why I Am Not a Muslim* (1995) at a local bookstore outside
New York City on September 12, 2001. A few months later, at the beginning
of 2002, in response to a column I had written puzzling through a C-SPAN
panel discussion of Islam, which was part double talk (from Islamic clerics)
and part fact-based logic (from Christian ministers), Andrew G. Bostom, a
medical professor at Brown University, wrote to ask whether he could send
me a collection of books by Bat Ye'or. He was finding that her historical research into jihad and dhimmitude was filling in the blanks on our contemporary quandaries.

Well, why not? He kindly sent several books my way: *The Dhimmi, The Decline of Eastern Christianity* and *Islam and Dhimmitude,* all keys from the exotic,
distant past to understanding our postmodern plight. Bostom had come upon
Bat Ye'or's works shortly after 9/11, a time when some among us were beginning to realize that what we were all hearing 24/7 on cable, on NPR, in *The
New York Times*, from all the experts—John Esposito, Karen Armstrong, Juan
Cole, ex-ambassadors to Saudi Arabia and the like—was out of sync with what
we were watching before our eyes. In other words, the narrative—"Islam is
peace"—was not supported by the evidence: Islam is violence. Islam is slavery
(Sudan). Islam is forced conversion (Egypt). Islam is child rape (Iran, Afghani-
stan, Saudi Arabia, South Yorkshire, too). Islam is pillage (Somalia). Islam is
religious cleansing (Iraq). Islam is death for apostasy (Swat Valley, Harvard
University, too[8]). Islam is censorship (everywhere). Islam is conquest (Cyprus,
Israel, Kosovo, Philippines, the 751 government-ID'd no-go zones of France[9]).
Such fact-based observations, of course, trigger charges of that sin of sins—
"Islamophobia" ("racism" being its domestic twin)—but does mere name-calling
("Islamophobe") make these serious crimes and their real victims go away?

In our world, yes. Over nearly a century of Big Lies we have learned to discount fact and disable logic. As in a frustration dream, the crimes, the victims,
and their suffering vanish in today's magic word, "Islamophobia." What
remains—slanderous allegations of "prejudice," permanent brands of "bias"—
triggers the revulsion reflex in the postmodern brain, still programmed to be
vigilant against racism, lynch mobs, the KKK, and the like. Extant or not, func-
tional or not, these usually faux stimuli create outrage Islam exploits as "Islamophobia." *Have you left no sense of decency?*

This pattern is very old. In pre-McCarthy times, the all-powerful word that
stopped the logic process cold was "Red-baiter." In 1938, J. B. Matthews, a
truth teller who would later work for Senator McCarthy and would himself be
publicly neutralized (slimed) for this same "crime," described "Red-baiting" as

"the best trick ever invented, short of a firing squad, for making short work of anybody who dares to object to communist theories and practices. If he is not effectively silenced, he is at least thoroughly discredited among the vast flock of citizens who enjoy thinking of themselves as liberals."[10]

Substitute "Islamophobia" for "Red-baiting" and the statement describes the fail-safe technique that has kept the facts of jihad—the consequences of jihad—under official wraps since 9/11, silencing and discrediting anybody who dares object to Islamic "theories and practices." Instead, we must ponder: "Why do they hate us?" This was the question public figures, the commentariat, the academy, even the birds in the trees called out to one another in those weeks and months as the battleground carnage in New York, Washington, and Pennsylvania cooled and was sorted. This was no mystery that reading about the hate for the "Other" codified in the Koran couldn't have readily solved, but experts by-passed the answer, many of them already deep into what Bertrand Russell might have called "the conspiracy of concealment," his 1920 phrase for the lies Western visitors to newly Bolshevik Russia considered necessary to make the nascent police state appear civilized in the eyes of the outside world.[11] At the same time, Russell made a memorable comparison between what was then exhausted Islam and high-riding Bolshevism.

> Bolshevism combines the characteristics of the French Revolution with those of the rise of Islam . . . Marx has taught that Communism is fatally predestined to come about; this produces a state of mind not unlike that of the early successors of Mahommet . . . Among religions, Bolshevism is to be reckoned with Mohammedanism rather than with Christianity and Buddhism. Christianity and Buddhism are primarily personal religions, with mystical doctrines and a love of contemplation. Mohammedanism and Bolshevism are practical, social, unspiritual, concerned to win the empire of this world.[12]

Eighty, ninety years later—in a time of rising Islam and not exactly exhausted but transformed Communism—a sound bite like that would get a pundit zapped on *Meet the Press* or CNN for insubordinate "Islamophobia," perhaps sending Fox News's Bill Kristol, for one, into ridicule mode over intimations of the coming Islamic empire known as the caliphate.[13] Meanwhile, just as pointing out Communism's stated goal to control the world was once a prompt for charges of "Red-baiting," now pointing out Islam's stated goal to impose its totalitarian system of religion, law, and politics onto the world is a prompt for charges of "Islamophobia."

Islam, we are told, has nothing to do with anything bad. How could it? Islam means "peace," said the forty-third president of the United States. No, in fact, Islam means "submission." There's a huge difference, and it explains why Islam celebrated the fall of the Twin Towers in Gaza, Kabul, and Queens. Dhimmitude, already evident in our society, goes a long way to explain why we didn't dare show that we had noticed.

What we were witnessing was the marshaling forces of the latest, greatest Big Lie. This was one Big Lie I didn't have to stumble across in an out-of-print book or extract from 1950s congressional testimony. I could watch it evolve close up and in real time as a matter of professional as well as national interest. I saw how, *pace* Communist penetration of yore, this Big Lie was actively pressed on us by cadres of agents of Islam and their own armies of useful fools: members of the Muslim Brotherhood fobbed off as advocates of a pluralistic, American Islam, the Iran Lobby, Saudi princelings, the international Islamic bloc now known as the Organization of Islamic Cooperation (OIC), the Bush administration, the Obama administration, practically anyone on a TV sound-stage. All "reasonable people," they peddled the same Big Lie: Islam is a religion of peace.

The history of the decade that followed, then, became a stuttering story of mongrel words and phrases (from "Islamofascism" to "violent extremism") and morphing suffixes ("ist," "ism"). It was a time of now-you-see-it, now-you-don't terminology (jihad, jihadist, sharia, mujahideen, shahid, taqqiyya, jizya, caliph-ate). Apt phrases became verboten ("Islamic terrorism," "Muslim violence," "Islamic jihad"), as did concepts uniquely or characteristically Islamic: religious supremacism, censorship, slavery, pederasty, "honor killings," "grooming," and totalitarianism, among others. We may have intuited that "apostasy" did not go out with Galileo, and that beheadings did not end with the French Revolution, but . . . *Islam is a religion of peace.* The real threat, we decided to believe, or thought we had no choice but to believe (or just didn't think), is "violent extremism."

Limiting our brains to this empty phrase, however, has done extreme vio-lence to our thought processes. Like a navy of Captain Hillses helming a fleet of *Arawa*s, we sail on, blind, deaf, and dumb. Hills only spent four years becom-ing brainwashed by paeans to "Uncle Joe" and Communism. We have spent more than a decade listening to propaganda about "Uncle Mo" and "the reli-gion of peace." Just as Captain Hills had no context to understand the fears of his human cargo bound for Gulag slavery and death, we have no context to discuss Islam and its designs on liberty, on conscience, on apostates, on elderly cartoonists in Scandinavia. At every level, we have censored the knowledge es-sential to such an understanding. After all, if the problem is "violent extrem-ism," what's the problem? Have a nice flight.

Here's the problem: "Violent extremism" is not terminology that informs or clarifies; it is what French scholar Alain Besançon has called "the language of ideology" and "official vocabulary." When the individual accepts this official ideological lexicon from authority with a capital *A,* he is lost. Besançon writes:

> The moment the individual accepts the language of ideology, he allows his mental world and his sense of self-respect to be hijacked along with the language. No matter how inadvertently he may have stumbled into the use of the official vocabulary, *he is now part of the ideology,* and has, in a manner of speaking, entered into a pact with the devil [emphasis added].[14]

The importance of this pact cannot be overestimated. At a certain point, the language of ideology binds the brain to ideology, "hijacking" thought, individualism, and self-respect along the way. Besançon was writing about the trap of twentieth-century totalitarianism. The comparison to Islam, however, is apt. Islam *is* totalitarian, sharing numerous attributes with Communism and Nazism both—blueprints for world domination, control of private and public life (including speech), demotion of despised groups to inferior status, one-party (or all Islamic parties) political systems. Once upon a time, such comparisons between Islam and totalitarianism formed an area of learned study mined by all manner of Western academics and students of history. Noted scholars in the first half of the twentieth century even used Islam's violent and fanatical example to explain the workings of Nazism and Communism.[15]

There is another pertinent comparison to be made: Both despotisms induce paralysis in the West. The Netherlands' Geert Wilders made this point explicit in a 2010 speech. Listing the striking similarities among Islam, Communism, and Nazism, Wilders said:

> There is one more striking parallel, but this is not a characteristic of the three political ideologies, but one of the West. It is the apparent inability of the West to see the danger . . . Our inability leads us to reject the logical and historical conclusions to be drawn from the facts, though we could and should know better. What is wrong with modern Western man that we make the same mistake over and over again?[16]

Nothing short of that pact with the devil invoked by Besançon begins to explain this problem. It was a soul-selling deal our forebears made with Communism as represented by its Soviet regime. We, as their heirs, must come to terms with it. We will continue to pay, just as Solzhenitsyn said we would, until we do. The lies will continue to redouble and compound, and the complicity, too, and thus become our own, and then our children's.

Wilders delivered this speech in Berlin one day before the tenth anniversary of the reunification of the two Germanys—divided from one another, of course, in that great "victory" of ours in World War II. It was a declaration against the Islamization of Germany, but it was also a declaration against all totalitarian creeds. Wilders invoked Soviet dissident Vladimir Bukovsky's belief that the West "never won the Cold War, never even fought it" because for most of the time the West appeased Communism and, as Bukovsky put it, "appeasers don't win wars." Wilders then said:

> Islam is the Communism of today. But, because of our failure to come clean with Communism, we are unable to deal with it, trapped as we are in the old Communist habit of deceit and double-speak that used to haunt the countries in the East *and that now haunts all of us* [emphasis added].[17]

Islam is the totalitarian threat of today. However, because we continue the "deceit and double-speak" we adopted in response to Communism, we are unable to deal with the new threat—the new Communism of today. We deal with Islam the same way we dealt with Communism: Having been subverted and undermined, we apologize and converge.

As Wilders asked, What is wrong with modern Western man? Did something happen to him? I think the answer is yes: Communism happened to him. Solomon aside, there was something novel under the Communist sun; under the shorter-lived Nazi sun, too. In his 1998 book *Century of Horrors: Communism, Nazism, and the Uniqueness of the Shoah,* Alain Besançon explains what that was: "Communism and Nazism set out to change something more fundamental than mores—that is, the very rule of morality, of our sense of good and evil. And in this, they committed acts unknown in prior human experience."[18]

And in this, our world was transformed. Besançon's focus on a discernible moral shift shines like a beam of light to reveal a switch in the continuum of human experience. It even offers something to hold on to, an anchor against answerless mental drift, in the search for a basis of understanding, maybe even a point from which to reclaim our moral bearings. "On or about December 1910 human character changed," Virginia Woolf once wrote, a line that became quite famous even if 1910 doesn't stand out to us as a monumental threshold, especially with World War I in the offing. In the end, though, she was only off by a decade or so.

Solzhenitsyn saw this same sea change sweep in with Communism. He wrote:

> Communism has never concealed the fact that it rejects all absolute concepts of morality.

So, too, does Islam, which makes lying obligatory in cases where lying advances Islam.

> It scoffs at any considerations of "good" and "evil" as indisputable categories. Communism considers morality to be relative . . . But I must say that in this respect, Communism has been very successful.

One man's terrorist is another man's freedom fighter.

He continued:

> It has infected the whole world with the belief in the relativity of good and evil. Today, many people apart from the Communists are carried away by this idea. Among progressive people, it is considered rather awkward to use seriously such words as "good" and "evil." Communism has managed to persuade all of us that these concepts are old-fashioned and laughable.[19]

Where "good" and "evil" are old-fashioned and laughable (and bracketed by quotation marks), moral relativism takes hold—Lenin's universal legacy.[20] Solzhenitsyn wondered what would happen next: "But if we are to be deprived of the concepts of good and evil, what will be left? Nothing but the manipulation of each other."[21]

The manipulation of each other through the manipulation of *narratives.* The fact is—can I say that?—facts no longer carry greater weight than Authority's narrative. That's what happens without immutable morality, without Good and Evil: Objective fact, reasoning powers, logical deduction, and sound judgment must *compete* with lies, with propaganda, with agitprop, with deception, with coercion, with power, with violence. Whoever's narrative is louder, bigger, stronger, or more dangerous is going to prevail.

Before Communism left the realm of theory to become manifest in a state in 1917, Good and Evil commanded a consensus as roughly immutable as any code observed by human beings can be. That would change, despite multitudes of rank-and-file Communists who undoubtedly believed they were supporting Good and opposing Evil. With the 1929 Depression, our confidence in free markets was shot; by the early 1930s, our deepest moral codes were under assault. Recognition in 1933 opened the floodgates. The U.S.-USSR relationship pitted a Judeo-Christian and primarily Anglo-Saxon notion of trust and bond against the ruthless expediency of a revolutionary and amoral regime. To initiate relations, the Terror Famine had to be ignored; a great moral crime on our part. To maintain relations, we had to shun the facts. For example, if it were a condition of recognition that the Russians cease and desist clandestine measures to overthrow the USA—and it was such a condition—then continued recognition in the face of continued clandestine measures to overthrow the USA was *wrong. It didn't make sense* according to the terms of the agreement. By rights, Soviet subversion inside the USA should have canceled or suspended the contract. Instead, in a world in which ideological means and ends were replacing rule of law—in a government increasingly penetrated by Soviet agents—it didn't make a bit of difference. So began the slipperiest slope ever to the slough of complete subversion.

The relationship between Soviet Russia and the West, then, was always predicated on lies: Soviet Russia told them . . . and then the West told them, too. It didn't have to have been that way. Not even two years after the recognition he'd championed, William C. Bullitt already foresaw the impossibility of normal relations with the *ab*normal regime. He had realized the USSR was, no matter what its leaders said to the contrary, still determined "to produce world revolution." His analysis of the Soviet state of mind was prescient:

> Diplomatic relations with friendly states are not regarded by the Soviet government as normal friendly relations but "armistice" relations and it is the conviction of the leaders of the Soviet Union that this "armistice" cannot possibly be ended by a definite peace, but only by a renewal of battle . . . Peace is looked upon merely as a happy respite in which future battles may be prepared.[22]

Bullitt was describing a Communist phenomenon, but I haven't seen a better definition of *hudna,* the Islamic term for temporary armistice, outside the *Islamic Encyclopedia.* Which, again, makes sense: Totalitarian Islam and Communism are both revolutionary movements that drive forward to impose their dominion on all the earth—"unceasing struggle with all other cultures," as Conquest put it in a phrase describing Communist Russia, but equally suitable to Islamic jihad.[23] Any halt in that drive, any pause in the struggle, is temporary. Such points of doctrine, however, fail to fit the preferred narrative of authority: Communism and Islam are both religions of peace. Orwell was already late to the party when in 1936 he observed the end of "neutral fact" and Koestler concurred. Human character—our nation's character—had already changed, or been changed.

I'm going to flip the calendar forward to 1969, when Yuri Besmenov, later known as Tomas Schuman, was contemplating his defection to the West. Born in 1939, Besmenov was a highly trained linguist who had never lived in a world with neutral fact or functioned without lies, big and small. As a KGB-trained "journalist" with Novosti, a joint creation of the Central Committee's agitprop department and the KGB, Besmenov was himself quite skilled at creating them—"changing perception," as he put it. For some extraordinary reason, Besmenov—possessing that "certain lucidity of heart and soul" that Solzhenitsyn said could still exist in societies "benumbed by . . . lies" (less so in the West[24])—was able to see through it all, including through himself and everyone around him. Later, he set down his remarkable thoughts at that moment:

> Observing the world-wide destruction of human minds caused by my motherland, unresisted and unpunished, and meditating about *how easily all that mindwarping could be stopped,* I wanted to believe that there, in the West, some people and organizations we call "reactionary circles" know the situation and how to deal with our subversion. They had done it, for some reason unknown to me at that time. But when needed, I thought, they would stop us for their own good [emphasis added].

Hard to know whether to laugh or cry. Defectors never seem to have imagined the extent to which Soviet efforts to subvert the West were already successful. He continued.

> Later, in India, I was surprised to realize that no one even thought we were doing anything wrong to their country. Are they blind and deaf? Or is there something that makes them unaware of impending danger? "I must defect and open their eyes," I thought.

We will meet the Americans and we will tell them.

"But," as Besmenov would conclude, "no one wanted either my information or to open up their eyes."[25]

Blind and deaf.

Why?

All these decades later, no one wants information or to open their eyes to the Muslim Brotherhood's self-described "civilization jihad," either.[26] It hurts our heads. It exhausts our limited lexicon of ideology. I always wonder whether it is the inhumanity of totalitarian ideologies that somehow drives us from full acknowledgment, as if we recoil from the abyss in which we perceive our complicity and winnowing self-respect. Fresh evidence, then, corroborating facts, and clarity of language become doubly, triply worse than any of the depredations or even inhumanity of the offending creed. Evidence exposes moral compromise, and, as we've seen, *nothing is worse than exposure.* It becomes a matter of self-preservation and a point of pride, then, to sunder the links between facts and conclusion. Welcome to the world of "PC."

And what is "PC"? The tag itself, I have come to realize, creates a linguistic cul-de-sac where we just park our brains. *"PC" is, gosh, "PC."* We look no further. Sure, the acronym "PC"—"political correctness"—conveys the idea that something is phony, forced, and ideologically, not logically, inspired, but it doesn't advertise its bona fide totalitarian provenance in the language of ideology, which, once accepted, once internalized, draws an individual into that ideological pact with the devil in which reasoning powers are lost. In other words, "PC" is just another label for Big Lies—little lies, too. It describes the systematic suppression of fact that advances and sustains the ideology of the State and its barricades in academia, media, and other cultural outposts. Big and Bigger Brother. It is a grievous offense against objectivity in every instance, from "chairperson" and "affirmative action" to "overseas contingency operations" and "blue on green" attacks, not to mention all the thoughts that go unexpressed altogether. These moral capitulations to ideological censorship ultimately block the flow of thought itself. Evidence is denigrated; logic is discarded—and it happened here.

Remember FDR's fond hopes for convergence? "PC" is one result, its origins in twentieth-century totalitarianism. Such ideology is not innate to Western republics. Indeed, the Cold War between the West and Communism was not a struggle between two ideologies as it is commonly framed. The Western approach, as Robert Conquest writes, "was not an ideological one at all." Western culture, he explains, "had, in a general way, a view of politics which included political liberty and the rule of law. It did not have a universal and exclusively defined mind-set."[27] Liberty is not a mind-set; it defies mind-set. That said, the struggle between the United States and the USSR was over ideology, all right—a struggle to resist the imposition of Communist ideology in the West, particularly following the debacle of World War II.

Then on 9/11 came the second totalitarian wave.

With our tragic past of deceit and double talk, no wonder we readily ceded the history, canon, and terminology of Islam for a new Big Lie, "Islam is peace." The government tells us "violent extremism" is what endangers us; what *reason* do we have to doubt it? We have no reason—capacity to reason, that is, not anymore. We have surrendered the tools of thought.

In his contribution to the famous 1949 collection of essays by ex-Communists titled *The God That Failed,* Arthur Koestler carefully illustrates how set language binds thought to ideology at the expense of evidence. He describes a conversation he had early in his Communist career with "Edgar," his Party contact, in which they discuss the front page of a Communist newspaper.

> "But every word on the front page is contradicted by the facts," I objected.
>
> Edgar gave me a tolerant smile. "You still have the mechanistic outlook, he said, and then proceeded to give me the dialectical interpretation of the facts . . .

> Gradually, I learned to distrust my mechanistic *preoccupation with facts* and to regard the world around me in the light of dialectical interpretation. It was a satisfactory and indeed blissful state; *once you had assimilated the technique, you were no longer disturbed by the facts* [emphasis added].[28]

Here, recounting his experience as a German Communist in the 1930s, Koestler is nonetheless describing the post-Communist, postmodern, post-9/11 American condition. It is the sinister overhaul of language and thought—so familiar!—that he personally engaged in, and that was *and is* the primary tool of Marxist and Islamic subversion. "Not only our thinking, but also our vocabulary was reconditioned," he explains. "Certain words were taboo."[29] Certain other words became telltales by which to identify dissenters or enemies. Literary, artistic, and musical tastes, he writes, were "similarly reconditioned" to support the renunciation of independent thought and logic necessary to submit to ideology.

> We cast off our intellectual baggage like passengers on a ship seized by panic, until it became reduced to the strictly necessary minimum of stock phrases, dialectical clichés and Marxist quotations . . . To be able to see several aspects of a problem and not only one, became a permanent cause of self-reproach. We craved to be single- and simple-minded.[30]

We crave this, too, or just go along with it, which is worse. And the U.S. government itself is happy to oblige:

> Don't Invoke Islam.
> Don't Harp on Muslim Identity.
> Avoid the Term 'Caliphate.'
> Never Use the Term 'Jihadist' or 'Mujahideen.'[31]

Such is the spawn of liberty's rendezvous with totalitarianism. In Roosevelt's hoped-for "convergence"—the rape of the West—we have become born liars, dupes, or both, our roots drawing from a tank of lies dug far deeper into our past than I ever used to imagine, back in a time when it seemed that "grown-ups," rational and moral actors, were still in charge. So much for "American exceptionalism," but so be it. The "Good War"? Please. The war to make the world safe for Gulags seems a little closer to the mark. The "moral clarity" of World War II we yearn for isn't just a canard but a psychodelic fantasy, testament to the staying power of one seductively potent placebo—the false narrative made vivid, lifelike, and indelible. "All we have to fear is fear itself"? No, it turns out there was much more to fear than that. The lies. The corrupting lies. Confess them all. Be done with "damage control" forever.

We lost World War II, wrote Martin Dies.

Yes.

We lost the Cold War, wrote Vladimir Bukovsky.

I would have to agree.

We even made everything worse in the process, writes one final iconoclast: British soldier and historian General J. F. C. Fuller.

Oh, great.

In 1949, Fuller wrote, "Though Germany was defeated and National Socialism overthrown, Russia and Stalinism took their place. Great Britain was bankrupted and her empire is now in a state of dissolution; and yearly America is spending billions of dollars to stem the Communist flood."[32]

He might well have added, America was also turning Europe pink and socialist in the process through Marshall Plan aid "because the Americans who ran it applied to European recovery methods of social planning which are anathema to most business men," enthused British Socialist R. H. S. Crossman in 1950.[33]

I can still feel pushback from decades of "Good War" conditioning: *But, but . . . how could Uncle Sam not have done everything possible to stop Hitler in Europe and save the Jews?* Well, you know what, America? Uncle Sam didn't do everything possible to stop Hitler in Europe; otherwise, the war might well have ended no later than 1943. Nor did Uncle Sam do everything to save the Jews—not the last million, not the last hundred. These blasted bits of history leave us . . . where?. Someplace, I'm afraid, with the poor fellow in Yeats's "Meru":

> Civilisation is hooped together, brought
> Under a rule, under the semblance of peace
> By manifold illusion; but man's life is thought,
> And he, despite his terror, cannot cease
> Ravening through century after century
> Ravening, raging, and uprooting that he may come
> Into the desolation of reality.

Having done a little ravening and uprooting of my own, I have to say I've come a long way from my freshman fall at Yale when I met a sunny-faced boy from Ohio who happened to tell me (can't recall why) that his parents—both of them, by the way, white-haired physicians—hated, but *hated, Franklin Roose-*

velt. In a way, maybe that's where this book began. In Freddy's household, Roosevelt's name was mud. L.A. born and Hollywood bred, I couldn't have been more puzzled. How could this be? My dad's first vote as a GI in northern Europe somewhere between D-day and the Bulge was for Roosevelt; my mom's family was Roosevelt all the way. I didn't get it, couldn't get it. Freddy came from Ohio—home, I later learned, of "Mr. Republican," Senator Robert Taft, son of President Taft, who entered national politics to try to guard the Constitution against the New Deal. (I lived in Taft entryway one year. Maybe not a harmonic convergence, but I like the connection.) Freddy also liked vanilla milkshakes. I remember putting that and his family's politics down to the exotica of the heartland. Even a quarter century later, when, at a used-book store in Vermont, I somewhat fatefully picked up a 1979 book titled *Roosevelt, Churchill, and the World War II Opposition: A Revisionist Autobiography* by George T. Eggleston, I could detect the residual radioactivity that wafted off the cover. Was I holding in my hands a book by a fascist, a Nazi? Or, maybe worse in the American context, an "isolationist"?

Isolationist yes, and, as an explanation of the point of view, intriguingly and even persuasively so.[34] In fact, I recommend the book to anyone interested in continuing this cultural reexamination. The process is vital not only to understanding our past but to mounting a successful rediscovery and restoration of "Americanism"—allegiance to the principles contained in the Declaration and the Constitution. Something is not right in this democratic republic, and it's getting worse.

Then again, is this a democratic republic?

That, too, becomes a trick question after peering past history's mirrors. In 1955, journalist and author John T. Flynn, one of the most famous and prolific critics of statism, collectivism, and Roosevelt (not necessarily in that order), argued in *The Decline of the American Republic* that following the Depression-triggered, war-entrenched Roosevelt-Truman revolution in spending, taxation, regimentation, and centralization known as the New Deal, and, later, less memorably, as the Fair Deal, the essential character of American society changed beyond recognition. The USA, Flynn wrote in that formative year of McDonald's, "Rock Around the Clock," and Disneyland, bore only "an external and superficial resemblance" to the republic that had existed for 144 years until 1933—and who even knew the difference by 1955 when Americans forty years of age (b. 1915) had no adult memory of anything different? The Constitution, of course, remained officially unchanged, Flynn noted. "It has been done by sheer usurpation of power by the federal government."[35]

As if to agree, Norman Thomas, perennial Socialist candidate for president, was moved to write in 1953, "Here in America more measures once praised or denounced as socialist have been adopted than once I should have thought possible short of a Socialist victory at the polls."[36]

Are you saying everyone who voted for X, Y, and Z were or are Socialists?

No, because I doubt that was the case. These legislators, however, almost without pause, voted for law after law that increased our reliance on, and our subservience to, the burgeoning state. Whether liberal-, Marxist-, Communist-, Socialist-, or Fascist-inspired—and there are strong parallels among these totalitarian systems, as Jonah Goldberg has argued compellingly in *Liberal Fascism*—our history since Roosevelt has been one of an expanding central government. (Even under Ronald Reagan, the federal government spending grew more than 3 percent.[37]) A state that took on the guise of paternalism in the early 1930s has become increasingly authoritarian, thuggish, even, and the citizens who sought or accepted that "helping hand" have become both wardlike and less free.

As far back as 1934, *The New York Times* trumpeted NEW DEAL PATERNALISM IMPERILS ALL INDIVIDUALISM.[38] The article describes a speech by Massachusetts governor Joseph Ely at a conference of America's governors. "There is no stopping short of the end of the road," Ely said, "and at the end of the road we shall have a socialistic state." Invoking Stalin in Russia, Mussolini in Italy, and Hitler in Germany—all newly minted dictators—Ely pointed out that where these despots ruled, "individualism had passed from the people to dictators making the people the 'children of government.'"

Echoes of de Tocqueville. One century earlier, the French visionary described the infantilizing effect of a paternalistic despotism in America. Imagining the "immense, protective power" of a state with "absolute" power, and likening such power to "parental authority," which keeps citizens in "perpetual childhood," he wondered, "Why should it not entirely relieve them from the trouble of thinking and all the cares of living?"[39] It would seem that the mortal blow against the "grown-up"—the free citizen—was struck, softly, once liberty was no longer paramount in this country, once ideology began to take precedence over facts, once we traded in the American ideal of "rugged individualism" for the material markers of "the American dream." If once upon a time Americans subscribed to our Founders' belief that our Creator endowed us with the right to life, liberty, and the pursuit of happiness, there came a time when we expected a package of perks—car, house, Play Station—to sweeten the deal. Suddenly, those perks became darn near an *entitlement,* an attitude entirely befitting the subjects in Tocqueville's absolute state. In fact, measured in material goods as it is, the contemporary "American dream" is a vision driven by the Marxist belief in the primacy of the economic.

From recognition to convergence.

No wonder Norman Thomas was tickled by the direction of the country in the Eisenhower years. By 1958, he was beside himself. "The United States is making greater strides toward socialism under Eisenhower than even under Roosevelt," he enthused.[40] By 1962, the man who had run for president on the Socialist ticket six times had concluded that "the difference between Democrats and Republicans is: Democrats have accepted the ideas of socialism cheerfully, while Republicans have accepted them reluctantly."[41] Just not by name. As Upton Sinclair put it in a 1951 letter to Thomas, "The American People will take Socialism, but they won't take the label."[42]

We take the Big Lie instead. Euphemism. Official vocabulary. Language of ideology. The "PC" pact with the devil. The Big Lie as big con. The narrative of authority. How to stand athwart false history and yell "Stop!"? The answer finally seems clear. If once it was vitally important to shore up America's bastions, something else is called for now. What's needed is a full-scale assault on those bastions of unreality, those safe houses of secrets, all in a painful but restorative effort to upend the narratives of authority, to break open the conspiracies of silence, which have endured through too many lifetimes. Put another way, it's time to avenge the victims and the truth tellers, the voiceless and the voices of one. It's time to avenge the American betrayal of Liberty herself.

NOTES

INTRODUCTION: "THE BEGINNING"

PAGES 1–7

1. Sam Tannenhaus, *Whittaker Chambers: A Biography* (New York: Modern Library, 1998), 96; Whittaker Chambers, *Witness* (New York: Random House, 1952), 337.
2. The details of Chambers's day in Washington come from Chambers, *Witness*, 335–40.
3. "Dr. Wirt's Statement on 'Brain Trust's Plans," *New York Times,* March 24, 1934.
4. "Quick End Planned for Wirt Inquiry," *New York Times,* March 31, 1934.
5. "Crowd at Hearing Fills Caucus Room," *New York Times,* April 11, 1934. The charges that Wirt was jailed as a German sympathizer would stand five days before Bulwinkle retracted them, noting cryptically that the false report "came to me by what any one would consider reliable sources." "Retracts Charge Against Dr. Wirt," *New York Times,* April 17, 1934.
6. "Dr. Wirt's Targets Swift in Denial," *New York Times,* April 11, 1934.
7. "Laughing Through," *Miami Daily News,* April 15, 1934.
8. "Big Crowd Meets Train," *New York Times,* April 14, 1934.
9. "Wirt Story Denied by Fellow-Diners," *New York Times,* April 18, 1934.
10. "Wirt Story Denied by Fellow-Diners," *New York Times,* April 18, 1934.
11. Barrows is noted in KGB archives, for instance, for helping to bring Laurence Duggan, a State Department official close to Assistant Secretary of State Sumner Welles, into espionage service to Stalin. The KGB record also chides her for serial affairs with Soviet representatives in Washington, first Boris Skvirsky, the USSR's unofficial representative, and then Ambassador Aleksandr Troyanovsky, the first Soviet ambassador. Almost unbelievably, Troyanovsky would host the first Soviet gala in Washington on the night of Wirt's testimony. Among the Soviet ambassador's guest list of five hundred were also two men Wirt had named: Rexford Tugwell and dinner party guest Laurence Todd. John Haynes, Harvey Klehr, and Alexander Vassiliev, *Spies: The Rise and Fall of the KGB in America* (New Haven and London: Yale University Press, 2009), 220, 528.
12. John Earl Haynes, comp., *Vassiliev Notebooks Concordance: Cover Names, Real Names, Abbreviations, Acronyms, Organizational Titles, Tradecraft Terminology* (2008), 88, available at http://www.wilsoncenter.org /publication/vassilie-notebook-concordance-file.
13. "Wirt Story Denied by Fellow-Diner," *New York Times,* April 18, 1934.
14. Investigation of Statements Made by Dr. William A. Wirt, 69.
15. "Wirt Story Denied by Fellow-Diners," *New York Times,* April 18, 1934.
16. "Wirt Story Denied by Fellow-Diners," *New York Times,* April 18, 1934.
17. Investigation of Statements Made by Dr. William A. Wirt, Minority Views, p.7.
18. "Wirt Sees Nation Going to Socialism," *New York Times,* May 1, 1934.
19. "O'Connor Admits Helping To Discredit Dr. Wirt," *The Observer Dispatch* (Utica), April 10, 1940.
20. Martin Dies, *Martin Dies' Story* (New York: Bookmailer, 1963), p. 33.

CHAPTER 1

1. A. Solzhenitsyn, *Warning to the West* (Farrar, Straus, & Giroux, 1976), p. 101.
2. Hans Christian Andersen, "The Emperor's New Clothes," *Hans Andersen's Fairy Tales: A New Translation by Reginald Spink* (London: J. M. Dent & Sons, 1958), 79–81.

3. Stephen C. Coughlin and I are coauthors of *Shariah: The Threat to America,* Report of Team B II (Center for Security Policy, 2010), with Lt. Gen. William "Jerry" Boykin, Lt. Gen. Harry Edward Soyster, Christine Brim, Amb. Henry F. Cooper, Michael Del Rosso, Frank J. Gaffney Jr., John Guandolo, Brian Kennedy, Clare M. Lopez, Adm. James A. "Ace" Lyons, Andrew C. McCarthy, Patrick Poole, Joseph E. Schmitz, Tom Trento, J. Michael Waller, R. James Woolsey, and David Yerushalmi.

4. Stephen Collins Coughlin, Major, Military Intelligence, USAR, " 'To Our Great Detriment': Ignoring What Extremists Say About Jihad," unclassified thesis, National Defense Intelligence College, July 2007.

5. See "Words That Work and Words That Don't: A Guide for Counterterrorism Communication," National Counterterrorism Center, March 14, 2008.

6. Spencer Ackerman, "FBI Purges Hundreds of Terrorism Documents in Islamophobia Probe," *Wired,* February 15, 2012, http://www.wired.com/dangerroom/2012/02/hundreds-fbi-documents-muslims/.

7. Memorandum from Chairman of the Joint Chiefs, April 24, 2012, http://tinyurl.com/8cjcpfq.

8. Pentagon spokesman Capt. John Kirby stated on Al Jazeera on or around May 10, 2012, "The concern here is not so much that we may be spinning down a cadre of individuals and creating these warped views but that again, it's not in keeping with—this material is not in keeping with our core values and is not in keeping with the strategy that we know we're out there executing." "US, Military Course 'Islam Is a Threat to America' Outlawed," http://www.youtube.com/watch?feature=player_embeded&v=Cy6y R3UJ2Dc.

9. Noah Shachtman and Spencer Ackerman, "U.S. Military Taught Officers: Use 'Hiroshima' Tactics for 'Total War' on Islam," *Wired,* May 10, 2012, http://www.wired.com/dangerroom/2012/05/total-war-islam /all/?pid=1200.

10. The slide cites the authoritative Koran sura (verse) 5:51, where Allah commands Muslims not to take Jews and Christians for friends; the authoritative hadith recorded by both Bukhari and Muslim (two authoritative Koranic commentators) that states Muslims will not enter paradise until the Muslims kill all the Jews; and another authoritative hadith that states Jesus will return at end of days to implement sharia, send all Christians to hell for failing to become Muslim, and kill all the Jews. In a memorandum of record shared with the author, Stephen C. Coughlin chronicled this chain of events surrounding the Dempsey-initiated purge of military training materials.

11. In 2008, following the largest terrorism-financing trial in U.S. history, the Holy Land Foundation and five of its leaders were convicted of providing material support to Hamas, a U.S.-designated terrorist group and Palestinian wing of the Muslim Brotherhood. Trial evidence revealed that the majority of Islamic organizations in the United States are affiliates of or associated with the Muslim Brotherhood. Many of these groups, including unindicted co-conspirators Islamic Society of North America (ISNA) and Council on American-Islamic Relations (CAIR), have been part of government "Muslim outreach" programs.

12. David Kilcullen, *Counterinsurgency in Iraq: Theory and Practice, 2007,* http://tinyurl.com/9xvuzlo.

13. COMISAF *Initial Assessment,* August 30, 2009, http://tinyurl.com/ko29sc.

14. Ibn Warraq, ed., *Leaving Islam: Apostates Speak Out* (Amherst, NY: Prometheus Books, 2003), 414. See the following Koranic principles, selected from Appendix A.

    The believers who stay at home . . . are not equal to those who fight for the cause of God with their good and their persons. (IV.95–96)

    Believers, do not choose the infidels rather than the faithful for your friends. (IV.144)

    O you who believe! Take not the Jews and Christians for friends. They are friends one to another. He among you who takes them for friends is one of them. (V.51)

    Make war on them until idolatory shall cease and God's religion shall reign supreme. (VIII.39)

    I will instill terror into the hearts of the Infidels, strike off their heads then, and strike off from them every fingertip. (VIII.12)

    Believers, when you meet the unbelievers preparing for battle do not turn your backs to them. [Anyone who does] shall incur the wrath of God and hell shall be his home: an evil dwelling indeed. (VII.15, 16)

    Believers, do not befriend your fathers or your brothers if they choose unbelief in preference to faith. Wrongdoers are those that befriend them. (IX.23)

    If you do not fight, He will punish you sternly, and replace you by other men. (IX.39)

    Prophet, make war on the unbelievers and the hypocrites and deal rigorously with them. Hell shall be their home: an evil fate. (IX.73)

    Do not yield to the unbelievers, but fight them strenuously with this Koran. (XXV.52)

    The unbelievers among the People of the Book and the pagans shall burn forever in the fire of Hell. They are the vilest of creatures. (XCVIII.6)

15. "Probe Targets clerk in London," *Washington Post,* October 28, 2001.

16. Ibn Warraq, *What the Koran Really Says* (Amherst, NY: Prometheus Books, 2002), 69.

17. Memorandum from Chairman of the Joint Chiefs, April 24, 2012, http://tinyurl.com/8cjcpfq.

18. Patrick S. Poole, "FBI Escorts Known Hamas Operative Through Top-Secret National Counterterrorism Center as 'Outreach' to Muslim Community," *Breitbart News,* September 27, 1010, http://tinyurl.com/8dfuvnt.

19. Patrick S. Poole, "Once Again, FBI's 'Muslim Outreach' Welcomes Terror-Tied Man," *PJ Media,* June 4, 2011, http://tinyurl.com/8lwpmct.

20. "Director of National Intelligence James Clapper: Muslim Brotherhood 'Largely Secular,' " *ABC News,* February 10, 2011, http://tinyurl.com/8ekyhj6.

21. Tina Magaard quoted and linked in Andrew G. Bostom, "Eurabia Versus Wilders Agonistes," *American Thinker,* April 29, 2012, http://tinyurl.com/943ak34.

22. See John David Lewis, " 'No Substitute for Victory': The Defeat of Islamic Totalitarianism," *The Objective Standard* 1, no. 4 (Winter 2006–7), http://www.theobjectivestandard.com/issues/2006-winter/no-substitute-for-victory.asp.

23. Dies, *Martin Dies' Story,* 144.

24. Andrew C. McCarthy, "Huma Abedin's Brotherhood Ties Are Not Just a Family Affair," *PJ Media,* July 27, 2012, http://pjmedia.com/andrewmccarthy/2012/07/27/huma-abedins-brotherhood-ties-are-not-just-a-family-affair.

25. Andrew C. McCarthy, "Fear the Muslim Brotherhood," *National Review Online,* January 31, 2011, http://www.nationalreview.com/articles/258419/fear-muslim-brotherhood-andrew-c-mccarthy?pg=2.

26. McCarthy, "Fear the Muslim Brotherhood."

27. "You Love Life and We Love Death," *Boston Globe,* March 14, 2004.

28. Andrew Bostom, "Why Hamas Loves Death (and Cease-Fires)," *American Thinker,* November 23, 2012, http://www.americanthinker.com/blog/2012/11/why_hamas_loves_death_and_cease_fires.html.

29. Diana West, "C-PAC and the 'Trojan' Brotherhood," syndicated column, February 11, 2011, http://www.dianawest.net/Home/tabid/36/EntryId/1686/C-PAC-and-the-Trojan-Brotherhood.aspx.

30. Diana West, "Pieces, Shards, Dust . . . Revolt?" blog entry, November 25, 2008, http://www.dianawest.net/Home/tabid/36/EntryId/603/Pieces-Shards-Dust-Revolt.aspx.

31. Edward Winslow, "Mourt's Relation," quoted in Mary Caroline Crawford, *Social Life in Old New England* (Boston: Little, Brown, 1915), 474.

32. West, "Pieces, Shards."

33. Robert Conquest, *The Dragons of Expectation: Reality and Delusion in the Course of History* (New York: Norton, 2005), 169.

34. Vladimir Bukovsky, *"The Power of Memory and Acknowledgment,"* *Cato's Letter* 8, no. 1 (Winter 2010): 2.

35. Paul Belien, "Former Soviet Dissident Warns for EU Dictatorship," *The Brussels Journal,* February 27, 2006, http://www.brusselsjournal.com/node/865; see also Vladimir Bukovsky and Pavel Stroilov, *EUUSSR: The Soviet Roots of European Integration* (Worcester Park, Surrey, UK: Sovereignty Publications, 2004).

36. Hans Vogel, "Twenty Years After . . . ," November 4, 2009, *Pravda,* http://english.pravda.ru/opinion/columnists/04-11-2009/110289-berlin_wall-0.

37. Conquest, *Dragons,* 167. Besides Soviet invasions of Hungary (1956) and Czechoslovakia (1968), there was the steady toll of individuals killed trying to cross from the east side of the Berlin Wall. There were also significant though unreported food riots (1962) and the mutiny of the warship *Storozhevoy* (1975) inside the USSR.

38. Ian Gallagher and Daniel Boffey, "EU's New 'Foreign Minister' Cathy Ashton Was Treasurer of CND." *Mail Online,* November 21, 2009, http://www.dailymail.co.uk/news/article-1229940/Cathy-Ashton-EUs-new-Foreign-Minister-Treasurer-CND.html. See also Pavel Stroilov, *Cold War & Peace Movement: The 'Peace Movement' in Britain in the Final Stages of the Cold War (mid-1970s–mid-1980s),* research paper commissioned by Gerard Batten, MEP, UK Independence Party, 2010. See: gerardbattenmep.co.uk/pamphlets/Peace02FEB10.pdf

39. Stroilov, *Cold War & Peace Movement,* 3.

40. Belien, "Former Soviet Dissident Warns."

41. "Batten Call to Block Commission," January 12, 2010, *UK Independence Party,* http://www.ukip.org/content/european-issues/1401-batten-call-to-block-commission. The six other commissioners are: Estonia's Siim Kallas, Slovakia's Maroš Šefčovič, the Czech Republic's Štefan Füle, Latvia's Andris Piebalgs, Slovenia's Janez Potočnik, and Hungary's László Andor. Their terms run through 2014.

42. The European Parliament mainly exists to vote on European Commission bills. It is not empowered to introduce legislation.

43. Jonah Goldberg, "What Kind of Socialist Is Barack Obama?" *Commentary,* May 2010.

44. The interview is available at http://www.youtube.com/watch?v=OkpdNtTgQNM.

45. Roger Kimball, "The Real Obama," *PJ Media,* October 27, 2008, http://pajamasmedia.com/rogerkimball/2008/10/27/the-real-obama-forget-the-constitution-economic-justice-demands-redistribution-of-wealth.

46. *Special Report with Brit Hume,* October 23, 2008, transcript available at http://www.foxnews.com/story/0,2933,443908,00.html.

47. Veronique de Rugy, "Bush's Regulatory Kiss-Off," *Reason,* January 2009, http://reason.com/archives/2008/12/10/bushs-regulatory-kiss-off.

48. Paul Kengor, "Why Obama's Communist Connections Are Not Headlines," *American Thinker,* September 4, 2012, http://www.americanthinker.com/2008/10/why_obamas_communist_connectio.html.

49. Jeff Zeleny, "The President Is on the Line to Follow Up on Socialism," *New York Times,* March 7, 2009, http://www.nytimes.com/2009/03/08/us/politics/08callback.html.

50. Kurtz quoting Hank De Zutter, "What Makes Obama Run?" *Chicago Reader,* December 7, 1995, http://www1.chicagoreader.com/obama/951208.

51. Kurtz changed his mind in his book *Radical-in-Chief: Barack Obama and the Untold Story of American Socialism* (New York: Threshold Editions, 2010), 6. "So when I began my post-campaign research for this book, my inclination was to downplay or dismiss evidence of explicit socialism in Obama's background. I thought the issue was an unprovable and unnecessary distraction. I was wrong. Evidence that suggests Obama is a socialist, I am now convinced, is real, important, and profoundly relevant to the present."

52. Adam Shaw, "Obama's Socialism," *American Thinker,* February 25, 2010, http://www.americanthinker.com/2010/02/obamas_socialism.html.

53. Andrew C. McCarthy, *The Grand Jihad* (New York: Encounter Books, 2010), 189.

54. Zeleny, "The President Is on the Line."

55. "Obama to Republicans: Stop Pretending Health Care Reform Is a 'Bolshevik Plot,'" January 29, 2010, *YouTube,* http://www.youtube.com/watch?v=RcRWS45gPzo.

56. M. K. Dziewanowski, *A History of Soviet Russia* (Englewood Cliffs, NJ: Prentice-Hall, 1979), 107.

57. Elizabeth Fee and Theodore M. Brown, eds., *Making Medical History: The Life and Times of Henry E. Sigerist* (Baltimore: Johns Hopkins University Press, 1997), 252.

CHAPTER 2

1. R. W. Apple Jr., "Washington-Moscow Name-Calling: What Does It Mean?" *New York Times,* February 5, 1981.

2. Christopher Andrew and Vasili Mitrokhin, *The Sword and the Shield: The Mitrokhin Archive and the Secret History of the KGB* (New York: Basic Books, 2001), 546.

3. Robert Conquest, *Reflections on a Ravaged Century* (New York: Norton, 2000), 155.

4. Nicholas S. Timasheff, *The Great Retreat: The Growth and Decline of Communism in Russia* (New York: Dutton, 1946), 192–203.

5. http://www.cpusa.org/a-way-out-of-the-deepening-crisis. Michael del Rosso pointed out this statement by CPUSA leader Sam Webb at the 29th National Convention of the Communist Party, USA, May 21–23, New York City: "What a difference between now and five years ago when we convened in Chicago! . . . Broadly speaking, our view of the general conditions of struggle and the strategic path forward is on the money. We make mistakes and acknowledge them. But we didn't make the big mistake—underestimating the danger of rightwing extremism in government and elsewhere. To the extent that we applied our strategy, we extended and deepened our mass connections, we contributed to the historic victory in 2008, we enhanced our presence and visibility, and we increased our membership. We didn't grow as much as we would have liked, but *we have a firm foundation on which to increase our size, visibility and readership of our publications in the period ahead"* (emphasis in original). Webb further described President Obama's reelection in 2012 as "the dawn of a new era." Sam Webb, "Democracy comes out on top on Nov. 6," *People's World,* November 6, 2012. See: http://peoplesworld.org/democracy-comes-out-on-top-on-nov/.

6. McCarthy, *Grand Jihad,* 14.

7. Adam B. Ulam, *The Rivals: America and Russia Since World War II* (New York: Penguin Books, 1971), 95.

8. Judge Kaufman's sentencing statement is available at http://www.law.umkc.edu/faculty/projects/ftrials/rosenb/ROS_SENT.HTM.

9. John Earl Haynes, Harvey Klehr, and Alexander Vassiliev, *Spies: The Rise and Fall of the KGB in America* (New Haven: Yale University Press, 2009), 143, 545. See also Herbert Romerstein and Eric Breindel, *The Venona Secrets* (Washington: Regnery, 2000), xv, 253.

10. Allen Weinstein and Alexander Vassiliev, *The Haunted Wood: Soviet Espionage in America—the Stalin Era* (New York: Modern Library, 2000), 344.

11. Bruce Cumings, *The Korean War: A History* (New York: Modern Library, 2011), 35. South Korea sustained roughly 1.3 million casualties, including 400,000 dead. North Korea suffered 2 million casualties, while 900,000 Chinese soldiers were killed.

12. http://www.nytimes.com/1991/04/29/opinion/essay-the-decline-of-the-east.html?scp=8&sq=gloat+Gorbachev&st=nyt.

13. The National Security Archive, online database, points out that the transcript it offers "is a translation of the Soviet record from the Gorbachev Foundation, since the U.S. memcons remain, astonishingly, still classified at the George H. W. Bush Library in Texas"; http://www.gwu.edu/~nsarchiv/NSAEBB/NSAEBB298/index.htm.

14. National Security Archive, "Bush and Gorbachev at Malta," http://www.gwu.edu/~nsarchiv/NSAEBB /NSAEBB298/index.htm, Document 10, Soviet Transcript of the Malta Summit, December 2–3, 1989, 10, 3.

15. http://query.nytimes.com/gst/fullpage.html?res=9C04EFDE1431F935A35751C1A9629C8B63.

16. Robert Buchar, ed., *And Reality Be Damned . . . Undoing America: What the Media Didn't Tell You About the End of the Cold War and the Fall of Communism in Europe* (New York: Eloquent Books, 2010), 6.

17. National Security Archive, "Bush and Gorbachev at Malta," http://www.gwu.edu/~nsarchiv/NSAEBB /NSAEBB298/index.htm, Document 8, Transcript of Gorbachev–John Paul II Meeting, Vatican City, December 1, 1989 [Transcribed notes by Aleksandr Yakovlev].

18. Soviet Transcript of the Malta Summit, 18.

19. Gregor Dallas, *1945: The War That Never Ended* (New Haven: Yale University Press, 2005), 576. "Stalin's policy through the last two years of the war and into the peace was an extension of the Nazi-Soviet Pact, with the Nazis conveniently excluded."

20. "Is the European Union the New Soviet Union?" Speech by Vladimir Bukovsky, February 28, 2002, http://www.scribd.com/doc/20956318/Bukovsky-Is-the-European-Union-the-New-Soviet-Union-Tran script-R.

21. Soviet Transcript of the Malta Summit, 18.

22. Philip Taubman, "Gorbachev's Gloomy America," *New York Times,* November 15, 1985. See also Joseph D. Douglass Jr., *Why the Soviets Cheat on Arms Control Treaties* (Washington: Pergamon-Brassey's, 1988), 13.

23. In FDR's first real public pitch for what would become Lend-Lease—his "arsenal of democracy" speech of December 29, 1940—he said, "There is no demand for sending an American expeditionary force outside our own borders. There is no intention by any member of your government to send such a force. You can therefore, nail, nail any talk about sending armies to Europe as deliberate untruth. Our national policy is not directed toward war. Its sole purpose is to keep war away from our country and away from our people"; http://www.americanrhetoric.com/speeches/fdrarsenalofdemocracy.html.

24. George Racey Jordan, *From Major Jordan's Diaries* (Belmont, MA: Western Islands, 1965), 67 (Jordan's book was originally published by Harcourt, Brace, 1952); John R. Deane, *The Strange Alliance: The Story of Our Efforts at Wartime Cooperation with Russia* (Bloomington: Indiana University Press, 1973), 94–95.

25. Martin J. Bollinger, *Stalin's Slave Ships: Kolyma, the Gulag Fleet, and the Role of the West* (Annapolis, MD: Naval Institute Press, 2003).

26. "Khrushchev Remembers," *Life,* December 4, 1970, 68. See also John Keegan, *The Second World War* (Penguin, 2005), 218.

27. Jordan, *Diaries,* 73.

28. George C. Herring, *Aid to Russia* (New York: Columbia University Press, 1973), xvii.

29. Jordan, *Diaries,* 99.

30. Jordan, *Diaries,* 20.

31. Hearings Regarding Shipments of Atomic Material to the Soviet Union During World War II (Washington: GPO, 1950), 909–10; Jordan, *Diaries,* 21.

32. Paul Johnson, *Modern Times: The World from the Twenties to the Eighties* (New York: Harper & Row, 1983), 386.

33. Louis Morton, *The Fall of the Philippines* (Washington: Center of Military History, 1953), 27, 49. Out of the 151,000 forces stationed in the Philippines in November 1941, 120,000 were Filipino and 31,000 were American.

34. Lord Moran, *Churchill: Taken from the Diaries of Lord Moran* (Boston: Houghton Mifflin, 1966), 41, 108, 499–500.

35. Johnson, *Modern Times,* 386.

36. Herring, *Aid to Russia,* 42, 56.

37. Robert Dallek, *Franklin D. Roosevelt and American Foreign Policy, 1932–1945* (New York: Oxford University Press, 1995), 338.

38. George T. Eggleston, *Roosevelt, Churchill, and the World War II Opposition: A Revisionist Autobiography* (Old Greenwich, CT: Devin-Adair, 1980), 155.

39. Gen. Douglas MacArthur, *Reminiscences* (New York: McGraw-Hill, 1964), 121. See also Eggleston, *Roosevelt, Churchill, and the World War II Opposition,* 153–54.

40. William Manchester, *American Caesar* (New York: Dell, 1978), 273.

41. Robert Sherwood, *The White House Papers of Harry L. Hopkins: An Intimate History, vol. 2, January 1942– July 1945* (Eyre & Spottiswoode, 1949), 634–35.

42. Andrew and Mitrokhin, *Sword and Shield,* 551.

43. Soviet Transcript of the Malta Summit, 16.

44. Soviet Transcript of the Malta Summit, 20.

45. The following discussion between Bush and Gorbachev about "Western values" appears in Soviet Transcript of the Malta Summit, 30–33.

46. http://bushlibrary.tamu.edu/research/public_papers.php?id=1297&year=&month=.

47. Freedom of the Press 2012, Freedom House, 17, http://www.freedomhouse.org/report/freedom=press/freedom=press=2012.

48. See the Committee to Protect Journalists Web site, http://cpj.org/killed/europe/russia/.

49. http://www.uscirf.gov/images/Annual%20Report%20of%20USCIRF%202012(2).pdf.

50. http://www.guardian.co.uk/world/2008/mar/03/russia.eu.

51. Vladimir Bukovsky, "The Power of Memory and Acknowledgement," *Cato's Letter,* 8, no. 1, (Winter 2010); 2.

52. http://en.rian.ru/analysis/20120209/171229834.html.

53. http://www.reuters.com/article/idUSTRE6501UF20100601.

54. Bukovsky, "The Power of Memory and Acknowledgement," 4.

55. Bukovsky, "The Power of Memory and Acknowledgement," 4–5.

56. John Laughland, *A History of Political Trials: From Charles I to Saddam Hussein* (Long Hanborough, Eng.: Peter Lang, 2008), 116.

57. Arkady Vaksberg, *Stalin's Prosecutor: The Life of Andrei Vyshinsky* (New York: Grove Press, 1991), 259.

58. Robert Conquest, *The Great Terror: A Reassessment* (New York: Oxford University Press, 2007).

59. Laughland, *Political Trials,* 116.

60. Vaksberg, *Stalin's Prosecutor,* 261; Telford Taylor, *The Anatomy of the Nuremberg Trials: A Personal Memoir* (New York: Knopf, 1992), 639.

61. Taylor, *Anatomy,* 192–93.

62. Taylor, *Anatomy,* 307.

63. John J. Dziak, *Chekisty: A History of the KGB* (New York: Ballantine Books, 1988), 203.

64. Taylor, *Anatomy,* 307.

65. Malcolm Muggeridge, *Things Past: An Anthology* (William Morrow, 1979), 135.

66. Laughland, *Political Trials,* 111.

67. Vaksberg, *Stalin's Prosecutor,* 101.

68. Conquest, *Dragons,* 169.

69. Laughland, *Political Trials,* 103.

CHAPTER 3

1. Victor Kravchenko, *I Chose Justice* (New York: Charles Scribner's Sons, 1950), 76. Vassili Lujna was one of many witnesses attesting to Soviet crimes on Kravchenko's behalf in his 1949 case accusing a French Communist publication of libeling him as a fabricator. Kravchenko won.

2. Aleksandr Solzhenitsyn, *The Mortal Danger: How Misconceptions About Russia Imperil America* (New York: Harper Colophon, 1980), 111.

3. As recently as September 2012, a CNN survey of historians and commentators placed FDR first for foreign policy; http://globalpublicsquare.blogs.cnn.com/2012/09/20/the-best-foreign-policy-presidents/.

4. Moran, *Churchill,* 837: "The President's feelings toward Winston were rather more complicated. To try to unravel them, I shall turn to a disturbing entry in my diary of those months [final year of war]. Hopkins, in a temper, blurted out that it did not seem just to the President that Winston should take all the credit as Leader of the Free World. Roosevelt had become jealous. Lord Halifax confirmed this when I put a direct question to him. Marshall told me about that time that the President did not look forward to Winston's visits to the White House. Winston would embark on endless discussions about his strategy, and he was always talking about the British Empire. The sad story ended at Yalta, where Winston became impatient with the President's apathy and indifference. He did not seem to realize that Roosevelt was a very sick man."

5. Chambers, *Witness,* 707.

6. John Earl Haynes and Harvey Klehr, *Venona: Decoding Soviet Espionage in America* (New Haven: Yale University Press, 1999), 171.

7. Chambers, *Witness,* 574. He was referring specifically to Truman's calling the Hiss case a "red herring" whose "political purpose was to distract attention from the sins of the 80th [Republican] Congress. For thousands of people that automatically outlawed the Case. To me, it meant that I was not only deprived of official good will in testifying against Communism; I must expect active hostility among most powerful sections of the Administration."

8. In *Martin Dies' Story,* 77–83, Dies discusses FDR's active role in thwarting his run for a U.S. Senate vacancy in 1941, and later the pressure the administration brought to bear to remove him from Congress in 1943–44. When some personal health matters came up, Dies, "disgusted and exhausted," announced his retirement. "I felt that the country had been given all the facts it needed to defeat Communism, and I asked myself: 'What more can I accomplish under a hostile Administration?'"

9. Dies, *Martin Dies' Story,* 145: "The President said, 'I do not regard the Communists as any present or future threat to our country, in fact, I look upon Russia as our strongest ally in the years to come. As I told you when you began your investigations [in 1938], you should confine yourself to Nazis and Fascists.'"

House Un-American Activities Committee investigator Robert Stripling corroborates Dies's account of that 1938 conversation. Dies, Stripling writes, returned from a White House visit in 1938 to tell the committee, "The President became very upset. He told me that no one was interested in Communism; that he had heard about it all his life but had seen nothing of it; that it was not a menace. *He urged me to concentrate on Nazism and Fascism and forget Communism.*" Robert Stripling, *The Red Plot Against America* (Drexel Hill, PA: Bell, 1949), 28–29, emphasis added. As noted by Dies (179) and elsewhere, at the Army-McCarthy hearings a witness let slip the fact that President Eisenhower participated in a White House meeting to consider how to halt McCarthy. Besides Eisenhower, presidential assistant Sherwood Adams, Attorney General William Rogers, Press Secretary James Haggerty, and presidential assistant General Wilton B. Persons were present. Vice President Richard Nixon was either present or available by telephone.

10. In the summer of 2012, Rep. Michele Bachmann (R-MN) and four House Republican colleagues asked inspectors general at five government agencies to investigate evidence of Muslim Brotherhood penetration. For this, Bachmann in particular was denounced—quite ignorantly, given McCarthy's vindication by the historical record—for "McCarthyism." Regarding contemporary ignorance about McCarthy, see M. Stanton Evans, "When Conservatives Parrot Liberal Lies About Joe McCarthy," *Human Events,* August 19, 2012, http://www.humanevents.com/2012/08/19/when-conservatives-parrot-liberal-lies-about-joe-mccarthy/.

11. Here, for starters, are ten McCarthy suspects M. Stanton Evans cites in the opening pages of *Blacklisted by History* (New York: Crown Forum, 2007) who have been identified as Soviet agents in the Venona archives: Solomon Adler, Cedric Belfrage, T. A. Bisson, V. Frank Coe, Lauchlin Currie, Harold Glasser, David Kerr, Mary Jane Keeney, Leonard Mins, Franz Neumann.

12. The "no decency" tag is probably the biggest bum rap of all time. To quote Stanton Evans (568): "Army Counsel Joseph Welch denounced McCarthy for outing Welch's assistant Frederick Fisher as a former member of a cited front group called the National Lawyers Guild. But *Welch himself* had publicly confirmed Fisher's former Guild membership weeks earlier in [a] *New York Times* story of April 16, 1945" (emphasis in original). Yet the rap lives on: http://billmoyers.com/wp-content/themes/billmoyers/tran script-print.php?post=7029.

13. Romerstein and Breindel, *Venona Secrets,* 454.

14. Evans, *Blacklisted by History,* 49.

15. Stripling, *Red Plot,* 23, 13.

16. Eugene Lyons, *The Red Decade: The Stalinist Penetration of America* (Indianapolis: Bobbs-Merrill, 1941), 11.

17. Stripling, *Red Plot,* 27.

18. Lyons, *Red Decade,* 11.

19. Stripling, *Red Plot,* 27.

20. Dies, *Martin Dies' Story,* 177.

21. Haynes, Klehr, and Vassiliev, *Spies,* 541.

22. Evans, *Blacklisted by History,* 7.

23. Eduard Mark, "Venona's Source 19 and the 'Trident' Conference of May 1943: Diplomacy or Espionage?" *Intelligence and National Security* 13, no. 2 (April 1998): 1–31, 2.

24. Evans, *Blacklisted by History,* 7.

25. Evans, *Blacklisted by History,* 7.

26. Evans, *Blacklisted by History,* 21. Evans notes a veritable cordon sanitaire against a reevaluation of McCarthy. "However, there has to date been no reevaluation of McCarthy's cases, or efforts to reassess his reputation based on the new disclosures. Despite occasional suggestions that he might have been onto something, the standard treatment of McCarthy and his charges rolls on today as negatively as ever. Indeed, the usual negative view not only prevails but is reinforced in some excellent studies of Venona, the Soviet archival sources, and other now-available records, without much indication the authors have made any particular study of McCarthy. To all appearances, these authors have simply rephrased the usual version of the story before proceeding on to the main business of their own researches."

27. Evans, *Blacklisted by History,* 21.

28. Victor Kravchenko, *I Chose Freedom: The Personal and Political Life of a Soviet Official* (New York: Charles Scribner's Sons, 1946), 304.

29. Kravchenko, *I Chose Freedom,* 304.

30. Kravchenko, *I Chose Freedom,* 305.

31. Haynes and Klehr would write a book about this denial called, appropriately enough, *In Denial: Historians, Communism, and Espionage* (San Francisco: Encounter Books, 2005).

32. Haynes and Klehr, *Venona,* 4, 7.

33. Haynes and Klehr tell us that partly due to the impact their initial archival revelations had on Senator Daniel Patrick Moynihan, and partly due to an institutional drive toward declassification, the Venona

cables—some 2,900 randomly decrypted and partly translated Soviet intelligence messages (out of hundreds of thousands)—began to be declassified by the U.S. government. Intelligence historians Jerrold and Leona Schecter see controversy over their revelations of Soviet infiltration of the Manhattan Project in their 1994 book with Soviet spymaster Pavel Sudoplatov, *Special Tasks,* as having helped midwife the release.

34. Chambers, *Witness,* 710. Jerrold and Leona Schecter, *Sacred Secrets: How Soviet Intelligence Operations Changed American History* (Washington DC: Brassey's Inc., 2002), 149, 156.
35. http://w.hnn.us/articles/1706.html#klehr.
36. Chambers, *Witness,* 707.
37. Haynes, Klehr, Vassiliev, *Spies,* 548.

CHAPTER 4

1. Lyons, *Red Decade,* 12.
2. Haynes, Klehr, and Vassiliev, *Spies,* 195.
3. Conquest, *Dragons,* 141.
4. Weinstein and Vassiliev, *Haunted Wood,* 340.
5. Roger Kimball summoned the phrase "the long march through the institutions," for the title of his book *The Long March.* While usually associated with Mao's path to power and cultural transformation, the phrase, Kimball writes, is attributed to Italian Marxist Antonio Gramsci, was later popularized by the German New Left's Rudi Dutschke, and was echoed by American student radicals to further revolutionary goals once violent overthrow became a nonstarter. Herbert Marcuse described the principle as "working against the institutions by working in them"—boring from within, a tactic embraced by revolutionaries from Alinsky to the Muslim Brotherhood.
6. Evans, *Blacklisted by History,* 124. Evans writes, "For the FBI, it [Bentley's testimony] was probably the single greatest data haul of the Cold War, rivaled only by *Venona.*"
7. Haynes, Klehr, and Vassiliev, *Spies,* 543.
8. Haynes and Klehr, *In Denial,* 210–12. Alger Hiss was a Soviet spy. Harry Bridges was an Australian labor leader whom the U.S. government unsuccessfully tried to deport as a secret Communist operative, which he denied under oath. Comintern files reveal that not only was Bridges a party member, he was elected to the Central Committee of the CPUSA. Millionaire Corliss Lamont was a socially prominent fellow traveler and Stalin sycophant. Meanwhile, at the University of Colorado, the Dalton Trumbo Free Speech Fountain spews forth the idea that this dedicated Stalinist believed in free speech for all, not just Communist Party Liners. See "Fountain of Lies" by University of Maryland history professor Art Eckstein for a partial history of Trumbo's enforcement of Party orthodoxy, http://archive.frontpagemag.com/readArticle.aspx?ARTID=9274.
9. Haynes, Klehr, and Vassiliev, *Spies,* 543–44.
10. Andrew and Mitrokhin, *Sword and Shield,* 546.
11. *FRUS* 1943, 3: 504.
12. http://tinyurl.com/8f9mjj9.
13. Robert C. Williams, *Russian Art and American Money, 1900–1940* (Cambridge: Harvard University Press, 1980), 249.
14. Williams, *Russian Art,* 246.
15. Williams, *Russian Art,* 246. Davies's edited letter of March 22, 1937, titled "Moscow's Shops and Theaters," appears on 130–31 in his book *Mission to Moscow.*
16. Williams, *Russian Art,* 254–56.
17. Tim Tzouliadis, *The Forsaken: An American Tragedy in Stalin's Russia* (New York: Penguin, 2008), 328. The museum lists it as *Holiday on a Collective Farm* by Sychkov.
18. Tzouliadis, *The Forsaken,* 120.
19. Williams, *Russian Art,* 240.
20. "Davies Predicts Victory in 1944," *New York Times,* January 30, 1943.
21. Todd Bennett, "Culture, Power, and *Mission to Moscow," Journal of American History* 88, no. 2 (September 2001): 489. In *I Chose Freedom,* 470–471, Kravchenko describes "perhaps my most harrowing evening in America" watching the movie *Mission to Moscow.* "I was grateful for the dark, which covered up the distress that, I am sure, was written on my face . . . No Soviet propaganda picture would have dared twist facts so recklessly out of their sockets . . .

"I had been through the purge. Though one of the least among the victims, I had suffered its indignities in my own flesh and spirit. Now in a Washington theatre I saw my own ordeal and that of my country being mocked in terms of caricature and falsification . . . When I emerged from the hours of my purgatory that evening I saw that I had drawn blood in my palms with my fingernails."
22. Timasheff, *Great Retreat,* 263.
23. Billingsley, *Hollywood Party,* 282.
24. Drawing from the testimony of a former high-ranking Czech Communist official, Maj. Gen. Jan Sejna, Joseph D. Douglass Jr. explores this horror in *Betrayed* (1st Books Library, 2002).

25. See Tzouliadis, *The Forsaken.*
26. Alexsandr I. Solzhenitsyn, *The Gulag Archipelago Two* (New York: Harper & Row, 1975), 632.
27. Billingsley, *Hollywood Party,* 64. M. B. B. Biskupski, *Hollywood's War with Poland, 1939–1945* (Lexington: University of Kentucky Press, 2009), 203.
28. Dalton Trumbo, "Getting into Focus," *The Worker,* May 5, 1946, quoted in Billingsley, *Hollywood Party,* 92–93.
29. John V. Fleming, *The Anti-Communist Manifestos: Four Books That Shaped the Cold War* (New York: Norton, 2009), 159.
30. Kravchenko, *I Choose Freedom,* 459, 461–62.
31. Edward Dmytryk, *Odd Man Out: A Memoir of the Hollywood Ten* (Carbondale: Southern Illinois University Press, 1996), 14.
32. Fleming, *Anti-Communist Manifestos.* The other three are Koestler's *Darkness at Noon* (1940), Kravechenko's *I Chose Freedom* (1946), and Chambers's *Witness* (1952).
33. Billingsley, *Hollywood Party*, 88, footnotes William L. O'Neill, *A Better World: The Great Schism: Stalinism and the American Intellectuals* (New York: Simon & Schuster, 1982), 78, which footnotes William Henry Chamberlin, "Where the News Ends," *New Leader,* August 22, 1942, 5.
34. *Partisan Review,* March–April 1942, 173.
35. The feature was short-lived; presumably publishing quickly stowed its "dangerous thoughts" for the duration. Having searched *PR*'s wartime editions, I found only one more entry for "Dangerous Thoughts" in the May–June 1942 issue, 271: the announcement by *Reader's Digest* that it would stop distributing free reprints of a December 1941 article by Max Eastman called "Stalin's American Power." *Digest* editors wrote, "Our decision is prompted by protests . . . against any unnecessary post-publication circulation of the article now that our own war effort is so closely connected with that of the Russian people." Despite the author's "express statement that 'common sense demands that we support' the Russian resistance to Hitler, we nevertheless feel that all doubts should be resolved against anything that might operate to disturb our essential war effort." In *PR*'s Summer 1944 issue, Orwell writes (281), "Russophile feeling [in London] is on the surface stronger than ever. It is now next door to impossible to get anything overtly anti-Russian printed. Anti-Russian books do appear, but mostly from Catholic publishing firms and always from a religious or frankly reactionary angle . . . The servility of the so-called intellectuals is astonishing. The Mission to Moscow film . . . was accepted here with hardly a murmur."
36. Amy Knight, *Beria: Stalin's First Lieutenant* (Princeton: Princeton University Press, 1993), 3.
37. Fleming, *Anti-Communist Manifestos,* 159–60
38. See note 13, chapter 3.
39. Andrew and Mitrokhin, *Sword and Shield,* 544. The authors further cite the bibliography of a praised academic study of Soviet foreign relations (1917–91) that, but for a Beria biography, lists no work on Soviet intelligence in more than 120 titles.
40. Dziak, *Chekisty,* xvii. Dziak also cites the "paucity of scholarly work on Soviet state security" (xv). He further notes his personal "distress" as a professor of Soviet intelligence and security on repeatedly finding students "had heretofore been taught about the Soviet system with no, or very little, reference to the gurantor of that system"—meaning the KGB (xvii).
41. Andrew and Mitrokhin, *Sword and Shield,* 545.
42. Andrew and Mitrokhin, *Sword and Shield,* 545.
43. Andrew and Mitrokhin, *Sword and Shield,* 545.
44. Andrew and Mitrokhin, *Sword and Shield,* 551.
45. Andrew and Mitrokhin, *Sword and Shield,* 667.
46. Joseph Alsop, "Kill-out by Stalin," *New York Times,* November 28, 1970.
47. Robert Conquest, *The Harvest of Sorrow: Soviet Collectivization and the Terror-Famine* (New York: Oxford University Press, 1986), 309.
48. *Witness, The God That Failed, I Chose Freedom, In Stalin's Secret Service,* etc.
49. Eugene Lyons, *Assignment in Utopia* (New York: Harcourt, Brace, 1937), 398.
50. Lyons, *Utopia,* 414–15. *The New Masses* was a leading Marxist publication.
51. Lyons, *Utopia,* 398.
52. S. J. Taylor, *Stalin's Apologist:* The New York Times's *Man in Moscow* (New York: Oxford University Press, 1990), 193–96. Cairns never returned to Russia; nor did his report see the light of day. Later, he would admit he'd been threatened "by powerful figures on the Left in Great Britain whom he believed at the time could do him great harm," Taylor writes. She names Beatrice Webb specifically; she and her husband, Sydney, were two of Stalin's most effective apologists for arguing that any misfortune Russian peasants suffered was all their own fault. Cairns's colleague on the trip, a German, published his scathing findings and was denounced as a fascist by *Pravda* and expelled from the USSR.
53. Lyons, *Utopia,* 398.
54. Lyons, *Utopia,* 392.

55. Lyons, *Utopia*, 392.
56. Lyons, *Utopia*, 400–401.
57. Lyons, *Utopia*, 414–15.
58. William Henry Chamberlin, *The Confessions of an Individualist* (New York: Macmillan, 1940), 88.
59. Muggeridge, *Things Past*, 44.
60. Lyons, *Utopia*, 418.
61. Conquest, *Harvest of Sorrow*, 308.
62. Written response to author's questions, July 21, 2011.
63. Orwell, *Essays* (New York: Everyman's Library, 2002), 439–41.
64. " 'Righteous' Aims Spur Bolsheviki," *New York Times*, March 1, 1933.
65. Muggeridge himself would memory-hole Jones, omitting him from subsequent accounts of the period for reasons or motivations unknown.
66. Lyons, *Utopia*, 575.
67. Lyons, *Utopia*, 575–76.
68. "Russians Hungry, but Not Starving," *New York Times*, March 31, 1933.
69. "Mr. Jones Replies," *New York Times*, May 13, 1933.
70. Conquest, *Harvest of Sorrow*, 344.
71. http://www.guardian.co.uk/books/2003/feb/15/featuresreviews.guardianreview23. It's worth noting this peculiar mechanism in action. In a 1969 review of *The Great Terror* in *The New York Review of Books*, Alexander Gerschenkron, a Harvard economics professor (who, his grandson later wrote, seriously believed Republicans were "morally flawed"), emphasized Conquest's failure to *understand* dictatorships "which must therefore create and continually recreate the stability conditions of its power." Still, he commends the research and accepts Conquest's assessment that Stalin caused twenty million deaths, calling it "a very reasonable estimate." None of it, however, colors his judgment. *It can't.* He writes, "The book must be read in its entirety, even though some tender souls will shrink from this close look into a chamber of horrors. But they should not and they need not. Brazen forgeries, improbable lies, cruel tortures, inhuman executions, barbarous treatment of prisoners—all this should be sickening. But it is much less so than one might expect. For the enormity of the crimes exceeds the capacity of the human mind to absorb the horror."
72. Conquest, *Harvest of Sorrow*, 322.
73. Conquest, *Dragons*, 141–42.
74. Conquest, *Dragons*, 142.
75. Vladimir Bukovsky, for one, has written extensively on the USSR's cynical manipulation and direction of the "peace movement," the unilateral (Western) nuclear freeze movement, and the campaign against the neutron bomb.
76. "John Le Carré Has a Surprising New Story to Tell," *Times of London*, September 14, 2008.
77. http://www.reaganfoundation.org/bw_detail.aspx?p=LMB4YGHF2&h1=0&h2=0&sw=&lm=berlinwall&args_a=cms&args_b=74&argsb=N&tx=1770.
78. Conquest, *Dragons*, 135.
79. "Gromyko News Conference: A 'Virtuoso Performance,' " *New York Times*, April 4, 1983.
80. John F. Burns, "Gromyko Rejects Reagan Arms Plan," April 3, 1983.

CHAPTER 5

1. Aleksandr Solzhenitsyn, *The Solzhenitsyn Reader: New and Essential Writings (1947–2005)* (Intercollegiate Studies Edition, 2006), 558.
2. *Thoughts from Maeterlinck* arranged and chosen by E.S.S. (Dodd, Mead, 1912), 29–30.
3. Conquest, *Great Terror*, 446.
4. Albert L. Weeks, *Russia's Life-Saver: Lend-Lease Aid to the USSR in World War II* (Lanham, MD: Lexington Books, 2004), 25.
5. See chapter 2.
6. Jordan, *From Major Jordan's Diaries*, 12.
7. W. L. White, *Report on the Russians* (New York: Harcourt, Brace, 1945), 124. In his 1950 book *America's Second Crusade* (Chicago: Regnery), 242–44, journalist William Henry Chamberlin described the "pro-Soviet hysteria" that drove widespread denunciations of White's by no means anti-Soviet (indeed, rather pro-Stalin) book in the spring of 1945. Chamberlin explains, "But what aroused the fury of many reviewers of the book was the author's frank, unsparing description of such negative sides of Soviet life as police terror, widespread employment of slave labor, gross discrepancy in the living standards of the higher bureaucrats and the masses of the people, and general poverty and backwardness. All these allegations were supported by a mass of corroborating evidence. But the feeling that Russia could do no wrong, that any criticism of Stalin's dictatorship was akin to treason, had taken a strong grip on the American wartime mind." After Pravda denounced it—"the standard stew from the fascist kitchen, with all its aroma of cal-

umnies, unpardonable ignorance and undisguised malice"—Chamberlin noted "many American reviewers echoed [Pravda's] sentiments, in slightly more sophisticated language. Sixteen American writers and journalists . . . signed on the dotted line an abusive denunciation of the book which was forwarded to Moscow by the National Council of American-Soviet Friendship," then led by pro-Soviet millionaire Corliss Lamont and identified as a Communist front group. Chamberlin continues, "I have dwelt at some length on this incident because it furnishes such clear proof of the mental subservience of many American intellectuals during the war to a foreign power, and to a totalitarian dictatorship at that. A muddled philosophy that might be called totalitarian liberalism came into fashion, with the Nation, the New Republic, and the newspaper PM as its main exponents. There was a tremendous revival of the prewar double standard of morals in judging those twin phenomena, communism and fascism."

8. White, *Report on the Russians,* 124.
9. Dallas, *1945,* 576.
10. Haynes, Klehr, and Vassiliev, *Spies,* 195–96.
11. Hanson Baldwin, *Great Mistakes of the War* (New York: Harper & Brothers, 1950), 9.
12. In *The New York Times,* February 14, 1943, Arthur Krock pointed out that OWI's *Victory* magazine called Hoover the candidate of "reactionaries" and featured a speech by Henry Wallace urging citizens to win "the people's revolution" that began with the War of Independence and included the Bolshevik Revolution of 1918.
13. Chesly Manly, *The Twenty-Year Revolution from Roosevelt to Eisenhower* (Chicago: Regnery, 1954), 113.
14. Arthur Krock reported in *The New York Times* on August 1, 1943 ("OWI's Critics Stirred by Broadcast on Italy"), that FDR himself "sternly rebuked" OWI's overseas division for Soviet-line broadcasts into Italy.
15. Evans, *Blacklisted by History.* 87.
16. Evans, *Blacklisted by History,* 90.
17. Romerstein and Breindel, *Venona Secrets,* 403, 433.
18. "Investigations: The Case Against IPR," *Time,* September 3, 1951, http://www.time.com/time/magazine/article/0,9171,821608-2,00.html.
19. Evans, *Blacklisted by History,* 393–95.
20. Evans, *Blacklisted by History,* 390–92.
21. Institute of Pacific Relations, Report Committee on the Judiciary, 82nd Congress, Hearings Held July 25, 1951–June 20, 1952, by the Internal Security Subcommittee, 38.
22. Arthur Herman, *Joseph McCarthy: Reexamining the Life and Legacy of America's Most Hated Senator* (New York: Free Press, 1999), 125.
23. Harvey Klehr and Ronald Radosh, *The Amerasia Spy Case: Prelude to McCarthyism* (Chapter Hill: University of North Carolina Press, 1996), 101.
24. Herman, *McCarthy,* 232.
25. "Report Cited to Back Charge by McCarthy," *New York Times,* December 20, 1950.
26. Karr shows up in both American and Soviet archives as a Soviet asset. Romerstein and Breindel (*Venona Secrets,* 158–59) report on a 1992 discovery of a KGB document by Yevgenia Albats that "showed that Karr had been regularly providing the KGB with information that was in turn relayed to the Central Committee of the Communist Party of the Soviet Union."
27. By contrast, Pearson didn't know whereof he spoke. "Of course, Dave [Karr], like a lot of youngsters, might have had Communist leanings or even been a party member," Pearson wrote in his diary. "But if I am any judge of human nature, he was cured of this long ago." *Drew Pearson Diaries, 1949–1959,* 75. Evans, *Blacklisted by History,* 44.
28. Evans, *Blacklisted by History,* 41; Haynes, Klehr, and Vassiliev, *Spies,* 190.
29. Evans, *Blacklisted by History,* 90.
30. Haynes, Klehr, and Vassiliev, *Spies,* 184–85; Haynes and Klehr, *Venona,* 78.
31. Evans, *Blacklisted by History,* 89; Romerstein and Breindel, *Venona Secrets,* 407.
32. Romerstein and Breindel, *Venona Secrets,* 169. Currie is further discussed in chapter 6.
33. Romerstein and Breindel, *Venona Secrets,* 169–72.
34. Evans, *Blacklisted by History,* 90. The Mihailovich story is further discussed in chapter 10.
35. Evans, *Blacklisted by History,* 90.
36. Haynes and Klehr, *Venona,* 198–201.
37. Haynes and Klehr, *Venona,* 325.
38. *WWII Behind Closed Doors: Stalin, the Nazis and the West* (New York: Vintage Books, 2010), 241.
39. Billingsley, *Hollywood Party,* 89.
40. Dennis J. Dunn, *Caught Between Roosevelt and Stalin: America's Ambassadors to Moscow* (Lexington: University Press of Kentucky, 1998), 141.
41. Timasheff, *Great Retreat,* 263.
42. Haynes and Klehr, *Venona,* 255–56. As we learn in Andrew and Mitrokhin's *Sword and Shield,* Solzhenitsyn, too, on leaving the USSR, drew a circle around him in Switzerland that was completely penetrated, including translators of his works (318).

43. Max Eastman conjured the term to describe Soviet defector Alexander Barmine. Alexander Barmine, *One Who Survived* (New York: G. P. Putnam's Sons, 1945), xii.

44. Jordan, *Diaries,* 47.

45. These lists came from the Soviets at Jordan's request.

46. Indeed, "the most famous brands of American industry [were used] in the service of the death camps," Tim Tzouliadis writes in *The Forsaken* (208), noting the crucial contributions of Lend-Lease, including Studebaker trucks and ice-breaking ships, that keep the flow of slave labor moving.

47. Hearings Regarding Shipments of Atomic Material to Russia During World War Two, House Committee on Un-American Activities, 81st Congress, December 7, 1949, testimony of Gen. Leslie R. Groves: "We didn't want this material shipped, yet they [officials from Lend-Lease] kept coming back and coming back" (947).

48. According to Jordan, "Lend-Lease," patents continued shipping to the USSR until 1949.

49. Jordan, *Diaries,* 11, 33. Regarding his claim about undocumented espionage workers, Jordan reproduces a letter by Maj. Gen. Follett Bradley that appeared in *The New York Times* on August 31, 1951. Bradley wrote, "Of my own personal knowledge I know that beginning early in 1942 Russian civilian and military agents were in our country in huge numbers. They were free to move about without restraint or check and, in order to visit our arsenals, depots, factories and proving grounds, they had only to make known their desires. Their authorized visits to military establishments numbered in the thousands. I also personally know that scores of Russians were permitted to enter American territory in 1942 without visas. I believe that over the war years this number was augmented at least by hundreds."

50. Victor Suvorov, *The Chief Culprit: Stalin's Grand Design to Start World War II* (Annapolis, MD: Naval Institute Press, 2008), 114–20. Suvorov argues that this military defeat stymied further Japanese aggression toward the USSR.

51. William H. Standley and Arthur A. Ageton, *Admiral Ambassador to Russia* (Chicago: Regnery, 1955), 221–35.

52. Jordan, *Diaries,* 149–150. The senior office was Lt. Col. J. D. McFarland, formerly an inspector for the Alaskan Wing of the Air Transport Command. Jordan quotes McFarland from an interview with the *Cincinnati Inquirer,* December 9, 1949: "I was in Great Falls every couple of weeks. Major Jordan repeatedly raised hell about uncontrolled deliveries going to Moscow.
"The Russians wanted no restrictions from the U.S. Army. Every time the issue got hot, they would telephone Washington, and they always had their way."

53. Jordan, *Diaries.* Jordan recounts the details of his one-man raid on Soviet secret cargo on 33–46.

54. Jordan, *Diaries,* 63. Jordan cites White's account of this wartime exchange in *Kansas City Star,* March 17, 1950.

55. Herring, *Aid to Russia,* xvi.

56. Hearings Regarding Shipment of Atomic Material to the Soviet Union During World War II, 1149.

57. Weeks, *Russia's Life-Saver,* 122. Weeks writes, "Some American experts also argue that a quantity of uranium was shipped through Great Falls to the Soviet Union . . . Some deny any such Russian conspiracy."

58. Jordan, *Diaries,* 1.

59. Jordan, *Diaries,* 63–64.

60. Richard Rhodes, *Dark Sun: The Making of the Hydrogen Bomb* (New York: Simon & Schuster, 1995), 96–100.

61. Jordan, *Diaries,* 48.

62. Rhodes, *Dark Sun,* 100.

63. Rhodes, *Dark Sun,* 592, 217–18.

64. Rhodes, *Dark Sun,* 121.

65. David J. Dallin, "The Kravchenko Case, A Personal Account," *Modern Age,* Summer 1962.

66. Dallin, "Kravchenko Case."

67. Haynes and Klehr, *Venona,* 253.

68. Walter Krivitsky was a senior Soviet intelligence official who defected in 1937; the cause of his death in a Washington hotel room in February 1941—suicide—is widely disbelieved. Similarly, the 1959 "suicide" of Paul Bang-Jensen in New York City remains suspicious. Bang-Jensen, a United Nations official from Denmark, refused to disclose the names of anonymous Hungarian witnesses to the Soviet invasion in Hungary in 1956. Both men had told their families that in the case of untimely demise, not to believe it could have been by suicide.

69. Robert Murphy, *Diplomat among Warriors: The Unique World of a Foreign Service Expert* (New York, Doubleday, 1964), 256.

70. Sherwood, *Hopkins,* 2:562.

71. Sherwood, *Hopkins,* 1:399.

72. "Harry L. Hopkins: Lender and Spender," *Life,* September 22, 1941, 93.

73. Sherwood, *Hopkins,* 1:448.

74. George McJimsey, *Harry Hopkins: Ally of the Poor and Defender of Democracy* (Cambridge: Harvard University Press, 1987), 360.

75. *FRUS,* The Tehran Conference, Roosevelt-Stalin Secret Meeting, December 1, 1943, 594. Martin Weil notes FDR's general political concerns about Senate ratification of the United Nations in *A Pretty Good Club: The Founding Fathers of the U.S. Foreign Service* (New York: Norton, 1978), 180.

76. Dallin, "Kravchenko Case."

77. McJimsey, *Hopkins,* 360. Sherwood makes no mention of the Kravchenko affair.

78. "Hopkins Backs a Third Term," *The Oelwein Daily Register,* June 16, 1939.

79. Chesley Manly, *Twenty-Year Revolution,* 95. Manly cites an article Hopkins wrote in *American Magazine,* July 1941.

80. Sherwood, *Hopkins,* 2:582–83.

81. "Addresses of Litvinov, Hopkins, and Green," *New York Times,* June 23, 1942.

82. Christina Krotkova, previously mentioned in the context of Soviet penetration of OWI.

83. Evans, *Blacklisted by History,* 86.

84. Haynes, Klehr, and Vassiliev, *Spies,* 26.

85. The cable comes to us via the KGB. Explanation in a nutshell: The British ambassador to Washington cabled the Foreign Office about Stettinius on November 27, 1944. His secret cable was "obtained" by a Soviet agent in London and conveyed to Stalin, Beria, and Molotov on December 12, 1944. Roughly half a century later, Alexander Vassiliev came across it in a KGB archive and copied it down in his famous notebooks. See Vassiliev, "Yellow Notebook No. #4, File 40935, Vol. 1, The US Government," viewable online at http://www.scribd.com/doc/84608440/Alexander-Vassiliev-Papers-Yellow-Notebook-No-4 -Translation.

86. Sherwood, *Hopkins,* 1:378.

87. *Life,* October 6, 1947, 68: Forrestal's "summons to Washington in 1940, which greatly surprised him, probably dated in part to the help he gave SEC in drawing up some of its new rules for Wall Street. It also resulted in part from his acquaintance with Harry Hopkins, whom he had met socially."

88. Weeks, *Russia's Life-Saver,* 22.

89. Sherwood, *Hopkins,* 1:268. Sherwood wrote: "It was obvious that Lend Lease should become the most vital element in the relations between the United States and all the Allied combatant nations and many neutrals as well, with the result that *more and more foreign missions in Washington were conducting, or attempting to conduct, their most important business directly with Hopkins,* thus bypassing the State Department (emphasis added).

90. Jean Edward Smith, *FDR* (New York: Random House, 2007), 583. Smith also notes that correspondence between FDR and Churchill and Stalin was "rarely seen in Foggy Bottom."

91. McJimsey, *Hopkins,* 241. Both Stimson and Hopkins recommended Leahy.

92. Evans, *Blacklisted by History,* 2.

93. Deane, *Strange Alliance,* 9. Quoted in *My Dear Mr. Stalin: The Complete Correspondence Between Franklin D. Roosevelt and Joseph V. Stalin,* ed. Susan Butler (New Haven: Yale University Press, 2005), 7.

94. Stettinius, "as far as anyone could tell," Martin Weil writes in *A Pretty Good Club* (142), "had no interest in policy. His sole objective was to please as many people as possible as often as possible"—chiefly his patrons President Roosevelt and "Deputy President" Hopkins.

95. Edward R. Stettinius Jr., *Lend-Lease: Weapon for Victory* (New York: Macmillan, 1944) 73.

96. http://www.ourdocuments.gov/doc.php?doc=71&page=transcript.

97. On February 16, 1943, FDR declared, "The defense of Saudi Arabia is vital to the defense of the United States." On December 31, 2005, George W. Bush declared the United States "has a vital interest in the success of a free Iraq." On December 1, 2009, Barack Obama declared it was in the United States' "vital interest" to send additional forces to Afghanistan.

98. Doris Kearns Goodwin, *No Ordinary Time: Franklin and Eleanor Roosevelt: The Home Front in War Time* (Touchstone, 1995), 193.

99. Goodwin, *No Ordinary Time,* 193. See also Sherwood, *Hopkins,* 1:223.

100. Goodwin, *No Ordinary Time,* 193.

101. Edward Jay Epstein, *Dossier: The Secret History of Armand Hammer* (New York: Random House, 1996), 135–56.

102. Sherwood, *Hopkins,* 2:224.

103. Evidence of Hopkins's work on behalf of the Kremlin will be fully discussed below.

104. Weeks, *Russia's Life-Saver,* 23.

105. Weil, *A Pretty Good Club,* 142.

106. Williams, *Russian Art and American Money,* 258.

107. Transcript of Tape 10, of conversations between Forrest Pogue and George C. Marshall, recorded January 22, 1957, 319.

108. McJimsey, *Hopkins,* 157.

109. Jordan, *Diaries,* 48–49.
110. Jordan, *Diaries,* 50.
111. Jordan, *Diaries,* 51.
112. Standley, 363. Faymonville, a.k.a "the Red General," was exposed as a Soviet asset and is discussed on page 183.
113. Christopher Andrew and Oleg Gordievsky, *KGB: The Inside Story* (New York: Harper Perennial, 1991), 287.
114. Haynes and Klehr, *Spies,* 258.
115. For details on Operation Snow, see Jerrold and Leona Schecter, *Sacred Secrets: How Soviet Intelligence Operations Changed American History* (Washington: 2002), 22–45.
116. Testimony by Elizabeth Bentley quoted in report, *Interlocking Subversion in Government Departments,* Senate Committee on the Judiciary, 83rd Congress, July 30, 1953, 30.
117. Andrew and Gordievsky, *KGB,* 287.
118. McJimsey, *Hopkins,* 52.
119. McJimsey, *Hopkins,* 74.
120. Dies, *Martin Dies' Story* 121.
121. David Ciepley, *Liberalism in the Shadow of Totalitarianism* (Cambridge: Harvard University Press, 2006), 76.
122. "Tugwell Sees End of Laissez-Faire," *New York Times,* February 16, 1934. See also http://www.bartleby.com/73/147.html.
123. McJimsey, *Hopkins,* 74–75.
124. Arthur M. Schlesinger Jr., *The Coming of the New Deal, 1933–1935* (Boston: Mariner Books, 2003), 40.
125. Schlesinger, *New Deal,* 49.
126. "Tugwell Sees End of Laissez-Faire."
127. Schlesinger, *New Deal,* 50.
128. Romerstein and Breindel, *Venona Secrets,* 212–13.
129. Andrew and Mitrokhin, *Sword and Shield,* 106.
130. Romerstein and Breindel, *Venona Secrets,* 214.
131. Andrew and Gordievsky, *KGB,* 287.
132. Andrew and Gordievsky, *KGB,* 287.
133. Andrew and Gordievsky, *KGB,* 350.
134. Andrew and Gordievsky, *KGB,* 290, 289.
135. Andrew and Mitrokhin, *Sword and Shield,* 111.
136. Eduard Mark, "Venona's Source 19 and the 'Trident' Conference of May 1943: Diplomacy or Espionage?" *Intelligence and National Security* 13, no. 2 (April 1998): 1–31, 15 quoted.
137. Andrew and Mitrokhin, *Sword and Shield,* 594.
138. Mark, "Venona's Source 19," 24.
139. Mark, "Venona's Source 19," 24.

CHAPTER 6

1. Soviet secret memorandum of 1931 as recounted by Igor Bogolepov in *Institute of Pacific Relations,* Report of the Committee of the Judiciary of the 82nd Congress, 2nd Session, Hearings Held July 25, 1951 to June 20, 1952 by the Internal Security Subcommittee, 31. Hereafter cited as IPR Report.
2. Buchar, editor, *And Reality Be Damned,* 85–86.
3. See Bryton Barron, *Inside the State Department* (New York: Comet Press, 1956), one of the first books, if not the first, to present evidence of Hiss's (and, in passing, Hopkins's) active role at Yalta. For a complete rendering of Alger Hiss's activities at Yalta, see also M. Stanton Evans and Herbert Romerstein's *Stalin's Secret Agents: The Subversion of Roosevelt's Government* (New York: Threshold Editions, 2012).
4. Fraser J. Harbutt, *Yalta 1945: Europe and America at the Crossroads* (Cambridge: Cambridge University Press, 2010), 232.
5. Elliot Rosen, *Roosevelt, the Great Depression and the Economics of Recovery* (University of Virginia, 2005), 172.
6. Romerstein and Breindel, *Venona Secrets,* 180–81.
7. Sherwood, *Hopkins,* 1:109.
8. Romerstein and Breindel, *Venona Secrets,* 181.
9. See Currie's intervention on behalf of Paul Hagen, for example, in chapter 5.
10. Romerstein and Breindel, *Venona Secrets,* 168.
11. Evans, *Blacklisted by History,* 374, 119.
12. Evans, *Blacklisted by History,* 119–21.
13. Evans, *Blacklisted by History,* 374.
14. IPR Report, 100.
15. IPR Report, 225.
16. Greenberg was also editor of IPR's magazine *Pacific Affairs.* IPR Report, p. 135.

17. See Peter B. Niblo, *Influence: The Soviet "Task" Leading to Pearl Harbor, the Iron Curtain, and the Cold War* (Elderberry Press, Oregon), 2002.
18. IPR Report, 228.
19. IPR Report via Evans, *Blacklisted by History*, 390–91.
20. Evans, *Blacklisted by History*, 395.
21. Evans, *Blacklisted by History*, 374.
22. Haynes and Klehr, *Venona*, 145.
23. Evans, *Blacklisted by History*, 375.
24. Evans, *Blacklisted by History*, 374.
25. "Currie and White Deny Under Oath They Aided Spies," *New York Times*, August 14, 1948.
26. Haynes and Klehr, *Venona*, 136.
27. Silvermaster file, vol. 7, http://education-research.org/csr/holdings/silvermaster/summaries.htm.
28. M. Stanton Evans called this FBI report, which also contains the real estate ad, to the author's attention.
29. Chambers, *Witness*, 600.
30. "Currie and White Deny Under Oath They Aided Spies."
31. Chambers, *Witness*, 601.
32. "Ruth Gerson, Justin Ginsburgh," *New York Times*, May 24, 2009.
33. Haynes and Klehr, *Venona*, 140; Earl Haynes, Klehr, and Vassiliev, *Spies*, 258. White's notes in Pumpkin Papers comes from IPR Report, 230.
34. Evans, *Blacklisted by History*, 373.
35. Pearson's lawyer estimated that some 275 lawsuits were filed against Pearson seeking more than $200 million in damages. Only one plaintiff ever collected. Review of *Drew Pearson: An Unauthorized Biography* by Oliver Pilat," *New York Times*, April 29, 1973.
36. Evans, *Blacklisted by History*, 111.
37. Laura Tyson Li, *Madame Chiang Kai-Shek: China's Eternal First Lady* (New York: Grove Press, 2006), 217.
38. Klehr and Radosh, *The* Amerasia *Spy Case*, 62.
39. Tyler Abell, ed., *Drew Pearson Diaries, 1949–1959* (New York: Holt, Rinehart & Winston, 1974), 166–67.
40. *Pearson Diaries*, 181.
41. Gen. Albert C. Wedemeyer, *Wedermeyer Reports!* (New York: Holt, 1958), 316–17. "It was all too typical of the general attitude in America, as influenced either by unwitting misrepresentations or by treasonable manipulators, that Drew Pearson should have referred to the Chinese Communists as 'the Northern Chinese.' " Typical, yes—but natural, given Communist influence.
42. Herman, *McCarthy*, 123.
43. See chapter 5.
44. The previous year, David Karr named a baby after Drew Pearson. *Drew Pearson Diaries*, 88.
45. Romerstein and Breindel, *Venona Secrets*, 139.
46. Evans, *Blacklisted by History*, 90.
47. Haynes, Klehr, and Vassiliev, *Spies*, 159–60. Allen, Tom Ricks reported, became an intelligence officer under Patton, one of few with clearance to read ULTRA. Ricks even wonders whether it might have been Allen who fed Pearson the notorious scoop on Patton slapping his shell-shocked soldiers, which helped end the career of the resolutely anti-Communist commander. See http://ricks.foreignpolicy.com/posts /2010/12/01/pattons_third_army_deputy_intel_officer_briefly_was_on_the_kgbs_payroll.
48. Herman, *McCarthy*, 232.
49. Krafsur worked under TASS Washington bureau chief Laurence Todd, of Wirt dinner party fame.
50. Haynes and Klehr, *Venona*, 242–44.
51. Alan Farnham, "Armand Hammer: Tinker, Traitor, Satyr, Spy," *Fortune*, November 11, 1996.
52. Schecter and Schecter, *Sacred Secrets*, 111.
53. Chambers, *Witness*, 574–75.
54. Schecter, *Sacred Secrets*, 143. Alger Hiss persistently raised the possibility that Chambers had long been in a mental institution. See *Witness*, 682–92.
55. Schecter, *Sacred Secrets*, 143.
56. Schecter, *Sacred Secrets*, 149.
57. Haynes and Klehr, *Venona*, 15.
58. Haynes and Klehr, *Venona*, 15.
59. The second source is Robert Louis Benson and Michael Warner, *Venona: Soviet Espionage and the American Response, 1939–1957* (Washington: National Security Agency, Central Intelligence Agency, 1996), xxiv, xxx. On xxiv, Benson and Warner write, "Truman's repeated denunciations of the charges against Hiss, White, and others—all of whom appear under cover names in decrypted messages translated before he left office in 1953—suggest that Truman either was never briefed on the Venona program or did not grasp its significance." Another possibility is that, he decided early on (see Schecter and Schecter) to ignore the facts/implications of the decrypted messages, and he stuck to it. Back to Benson and Warner: "Although it

seems odd that Truman might not have been told, no definitive evidence has emerged to show that he was. In any event, Truman always insisted that Republicans had trumped up the loyalty issue and that wartime espionage had been insignificant and well contained by American authorities."

60. Robert Novak and Haynes and Klehr duked it out, academically speaking, in the pages of *The Weekly Standard* in June and July, 2003. I agree with Novak and the Schecters. The exchange is also available on-line at: http://hnn.us/articles/1706.html.

61. Schecter and Schecter, *Sacred Secrets,* 146.

62. Daniel Patrick Moynihan, *Secrecy: The American Experience* (New Haven: Yale University Press, 1999), 70–71.

63. I'm not aware of new records to bolster Moynihan's and Haynes and Klehr's contention. Curiously, when Moynihan wrote a new preface to *Secrecy* for the 1999 paperback edition, he highlighted the Truman-as-Venona-innocent tale, noting General Bradley's role as gatekeeper and *therefore roadblock on Venona information* (which I think is wishful thinking, not a logical deduction), quoting Haynes and Klehr for additional support: "The evidence is not entirely clear, but it appears that Army Chief of Staff Omar Bradley . . . decided to deny President Truman direct knowledge of the Venona Project." Talk about circular arguments: The Haynes and Klehr quotation that Moynihan uses here footnotes Moynihan himself— *Secrecy,* 70–71!

64. http://www.nsa.gov/about/cryptologic_heritage/hall_of_honor/2008/kirby.shtml.

65. Benson and Warner, *Venona,* xxvi–xxvii.

66. Schecter and Schecter, *Sacred Secrets,* 149. The authors footnote this statement to a March 5, 1999, interview with Kirby plus "Kirby's handwritten notes."

67. This isn't dissimilar from current strategy to consider everyone a suspect rather than identifying the doctrinal Islamic nature of the threat.

68. Novak wrote that Kirby's assertions that Truman knew are based on notes he made *at the time* he worked on Venona, contradicting the Klehr and Haynes dismissal of Kirby's recollections "fifty years after the event."

69. Haynes and Klehr, *Venona,* 11–12.

70. Dies, *Martin Dies' Story,* 144

71. "Earle Reports Ban on Katyn Evidence," *New York Times,* November 14, 1952.

72. Schecter and Schecter, *Sacred Secrets,* 149.

73. Evans, *Blacklisted by History,* 77.

74. "Bricker Attacks Foreign Influence," *New York Times,* October 31, 1944.

75. Baldwin, *Great Mistakes of the War,* 9.

76. Robert H. Jackson, "Communism in America," *New York Times,* May 21, 1950.

77. For example, CPUSA policy shifted with ups and downs of the Nazi-Soviet Pact.

78. Haynes and Klehr, *In Denial,* 8.

79. George Orwell, *1984,* (New York: Signet Classic, 1977), 80.

80. Conrad Black, *Franklin Delano Roosevelt: Champion of Freedom* (New York: Public Affairs, 2005), 950. This book, too, is devoid of Venona revelation, although Haynes and Klehr's *Venona* is listed in the bibliography.

81. August 4, 1948, http://tinyurl.com/9jdjtrh.

82. Haynes, Klehr, and Vassiliev, *Spies,* 427.

83. Haynes and Klehr, *In Denial,* 4.

84. Susan C. W. Abbotson, ed., *Masterpieces of 20th-Century American Drama* (Westport, CT: Greenwood, 2005), 77.

85. Chambers, *Witness,* 741–42.

86. See chapter 1, "Case Closed," Haynes, Klehr, and Vassiliev, *Spies.*

87. Chambers, *Witness,* 556–57.

88. Lyons, *Red Decade,* 309–10.

89. Lyons, *Red Decade,* 47.

90. Dies, *Martin Dies' Story,* 40.

91. Lyons, *Red Decade,* 298–99.

92. Niblo, *Influence,* 55.

93. Chambers, *Witness,* 549–50.

94. Keith Windschuttle, *The Killing of History: How Literary Critics and Social Theorists Are Murdering Our Past* (San Francisco: Encounter, 2000), ix.

CHAPTER 7

1. Conquest, *Great Terror,* 463.

2. Charles A. Beard, *President Roosevelt and the Coming of the War, 1941: A Study in Appearances and Realities* (New Haven: Yale University Press, 1948), 577.

3. "Washington Success Story," *New York Times,* July 26, 1942.

4. In the Harry L. Hopkins Papers at Georgetown University, the author discovered a letter dated August 7, 1941, apparently typed by Hopkins himself (there are no secretarial initials), noting his recent meeting with Stalin. It is to General Hastings Lionel "Pug" Ismay, Churchill's top military advisor. It begins "Dear Pug," and it is signed, "Ever so gratefully yours, H.H." Box 60, Folder 9.

5. Hearings Regarding Shipment of Atomic Materials to the Soviet Union During World War II, House Committee on Un-American Activities, 81st Congress, 1049, 1149.

6. Sherwood, *Hopkins,* 1:388.

7. Romerstein and Breindel, *Venona Secrets,* 217–18.

8. To be discussed at length.

9. Andrew and Gordievsky, *KGB,* 287.

10. John Keegan, "Necessary or Not, Dresden Remains a Topic of Anguish," *Telegraph,* October 31, 2005; Niblo, *Influence,* 124.

11. Victor Klemperer records their escape in the second of his three volumes of diaries.

12. Sherwood, *Hopkins,* 2:920–21.

13. Dunn, *Caught Between Roosevelt and Stalin,* 93.

14. Dunn, *Caught Between Roosevelt and Stalin,* 132, quoting Hopkins's biographer McJimsey.

15. Standley and Ageton, *Admiral Ambassador to Russia,* 314.

16. Dunn, *Caught Between Roosevelt and Stalin,* 128.

17. Sherwood, *Hopkins,* 2:399.

18. Sherwood writes in his biography preface of the forty filing cabinets in the Hopkins house and "a great many more in a warehouse, the latter being records of the New Deal, which I have never seen." Sidney Hyman organized the papers, sorting them into folders—"Casablance Conference," "Aid to Russia," etc.—before Sherwood arrived, making Hyman the editor of Hopkins's papers, not Sherwood.

19. *Newsweek,* December 19, 1949, quoted in Jordan's 1950 congressional testimony, 1169.

20. Sherwood, *Hopkins,* 1:155–57, 2:701, 1:181.

21. Sherwood, *Hopkins,* 1:16.

22. Andrew and Mitrokhin, *Sword and Shield,* 111.

23. Andrew and Mitrokhin, *Sword and Shield,* 594.

24. Harvey Klehr, John Earl Haynes, and Fridrikh Igorevich Firsov, *The Secret World of American Communism* (New Haven: Yale University Press, 1995), 216.

25. Romerstein and Breindel, *Venona Secrets,* 545–46.

26. Romerstein and Breindel, *Venona Secrets,* 255–57.

27. Hearings 1950, Shipment of Atomic Material, 1163

28. Benson and Warner (eds.), *VENONA,* 49–50.

29. Sherwood, *Hopkins,* 2:402.

30. When Maj. Gen. John R. Deane, U.S. ambassador in Moscow, learned that the Soviets were stockpiling surplus diesel engines and ordering more at a time when these same engines were in scarce supply for landing craft designated for OVERLORD, Deane, already aboil over similarly urgent but unexplained Soviet demands for increases in aluminum, nickel, copper wire, and alcohol, cabled the Joint Chiefs of Staff back in Washington his recommendation that before approving allocations to Moscow the United States obtain one, good, Soviet reason for sending the stuff. How reasonable. Deane wasn't urging a cutoff in a fit of pique; simply justification. General Marshall cabled his approval of Deane's recommendation. Hopkins's man in Moscow, Averell Harriman, however, told Hopkins about the Deane logjam and received "what amounted to instructions to attach no strings to our aid to Russia," Deane wrote. All of the extra supplies (including diesel engines) went through. Deane, *Strange Alliance,* 96–98.

31. "Forrestal," *Life,* October 6, 1947, 68.

32. See Russell Kirk and James McClellan, *The Political Principles of Robert A Taft* (New York: Fleet Press Corporation, 1967). The authors underscore the "feebleness of party principles" that marked both the Republican and Democratic parties before the New Deal, which endowed the Democratic Party with "a strong ideological cast." Arthur Krock quotation from Weil, *A Pretty Good Club,* 85–86.

33. Joseph D. Douglass Jr., *Why the Soviets Violate Arms Control Treaties* (Washington: Pergamon-Brassey's, 1988), 18.

34. Dies, *Martin Dies' Story,* 144–48; Robert I. Gannon, S.J., *The Cardinal Spellman Story* (Garden City, NY: Doubleday, 1962), pp. 222–25.

35. Dunn, *Caught Between Roosevelt and Stalin,* 281, note 17. In Dunn's interview with Harriman, Dunn writes, Harriman "emphasized the importance of the theory of convergence in explaining Roosevelt's policies." Sumner Welles, *Where Are We Heading?* (New York: Harper & Brothers, 1946), 37–38: FDR "told me that he did believe that if one took the figure 100 as representing the difference between American democracy and Soviet Communism in 1917, with the United States at 100 and the Soviet Union at 0, American democracy might eventually reach the figure of 60 and the Soviet system might reach the figure of 40 . . . He regarded this trend as making it more likely that no fundamental conflict between the two

countries need ever become inevitable, *provided Soviet Communism had permanently abandoned its doctrine of world revolution"* (emphasis added). This last provision, Bullitt tells us, is what Harry Hopkins told him.

36. Weil, *A Pretty Good Club,* 93. Some files were saved and later went to the CIA.

37. Weil, *A Pretty Good Club,* 134–35.

38. Weil, *A Pretty Good Club,* 106. Weil notes George Kennan "echoed these feelings in a letter he wrote to Henderson" two days after the German invasion of Russia.

39. Evans, *Blacklisted by History,* 81–82.

40. Orville H. Bullitt, ed., *For the President, Personal and Secret: Correspondence Between Franklin D. Roosevelt and William C. Bullitt* (Boston: Houghton Mifflin, 1972), 57.

41. Excerpts from testimony of Dr. D. H. Dubrowsky, former head of Russian Red Cross. See Dies, *Martin Dies' Story,* 223.

42. Litvinov letter of agreement on terms of recognition reproduced in full in Dies, *Martin Dies' Story,* 221.

43. Herbert Hoover, *Freedom Betrayed: Herbert Hoover's Secret History of the Second World War and Its Aftermath,* edited and with an introduction by George H. Nash (Stanford, CA: Hoover Institution Press, 2011), 24–29. Hoover notes (25) that on becoming president, FDR "had knowledge of two current glaring examples of Communist conspiracy specifically directed against the United States. These were the so-called 'Bonus March' of 1932 and the flooding of the world with counterfeit American money printed in Moscow and used for Communist purposes."

44. Solzhenitsyn, *Warning to the West,* 19–20. Totaling executions and victims of civil repression including pogroms between 1860 and 1914 in Czarist Russia, Robert Conquest writes, "We can hardly reach a figure of twenty thousand odd. The current estimate for executions alone in the two-year period 1937–1938 is just under two million. In terms of dialectic, this is surely an overwhelming case of the quantitative becoming the qualitative." *Reflections on a Ravaged Century* (New York: Norton, 2000), 86.

45. Conquest, *Great Terror,* 470.

46. Conquest, *Great Terror,* 470.

47. Bullitt, *Correspondence,* 58.

48. There were two final straws for Bullitt: the blood purges after the December 1934 murder of Kirov, which, he wrote FDR on May 1, 1935 (116), intensified "the terror, always present, . . . to such a pitch that the least of the Muscovites, as well as the greatest, is in fear"; and, finally, the 1935 Moscow meeting of the world's Communist Parties in which the CPUSA leaders took leading roles. As Dunn notes (*Caught Between Roosevelt and Stalin,* 49), "This not only proved that [the Soviets] still pursued the goal of world revolution, but it also proved that they were breaking their promise made in the letters exchanged between Roosevelt and Litvinov in November 1933 which stipulated that Moscow would have nothing to do with the American Communist Party."

49. Bullitt, *Correspondence,* 130–31.

50. Standley, *Admiral Ambassador,* 308.

51. Douglass, *Why the Soviets Violate Arms Control Treaties,* vii, 85.

52. Dunn, *Caught Between Roosevelt and Stalin,* 52.

53. Bullitt, *Correspondence.* See xix for Kennan's assessment; see 575–90 for the January 29, 1943 letter.

54. See chapter 5.

55. Bullitt, *Correspondence,* 577.

56. William C. Bullitt, "How We Won the War and Lost the Peace," *Life,* August 30, 1948, 94.

57. Bullitt, *Correspondence,* 578.

58. Evans, *Blacklisted by History,* 478–90.

59. Charles E. Bohlen, *Witness to History, 1929–1969* (New York: Norton, 1973), 126.

60. Kravchenko, *I Chose Freedom,* 467–68.

61. http://tinyurl.com/8fz842e.

62. Lyons, *Assignment in Utopia,* 572.

63. Thaddeus Wittlin, *Time Stopped at 6:30: The Untold Story of the Katyn Massacre* (Indianapolis: Bobbs-Merrill, 1965). Stalin endlessly stonewalled Polish and Allied officials seeking information on missing Poles; see 223–32.

64. Schecter and Schecter, *Sacred Secrets,* 64.

65. The Katyn Forest Massacre, Final Report, 82nd Congress, 2nd Session, 10.

66. Rees, *WWII,* 184.

67. Rees, *WWII,* 184.

68. David Carlton, *Churchill and the Soviet Union* (Manchester: Manchester University Press, 2000), 106.

69. Katyn Final Report, 19.

70. McJimsey, *Hopkins,* 293.

71. Excerpts of O'Malley's report come from Rees, *WWII,* 186–89.

72. Solzhenitsyn, *Warning to the West,* 21.

73. Dunn, *Caught Between Roosevelt and Stalin,* 105.

74. Rees, *WWII,* 190.

75. David Irving, *Nuremberg* (N.P.: Focal Point Publications, 1999), 62.

76. Solzhenitsyn, *Warning to the West*, 19–20.

77. Kravchenko, *I Chose Freedom*, 466–67.

78. Rees, *WWII*, 191–92.

79. Standley, *Admiral Ambassador*, 363.

80. *FRUS: The Conferences at Washington and Quebec, 1943*, 624–27. See also Manly, *Twenty-Year Revolution*, 115–16.

81. Schecter and Schecter, *Sacred Secrets*, 98–100.

82. Haynes and Klehr, *Venona*, 44–45.

83. McJimsey, *Hopkins*, 293.

84. Pennsylvania Historical and Museum Commission, http://tinyurl.com/8ozefca.

85. George H. Earle, "F.D.R.'s Tragic Mistake!" *Confidential*, August 1958, 16.

86. Katyn Forest Massacre Hearings, 2197.

87. Katyn Forest Massacre Hearings, 2204.

88. Katyn Forest Massacre Hearings, 2205.

89. Katyn Forest Massacre Hearings, 2211–212.

90. Letter from Earle to FDR, June 11, 1944, Katyn Forest Massacre Hearings, 2199.

91. Romerstein and Breindel, *Venona Secrets*, 217–18, In this example, General F. L. Anderson notes in a memo that Hopkins stated he would withhold from FDR cables from Churchill and the U.S. ambassador to London favoring air support for a Polish uprising.

92. Joseph Persico, *Roosevelt's Secret War: FDR and World War II Espionage* (New York: Random House, 2002), 385.

93. A facsimile of the president's letter is reproduced in "F.D.R.'s Tragic Mistake" by George H. Earle, *Confidential*, August 1958.

94. Rees, *WWII*, 249–50.

95. Julius Epstein, "The Mysteries of the Van Vliet Report: A Case History," http://tinyurl.com/8vad5yy.

96. Ibid. On September 18, 1950, the Department of Defense finally released a dossier of previously classified documents relating to the Katyn Forest Massacre. Julius Epstein explains its importance: "With the release of this report, our government indicates for the first time that it does not any longer believe in Stalin's lies about the German guilt. This is of tremendous importance in view of the fact that the government, through its Office of War Information, disseminated for years Stalin's lies about Katyn, and our present *Voice of America* has always rejected [efforts] to tell the world the truth about Katyn. This persistence in not telling the truth about Katyn went so far that the *Voice* even forced Count Joseph Czapski, one of the few survivors of the Russian massacre of Polish officers, to omit any mention of the word and the facts of Katyn when he was invited to broadcast in Polish to his Polish brethren."

97. Herbert Romerstein, "Coverup for Those Who Carried Out Mass Murder," *Polska*, March 8, 2008, accessed online at http://victimsofcommunism.org/media/article.php?article=3738. Romerstein notes that while the State Department claimed to have no record of receipt of the 1945 Van Vliet Report (and the army claimed to have no carbon copies), "it is interesting to note that the report went to that part of the State Department headed by Alger Hiss. We now know that Alger Hiss was a Soviet spy. So we can understand the disappearance of the document."

98. Final Report of the Select Committee to Conduct an Investigation and Study of the Facts, Evidence, and Circumstance on the Massacre at Katyn Forest, 8.

99. "New Security Charter Seems to Be Assured," *New York Times*, May 20, 1945.

100. "San Francisco Outlook: Hope of Banning War Stirs World Despite History's Somber Teaching," *New York Times*, May 21, 1945.

101. Final Report, Katyn Massacre, 8.

102. "How Has the United States Met Its Major Challenges Since 1945?" *Commentary*, November 1985.

103. Romerstein, "Coverup."

104. Evans, *Blacklisted by History*, 83.

105. Evans, *Blacklisted by History*, 83.

106. See Wittlin, *Time Stopped*, 276–84, for details on Krivosertsov's life and death.

CHAPTER 8

1. Conquest, *Harvest of Sorrow*, 314.

2. Standley and Ageton, *Admiral Ambassador*, 276. Willkie, the GOP's presidential candidate in 1940, was addressing Stalin's primo fixer, Andrei Vyshinsky, in 1942.

3. Solzhenitsyn, *Warning to the West*, 133.

4. Solzhenitsyn objected to the word "anti-Communism." He wrote, "It makes it appear as though Communism were something original, fundamental. Therefore, it is taken as the point of departure, and anti-Communism is defined in relation to Communism . . . The primary, the eternal concept is humanity, and

Communism is anti-humanity. Whoever says 'anti-Communism' is saying, in effect, 'anti-anti-humanity.' A poor construction. So we should say: That which is against Communism is for humanity. Not to accept, but to reject this inhuman Communist ideology is simply to be a human being. Such a rejection is more than a political act. It is a protest of our souls against those who would have us forget the concept of good and evil." *Warning to the West,* 58–59.

5. Solzhenitsyn, *Warning to the West,* 19–20.

6. Aleksandr I. Solzhenitsyn, *The Oak and the Calf: Sketches of Literary Life in the Soviet Union* (New York: Harper & Row, 1980), 10.

7. Michael Scammell, ed., *The Solzhenitsyn Files: Secret Soviet Documents Reveal One Man's Fight Against the Monolith* (Chicago: Edition q, 1995).

8. Elia Kazan, *A Life* (New York: Anchor Books, 1988), 459.

9. Kazan, *A Life,* 464, 459.

10. Paul Kengor, *Dupes: How America's Adversaries Have Manipulated Progressives for a Century* (Wilmington, DE: Intercollegiate Studies Institute, 2010), 521.

11. See "Justice Jackson on Communism in America," *New York Times,* May 21, 1950. Jackson distinguishes between the Communist Party and all other U.S. political parties in his concurrence with the Supreme Court ruling upholding Taft-Hartley. For example, noting that no other parties are secret, disciplined organizations, he writes, "Membership in the Communist Party is totally different. The party is a secret conclave. Members are admitted only upon acceptance as reliable and after indoctrination in its policies . . . Moreover, each pledges unconditional obedience to party authority. . . ."

12. Dmytryk, *Odd Man Out,* 158.

13. Lyons, *Red Decade,* 184.

14. *Village Voice,* March 16, 1999; Maureen Dowd, "Streetcar Named Betrayal," *New York Times,* February 24, 1999; Gordon quotation in "Elia Kazan; Feted but Not Forgiven," *Christian Science Monitor,* March 10, 1999; Polonsky quotation in *Entertainment Weekly,* February 5, 1999.

15. "Gold Field Prisoner," *New York Times,* October 30, 1949.

16. "Workers in Chains," *New York Times,* June 17, 1951. Dallin assisted Kravchenko on his defection.

17. "Mr. Dallin Among the Scholars," *Modern Age,* Winter 1960–61, http://tinyurl.com/8dxv9tr.

18. Lyons, *Red Decade,* 184.

19. Solzhenitsyn, *The Gulag Archipelago Three* (New York: Harper & Row, 1978), 28, via Dallas, *1945,* 457. Time magazine perceived the double standard as early as December 1934 in a report about Stalin's blood purge following the assassination of Kirov, writing, "Since President Roosevelt cast the cloak of his popularity over Dictator Stalin by recognizing the Soviet Union, the U.S. Press last week breathed no such denunciation as at Adolf Hitler's 'blood purge.' " *Time,* December 17, 1934.

20. Of note is a 1951 tribunal in Brussels where survivors of Nazi concentration camps put the concentration camp system of the Soviet Union "on trial" by hearing testimony of Gulag survivors of inhuman cruelties. The verdict? Guilty. See http://tinyurl.com/8d3r88z.

21. Indeed, his Swiss ménage was penetrated by Communist agents.

22. Andrew and Mitrokhin, *Sword and Shield,* 311, 317–20.

23. Douglass, *Why the Soviets Violate Arms Control Treaties,* 9–10. Among others, Douglass cites John W. Finney, "Brezhnev Said to Assure East Europe that Accords with West Are a Tactic," *New York Times,* September 17, 1973, and William Beecher, "Brezhnev Termed Détente a Ruse, 1973 Report Said," *Boston Globe,* February 11, 1977. Both articles refer to a British intelligence report on a secret spring 1973 meeting in Prague where Brezhnev described détente as a strategy to serve world Communist interests: "We are achieving with detente what our predecessors have been unable to achieve using the mailed fist."

24. Beecher, "Brezhnev Termed Détente a Ruse."

25. Claire Sterling, *The Terror Network: The Secret War of International Terrorism* (New York: Holt, Rinehart & Winston, 1981), 293. Simultaneously, the Soviets were expanding the international drug trade with similar deniability, as Joseph D. Douglass Jr. would write in his groundbreaking book *Red Cocaine: The Drugging of America* (Atlanta: Clarion House, 1990), an exposé of pharmacological Soviet aggression post–Cold Warriors refused to confront.

26. Conquest, *Dragons,* 99.

27. Henry Kissinger, *Years of Renewal: The Concluding Volume of His Memoirs* (New York: Simon & Schuster, 1999), 650.

28. Sterling, *Terror Network,* 2.

29. A. Solzhenitsyn, *Warning to the West,* 22.

30. 2 + 2 = 5 was the equation Orwell made famous in *1984,* which was undoubtedly borrowed from Eugene Lyons's chapter of the same name in *Assignment in Utopia.*

31. http://nobelprize.org/nobel_prizes/literature/laureates/1970/solzhenitsyn-autobio.html.

32. There is a sickening point of comparison between this repatriation policy, born of Yalta, and a secret agreement between the Nazis and the Soviets to return to each other either German Marxists who

had sought refuge in Soviet Russia, or anti-Communist Russians who had sought refuge in Germany. Two main differences: The numbers of those returned were insignificant in the Nazi-to-Soviet example; and in the British and American case, we didn't get thousands of our hostages back in return. See chapter 11.

33. Nikolai Tolstoy, *The Secret Betrayal* (New York: Charles Scribner's Sons, 1977); Julius Epstein, *Operation Keelhaul: The Story of Forced Repatriation* (Old Greenwich, CT: Devin-Adair, 1973).

34. Nikolai Tolstoy, Letter to the Editor, *TLS,* October 27, 2010.

35. Barron, *Inside the State Department* (New York: Comet Press, 1956), 18.

36. Pavel Sudoplatov and Anatoli Sudoplatov with Jerrold L. and Leona P. Schecter, *Special Tasks: The Memoirs of an Unwanted Witness, a Soviet Spymaster* (Boston: Little, Brown, 1994), 227.

37. Romerstein and Breindel, *Venona Secrets,* 136–37.

38. See chapter 7.

39. Epstein, *Operation Keelhaul,* 27, 53.

40. Aleksandr I. Solzhenitsyn, *The Gulag Archipelago, 1918–1956: An Experiment in Literary Investigation, I–II* (New York: Harper & Row, 1973), 85. Solzhenitsyn notes that not until 1973—in the *Sunday Oklahoman* of January 21—was an article by Julius Epstein published. Julius Epstein, as noted and saluted above, was one of our great truth tellers. It was his investigative journalism that prompted the 1951 congressional hearings on the official suppression of the Katyn Massacre that were crucial to the reestablishment and preservation of the historical record.

41. Epstein, *Operation Keelhaul,* 213–14.

42. Epstein, *Operation Keelhaul,* "Introduction" by Bertram D. Wolfe, viii.

43. Epstein, *Operation Keelhaul,* 92–93.

44. Epstein, *Operation Keelhaul,* 97.

45. Epstein, *Operation Keelhaul,* 63.

46. Epstein, *Operation Keelhaul,* 62.

47. Patton, at Eisennhower's order, was cooling his heels outside Prague, waiting for the Red Army to enter Prague, but Vlasov was there first; Epstein, 64–65, sourcing a report in *The Saturday Evening Post* by a reporter in Prague.

48. Solzhenitsyn, *Warning to the West,* 22.

49. *Time,* December 17, 1934, quoted in Tzouliadis, *The Forsaken,* 76.

50. James Allan, *No Citation* (London: Tandem Books, 1965).

51. Baldwin, *Great Mistakes of the War,* 45–57. About Berlin, Baldwin writes, "General Eisenhower's own inclinations about Berlin apparently had full support in Washington; Edgar Ansel Mowrer reports in *The Nightmare of American Foreign Policy* that he had been personally told by the White House that 'the Joint Chiefs of Staff advised Truman to let the Russians take Berlin.' "

52. This included thousands of refugees of the Russian Revolution who had never been Soviet citizens and were not covered by the Yalta Agreement. See Tolstoy, *Secret Betrayal,* 19–20. Tolstoy describes the millions of Russians who came West during the war as forced workers, POWs, or refugees, at 26–41. Among them were nearly one million Russian and other anti-Soviet men who joined the German enemy of their Soviet enemy. As Tolstoy puts it on 101, this made for an extreme peculiarity in the annals of war: "The USSR alone of all the Allies had provided the enemy with thousands of recruits." This was more than an embarrassmen; it was a massive cut at Soviet prestige. It was Soviet policy to deny such a "problem" existed, although this became difficult as Russians in German uniforms started massing by the thousands in British and American POW camps after D-day. The Soviet regime fully expected these men and their families to pay for their anti-Soviet actions; additionally, it feared as a matter of its own survival the existence of an armed, anti-Soviet army in the West. Repatriation was their answer to which the British and Americans acquiesced,

53. Evans, *Blacklisted by History,* 90.

54. A photograph is captioned "Greenhouse vitamins for Miners." The subhead reads, "We visited goldmines operated by Dalstroi in the valley of the Kolyma River . . . It was interesting to find, instead of the sin, gin, and brawling of an old-time gold rush, extensive greenhouses growing tomatoes, cucmbers and even melons, to make sure the hardy miners got enough vitamins!" (657) As Tim Tzouliadis points out in *The Forsaken* (222), these miners in the photograph were not what they seemed. He writes, "Judging from their physical condition, these strong 'healthy miners' could only have been NKVD guards playing the part for the American visitors . . . While the persecutors took on the role of the persecuted for a few hours, the real miners waited hidden in the shadows, worked close to death . . . Their faces would never grace the pages of the *National Geographic.*"

55. Tzouliadis, *The Forsaken,* 220–21. According to the IPR Report, Lauchlin Currie got Lattimore the gig traveling as a senior adviser to Wallace.

56. *Life,* August 30, 1948, 94; Kravchenko, *I Chose Freedom,* 471.

57. Nigel Cawthorne, *The Iron Cage: Are British POWs Still Alive in Siberia?* (London: Fourth Estate, 1994), 114–15.

58. Tolstoy, *Secret Betrayal*, 305.

59. Kravchenko, *I Chose Freedom*, 468.

60. Solzhenitsyn, *Warning to the West*, 44–45.

61. Andrew and Mitrokhin, *Sword and Shield*, 320–21.

62. Tzouliadis, *The Forsaken*, 56–57.

63. Conquest, *Harvest of Sorrow*, 309.

64. Dunn, *Caught Between Roosevelt and Stalin*, 37.

65. Weil, *A Pretty Good Club*, 70.

66. Weil, *A Pretty Good Club*, 106.

67. Dunn, *Caught Between Roosevelt and Stalin*, 137

68. Bullitt, *Correspondence*, 522.

69. Weil, *A Pretty Good Club*, 91–92.

70. Evans, *Blacklisted by History*, 83–84.

71. Weil, *A Pretty Good Club*, 92–93, 283.

72. See chapter 1.

73. Dies, *Martin Dies' Story*, 64.

74. Dies, *Martin Dies' Story*, 62–63. Dies notes that the highest membership serial number his committee ever came across was 195,762. "Given that Communists strive for quality, rather than quantity, it was amazing that they had been able to grow from 10,000 aliens in 1919 to nearly 200,000 members in 1938, mostly native born or naturalized citizens."

75. Weil, *A Pretty Good Club*, 139.

76. Weil, *A Pretty Good Club*, 139.

77. See chapter 3.

78. Weinstein and Vassiliev, *Haunted Wood*, 343–44.

CHAPTER 9

1. On opening, the National D-day Memorial in Bedford, Virginia—a town that lost more Americans per capita on D-day than any other—unveiled busts of FDR, Truman, Churchill, Chiang Kai-shek, and Stalin. Stalin's inclusion sparked anger, editorials, a petition, and, finally, board action to remove all of the leaders from public display. http://www2.newsadvance.com/news/2010/sep/28/d-day-memorial-remove-busts-stalin-other-allied-fi-ar-530016/.

2. Suvorov, *Chief Culprit*, xi.

3. Bohlen, *Witness to History*, 126.

4. Suvorov, *Chief Culprit*, xi.

5. Suvorov, *Chief Culprit*, xiii.

6. Dies, *Martin Dies' Story*, 11.

7. Gen. Mark W. Clark, *Calculated Risk* (New York: Enigma Books, 2007), 389.

8. Wedemeyer, *Wedemeyer Reports!* 405–32.

9. William C. Bullitt, "How We Won the War and Lost the Peace," *Life*, August 30, 1948.

10. Dwight D. Eisenhower, *Crusade in Europe* (Garden City, NY: Doubleday, 1948), 396.

11. See, for example, Rafael Medoff, "The Roosevelt Administration, David Ben-Gurion and the Failure to Bomb Auschwitz," http://www.wymaninstitute.org/special-reports/.

12. Dallas, *1945*, 413–14.

13. Suvorov makes a compelling argument that the Soviets were caught off guard in an offensive position while preparing to strike at Germany themselves.

14. "Chinese Ask Russia for Second Front," *New York Times*, June 14, 1943.

15. Notwithstanding the Soviets' "secret" blitzkrieg in Mongolia in August 1939 that destroyed Japan's 6th Army. See Suvorov, *Chief Culprit*, 114–20.

16. Manchester, *American Caesar*, 241. Initially, army brass (including Marshall) and FDR found MacArthur's proposal to bring Russia into the Pacific War persuasive; with Japan knocked out, all Allied forces could turn to captive Europe. FDR wired Moscow to convene a conference. "Stalin's reply was cool. He preferred, he said, to defer judgment on the matter until spring. Studying his reply, Marshall and Stark decided it would be unwise to press the issue."

17. Winston S. Churchill, *The Grand Alliance* (Boston: Houghton Mifflin, 1950), 605.

18. Schecter and Leona Schecter, *Sacred Secrets*, chapter 2, "Operation Snow," 22–45.

19. Niblo, *Influence*, 101. Niblo agrees with Adm. Edwin Layton that the Soviets probably knew of the attack given that the Japanese strike force, steaming toward Hawaii with instructions to sink anything in its path, permitted a Soviet-flagged freighter, *Uritsky*, loaded with Lend-Lease goods, to sail unharmed. Admiral Layton writes in *"And I Was There": Pearl Harbor and Midway*, "This raises the probability that Uritsky's course must have been given to the Japanese by the Russians themselves. This deduction then leads to the logical assumption that that Soviet intelligence knew precise details of the course to be take across the

Northern Pacific by Nagamo's striking force." Rear Admiral Edwin T. Layton, U.S.N. (ret.), with Captain John Pineau, U.S.N.R. (ret.), and John Costello, *"And I Was There": Pearl Harbor and Midway—Breaking the Secrets* (Old Saybrook, CT: Konecky and Konecky, 1985), 221.

20. Schecter and Schecter, *Sacred Secrets,* 37.
21. Schecter and Schecter, *Sacred Secrets,* 44.
22. Manly, *Twenty-Year Revolution,* 114.
23. Baldwin, *Great Mistakes of the War,* 30.
24. Manchester, *American Caesar,* 240, 270.
25. Manchester, *American Caesar,* 279.
26. Sherwood, *Hopkins,* 2:548. Sherwood writes, "In one convoy [to Murmansk] twenty-one out of thirty-three ships were sunk."
27. Transcript of Lend-Lease Act of 1941, http://www.ourdocuments.gov/doc.php?doc=71&page=transcript.
28. Lyons, *Red Decade,* 240.
29. McJimsey, *Hopkins,* 190.
30. Sherwood, *Hopkins,* 1:400.
31. Herring, *Aid to Russia,* 46.
32. Sherwood, *Hopkins,* 1:449. Chesly Manly discusses this paradox in *Twenty-Year Revolution,* 114–15.
33. Sherwood, *Hopkins,* 2:542.
34. Writing in 1958, General Wedemeyer, a member of the first joint strategic planning group in early 1942, defended Marshall and rejected the notion that the "second front" was conceived with anything but Western interests at heart. "From my own knowledge I can state categorically that the BOLERO-ROUNDUP conception was aimed at winning the war on preferential terms for the West. See *Wedemeyer Reports!* 153–54.
35. "Drive in North Africa Not Enough," *New York Times,* October 28, 1942.
36. "Shock Troops Lead, Simultaneous Landings Made Before Dawn at Numerous Points," *New York Times,* November 8, 1942; see FDR's statement announcing "second front" at http://www.ibiblio.org/pha/policy/1942/421107b.html.
37. "Stalin Still Insisting on That Second Front," *New York Times,* November 8, 1942.
38. "Stalin Says Drives in Africa Turn War in Favor of Allies," *New York Times,* November 14, 1942.
39. Figures come from Mark Clark's memoir, *Calculated Risk,* 290.
40. Moran, *Churchill,* 155. According to Moran, it was at Tehran where Churchill first realized that "if he wanted to help the countries of Eastern Europe he must get there before the Red Army."
41. Sherwood, *Hopkins,* 2:790.
42. Sherwood, Hopkins, 2:769. "During these days at Cairo, Hopkins formed a friendship with Charles E. Bohlen. . . . Hopkins asked him all manner of questions about the Soviet Union, and was surprised and impressed by the objectivity and lack of bias as well as by the considerable scholarship revealed in his answers . . . Hopkins subsequently persuaded the president to appoint Bohlen to a post in the White House where he would act as a liaison officer with the State Department . . ."
43. Bohlen, *Witness to History,* 148.
44. "Was Stalin (the Terrible) Really a Great Man? A Conversation with Averell Harriman," *Encounter,* November, 1981, 24.
45. Harry C. Butcher, *My Three Years with Eisenhower: The Personal Diary of Captain Harry C. Butcher, USNR, Naval Aide to General Eisenhower, 1942–1945* (New York: Simon & Schuster, 1946), 447–48.
46. These Eisenhower quotations come from *FRUS: The Conferences at Cairo and Tehran, 1943* (published 1961), 359–61.
47. Baldwin, *Great Mistakes of the War,* 38–39. Eaker explained that from an air point of view it would be "easier to support a trans-Adriatic operation than the invasion of southern France. The bases, he pointed out, had already been established in Italy . . . But the southern France operation would have to be supported from new bases in Corsica. After the meeting was over, General Marshall commented . . . to General Eaker: "You've been too damned long with the British."
48. See Moran, *Churchill,* for an eyewitness account of Hopkins's Churchill-rage.
49. Eisenhower, *Crusade in Europe,* 198–200.
50. Baldwin, *Great Mistakes of the War,* 56–57. "General Eisenhower's own inclinations about Berlin apparently had the full support of Washington; Edgar Ansel Mowrer reports in *The Nightmare of American Foreign Policy* that he had been personally told by the White House that 'the Joint Chiefs of Staff advised Truman to let the Russians take Berlin.' President Truman, new to the White House and without much background about the past nuances of our politico-military policies, apparently acceded." Joint Chiefs = Marshall. Marshall = Hopkins?
51. "Allied Front in Italy Not So Far from Reich," *New York Times,* September 12, 1943.
52. Gannon, *Cardinal Spellman Story,* 224.
53. Dunn, *Caught Between Roosevelt and Stalin,* 195–96.
54. Clark, *Calculated Risk,* 203.

55. "St. Exupery Lost on Flying Mission," *New York Times,* August 10, 1944.

56. Clark, *Calculated Risk,* 294.

57. Dunn, *Caught Between Roosevelt and Stalin,* 196.

58. Somehow Hopkins's coaching of Molotov to circumvent American military advice didn't make it into Sherwood. See Mark, "Venona's Source," 20.

59. "Mr. Molotoff Came to Plead for a Second Front," *New York Times,* June 13, 1942.

60. Sherwood, *Hopkins,* 2:610.

61. Sherwood, *Hopkins,* 2:615.

62. Schecter and Schecter, *Sacred Secrets,* 90.

63. Standley and Ageton, *Admiral Ambassador,* 271.

64. "Our Indispensable Fronts," *New York Times,* February 25, 1943.

65. "Second Front Lag Is Denied By Knox," *New York Times,* June 23, 1943.

66. Moran, *Churchill,* 102.

67. "Zero Hour," *New York Times,* July 11, 1943.

68. "Russians Cheer Landing as Aid to the Red Army," *New York Times,* July 11, 1943.

69. McJimsey, *Hopkins,* 299.

70. Moran, *Churchill,* 142.

71. Moran, *Churchill,* 140–42.

72. *FRUS: The Conferences at Cairo and Tehran, 1943* (published 1961), 493.

73. *FRUS: Cairo and Tehran,* 494. "Marshal Stalin said that he favored the operation in Southern France particularly as he thought Turkey would not enter the war. He repeated that he thought Turkey would not enter the war." You better believe Turkey wouldn't enter the war. Lord Moran tells us (157) that Churchill tried desperately to bring Turkey in. "Inonu had made it clear that it is Russia, not Germany that the Turks fear. They fear that if Russians come to their assistance they will remain; once the Kremlin has her troops in command of the Straits, only force will displace them."

74. Clark, *Calculated Risk,* 293–95.

75. Sherwood, *Hopkins,* 2:775.

76. From Sherwood, *Hopkins,* 1:202–3: "Columnist Marquis Childs wrote: Should the President on a dull day suggest casually to his friend and confidant Harry L. Hopkins that the national welfare would be served if Mr. Hopkins were to jump off the Washington Monument, the appointed hour would find Mr. Hopkins poised for the plunge. Whether with or without parachute would depend on what the President seemed to have had in mind.

Mr. Hopkins would know about that, because he has made a career of understanding, sensing, divining, often guessing—and usually guessing right—what is in Franklin Roosevelt's mind. It is a career that has taken him from the dull routine of social-service work to the upper reaches of diplomacy, where he has had a thrilling preview of the shape of things to come. And, what is more, history may show that he was one of the shapers."

77. Sherwood, *Hopkins,* 2:775.

78. Manly, *Twenty-Year Revolution,* 121.

79. Sherwood, *Hopkins,* 2:783.

80. Bohlen, *Witness to History,* 148.

81. *FRUS: Cairo and Tehran,* 563–64.

82. Sherwood, *Hopkins,* 2:788. On December 1, 1943, the last day of the conference, the Prime Minister put in a final plug for an assault on Rhodes and Hopkins went into smack-down mode. In fact, as Sherwood writes, "Hopkins was so anxious to have the record straight that he wrote his own version of his comments for inclusion in the minutes," disowning Churchill's remarks every way possible: "It should be clearly understood that the American side believe that there are no landing-craft available for an attack on Rhodes—and, more important, still, that even if the landing-craft were available—no decision has been reached as to whether or not the landing craft could not be used to better advantage in some other operation."

83. Moran, *Churchill,* 155.

84. Wedemeyer, *Wedemeyer Reports!* 96.

CHAPTER 10

1. Wedemeyer, *Wedemeyer Reports!* 92.

2. After meeting with Stalin in Moscow on May 28, 1945, Hopkins told Truman that Stalin "prefers to go through with unconditional surrender" regarding Japan. "However, he feels that if we stick to unconditional surrender the Japs will not give up and we will have to destroy them as we did Germany." Sherwood, *Hopkins,* 2:892–93.

3. Manly, *Twenty-Year Revolution,* 123. Allen Dulles, *Germany's Underground* (New York: Macmillan, 1947), 22.

4. Dulles, *Underground,* 140.

5. Dulles, *Underground,* 165.

6. Dulles, *Underground,* 136. This cable was written in April 1944.

7. "Full Story of Anti-Hitler Plot Shows That Allies Refused to Assist," *New York Times,* March 18, 1946.

8. "Gen. Menzies, Ex-British Intelligence Chief, Dies," *New York Times,* May 31, 1968.

9. Dulles, *Underground,* 24–25.

10. "Eisenhower Praises Anti-Nazi Resistance," *New York Times,* May 11, 1945.

11. Peter Hoffman, *The History of the German Resistance, 1933–1945,* 3rd English ed. (Montreal: McGill-Queen's University Press, 2001), xiii.

12. "Canaris Hanging Related," *New York Times,* October 11, 1952.

13. "Lubavitch Jews Want Admiral Canaris Honoured by Yad Vashem," *Agence France Presse,* August 6, 2009, http://www.ejpress.org/article/38250. "Following historical research we have established that Admiral Canaris saved Rabbi Yosef Schneerson—sixth in that lineage—and 500 other Jews from the Warsaw ghetto," said [Rabbi Benjamin] Lipshitz."

14. Czeslaw Milosz, *The Captive Mind* (New York: Vintage Books, 1981), 126.

15. Ian Colvin, *Hitler's Secret Enemy* (London: Pan Books, 1957). It was Sir Christopher Warren, undersecretary of the British Foreign Office, who first told Colvin of Canaris's aid to the British. Colvin's book was later endorsed by Gen. L. Rivet of the Deuxième Bureau, France's military intelligence organization.

16. Colvin, *Canaris,* 7.

17. Wedemeyer, *Wedemeyer Reports!* 418.

18. Box 61, Folder 4, Harry Hopkins Papers, Georgetown University Library.

19. See chapter 7 for more about Sidney "Harry-Doesn't-Know-Uranium-from-Geranium" Hyman. There is only one passing mention of Earle in the Sherwood Hopkins biography.

20. Richard Harris Smith, *OSS: The Secret History of America's First Central Intelligence Agency* (Guilford, CT: Lyons Press, 2005), 368, quoting *Secret and Personal,* by F. W. Winterbotham (New York: HarperCollins, 1969), 162.

21. Schecter and Schecter, *Sacred Secrets,* 93–97.

22. Butler, *My Dear Mr. Stalin,* 119.

23. Weil, *A Pretty Good Club,* 134–35.

24. Dunn, *Caught Between Roosevelt and Stalin,* 181.

25. George H. Earle, "F.D.R.'s Tragic Mistake," *Confidential,* August 1958, 19.

26. Two weeks after Canaris made the Paris trip, the answer from Churchill came back: unconditional surrender. Larry Collins and Dominique Lapierre, *Is Paris Burning? How Paris Miraculously Escaped Hitler's Sentence of Death in August 1944* (New York: Grand Central Publishing, 1991), 5.

27. Vassiliev's White Notebook No. 3 notes (133) that Neumann's KGB recruitment was approved on January 2, 1943. In 1942, Vassiliev's notes also reveal, three still unidentified KGB agents considered Neumann "pro-Soviet."

28. Jürgen Heideking and Christof Mauch, eds., *American Intelligence and the German Resistance to Hitler: A Documentary History* (Boulder, CO: Westview Press, 1996), 267.

29. Haynes, Klehr, and Vassiliev, *Spies,* 308, 305.

30. Alexander Vassiliev Papers, White Notebook No. 1 Translation, 51, http://www.scribd.com/doc/84608249/Alexander-Vassiliev-Papers-White-Notebook-No-1-Translation.

31. Their names, unasterisked, stud the index of the tome *Postwar Foreign Policy Preparation, 1939–1945* (Department of State, Publication 3580, 1950).

32. Stripling, *Red Plot Against America,* 35–36.

33. Niblo, *Influence,* 75.

34. Sherwood, *Hopkins,* 2:693.

35. *FRUS: Casablanca* wasn't published until 1968—twenty-five years after the conference!

36. Without delving into CFR's reputation among so-called conspiracy theorists (were they at least half right all along?), I will note that the online history of CFR to this day describes Soviet military intelligence agent Alger Hiss on joining the group after World War II as "a newly elected member sympathetic to the left wing of the Democratic Party"; http://www.cfr.org/about/history/cfr/first_transformation.html.

37. *FRUS: The Conferences at Washington, 1941–1942, and Casablanca, 1943,* 506.

38. McJimsey, *Hopkins,* 277. *FRUS: Washington and Casablanca,* 703.

39. Wedemeyer, *Wedemeyer Reports!* 96.

40. Wedemeyer, *Wedemeyer Reports!* 95.

41. This list includes British prime minister Winston Churchill, British foreign minister Anthony Eden, Secretary of State Cordell Hull, and soon-to-be U.S. Ambassador to Moscow W. Averell Harriman. See *The Memoirs of Cordell Hull, vol. 11* (New York: Macmillan, 1948), 1570, 1575. See also W. Averell Harriman and Elie Abel, *Special Envoy to Churchill and Stalin, 1941–1946* (New York: Random House, 1975), 189. In 1948, Eisenhower calls the unconditional surrender announcement of 1943 "extraordinarily pleasing to me," but he himself sought modifications in 1944 to counter "German propaganda . . . interpreting the

words "unconditional surrender" to strengthen the morale of the German Army and people." See Hull, *Memoirs*, 1578. See also Butcher, *My Three Years with Eisenhower*, 518. Butcher further wrote, "Any military person knows there are conditions to every surrender . . . Our psychological experts believe we would be wiser if we created a mood of acceptance of surrender in the German army which would make possible a collapse of resistance."

42. B. H. Liddell Hart, *The German Generals Talk* (New York: William Morrow, 1948), 292–93; see also Manly, *Twenty-Year Revolution*, 122–23.

43. Biskupski, *Hollywood's War with Poland*, 74, 155–56.

44. Biskupski, *Hollywood's War with Poland*, 77, 263.

45. Stanislaw Mikolajczyk, *The Rape of Poland* (New York: Whittlesey House, 1948), 25.

46. Evans, *Blacklisted by History*, 95–97.

47. Julian Wadleigh admitted in court that he passed four hundred to five hundred secret State Department documents to the Soviets. See Romerstein and Breindel, *Venona Secrets*, 130.

48. On this State Department committee list appear three of the four lucky recipients of fine Bokhara rugs Whittaker Chambers delivered on behalf of the Kremlin for services rendered for the Communist cause: Hiss, Wadleigh, and White. George Silverman was the fourth. See Romerstein and Breindel, *Venona Secrets*, 117.

49. *Postwar Foreign Policy Preparation, 1939–1945*, 76.

50. Hull, *Memoirs*, 1570–71.

51. McJimsey, *Hopkins*, 278–79.

52. Klaus P. Fischer, *Hitler and America* (Philadelphia: University of Pennsylvania Press, 2011), 237.

53. Hoffman, *The History of the German Resistance, 1933–1945*, 214–15, 596.

54. Earle, "FDR's Tragic Mistake!" *Confidential*, 18.

55. Earle, "FDR's Tragic Mistake!" 56.

56. Earle, "FDR's Tragic Mistake!" 56–57.

57. I say "Roosevelt White House" rather than "Roosevelt administration" because Secretary of State Cordell Hull and Secretary of War Henry L. Stimson vehemently opposed the Morgenthau Plan, and were angered also at the "high-handed procedure" by which Morgenthau "conducted negotiations" at the 1944 Quebec Conference "on a matter of primary concern to the State and War Departments, without consultation with us." See Hull, *Memoirs*, 1615.

58. These quotations on the impact of the Morgenthau Plan on German morale come from John Dietrich, *The Morgenthau Plan: Soviet Influence on American Postwar Policy* (New York: Algora Publishing, 2002), 69–70.

59. Dietrich, *Morgenthau Plan*, 70–71.

60. Ernie Pyle, *Here Is Your War* (New York: World Publishing, 1945), 240–42.

61. Geoffrey T. Hellman, "Profiles—House Guest II," *New Yorker*, August 14, 1943, 35.

62. The Schecters found a copy of the Morgenthau Plan in Soviet archives with "Soviet comments" noting Western opponents including Churchill, the Catholic Church, Republicans, businesses, and banks. See *Sacred Secrets*, 124.

63. Bentley testimony of May 29, 1952, *Interlocking Subversion in Government Departments*, Report of the Subcommittee to Investigate the Administration of the Internal Security Act and Other Internal Security Laws to the Committee on the Judiciary, United States Senate, 83rd Congress, 1st Session, July 30, 1953, http://www.archive.org/stream/interlockingsubv1953unit/interlockingsubv1953unit_djvu.txt.

64. Douglas Waller, *Wild Bill Donovan: The Spymaster Who Created the OSS and Modern American Espionage* (New York: Free Press, 2011), 191–92.

65. As a Royal Marine, Ian Colvin was himself in discussions with British intelligence about a possible mission to contact Canaris, "but," Colvin wrote, "other councils in the end prevailed.
   "I am sorry I cannot send you to meet Admiral Canaris," said the senior intelligence officer with whom I had been discussing the project in October 1942, "but the Foreign Office says we have to be awfully careful not to offend the Russians." *Canaris*, 148.

66. Smith, *OSS*, 368.

67. "Gen. Menzies, Ex-British Intelligence Chief, Dies," *New York Times*, May 31, 1968.

68. Sudoplatov and Sudoplatov, *Special Tasks*, 115–16.

69. Heideking and Mauch, *American Intelligence*, 130–42.

70. Heideking and Mauch, *American Intelligence*, 139.

71. The Berle incident is related in Christof Mauch, *The Shadow War Against Hitler* (New York: Columbia University Press, 2003), 64–65.

72. Mauch, *Shadow War*, 64–65.

73. Mauch, *Shadow War*, 248.

74. Heideking and Mauch, *American Intelligence*, 136.

75. Heideking and Mauch, *American Intelligence*, 144.

76. Heideking and Mauch, *American Intelligence*, 143–44.

77. Heideking and Mauch, *American Intelligence,* 145.
78. Francis Biddle Papers: Series 2, Correspondence: Chronological, Box 6, Folder 45, Georgetown Special Collections.

CHAPTER 11

1. http://frontpagemag.com/2011/07/22/symposium-why-we-left-our-pows-behind/. Joseph D. Douglass Jr. is the author of *Betrayed,* a comprehensive history of U.S. POWs left behind in Communist captivity. He is also the author of *Red Cocaine,* a shocking account of the Communist strategy to undermine the West with illegal narcotics.
2. White House press conference, June 16, 1992.
3. *An Examination of Policy Toward POW/MIA,* U.S. Senate Foreign Relations Committee Minority Staff, May 23, 1991, 16. This report is available at: www.scribd.com/doc/82455046/An-Examination-of-US-Policy-Towards-POW-MIAs-1991.
4. The term "concentration camp" had been used during World War I, Solzhenitsyn tells us, "but here in 1918 it was for the first time applied to the citizens of one's own country." *Gulag Archipelago,* 2:17.
5. Senate Minority POW/MIA Report, 16–17.
6. Solzhenitsyn, *Warning to the West,* 17.
7. Tzouliadis, *The Forsaken,* 255.
8. "Group Is Called Communist Front," *New York Times,* February 9, 1956.
9. "Threat of Atomic War Held Basis of Misunderstanding with Soviets," *New York Times,* November 15, 1945.
10. Tzouliadis, *The Forsaken,* 253.
11. M. Stanton Evans and Herbert Romerstein posit in *Stalin's Secret Agents* that the feeble FDR may not have even comprehended the secret agreements at Yalta he signed.
12. Sherwood, *Hopkins,* 2:864.
13. Harriman and Abel, *Special Envoy,* 430.
14. Butler, *My Dear Mr. Stalin,* 298–99.
15. Cawthorne, *Iron Cage,* 5.
16. Butler, *My Dear Mr. Stalin,* 299.
17. Harriman and Abel, *Special Envoy,* 430; Polish report in Deane, *Strange Alliance,* 191.
18. Harriman and Abel, *Special Envoy,* 424–25.
19. Cable classified URGENT, TOP SECRET, "A Personal Message for the President, From U.S. Ambassador to Russia, W. Averell Harriman," March 8, 1945. It is quoted in the Senate Minority POW/MIA Report, 31.
20. See note 19. This March 8, 1945, cable is also excerpted in Harriman's memoir, *Special Envoy,* 420–21.
21. Harriman and Abel, *Special Envoy,* 426.
22. It's worth recalling the aide-mémoire Cardinal Spellman wrote up after meeting with FDR on September 3, 1943. With Russian armies still well inside Russia, FDR tells Spellman, "there is no point to oppose the desires of Stalin because he has the power to get them anyhow. So better give them gracefully." FDR went on to tick off all of the nations of Europe he was ceding to the USSR—before Tehran, before Yalta: Finland, the Baltics, the "Eastern half" of Poland, Bessarabia. *"There will be no opposition to a Russian-dominated Communist Austrian regime,"* FDR said. *"No plebiscite is to be expected in Czecho-Slovakia."* What comes through is the sound of regurgitated agitprop. To wit: FDR said it's "improbable" to get Stalin to pledge not to extend Soviet territory past a certain line; the population of Eastern Poland "wants to become Russian"; the USSR is "expected" to engineer Communist regimes in Europe; "Communist Regimes would expand but what can we do about it." FDR continues, "We should not overlook the magnificent achievements of Russia. Their finances are sound." FDR as five-year-plan flack, too? Then, "Be it as it may . . . the U.S. and Britain cannot fight the Russians. The Russian production is so big that the American help, except for trucks, is negligible." Maybe the president hadn't heard of Lend-Lease.
23. Cable, "To: Edward R. Stettinius, Jr., U.S. Secretary of State, From: Ambassador Harriman in Moscow, No. PH-1449," March 14, 1945. Quoted in the 1991 Senate Minority Report on POWs, Sections 3–9 and 3–10.
24. Winston S. Churchill, *Triumph and Tragedy* (Boston: Houghton Mifflin, 1953), 429.
25. Butler, *My Dear Mr. Stalin,* 300.
26. After Yalta, Hopkins never saw FDR again.
27. Harriman and Abel, *Special Envoy,* 422.
28. Deane, *Strange Alliance,* 190. "The reason for this was that the Soviet leaders did not want American or British officers within Poland where they could observe the methods being used to bring Poland under the domination of the Soviet Union. The world was led to believe that the Poles were so enthusiastically happy at their deliverance from the Germans that they wanted nothing more than to embrace their Russian liberators, including their ideology."
29. As a Russian speaker, Captain Hills remained involved in the British end of repatriation, witnessing many Soviet atrocities.

30. Butler, *My Dear Mr. Stalin,* 301–02.
31. Deane, *Strange Alliance,* 186.
32. Michael Beschloss, *The Conquerors: Roosevelt, Truman and the Destruction of Hitler's Germany* (New York: Simon & Schuster, 2002), 83.
33. Weil, *A Pretty Good Club,* 189.
34. Churchill, *Triumph and Tragedy,* 419.
35. Beschloss, *Conquerors,* 196.
36. Barron, *Inside the State Department,* 44.
37. Barron, *Inside the State Department,* 53. See also chapter 2, "The Role of Alger Hiss and Others Like Him," 15–36.
38. Sherwood, *Hopkins,* 2:867.
39. Harriman, *Special Envoy,* 421–22.
40. Harriman, *Special Envoy,* 422.
41. Rees, *WWII,* 249–50.
42. http://quod.lib.umich.edu/h/hiss/hiss1111.0100.004/2?page=root;rgn=full+text;size=100;view=image.
43. Tzouliadis, *The Forsaken,* 255–56.
44. Tzouliadis, *The Forsaken,* 256–57.
45. The Soviets would make good propaganda use of having liberated these cities in Communist coups in Czechoslovakia and in Austria. Baldwin, *Great Mistakes of the War* (Harper & Brothers, 1950), pp. 45–57.
46. Kent Cooper, *The Right to Know: An Exposition of the Evils of News Suppression and Propaganda* (New York: Farrar, Straus, 1956), 205.
47. Cooper, *Right to Know,* 207–8.
48. Baldwin, *Great Mistakes of the War,* 49, 51.
49. Edward Kennedy, "I'd Do It Again," *The Atlantic,* August 1948, 41.
50. Cooper, *Right to Know,* 206.
51. Cooper, *Right to Know,* 208.
52. Senate Minority POW/MIA Report, 39. "SHAEF Asks Russians About Freed PW's," Associated Press dispatch, ADVANCE HEADQUARTERS, Reims, France, May 12, 1945.
53. Report, "From: Major General R. W. Barker, Subject: Report on conference with Russian Officials Relative to the Repatriation of Prisoners of War and Displaced Persons, To: The Chief of Staff, Supreme Headquarters, AEF (Allied European Forces)," May 23, 1945. Quoted in Senate POW/MIA Minority Report, 41.
54. *FRUS: The Conference of Berlin (the Potsdam Conference), 1945,* 70–71.
55. *FRUS: Potsdam,* 38.
56. *FRUS: Potsdam,* 57–59.
57. Stalin wouldn't even release the sixteen Poles. Churchill, *Triumph and Tragedy,* 498: "Nothing more was heard of the [Polish] victims of the trap until the case opened against them on June 18. It was conducted in the usual Communist manner. The prisoners were accused of subversion, terrorism, and espionage and all but one admitted wholly or in part the charges against them. Thirteen were found guilty, and sentenced to terms of imprisonment ranging from four months to ten years, and three were acquitted. This was in fact the judicial liquidation of the Polish Underground which had fought so heroically against Hitler. The rank and file had already died in the streets of Warsaw."
58. Senate Minority POW/MIA Report, 42.
59. Senate Minority POW/MIA Report, 41.
60. Cable, "To: AGWAR, From: SHAEF FORWARD, SIGNED EISENHOWER, REF. No. FWD-23059," June 1, 1945. Quoted in Senate Minority POW/MIA Report, 42.
61. Jean Edward Smith, *Eisenhower in War and Peace* (New York: Random House, 2012).
62. Senate Minority POW/MIA Report, 42–43.
63. Bukovsky, "The Power of Memory and Acknowledgment."
64. Tzouliadis, *The Forsaken,* 339.
65. Senate Minority POW/MIA Report, 43. See "10,000 Ex-Captives Coming by Week-End; Army Sees All in Europe Accounted For," *New York Times,* June 1, 1945.
66. Senate Minority POW/MIA Report, 43.
67. Cawthorne, *Iron Cage,* 3.
68. "Ex-U.S. Envoy Says Yeltsin Misspoke on M.I.A.'s," *New York Times,* June 27, 1992.
69. Tzouliadis, *The Forsaken,* 291.
70. Wringer report, 51-B-13005A, http://lcweb2.loc.gov/frd/wringer/.
71. Senate Minority POW/MIA Report, 49.
72. Joseph D. Douglass Jr., *Betrayed* (1st Book Library, 2002). Douglass credits researchers John M. G. Brown and Tom Ashworth with first recounting this history of abandonment.

73. http://www.villagevoice.com/content/printVersion/181282/.
74. Sydney Schanberg, "Silent Treatment," *The American Conservative,* July 1, 2010, http://conservative.com/articles/silent-treatment/.
75. The first half of *Betrayed* reports on the experiences of Gen. Jan Sejna, a very high-ra[...] munist official who defected in 1968. Sejna revealed the extent to which thousands of prisoners, [...] American POWs, were used as human guinea pigs for Communist "medical experiments."
76. "Official Says Hundreds of U.S. Citizens Likely Died in Soviet Gulags," CNN, February 11, 2005. See at: http://articles.cnn.com/2005-02-11/us/gulag.report_1_gulag-system-pentagon-report-camps?_s=PM:US.
77. *Washington Post,* September 15, 1990, A21.
78. Known as "Memoirs," this interview was obtained by the U.S. Russia Joint Commission on POW/MIA and Defense Personnel POW/Missing Personnel Office; http://www.nationalalliance.org/korea/memoirs.htm.
79. Jordan, *Diaries,* 29.
80. Bollinger, *Stalin's Slave Ships,* 108–9. On assessing the Soviet merchant fleet as inadequate for transporting Lend-Lease equipment across the Pacific, the United States transferred to Soviet control "about a hundred older merchant ships [and] thirty-eight new Liberty ships and five more advanced Victory ships, all built in the 1940s . . . It seems clear that the cargo included forced laborers and that the destinations included Magadan." Bollinger continues, "There are a number of reports that the Soviets used some of these ships after the war to transfer prisoners to the Kolyma camps, including perhaps U.S. military personnel."

CHAPTER 12

1. Igor Shafarevich, *The Socialist Phenomenon* (New York: Harper & Row, 1980), 269.
2. Tomas Schuman, *World Thought Police* (Los Angeles: NATA Almanac, 1986), 5.
3. Muggeridge, *Things Past,* 226.
4. This idea grew into *The Death of the Grown-Up* (New York: St. Martin's, 2007).
5. Geert Wilders, speech at Cornerstone Church, Nashville, Tennessee, May 12, 2011.
6. For a textbook example of how Islamic violence effectively advances Islamic law, see my discussion of the 2006 Airplane Plot at http://tinyurl.com/8mtupw3.
7. http://www.dailymail.co.uk/news/article-2128788/London-university-considers-stopping-sale-immoral-alcohol-campus-offends-Muslim-students.html. Muslims comprise an estimated 20 percent of London Metropolitan University.
8. Diana West, "Shariah Goes to Harvard," *Washington Times,* April 24, 2009.
9. http://sig.ville.gouv.fr/Atlas/ZUS/.
10. J. B Matthews, *Odyssey of a Fellow Traveler* (Belmont, MA: American Opinion Reprints, 1961), 110.
11. Ibn Warraq, *Why I Am Not a Muslim* (Amherst, NY: Prometheus, 1995), 30; Betrand Russell, *The Practice and Theory of Bolshevism* (Project Gutenberg E-book, 2005), 165.
12. Russell, *Autobiography,* 5.
13. http://www.wnd.com/2011/02/267817/. Despite commentators' derision, the caliphate polls well in the Islamic world. In 2007, University of Maryland/WorldPublicOpinion.org polled four Muslim countries: Egypt, Pakistan, Indonesia and Morocco. By large majorities, Muslims favored the application of sharia and uniting Islam in a caliphate. http://tinyurl.com/99zs9eu.
14. Alain Besançon quoted in Conquest, *Reflections on a Ravaged Century,* 112–13.
15. Ibn Warraq, *Virgins? What Virgins? And Other Essays* (Amherst, NY: Prometheus, 2010), 289–95; Andrew Bostom, "Geert Wilders, Western Sages, and Totalitarian Islam," http://pjmedia.com/blog/geert-wilders-western-sages-and-totalitarian-islam/.
16. http://www.pvv.nl/index.php/component/content/article/36-geert-wilders/3586-speech-geert-wilders-berlijn.html.
17. See note 16.
18. Alain Besançon, *A Century of Horrors: Communism, Nazism, and the Uniqueness of the Shoah* (Wilmington, DE: ISI Books, 2007), p. 36.
19. Solzhenitsyn, *Warning to the West,* 57–58.
20. Lenin wrote, "Our morality is entirely subjugated to the interests of the class struggle of the proletariat"— i.e., Lenin himself. He also wrote, "We do not believe in eternal morality, and we expose all the fables about morality." See Matthews, "Odyssey of a Fellow Traveler," 104. Matthews also quotes a letter from a Marxist friend who wrote (105), " 'Right' is a relative term, with many connotations. Being on the right *side* is more important by far than doing the precisely right thing in a given instance."
21. Solzhenitsyn, *Warning to the West,* 58.
22. Dunn, *Caught Between Roosevelt and Stalin,* 50.
23. Conquest, *Dragons,* 169.
24. Solzhenitsyn, *Warning to the West,* 125–26.
25. Schuman (Besmenov), *World Thought Police,* 2.

26. "An Explanatory Memorandum on the Strategic Goal for the Group in North America," http://tinyurl .com/8ggj23l.

27. Conquest, *Ravaged Century,* 155.

28. Richard Crossman, ed., *The God That Failed* (New York: Columbia University Press, 2001), 34.

29. Crossman, *God That Failed,* 45.

30. Crossman, *God That Failed,* 50.

31. "Words that Work and Words that Don't: A Guide for Counterterrorism Communication," National Counterterrorism Center, March 14, 2008.

32. Manly, *Twenty-Year Revolution,* 79.

33. R. H. S. Crossman, "Agreeing to Disagree," *The Nation,* December 16, 1950.

34. Eggleston, *Roosevelt, Churchill, and the World War II Opposition.*

35. John T. Flynn, *The Decline of the American Republic: And How to Rebuild It* (New York: Devin-Adair, 1955), 4, 45.

36. Raymond F. Gregory, *Norman Thomas: The Great Dissenter* (New York: Algora Publishing, 2008), 241.

37. Murray N. Rothbard, "The Myth of Reaganomics," http://mises.org/daily/1544.

38. "Socialism Threat Seen by Ely in NRA," *New York Times,* July 28, 1934.

39. Alexis de Toqueville, *Democracy in America* (New York: Harper Perennial, 1988), 691–92.

40. Raymond Moley, "Thomas Sings Hosanna for Ike's Course," *Kittanny Simpson Leader Times*, May 6, 1957. In his syndicated column, ex-New Dealer Moley was quoting a recent interview with Thomas conducted by the college newspaper, *The Harvard Times Republican.* Moley further quoted Grayson Kirk, Eisenhower's successor as president of Columbia, as describing the "danger" that "we shall begin to develop government as an instrument of welfare [and] lose, in the process, some of our own stamina, self-reliance and individual initiative."

41. Attributed to Norman Thomas by W. Cleon Skousen, Letter to the Editor, *Schenectady Gazette*, January 3, 1979.

42. Leon A. Harris, *Upton Sinclair: American Rebel* (New York: Crowell, 1975), 351.

INDEX